S0-ABQ-798

Fodor's

ESSENTIAL THAILAND

Welcome to Thailand

Thailand conjures images of white sand beaches and cerulean waters, peaceful temples, and lush mountain jungles. In Bangkok, a 21st-century playground, the scent of spicy street food fills the air, and the Grand Palace recalls the country's traditions. Outside the capital, the wonders of the countryside enchant, whether you are trekking to remote villages in the northern hills, exploring Ayutthaya's splendid ruins, or diving in the waters of the idyllic southern coast. The unique spirit of the Thai people—this is the "land of smiles," after all—adds warmth to any visit.

TOP REASONS TO GO

★ **Beaches:** Pristine strands and hidden coves bring vacation daydreams alive.

★ **Food:** Rich curries, sour-spicy tom yum soup, and tasty pad thai are worth savoring.

★ **Architecture:** Resplendent stupas and pagodas evoke the glory of ancient kingdoms.

★ **Spas:** Luxurious retreats offer indulgences such as world-renowned Thai massage.

★ **Trekking:** A trek to a remote mountain village to visit hill tribes is a memorable experience.

★ **Shopping:** Iconic night markets sell everything from hand-carved crafts to handbags.

Contents

Fodor's Features

MAPS

Chapter 1

EXPERIENCE THAILAND

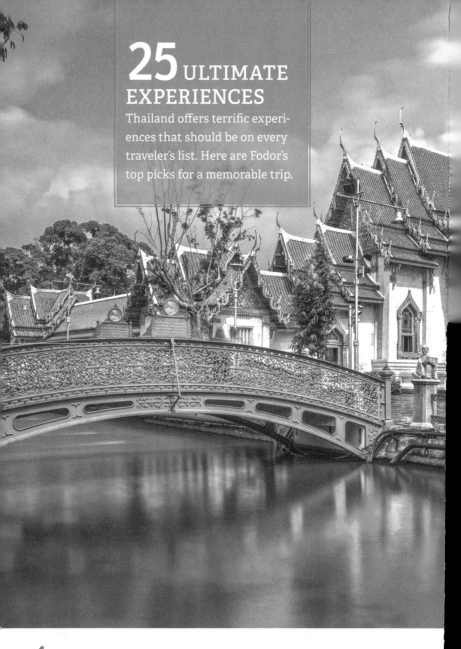

25 ULTIMATE EXPERIENCES

Thailand offers terrific experiences that should be on every traveler's list. Here are Fodor's top picks for a memorable trip.

1 Bangkok's Famous Temples

There are more than 400 temples in Bangkok so start with the famous ones: Wat Phra Kaew (Temple of the Emerald Buddha), in the Grand Palace; Wat Pho or Temple of the Reclining Buddha; and Wat Benchamabophit, covered in marble and featured on the 5 baht coin. (Ch. 3)

2 Kanchanaburi

Just a few hours by train from Bangkok, you can swim and explore the the waterfall in Erawan National Park, then visit the Bridge on the River Kwai. (Ch. 4)

3 The Hill Tribes

Thailand's hill tribes live in the mountainous regions of the north. Avoid the tourist traps and book a guide to take you to more remote villages. (Ch. 8)

4 Festivals

Experience Thailand's rich traditions at a festival like Yi Peng, when candlelit lanterns are released into the sky and river along with the previous year's misfortunes. (Ch. 7)

5 Ayutthaya

Destroyed in the late 1700s, the Thai- and Khmer-style ruins of Thailand's second capital now form Ayutthaya Historical Park and evoke the city's lost grandeur. (Ch. 4)

6 Island-Hopping Around Krabi

Hire a longtail boat to explore breathtaking scenery, white sandy beaches, turquoise waters, limestone cliffs, and incredible coral reefs. (Ch. 6)

7 Doi Inthanon

Thailand's highest peak rises majestically over a national park of staggering beauty, popular with birders, nature lovers, and hikers day-tripping from Chiang Mai. (Ch. 7)

8 Snorkel and Dive

Thailand's Andaman Coast offers some of the best snorkeling and dive sites in the world with crystal clear waters, abundant marine life, and spectacular underwater scenery. (Ch. 6)

9 Mae Hong Son Loop

Thailand's famous trail runs from Chaing Mai to Mae Hong Son via Pai and winds through spectacular mountain scenery along the way. (Ch. 8)

10 Thai Massage

Widely available in temples, markets, jungle hideaways, and luxury resorts, Thai massage treatments can be rigorous, even painful but, pleasant.

11 Floating Markets

Vendors in straw hats peddle everything from caramelized crickets and samurai swords to herbal potions and silk at floating markets like Damnoen Saduak. (Ch. 4)

12 Pai

A popular stop along the Mae Hong Son Loop, this peaceful town ensconced in nature has a WWII Memorial Bridge, caves, a canyon, and a hippy scene. (Ch. 8)

13 Khao Sok National Park

One of the most spectacular landscapes in Thailand, remote Khao Sok offers lush greenery with rare flora and fauna and towering mountain ranges. (Ch. 5)

14 Khao San Road

Touristy and crowded with overpriced souvenirs, Bangkok's most famous shopping thoroughfare is still a must with its hustle and bustle, lively bars, and street food. (Ch. 3)

15 Sky Bar

Bangkok is famous for its rooftop bars, especially Sky Bar, with its breathtaking views of the Chaophraya River and a cocktail named for *The Hangover* movie filmed here. (Ch. 3)

16 Silk

Chiang Mai and silk are synonymous and at several workrooms along San Kamphaeng Road, you can learn how silk is made and buy quality silk clothing and home decor items. (Ch. 7)

17 Similan and Surin Islands

Unspoiled beaches and crystal-blue waters with a diversity of marine life, these remote island paradises are popular for diving, fishing, and hiking. (Ch. 6)

18 Cooking Class

Learn a few fundamentals and the history of Thai cuisine while you master an authentic green curry, a hot-and-spicy soup, or pad thai. (Ch. 3)

19 Sukhothai

This ancient city's impressive 13th-century ruins with Khmer- and Hindu-influenced sculpture and architecture are relatively unspoiled by the ages. (Ch. 8)

20 Lopburi Monkeys

Lopburi has an unusually large monkey population and they like to gather around monuments like Phra Prang Sam Yot. They also like to steal your food or shoes! (Ch. 4)

21 Chiang Mai

Northern Thailand's largest city offers significant temples, trekking trails that lead to the hill tribes, and bustling night markets that are a riot of sounds and smells. (Ch. 7)

22 Koh Chang

Mountainous Koh Chang, or Elephant Island, is part of a national park and many of its beaches and villages are only accessible by boat, making them unspoiled paradises. (Ch. 5)

23 Phetchaburi

Khao Long Cave overflows with Buddhas, including a 32-ft reclining Buddha, and is best visited in the morning when the sun reflects off of the brass icons. (Ch. 4)

24 Chiang Rai

This city is a must for its access to the Golden Triangle and the surrounding hill tribes, as well as its glistening and spectacular White Temple, Wat Rong Khun. (Ch. 8)

25 Street Food

Join locals gathered around street stalls slurping noodles; devouring curries, sticky rice, and spicy som tam; and snacking on panfried insects. (Ch. 3)

WHAT'S WHERE

1 Bangkok. In this city of contrasts where old-world charm meets futuristic luxury, you can dine at street stalls or ritzy restaurants, visit the jaw-dropping Grand Palace, and shop at Chatuchak Weekend Market or Pathumwan's designer malls. At night, there are hip mega-clubs as well as quiet romantic restaurants and wine bars.

2 Around Bangkok. Petchaburi and Ayutthaya have ancient temples, while Thailand's oldest city, Nakhon Pathom, is home to Phra Pathom Chedi, the world's tallest Buddhist stupa.

3 The Gulf Coast Beaches. Thailand's two shores have alternating monsoon seasons, so there's always great beach weather *somewhere*. The gulf has Pattaya's nightlife and the island trio of Koh Samui (good sailing), Koh Pha Ngan (full-moon revelry), and Koh Tao (diving).

4 Phuket and the Andaman Coast. Highlights of this spectacular coastal region include Phuket, Phang Nga Bay (with James Bond Island aka Koh Tapu), and Krabi,

which is a paradise for divers and rock climbers.

5 Chiang Mai. This moat-encircled city is riddled with temples and markets and deserves a lingering stop in any tour of the north. Wander the narrow alleys and brick roads of the Old City, then dine in the university area alive with hip crowds.

6 Northern Thailand. Chiang Rai is a chill regional center and the gateway to the Golden Triangle, where Laos, Myanmar (Burma), and Thailand meet. Thailand's first capital, Sukhothai, has carefully restored ruins.

7 Cambodia. No Southeast Asia trip is complete without a visit to the temple ruins of Angkor in Siem Reap. The capital, Phnom Penh, is a vibrant city with a thriving food scene. There is also plenty to interest hikers, birders, and wildlife buffs.

8 Laos. Photogenic rivers, mountainous countryside, and the dreamy feeling of going back in time are major reasons to visit. World Heritage sites Luang Prabang and Champasak have beautiful temples and the Plain of Jars will wow anyone.

What to Eat and Drink in Thailand

PANANG (PEANUT) CURRY
Panang curry uses fragrant red curry as a base and adds ground peanuts for creaminess and depth. A topping of basil and strips of fragrant Makrut lime leaf contrast the peanutty stick-to-your-ribs aspect of this dish. Thick, sweet, tasty, and commonly paired with chicken.

FRESH POMEGRANATE JUICE
Juice stands abound in the street markets of Thailand, and no juice is quite as easy to spot as that of the pomegranate. Squeezed fresh, it's tart, blood-red, and quenching. Some stands may sell pre-squeezed juice or may add in other flavors or juices. If you want to make sure you get the real stuff, find a stand that makes the juice in front of you.

PANDAN CAKE
This treat combines the comfort and familiarity of sponge cake with the distinctly Southeast Asian addition of the juice of the beloved pandan plant, which is extracted by squeezing or pulverizing the long, narrow leaves. Added to pound cake, it provides a shock of green color and a very pleasant aroma.

THAI ICED COFFEE OR TEA
Thai coffee, poured over ice and mixed with thick, sweetened condensed milk, is a favorite thirst quencher in this hot climate. For a similar dose of caffeine and sugar, with a bit more nuance, try *cha yen*, or iced Thai tea. Both of these are easy to find at drink stands and market stalls.

BASIL CHICKEN WITH FRIED EGG

Tossed in a smoking wok with chicken and chilies, basil holds both its texture and flavor to produce a fragrant, herbal stir fry that knocks the socks off of any sad carryout you've had in the past. Park yourself on a stool built for a toddler and always get the fried egg.

KHAO PHAT

Thai fried rice takes on many forms depending on available ingredients and personal preference. What is consistent is that it's made with jasmine rice and has a decidedly Thai flavor palate, meaning you'll find fish sauce, eggs, garlic, onions, and often chopped herbs.

ROLLED ICE CREAM

This Instagram-friendly dessert was born on the streets of Thailand. Soft, near-liquid ice cream is spread on a chilled metal surface and scraped into tightly coiled rolls of deliciousness. Yes, it is super-touristy, but it's also the perfect way to cool down on a sultry Thai night.

Mango sticky rice

LARB

At its core, larb is a simple dish made from finely chopped or ground meat (such as chicken) tossed with chopped mint and cilantro, onion, and chilies, and spritzed with lime juice. Eaten with rice or scooped up with lettuce, it's a wonderful meal and is something you'll seek again and again.

THAI BEER

Singha or Chang are great examples of the kind of beer found all across Asia—light, golden, and easily quaffable and the perfect match for hot and humid weather and flavorful, spicy food.

MANGO STICKY RICE

That most ubiquitous of Thai desserts, mango sticky rice is a pile of sweet and starchy short-grain rice topped by fresh mango, drizzled with sweetened coconut milk, and often studded with puffed rice. Don't be surprised if the mango is wildly better than anything you've had in the past—India and Southeast Asia produce some of the best mangoes in the world, including varieties that are too fragile to ship to other places. Eat it while you can; it's not going to be this good back home.

What to Buy in Thailand

COCONUT EVERYTHING
Straw-ready fresh coconuts are on the menu at most Thai restaurants and often sold on the beach and on the street. The country's production of coconuts—more than 750,000 tons annually—means grocery shelves are laden with fresh coconut water, shredded coconut, chips, milk, moisturizer, candy, baked goods, ice cream, and coconut oil.

PARASOLS
Save for a few months in northern Thailand, it's always hot and the sun is *strong*. In addition to sunscreen, make like the Thais and use a parasol to protect yourself. You can find them at markets in Bangkok and Phuket, and Bo Sang, just outside Chiang Mai's city center, is umbrella central.

HILL TRIBE HANDICRAFTS
Hill tribe handicrafts abound in Chiang Mai, and these purses, clothing, home goods, and silver jewelry make great gifts. For bolts of hill tribe fabric, trim, embroidery, and beads, go to Chiang Mai's fabric district and look for stalls run by hill tribe women. Or hire a guide and drive out to villages deep in the countryside to buy textiles directly from them.

COTTON TEXTILES
Thai silk gets most of the attention, but skilled artisans in Thailand also produce beautiful cotton textiles. It has a few advantages over silk: it's less costly, it's heartier, and it's more versatile. The patterns vary; you'll find slim stripes, batik, and *mudmee* (Thai ikat).

LOCAL ALCOHOL
Among the country's many craft beers are Full Moon and its popular Chalawan Pale Ale, Taopiphop and its saison, and Dirty Forty's light-bodied pilsner, all stocked in convenience stores. For local rum, look for Chalong Bay and Magic Alambicrum brands. For gin, Bangkok-brewed Iron Balls gin.

SPICES

All grocery stores sell a good selection of spices, and Bangkok's Little India, Pahurat, has various spice shops. Look for curry paste, Kaffir leaves, and galangal for curries, lemongrass for soups and curries, pandan leaves for desserts, and bird's eye chili and crushed chili for everything.

BEAUTY PRODUCTS

Thai beauty products may not get as much attention as Korean or French, but you should still plan to shop. Look for Sunsilk hair masks, Water Angel masks, Smooth E cleansers, and Lansing eye creams and serums. Read packaging carefully, as some products have whitening cream in them. Shop chain pharmacies, Siam Center mall, Beauty Buffet, and Oriental Princess.

WOOD FURNITURE AND ACCESSORIES

Carved wood sculptures and pretty baskets made of water hyacinth are widely available, but for wooden furniture and accessories, head to Chiang Mai. Drive out to Baan Tawai Village in Han Dong, where vendors sell custom teak and mango furniture and can arrange shipping.

COFFEE

Thailand grows Arabica beans in the north and Robusta in the south, with Arabica being the most popular. Go to Chiang Mai or Chiang Rai and arrange a coffee tour where you can buy beans directly from farmers and sip their brews on the spot. If you just want to sip a good cup and bring home a few bags of excellent beans, hit up specialty coffee shops in Chiang Mai and Bangkok.

SILK

You can buy pretty scarves at most markets but don't pay for authentic silk when you're likely getting polyester. In Bangkok, the Museum of Textiles and Jim Thompson House are reputable places to buy silk, as is Lamphun outside Chiang Mai.

Best Festivals in Thailand

YI PENG, NOVEMBER

This Chiang Mai festival of lanterns features the release of thousands of candlelit lanterns into the night sky in a magical scene that will take your breath—and the previous year's bad luck and misfortunes—away. Highlights include candlelit streets and Buddhist purification ceremonies.

UBON RATCHATHANI CANDLE FESTIVAL, JULY

Held at Thung Si Muang, this candle-carving festival marks the beginning of Buddhist Lent. Historically, monks carved ornate designs into donated candles. Today, there are competitions, festivities, and a procession that includes giant candles and the Royal Candle.

LOY KRATONG, NOVEMBER

This festival of lights falls on the full moon, and marks the end of the rainy season. Participants release lotus-shaped lanterns onto rivers to signify a release of past negative thoughts. The best places to witness this sacred ritual are Bangkok, Chiang Mai, and Old Sukhothai.

SONGKRAN, APRIL

Thailand's biggest and wettest festival marks the beginning of the Thai New Year on the Buddhist calendar. During this time locals and visitors throw buckets of water on each other, spray passersby with water pistols, and catapult water balloons. Although less fun, it's also customary to spend time with your elders.

FULL MOON PARTY, MONTHLY

This is one of Thailand's most notorious festivals held on the island of Koh Phangan, next to Koh Samui. This rowdy all-night dance party starts at sunset on Haad Rin Beach and continues until dawn with a variety of music, dancers, and fire performers.

WONDERFRUIT MUSIC AND ARTS FESTIVAL, DECEMBER

Music lovers and free spirits flock to The Fields at Siam Country Club in the seaside city of Pattaya for Thailand's high-concept, eco-friendly Burning Man. Events include musical performances from a mix of international and local acts, interactive art installations, banquets by award-winning chefs, workshops on everything from wellness to sustainable architecture, and more. The four-day, carefully curated festival of experiences is 24 hours a day, cashless, and plastic-free.

A parade float in Chiang Mai's Flower Festival.

VEGETARIAN FESTIVAL, OCTOBER

This nine-day holiday from meat and other indulgences is an act of purification in the Chinese community and taken to extremes in Phuket, where acts like walking barefoot on hot coals, putting swords through cheeks, and other acts of self-mutilation represent carrying the sins of the community. Rituals are accompanied by fireworks, drums, processions, and delicious vegetarian cuisine. Not for the weak of heart or stomach.

CHIANG MAI FLOWER FESTIVAL, FEBRUARY

A three-day floral extravaganza to mark the end of the cold season, this colorful celebration held in Chiang Mai features the local Damask rose and extravagant displays of white and yellow chrysanthemums. The not-to-miss activity is the Saturday morning parade with blooming floats and dancers.

BIG MOUNTAIN MUSIC FESTIVAL, DECEMBER

Thailand's largest and most popular music festival brings more than 70,000 people to The Ocean Khao Yai in Phetchaburi Province. Over the course of two days, there are more than 200 performers on nine stages, including musicians and acts from around the world. Thai bands and artists prevail at BNFF, including Luk-Thung country music, Moh-Lam folk songs, and also modern genres.

CHINESE NEW YEAR, JANUARY OR FEBRUARY

Yaowaraj, Bangkok's Chinatown, is the place to be for the giant annual party in the street to kick off Chinese New Year. Ornate dragon dancers, firecrackers, and elaborate, delicious Chinese banquets are everywhere, and people are dressed in red to ward off Nien, a mythical beast.

Best Temples and Ruins in Thailand

DOI SUTHEP
Legend has it that this gilded temple inside Chiang Mai's Doi Suthep National Park was built here in the late 14th century because an elephant carrying religious relics from Chiang Mai climbed up to the 3,542-foot summit and decided to stay. To get here, climb 304 steps, the staircase flanked by 16th-century balustrades in the shape of nagas (mythical snakes), or hop on the funicular.

WAT BENCHAMABOPHIT
Built in 1899 and designed by the half-brother of then-king Chulalongkorn, this active temple with resident monks is one of Thailand's most dazzling temples with its glorious Italian Carrara marble courtyard, pillars, and its stepped-out roof and ornate finials.

AYUTTHAYA
Ayutthaya was the capital of Thailand (then Siam) for more than 400 years, until it was succeeded by Bangkok in the 18th century. Despite its destruction by the Burmese in 1767, many of the stupas, temples, and carvings that fill the Historic City of Ayutthaya, a UNESCO World Heritage Site, are remarkably well preserved.

LOPBURI
The ancient city of Lopburi, now inhabited by a lively population of monkeys, features important ruins from the 12th century onward, when Lopburi (then Lavo) became part of the Khmer empire. Of special note are Wat Phra Sri Rattana Mahathat (12C), Prang Sam Yot (early 13C), and Bahn Vichien (17C).

SANCTUARY OF TRUTH
Part temple, part art installation, and part cultural monument, construction on this temple in Pattaya began in 1981 and isn't done yet, though tours are possible. The building is made completely out of wood, and covered in carvings of Thai, Khmer, Chinese, and Indian religious iconography.

WAT KU TAO
This rarely visited temple in Chiang Mai was built in 1613 to inter the remains of Tharawadi Min, son of King Bayin-naung, who ruled the then-Lanna kingdom from 1578 to 1607. The temple incorporates Burmese design elements and a distinctive chedi (stupa) made up of five stone spheres, rising largest to smallest.

WAT ARUN
The sparkling Temple of Dawn, bedecked in a mosaic of broken porcelain, is one of Bangkok's most breathtaking sights. It's named after the Hindu god Aruna, often personified as the glow of the rising sun, and its most iridescent moments are at sunrise and dusk, when the light reflects off the Chao Phraya River.

WAT RONG KHUN
Chiang Rai's striking white Marble Temple is a symbol of modern Thailand: a glittering contemporary art installation by Chaloemchai Kositpipat, built in the late 1990s to look like a Buddhist temple. The temple's intricately carved exterior is white to symbolize Buddha's purity.

SUKHOTHAI HISTORI-CAL PARK
A massive, late-20th-century restoration project created the impressive Sukhothai Historical Park, a UNESCO World Heritage Site that comprises the partially restored ruins of historical sites across five zones. The central zone was the royal part of the city and contains 21 temples interspersed among lotus-covered pools, canals, and greenery.

WAT PHO
Just off the Chao Phraya River, next to Bangkok's Grand Palace, this temple is home to a 150-foot gold reclining Buddha with 10-foot feet inlaid in mother-of-pearl. The complex also holds Bangkok's oldest university, with a monk-run Thai massage school.

Best Temples and Ruins in Cambodia and Laos

WAT OUNALOM, CAMBODIA

This 15th-century temple is admired for its beauty and respected as the center for Cambodian Buddhism. The highlight is a cheddai dating to Angkorian times and said to contain hair from one of the Buddha's eyebrows.

PLAIN OF JARS, LAOS

Little is known of the people who carved the hundreds, possibly thousands, of huge sandstone containers strewn across fields around the town of Phonsavan. These giant ancient vessels are swathed in mystery and surrounded by country-side that is scarred by the "Secret War."

PHA THAT LUANG, LAOS

This 147-foot-high, gilded stupa is the nation's most important cultural symbol, representing the unity of the Lao people. Built in 1566 by King Setthathirat to guard a relic of the Buddha's hair, the complex includes two brilliantly decorated temple halls and a long reclining Buddha.

PAK OU CAVES, LAOS

Set in limestone cliffs above where the rivers Mekong and Nam Ou meet, these two caves are filled with thousands of 16th-century Buddha statues. Both caves are reached by staircases, so the climb isn't difficult; your entrance fee includes a guide and flashlight, which you'll need for the dark upper cave. It's best to arrive via a tranquil boat ride along the Mekong.

WAT PHOU, LAOS

Wat Phou translates to Mountain Temple, and it's built on three levels, with 11th to 13th century ruins on the lower and middle. This was originally a Hindu temple, later converted to Buddhism, so you'll see carvings on the lintels of deities Vishnu and Shiva. While level two has most of the impressive ruins, it's up top that you'll find the sanctuary, impressive stone carvings of an elephant and a crocodile, and views to the Mekong.

ANGKOR WAT, CAMBODIA

Arguably the most famous temple in Cambodia, if not all of Asia, Angkor Wat is one of approximately 50 temples within the Angkor Archeological Park, a UNESCO World Heritage Site. It has impressed visitors for nearly 1,000 years, with construction dating from sometime between BC 1113 and 1150. Originally a Hindu temple dedicated to Vishnu, Angkor Wat was converted to a Buddhist temple in the 14th century and later served as the capital of the Khmer empire.

The Banyon temple in Angkor, Cambodia.

TA PROHM, CAMBODIA
This expansive Buddhist temple near Tonle Bati, outside Phnom Penh, was first built around the mid-12th century and while it is maintained like all Angkor temples, the undisturbed roots of large banyan, fig, and kapok trees appear to grasp it mightily. Wooden walkways have been installed around the jungle's attempts to reclaim the temple.

BAYON, CAMBODIA
It's ok to feel uneasy at Bayon—with over 200 smiling stone faces staring at you, this Buddhist shrine is unlike anywhere else. Scholars believe the faces are all representations of Jayavarman VII, a powerful Khmer king of the late 12th century, and perhaps are a testament to the power of ego. Many well-preserved mythological scenes are still visible in the temple's bas-reliefs.

PHNOM BANAN, CAMBODIA
Despite years of neglect and pillaging, this Angkor-era mountaintop temple is still worth a visit for its stunning views and intricate carvings. From the top of the temple, gaze out over lush rice fields, traditional villages, and dramatic mountains. Notable architectural features include carved lintels above doorways, and the five distinctive, intact towers of the temple, a key architectural element of Khmer temple design.

BUDDHA PARK, LAOS
Created by a shaman-artist in the 1950s, this delightful park just outside Vientiane features some 200 Buddhist and Hindu sculptures in all sizes and poses. Enter the mouth of a demon head and climb its three floors—representing hell, heaven, and Earth—for great views.

Best Natural Wonders in Cambodia and Laos

TONLE SAP LAKE, CAMBODIA
One of Southeast Asia's biggest lakes, the Tonle Sap swells and shrinks seasonally based on fluctuations in the Mekong's water levels. Once a year, the lake's tributary experiences a reversal of flow that Cambodians celebrate with an exciting festival, Bon Om Touk, in November.

KOH RONG, CAMBODIA
One of the biggest islands off the southwest Cambodian coast still resists major development, and boasts 23 soft sand beaches where the bungalows and small resorts prefer to remain low-key. Find dense jungle with great trekking and over 15 dive sites and stretches of reef offshore.

THE MEKONG RIVER, LAOS
The Mekong River has been Laos's lifeline for centuries and the stretch from Huay Xai to Luang Prabang remains the most popular way to experience the slow lifestyle of local river communities. The two-day trip stops in the village of Pak Beng before docking at Luang Prabang.

PHONGSALY, LAOS
This remote, less trafficked extreme northern corner of an already quiet country has some of Laos's most spectacular mountains, as well as dense forests containing an abundance of animal, bird, insect, and plant life. Trekking to the remote villages through these forest-covered roads and past rushing rivers is as close to the thrill of exploring virgin territory as it comes.

THAM KHONG LOR CAVE, LAOS
Over 200 miles south of Vientiane, the bustling Mekong River port of Tha Khek is known for its access to stunning surrounding countryside and access to natural attractions in Phu Hin Bun National Park, including the Blue Lagoon and the phenomenal Thanm Khong Lor cave. Riding a narrow boat through the dark, impressively long cave for up to an hour and then emerging to a wide green river, framed by lush green vegetation and limestone cliffs—and maybe buffalo cooling in the water—is an otherworldly experience.

TAD KOUANG SI FALLS, LAOS
An hour tuk-tuk ride from Luang Prabang, these stunning tiered falls offer cascades of milky-blue waters tumbling from lush jungle into perfectly formed pools where visitors can take a refreshing dip. Hike to the top where you will find quieter pools, incredible views of Lao countryside, and beautiful forest.

Kuang Si Falls, Laos

YEAK LAOM LAKE, CAMBODIA

This mystical lake, sacred to the Khmer Loeu hill tribes, occupies a volcanic crater and is bordered by lush jungle. The emerald-hued lake is almost perfectly round, extremely clear, and very clean. There are hammocks in huts lining its shore and wooden jetties from which to launch yourself into the cool waters. Nature trails wind along the lakeside. A walk around the perimeter takes about forty minutes. Midway along the track, at the western end of the lake, there is a small visitor center where you can find local handicrafts; proceeds go directly to the local communities.

KAMPI (NEAR KRATIE), CAMBODIA

The stretch of the Mekong running from Kampi, just north of Kratie, all the way to Laos is populated with the endangered freshwater Irrawaddy dolphins. Catching a glimpse of these rare creatures is thrilling.

VIRACHEY NATIONAL PARK, CAMBODIA

A lush scenic jungle, best experienced on a tour so that you can spot rare wildlife, this park is home to an impressive two-tier waterfall, Bu Sra waterfall, a pristine and popular bathing and picnic spot. In Bang Lung, book at least a three-day trek led by English-speaking rangers for an authentic jungle experience.

KULEN MOUNTAIN, CAMBODIA

This most sacred mountain in Cambodia, north of Angkor Wat, is a rewarding spot for a day hike with gorgeous water-falls, archaeological sites such as the River of a Thousand Lingas which is strewn with phallic carvings, and the giant reclining Buddha in Preah Ang Thom.

Introduction to Thai Architecture

You'd be hard-pressed to find a visitor to Thailand who doesn't spend at least a little time staring in amazement at the country's glittering wats and ornate palaces—and the elegant sculptures of the mythical beasts that protect them.

WATS

Wat is the Thai name for what can range from a simple ordination hall for monks and nuns to a huge sprawling complex comprising libraries, bell towers, and meditation rooms. Usually the focal point for a community, it's not unusual for a wat to also be the grounds for village fêtes and festivals. Although most wats you come across symbolize some aspect of Thai-style Theravada Buddhism, examples of other architectural styles are relatively easy to find: Khmer ruins dot the Isan countryside to the east, while northern Thailand showcases many Burmese-style temples.

Wats are erected as acts of merit—allowing the donor to improve his karma and perhaps be reborn as a higher being—or in memory of great events. You can tell much about a wat's origin by its name. A wat *luang* (royal wat), for example, was constructed or restored by royals and may have the words *rat, raja,* or *racha* in its name (e.g., Ratburana or Rajapradit). The word *phra* may indicate that a wat

contains an image of the Buddha. Wats that contain an important relic of the Buddha have the words *maha* (great) and *that* (relic) in their names. Thailand's nine major wat mahathats are in Chiang Rai, Chai Nat, Sukhothai, Phisanulk, Ayutthaya, Bangkok, Yasothon, Phetchaburi, and Nakhon Si Thammarat.

Thai wats, especially in the later periods, were seldom planned as entire units, so they often appear disjointed and crowded. To appreciate a wat's beauty you often have to look at its individual buildings.

Perhaps the most recognizable feature of a wat, and certainly a useful landmark when hunting them down, is the towering conelike *chedi*. Originally used to hold relics of the Buddha (hair, bones, or even nails), chedis can now be built by anyone with enough cash to house their ashes. At the base of the chedi you can find three platforms representing hell, Earth, and heaven, while the 33 Buddhist heavens are symbolized at the top of the tallest spire by a number of rings.

The main buildings of a wat are the *bot*, which contains a Buddha image and functions as congregation and ordination hall for the monks, and the *viharn*, which serves a similar function, but will hold the most important Buddha image. Standard bot and viharn roofs will feature three steeply curved levels featuring red, gold, and green tiles; the outer walls range from highly decorated to simply whitewashed.

Other noticeable features include the *mondop, prang,* and *ho trai.* Usually square with a pyramid-shape roof, the mondop is reminiscent of Indian temple architecture and serves as a kind of storeroom for holy artifacts, books, and ceremonial objects. The prang is a tall tower similar to the chedi, which came to Thailand by way of the Khmer empire and is used to store images of the Buddha. Easily identifiable by its stilts or raised platform, the ho trai is a library for holy scriptures.

Roofs, which are covered in glazed clay tiles or wooden shakes, generally consist of three overlapping sections, with the lower roof set at gentle slopes, increasing to a topmost roof with a pitch of 60 degrees. Eave brackets in the form of a *naga* (snakes believed to control the irrigation waters of rice fields) with its head at the bottom often support the lower edges of the roofs. Along the eaves of many roofs are a row of small brass bells with clappers attached to thin brass pieces shaped like Bodhi tree leaves.

During the early Ayutthaya period (1350–1767), wat interiors were illuminated by the light passing through vertical slits in the walls (wider, more elaborate windows would have compromised the strength of the walls and, thus, the integrity of the structure). In the Bangkok period (1767–1932), the slits were replaced by proper windows set below wide lintels that supported the upper portions of the brick walls. There are usually five, seven, or nine windows on a side in accordance with the Thai preference for odd numbers. The entrance doors are in the end wall facing the Buddha image; narrower doors may flank the entrance door.

PALACES
The Grand Palace has been the official residence of the Kings of Siam (and later Thailand) since 1782. Shots of the palace with its gleaming spires flood-lighted up at night fill every postcard stand, and it's arguably Bangkok's single most important tourist attraction.

Built in 1782 when King Rama I chose Bangkok as Siam's new capital, the Grand Palace is the only remaining example of early Ratanakosin architecture—Rama II and III chose not to initiate any large-scale construction projects in the face of economic hardship. A primarily functional collection of buildings, the compound contains the Royal Thai Decorations and Coin Pavilion, the Museum of Fine Art, and the Weapons Museum.

Also worth checking out while in the capital is what is believed to be the world's largest golden teak-wood building. The three-story Vimanmek Palace was moved from Chonburi in the east to Bangkok's Dusit Palace, and contains jewelry and gifts given as presents from around the world.

Rama IV led the revival of palace construction in the second half of the 19th century, overseeing the building of several royal getaways. Perhaps the most impressive of these is Phra Nakhon Khiri in the southern town of Phetchaburi. Known locally as Khao Wang, the palace sits atop a mountain with wonderful panoramic views. Sharing its mountain home are various wat, halls, and thousands of macaque monkeys. Klai Kangwon in nearby Hua Hin is still used as a seaside getaway for the royal family and as a base when they visit southern provinces. Built in 1926 by Rama VI, the two-story concrete palace's name translates as Far From Worries and was built in the style of European châteaux.

HOUSES
Traditional Thai houses are usually very simple and essentially boil down to three basic components: stilts, a deck, and a sloping roof. Heavy, annual monsoon rains all over the country necessitate that living quarters be raised on stilts to escape flooding; in the dry season the space under the house is typically used as storage for farming equipment or other machinery. The deck of the house is essentially the living room—it's where you can find families eating, cooking, and just plain relaxing.

As with wats, it's often the roofs of houses that are the most interesting. Lanna-style (northern Thailand) roofs, usually thatched or tiled, are thought to have evolved from the Thai people's roots in southern China, where steeply pitched roofs would have been needed to combat heavy snows. Although there's no real chance of a snowball fight in Thailand, the gradient and overhang allows for quick runoff of the rains and welcome shade from the sun.

These basics are fairly uniform throughout the country, with a few small adjustments to accommodate different climates. For example, roofs are steepest in areas with more intense weather patterns, like the Central Plains, and northern Thai houses have smaller windows to conserve heat better.

Thai Massage

Thai massage, once only available at temples or tiny shophouses, has become much more popular in recent years. You'll find masseurs and masseuses at work all over the country—in bustling markets, at boutique spas, and in jungle hideaways.

Today massage is a pleasant and relaxing part of Thai culture, and you may see locals giving casual shoulder, back, and arm massages to their friends. But *nuad paen boran* (ancient massage) is also a branch of traditional Thai medicine. Originally it was taught and performed in Thai temples, which were historically places of physical—as well as spiritual—healing.

Traditional massage combines acupressure, reflexology, yoga, and meditation. Practitioners believe that 10 energy lines, called *sip sen,* link the body's meridian points. Blocked lines may lead to physical or spiritual ailments. Massage is thought to unblock the energy lines, clearing toxins and restoring balance to the body.

WHERE TO GET MASSAGE

Outdoors: At markets, on beaches, and at temple fairs, masseurs and masseuses set up shop alongside street vendors. On the beach you'll lie on a mat; at the market you'll probably be seated in a streetside plastic or lounge chair set up for foot massage. Prices vary—a one-hour foot massage might cost as little as B100 at a temple fair or B250 on a popular beach.

Resort and Hotel Spas: For five-star pampering, head to upscale hotels and resorts, whose luxurious, tranquil spas offer an extensive array of massages, including Swedish massage, plus other treatments like tai chi and new-age therapies. Expect to pay at least B2,500 or more for an hour-long massage at a top

Bangkok hotel—a lot by Thai standards, but still less than what you'd pay back home.

Restrooms: In a few clubs and bars (both gay and straight), some visitors are alarmed when men's restroom attendants start massaging their shoulders as they stand at the urinal. If you don't like it, ask them to stop (*mai ow, kup*). Otherwise, a B10 tip is welcome.

Shophouses: These ubiquitous massage parlors offer no-frills service. Expect to share a room with other patrons (curtains separate the cots); if you're getting a foot massage, you may be seated in the shop window. There's often music, TV, or chatter in the background. A two-hour massage costs at least B400. Though many shophouses are legitimate businesses, some offer "extra" sexual services. To avoid embarrassing misunderstandings, steer clear of treatments with suggestive names, like "special" or "full body" massage. You can also ask the concierge at your hotel to recommend a reputable place.

Temples: Some temples still have massage facilities, and massages are often provided to the elderly at no charge. At Wat Pho in Bangkok you can receive a massage in an open-air pavilion for B420 an hour.

Urban Spas: A growing phenomenon, urban spas are more upscale than shophouse parlors. They're often located in old Thai houses, with contemporary Asian-style private treatment rooms. You'll have more options here: simple Thai massage is still on the menu (for B1,000 and up per hour), along with body scrubs, facials, and various other treatments.

THE MOVES

Thai massage is an extremely rigorous, sometimes painful experience, and people with back, neck, or joint problems should not undergo it without seeking medical advice first. But it can also be very pleasurable. It's okay to ask if you want softer pressure (*bow bow, kup/ka*).

Massage artists primarily work with their hands, but they sometimes use elbows, knees, and feet to perform deep-tissue kneading. They occasionally apply balm to ease muscle aches, but they traditionally don't use oil. They may push and pull your body through a series of often contorted yogic stretching movements. There's normally a set sequence: you start lying on your back and the massage artist will work from your feet through your legs, arms, hands, and fingers. Then you turn over for legs, back, neck, head, and face. At the end the masseur will stretch your back across his or her upturned knees. Some people find that they have better flexibility after a massage, in addition to relief from muscular aches.

Massages are booked by the hour, and aficionados say two hours is best to get the full benefit. In most shophouse parlors the masseuse will first bathe your feet and then give you a pair of pajamas to wear. Spas have shower facilities. You can remove your underwear or not—whatever makes you comfortable.

The standard varies enormously. If you find a masseur or masseuse you like, take his or her name (sometimes they'll have an identifying number as well) and return to that person the next time.

TIPPING

Tipping is customary. There aren't hard-and-fast rules about how much to tip, but B50 to B150 at a shophouse, and 10% to 20% in a spa, is about right.

ALTERNATIVE MASSAGE

Foot massage: This popular treatment is typically a half-hour or hour-long massage of the feet and lower legs, usually with oil or balm. Foot massage is based on the reflexology principle that manipulating pressure points in the feet can relieve disorders in other parts of the body.

Oil Massage: Most parlors and spas now offer oil massage, which is a gentler treatment based on Swedish massage and doesn't involve stretching. Masseurs will sometimes use oils with delicious aromas, such as lemongrass or jasmine.

LEARN THE ART OF MASSAGE

Bangkok's Wat Pho is an acknowledged instruction center with an almost 200-year pedigree. A five-day, 30-hour course costs B9,500. You can get more information on their website (*www.watpomassage.com*). The Thai Massage School in Chiang Mai (*www.tmcschool.com*) is also good. Many shophouse parlors in both cities now also offer courses (a one-hour session at a Khao San Road shophouse costs about B250).

Thailand Today

ROYALTY AND THE GOVERNMENT

Thailand is a constitutional monarchy, in which the prime minister is head of government and the king head of state; in practice, the country is at present ruled by the government. Beloved King Bhumibol Adulyadej (King Rama IX), the world's longest-reigning head of state, died in October 2016 and the country was in mourning for a year. He was succeeded by his only son, Prince Vajiralongkorn. Politically, Thailand is a country divided and recent years have seen a fair amount of chaos. Prayuth Chan-ocha remains prime minister of Thailand after winning a 2019 election mired in controversial delays and irregularities. In early 2020, student activists began organizing thousands-strong rallies making unprecedented demands for monarchy reform and the government to step down. Several clashes between protesters and police have occurred, and the imprisonment of activists for violating lèse-majesté laws have led to high criticism of the current Thai government from international human rights organizations. Note that Thailand's politics barely impact tourism, save for protests in Bangkok leading to traffic jams.

ETHNIC DIVERSITY

Throughout its history, Thailand has absorbed countless cultural influences, and is home to groups with Chinese, Tibetan, Lao, Khmer, Malaysian, Burmese, and other origins. Migrating tribes from modern-day China, Cambodia, Myanmar, and the Malay Peninsula were the region's earliest inhabitants. Ancient trade routes meant constant contact with merchants traveling from India, China, and other parts of Southeast Asia. Conflicts and treaties continue to alter the country's borders and ethnicity. Contemporary Thailand's cultural richness comes from its ethnic diversity. Though Buddhism is the predominant religion, Hindu and animist influences abound, and there's a significant Muslim population in the south. Malay is spoken in the southern provinces, Lao and Khmer dialects of Thai are spoken in the northeast, and the hill tribes have their own dialects as well.

MYSTICISM

Many Thais believe in astrology and supernatural energy. The animist element of Thai spirituality dictates that everything, from buildings to trees, has a spirit. With so many spirits and forces out there, it's no surprise that appeasing them is a daily consideration. Thais often wear amulets blessed by monks to ward off evil, and they believe that tattoos, often of real or mythical animals or magic spells, bring strength and protect the wearer. Car license plates with lucky numbers (such as multiple nines) sell for thousands of baht; important events, such as weddings, house moves, and even births, are arranged, when possible, to fall on auspicious days, which are either divined by shamans or consist of lucky numbers. Newspapers solemnly report that politicians have consulted their favorite astrologers before making critical policy decisions. Businesses erect shrines to powerful deities outside their premises, sometimes positioned to repel the power of their rivals' shrines.

THE IMPORTANCE OF SANUK

That's the word for Thai fun. Thais believe that every activity should be fun—work, play, even funerals. Of course, this isn't always practical, but it's a worthy aim. Thais enjoy being together in large parties, making lots of noise, and—as sanuk nearly always involves food—eating. They are also guided by a number of other behavior principles. Many, such as *jai yen* (cool heart) and *mai pen rai* (never mind), are rooted in the Buddhist philosophies of detachment, and result in a nonconfrontational demeanor and an easygoing attitude. Giving and sharing are important, since being generous is an act of merit making, a way of storing up points for protection in this life and in future lives.

ART, CREATIVITY, AND FUN

Thailand has always had a flair for art, creativity, and fun. You'll find that today in everything from fashion to interior design to the clever ads blaring across BTS stations as you wait for your train. Sophisticated Thai architects and designers create some of the world's most inviting spaces, using a mix of traditional materials (teak, silk, stone, clay) with modern elements and elegant styling. Visit a chic spa for a perfect example of this. This is a country oriented toward youth, and young Thais are as hip and connected as ever, wearing the trendiest clothes and obsessing with the latest digital devices. There's a rapidly growing contemporary art scene scattered across Bangkok (check out the Museum of Contemporary Art and the Bangkok Art and Culture Centre) and in the university area of Chiang Mai.

Food in Thailand is always trendy, and city chefs are adept at mixing Thai flavors with other cuisines, though that hasn't displaced the myriad street stalls slinging delicious, inexpensive Thai comfort fare; street eats never go out of style, with several stalls attracting international awards and attention. Bangkok's drinking scene has evolved in recent years, too, to include an influx of wine bars and craft beer venues that cater to locals and foreigners alike. And perhaps no other metropolis on earth has quite the collection of rooftop sky bars as

Bangkok—don't miss a cocktail on an open-air patio 30 floors or more above the cacophony below.

If alcohol isn't your thing, Thailand is awash with slick third-wave coffee shops catering to java connoisseurs. These days you'll never have to go without that work-of-art cappuccino in a Thai city. But some things never change. Bangkok is—and likely always will be—a city to experience on the street. There's no better way to get a feel for Bangkok than to spend the day jostling with crowds on the sidewalks, grazing from one food stall to the next, people-watching all the way. Too hot? Tired feet? There's always an air-conditioned shopping mall around the next corner. Step inside and catch an ear-splittingly loud blockbuster movie before heading back into the chaos. Another thing never seems to change in Thailand: despite the country's repeated, ongoing political troubles, tourism and development seem never to stop. Thailand is consistently a favorite pick among foreign visitors, year after year.

IMPACT OF COVID-19 ON THAILAND

Thailand was hit hard by COVID-19. The government imposed a state of alarm, closed its borders, and enforced heavy restrictions. All of this had a huge effect on an economy that relies heavily on tourism. In late 2021, international travelers began to be allowed to enter Thailand again and the country looks optimistically toward a revival of tourism.

What to Read and Watch

PREMIKA

This gloriously absurd Thai horror-comedy romp by Thai director Siwakorn Jarupongpa boldly asks the question: What if being bad at karaoke had consequences? *Deadly* consequences.

TROPICAL MALADY

This Cannes Jury Prize winner by one of Thailand's leading experimental film-makers, Apichatpong Weerasethakul, is a blissfully unconventional work and a beguiling meditation on love and the animalistic nature of mankind.

THE OVERTURE

Based on the life of legendary court musician and master of the *ranad-ek* (Thai xylophone) Luang Pradit Pairo, this 2004 period drama takes place in the late 19th-century through the 1930s, when the playing of such music was banned by the government.

SHUTTER

After fleeing from the scene of a hit-and-run, a Bangkok photographer, Tun, and his frightened wife, Jane, are haunted by a ghostly figure that appears in the background of his pictures. Unrelenting dread permeates every frame of this 2004 horror movie from Thai filmmakers Banjong Pisanthanakun and Parkpoom Wongpoom.

ONG BAK: MUAY THAI WARRIOR

No CGI. No wires. Just inventive stunts and world-class fight choreography. The plot follows Ting (Tony Jaa) as he leaves his rural home for the big city of Bangkok in order to retrieve the stolen head of a sacred Buddha statue. Jaa's martial arts skills here drew comparisons to Bruce Lee and Jackie Chan.

THE LIONESS IN BLOOM: MODERN THAI FICTION ABOUT WOMEN

The short stories and excerpted novels in this collection explore topics as diverse as their Thai authors. Some are humorous and witty, some are bleak and heartbreaking. But they all provide a well-rounded look at what womanhood means to the women of Thailand.

FOUR REIGNS BY KUKRIT PRAMOJ

This historical novel follows the life of Phloi, who arrives at the royal palace as a young girl and minor courtier, and follows her as she experiences the reigns of four Chakri Kings. As Phloi observes the massive upheaval that culminated in the 1932 coup that forced the dissolution of the monarchy, she must figure out how she, too, must adapt to the new age.

HUSH! A THAI LULLABY BY MINFONG HO

In this atmospheric Caldecott Honor–winning children's book, written in verse and charmingly illustrated, a mother entreats the animals that surround her home to be quiet and still as her baby sleeps. By book's end the mother and all the animals are sleeping but baby, of course, is wide-awake.

JASMINE NIGHTS BY S. P. SOMTOW

This semi-autobiographical novel, set in the early 1960s, follows a young boy named Justin (nicknamed Little Frog) as he navigates between two lives. One is on his family's estate where he lives in the care of his eccentric aunts. The other takes him into a ruined house where he makes a game weaving science fiction, Homer, and spirits out of Thai mythology.

SIGHTSEEING BY RATTAWUT LAPCHAROENSAP

This collection of short stories marks the debut of Rattawut Lapcharoensap, a Thai-American writer who was only 26 at the time of its publication. Set in contemporary Thailand, Lapcharoensap's characters are sharply drawn and his stories illuminate the beauty in even the bleakest of places.

COUPS & THE KING
THAILAND'S TURBULENT HISTORY

by Karen Coates

Thais share a reverence for their king, Bhumibol Adulyadej, who has been the nation's moral leader and a unifying figure since 1946. Thais are united by a respect for their king—King Rama X who ascended the throne in late 2016 after the death of his father—a deep pride in their country, a constitutional monarchy and the only Southeast Asian nation never colonized by Europeans. But this hasn't stopped political turmoil from roiling beneath the surface and erupting.

Though northeastern Thailand has been inhabited for about 2,500 years, it wasn't until 1238 that Thai princes drove the Cambodian Khmers out of central Thailand and established

Sukhothai, the first centralized Thai state. There was conflict again in the late 14th century, when the rival state of Ayutthaya conquered Sukhothai. After over 400 years of power, Ayutthaya in turn was defeated by the Burmese in the late 18th century, and the Thais established a new capital in Bangkok.

As European influence in Southeast Asia grew, Thailand alternated between periods of isolation and openness to foreign trade and ideas. Western-style democracy was one idea that took hold in the early 20th century. But since then a pattern has emerged in Thai politics: a prime minister is elected, allegations of corruption surface, the public protests, and the leader is ousted.

King Rama V
(1853–1910)
and family

TIMELINE

4,000–2,000 BC Rice first cultivated in Thailand

1238
Sukhothai kingdom
founded

1350
Ayutthaya kingdom
founded

4000 BC   1200   1300   1400

(top) Pottery found at Ban Chiang; (left) stone face at Bayon in Angkor Thom, Cambodia; (bottom) Khmer elephant-shaped box.

Bronze & Rice

4000–2000 BC

Scientists think that northeastern Thailand was a hotbed for agricultural innovation. In fact, the Mon people from modern-day Myanmar who settled in Ban Chiang may have been Asia's first farmers. Archaeologists have found ancient pottery, bronze rings, spearheads, bracelets, and axes.

Great Migrations

500–1400

Historians believe the Thais' ancestors were the ethnic Tai people of southern China. The Tai migrated south into modern-day Thailand in waves, but the biggest southern push came after the Mongols invaded their kingdom in the 13th century. The fleeing Tai settled in the Mekong River Valley, inventing elaborate agricultural systems to farm rice. Around this time, the Khmers of what is today called Cambodia were extending the Angkor empire west into Thailand.

Sukhothai & the Golden Age

1238–1438

In 1238 chieftains established the first Thai kingdom at Sukhothai in central Thailand, kicking out the Khmer overlords. The Sukhothai kingdom united many Thai settlements and marked the beginning of a prosperous era when, legend has it, the rivers were full of fish, and the paddies were lush with rice. In the late 13th century, King Ramkhamhaeng created a writing system that is the basis of the modern Thai alphabet.

1511
Portuguese
arrive

1782
Capital moves to Bangkok
1767
Ayutthaya falls to Burmese invaders

1500 1600 1700

In Focus | COUPS & THE KING

(left) Interior of Wat Po, Bangkok; (top) Royal jewelry from Ayutthaya; (bottom) Buddha statue from Ayutthaya.

Ayutthaya Kingdom

1350–1767

King Ramathibodi founded the kingdom of Ayutthaya, 45 miles up the Chao Phraya River from Bangkok, in 1350 and took over Sukhothai 25 years later. The king made Theravada Buddhism the kingdom's official religion and established the Dharmashastra, a legal code with roots in Hindu Indian texts. Ayutthaya, a city of canals and golden temples, became wealthy and prominent.

European Influence

1511–1800S

The Portuguese were the first Europeans to arrive in Thailand, establishing an embassy in Ayutthaya in 1511. But they brought more than ambassadors: The Portuguese also brought the first chilies to the country, making a huge contribution to Thai cuisine.

Over the following centuries of European trade and relations, Thailand's kings charted a sometimes tenuous course of autonomy as their neighbors were colonized by the Portuguese, Dutch, English, and French.

Burmese Invasion & New Beginnings

1767–1809

In 1767 the Burmese sacked Ayutthaya, destroying palaces, temples, artwork, and written records. But within two years, General Phraya Taksin ran out the Burmese and established a new capital at Thonburi, which is today a part of Bangkok. Taksin became king but was forced from power and executed in 1782. After this coup, Buddha Yodfa Chulaloke the Great (known as Rama I) took control. He moved the capital across the river, where he built the Grand Palace in the image of past Thai kingdoms.

(left) King Mongkut with queen;
(top) *The King and I*;
(bottom) 19th-century tin coin.

The King and I & Beyond

1851–1931

In 1862, Anna Leonowens, an English schoolteacher, traveled to Bangkok with her son to serve as royal governess to King Mongkut's wives and children. Leonowens's memoirs inspired Margaret Landon's controversial novel Anna and the King of Siam, which in turn was the basis for the well-known Broadway musical The King and I and the subsequent film.

Thais were deeply offended by the film, which portrays the king as foolish and barbaric; The King and I was consequently banned in Thailand. A 1999 remake, Anna and the King, followed Leonowens's version of the story more closely, but Thais, who are extremely devoted to their royal family, still found this version culturally insensitive.

Mongkut (or Rama IV) earned the nickname "Father of Science and Technology" for his efforts to modernize the country. He signed a trade treaty with Great Britain, warding off other colonial powers while opening Thailand to foreign innovation.

After Rama IV's death in 1868, his son Chulalongkorn became king. Also called "Rama the Great," Chulalongkorn is credited with preserving Thailand's independence and abolishing slavery.

Constitutional Era

1932–41

Thailand moved toward Western-style democracy when young intellectuals staged a bloodless coup against King Prajadhipok (Rama VII) in 1931. Thailand's first constitution was signed that year and parliamentary elections were held the next. In the new system—a constitutional monarchy similar to England's—the king is still head of state, but he doesn't have much legal power.

In 1939 the government changed the country's name from Siam to Thailand. The new name refers to the Tai people; Tai also means "free" in Thai.

1939 Siam renamed Thailand | 1942 Alliance formed with Japan
1944 Phibun ousted
1932 First elections held | 1946 Rama IX crowned | 1959–75 Vietnam War

1925   1950   1975

(left) Bridge over the River Kwai; (top) U.S. pilot in Vietnam; (bottom) Postage stamp c. 1950 featuring king Bhumibol Adulyadej.

World War II

1941–46

In 1941, Japan helped Thailand win a territorial conflict with France over parts of French Indochina (modern-day Cambodia, Laos, and Vietnam.) Later that year, the Japanese demanded free passage through Thailand so that they could attack Malaya and Burma. In 1942, under the leadership of Phibun, a military general elected prime minister in 1938, Thailand formed an alliance with Japan.

The Japanese conquered Burma and began to construct the Thailand–Burma "Death Railway," so named because over 100,000 Asian forced-laborers and Allied POWs died while working on it. Meanwhile, an underground resistance called Seri Thai gathered strength as Thais turned against the Phibun regime and the Japanese occupation. Phibun was ousted in 1944 and replaced by a government friendly to the Allies.

In 1946 King Rama VIII was murdered. He was succeeded by his brother, the beloved Bhumibol Adulyadej (Rama IX), who was the world's longest serving head of state until his death in late 2016.

The Vietnam War

1961–75

While publicly staying neutral, the Thai government let the U.S. Air Force use bases throughout Thailand to bomb Laos and Cambodia between 1961 and 1975. Meanwhile, Bangkok and Thailand's beaches became playgrounds to thousands of soldiers on leave. The Westernization of Thai popular culture has roots in the Vietnam era, when restaurants and bars catered to beer- and Coke-drinking Americans.

TIMELINE

1973–81 Violence against students and activists

1985

1995

1997
Asian Financial Crisis

2001
Thaksin
Shinawatra
elected

2006
Thaksin
outsted

(left) Protesters occupying the Government House garden. Bangkok, September 3rd 2008; (top) Banner demanding that ousted P.M. Thaksin Shinawatra and his wife return to Thailand to stand trial; (bottom) Samak Sundaravej.

1973–PRESENT

Unrest

A new democracy movement gained force in 1973, when protesters charged the streets of Bangkok after students were arrested on antigovernment charges. On October 14, protests erupted into bloody street battles, killing dozens. More violent outbreaks occurred on October 6th, 1976, and again in "Black May" of 1992, when a military crackdown resulted in more than 50 deaths.

In 2001, billionaire Thaksin Shinawatra was elected prime minister on a platform of economic growth and rural development. The year after he was elected, he dissolved the liaison between the Muslim southern provinces and the largely Buddhist administration in Bangkok, rekindling bloody unrest after years of quiet. The situation escalated until insurgents attacked a Thai army arsenal in early 2004; thousands have been killed in frequent outbursts of violence in southern Thailand.

In September 2006, Thaksin was ousted by a junta, which controlled the country until voters approved a new constitution and elected Samak Sundaravej prime minister. He was forced to resign months later and was quickly replaced by Somchai Wongsawat, Thaksin's brother-in-law.

The protests did not end there. In late 2008 Somchai was forced to step down, and Parliament voted in Abhisit Vejjajiva, leader of the opposition party. Since 2011, anti-government protests have increased, and 2014 saw a coup d'etat and the establishment of a military junta. Thailand's long voyage toward democracy is ongoing.

In 2016, King Bhumibol Adulyadej (Rama IX), the world's longest reigning monarch, died at age 88 after a long illness. The King was immensely popular and commanded great love and respect during his reign. He was seen as a leader who skillfully charted a course that put the monarchy at the center of Thai society, even as the country lurched between political crises and military coups. After a year of mourning, Bhumibol's son and successor, King Rama X or King Maha Vajiralongkorn Bodindradebayavarangkun ascended the throne.

Chapter 2

TRAVEL SMART

Updated by
Barbara Woolsey

★ **CAPITAL:**
Bangkok

👥 **POPULATION:**
70,006,389

$ **CURRENCY:**
Baht

☎ **COUNTRY CODE:**
66

⚠ **EMERGENCIES:**
191

🚗 **DRIVING:**
On the left

⚡ **ELECTRICITY:**
220 volts/50 cycles; wall
outlets take either two flat
prongs or two round prongs

💬 **LANGUAGE:**
Thai

🕐 **TIME:**
12 hours ahead of
New York; 15 hours
ahead of Los Angeles

🌐 **WEB RESOURCES:**
www.tourismthailand.org
www.bangkokpost.com

Know Before You Go

Should you tip? When can you eat? Do you need to plan ahead for the major attractions or can you just show up? We've got answers and a few tips to help you make the most of your visit to this beautiful country.

COVER UP, LADIES

If you're a female traveler, you may be asked to cover your shoulders or knees as a sign of respect at sacred sites. There are also certain beliefs in the Buddhist culture that prohibit women from entering specific temples entirely, as their menstrual cycles are considered unholy. Female travelers should also avoid touching or sitting next to monks.

WATCH WHAT YOU SAY

Any insult against the king or monarchy is an insult against the national religion and patrimony and an illegal offense punishable by jail time. If you don't have something nice to say about the king or his relatives, don't say anything at all.

USE YOUR RIGHT HAND

When possible do not give or receive anything with your left hand; use your right hand and support it lightly at the elbow with your left hand to show greater respect.

REMOVE YOUR SHOES

Always remove your shoes when you enter a home. Do not step over a seated person's legs. Don't point your feet at anyone; keep them on the floor, and take care not to show the soles of your feet (as the lowest part of the body, they are seen by Buddhists as the least holy).

ELEPHANT ENCOUNTERS ARE A NO-NO

You may have visions of riding an elephant through the jungle but a debate is raging in Thailand, and internationally, as to the ethics of such animal interactions so you may want to reconsider that selfie. Tourism perpetuates the captivity of elephants but it also helps fund their care so you see the dilemma. Check your conscience and consider the welfare of these gentle giants before signing up for any kind of animal interaction. If you want to see an elephant in real life, it may be best to visit or volunteer with an organization that is working to rehabilitate these elephants, like the Elephant Nature Park in Chiang Mai. There are also a growing number of sanctuaries where you can observe rescued elephants; ask questions to ensure an ethical experience.

BARGAIN

You will likely spend a pretty penny sorting through handmade treasures to bring a little bit of Thailand home with you but know that the price is often negotiable and Thais respect a good bargainer. Begin by allowing the vendor to make the first offer, and then ask if there is a better price available. Your counter offer should be for about 30% less. From there, you have room to negotiate. If the vendor won't compromise, walking away might do the trick. It is important to note, however, that most vendors make their income from selling these products, so while you shouldn't be short-changed yourself, you also don't want to insult them with a ridiculously low wager. Also, please don't bargain unless you plan to buy.

DON'T DRINK FROM THE TAP

Though you might see locals sipping tap water, there's a good chance your digestive system isn't adjusted to the enzymes present in Thai water. We suggest opting for the bottled stuff, and using bottled or boiled water to brush your teeth.

TAKE THREE

Thais don't like anything done in twos, a number associated with death. Hence, you should buy three mangoes, not two, and stairways have odd numbers of stairs.

SLOW DOWN

Thais aim to live with a "cool heart" or *jai yen*—free from emotional extremes. Since being in a hurry shows an obvious lack of calm, they don't rush and aren't always punctual. Try to leave space in your itinerary for this relaxed attitude, since something will invariably happen to slow your progress.

PARK YOURSELF HERE

Thailand has 127 land and marine national parks with many rare species of flora and fauna. The National Park Wildlife and Plant Conservation Department (*www.portal.dnp.go.th*) has some useful information on facilities, animal-spotting opportunities, notable features like waterfalls, and available cabin rentals or camping areas (you can book accommodation online), plus weather news and updates on which areas are closed. The more easily navigable site, *www.thaina-tionalparks.com*, has even more information.

KID FRIENDLY

Thais dote on kids, so chances are you'll get extra help and attention when traveling with them, and the experience should be relatively problem-free. Powdered, canned, and pasteurized milk are readily available. Stomach bugs and infections thrive in the tropical climate. Basic cleanliness—washing hands frequently and making sure any cuts are

treated with antibacterial ointment and covered—is the best protection against bacteria. Be careful while walking along sidewalks, where open manhole covers and people riding motor-bikes can be hazardous.

THAI MASSAGE

Thai massage is an extremely rigorous, sometimes painful experi-ence, and people with back, neck, or joint problems should not undergo it without seeking medical advice first. But it can also increase flexibility and provide relief to aches and pains. It's okay to ask if you want softer pressure (bow bow, kup/ka). Massages are booked by the hour, and aficionados say two hours is best to get the full benefit. In most shophouse parlors the masseuse will first bathe your feet and then give you a pair of pajamas to wear. You can remove your underwear or not—whatever makes you comfortable.

BATHHOUSE "MASSAGE"

Often classically ornate with names like Posei-don or similar, barnlike bathhouses and saunas are fronts for prostitution. They offer the euphemis-tic "massage" for which Thailand has had a reputa-tion since the Vietnam War. Luckily, they're fairly easy to avoid—masseuses are usually on display behind a glass partition, and the treatment menu will include options like "soapy massage."

PAUSE FOR THE ANTHEM

The national anthem is played twice a day, at 8 am and 6 pm. Every TV and radio station plays it, and it will be played over government building speaker systems, at the sky train and underground in Bangkok, bus stations, in parks, and in most other public places. Stop what you are doing and stand in silence. It takes less than a minute and is a small way to show respect to the Thai people and to the country you are visiting.

DON'T BUY ANYTHING WITH THE BUDDHA ON IT

While it isn't likely that you'll be arrested for buying a key chain featuring the image of the Buddha, you will notice signs through-out various cities that warn against disrespecting this Thai leader. Merchants who print his image on anything—from T-shirts to handbags and magnets—must source these goods from other countries, since Thailand bans the practice. If you want to be mindful of the rules of the region, it's recommended to avoid funding this form of sales. Also, don't get a tattoo of the Buddha; it's consid-ered sacrilegious. If you're planning on buying Buddha statues (over 5 inches tall) you will need to apply for an export permit from the Office of the National Museum. Plan ahead and allow 4 to 5 days for the process. Some shop owners will help you with this process.

Getting Here and Around

Thailand is a long country, geographically, stretching some 1,100 miles north to south. Bangkok is a major Asian travel hub, so you'll likely begin your trip by flying into the capital. Relatively affordable flights are available from Bangkok to every major city in the country, and if you're strapped for time, flying is convenient and generally inexpensive. Train travel, however, where available, can be an enjoyable sightseeing experience if you're not in a rush, and Thailand also has a comprehensive bus system.

Air

Bangkok is 17 hours from San Francisco, 18 hours from Seattle and Vancouver, 20 hours from Chicago, 22 hours from New York, and 10 hours from Sydney. Be sure to check your itinerary carefully if you are flying out of Bangkok—most low-cost carriers and domestic flights operate out of Don Mueang Airport, while Suvarnabhumi Airport remains the international hub. On popular tourist routes during peak holiday times, domestic flights in Thailand are often fully booked. Make sure you reserve well in advance of your travel date.

AIRPORTS

Thailand's gateway to the world, Bangkok, has two airports: Suvarnabhumi (pronounced *soo-wanna-poom*) International Airport (BKK), 30 km (18 miles) southeast of town, and Don Mueang International Airport (DMK), 25 km (15 miles) north of central Bangkok. Don Mueang is Bangkok's secondary international airport, handling both domestic and international flights and mostly low-cost carriers. Neither airport is close to the city, but both offer shuttle links and/or bus and taxi service throughout Bangkok. The smoothest ride to Suvarnabhumi is the Airport Rail Link, connecting the airport to the Skytrain and key areas of the city.

Chiang Mai International Airport, which lies on the edge of that city, has a large new terminal to handle the recent sharp increases in national and regional air traffic. Phuket airport is Thailand's third busiest airport (especially in summer) and is a major link to the southern beaches region, particularly the islands of the Andaman Coast.

Bangkok Airways owns and runs airports in Sukhothai, Trat, and Koh Samui. They have the only flights to these destinations, which can be expensive in high season.

AIRPORT TRANSFERS

Shuttle service is available between Suvarnabhumi and Don Mueang airports. Bus service starts at 5 am and ends at midnight. Be warned that the transfer could take between 50 minutes to two hours depending on traffic. Other transportation options between the two airports include Uber and taxi. A taxi fare will run about B350 on the meter.

Bus

Thai buses are cheap and faster than trains, and reach every corner of the country. There are usually two to three buses a day on most routes and several daily (or even hourly) buses on popular routes between major towns. Most buses leave in the morning, with a few other runs spaced out in the afternoon and evening. Buses leave in the evening for long overnight trips. Overnight buses are very popular with Thais, and they're a more efficient use of time, but they do crash with disturbing regularity, and many expats avoid them.

Avoid taking private bus company trips from the Khao San Road area. The buses are not as comfortable as public buses, they take longer, and they usually try to trap you at an affiliated hotel once you reach your destination. This is particularly the case for cross-border travel into Cambodia. There have also been many reports of rip-offs, scams, and luggage thefts on these buses over the years.

There are, generally speaking, three classes of bus service: cheap, no-frills locals on short routes that stop at every road crossing and for anyone who waves them down; second- and first-class buses on specific routes that have air-conditioning, toilets (sometimes), and loud chop-socky movies (too often); and VIP buses that provide nonstop service between major bus stations and have comfortable seats, drinks, snacks, air-conditioning, and movies. If you're setting out on a long bus journey, it's worth inquiring about the onboard entertainment—14 hours on a bus with continuous Thai pop karaoke VCDs can be torturous. Air-conditioned buses are usually so cold that you'll want an extra sweater. On local buses, space at the back fills up fast with all kinds of oversize luggage, so it's best to sit toward the middle or the front.

Bangkok has three main bus stations, serving routes to the north (Mo Chit), south (Southern Terminal), and east (Ekamai). Chiang Mai has one major terminal. All have telephone information lines, but the operators rarely speak English. It's best to buy tickets at the bus station, where the bigger bus companies have ticket windows. Thais usually just head to the station an hour before they'd

like to leave; you may want to go a day early to be sure you get a ticket if your plans aren't flexible—especially if you hope to get VIP tickets. Travel agents can sometimes get tickets for you, but often the fee is more than half the cost of the ticket. All fares are paid in cash.

 ## Car

Car travel in Thailand has its ups and downs. Major thoroughfares tend to be congested, but the limited number of roads and the straightforward layout of cities combine to make navigation relatively easy. The exception, of course, is Bangkok. Avoid negotiating that tangled mass of traffic-clogged streets by hiring a driver.

Cars are available for rent in Bangkok and major tourist destinations. Nevertheless, even outside Bangkok hiring a driver is a small price to pay for peace of mind. If a foreigner is involved in an automobile accident, he or she—not the Thai—is likely to be judged at fault, no matter who hit whom.

If you do decide to rent a car, know that traffic laws are routinely disregarded. Bigger vehicles have the unspoken right-of-way, motorcyclists seem to think they are invincible, and bicyclists often don't look around them.

Rental-company rates in Thailand begin at about $40 a day for a jeep or $50 for an economy car with unlimited mileage. It's better to make your car-rental reservations when you arrive in Thailand, as you can usually secure a discount.

You must have an International Driving Permit (IDP) to drive or rent a car in Thailand. IDPs are not difficult to obtain, and

Getting Here and Around

having one in your wallet may save you from unwanted headaches dealing with local authorities. Check the AAA website for more info as well as for IDPs ($20) themselves.

Motorcycle

Many people rent small motorcycles to get around the countryside or the islands. A Thai city is not the place to learn how to drive a motorcycle. Phuket in particular is unforgiving to novices—don't think of driving one around there unless you are experienced. Motorcycles skid easily on wet or gravel roads. On Koh Samui a sign posts the year's count of foreigners who never made it home from their vacations because of such accidents. When driving a motorbike, make sure your vehicle has a rectangular sticker showing up-to-date insurance and registration. The sticker should be pasted somewhere toward the front of the bike, with the Buddhist year in big, bold numbers. You can rent smaller 100cc to 125cc motorcycles for only a few dollars a day. Dirt bikes and bigger road bikes, 250cc and above, start at about $25 per day.

🚕 Taxi

Most Thai taxis now have meters installed, and these are the ones tourists should take. (Nevertheless, the drivers of Chiang Mai's small fleet of "meter" taxis often demand flat fees instead. Bargain.) Taxis waiting at attractions are more likely to demand a high flat fare than those flagged down on the street. Never enter any taxi until the price has been established or the driver agrees to use the meter. Whenever possible, ask at your hotel front desk what the approximate fare should be. If you flag down a meter taxi and the driver refuses to use the meter, you can try to negotiate a better fare or simply get out. If you negotiate too much, he will simply take you on a long route to jack the meter price up. On the Grab app, you can also book taxis and private drivers for reasonable fixed prices.

Train

Though they're a bit slower and generally more expensive than buses, trains are comfortable and safe. They go to (or close to) most major tourist destinations, and many go through areas where major roads don't. The State Railway of Thailand has four lines, all of which terminate in Bangkok. Hua Lamphong is Bangkok's main terminal; you can book tickets for any route in the country there. (Chiang Mai's station is another major hub, where you can also buy tickets for any route.)

TRAIN ROUTES

The Northern Line connects Bangkok with Chiang Mai, passing through Ayutthaya, Phitsanulok, and Sukhothai. The Northeastern Line travels up to Nong Khai, on the Laotian border (across from Vientiane), and has a branch that goes east to Ubon Ratchathani. The Southern Line goes all the way south through Surat Thani (get off here for Koh Samui) to the Malaysian border and on to Kuala Lumpur and Singapore, a journey that takes 37 hours. The Eastern Line splits and goes to both Pattaya and Aranyaprathet on the Cambodian border. A short line also connects Bangkok with Nam Tok to the west, passing through Kanchanaburi and the bridge over the River Kwai along the way. (There's no train to Phuket; you have to go to the Phun Phin station, about 14 km [9 miles] from Surat Thani and change to a bus.)

TICKETS AND RAIL PASSES

The State Railway of Thailand offers two types of rail passes. Both are valid for 20 days of unlimited travel on all trains in either second or third class. The cheaper of the two does not include supplementary charges such as air-conditioning and berths. Ask at Bangkok's Hualamphong Station for up-to-date prices and purchasing; if the train is your primary mode of transportation, it may be worth it.

Even if you purchase a rail pass, you're not guaranteed seats on any particular train; you'll need to book these ahead of time through a travel agent or by visiting the advance booking office of the nearest train station. Seat reservations are required on some trains and are strongly advised on long-distance routes, especially if you want a sleeper on the Bangkok–to–Chiang Mai trip. Bangkok to Chiang Mai and other popular routes need to be booked several days in advance, especially during the popular tourist season between November and January, as well as during the Thai New Year in April. Tickets for shorter, less frequented routes can be bought a day in advance or, sometimes, right at the station before departure. Most travel agencies have information on train schedules, and many will book seats for you for a small fee, saving you a trip to the station.

The State Railway of Thailand's rather basic website (*www.railway.co.th*) has timetables, routes, available seats, and a booking system that doesn't always work. The British-based website Seat 61 (*www.seat61.com*) also has lots of helpful information about train travel in Thailand.

 # Tuk-Tuk

So-called because of their flatulent sound, these three-wheel cabs can be a more rapid form of travel through congested traffic. All tuk-tuk operators drive as if chased by hellhounds. Tuk-tuks are not very comfortable, require hard bargaining skills, are noisy, are very polluting, and subject you to the polluted air they create—so they're best used for short journeys, if at all.

If a tuk-tuk driver rolls up and offers to drive you to the other side of Bangkok for B20, think twice before accepting, because you will definitely be getting more than you bargained for. By dragging you along to his friend's gem store, tailor's shop, or handicraft showroom, he'll usually get a petrol voucher as commission. He'll tell you that all you need to do to help him put rice on his family's table is take a five-minute look around. Sometimes that's accurate, but sometimes you'll find it difficult to leave without buying something.

Essentials

🍽 Dining

Thai food is eaten with a fork and spoon; the fork is used like a plow to push food into the spoon. Chopsticks are used only for Chinese food and noodle dishes. After you have finished eating, place utensils on the plate at the 5:25 position to show you are finished.

If you want to catch a waiter's attention, use the all-purpose polite word, *krup* if you are a man and *ka* if you are a woman. Beckoning with a hand and fingers pointed upward is considered rude; point your fingers downward instead.

What It Costs in Thai Baht

$	$$	$$$	$$$$
RESTAURANTS			
under B200	B200– B300	B301– B400	over B400

MEALS AND MEALTIMES

Thai cuisine's distinctive flavor comes particularly from the use of fresh Thai basil, lemongrass, tamarind, lime, and citrus leaves. You can ask for your dish not spicy *mai ped* or just a little spicy *niknoy ped*.

Restaurant hours vary, but Thais eat at all times of day, and in cities you will find eateries open through the night. In Thailand breakfast outside the hotel often means noodle soup or congee. Street vendors also sell coffee, although die-hard caffeine addicts may not get enough of a fix; Thai coffee isn't simply coffee, but a combination of ground beans with nuts and spices.

The lunch hour is long—roughly 11:30 to 2—in smaller towns and rural areas, a holdover from when Thailand was primarily a country of rice farmers and everyone napped during the hottest hours of the day.

PAYING

Expect to pay for most meals in cash, particularly at small, local restaurants and street vendors. Most hotels and restaurants in metropolitan areas do often accept major credit cards.

WINES, BEER, AND SPIRITS

Singha, Tiger, and Heineken are at the top end of Thailand's beer market, while Chang, Leo, and a host of other brands fight it out for the budget drinkers. It's also becoming more common to find imports and craft beer at cosmopolitan bars.

Rice whisky, which tastes sweet and has a whopping 35% alcohol content, is another Thai favorite. It tastes and mixes more like rum than whisky. Mekong and Hong Thong are by far the most popular. Thais mix their rice whisky with soda water.

Expect to pay handsomely for wine and cocktails in Thailand because of taxes levied in 2017.

📍 Etiquette

Don't speak ill about the king or monarchy; it's not only insulting but also an illegal offense punishable by jail time.

Thais aim to live with a "cool heart" or *jai yen*—free from emotional extremes. Since being in a hurry shows an obvious lack of calm, they don't rush and aren't always punctual. Try to leave space in your itinerary for this relaxed attitude, since something will invariably happen to slow your progress.

Always remove your shoes when you enter a home. Do not step over a seated person's legs. Don't point your feet at anyone; keep them on the floor, and take care not to show the soles of your feet (as the lowest part of the body, they are seen by Buddhists as the least holy). Never touch a person's head, even a child's (the head is the most sacred part of the body in Buddhist cultures), and avoid touching a monk if you're a woman.

When possible do not give or receive anything with your left hand; use your right hand and support it lightly at the elbow with your left hand to show greater respect. Don't be touchy-feely in public. Speak softly and politely—a calm demeanor always accomplishes more than a hot-headed attitude. Displays of anger, raised voices, or even very direct speech are considered bad form.

Thais don't like anything done in twos, a number associated with death. Hence, you should buy three mangoes, not two; stairways have odd numbers of stairs.

Thais are devout Buddhists, and it's important for visitors to respect the religion. Cover your arms and legs (no shorts or tank tops) or you might be denied access to temples and other sacred attractions and be respectful.

➕ Health

The most common vacation sickness in Thailand is traveler's diarrhea. You can take some solace in knowing that it is also the most common affliction of the locals. It generally comes from eating contaminated food, be it fruit, veggies, or badly prepared or stored foods—really anything. It can also be triggered by a change in diet. Avoid ice unless you know it comes from clean water, uncooked or undercooked foods (particularly seafood, sometimes served raw in salads), and unpasteurized dairy products.

■ TIP→ **Drink only bottled water or water that has been boiled for at least 20 minutes, even when brushing your teeth.**

The water served in pitchers at small restaurants or in hotel rooms is generally safe, as it is either boiled or from a larger bottle of purified water, though if you have any suspicions about its origins, it's best to go with your gut feeling.

The best way to treat "Bangkok belly" is to wait for it to pass. Take Pepto-Bismol to help ease your discomfort, and if you must travel, take Imodium (known generically as loperamide), which will immobilize your lower gut and everything in it. It doesn't cure the problem, but postpones it until a more convenient time. Note that if you have a serious stomach sickness, taking Imodium can occasionally intensify the problem. If at any time you get a high fever with stomach sickness, find a doctor.

If you have frequent, watery diarrhea for more than two days, see a doctor. Days of sickness can leave you seriously dehydrated and weak in the tropics.

In any case, drink plenty of purified water or tea—chamomile, lemongrass, and ginger are good choices. In severe cases rehydrate yourself with a salt-sugar solution (½ teaspoon salt and 4 tablespoons sugar per quart of water) or rehydration salts, available at any pharmacy.

Malaria and dengue fever are fairly rare in well-traveled areas. Malarial mosquitoes generally fly from dusk to dawn, while dengue carriers do the opposite; both are most numerous during the rainy season,

Essentials

as they breed in stagnant water. However, avian flu is a persistent, seasonal concern.

The best policy is to avoid being bitten. To that end, wear light-colored clothing and some form of insect repellent (preferably containing DEET) on any exposed skin when out and about in the mornings and evenings, especially during the rainy season. Make sure that hotel rooms have air-conditioning, mosquito nets over the bed, good screens over windows, or some combination thereof. You can also use a bug spray (available everywhere) in your room before heading out to dinner, and return to a bug-free room.

■ TIP➡ **The ubiquitous bottles of menthol-scented Siang Pure Oil both ward off mosquitoes and stop the incessant itching of bites.**

Dengue fever tends to appear with a sudden high fever, sweating, headache, joint and muscle pain (where it got the name "breakbone fever"), and nausea. A rash of red spots on the chest or legs is a telltale sign. Malaria symptoms include fever, chills, headache, sweating, diarrhea, and abdominal pain. A key sign is the recurrent nature of the symptoms, coming in waves every day or two.

Find a doctor immediately if you think you may have either disease. In Thailand the test for both is quick and accurate, and the doctors are accustomed to treating these diseases. Left untreated, both diseases can quickly become serious, possibly fatal. Even when properly treated, dengue has a long recovery period, leaving the victim debilitated for weeks, sometimes months.

 Immunizations

We strongly recommend the hepatitis A vaccination as well as typhoid for entering Thailand. You should also make sure your tetanus and polio vaccinations are up-to-date, as well as measles, mumps, and rubella. With COVID-19 a continuing problem at the time of writing, make sure to check the current vaccination requirements for entry to Thailand.

Malaria and dengue fever are also possible (though remote) risks as you move out of the main tourist areas. There is much debate about whether travelers headed to Thailand should take malarial prophylactics. Though many doctors recommend that you take antimalarials, many health-care workers in Thailand believe they can do more harm than good: they can have side effects, they are not 100% effective, they can mask the symptoms of the disease if you do contract it, and they can make treatment more complicated. Consult your physician, see what medications your insurance will cover, and do what makes you feel most comfortable.

There are no prophylactics available for dengue fever. The best way to prevent mosquito-borne illness is to protect yourself against mosquitoes as much as possible.

According to the U.S. government's National Centers for Disease Control (CDC) there's also a risk of hepatitis B, rabies, and Japanese encephalitis in rural areas of Thailand, as well as drug-resistant malaria near the Myanmar border and in parts of Cambodia. In most urban or easily accessible areas you need not worry. Nevertheless, if you plan to visit remote regions or stay for more than six weeks, check with the CDC's International Travelers Hotline.

Lodging

In smaller towns hotels may be fairly simple, but they will usually be clean and inexpensive. In major cities or resort areas there are hotels to fit all price categories. The least-expensive places may have a fan rather than air-conditioning. Breakfast is sometimes included in the room rate at hotels and guesthouses.

During the peak tourist season, hotels are often fully booked and rates are at their highest. During holidays, such as between December 30 and January 2, Chinese New Year (in January or February, depending on the year), and Songkran (the Thai New Year in April), rates climb even higher, and reservations are difficult on short notice. Weekday rates at some resorts are often lower, and virtually all hotels will discount their rooms if not fully booked. You often can get a deal by booking mid- to upper-range hotel rooms through Thai travel agents. They get a deeply discounted rate, part of which they then pass on to you.

Don't be reticent about asking for a special rate. Though it may feel awkward to haggle, because hotel prices elsewhere aren't negotiable, this practice is perfectly normal in Thailand. Often it will get you nothing, but occasionally it can save you up to 50% if you catch a manager in the right mood with a bunch of empty rooms.

What It Costs in Thai Baht

	$	$$	$$$	$$$$
HOTELS				
	under B2,000	B2,001–B4,000	B4,001–B6,000	over B6,000

APARTMENT AND HOUSE RENTALS

It is possible to rent apartments or houses for longer stays in most places in Thailand. Bangkok, Chiang Mai, Phuket, and Pattaya in particular have large expat and long-term tourist communities. Also, many hotels and guesthouses are willing to offer greatly reduced rates for long-term guests. Agents are available in all big cities and are used to helping foreigners. Listings websites such as Airbnb ⊕ *www.airbnb.com*, 9apartment ⊕ *www.en.9apartment.com*, or ThaiApartment ⊕ *www.thaiapartment.com* are good resources for rentals.

GUESTHOUSES

Though the "guesthouse" label is tacked onto accommodations of all sizes and prices, guesthouses are generally smaller, cheaper, and more casual than hotels. They are often family-run, with small restaurants. The least-expensive rooms often have shared baths, and linens may not be included. At the other end of the spectrum, $35 will get you a room with all the amenities—air-conditioning, cable TV, en suite bathrooms, even Internet access—just about everywhere.

Even if you're traveling on a strict budget, make sure your room has window screens or a mosquito net.

HOTELS

Thai luxury hotels are among the best in the world. At the other end of the scale, budget lodgings are simple and basic—a room with little more than a bed. Expect any room costing more than the equivalent of $35 a night to come with hot water, air-conditioning, and a TV. Southeast Asian hotels traditionally have two twin beds. Make sure to ask for one big bed if that is your preference, though this can be two twins pushed together.

Essentials

💿 Packing

BREATHABLE CLOTHING

The climate is hot and humid so you will want to pack clothes made of breathable fabrics like light cotton or linen. Drip-dry clothing is an especially good idea, because the tropical sun and high humidity encourage frequent changes of clothing. Lightweight but long-sleeve shirts and long pants will come in handy for visiting temples and also provide protection against insect bites.

WATERPROOF GEAR

If traveling in the rainy season a lightweight rain jacket or waterproof poncho is essential. If you plan to partake of water activites or just to spend a lot of time on the beach, bring a waterproof bag to keep your camera, phone, and wallet dry; it will also come in handy during the rainy season.

PRACTICAL SHOES

The paths leading to temples can be rough, so bring sturdy walking shoes. Slip-ons are preferable to lace-up shoes, as they must be removed before you enter shrines and temples.

SUNSCREEN AND A HAT

The tropical sun is powerful, and its effects long-lasting (and painful) so bring a hat and UV-protection sunglasses and sunscreen. Don't let a rainy season forecast fool you; you will still need to be protected from the sun.

A SARONG

Out of respect for the Buddhist culture, women are expected to cover up in temples. Pack a sarong to tie over shorts in such situations. It will also come in handy on the beach and as a head cover during tropical heat.

INSECT REPELLANT

As with most hot and humid countries, you will find a lot of mosquitos in Thailand. DEET-based insect repellent is preferable to avoid being bitten.

ANTI-DIARRHEAL PILLS

To be safe, pack "Bangkok Belly" busters such as Imodium (known generically as Loperamide) and soothers such as Pepto-Bismol, as well as rehydration salts or solution such as Gastrolyte. Activated charcoal can also be helpful.

POWER ADAPTER AND VPN

Thai power outlets most commonly feature two-prong round or flat sockets; pack a universal travel power adapter to avoid complications. If you're planning to work or stay connected while you travel, a portable VPN will ensure you won't get blocked from accessing certain sites. It also protects your passwords, credit cards, and identity while you travel.

🌐 Passport and Visas

U.S. citizens arriving by air need only a valid passport, not a prearranged visa, to visit Thailand for less than 30 days. Technically, travelers need an outgoing ticket and "adequate finances" for the duration of their Thailand stay to receive a 30-day stamp upon entry, though authorities in Bangkok rarely check your finances. They do occasionally ask to see an outbound ticket.

If you want to stay longer than one month, you can apply for a 60-day tourist visa through a Royal Thai embassy. The embassy in Washington, D.C., charges about $40 for this visa, and you'll need to show them a round-trip ticket and a current bank statement to prove you can afford the trip. Be sure to apply for the correct number of entries; for example, if you're going to Laos for a few days in the middle of your stay, you'll need to apply for two Thailand entries.

Tourist visas can also be extended one month at a time once you're in Thailand. You must apply in person at a Thai immigration office; expect the process to take a day.

If you overstay your visa by a day or two, you'll have to pay a B500 fine for each day overstayed when you leave the country.

■ TIP→ **Tourists who arrive in Thailand by land from a neighboring country are now only eligible for a 30-day visa on arrival twice per year.**

🛑 Safety

You should avoid travel in the four southern provinces closest to the Malaysian border: Yala, Pattani, Songkhla, and Narathiwat. A low-grade and seemingly endless insurgency there, which began in 2004, has led to thousands of deaths and injuries. Tourist centers, shopping malls, restaurants, trains, and the airport at Hat Yai have been targeted in bombings. Fear permeates both Buddhist and Muslim communities in these southern provinces; often locals have no idea who is attacking or why. Residents avoid driving at night, shops close early, and southern towns turn eerily quiet by sundown.

Thailand is generally a safe country, and millions of foreigners visit each year without incident. That said, use common sense: be careful at night, particularly in poorly lighted areas or on quiet beaches, watch your valuables in crowded areas, and keep valuables in your hotel safe.

Crooks generally try to relieve you of cash through crimes of convenience or negligence, not violence.

■ TIP→ **A great little invention is the metal doorknob cup that can be found at Thai hardware shops. It covers your doorknob and locks it in place with a padlock, keeping anyone from using a spare key or even twisting the knob to get into your room. A good B300 investment, it's usable anywhere.**

Guesthouses offer commission for customers brought in by drivers, so be wary of anyone telling you that the place where you booked a room is suddenly full. Smile and be courteous, but be firm about where you want to go. If the driver doesn't immediately take you where you want to go, get another taxi.

Thailand's most famous danger comes from the ocean. The Asian tsunami hit the Andaman Coast in December 2004 and killed more than 5,300 people in Thailand. Reports from the areas hit show that many people could have been saved if they had known how to recognize the signs of an impending tsunami, or if an evacuation plan had been in place. Tsunamis are rare and very unpredictable. It's highly unlikely you'll experience one, but if you plan to stay in a beach resort, ask about their tsunami plan. If you feel an earthquake, leave any waterside area. Remember, a tsunami is a series of waves that could go on for hours.

■ TIP→ **Pay attention to the ocean: If you see all of the water race off the beach, evacuate immediately and head for high ground.**

Essentials

Taxes

A 7% (and sometimes more) value-added tax (V.A.T.) is built into the price of all goods and services, including restaurant meals. You can reclaim some of this tax on high-price items purchased at stores that are part of the V.A.T. refund program at the airport upon leaving the country. You cannot claim the V.A.T. refund when leaving Thailand by land at a border crossing. Shops that offer this refund will have a sign displayed; ask shopkeepers to fill out the necessary forms and make sure you keep your receipts. You'll have to fill out additional forms at the airport.

V.A.T. purchases at each shop you visit must total more than B2,000 before they can fill out the necessary forms. The total amount claimed for refund upon leaving the country cannot be less than B5,000. You must depart the country from an international airport, where you finish claiming your refund at the V.A.T. Refund Counter—allow an extra hour at the airport for this process. You cannot claim V.A.T. refunds for gemstones.

For refunds less than B30,000 you can receive the money in cash at the airport or have it wired to a bank account or to a credit card, both for a B100 fee. Refunds over B30,000 are paid either to a bank account or credit card for a B100 fee.

Tipping

Tipping is not a local custom, but it is expected of foreigners, especially at larger hotels and restaurants and for taxi rides. If you feel the service has been less than stellar, you are under no obligation to leave a tip.

In Thailand tips are generally given for good service, except when a price has been negotiated in advance. With metered taxis in Bangkok, however, the custom is to round the fare up to the nearest B5. Hotel porters expect at least a B20 tip, and hotel staff who have given good service are usually tipped. A 10% tip is appreciated at a restaurant when no service charge has been added to the bill.

When to Go

HIGH SEASON
Thailand's high season runs from late November to February and is perfect for everything: the beaches in the south, trekking in the north, or exploring Bangkok. The northern nights are chilly in winter, generally in the 50s, but as low as freezing.

LOW SEASON
Thailand is at its hottest from March to May. Pollution in the north can reach dangerous levels toward the end of the dry season in March and April. By April you can find good hotel deals, if you can stand the heat, though some hotels in less touristy areas shut down for the hot season.

SHOULDER SEASON
Thailand's rainy season starts in June and continues through the first half of November. City sightseeing is okay during these months but flooding can make rural areas inaccessible, and it's not a reliable time to plan a trek.

Contacts

Air

AIRPORTS Airports of Thailand. ⊕ *www. airportthai.co.th.* **Don Mueang Airport.** ⊕ *www. donmueangairport.com.* **Suvarnabhumi Airport.** ✉ *Bangkok* ⊕ *www.bang-kokairportonline.com.*

Embassies

Most nations maintain diplomatic relations with Thailand and have embassies in Bangkok; a few have consulates also in Chiang Mai.

IN BANGKOK U.S. Embassy. ✉ *95 Wireless Rd., Bangkok* ☎ *02/205–4000* ⊕ *th. usembassy.gov.*

IN CHIANG MAI U.S. Consulate. ✉ *387 Wichayanon Rd., Chiang Mai* ☎ *053/107700* ⊕ *th.usembassy.gov/ embassy-consulate/ chiang-mai.*

IN PHNOM PENH, CAMBODIA U.S. Embassy. ☎ *023/728000* ⊕ *kh.usem-bassy.gov.*

IN VIENTIANE, LAOS U.S. Embassy. ✉ *Thadeua Rd., Km 9, Ban Somvang Tai, Hatsayfong District* ☎ *21/487000* ⊕ *la.usem-bassy.gov.*

Train

Chiang Mai Railway Station. ☎ *05/324–5363* ⊕ *www. thairailways.com/train-sta-tion.chiangmai.html.* **Hua Lamphong Railway Station.** ✉ *Hua Lamphong Railway Station, Bangkok* ☎ *1690 railway call center* ⊕ *www.thairailways.com/ train-station.bangkok.html.* **State Railway of Thailand.** ⊕ *www.railway.co.th/ main/index_en.html.*

Travel Agents

Thailand-based travel agents can be useful if you're trying to pack a lot into a short trip. The 24-hour support many agents offer is particularly helpful if things go wrong, such as when internal flights are delayed.

Asian Oasis. ☎ *66/888–097047* ⊕ *www.asian-oa-sis.com.* **Asian Trails.** ☎ *66/262–62000* ⊕ *www. asiantrails.travel.* **Diethelm Travel.** ☎ *66/266–07000* ⊕ *www.diethelmtravel. com/thailand.* **EXO Travel.** ☎ *66/263–39060 in Bang-kok* ⊕ *www.exotravel. com.*

Visitor Information

CONTACTS Tourism Author-ity of Thailand (TAT). ☎ *1672 Thailand contact center, 323/461–9814 in Los Angeles, 212/432–0433 in New York* ⊕ *www. tourismthailand.org.* **National Park Wildlife and Plant Conservation Depart-ment** ⊕ *www.portal.dnp. go.th.* **Thai National Parks** ⊕ *www.thainationalparks. com.*

Great Itineraries

Highlights of Thailand: Bangkok, Beaches, and the North

10 DAYS

To get the most out of your Thailand vacation, decide what you'd particularly like to do—party in the big city, lie on the beach, go trekking, etc.—and arrange your trip around the region best suited for that activity. There's so much to offer, you'll barely scratch the surface in two weeks. If you don't know where to start, the following itinerary will allow you to see three very different areas of the country without requiring too many marathon travel days.

Almost every trip to Thailand begins in **Bangkok,** which is a good place to linger for a day or two, because some of the country's most astounding sights can be found in and around the **Old City.** You'll probably be exhausted by the pace in a few days, so head down to the beach, to swim in clear seas and sip cocktails on the beach. After relaxing for a few days, you'll be ready for more adventures, so head to Thailand's second city, **Chiang Mai.** The surrounding countryside is beautiful, and even a short stay will give you a chance to visit centuries-old architecture and explore the lush forests of Doi Inthanon National Park.

DAYS 1 AND 2: BANGKOK

Experience the Old Thailand within this modern megalopolis by beginning with a tour of **Bangkok's Old City** and visiting the stunning **Grand Palace** and **Wat Pho's Reclining Buddha.** Later in the day, hire a longtail boat and spend a couple of hours exploring the canals. On the river you'll catch a glimpse of how city people lived until just a few decades ago, in wooden stilt houses along the water's edge. For a casual evening, head to the backpacker hangout of **Khao San Road** for a cheap dinner and bar-hopping. For something fancy, take a ferry to the **Mandarin Oriental Hotel** for riverside cocktails and dinner at Le Normandie.

Start Day 2 with the sights and smells of **Chinatown,** sampling some of the delicious food along the way. Then head to **Jim Thompson's House,** the silk mogul's former home and a fine example of a traditional teak abode, with antiques displayed inside. If you're up for more shopping, the malls near **Siam Square** are great browsing territory for local and international fashion, jewelry, and accessories. CentralWorld, touted as "the largest lifestyle shopping destination," includes some 500 shops, 50 restaurants, 21 movie theaters, an office tower, a hotel, and more. Later grab a meal at **Ban Khun Mae**—tasty if a bit touristy—or elsewhere. Then if you've energy left, head over to **Lumphini Stadium** for a Thai boxing match.

DAYS 3 TO 5: THE BEACHES

Most island destinations are within a few hours flying time from Bangkok. It's roughly an hour to Samui or Trat (jumping-off point for Koh Chang); an hour and 20 minutes to Phuket and Krabi. Hua Hin is roughly a 3½-hour drive, a 3½ to 4½-hour railway journey, or a 4½-hour bus ride from Bangkok.

Get an early start and head to the beach regions. The choices are numerous, but **Koh Samui, Phuket,** and **Krabi** are all good bets if time is short because of the direct daily flights that connect them with Bangkok. Peaceful **Khao Lak** is only a two-hour drive from the bustle of Phuket, and **Koh Chang** is just a couple of hours by ferry from Trat Airport. Closer to Bangkok are **Koh Samet** (reached by

4 to 4½-hour drive and 30-minute ferry) and **Hua Hin** reachable by car. But if you have at least three days to spare, you can go almost anywhere that piques your interest—just make sure the time spent traveling doesn't overshadow the time spent relaxing.

Samui, Phuket, and Krabi are also good choices because of the variety of activities each offers. Though **Samui** has traditionally been backpacker terrain, there are now a number of spa retreats on the island. You can also hike to a waterfall, careen down a treetop zipline, or take a side trip to **Ang Thong National Marine Park.** There are dive shops on all the islands, with a number on **Phuket.** These offer diving and sometimes snorkeling trips to nearby reefs. There's great sailing around Phuket, too. On **Krabi** you can enjoy a relaxing afternoon and cheap beachside massage at gorgeous **Phra Nang Beach**; go rock climbing on limestone cliffs; kayak from bay to bay; and watch the glorious sunset from nearby **Railay Beach.**

DAY 6: CHIANG MAI

Chiang Mai is 1 hour by air, about 10 hours by bus or 12 to 15 hours by train from Bangkok.

Though it shouldn't be a terribly taxing day, getting to **Chiang Mai** requires some travel time, so get an early start. Wherever you are, you'll most likely have to make a connecting flight in Bangkok. If you play your cards right, you should be in Chiang Mai in time to check into your hotel and grab a late lunch. Afterward stroll around the **Old City,** and in the evening go shopping at the night market or for a drink in trendy Nimmanhaemin Road, the university area.

DAY 7: CHIANG MAI

If traveling by saengthaew, allow one hour from downtown Chiang Mai to Doi Suthep; if traveling by motorcycle or private car, allow ½ hour each way.

Spend the day exploring the city and visiting the dazzling hilltop wat of **Doi Suthep.** Ring the dozens of bells surrounding the main building for good luck. On the way back to Chiang Mai, drop in at the seven-spired temple called **Wat Chedi Yot.** Chiang Mai is famous for its massage and cooking schools, so if you're interested in trying a class in either—or just getting a massage—this is the place to do it.

Great Itineraries

DAY 8: LAMPANG

Lampang is 60 miles outside Chiang Mai, and the elephant center is midway between. Allow a full day.

An easy side trip from Chiang Mai, **Lampang** has some beautiful wooden-house architecture and a sedate way of getting around, in pony-drawn carriages.

A short ride out of town is one of northern Thailand's most revered temples, **Wat Phra That Lampang Luang,** which contains the country's oldest wooden building. It's an excellent example of classic Lanna architecture. Stroll through Kad Kong Ta market, eyeing pretty teak houses and munching on street fare.

DAY 9: AROUND CHIANG MAI

30 minutes to 1 hour from central Chiang Mai, depending on traffic.

Your last day in the region can be spent in a variety of ways. Shoppers can take taxis to the nearby **Hang Dong** district with furniture and art shops as well as handicrafts villages such as **Baan Tawai**; or to **Lamphun,** which has some pre-Thai-era temple architecture from the 7th century. Active types can head to **Doi Inthanon National Park,** where there are great views across the mountains toward Myanmar, plus bird-watching, hiking to waterfalls, and wildlife that includes Asiatic black bears.

DAY 10: BANGKOK

Head back to Bangkok. If you're not flying home the moment you step off the plane from Chiang Mai, spend your final day in the city doing some last-minute shopping at the city's numerous markets or just relax in **Lumphini Park.**

Three-Country Tour

14 DAYS

It's possible to see three countries in two weeks, if you concentrate on a few highlights and are prepared to fly all over. Do you want to focus on cultural sites and cities? Do you need a few relaxing days at the beach? Determine your priorities first, then set your itinerary. Here is one possible route that will hit a bit of everything—Bangkok buzz, ancient temples, quiet beaches, and more.

DAY 1 BANGKOK

Follow Days 1 or 2 of the Essential Thailand itinerary.

DAYS 2–4 CHIANG MAI

1 hour 15 minutes from Bangkok. There are 45-plus direct flights daily.

Take an early evening flight from Bangkok and head to dinner and drinks on the ever-popular Nimmanhaemin Road, where Chiang Mai's students and trendy types hang out. The next day, tour the city's famous ancient temples including Wat Phra Singh, breaking for a tasty street-side lunch of *khao soi* (egg noodle curry) at Khao Soi Khun Yai. If you've got energy this afternoon, hire a car or catch a sangthaew up to Doi Suthep, the mountain temple overlooking the city. On the way stop at Studio Naenna to snap up beautiful textiles. If the weather is clear, it's a great spot to experience sunset. Eat dinner at one of the restaurants along the base of the mountain, or head back into the Old City. Overnight at Bussaba Bed and Breakfast Lodge for good value and local flavor.

The next day, hire a car for the two-hour drive to Doi Inthanon National Park. It can be a good 10-degrees cooler up here, where hiking trails, waterfalls and viewpoints beckon. Lunch at one of the local joints on the road leading up to the park.

DAYS 5–7 CHIANG MAI– LUANG PRABANG

1 hour 10 minutes. Book early on the one direct flight (Sun., Mon., Wed., Fri.).

Stop by Overstand Coffee for an Aussie brunch before your afternoon flight to Luang Prabang. You'll be there in time for a sunset drink on the Mekong. The entire UNESCO World Heritage city is accessible by foot, so wear sturdy shoes and plan full days of walking. Rise early on Day 7 (just before sunrise) to catch the parade of Buddhist monks out for their morning alms. Afterward you'll find enough temples, shops, and restaurants to keep you busy in the historical district. Spend a day taking in the views from Phu Si Hill, getting a massage at one of the town's many spas and perhaps trying your hand at a Lao cooking class. You can take a ferryboat across the Mekong and explore some of the old temple ruins directly across from the Luang Prabang Peninsula. Another option is to hire a boat upriver to the Pak Ou Caves, filled with Buddha statues. Plan on a full afternoon. After a riverside dinner, wander through the handicrafts market that sets up along Sisavangvong Road. Stay in the 3 Nagas Boutique hotel, in a UNESCO Heritage–protected mansion, or splash out on the Amantaka resort for your final night.

DAYS 8–10: LUANG PRABANG–SIEM REAP

1 hour 25 minutes. Book early on the one direct flight flight (Mon., Wed.–Sat.).

You'll want to arrange a tour of the Angkor Archaeological Park as soon as you arrive. (Any hotel can help you, or book

Tips

Temples and royal buildings, such as Bangkok's Grand Palace, require modest dress (no shorts or tank tops).

Take a taxi to the Grand Palace or an express boat to nearby Tha Chang Pier. Wat Pho is a 10-minute walk south. Hire a longtail boat to get to the canals and back at Tha Chang Pier. Khao San Road is a short taxi ride from the pier.

Bangkok Airways owns the airport at Koh Samui, and flights there are relatively expensive due to taxes. Bangkok Airways runs most of the many daily flights, and these are slightly lower in price than Thai Airways. Nok Air, AirAsia, and Thai Lion also offer cheap flights to nearby Surat Thani or Nakhon Si Thammarat, from which you can take a ferry to the island.

Late November through April is the best time to explore the Andaman Coast. For the Gulf Coast there's good weather from late November until August.

Hotels in the south are frequently packed during high season and Thai holidays, so book in advance.

direct with any tuk-tuk driver you see; one of the best ways to see the temples is to hire a tuk-tuk, so you can experience the scenes in open-air style.) Many visitors choose to spend at least one sunrise at Angkor Wat and one sunset on the hilltop Phnom Bakheng. The temple complex is vast, so talk to your guide, pick up one of the many freely available printed

Great Itineraries

temple pamphlets, and design the itinerary that best suits your interests. If you have time after the second day at Angkor Wat, wander the old city and shop at the Psa Chas market. On your last night in Siem Reap, savor a modern Cambodian meal at Cuisine Wat Damnak.

DAYS 11–13: SIEM REAP–PHUKET

1 hour 30 minutes. Book early on the one direct flight (Sun., Mon., Wed., Fri.).

After multiple days pounding the grounds of temples, it's time for sand, sun (and shade!). Swim in crystal clear waters and laze under palm trees, fresh coconut in hand. The snorkeling and diving around Phuket are excellent, and any dive shop in town can arrange an excursion. You can also snorkel off Kata and Kata Noi beaches, but watch the current.

DAY 14: PHUKET–BANGKOK

1 hour 25 minutes. There are 40-plus direct flights daily.

Catch a flight to Bangkok, and connect to your flight home or spend another night shopping-eating-sightseeing in Thailand's scintillating capital city.

Chapter 3

BANGKOK

Updated by
Joe Cummings

👁 Sights	🍴 Restaurants	🛏 Hotels	🛍 Shopping	🍸 Nightlife
★★★★★	★★★★★	★★★★☆	★★★★☆	★★★★☆

WELCOME TO BANGKOK

TOP REASONS TO GO

★ **The Canals:** Bangkok is called the "Venice of the East," and while boat tours are a bit touristy, the sights, from Ayutthaya-era wats to bizarre riverside dwellings, are rare and wonderful.

★ **Street Food:** Bangkok may have the best street food in the world. Don't be afraid to sample the more exotic offerings. They're often fresher and better than the food you'd get at a hotel restaurant.

★ **Amazing Shopping:** Some of Asia's most high-tech malls sell high-end designer goods in amazing settings.

★ **Sky-High Sipping:** "Bar with a view" is taken to the extreme when you sip martinis in open-air spaces atop lofty towers.

★ **Temple-Gazing:** From the venerable Wat Pho to its many smaller wats, Bangkok's collection of temples is hard to top.

Bangkok's endless maze of streets is part of its fascination and its complexity—getting around a labyrinth is never easy. Although the S-curve of the Chao Phraya River can throw you off base, it's actually a good landmark. Most of the popular sights are close to the river, and you can use it to get swiftly from one place to another. The BTS Skytrain and MRT subway will help you navigate and get around quickly.

1 The Old City. The Old City is the historic heart of Bangkok and home to opulent temples like Wat Pho.

2 Banglamphu. North of the Old City, Banglamphu is known for pleasant strolls, diverse restaurants and vendors, and its famous backpacker hub—Khao San Road—which becomes a frenetic market by night and a huge water fight during Thai New Year (mid-April).

3 Thonburi. Across the river from the Old City is Thonburi, a mostly residential neighborhood, whose most notable attractions are the Royal Barge Museum and the spectacular Wat Arun.

4 Dusit. North of Banglamphu is this royal district, where elegant buildings line wide avenues. Dusit Park is one of the city's most appealing green spaces.

5 Northern Bangkok. This area includes the Victory Monument and all points north, such as the famous Chatuchak Weekend Market, the northern bus station of Mo

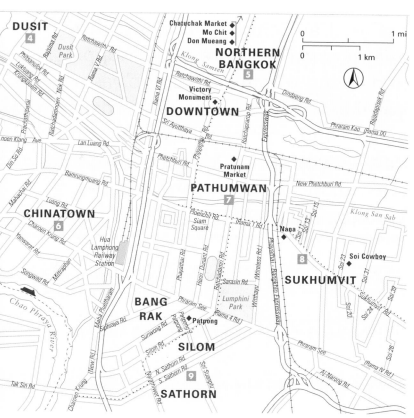

Chit, and the budget air terminal at Don Mueang.

6 Chinatown. East of the Old City in labyrinthine Chinatown are shops selling Buddhas and spices. The open-air markets and street food vendors here are among Bangkok's most vibrant.

7 Pathumwan. This area, which can be considered Bangkok's downtown, is home to the city's greatest

collection of shopping malls as well as the popular Pratunam clothing market.

8 Sukhumvit. A bustling district filled with high-end restaurants, hotels, and shops, as well as the red-light areas of Nana and Soi Cowboy.

9 Silom, Sathorn, and Bang Rak. In this busy area you'll find Lumpini Park, Bangkok's oldest and

largest park; it's a pleasant space to escape the harried pace of the city. The Silom area has many bars and restaurants, and the infamous red-light district of Patpong. At the east end of Bang Rak lies the Chao Phraya River and many opulent hotels.

Bangkok, also known as the City of Angels and the Venice of the East, will hit you like a ton of bricks. Hot, polluted, and chaotic, it thrills with energy, and the sightseeing, shopping, and eating possibilities are so vast that you'll have little time to rest. When you do find a moment, though, you can pamper yourself at spas, skyline-view bars, luxurious hotels, and excellent restaurants.

The city is a mesmerizing blend of old and new, East and West, and dizzying contradictions. Temples and red-light districts, languid canals and permanent gridlock, street-side vendors and chic upscale eateries, all exist side by side. Bangkok rarely fails to make an impression, and yes, you might need to spend a few days on the beach to recover from it all.

The Grand Palace, Wat Pho, and Wat Phra Kaew (Temple of the Emerald Buddha) are tops on most visitors' itineraries, but lesser-known temples, such as Wat Benchamabophit, the golden stupa of Wat Saket, and Wat Suthat also merit a look. Besides temples, there are plenty of niche touring possibilities. Take in a venom-extraction and python-feeding show at the snake farm at the Queen Saovabha Memorial Institute, or go to the nearby Jim Thompson House to learn all about the famed Thai silk industry. If architecture appeals to you, there is the Suan Pakkad Palace with its antique-teak-house collection.

The Old City is a major destination for travelers, as it's home to opulent temples like Wat Pho and Wat Phra Kaew. Across the river is Thonburi, made up of working-class and middle-income neighborhoods, and historic riverside sites such as Wat Arun (Temple of the Dawn). At the northern tip of the Old City is Banglamphu, one of Bangkok's older market and residential neighborhoods. It's best known now for Khao San Road, a backpacker hangout, though the neighborhood has much more to offer, especially when it comes to street food. North of Banglamphu is Dusit, the royal district since the days of Rama V.

East of the Old City is Chinatown, a labyrinth of streets with restaurants, shops, street vendors, and warehouses. Chinatown deserves at least a day on every travel itinerary—be sure to check out the sprawling Flower Market, hipster bars on Soi Nana and Charoen Krung Road, and Chinese-Thai seafood restaurants on Yaowarat Road. Farther down the Chao Phraya River is bustling Silom Road, a major commercial district. Patpong, the most famous of several red-light districts, is also here. Bang Rak is home to some of the city's leading hotels: the Mandarin Oriental, the Royal Orchid Sheraton, and the Shangri-La. To the north of Rama IV Road is one of Bangkok's largest green areas, Lumpini Park.

Continue northeast and you reach Sukhumvit Road, eastern Bangkok's main vein. Thong Lor, a road running north of Sukhumvit, is an "in" neighborhood for restaurants and nightlife. The Nana and Asok areas of Sukhumvit are home to red-light entertainment districts (Nana and Soi Cowboy) that are busier than Patpong. Farther south is the Sathorn district, where a smattering of trendy bars and eateries have also opened in recent years.

In all these neighborhoods you will find cuisine unrivaled for spice, taste, and variation. From multicourse meals to small bites from street vendors, the one constant here is food that's fresh and delicious at every level. You can lunch on superlative roast duck or wonton noodles on a street corner, and dine that evening on the sophisticated creations of world-class chefs. Your choices are by no means limited to spicy Thai either. There are excellent French and Italian restaurants, and many other cuisines.

Planning

When to Go

From late October to late February, when Bangkok is at its coolest (85°F) and driest, is the best time to visit. By April the humidity and heat create a sticky stew that lasts until the rains begin in late June. The city cools down slightly during the June through October rainy season, but it can still be uncomfortably hot.

Planning Your Time

Bangkok's sights are very spread out and the heat, traffic, and chaos can be overwhelming. No wonder, then, that many visitors to Thailand quickly repair south to the islands. That said, two full days are the minimum for getting a quick fix of the country's dynamic capital, and three would be better. You just need to pace yourself. The BTS Skytrain, MRT subway, and river ferries will help you dodge some of the traffic, but the heat and urban sprawl can exhaust you. Don't try to pack too much into one day and you'll have more fun. Plan on half a day to take in the Grand Palace and Wat Pho and another half to visit one or two other nearby sights. Later enjoy a meal along the riverside and have a drink at a skyscraper's rooftop bar. Another day could be well spent exploring Chinatown in the morning and the Jim Thompson House or Queen Saovabha Memorial Institute in the afternoon, followed by a dinner cruise on the river. Food lovers can take an extra day to explore the markets and hole-in-the-wall restaurants. If in town on the weekend, be sure to visit Chatuchak Weekend Market.

Getting Here and Around

Bangkok has two main airports, multiple bus terminals, and a centrally located main railway station. Planes, buses, and trains connect Bangkok to all of Thailand's major cities and towns. Bangkok is large, so once here remember to pace yourself and take a break to escape the midday heat. The traffic is unbearable, so do yourself a favor and skip driving in the city.

AIR

Bangkok's Suvarnabhumi International Airport (pronounced "Su-wan-na-poom") is about 30 km (18 miles) southeast of the city center. About 25 km (16 miles) north of the city is the former international airport, Don Mueang, which now receives many domestic as well as some international flights and has become the terminal for budget airlines. A free shuttle service connects the two airports.

AIRPORTS Don Mueang International Airport. ✉ *222 Vipavadee Rangsit Rd.* ☎ *02/535–1192* ⊕ *donmueang.airportthai. co.th* Ⓜ *MRT: Chatuchak Park; BTS: Mo Chit, then taxi.***Suvarnabhumi International Airport.** ✉ *999 Moo 1, Nong Prue, Bang Phli District, Samut Prakan* ☎ *02/132– 1888* ⊕ *suvarnabhumi.airportthai.co.th* Ⓜ *Airport Link: Suvarnabhumi.*

AIRPORT TRANSFERS

Inexpensive and available around the clock, taxis are the most convenient way to get between downtown and the airport.

■**TIP**➜ **Make sure to have some baht on hand to pay for your taxi.**

At Suvarnabhumi International Airport, get a taxi by heading to one of the taxi counters on Level 1, near Entrances 3, 4, 7, and 8. Take a number and state your destination to the dispatcher, who will lead you to your taxi. Allow 30 to 90 minutes to get downtown, depending on traffic and if your driver takes the expressway (you may want to request this to shorten the journey). A trip downtown will cost between B250 and B400, plus a B50 airport surcharge and any expressway tolls.

■**TIP**➜ **Avoid drivers who insist on a fixed price or refuse to turn on their meters.**

The Airport Rail Link system from Suvarnabhumi is your best option during rush hour. The express train (B150) takes 15 minutes to reach Makkasan Terminal, next to the Phetchaburi MRT subway stop. The regular commuter train (B15 to B45 depending on where you get off) takes about 26 minutes to the BTS Phaya Thai Station, convenient for those staying on the Skytrain line. The entrance to the system is on the airport's lower level.

Buses and minivans headed for Bangkok depart from the Airport Bus Station, which is reached in 10 minutes via a free shuttle bus you can catch at the front of the airport.

From Don Mueang International Airport, taxis leave from a parking lot in front of the Arrivals area on the ground floor. A B50 surcharge applies here as well. Taxis from Don Mueang to central Bangkok run around B200 to B350, plus B70 to B120 for toll charges if you ask the driver to use the tollway system.

CONTACTS Airport Rail Link. ✉ *Makkasan Station, New Petchaburi Rd.* ☎ *02/308–5600* ⊕ *www.srtet.co.th* Ⓜ *MRT: Petchaburi; BTS: Phaya Thai.* **Suvarnabhumi Airport Bus Station.** ✉ *999 Bang Phli Yai, Bang Phli District, Samut Prakan* ☎ *02/086–3242391* ⊕ *suvarnabhumi.airportthai.co.th.*

BOAT

The Chao Phraya River is a great way to bypass the traffic that clogs most of the city. Vessels operated by the Chao Phraya Express Boat service (fares from B13 to B32, depending on distance) can get crowded, especially at peak times, but they're still far more pleasant than sitting in a taxi as it navigates bumper-to-bumper traffic. The company also operates a hop-on, hop-off tourist boat that serves nine piers near sightseeing attractions. A one-day pass (B180) for this boat can also be used to board express boats.

CONTACTS Chao Phraya Express Boat. ✉ *99 Mu 3 Bang Si Muang* ☎ *244–93000, 244–58888 hotline* ⊕ *www.chaophraya-expressboat.com.*

BUS

Getting Here: Bangkok has three major terminals for buses headed from other parts of the country. Buses to and from Hua Hin, Koh Samui, Phuket, and points south and west arrive at the Southern Bus Terminal, in Thonburi. The Eastern Bus Terminal, called Ekkamai, is for buses

Tuk-Tuks

Though colorful three-wheeled tuk-tuks are somewhat of a symbol of Bangkok, they're really only a good option when traffic is light—otherwise you can end up sitting in gridlock, sweating, and sucking in car fumes. They're also unmetered, their drivers prone to overcharging; unless you are good at bargaining, you may well end up paying more for a tuk-tuk than for a metered taxi. Some tuk-tuk drivers drive like madmen, and an accident in a tuk-tuk can be scary. Expats are loath to enter a tuk-tuk, but for many tourists, a trip to Bangkok isn't complete without a ride.

■TIP→ Watch out for unscrupulous tuk-tuk drivers who offer cut-rate tours, then take you directly to jewelry and clothing shops that pay them a commission.

If a trip to Bangkok does not seem complete without a tuk-tuk adventure, pay half of what the driver suggests, insist on being taken to your destination, and hold on for dear life.

headed to and from Pattaya, Rayong, Trat, and other eastern provinces. Buses to and from Chiang Mai and points north arrive at the Northern Bus Terminal in Chatuchak. Minivans to nearby destinations like Hua Hin, Cha-am, Pattaya, Kanchanaburi, and elsewhere depart from Victory Monument.

Bus companies generally sell tickets on a first-come, first-served basis. This is seldom a problem because service is frequent. The most comfortable buses are those of Nakhon Chai Air, which has its own terminal near Mo Chit. Nakhon Chai connects Bangkok with many destinations within Thailand.

Getting Around: Bangkok Mass Transit Authority provides bus service in the city. For a fare of B8 to B10 on non-air-conditioned buses and B13 to B25 on air-conditioned ones, you can travel virtually anywhere in Bangkok. Air-conditioned microbuses charge B25. Most buses operate from 5 am to around 11 pm, but a few routes operate around the clock. You can pick up a route map at most bookstalls for B35, or just ask locals which bus is headed to your destination.

CONTACTS Bangkok Mass Transit Authority (BMTA). ✉ 131 Watthanatham Rd., Huay Khwang, Huai Khwang ☏ 1348 hotline ⊕ www.bmta.co.th. **Bangkok Southern Bus Station (Sai Tai Mai).** ✉ 2/2, Borommaratchachonnani Rd, Chim Phli, Taling Chan, Bangkok ☏ 02/894–6122 ⊕ www.transitbangkok.com. **Bangkok Bus Terminal (Chatuchak).** ✉ Kamphaeng Phet 2 Rd., Chatuchak ☏ 02/936–2852, 02/064–8060265 mobile number ⊕ www.transitbangkok.com Ⓜ MRT: Chatuchak Park. **Nakhon Chai Air Bus Station.** ✉ 333 Chatuchak Rd., Chatuchak, Chatuchak ☏ 1624 call center, 02/939–4999 ⊕ www.nca.co.th Ⓜ MRT: Chatuchak Park; BTS: Mo Chit.

BTS SKYTRAIN AND MRT SUBWAY

The BTS Skytrain, an elevated city rail system, covers a huge portion of the capital, and is a fast and convenient way to move through the city. Rates run between B16 and B59, and the trains from 6 am to midnight daily. The MRT subway system complements the BTS as a way to get around, and has expanded to cover a greater portion of the city in recent years, including Chinatown and the old city. The subway operates daily

72

from 6 am until midnight. Fares run from B16 to B70. Although the Skytrain and subway are separate entities and use different fare and ticketing systems, the two connect at three points: Sala Daeng Station and Silom Station, Asok Station and Sukhumvit Station, and Mo Chit Station and Chatuchak Station.

■ TIP→ **If you are traveling between two points along the route, BTS is by far the best way to go.**

■ TIP→ **During rush hour, long lines are common at ticket machines, especially at busier stations. Buying reloadable cards for the BTS for an initial issuing fee of B100, or for the MRT for a B50 deposit plus B30 issuing fee, each can save you time waiting. Cards can be returned at ticket offices for a refund on unused fares.**

CONTACTS BTS Skytrain. ⊠ *BTS Building, 1000 Phahonyothin Rd., Chatuchak* ☎ *261–77300, 261–77341 tourist information* ⊕ *www.bts.co.th* Ⓜ *MRT: Chatuchak Park.***MRT Bangkok Metro.** ⊠ *189 Rama IX Rd., Huay Khwang* ☎ *02/624–5200* ⊕ *www.bemplc.co.th.*

TAXI AND RIDE-SHARING

Taxis can be an economical way to get around, provided you don't hit gridlock. Most taxis have meters, so avoid drivers whose cabs lack one or who claim that it is broken. The rate for the first 1 km (½ mile) is B35, with an additional B5 for every kilometer after that; a 5-km (3-mile) journey costs about B60. There's a B50 surcharge for all taxi journeys originating at either of Bangkok's airports, Don Mueang or Suvarnabhumi.

With Grab, a local ride-sharing app that you can download on your phone, you can easily book taxis, private cars, and vans. Fares for booked taxis are slightly higher than for taxis flagged on the street. However, since you can enter your exact destination into the app using Google Maps, it's less confusing than dealing with a street taxi if you don't know the city well.

■ TIP→ **Ask your concierge to write the name of your destination and its cross streets in Thai.**

COMPANIES Alpha Taxis. ☎ *014/585–8585* ⊕ *www.alphataxis.fr.***Taxis G7.** ☎ *3607 €0.45/min, 014/127–6699 for service in English* ⊕ *www.g7.fr.*

TRAIN

The main train station is Bangkok Railway Station, more commonly known as Hua Lamphong, located near Chinatown and accessible by MRT. Trains here connect Bangkok and many destinations within Thailand. At some point in 2022, however, the Bangkok hub will move to Bang Sue Grand Station further north in the city.

CONTACTS Bangkok Railway Station (Hualamphong Railway Station). ⊠ *Rongmuang Rd., Pathumwan* ☎ *1690 hotline,* ⊕ *www.railway.co.th* Ⓜ *MRT: Hua Lamphong.*

Health and Safety

For a city of its size, Bangkok is relatively safe; however, you still need to practice common sense. Don't accept food or drinks from strangers, as there have been reports of people being drugged and robbed. If you plan to enjoy a massage in your hotel room, put your valuables in the safe. Bangkok is no more dangerous for women than any other major city, but it's still best to avoid walking alone at night (take a taxi if you're out late).

■ TIP→ **Beware of hustlers who claim that your hotel is overbooked.**

They'll try to convince you to switch to one that pays them a commission. Also avoid anyone trying to sell you on an overpriced taxi or limo. Proceed to the taxi stand; these taxis will use a meter.

Contact the Tourist Police first in an emergency. For medical attention,

Bumrungrad Hospital and BNH Hospital are considered the best.

Money Matters

Major banks all exchange foreign currency, and most have easily accessible ATMs that accept foreign bank cards. Currency-exchange offices are common, but don't wait until the last minute. It's distressing to try to find one when you're out of baht.

Restaurants

Thais are passionate about food, and love discovering out-of-the-way shops that prepare unexpectedly tasty dishes. Nowhere is this truer—or more feasible—than in Bangkok. The city's residents always seem to be eating, so the tastes and smells of Thailand's cuisine surround you day and night. That said, Bangkok's restaurant scene is also a minefield, largely because the relationship between price and quality at times seems almost inverse. For every hole-in-the-wall gem serving the best sticky rice, *larb* (meat salad), and *som tam* (the hot-and-sour green-papaya salad that is the ultimate Thai staple) you've ever had, there's an overpriced hotel restaurant serving touristy, toned-down fare. In general the best Thai food is found at the most bare-bones, even run-down restaurants, although there are famous, upscale places providing experimental twists.

If you want a break from Thai food, many other world cuisines are represented. Best among them is Chinese, although Japanese, Korean, Italian, and Indian are well represented as well. The city's ubiquitous noodle shops have their roots in China, as do roast-meat purveyors, whose historical inspiration was Cantonese. Western fare tends to suffer from the distance, although in the past decade some excellent trendy Western eateries have opened.

As with anything in Bangkok, travel time is a major consideration when choosing a restaurant. If you're short on time or patience, choose a place that's an easy walk from a BTS or MRT station.

■ TIP→ **The easiest way to reach a riverside eatery is often on a Chao Phraya River express boat.**

What It Costs in Baht

$	$$	$$$	$$$$
AT DINNER			
under B200	B200–B400	B401–B500	over B500

Hotels

Bangkok offers a staggering range of lodging choices, and even some of the best rooms are affordable to travelers on a budget. The city has nearly 500 hotels and guesthouses, and the number is growing. Competition keeps prices below the international average, and Thailand's legendary service orientation means you'll often feel more pampered here than in many other cities.

For first-class lodging, few cities in the world rival Bangkok. In recent years the Mandarin Oriental, Anantara Siam, The Siam, St. Regis, The Peninsula, Shangri-La, and a handful of others have been repeatedly rated among the best in the world, with newer players like the Capella and Sofitel So receiving major accolades. If there were a similar comparison of the world's boutique hotels, Bangkok's would be near the top, too. These high-end hotels are surprisingly affordable, with rates comparable to standard hotels in New York or London. Business hotels also have fine service, excellent restaurants, and amenities like health clubs and spas.

Wherever you stay, remember that prices fluctuate enormously, and that huge discounts are the order of the day. Internet discounts are widely available, and booking online can often save you up to several thousand baht.

■ TIP→ **Always ask for a better price, even when you are checking in.**

Deals may be more difficult to come by during the high season from November through February, but during low season they're plentiful.

What It Costs in Baht			
$	$$	$$$	$$$$
FOR TWO PEOPLE			
under B2,000	B2,000– B4,000	B4,001– B6,000	over B6,000

Hotels are concentrated in four areas: in Silom and Bang Rak (home to many riverfront hotels); around Siam Square and along Phetchaburi Road in Pathumwan; along Sukhumvit Road, which has the greatest number of hotels and an abundance of restaurants and nightlife; and in the Chinatown and the Old City neighborhoods, which have a smaller number of properties, most of which are affordable. Backpackers often head to Khao San Road, also home to some newer, more upmarket guesthouses.

Nightlife

The city that was once notorious for its raunchy sex trade now entertains an ever-growing class of professionals hungry for thumping dance clubs, trendy cocktail lounges, and swanky rooftop bars. Most bars and clubs close around 2 am, though nighthawks can probably find a place or two open until 5 or 6 am.

There are a few notable nightlife sections: the area off Sukhumvit Soi 55 (also called Soi Thonglor) is full of bars and nightclubs, and trendy and happening new places are springing up around

Sathorn Road and the adjoining Suan Phlu. Talat Noi, a neighborhood along Charoen Krung Rd. and Rama IV Rd. has lately become a nightlife focus as well with an influx of young Thais opening hipster bars and cafes.

If you want to take a walk on the wild side, Bangkok still has three surviving red-light districts: Patpong, Nana Plaza, and Soi Cowboy. Patpong, the largest and most touristy, includes two streets that run between Surawong and Silom roads. Nana Plaza, at Sukhumvit Soi 4, is packed with three floors of hostess bars, go-go clubs, and "ladyboy" clubs. Soi Cowboy, off Sukhumvit Road at Soi 21 (the Asok intersection), is where many expats go, finding it more relaxed and less of a tourist trap than Patpong or Nana.

Even though it may not seem like it, live sex shows are officially banned and prostitution is illegal. The government doesn't always turn a blind eye, so exercise caution and common sense.

Performing Arts

A contemporary arts scene is relatively new to Thailand, but the last 20 years has seen great changes in the fine arts: artists are branching out into all kinds of media, and modern sculpture and artworks can be found in office buildings, parks, and public spaces. Music options range from piano concertos and symphonies to rock concerts and blues-and-jazz festivals.

Bangkok offers a variety of theater and dance performances, among them traditional puppet shows and masked dance dramas known as *khon*. For Thais classical dance is more than graceful movements. The dances depict tales from the religious epic *Ramakien*. Performances are accompanied by a *piphat* orchestra, led by the *pii*, a double-reed woodwind

Where Should I Stay?

	Neighborhood Vibe	Pros	Cons
The Old City and Banglamphu	These central neighborhoods are the historic heart of the city. They're full of places to stay in all price ranges.	Tons of dining and lodging options here to match any budget; you'll be near major attractions like the Grand Palace.	May feel chaotic and touristy to others. Not easily accessible by MRT or BTS. Not the cheapest part of town.
Thonburi	You'll rub elbows with the locals in this very Thai neighborhood across the river from the Old City.	Secluded from the noise and chaos; stellar river views. Some parts of Thonburi are now well served by BTS and MRT.	Everything else is on the other side of the Chao Phraya, so expect to take the ferry a lot and spend more on taxis.
Dusit and Northern Bangkok	This relatively quiet business and residential neighborhood has plenty of local culture but few tourist attractions.	This is the closest neighborhood to Don Mueang, the domestic and low-budget carrier airport—helpful if you have an early flight.	It's a ways from downtown, which means you'll spend a lot on taxis getting to the city center. Public transportation options are limited.
Chinatown	The chaos of Chinatown isn't for everybody. You'll be inundated by the sights and sounds.	There are some good hotel deals, the food is great, and the street markets are fascinating. Has four MRT stations.	Hectic and not the most tourist-friendly part of town. Limited hotel selection, terrible daytime traffic.
Pathumwan	The neighborhood that makes up Bangkok's "downtown," this sprawling area is full of markets and megamalls and has several tourist attractions.	A shopper's paradise, and relatively convenient to MRT and BTS. Many superposh hotels; this is the place to stay if you're traveling in style.	Horrible traffic—you'll run up a taxi tab sitting in gridlock. Most options are pricey and may be noisy, because there's lots of nightlife nearby.
Sukhumvit	This central tourist- and expat-heavy neighborhood is a major nightlife zone, with everything from Irish pubs to hostess bars. Lots of good restaurants.	If you want to party, this is the place to be, with a wide range of hotels and convenient public transit.	Fast-paced and noisy. You may run into some shady dealings, though there are plenty of classy establishments, too.
Silom, Sathorn, and Bang Rak	This central area is the city's biggest business hub and has the greatest concentration of restaurants. Nightlife options are more creative than along Sukhumvit.	Popular with travelers, so lots of comfortable restaurants and bars. Convenient MRT–BTS connection.	Lots of traffic. Not the most authentic Thai experience, and because it's a business district, there's a lot concrete.

which sounds a bit like an oboe, as well as a range of gongs and percussion instruments. In addition to conventional theaters, a few upscale tourist-oriented restaurants present classical dance.

Activities

Thailand has an abundance of outdoor activities, but it's often difficult to find any within Bangkok. Due to elevated temperatures, Bangkok residents generally head to the malls on weekends to cool off. Soccer is immensely popular, and the Thai Premier League has matches at several stadiums around town during the season. Bangkok offers visitors one of the most intense spectator sports in the world, *Muay Thai* (Thai kickboxing), considered Thailand's national sport and provisionally accepted for the 2024 Olympics. Seeing a professional match is a quintessential Bangkok experience.

Shopping

Many tourists are drawn to Bangkok for its relatively cheap silk, gems, and tailor-made clothes. But there are many other goods worth seeking out: quality silverware, fine porcelain, sturdy bronzeware, and handmade leather goods—all at prices well below those in Western shops. The already reduced prices can often be haggled down even further—haggling is mainly reserved for markets, but shopkeepers will let you know if they're willing to discount, especially if you start walking away.

Don't be fooled by a tuk-tuk driver offering to take you to a shop. Shop owners pay drivers a commission to lure in unsuspecting tourists.

■ TIP➜ **Patronizing reputable dealers will help you avoid getting scammed on big-ticket items like jewelry.**

Thai antiques and old images of the Buddha require a special export license; check out the Thai Board of Investment's website for rules on exporting and applications to do so.

The city's most popular shopping areas are along **Silom Road and Surawong Road,** where you can find quality silk; **Sukhumvit Road,** which is rich in leather goods; **Yaowarat Road in Chinatown,** where gold trinkets abound; and along **Oriental Lane and Charoen Krung (New Road),** where there are many antiques shops. The shops around **Siam Square** and at **River City** attract both Thais and foreigners. If you're knowledgeable about fabric, you can find bargains at the textile merchants who compete along Pahurat Road in Chinatown and the **Pratunam neighborhood off Phetchaburi Road.** You can even take the raw material to a tailor and have something made.

Visitor Information

Tourist Authority of Thailand
✉ *1600 New Phetchaburi Rd., Makkasan, Ratchathewi* ☎ *02/250–5500, 1672 call center* ⊕ *www.tourismthailand. org* Ⓜ *MRT: Phetchaburi.*

The Old City

 Sights

City Pillar Shrine
HISTORIC SIGHT | Somewhat in the shadow of grander nearby attractions like the Grand Palace and the Temple of the Emerald Buddha, this shrine is one of the most historically and culturally significant sites in the city. Just east of the Grand Palace compound, the City Pillar Shrine contains the foundation stone (Lak Muang) from which all distances in Thailand are measured. The stone is believed to be inhabited by a spirit that guards

Two Days in Bangkok

You could spend weeks in Bangkok and not get bored but, especially if you have limited time, planning around Bangkok's traffic is a must. Look for sights near public transportation or close enough to one another to visit on the same day, and don't assume that taxis will be faster than the BTS or MRT. You can see a lot in a few days.

Start your first day with the most famous of all Bangkok sights, the Grand Palace. In the same complex is the gorgeously ornate Wat Phra Kaew. Not far south of the Grand Palace is Bangkok's oldest and largest temple, Wat Pho, famous for its enormous Reclining Buddha and for being a great place for a traditional Thai massage. Later take the ferry up to Banglamphu (get off at the Phra Athit pier), where you can enjoy a river walk at Santichaiprakarn Park and the Phra

Sumen Fort before checking out the hip restaurants and bars that front Phra Athit Road, which parallels the river. From here lively Khao San Road and all of its shopping are just a short stroll away.

The next day start out in Chinatown, where you can spend hours browsing the food and spice markets, peeking into temples and shops, and just absorbing the atmosphere. Next work your way to the Chao Phraya River, ferry down to the Saphan Taksin Pier, and take a *klong* (canal) tour, which will give you a glimpse of the fascinating canal life in Bangkok. If it's a weekend, head to Kukrit Pramoj Heritage House; if it's a weekday, visit the Jim Thompson House. Take the BTS in the evening either to Silom or Sukhumvit Road, where great restaurants and bars await.

3

Bangkok THE OLD CITY

---

the well-being of Bangkok. The shrine is free to enter and frequented by locals who come here to pray, so behave and dress respectfully (knees and shoulders should be covered). ⊠ *2 Lak Muang Rd., Phra Nakhon* ⊹ *East of the Grand Palace compound* Ⓜ *MRT: Sanam Chai.*

Democracy Monument
MONUMENT | One of Bangkok's biggest and best-known landmarks, the monument anchors a large traffic circle three blocks from the eastern end of Khao San Road. Not frequented much by tourists, it commemorates the establishment of a constitutional monarchy in Thailand in 1932. ⊠ *Ratchadamnoen Rd., at Dinso Rd., Old City* 🎟 *Free.*

Giant Swing (Sao Ching Cha)
HISTORIC SIGHT | Originally built by King Rama I in 1784, this towering 27-meter (88-foot) wood structure has a great

backstory but today it is just a random photo op. If you find yourself posing in front of it, or just walking by, know that it was once used in Hindu ceremonies where teams of men would launch themselves into the air and catch gold coins with their teeth; slingshotting them to good fortunes on heaven and Earth. The competitions were banned in 1935 after several fell to untimely deaths. ⊠ *Bamrung Muang Rd., Phra Nakhon.*

★ Grand Palace
CASTLE/PALACE | This is one of Bangkok's most revered spots and one of its most visited. King Rama I built this walled city in 1782, when he moved the capital across the river from Thonburi. The palace and adjoining structures only got more opulent as subsequent monarchs added their own touches. The grounds are open to visitors, but the buildings

are not. They're used only for state occasions and royal ceremonies. On rare occasions, rooms in the Chakri Maha Prasat Palace—considered the official residence of the king, even though he does not live here—are sometimes open to visitors. Admission for the complex includes entrance to Dusit Palace Park. Note, proper attire (no flip-flops, shorts, or bare shoulders or midriffs) is required, if you forget, you will be loaned unflattering but more demure shirts and shoes at the entrance (deposit required). You can buy tickets online. ⊠ *Sanam Chai and Na Phra Lan Rd., Old City* ✛ *A few hundred meters east of Tha Chang ferry pier* ☎ *026–235500* ⊕ *www.royalgrandpalace.th* ☞ *B500, includes admission to Wat Phra Kaew and Queen Sirikit Museum of Textile, which are within the Grand Palace compound.* Ⓜ *MRT: Sanam Chai.*

National Gallery

ART MUSEUM | Although it doesn't get nearly as much attention as the National Museum, the gallery has a permanent collection of modern and traditional Thai art that is worth seeking out. There are also frequent temporary shows from around the country and abroad. To get to the gallery, walk down Na Phra That Road, past the National Theater and toward the river. Go under the bridge, then turn right and walk about 200 meters (650 feet); the gallery is on your left. The building used to house the royal mint. ⊠ *4 Chao Fa Rd., Phra Nakhon* ☎ *02/282–8525* ⊕ *www.finearts.go.th/museumnationalgallery* ☞ *B200* ◷ *Closed Mon. and Tues.*

National Museum

HISTORY MUSEUM | There's no better place to acquaint yourself with Thai history than the National Museum, which also holds one of the world's best collections of Southeast Asian art. The exhibitions of Thai artworks and artifacts begin with the ceramic utensils and bronzeware of northeastern Thailand's Ban Chiang

culture (2000–900 BC). Most of the masterpieces from the northern provinces are displayed here, not in museums there. ■**TIP**➔ **Free guided tours in English take place on Wednesday and Thursday, usually at 9:30 am.** ⊠ *4 Na Phra That Rd., Phra Nakhon* ☎ *02/241333* ⊕ *www.mynmv.com/national-museum-bangkok* ☞ *B200* ◷ *Closed Mon. and Tues.* Ⓜ *MRT: Hua Lamphong.*

October 14 Memorial

MONUMENT | The memorial honors Thais killed during a student-led uprising against military rule. That revolt began on October 14, 1973, and tributes to people killed in October 1976 and May 1992 in similar protests have also been incorporated. Although most of the inscriptions are written in Thai, the memorial is a sobering sight, especially being so close to the Democracy Monument, which acknowledges the establishment of the constitutional monarchy. Traffic is always whizzing about, the gate is often closed, and there seem to be no regular hours, though there are painting exhibitions at times. ⊠ *Ratchadamnoen and Tanao Rds., Phra Nakhon* ✛ *2½ blocks west of Democracy Monument* ☞ *Free.*

Queen Sirikit Museum of Textiles

OTHER MUSEUM | Within the Grand Palace complex, in the old Ministry of Finance building, this interesting little museum tells the story of Thai silk through a lovely display of the current queen's most celebrated outfits. There are daily silk-making demonstrations, and a particularly good gift shop. ⊠ *Grand Palace, Na Phralan Rd., Old City* ✛ *Just inside main visitors' gate, Grand Palace* ☎ *02/259430, 02/259420* ⊕ *www.qsmtthailand.org* ✉ *Included in Grand Palace ticket, or B150 for museum alone* Ⓜ *MRT: Sanam Chai.*

★ Wat Pho (*Temple of the Reclining Buddha*)

RELIGIOUS BUILDING | The city's largest wat has what is perhaps the most majestic representation of the Buddha in Bangkok. The 150-foot sculpture, covered with gold, is so large it fills an entire *viharn.* Especially noteworthy are the mammoth statue's 10-foot feet, with the 108 auspicious signs of the Buddha inlaid in mother-of-pearl. Many people ring the bells surrounding the image for good luck. Behind the *viharn* holding the Reclining Buddha is Bangkok's oldest university. A century before Bangkok was established as the capital, a monastery was founded here to teach traditional medicine. Around the walls are marble plaques inscribed with formulas for herbal cures, and stone sculptures squat in various postures demonstrating techniques for relieving pain. The monks still practice ancient cures, and the massage school is now famous. Thai massages (which can actually be painful, though therapeutic) cost around B400 for one hour. Appointments aren't necessary—you usually won't have to wait long if you just show up. Massage therapy courses of up to 200 hours are also available at a clinic nearby the temple. ⊠ *Chetuphon Rd., Old City* ☎ *083–0577100* ⊕ *www.watpho. com* ✉ *B100* Ⓜ *MRT: Sanam Chai.*

★ Wat Phra Kaew (*Temple of the Emerald Buddha*)

RELIGIOUS BUILDING | This is the most sacred temple in the kingdom and no single structure within the Grand Palace elicits such awe, and no other wat in Thailand is so ornate or so embellished with glittering gold. As you enter the compound, take note of the 20-foot-tall statues of fearsome creatures in traditional battle attire standing guard. Turn right as you enter the compound, where the inner walls are lively murals depicting Thailand's national epic the *Ramakien.* Several *kinnaree* (half-woman, half-lion creatures) stand guard outside the main chapel, which has a gilded three-tier roof. Inside sits the Emerald Buddha. This most venerated image of Lord Buddha is carved from a single piece of green jasper 26 inches high. ⊠ *Sanam Chai and Na Phra Lan Rds., Old City* ✛ *Near Tha Chang ferry pier* ☎ *02/243290* ⊕ *www. royalgrandpalace.th/en/home* ✉ *B500, includes admission to Grand Palace and Queen Sirikit Museum of Textile, which are within the Grand Palace compound.* Ⓜ *MRT: Sanam Chai.*

Wat Saket

RELIGIOUS BUILDING | A well-known landmark, the towering gold stupa of Wat Saket, also known as the Golden Mount, was once the highest point in the city. King Rama III began construction of this temple, but it wasn't completed until the reign of Rama V. On a clear day the view from the top is magnificent. Every November, during the Loi Krathong festival, the temple hosts a popular fair with food stalls and performances. ◼ **TIP→ To reach the gilded chedi you must ascend an exhausting 318 steps, so don't attempt the climb on a hot afternoon.** ⊠ *Chakkaphatdi Phong Rd., Old City* ☎ *065–0103131* ✉ *B50* Ⓜ *MRT: Sam Yot, then taxi.*

Wat Suthat

RELIGIOUS BUILDING | Built between the reigns of kings Rama I and Rama III, this highly venerated royal temple houses Thailand's largest surviving Sukhothai-period bronze Buddha, along with intensely colored murals depicting scenes from Buddhist mythology. The ashes of Rama VIII (Ananda Mahidol) are interred in the base of the huge Buddha. ⊠ *146 Bamrung Meuang Rd., Old City* ☏ *02/622–2819* Ⓜ *MRT: Sam Yot, then walk.*

Restaurants

The Old City has every type of restaurant, including many small shophouses serving excellent Thai food.

Krua Apsorn

$$ | THAI | This small shophouse restaurant is a truly capable all-round Thai eatery, a rarity in a neighborhood where you're generally better off eating at places that specialize in one or two dishes. Recommended plates include *nuea pu phat phrik lueang* (crabmeat stir-fried with yellow chili) and *kaeng khiaw-wan look chin pla krai* (green curry with fish balls). **Known for:** convenient to key Old City tourist sights; consistently good food; crab meat with yellow peppers. Ⓢ *Average main: 200* ⊠ *169 Dinso Rd., Old City* ☏ *02/685–4531* ⊕ *www.kruaapsorn.com* ⊘ *Closed Sun.* Ⓜ *MRT: Sam Yot, then taxi.*

Methavalai Sorndaeng

$$ | THAI | Serving exceptional traditional Thai food for more than 60 years, Sorndaeng features white tablecloths, lacy curtains, and black-trousered waiters. Fans say the restaurant makes the best *thawt man plaa* (fried spicy fish cakes) in the city. **Known for:** upscale atmosphere; sophisticated presentation; lunchtime busy with government workers. Ⓢ *Average main: 400* ⊠ *78/2 Ratchadamnoen Klang Rd., Old City* ☏ *02/224–3088* Ⓜ *MRT: Sam Yot, then taxi.*

★ Raan Jay Fai

$$$$ | THAI | To enjoy chef Jay Fai's Michelin-award-winning dishes at her small open-air eatery, plan in advance or be prepared for upwards of a three-hour wait. Reservations via email or phone are possible, although response may be slow; you can also try showing up when the restaurant opens at 10 am, and put your name on a waiting list. **Known for:** cult following; pad khee mao (drunken noodles); lump crabmeat with curry. Ⓢ *Average main: B1,000* ⊠ *327 Mahachai Rd., Phra Nakhon* ☏ *02/223–9384* ⊘ *Closed Mon. and Tue.* Ⓜ *MRT: Sam Yot, then taxi.*

🛏 Hotels

The Bhuthorn

$$$ | HOTEL | This century-old shophouse in the historic Samphraeng neighborhood has been lovingly restored by an artistic Thai couple and has three guest rooms. **Pros:** walking distance to prime Bangkok sights; excellent restaurants nearby; personalized service. **Cons:** somewhat congested neighborhood; books up quickly; doesn't have the amenities of a big hotel. Ⓢ *Rooms from: 5,000* ⊠ *96-98 Phraeng Phuthorn Rd., Old City* ☏ *04/364–4595, 02/622–2270* ⊕ *www.thebhuthorn.com* ❌ *Free Breakfast* ⤳ *3 rooms* Ⓜ *MRT: Sam Yot, then taxi.*

★ Chakrabongse Villas & Residences

$$$$ | B&B/INN | On the riverbank close to Wat Pho, Chakrabongse Villas offers four Thai-themed luxury suites in reconstructed traditional Thai homes, along with three Moroccan-inspired rooms, on the grounds of Chakrabongse House, which was built in 1908 for Prince Chakrabongse. **Pros:** large discounts during low season; unique hotel experience; beautiful surroundings. **Cons:** feels isolated; fills up quickly; extremely expensive. Ⓢ *Rooms from: B6,700* ⊠ *396 Maharaj Rd., Phra Nakhon* ☏ *02/222–1290*

chakrabongsevillas.com ¶◎¶ *No Meals*
🍴 *4 suites, 3 three rooms* Ⓜ *BTS:
Saphan Taksin, then river ferry.*

Phranakorn-Nornlen Hotel
$$ | **HOTEL** | Ideal for travelers seeking an artsy, off-the-beaten-track experience, this cute boutique guesthouse is in the old Phra Nakhon district. **Pros:** in a real Bangkok neighborhood well off the tourist track; artsy setting; friendly and helpful staff. **Cons:** difficult to find; far from Skytrain and subway; lacks pool, gym, and other hotel amenities. $ *Rooms from: B2,500* ✉ *46 Thewet, Soi 1, Phranakorn, Bangkhunprom, Krung-kasem, Phra Nakhon* ☎ *02/628–8188* *www.facebook.com/Phranakorn-Nornlen-10157596094* ¶◎¶ *Free Breakfast* 🍴 *30 rooms.*

Riva Arun Bangkok
$$ | **HOTEL** | This luxurious boutique hotel overlooking the Chao Phraya River is all about elegant modern furnishings, perfect for couples seeking a romantic escape. **Pros:** quiet and tucked down an alley; near to Grand Palace and other attractions; rooftop restaurant. **Cons:** expensive; far from city center; very limited occupancy. $ *Rooms from: B3,000* ✉ *392/25-28 Maharaj Rd., Phra Nakhon* ☎ *02/221–1188* *www.rivaarunbangkok.com* ¶◎¶ *No Meals* 🍴 *25 rooms.*

Sala Rattanakosin
$$ | **HOTEL** | Hidden down an alley filled with shophouses, this upcycled building features lovely rooms with views of Wat Pho and Wat Arun twinkling against the river. **Pros:** among newer accommodations in the area; excellent views; near Grand Palace and other attractions. **Cons:** rooms book up fast; on the expensive side; far from city center. $ *Rooms from: B3,600* ✉ *39 Maha Rat Rd., Phra Nakhon* ☎ *02/231–2589* *www.salarattanakosin.com* ¶◎¶ *No Meals* 🍴 *16 rooms* Ⓜ *MRT: Sanam Chai.*

★ The Siam Hotel
$$$$ | **RESORT** | Old Hollywood meets art deco at this family-owned property on the Chao Phraya, where ultraluxurious design pays homage to the postcolonial, early-1900s era of King Rama V, with black-and-white striped chairs and a library lined with limited-edition tomes. **Pros:** whimsical design; minutes from Grand Palace via private riverboat; exclusive, serene, and private. **Cons:** a long way from public transportation; very pricey; far from nightlife. $ *Rooms from: B12,324* ✉ *3/2 Thanon Khao, Vachirapa-yaabal, Dusit* ☎ *02/206–6999* *www.thesiamhotel.com* ¶◎¶ *Free Breakfast* 🍴 *28 suites, 10 villas, 1 cottage* Ⓜ *BTS: Saphan Taksin, then hotel's private boat.*

 Performing Arts

THEATER AND DANCE
National Theatre
FOLK/TRADITIONAL DANCE | Classical Thai dance-drama known as *khon* can usually be seen here on Fridays and Saturdays at 1:30 and 5 pm. ✉ *2 Rachini Rd, Phraborom Maharatchawang, Old City* ☎ *02/224–1342* *ntt.finearts.go.th* 🎫 *From B60* 🕐 *Closed Mon. and Tues.*

Sala Chalerm Krung Royal Theatre
FOLK/TRADITIONAL DANCE | **FAMILY** | A former student at the École des Beaux-Arts in Paris designed this theater, which opened in 1933, in a style that might best be described as Thai deco. The venue hosts traditional *khon* dance-drama Monday through Friday, five times a day starting at 10:30 am. ✉ *66 Charoen Krung Rd., Wang Burapha, Phra Nakhon* ☎ *02/224–4499, 02/225–8757* *www.salachalermkrung.com* 🎫 *B400* Ⓜ *BTS: Saphan Taksin.*

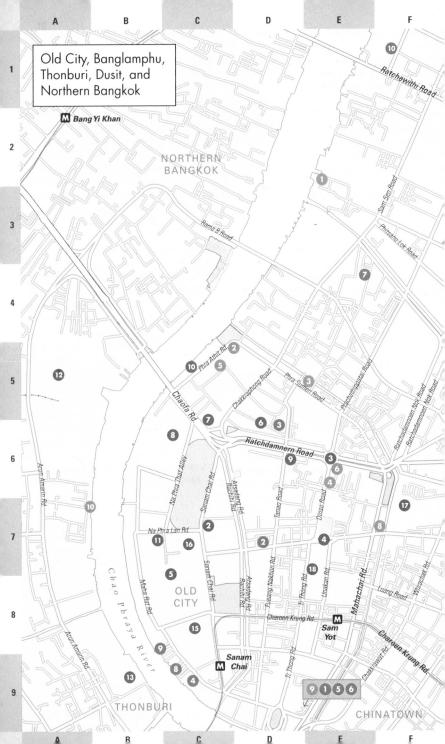

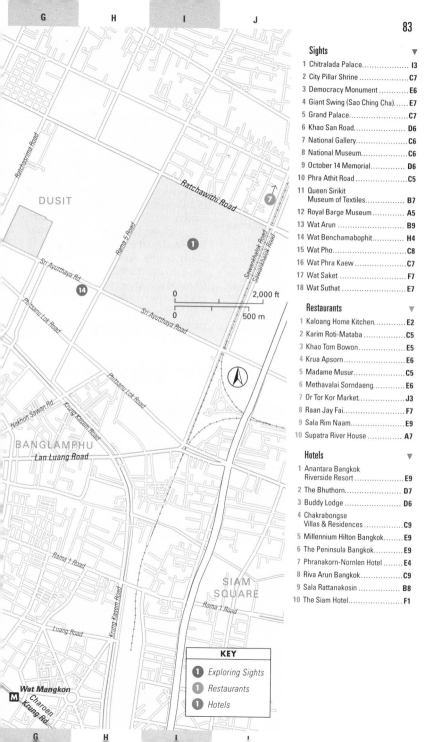

Sights ▼

Restaurants ▼

Hotels ▼

KEY

1 *Exploring Sights*

1 *Restaurants*

1 *Hotels*

Shopping

JEWELRY

Thailand is known for its sparkling gems, and the country exports more colored stones than anywhere in the world. You'll find things you wouldn't find at home, and prices are far lower than in the United States. There are countless jewelry stores on Silom and Surawong roads. Scams are common, though, so it's best to stick with established businesses.

■ TIP➔ **Deals that seem too good to be true probably are.**

Johny's Gems

JEWELRY & WATCHES | If you call first, this long-established firm will send a car—a common practice of the city's better stores—to bring you to the shop near Wat Phra Kaew. The selection is massive, and you can order custom-designed pieces. ✉ *199 Fuengnakorn Rd., Phra Nakhon* ☎ *02/224–4065* ⊕ *www.johnysgems.com* ⊗ *Closed Sun.* Ⓜ *MRT: Sam Yot, then walk 4 blocks or take taxi.*

Lin Jewelers

JEWELRY & WATCHES | The jewelry sold at this highly respected shop is more expensive than average, but so is the quality. ✉ *9 Charoen Krung, Soi 38, Bang Rak* ☎ *02/234–2819, 06/366–99636* ⊕ *www.linjewelers.com* Ⓜ *BTS: Saphan Taksin.*

Banglamphu

In the northern part of the Old City, Banglamphu offers pleasant strolls, interesting markets, and Khao San Road, one of the world's best-known backpacker hubs. Visitors from dozens of countries populate the scene year-round, served by an equally diverse selection of restaurants and street vendors.

Sights

Khao San Road

STREET | This thoroughfare dates back to a time when it was primarily occupied by rice vendors, hence the name Khao San, which means "milled rice." Since the mid-1980s the road and surrounding neighborhood have become the world's most well-known backpacking scene. More recently, the Thais have attempted to make it trendy, adding more upscale accommodation amid the ubiquitous low-budget guesthouses, and turning Khao San Road itself into a pedestrian-only street. There's a plethora of Western and Thai restaurants in the area, most of which are rather mediocre. The road has become popular as well with Thais, who frequent the bars, especially on weekends. Early evening is the best time to stroll or sit back and people-watch. The frenetic activity can, depending on your perspective, be infectious or overwhelming. During Songkran, the Thai New Year, in mid-April, Khao San turns into one huge wet-and-wild water fight. Join in the fun only if you don't mind being completely soaked. ✉ *Khao San Rd., Banglamphu* ✢ *Between Chakrapong and Tanao Rds.; head southeast from Phra Athit ferry pier.*

Phra Athit Road

STREET | Chao Phraya breezes cool the short path that leads from the Phra Athit ferry pier to Santichaiprakarn Park, a tree-lined spot at the northern end of Phra Athit Road. The park, a delightful place to sit and watch the river, contains **Phra Sumen Fort,** one of the two remaining forts of the original 14 built under King Rama I. Some of the buildings along Phra Athit Road itself date back more than 100 years. At night the street, a favorite of university students, comes alive with little bars and restaurants hosting live music. ✉ *Phra Athit Rd., Banglamphu* ✢ *Take taxi, or Chao Phraya ferry to Phra Athit pier.*

Cooking Classes

A Thai cooking class can be a great way to spend a half day—or longer. You won't become an expert, but you can learn a few fundamentals and some of the history of Thai cuisine. You can also find specialty classes that focus on things like fruit carving (where the first lesson learned is that it's more difficult than it looks) or hot-and-spicy soups. All cooking schools concentrate on practical dishes that students will be able to make at home, usually with spices that are internationally available, and all revolve around the fun of eating something you cooked (at least partly) yourself.

■ TIP→ **Book cooking classes ahead of time, as they fill up fast.**

Most classes are small enough to allow individual attention and time for questions. Prices vary from B2,000 to more than B10,000.

Blue Elephant Cooking School. Long a favorite, and connected with the same-named restaurant, this school has a very friendly staff. The Thai dishes taught here are heavily Westernized. ✉ *233 S. Sathorn Rd., Sathorn* ☎ *267–39353* 🌐 *www.blueelephant.com* 🎫 *From B2,800 per half day* [M] *BTS: Surasak.*

Cooking with Poo & Friends. Khun Poo and her assistant instructors offer a grassroots approach to Thai culinary lessons, at a location near the massive Khlong Toey Market, one of the largest fresh produce markets in the world. Small-group classes cost 1,500 baht and last three to four hours, including a market trip to source ingredients. ✉ *Khlong Toey Market, Klong Toey* ☎ *08/768–63714* 🌐 *www.cookingwith-poo.com* 🎫 *B1,500* [M] *MRT: Khlong Toey, then taxi. BTS: Ekamai, then taxi.*

Oriental Thai Cooking School. The cooking school at the Mandarin Oriental hotel is Bangkok's most established and expensive, but the classes are fun and informative, and the dishes tend to be authentic. Classes are taught in a beautiful century-old house across the river from the hotel. A visit to a local market is part of the program. ✉ *Mandarin Oriental, 48 Oriental Ave., Bang Rak* ☎ *02/659–9000* 🌐 *www.mandarinoriental.com/bangkok/chao-phraya-river/luxury-hotel/experiences* 🎫 *B5,300 per person, two-person minimum* [M] *BTS: Saphan Taksin then hotel boat.*

🍴 Restaurants

Touristy Khao San Road is north of the Old City, though the tame Thai food available in this backpacker mecca is nothing to go out of your way for. Don't be afraid to sample the street food in the alleyways away from Khao San Road—it often makes for a memorable meal. Generally speaking, the better, more authentic eateries in Banglamphu are found along Dinso and Tanao Roads.

Karim Roti-Mataba

$ | **INDIAN** | In a century-old building across from Santichaiprakarn Park on the Chao Phraya, a short walk from Khao San Road, this little two-story restaurant serves Indian and Thai-Muslim cuisine. The specialty, as the name suggests, is sizzling *mataba,* unleavened flatbread filled with your choice of vegetables, chicken, beef, fish, or seafood. **Known for:** popular with tourists; Thai-Muslim dishes like Massaman curry; air-conditioned seating. [$] *Average main: B44* ✉ *136 Phra*

Athit Rd., Banglamphu ☎ *02/282–2119* ⊕ *www.roti-mataba.net* ⊟ *No credit cards* Ⓜ *Chao Phraya River Express: Phra Athit Pier.*

Khao Tom Bowon

$$ | THAI | Across the street from Wat Bowonniwet, this humble eatery is famed for high-quality *khao tom,* rice soup served with a wide variety of Chinese-Thai dishes, including excellent *phat phak bung* (water spinach stir-fried with chili and garlic), *jap chai* (mixed-vegetable stew), and *pet phalo* (five-spice duck in gravy). This is a good late-night eating choice, since it's open daily from 5 pm to 3 am. **Known for:** open very late; local favorite; khao tom. Ⓢ *Average main: 200* ⊠ *243 Phra Sumen Rd., Banglamphu* ⊹ *Northeast of Khao San Rd.* ☎ *02/629–1739* ⊟ *No credit cards.*

Madame Musur

$$ | THAI | The only restaurant in Banglamphu focusing on northern Thai cuisine is tucked away in a quiet corner of Rambutri Road not far from Khao San. *Khao soi,* a northern Thai dish of egg noodles in a mild curry broth, is a house specialty. **Known for:** amazing khao soi; atmospheric bamboo furniture; convenient location to Khao San Road. Ⓢ *Average main: 350* ⊠ *41 Rambutri Rd., Banglamphu* ☎ *02/281–4238* ⊕ *www.facebook.com/madamemusur* ⊘ *Closed Mon.*

Hotels

Buddy Lodge

$ | HOTEL | This colonial-style semi-boutique hotel has contributed greatly to the upgrading of Khao San Road. **Pros:** rooftop pool; happening location; comfortable rooms. **Cons:** no MRT or BTS access; nothing fancy; high price for Khao San Road. Ⓢ *Rooms from: B1,598* ⊠ *265 Khao San Rd., Banglamphu* ☎ *02/629–4477* ⊕ *www.buddylodge.com* ☥⊙ *No Meals* ⤸ *76 rooms.*

Nightlife

Khao San Road, along with most nearby streets in the neighborhood, is abuzz with bars and cafes that stay open late into the night. There are also a couple of long-standing music venues.

LIVE MUSIC

Adhere The 13th Blues Bar

LIVE MUSIC | This small, narrow shophouse bar has been hosting top-shelf blues and R&B bands for two decades. ⊠ *13 Samsen Rd., Banglamphu* ☎ *08/976–94613* ⊕ *www.facebook.com/adhere13thbluesbar* ⊘ *Closed Mon. and Tues.*

Brick Bar

LIVE MUSIC | Behind Buddy Lodge on Khao San itself, Brick Bar is a longtime venue known for nightly live music, often ska or reggae. It can fit a pretty big crowd. ⊠ *265 Khao San Rd., Banglamphu.*

Brown Sugar

LIVE MUSIC | A good place to check out live jazz and the occasional blues band, the smoky Brown Sugar has been in business for over three decades. ⊠ *469 Phra Sumen Rd., Banglamphu* ☎ *06/379–49895, 02/282–0396* ⊕ *www.facebook.com/brownsugarbangkok* ⊘ *Closed Mon.*

Shopping

FOOD

Nittaya Thai Curry

FOOD | If you're thinking about bringing home a taste of Thailand, Nittaya Thai Curry shop has premade curry pastes packed in durable pouches so that you can make authentic Thai curry in your own kitchen. ⊠ *136-40 Chakrabongse Rd., Banglamphu* ☎ *02/281–8214.*

MARKETS

Khao San Road

MARKET | Yes, this is backpacker central, with harem pants and cheesy souvenirs for sale, and lots of cheap pad Thai street food, but the people-watching can be entertaining. ✉ *Khao San Rd., Banglamphu* ✥ *Between Chakrapong and Tanao Rds.; head southeast from Phra Athit ferry pier.*

Thonburi

Crisscrossed by canals, Thonburi is an atmospheric area to take a ride along the city's ancient waterways and fully appreciate the wonderful "Thai-ness" of Bangkok. The Chao Phraya riverbank is undergoing major retail and condo development, but the dozens of canals winding deep into Thonburi are still lined with old wooden homes and temples.

Sights

Royal Barge Museum

OTHER MUSEUM | Splendid ceremonial barges are berthed on the Thonburi side of the Chao Phraya River. The boats, carved in the early part of the 19th century, take the form of mythical creatures in the *Ramakien.* The most impressive is the red-and-gold royal vessel called *Suphannahongse* (Golden Swan), used by the king on special occasions. Carved from a single piece of teak, it measures about 150 feet and weighs more than 15 tons. Fifty oarsmen propel it along the river, accompanied by flag wavers, two coxswains, and a rhythm-keeper. The museum is challenging to find, so you may want to join a tour or find a taxi driver who knows the area. **TIP→ Steer clear of scam artists offering tours or claiming that the museum is closed.** ✉ *80/1 Arun Amarin Rd., Thonburi* ✥ *Chao Phraya River Express Boat to Phra Pinklao Pier, then taxi to the museum.* ☎ *02/424–0004* 🌐 *www.finearts.go.th/museumroyalbarges* 🎟 *B100.*

★ **Wat Arun** (*Temple of Dawn*)

RELIGIOUS BUILDING | This riverside spot is inspiring at sunrise, but it's even more marvelous toward dusk, when the setting sun throws amber tones over the entire area. In front of the monastery facing the river is a square courtyard containing an impressive 341-feet tall *prang* (Khmer-style tower), surrounded by four smaller ones. All five prangs are covered in mosaics assembled from broken Chinese porcelain originally used as ballast on ships coming from China. Energetic visitors can climb the steep steps about halfway up the main tower overlooking the Chao Phraya; the less ambitious can linger in the small riverside park. ✉ *34 Arun Amarin Rd., Thonburi* ✥ *Chao Phraya River Express Boat to Tha Tien Pier, then cross-river ferry to Wat Arun.* ☎ *02/466–3167* 🌐 *www.watarun1.com/en* 🎟 *B50.*

Restaurants

In Thonburi you'll find restaurants with incredible river views, as well as dinner cruises. The latter are a lovely way to see the city, though the food is usually rather mediocre. *See the Dinner Cruises box for more info.*

Sala Rim Naam

$$$$ | **THAI** | Come to Sala Rim Naam—part of the Mandarin Oriental hotel but across the river—to soak up the atmosphere, which includes a classical Thai dancing show nightly at 7:45 pm in an indoor pavilion, or to enjoy the romantic mood of alfresco tables overlooking the river. The renditions of Thai food are rather Westernized, but the set dinners, buffet lunches, and à la carte menus offer plenty of choices. **TIP→ There is a complimentary shuttle boat across the Chao Phraya River from the Mandarin Oriental Hotel. Known for:** extensive menu; Thai dancing shows; riverside terrace. [$] *Average main: B1,000* ✉ *48 Oriental Ave., Thonburi* ☎ *02/659–9000* 🌐 *www.mandarinoriental.com/bangkok* [M] *BTS: Saphan Taksin, then hotel boat.*

Supatra River House

$$ | THAI | Located on the Chao Phraya River across from the Grand Palace, this charming restaurant is in the former home of Khunying Supatra, founder of Bangkok's express boat business. A free ferry from Maharaj Pier shuttles diners back and forth to enjoy impressive views and Thai cuisine, with multicourse prixe-fixe meals and à la carte options. **Known for:** steamed sea bass in soy or spicy lemon; riverside terrace; great for sunsets. $ *Average main: B330* ⊠ *266 Soi Wat Rakhang, Arunamarin Rd., Siriraj* ☎ *02/411–0305, 08/630–32811* ⊕ *www. bangkokriver.com/place/supatra-river-house/* Ⓜ *BTS: Saphan Taksin, then river ferry.*

 ## Hotels

Anantara Bangkok Riverside Resort

$$$$ | RESORT | Getting to the Anantara is a pleasant adventure in itself—free boats shuttle guests down the Chao Phraya from Saphan Taksin Pier—and once there, the large pool and garden area on the riverside make you feel a long way from downtown's bustle. **Pros:** great service; resort feel; lots of activities. **Cons:** may feel too secluded; a hassle to get into the city; not all rooms have views. $ *Rooms from: B7,920* ⊠ *257/1–3 Charoen Nakhon Rd., Thonburi* ☎ *02/365–9110* ⊕ *www. anantara.com/en/riverside-bangkok* Ⓜ *No Meals* ⤍ *281 guest rooms and 95 suites* Ⓜ *BTS: Saphan Taksin, then hotel boat.*

★ Millenium Hilton Bangkok

$$$$ | HOTEL | Lording over the Chao Phraya, this flagship Hilton designed with cutting-edge flair competes successfully with Bangkok's other hotel giants but has far lower rates. **Pros:** all rooms have city and river views; snazzy amenities; cool pool area. **Cons:** across the river from downtown pursuits; rooms somewhat small; ferry service takes time. $ *Rooms from: B2,280* ⊠ *123 Charoen Nakhon Rd., Klong San* ☎ *02/442–2000* ⊕ *www. hilton.com/en/hotels/bkkhitw-millenni-um-hilton-bangkok* Ⓜ *Free Breakfast* ⤍ *533 rooms* Ⓜ *BTS: Saphan Taksin.*

The Peninsula Bangkok

$$$$ | HOTEL | The rooms at the Peninsula have plenty of high-tech gadgets, among them bathrooms with hands-free phones and mist-free TV screens, and bedside controls that dim the lights and close the curtains. **Pros:** awesome views; beautiful pool; exceptional service. **Cons:** on-site dining not very good; most attractions are across the river; outrageously expensive for Bangkok. $ *Rooms from: B9,200* ⊠ *333 Charoen Nakhon Rd., Klong San* ☎ *02/020–2888* ⊕ *www.peninsula.com/ en/bangkok/5-star-luxury-hotel-riverside* Ⓜ *No Meals* ⤍ *370 rooms and suites* Ⓜ *BTS: Saphan Taksin.*

 ## Nightlife

The best reason to visit Thonburi is to take in the river views at some of the fancier hotel bars.

BARS AND PUBS

Longtail by the River

This bar distinguishes itself with a tropical feel that is generally elusive in Bangkok—you can drink your cocktails by the river, either in a traditional sala or on outdoor sofas. To get here you need to sail about 30 minutes from Saphan Taksin Pier on one of the Anantara resort's dedicated boats, which can be quite pleasant on a nice evening. ⊠ *Anantara Bangkok Riverside, 257 Charoen Nakhon Rd., Samrae Thonburi, Thonburi* ☎ *02/476–0022* ⊕ *www.anantara. com/en/riverside-bangkok/restaurants/ longtail-bar.*

Shopping

IconSiam

MALL | Opened in 2018 on the banks of the Chao Phraya River, IconSiam is one of the largest shopping malls in Asia. The sleek, multilevel, air-conditioned space is filled with shops and restaurants, including the first Apple Store in Thailand and Michelin-starred Blue by Alain Ducasse. There's also a 14-theater cineplex and a huge food court designed to resemble a floating market. ✉ *299 Charoen Nakhon Rd., Klong San* ☎ *02/495–7080* 🌐 *www.iconsiam.com* [M] *BTS: Krung Thonburi; free shuttle boat from Sathorn Pier and from nearby riverside hotels.*

Dusit and Northern Bangkok

More than any other neighborhood in the city, this area north of Banglamphu seems calm and orderly. Its tree-shaded boulevards and elegant buildings befit the district that holds Dusit Palace, a compound of residences that's been home to every Thai king since Rama V. The first of the country's monarchs to visit Europe, Rama V based the neighborhood's layout on foreign cities he had visited. Dusit is a sprawling area, but the major attractions are fairly close together.

Sights

Chitralada Palace

CASTLE/PALACE | All Thai kings since Rama V have resided at this sprawling palace compound, where the residential part of the property is sometimes referred to as Chitralada Royal Villa. Although it's closed to the public, the surrounding walls and moat are a lovely sight, especially when lighted to celebrate royal-related holidays. The extensive grounds shelter a small herd of royal white elephants and a farm established by the late Rama IX, although these can't be seen from outside. A small, beautifully designed train station reserved for royal use can be seen along the rail line parallel to Kamphaeng Phet 5 Road. ✉ *Ratchawithi Rd. and Rama V Rd., Dusit* [M] *BTS: Victory Monument (take a taxi from the station).*

Wat Benchamabophit (*Marble Temple*)

RELIGIOUS BUILDING | Built in 1899, this wat is a favorite with photographers because of its open spaces and bright, shining marble. Fifty-two Buddha statues of various styles surround the courtyard, the magnificent interior has crossbeams of lacquer and gold, and an exquisite, bronze seated Buddha is the focal point of the ordination hall's main altar. But Wat Benchamabophit is more than a glorious structure. The monastery here is a seat of learning that appeals to Buddhist monks with intellectual yearnings. ✉ *Rama V Rd., Dusit* ☎ *02/282–9686* 🎫 *B50* [M] *BTS: Victory Monument (take a taxi from station).*

Restaurants

Northern Bangkok is worth dining in only if you happen to be in the neighborhood for sightseeing, or if you really want to get to a part of the the city that's off the beaten track.

Kaloang Home Kitchen

$$ | **THAI** | An alley near the National Library leads to this off-the-beaten-track restaurant on a ramshackle pier overlooking the Chao Phraya River. Kaloang Home Kitchen might not look like much with its plastic seats and simple tables, but it's a local favorite for waterfront breezes that keeping things comfortably cool, as well as generous grilled seafood platters and giant river prawns. **Known for:** well-priced seafood; no-frills dining; riverside location. [$] *Average main: B250* ✉ *2 Sri Ayutthaya Rd., Dusit* ☎ *02/281–9228,* 🌐 *www.kaloanghome.com.*

Continued on page 98

The
Grand Palace

Thais regard their royal family with great respect, so it's no surprise that they hold the Grand Palace in high esteem. But the main attraction here is not a royal residence—it's Wat Phra Kaew (Temple of the Emerald Buddha), the home King Rama I built for the country's most revered idol. The temple is a reminder that in a country where everyone bows to the king, even the king bows to the Buddha.

by Lee Middleton

When Rama I was crowned in 1782, he wanted to celebrate the kingdom's renewed power. He moved the capital to Bangkok and set out to exceed the grandeur of Ayutthaya, once one of Asia's finest cities. The result was the dazzling Grand Palace compound, protected by a high white wall over a mile long. Rama I both ruled from and lived in the palace. Indeed, the royal family resided here until 1946, and each king who came to power added to the compound, leaving a mark of his rule and the era. Today, the Grand Palace compound's official use is for state occasions and ceremonies like coronations. The current monarch, King Maha Vajiralongkorn(Rama X), lives in Chitralada Palace which is closed to the public and is in Bangkok's Dusit District, northeast of the palace.

GRAND PALACE COMPOUND

The palace grounds and Wat Phra Kaew are open to visitors, but many of the buildings in the complex are not. If you arrive by boat, you will land at Chiang Pier (tha Chang). Make your way to the main entrance on Na Phra Lan Road. **Wat Phra Kaew** is the best place to begin your tour. Other highlights are **Phra Thinang Amarin Winichai Mahaisun** (Amarinda Winichai Throne Hall), **Chakri Maha Prasat** (Grand Palace Hall), **Dusit Maha Prasat** (Audience Hall), **Phra Thinang Borom Phiman** (Borom Phiman Mansion), and the **Wat Phra Kaew Museum**.

Mural at the Grand Palace.

Phra Thinang Borom Phiman

5

1 **Wat Phra Kaew**

PRASAT PHRA DHEPBIDORN

HOR PHRA MONTHIAN DHARMA

PHRA MONDOP

PHRA WIHARN YOD

HOR PHRA NAGA

PHRA SIRATANA CHEDI

Shop

SALA SAHADAYA

MAIN ENTRANCE

TEXTILE MUSEUM

Na Phra lan Road

1 Wat Phra Kaew. King Rama I built Wat Phra Kaew—now regarded as Thailand's most sacred temple—in 1785. The main building, called ubosoth, houses the Emerald Buddha. The ubosoth has three doors; only the king and queen are allowed to enter through the central door.

2 Phra Thinang Amarin Winichai Mahaisun. The only part of Rama I's original residence that's open to visitors is used today for royal events such as the king's birthday celebration. Inside this audience hall are an antique boat-shaped throne from Rama I's reign that's now used to hold Buddha images during ceremonies, and a second throne with a nine-tiered white canopy where the king sits. At the entrance, you'll see gold-topped red poles once used by royal guests to tether their elephants.

Golden statue.

Wat Phra Kaew.

3 Chakri Maha Prasat. Rama V's residence, built in 1882, is the largest of the palace buildings. The hybrid Thai–European style was a compromise between Rama V, who wanted a neoclassical palace with a domed roof, and his advisors, who thought such a blatantly European design was inappropriate. Rama V agreed to a Thai-style roof; Thais nicknamed the building farang sai chada or "the westerner wearing a Thai hat."

4 Dusit Maha Prasat. Built in 1784, the Audience Hall contains Rama I's original teak and mother-of-pearl throne. Today the hall is where Thais view royal remains, which are placed here temporarily in a golden urn.

5 Phra Thinang Borom Phiman. King Rama V built this French-style palace for his son (the future Rama VI) in 1903. Though later kings did not use the palace much, today visiting dignitaries stay here.

6 Wat Phra Kaew Museum. Stop by after touring the compound to learn about the restoration of the palace and to see the seasonal robes of the Emerald Buddha. Labels are in Thai, but free English tours occur regularly.

PHRA THINANG BUDDHA RATANA STARN

PHRA THINANG SRIDHALA PIROMYA

2 Phra Thinang Amarin Winichai Mahaisun

PHRA THINANG MOONSTARN BAROMART

Inner Palace Area (Closed To Public)

PHRA THINANG SOMUT DEVARAJ UBBAT

PHRA THINANG PHIMAN RATAYA

Ticket

PHIMANCHAISRI GATE

3 Chakri Maha Prasat

4 Dusit Maha Prasat

APHONPIMOK PHASAT PAVILION

SALA LUKHUM

Wat Phra Kaew Museum

6

CHANG PIER

Elephants, or chang, symbolize independence, power, and luck in Thai culture. Kings once rode them into battle, and the palace even included a department to care for royal elephants. This pier is named for the kings' beasts, which were bathed here. Many elephant statues also grace the complex grounds. Notice how smooth the tops of their heads are—Thais rub the heads of elephants for luck.

Chang Pier

TOURING TIPS

■ Free guided tours of the compound are usually available in English at 10:00, 10:30, 1:30, and 2:00 daily; confirm at the ticket office. Personal audio guides are available for B200 plus a passport or credit card as a deposit.

■ The best way to get here is to take the Skytrain to Taksin Station and then board the Chao Phraya River Express boat to Chang Pier. It's a short walk from the pier to the palace entrance. You can also take a taxi to the Grand Palace but you may end up wasting time in traffic or getting ripped off.

■ Don't listen to men loitering outside the grounds who claim that the compound is closed for a Buddhist holiday or for cleaning, or who offer to show you the "Lucky Buddha" or take you on a special tour. These phony guides will ultimately lead you to a gift shop where they receive a commission.

■ Allow half a day to tour the complex. You'll probably want to spend three hours in Wat Phra Kaew and the other buildings, and another half-hour in the museums.

■ Wat Phra Kaew is actually worth two visits: one on a weekday (when crowds are thinner and you can explore at a leisurely pace) and another on a Sunday or public holiday, when the smell of flowers and incense and the murmur of prayer evoke the spirituality of the place.

⊠ Sana Chai Rd., Old City
☎ 02/224–1833
💴 B500, admission includes entrance to Wat Phra Kaew, The Royal Thai Decorations & Coins Pavilion, and Museum of Textiles.
🕙 Daily 8:30–3:30.

The Grand Palace.

WAT PHRA KAEW

Yaksha.

As you enter the temple compound, you'll see 20-foot-tall statues of fearsome creatures in battle attire. These are *yakshas*—guardians who protect the Emerald Buddha from evil spirits. Turn right to see the murals depicting the *Ramakien* epic. Inside the main chapel, which is quiet and heavy with the scent of incense, you'll find the Emerald Buddha.

THE RAMAKIEN

The *Ramakien* is the 2,000-year-old Thai adaptation of the famous Indian epic the *Ramayana,* which dates from around 400 BC. Beginning at the temple's north gate (across from Phra Wihan Yot [the Spired Hall]) and continuing clockwise around the cloister, 178 mural panels illustrate the story, which, like most epics, is about the struggle between good and evil. It begins with the founding of Ayutthaya (City of the Gods) and Lanka (City of the Demons) and focuses on the trials and tribulations of Ayutthaya's Prince Rama: his expulsion from his own kingdom; the abduction of his wife, Sita; and his eventual triumph over the demon Tosakan.

Sita's Abduction

Rama's wife Sita is abducted by the evil demon king, Tosakan, ruler of Lanka. Disguising himself as a deer, Tosakan lures Sita to his palace. A battle ensues, forming a large part of the long and detailed epic, which concludes when Rama rescues Sita.

Section of *Ramakien*.

THE APSONSI

The beautiful gilded figures on the upper terraces of Wat Phra Kaew are *apsonsi*—mythical half-angel, half-lion creatures who guard the temple. According to Thai mythology, apsonsi inhabit the Himavant Forest, which is the realm between earth and the heavens.

Ramakien battle scene.

Aponsi.

THE EMERALD BUDDHA

Thailand's most sacred Buddha image is made of a single piece of jade and is only 31 inches tall. The statue, which historians believe was sculpted in Thailand in the 14th or 15th century, was at one point covered in plaster; in 1434 it was discovered in Chiang Rai as the plaster began to flake.

When the king of nearby Chiang Mai heard about the jade Buddha, he demanded it be brought to him. According to legend, the statue was sent to the king three times, but each time the elephant transporting it veered off to Lampang, 60 miles southeast of Chiang Mai. Finally the king came to the Buddha, building a temple at that spot.

The Buddha was kept at various temples in northern Thailand until Laotian invaders stole it in 1552. It stayed in Laos until the 18th century, when King Rama I captured Vientiane, the capital, reclaimed the statue, and brought it to Bangkok.

Perched in a gilded box high above the altar, the diminutive statue is difficult to see. This doesn't deter Thai Buddhists, who believe that praying before the Emerald Buddha will earn them spiritual merit, helping to ensure a better rebirth in the next life.

The king is the only person allowed to touch the Emerald Buddha. Three times a year, he changes the Buddha's robes in a ceremony to bring good fortune for the coming season. The Buddha's hot season attire includes a gold crown and jewels; in the rainy season, it wears a headdress of gold, enamel, and sapphires; and, in the

Emerald Buddha in hot season outfit.

cool season, it's adorned in a mesh robe of gold beads.

Most Thais make an offering to the Buddha when they visit the temple. Inexpensive offerings, for sale outside the temple, generally include three joss sticks, a candle, and a thin piece of gold leaf stuck on a sheet of paper. At some wats, Thais stick gold leaves on the Buddha, but since that's not possible here, keep it as a souvenir or attach it to another sacred image (some elephant statues have gold leaves on their heads.) Light the candle from others that are already burning on the front alter, then light the incense with your candle.

WHAT'S A WAT?

A wat is a Buddhist temple or monastery, typically made up of a collection of shrines and structures in an enclosed courtyard, rather than a single building. Traditionally, monks reside in wats, but Wat Phra Kaew is a ceremonial temple, not a place of Buddhist study, so monks don't live here.

HONORING THE EMERALD BUDDHA

Thais usually follow an offering with three prostrations, or bows, to the Buddha. To prostrate, sit facing the Buddha with your legs folded or your feet tucked under you—then follow the sequence below. After prostrating you can sit in front of the Buddha in prayer or meditation for as long as you like.

1) Hold your hands together in a *wai* (palms together, fingers pointing up) at your heart.

2) Bring the *wai* up to touch your forehead.

3) Place your palms on the ground and bow your forehead until it's touching the ground between them.

4) Sit up, bring your hands back into a *wai* in front of your heart, and repeat.

TEMPLE ETIQUETTE

Even if you don't want to make an offering, pray, or prostrate, it's OK to linger in the temple or sit down. Here are a few other things to keep in mind:

■ Appropriate dress—long-sleeved shirts and long pants or skirts—is required. Open-toed shoes must be "closed" by wearing socks. If you've come scantily clad, you can rent a sarong at the palace.

■ Never point—with your hands or your feet—at the Emerald Buddha, other sacred objects, or even another person. If you sit down in the temple, make sure not to accidentally point your feet in the Buddha's direction.

■ When walking around religious monuments, try to move in a clockwise direction. Thais believe that the right side of the body is superior to the left, so it's more respectful to keep your right side closer to sacred objects.

■ Keep your head below the Buddha and anything else sacred. Thais will often bend their knees and lower their heads when walking past a group of older people or monks; it's a gesture of respect even if their heads aren't technically below the monks'.

Offerings.

Bargaining in Bangkok

Even if you've honed your bargaining skills in other countries, you might still come up empty-handed in Thailand. The aggressive techniques that work well in say, Delhi, won't get you very far in Bangkok. One of the highest compliments you can pay for any activity in the Land of Smiles is calling it *sanuk* (fun), and haggling is no exception. Thais love to joke and tease, so approach each bargaining situation playfully. Nevertheless, be aware that Thais are also sensitive to "losing face," so make sure you remain pleasant and respectful throughout the transaction.

As you enter a market stall, smile and acknowledge the proprietor. When something catches your eye, inquire politely about the price, but don't immediately counter. Keep your voice low—you're more likely to get a deal if

it's not announced to the whole shop—then ask for a price just slightly below what you want. Don't get too cavalier with your counteroffer—Thai sellers generally price their wares in a range they view as fair, so asking to cut the initial price in half will most likely be seen as an insult and might end the discussion abruptly. In most cases the best you can hope for is a 20% to 30% discount.

If the price the shopkeeper offers in return is still high, turn your smile up another watt and say something like, "Can you discount more?" If the answer is no, your last recourse is to say thank you and walk away. If you are called back, the price is still negotiable; if you aren't, maybe the last price quoted wasn't such a bad one after all.

★ Or Tor Kor Market

$ | **THAI** | **FAMILY** | Inundated with colors, sounds, and smells, this is where Bangkok's top Thai chefs shop for quality produce, herbs, and cooking gear. The market's food court is a legendary spot where spicy Thai fare is scooped onto plastic plates; you pick up the cutlery from trays, and grab a seat at one of the tables in the center. **Known for:** raw and cooked seafood; traditional Thai-market atmosphere; fresh tropical fruits and vegetables. $ *Average main: B100* ✉ *101 Kamphaeng Phet Rd., Chatuchak* ☎ *02/279–2080* ⊕ *www.mof.or.th* ⚌ *No credit cards* Ⓜ *MRT: Chatuchak Park; BTS: Saphan Kwai or Mo Chit.*

Nightlife

There aren't that many nightlife spots frequented by foreigners around here, but the area around Victory Monument is home to the long-running Saxophone Pub, along with a smattering of good bars along the nearby Soi Rangnam.

BARS AND PUBS

Saxophone Pub

LIVE MUSIC | Popular with locals and expats for over 30 years, the spacious Saxophone hosts some of Thailand's best rhythm and blues, jazz, blues, rock, reggae, and ska bands. There are bars on each of the three floors. ✉ *3/8 Phayathai Rd., Victory Monument* ☎ *02/246–5472* ⊕ *www.saxophonepub.com* Ⓜ *BTS: Victory Monument.*

Performing Arts

THEATER AND DANCE

Siam Niramit

This 2,000-seat theater presents *Journey to the Enchanted Kingdom of Siam,* a history of Thailand told in words and music. The 80-minute performance begins at 8 pm nightly. ⊠ *19 Tiamruammit Rd., Huai Khwang* ☎ *02/649–9222* ⊕ *www. siamniramit.com* 💲 *B1,500; with dinner B1,850* Ⓜ *MRT: Thailand Cultural Center.*

Thailand Cultural Center

The center hosts local and international performing artists, including opera companies, symphony orchestras, and modern dance and ballet troupes. ⊠ *14 Thiam Ruammit Rd, Huai Khwang* ☎ *02/247–0028* ⊕ *www.facebook.com/ ThailandCulturalCentre/* Ⓜ *MRT: Thai Cultural Center.*

🛍 Shopping

DUTY-FREE SHOPPING

King Power International Group

DUTY-FREE | If you want the convenience of duty-free shopping, try King Power. You choose and pay for the items at the shop or online, then pick them up at Suvarnabhumi Airport when you depart Thailand (or simply take them with you). You need your passport and an airline ticket, and you need to make your purchase at least eight hours before leaving the country. The airport branch is open 24 hours. ⊠ *King Power Complex, 8/2 Rangnam Rd., Phayathai, Ratchathewi* ☎ *1631 contact center, 02/205–8888* ⊕ *www.kingpower.com* Ⓜ *BTS: Victory Monument.*

MARKETS

★ Chatuchak Weekend Market

MARKET | You can buy just about anything at the city's largest market, including silk items in a *mudmee* (tie-dyed before weaving) design that would sell for five times the price in the United States.

Despite its name the market is open daily, though it's best to come on Friday or the weekend—in the morning before the place gets too crowded and hot. An afternoon at JJ, as it is known by locals ("ch" is pronounced "jha" in Thai, so phonetically Chatuchak is Jatujak), is not for the faint of heart: up to 200,000 people visit each day, and there are more than 15,000 vendors. Keep your bearings by remembering that the outer ring has mainly new clothing and shoes, with some plants, garden supplies, and home decor. The next ring is primarily used (and some new) clothing and shoes plus accessories like jewelry, belts, and bags. Farther in are pottery, antiques, furniture, dried goods, and live animals. Be prepared with bottles of water, comfortable shoes, and make sure to print out a copy of the map of the market from the website. Strategically placed food vendors mean you don't have to stop shopping to grab a bite. ⊠ *Phaholyothin Rd., Chatuchak* ⊕ *www.chatuchakmarket.org* Ⓜ *MRT: Chatuchak Park; BTS: Mo Chit.*

Chinatown

Chinatown is Bangkok's oldest residential neighborhood, bustling with markets, teahouses, restaurants, and, more recently, art galleries, hip cafes, and trendy bars. Like much of the Old City, Chinatown is a great place to explore on foot. Meandering through the maze of alleys, and ducking into herb shops and temples along the way is a great way to pass an afternoon, though the constant crowd, especially on hot days, can be wearying.

Yaowarat Road, crowded with gold shops and excellent restaurants, is the main thoroughfare. Pahurat Road, Bangkok's "Little India," is full of textile shops, some quite literally underground. Many of the Indian merchant families on this street have been here for generations.

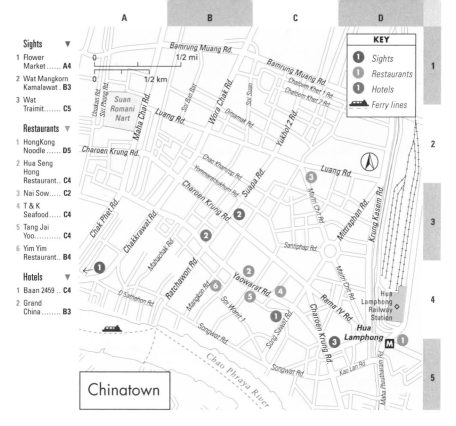

Chinatown

Sights ▼

1 Flower Market **A4**

2 Wat Mangkorn Kamalawat . **B3**

3 Wat Traimit **C5**

Restaurants ▼

1 HongKong Noodle **D5**

2 Hua Seng Hong Restaurant.. **C4**

3 Nai Sow..... **C2**

4 T & K Seafood..... **C4**

5 Tang Jai Yoo........... **C4**

6 Yim Yim Restaurant.. **B4**

Hotels ▼

1 Baan 2459 .. **C4**

2 Grand China **B3**

KEY

1 Sights

1 Restaurants

1 Hotels

Ferry lines

■ **TIP**→ **Getting to Chinatown is easiest via MRT Wat Mangkhon station.**

The amount of traffic in this area cannot be overemphasized: avoid taking a taxi into the neighborhood during the day if you can help it.

◉ Sights

★ **Flower Market** (*Pak Khlong Talat*)
MARKET | Also known as Pak Khlong Talat, the Flower Market covers several city blocks near the river and is filled with flower vendors busy around the clock. It's most interesting at night when more deliveries are heading in and out. This is where individuals and buyers for restaurants, hotels, and other businesses purchase their flowers and bargain prices. Just stroll into the warehouse areas

and watch the action. Many vendors only sell flowers in bulk, but others sell small bundles or even individual flowers. As everywhere else where Thais do business, there are plenty of street stalls selling food. This very photogenic area that sees few tourists is well worth a visit. ⊠ *Chakraphet Rd., between Pripatt and Yod Fa Rds., Phra Nakhon* Ⓜ *MRT: Sanam Chai.*

Wat Mangkhon Kamalawat (*Neng Noi Yee*)
RELIGIOUS BUILDING | In classic Chinese style, this 150-year-old temple has a glazed ceramic roof topped with fearsome dragons. Known in Chinese as Leng Noi Yee, the central shrines contain not only statues of Buddha but other art that incorporate Confucian and Taoist elements. The wat is especially colorful during Chinese New Year, when

Bangkok's Skytrain and Subway

The BTS Skytrain transformed the city when it opened on the late King Bhumibol's birthday in 1999. It now has 60 stations on two lines that intersect at Siam Square. Although the BTS bypasses many parts of the city, it is the speediest way to travel when its route coincides with yours. The fare is B16 to B59, depending on how far you plan to travel, and trains run from 6 am to midnight. The cars are impressively clean and efficient, although they can get tremendously crowded at rush hour. Stations are generally about three minutes apart, so a trip from Chong Nonsi to National Stadium, which is four stations away, will take less than 12 minutes. The MRT subway, which opened its first two lines in 2004, has a total of 54 stations so far. Three more MRT lines are slated to begin operation in 2022, followed by a fourth in coming years. The BTS and MRT intersect at three stations—Chatuchak Park, Sukhumvit, and Saladaeng. MRT fares range from B14 to B70. Many sights spread far apart in the metropolis are near a BTS or MRT station.

thousands of Thais visit the temple to burn incense to pay respect and make merit. ✉ *423 Charoen Krung Rd., Pom Prap Sattru Phai* ☎ *02/222–23975* Ⓜ *MRT: Wat Mangkhon.*

★ **Wat Traimit** (*Temple of the Golden Buddha*)

RELIGIOUS BUILDING | While this temple isn't especially notable for its architecture, off to its side is a small chapel containing the world's largest solid-gold Buddha, cast about nine centuries ago in the Sukhothai style. Weighing 5½ tons and standing 10 feet high, the statue is considered a symbol of strength and power. It's believed that the statue was brought first to Ayutthaya. When the Burmese were about to sack the city, it was covered in plaster. Two centuries later, still in plaster, it was thought to be worth very little; when it was being moved to a new Bangkok temple in the 1950s, it slipped from a crane and was left in the mud by the workmen. In the morning a temple monk, who had dreamed that the statue was divinely inspired, went to see it. Through a crack in the plaster, he saw a glint of yellow. In addition to the Buddha, Wat Traimit's museum devoted to Thai-Chinese history is worth checking out. ✉ *661 Traimit Rd., Samphanthawong* ☎ *08/900–22700* ✉ *B40 for statue, B100 for museum* Ⓜ *MRT: Hua Lamphong.*

🍴 Restaurants

Bangkok's Chinatown is known for its food. The neighborhood draws huge crowds of Thais who spend big bucks on specialties like shark's fin and bird's nest, but you'll also find excellent restaurants serving regional Chinese cuisines such as Chao Zhou or Sichuan, along with traditional Thai food and a sprinkling of international cafes. In the middle of Chinatown, just off Yaowarat, there's a massive Indian fabric market known as Phahurat, and many Indian restaurants do business nearby. Don't overlook Chinatown's street food, the noodle and dumpling shops, and the fruit and spice markets.

HongKong Noodle

$ | **CHINESE** | This famous noodle shop outside the Hua Lamphong railway station is perfectly placed for a quick meal when you first get into Chinatown or on the way out. Thanks to an air-conditioned second floor, it's a little comfier than your average noodle stand, but still quite cheap, and the window offers great people-watching on the street below. **Known for:** noodles and dim sum; convenient location; cheap and satisfying dishes. [$] *Average main: B100* ✉ *513–514 Rong Muang Rd., at Rama IV, Pathumwan* ☎ *02/613–8977* 🌐 *www.hkn.co.th* [M] *MRT: Hua Lamphong.*

Hua Seng Hong Restaurant

$$ | **CHINESE** | In business since 1956, this expensive but worthwhile Chinatown classic takes you straight to Hong Kong with its excellent Cantonese roast meats, dim sum, and service that is authentically brusque. Hua Seng Hong has other locations across Bangkok, including at CentralWorld mall in the city center, but this is the original and most beloved for its bustling atmosphere—from inside to outside on Chinatown's main vein, Yaowarat Road. **Known for:** combo specials and à la carte; delicious fatty duck; goose foot–and–abalone stew. [$] *Average main: B350* ✉ *371–373 Yaowarat Rd., Samphanthawong* ☎ *02/222–7053* 🌐 *www.huasenghong.co.th.*

Nai Sow

$$ | **ASIAN** | This unassuming restaurant next to Wat Plaplachai has a steady clientele thanks to fast service and consistently excellent Chinese-Thai dishes prepared according to the owner's secret family recipes. The lighting and decor are lacking, but that can be forgiven when you taste the traditional *tom yum goong* (spicy, hot and sour shrimp soup), which some deem to be the city's best. **Known for:** specialties such as tom yum goong and the deep-fried taro dessert; family business; very busy with no reservations accepted. [$] *Average main: B320* ✉ *3/1 Maitrichit Rd., Pom Prap Sattru Phai* ☎ *02/222–1539* [M] *MRT: Wat Mongkhon.*

★ **T & K Seafood**

$$ | **THAI** | Proudly displaying the freshest catches on ice out front, this enormous and popular seafood restaurant opens daily at 4 pm and serves until as late as 1:30 am. Make your way through the evening crowds and take a number to secure your table—either on the sidewalk or inside. **Known for:** seating right on Yaowarat Road; fresh shellfish like mussels and razor clams; classic Thai dishes like yellow curry crab. [$] *Average main: B300* ✉ *49–51 Phadungdao Rd., Samphanthawong* ☎ *02/222–34519* 🌐 *www.facebook.com/tkseafood* ⏲ *No lunch* [M] *MRT: Wat Mangkhon.*

Tang Jai Yoo

$$ | **CHINESE** | This open-air seafood restaurant is full of festive round tables and tanks containing live whole crabs, lobsters, and sea leech ready to be cooked in traditional Thai-Chinese style. There are lots of à la carte options from land and sea, but ordering off one of the many set menus is the best way to sample a variety of dishes. **Known for:** traditional Thai-Chinese; stewed turtle soup; whole roasted suckling pig. [$] *Average main: B300* ✉ *85–89 Yaowapanit Rd., Samphanthawong* ☎ *02/224–2167* [M] *MRT: Wat Mangkhon.*

Yim Yim Restaurant

$$ | **CHINESE** | This second-floor restaurant has been serving Chao Zhou cuisine for more than 70 years and though it lacks the elegance of the hotel restaurants in the area—the dining room is simple and you have to walk through the dishwashing room to reach the bathroom—it's a solid option in the heart of Chinatown. The Chinese-style sashimi and the fresh crab claws with ginger are excellent, but if you're feeling bold, try the ham with goatskin dipped in rice vinegar. **Known for:** authentic Chao Zhou Chinese; simple decor; relaxed atmosphere. [$] *Average main: B300* ✉ *89 Yaowa Phanit Rd., off Yaowarat Rd. near intersection with Ratchawong Rd., Samphanthawong* ☎ *02/224–2203* 🌐 *www.facebook.com/yimyim.restaurant* [M] *MRT: Wat Mangkhon.*

Hotels

Baan 2459

$$$ | **HOTEL** | Originally a mansion built in 1916 by the Vadanyakul family, this stately building has had incarnations as a Chinese newspaper printing press, a teahouse, and a warehouse before being turned into a boutique hotel in the heart of Chinatown. **Pros:** historic neighborhood; personalized service; walking distance from MRT. **Cons:** often full; teahouse attracts a lot of nonguests; hard to find. [$] *Rooms from: 5,395* ✉ *98 Soi Phat Sai, off Songsawat Rd., Samphanthawong* ☎ *08/239–32459* 🌐 *www.facebook.com/baan2459* 🍴 *No Meals* 🛏 *4 suites* [M] *MRT: Wat Mangkhon.*

Grand China

$ | **HOTEL** | This Chinatown hotel occupies the top two-thirds of a 25-story tower and while the rooms are somewhat plain they do have panoramic city views. **Pros:** lots of Chinese and Thai food nearby; great city and river views; convenient to the MRT. **Cons:** daytime traffic can be congested; neighborhood not overly tourist-friendly; popular with big groups. [$] *Rooms from: B1,023* ✉ *215 Yaowarat Rd., Samphanthawong* ☎ *02/224–9977* 🌐 *www.grandchina.com* 🍴 *No Meals* 🛏 *155 rooms, 22 suites* [M] *MRT: Wat Mangkhon.*

Shopping

MARKETS

Phahurat Market

MARKET | The Little India market near Chinatown is known for its bargain textiles. A man with a microphone announces when items at a particular stall will be sold at half price, and shoppers surge over to bid. It's best to come in the evening, when it's cooler and many street vendors sell snacks. ✉ *Phahurat Rd., Phra Nakhon* ⊕ *Near intersection of Chakraphet Rd., after Yaowarat* [M] *MRT: Sam Yot.*

Sampeng Lane Market

MARKET | Sampeng Lane, a narrow road running parallel to Yaowarat Road and bisecting Chinatown and Phahurat, is home to the city's oldest continually operating market. The Chinatown half of Sampeng is lined with shops selling wholesale beauty salon accessories, pens, stickers, household wares, and small electronics. Once it enters Phahurat, the lane becomes a fabric center mostly rung by by Sikh merchants. Weekends are ultracrowded. ✉ *Soi Sampeng (Soi Wanit 1), Samphanthawong* ⊕ *Off Yaowarat Rd.* [M] *MRT: Wat Mangkhon; Chao Phraya River Express Boat: Ratchawong Pier.*

Pathumwan

Bangkok has many commercial areas that blend into each other, but Pathumwan, which encompasses two major shopping areas (Siam Square and the Rajaprasong Junction), along with important attractions such as Erawan Shrine and the Jim Thompson House, is the closest thing to a real "downtown" in Central Bangkok. Gaysorn Village (for luxury goods) and the gigantic CentralWorld mall are at Rajaprasong Junction, the intersection of Ratchadamri and Ploenchit roads. Just east of this intersection on Ploenchit Rd. and Soi Chidlom stands Bangkok's flagship Central Department Store, and the ultraupscale Central Embassy mall is next door.

Over at Siam Square are the Siam Paragon, Siam Discovery, and Siam Center malls. Just north of Pathumwan in Ratchathewi, the Pratunam neighborhood is famed for Pantip Plaza—Thailand's biggest computer center, with five floors of computer stores—and the Pratunam Market garment district.

TIP→ See Shopping, below, for more about these malls and markets.

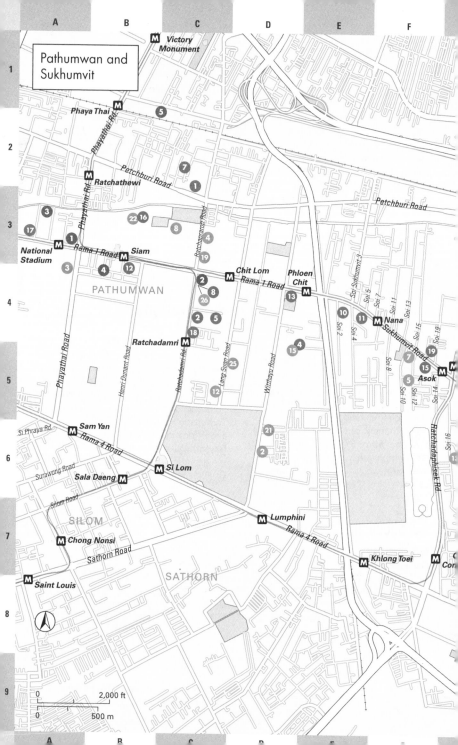

KEY

1 Exploring Sights
1 Restaurants
1 Hotels

Sights ▼

1 Bangkok Art and
  Culture Centre........... **A3**
2 Erawan Shrine **C4**
3 Jim Thompson House
  Museum **A3**
4 Siam Square............. **B4**
5 Suan Pakkad Palace ... **B2**

Restaurants ▼

1 Appia..................... **H5**
2 Baan Thai
  Family Recipes......... **D6**
3 Ban Khun Mae.......... **A4**
4 Big C Supercenter
  Ratchadamri.............. **C3**
5 Cabbages &
  Condoms.................. **F5**
6 The Commons
  Thonglor **I7**
7 Doo Rae.................... **F5**
8 Dynasty **C3**
9 55 Pochana.............. **I7**
10 Isao...................... **G5**
11 Je Ngor **G6**
12 Khrua Nai Baan
   (Home Kitchen) **C5**
13 Kuppa **G6**
14 Le Dalat................. **G4**
15 Liu **D5**
16 The Local **G4**
17 Ministry of Crab.......... **H5**
18 My Choice **I8**
19 Paste Restaurant **C3**
20 Peppina **H5**
21 Polo Fried Chicken...... **D6**
22 Sra Bua by Kiin Kiin..... **B3**
23 Sri Trat **H5**
24 Supanniga
   Eating Room.............. **I7**
25 Vaso...................... **C5**
26 You & Mee............... **C4**

Hotels ▼

1 Amari Watergate **C2**
2 Anantara Siam
  Bangkok **C4**
3 Bangkok Marriott Hotel
  Sukhumvit **I7**
4 Conrad Bangkok........ **D5**
5 Courtyard by Marriott
  Bangkok **C4**
6 The Davis Bangkok..... **G7**
7 First House **C2**
8 Grand Hyatt Erawan..... **C4**
9 Indochinoise
  Residence **I6**
10 J. W. Marriott Hotel
   Bangkok **E4**
11 The Landmark
   Bangkok **E4**
12 Novotel Bangkok on
   Siam Square............. **B4**
13 The Okura Prestige
   Bangkok **D4**
14 Pullman Bangkok
   Grande Sukhumvit...... **G4**
15 Sheraton Grande
   Sukhumvit **F5**
16 Siam Kempinski......... **B3**
17 Siam@Siam **A3**
18 The St. Regis
   Bangkok **C4**
19 The Westin Grande
   Sukhumvit **F5**

Sights

Bangkok Art and Culture Centre (*BACC*)

ART GALLERY | The large, striking white building opened in 2008 and is the main showcase for cutting-edge contemporary art, music, theater, and film in Bangkok. Past exhibitions have included work by Thai and international artists. Inside, the curving stairway of the central atrium is reminiscent of the Guggenheim in New York City. ⊠ *939 Rama I Rd., Pathumwan* ☎ *02/214–6630* ⊕ *en.bacc.or.th* 🎟 *Free* ⊘ *Closed Mon.* Ⓜ *BTS: National Stadium.*

Erawan Shrine (*San Phra Phrom*)

RELIGIOUS BUILDING | Completed in 1956, this is not a particularly old shrine by Bangkok standards, but it's one of the more active and highly revered ones, with many people stopping by on their way home to pray to a gleaming image of Brahma, the Hindu creator god. Thai dancers in traditional dress and a small orchestra perform for a fee to increase the likelihood that your wish will be granted. Even with a traffic jam right outside the gates, the mix of burning incense, dancers, and worshippers is an intoxicating sight. Entry is free, but many leave a small donation. There are also fantastic views of the shrine from the Rajaprasong Skywalk up above, from where many visitors take pictures. ⊠ *Ratchadamri and Ploenchit Rds., Pathumwan* 🎟 *Free (small donation customary)* Ⓜ *BTS: Chidlom.*

★ **Jim Thompson House Museum**

HISTORIC HOME | After starting his career as an architect in New York City, Jim Thompson ended up in Thailand at the end of World War II after a stint at the Office of Strategic Services, the predecessor to the CIA. He eventually moved into the silk business and is credited with revitalizing the industry in Thailand. This alone would have made him a legend, but his former home is also a national treasure. Thompson imported parts of several up-country buildings, some over a century old, to construct his compound. Three of six are still exactly the same as their originals, including details of the interior layout. With true appreciation and a connoisseur's eye, Thompson furnished the homes with what are now priceless pieces of Southeast Asian art. Adding to Thompson's notoriety is his disappearance: in 1967 he went to the Malaysian Cameron Highlands for a quiet holiday and was never heard from again. The entrance to the house is easy to miss—it's at the end of an unprepossessing lane, leading north off Rama I Road, west of Phayathai Road (the house is on your left). A good landmark is the BTS National Stadium station—the house is north of the station, just down the street from it. An informative 30-minute guided tour starts every 15 minutes and is included in the admission fee. ■ TIP→ **The grounds also include a silk and souvenir shop and a restaurant that's great for a coffee or cold-drink break.** ⊠ *Soi Kasem San 2, Rama I Rd., Pathumwan* ☎ *02/216–7368* ⊕ *www.jimthompsonhouse.com* 🎟 *B200* Ⓜ *BTS: National Stadium.*

Siam Square

STORE/MALL | Fashion, education, and diverse shopping converge in glitzy Siam Square in the heart of downtown. Thailand's most prestigious college, Chulalongkorn University, is here, along with neon-splashed malls, designer boutiques and trendy restaurants. At night along the sidewalk, a bohemian and latest-fashions outdoor market scene unfolds. ⊠ *Rama I Rd., Pathumwan* ⊕ *www.facebook.com/SiamSquareOfficial* Ⓜ *BTS: Siam.*

Suan Pakkad Palace

CASTLE/PALACE | Eight antique teak houses built high on columns sit amid the undulating lawns and shimmering lotus pools of this lush complex. The houses, which exhibit porcelain, stone heads, traditional paintings, and Buddha statues, were dismantled at their original sites

Roaming the Waterways

Bangkok used to be known as the "Venice of the East," but many of the *khlong* (canals) that once distinguished this area have been paved over. Traveling along the few remaining waterways, however, is one of the city's delights. You'll see houses on stilts, women washing clothes, and kids going for a swim. Traditional wooden canal boats are a fun way to get around town.

Khlong Saen Saeb, just north of Phetchaburi Road, is the main east-west boat route for Bangkok proper (as opposed to Thonburi, home to a greater number of canals). This canal runs 18 miles long and sees up to 18,000 passengers a day. The fare ranges from B10 to B20, depending on the distance, and during rush hour boats pull up to piers at one-minute intervals. Klong boats provide easy access to the Jim Thompson House and are a handy alternative way to get to Khao San Road during rush hour. The last stop is Phan Fa Pier, which is about a 15-minute walk from the eastern end of Khao San Road.

Chao Phraya River Express Boats (sometimes called river buses) ply the Chao Phraya River from north to south. The fare for these express boats is based on how far you travel, ranging from B13 to B50. The river can be an efficient way to get around as well as a sightseeing opportunity. The express boats travel specific routes from about 6 am to 7 pm. These boats stop at every pier and will take you all the way to

Nonthaburi, where you'll find quaint, car-free Koh Kret, an inhabited island in the river. A pleasant afternoon trip when the city gets too hot, the island has a Mon community and specializes in pottery.

Under the BTS Saphan Taksin station, there is a ferry pier where passengers can cross the river to Thonburi for B3. Many hotels run their own boats from the pier at Saphan Taksin. From here you can get to the Grand Palace in about 10 minutes and the other side of Krungthon Bridge in about 15 minutes.

A Chao Phraya Tourist Boat day pass provides a fun introduction to the river, and at B180 for the day it's a bargain. One advantage of the tourist boat is that while traveling from place to place there's a running commentary in English about the historic sights along the river. The tourist boat starts at Saphan Taksin Pier, but you can pick it up at any of the piers where it stops, and you can get on and off as often as you like.

Longtail boats, so called for the extra-long propeller shaft that extends behind the stern, operate like taxis. Boatmen will take you anywhere you want to go for B400 to B600 per hour. The best place to hire these boats is at the Saphan Taksin Pier. A private trip up the old klongs to the Royal Barge Museum and the Khoo Wiang Floating Market starts at the Chang Pier near the Grand Palace. Longtails usually stop running at 6 pm.

and reassembled here. At the back of the garden is the serene Lacquer Pavilion, worth a look for its gold-covered paneling with scenes from the life of the Buddha. Academics and historians debate how old the murals are—whether they're from the reign of King Narai (1656–88) or from the first reign of the current Chakri Dynasty, founded by King Rama I (1782– 1809). ⊠ *352–354 Sri Ayutthaya Rd., Ratchathewi* 🕾 *02/245–4934* ⊕ *www. suanpakkad.com* 🖾 *B100* Ⓜ *BTS: Phaya Thai (10-min walk east of station).*

🍴 Restaurants

Unimaginably busy Pathumwan, which includes Siam Square, has a little bit of everything, from humble lunch stops to power-dining extravaganzas.

Baan Thai Family Recipes

$$ | THAI | Close to Lumpini Park on Withayu Road, Baan takes recipes that have been handed down through generations and takes them up a notch by using top-line ingredients and fine-dining presentations. Signature dishes include braised beef curry, spicy five-spiced egg stew, and stir-fried, minced dry-aged beef in spicy holy basil. **Known for:** good wine selection; spicy pad kra phao; updated homestyle cooking. $ *Average main: 350* ⊠ *139/5 Withayu Rd., Pathumwan* 🕾 *02/655–8995* ⊕ *baanbkk.com* Ⓜ *MRT: Lumpini.*

Ban Khun Mae

$$ | THAI | FAMILY | Casually upmarket and aimed at tourists, this decades-old restaurant formerly in Siam Square serves authentic Thai cuisine in an atmosphere a few notches above that of the simple family restaurants. What's best about Ban Khun Mae is a large dining area filled with big round tables, warm wood, and a few antique decorations, offering a comfortable and airy feel perfect for post-shopping relaxation. **Known for:** good wine list; specialties like marinated

chicken in pandan leaves; decor resembling a traditional Thai home. $ *Average main: B200* ⊠ *MBK Center, 2nd floor, 444 Phayathai Rd., Pratunam* 🕾 *08/099– 84756* ⊕ *www.bankhunmae.com* Ⓜ *BTS: National Stadium.*

Big C Supercenter Ratchadamri

$ | THAI | The food court on the fifth floor of the Big C shopping mall offers a staggering selection of authentic Thai (and a few Chinese and Korean) dishes at rock-bottom prices, with virtually nothing exceeding B80. Prepay at the cashier station and get a debit card, then order at whatever counter you wish; the balance is refundable at the end. **Known for:** cheap yet satisfying eats; cafeteria-style service; Thai street food like spicy soups, and rice and noodle dishes. $ *Average main: B60* ⊠ *Big C Supercenter Ratchadamri, 97/11 Ratchadamri Rd., Pathumwan* ⊹ *Opposite CentralWorld* 🕾 *02/250–4888* ⊕ *www.bigc.co.th* Ⓜ *BTS: Chidlom.*

Dynasty

$$$$ | CHINESE | This restaurant has long been a favorite among government ministers and corporate executives, both for its outstanding Cantonese cuisine and its private areas, perfect for business lunches or romantic dinners. The main dining room is elegant, with crimson carpeting, carved screens, lacquer furniture, and porcelain objets d'art. **Known for:** dim sum; fantastic Peking duck; seasonal specialties like Taiwanese eels. $ *Average main: B1000* ⊠ *Centara Grand at Central Plaza Lad Phrao, 1695 Phaholyothin Rd., Chatuchak* 🕾 *02/541– 1234* ⊕ *www.centarahotelsresorts.com/ centaragrand/cglb/restaurant/dynasty-chinese-restaurant* Ⓜ *MRT: Phahon Yothin.*

Khrua Nai Baan (Home Kitchen)

$ | THAI | FAMILY | A real hole-in-the-wall where friends gather to enjoy great meals together, this long-running eatery turns out excellent Thai-Chinese cuisine in a simple dining room. All the classics everyone should try at least once on a

Bangkok trip are served here at reasonable prices, making it a favorite among the Thais and expats who live and work on laid-back Soi Lang Suan. **Known for:** close to Lumpini Park; traditional Thai dishes like tom yum goong and oyster omelet; great value. $ *Average main: B150* ⊠ *90/2 Soi Lang Suan, Pathumwan* ✛ *Just north of Lumphini Park* ☏ *02/255–8947* ⊕ *www.khruanaibaan.com* Ⓜ *MRT: Lumphini; BTS: Chidlom.*

Liu

$$$ | **CHINESE** | **FAMILY** | You'll want to be spotted at this so-called "neoclassic Chinese" restaurant in the Hilton hotel, where the contemporary-focused concept and design come from the creator of the equally snazzy Green T. House in Beijing. **Known for:** dim sum lunches; Chinese cuisine fusing different regional styles; dishes with fried frogs' legs. $ *Average main: B450* ⊠ *Conrad Bangkok, 87 Wittayu (Wireless Rd.), Pathumwan* ☏ *02/690–9999* ⊕ *www.hilton.com/en/hotels/bkkcici-conrad-bangkok* Ⓜ *BTS: Ploenchit.*

★ Paste Restaurant

$$$$ | **THAI** | The Michelin-award-winning Paste, an upscale, intimate eatery run by the experienced Australian-Thai husband-and-wife team, Bee Satongun and Jason Bailey, elevates traditional Thai food and flavors to a whole new level with fresh produce and technical flair. It's on the top floor of the high-end Gaysorn Village shopping mall, and open for lunch and dinner, with à la carte and multiple tasting menus available. **Known for:** historical and royal inspirations; plentiful vegetarian options; extensive wine list. $ *Average main: B900* ⊠ *Gaysorn Village, 999 Ploenchit Rd. at Ratchadamri Rd., 3rd fl., Pathumwan* ☏ *02/656–1003* ⊕ *pastebangkok.com* 🍴 *Smart casual* Ⓜ *BTS: Chidlom.*

Polo Fried Chicken

$ | **THAI** | This legendary restaurant has been delighting diners with its fried chicken seasoned with black pepper and plenty of golden-brown garlic for more than 50 years. The restaurant is a bit hard to find—as you enter Soi Polo (Soi Sanam Khli), it's about 50 yards in on your left. **Known for:** awarded Michelin Bib Gourmand status in 2021; delicious sides like sticky rice and papaya salad; frequented by Thais and foreigners alike. $ *Average main: B150* ⊠ *137/1–2 Soi Polo (Soi Sanam Khli), Pathumwan* ✛ *Off Wittayu (Wireless Rd.)* ☏ *02/655–8489* Ⓜ *BTS: Ploenchit; BTS Lumpini.*

★ Sra Bua by Kiin Kiin

$$$$ | **THAI** | Luxurious and utterly unique, this restaurant upends conventional wisdom about Thai cuisine and technique. Chef Henrik Yde-Andersen's tasting menus, priced starting at B1,850 for dinner, represent a veritable catalog of Thai flavors and dishes, though through the iterations of foams, emulsions, powders, and plenty of smoky liquid nitrogen. **Known for:** experimental Thai cuisine; molecular gastronomy; winner of many fine-dining awards. $ *Average main: B900* ⊠ *Siam Kempinski, 991/9 Rama I Rd., Pathumwan* ☏ *02/162–9000* ⊕ *www.srabuabykiinkiin.com/en* 🍴 *Smart casual* Ⓜ *BTS: Siam.*

Vaso

$$ | **SPANISH** | In the ultramodern Velaa Sindhorn community mall on Soi Lang Suan, Vaso has an oval-shaped bar—no tables—surrounding an open kitchen that serves modern Spanish tapas and shared plates, including fresh oysters and imported Iberico jam. The short, well-curated wine list includes cava, Spain's bubbly equivalent to prosecco or Champagne. **Known for:** tapas; lively ambience; cava (Spanish bubbly). $ *Average main: 350* ⊠ *Velaa Sindhorn, 87 Soi Lang Suan, Pathumwan* ☏ *09/891–44664* ⊕ *www.vasobangkok.com* Ⓜ *BTS: Chidlom.*

You & Mee

$$ | **THAI** | Hotel restaurants in Bangkok often disappoint, but this casual street-kitchen–inspired spot at the Grand Hyatt Erawan serves high-quality Thai food—particularly northern Thai dishes—at reasonable prices. Come for the good range of noodles, curries, and congee, served à la carte or as buffet options, with premium add-ons such as lobster, crab, and braised beef available. ■ **TIP→ There's a curry buffet at lunch and dinner for B550 and B650 respectively.** **Known for:** central location; northern dishes like khao soi; fast service. [$] *Average main: B230* ✉ *Grand Hyatt Erawan, 494 Ratchadamri Rd., Pathumwan* ☎ *02/254–1234* 🌐 *bangkok.grand.hyatt.com* [M] *BTS: Chidlom.*

Hotels

Amari Watergate

$$ | **HOTEL** | The spacious and comfortable rooms at the Amari chain's Bangkok flagship are swathed in silks and other rich fabrics. **Pros:** massive pool; many amenities; executive floor. **Cons:** impersonal feel; restaurants are average; busy front desk. [$] *Rooms from: B3,170* ✉ *847 Phetchaburi Rd., Pathumwan* ☎ *02/653–9000* 🌐 *www.amari.com/watergate* 🍴 *No Meals* 🛏 *564 rooms and suites* [M] *Airport Link: Ratchaprarop, then taxi; BTS: Siam.*

Anantara Siam Bangkok

$$$ | **HOTEL** | One of Bangkok's most elegant hotels, the Anantara Siam is not only popular with visitors but attracts local society for morning coffee and afternoon high tea in the palatial lobby, decorated with silk murals hand-painted by Paiboon Suwanankudt, Thailand's greatest living traditional muralist. **Pros:** magnificent tearoom; accessible location; great pool. **Cons:** not all rooms have nice views; decor verges on stuffy; extremely pricey in season. [$] *Rooms from: B5,202* ✉ *155 Ratchadamri Rd., Pathumwan* ☎ *02/126–8866* 🌐 *siam-bangkok.anantara.com* 🍴 *Free Breakfast* 🛏 *354 rooms, 19 suites* [M] *BTS: Ratchadamri.*

Conrad Bangkok

$$ | **HOTEL** | Though this hotel is one of the largest in Bangkok, the service doesn't suffer—the staff is attentive, and the beautifully designed rooms are perfect down to the smallest detail. **Pros:** sprawling pool area; attentive staff; fun nightlife. **Cons:** far from the main road; huge; attached shopping mall attracts outside visitors. [$] *Rooms from: B3,173* ✉ *87 Withayu (Wireless Rd.), Pathumwan* ☎ *02/690–9999* 🌐 *www.hilton.com* 🍴 *No Meals* 🛏 *391 rooms, 20 suites* [M] *BTS: Ploenchit.*

Courtyard by Marriott Bangkok

$ | **HOTEL** | Although it lacks the luxury of Bangkok's high-end lodgings, this reasonably priced Marriott property is well located and has attractive furnishings. **Pros:** convenient location; good value; family-friendly. **Cons:** not as luxurious as other Marriotts; a bit unremarkable; just the standard amenities. [$] *Rooms from: B1,176* ✉ *155/1 Soi Mahadlekluang 1, Soi Lang Suan, Pathumwan* ☎ *02/690–1888* 🌐 *www.marriott.com/hotels/travel/bkkcy-courtyard-bangkok* 🍴 *Free Breakfast* 🛏 *316 rooms* [M] *BTS: Ratchadamri.*

First House

$ | **HOTEL** | Tucked behind the Pratunam Market, this bright and cheery lodging in the bustling garment district is an excellent value. **Pros:** close to Airport Rail Link station Ratchaprarop; reasonably priced; attractive rooms. **Cons:** neighborhood on the noisy side; not much natural light in rooms; no Skytrain or metro station nearby. [$] *Rooms from: B1,564* ✉ *14/20–29 Phetchaburi Rd., Soi 19, Ratchathewi* ☎ *02/254–3101* 🌐 *www.firsthousebkk.com* 🍴 *No Meals* 🛏 *100 rooms* [M] *Airport Link: Ratchaprarop.*

Motorcycle Taxis

At many *sois* (side streets) you will find clusters of motorcycle taxis whose orange-vested drivers will take you anywhere in Bangkok, although they're best for short trips within a neighborhood. Many of these drivers know their way around their neighborhood better than taxi drivers. Fares are not negotiable—the drivers have set rates to nearby points, usually a bit less than a taxi. Motorcycles can be dangerous; helmets, when available, are often nothing more than a thin piece of plastic without a chin strap. The risks and discomforts limit their desirability, but motorcycles can be the best way to get around Bangkok if you're in a hurry and if the traffic is bad. Motorcycle taxis can also be hailed on the Grab app for cheaper than at stands, but often drivers don't speak much English, making pickups difficult if for some reason you can't find each other.

Grand Hyatt Erawan
$$ | **HOTEL** | This stylish hotel, filled with modern Thai art is right next to the auspicious Erawan Shrine. **Pros:** nine restaurants; world-class spa; easy access to many points in the city. **Cons:** often high occupancy; huge; very busy lobby. [$] *Rooms from: B3,429* ✉ *494 Ratchadamri Rd., Pathumwan* ☎ *02/254–1234* 🌐 *www.hyatt.com* 🛏 *380 rooms, 44 suites* 🍴 *Free Breakfast* [M] *BTS: Chidlom.*

Novotel Bangkok on Siam Square
$ | **HOTEL** | Convenient to shopping, dining, and entertainment, this sprawling hotel is a short walk from the BTS Siam station, which puts much of the city within reach. **Pros:** cozy rooms; good service; convenient location. **Cons:** busy front desk; not many in-room amenities; large lobby with music stage and lots of action. [$] *Rooms from: B1,467* ✉ *392/44 Siam Square, Soi 6, Pathumwan* ☎ *02/209–8888* 🌐 *www.novotelbkk.com* 🍴 *No Meals* 🛏 *425 rooms* [M] *BTS: Siam.*

★ **The Okura Prestige Bangkok**
$$ | **HOTEL** | The Okura Prestige stands out among the other 5-star hotels in Bangkok for its sleek minimalism and Japanese touches like comfy cotton yukata robes in every room, as well as high-tech amenities, impressive downtown views, and a gorgeous 25th-floor infinity pool. **Pros:** excellent restaurants; chic Japanese design; direct link to BTS. **Cons:** lobby not located on ground floor; pricey rooms; not suitable for families. [$] *Rooms from: B3,399* ✉ *57 Witthayu Rd., Pathumwan* ☎ *02/687–9000* 🌐 *www.okurabangkok.com* 🍴 *No Meals* 🛏 *240 rooms* [M] *BTS: Ploen Chit.*

Siam@Siam
$$ | **HOTEL** | This boutique design hotel is definitely where the cool kids stay, but even those traveling with actual kids will feel welcome. **Pros:** creative rooms; great location; superhip crowd. **Cons:** some rooms have little natural light; can be noisy; decor might not be to everyone's taste. [$] *Rooms from: B2,588* ✉ *865 Rama I Rd., Wang Mai, Pathumwan* ☎ *02/217–3000* 🌐 *www.siamatsiam.com* 🍴 *Free Breakfast* 🛏 *203 rooms* [M] *BTS: Siam.*

Siam Kempinski
$$$ | **HOTEL** | The palatial Siam Kempinski combines sheer elegance with the feel of an escapist resort in the middle of the city. **Pros:** notable restaurants; central

location; some rooms have direct pool access. **Cons:** no direct mall access from lobby; pricey; standard room rate doesn't include breakfast. [$] *Rooms from: B6,000* ✉ *991/9 Rama I Rd., Pathumwan* ☎ *02/162–9000* 🌐 *www.kempinski.com/bangkok* 🍴 *Free Breakfast* 🛏 *303 rooms* [M] *BTS: Siam.*

★ The St. Regis Bangkok

$$$$ | HOTEL | The first hotel in Thailand to offer guests around-the-clock personal butler service, the St. Regis is all about pampering. **Pros:** centrally located; rooftop pool; elegant rooms. **Cons:** lobby not on ground floor; can be a bit stuffy; expensive rates. [$] *Rooms from: B7,270* ✉ *159 Ratchadamri, Pathumwan* ☎ *02/207–7777* 🌐 *www.marriott.com/hotels/travel/bkkxr-the-st-regis-bangkok* 🍴 *Free Breakfast* 🛏 *176 rooms and 52 suites* [M] *BTS: Ratchadamri.*

Nightlife

The bustling downtown heart of Bangkok has fewer nightlife spots than you'd imagine, other than chic luxury hotel bars. The Diplomat Bar at the Conrad Bangkok has live jazz most nights, while the St. Regis Bar, on the 12th floor of The St. Regis Bangkok, has aerial views of the golf course at the Royal Bangkok Sports Club and classic cocktails.

BARS AND PUBS

Diplomat Bar

BARS | Inside the Conrad Bangkok, this relaxed yet sophisticated bar offers well-made cocktails, plus a good wine and Champagne selection. The 5 pm to 8 pm happy hour is popular with staff from local embassies. Jazz ensembles perform live nightly except Sunday. ✉ *Conrad Bangkok, Withayu Rd., Pathumwan* ☎ *02/690–9244* 🌐 *www.hilton.com/en/hotels/bkkcici-conrad-bangkok/dining* 🕒 *Sun.* [M] *BTS: Ploenchit, then free shuttle or walk.*

★ St. Regis Bar

From this 12th-floor bar that overlooks the Royal Bangkok Sports Club, you can watch the horse races while sipping a Siam Mary, the Bangkok version of the Bloody Mary. The bar continues the age-old St. Regis tradition of Champagne sabering (opening a bottle using a saber), displayed nightly at 6. The afternoon tea here, with tiers of colorful treats, is also impeccable. ✉ *The St. Regis Bangkok, 159 Ratchadamri Rd., Pathumwan* ☎ *02/207–7777* 🌐 *www.stregis.com/bangkok* [M] *Skytrain: Ratchadamri.*

Shopping

CLOTHING AND FABRICS

There are two types of fabrics worth seeking out in Bangkok: *mudmee* (tie-dyed) silk, produced in the northeastern part of the country, and Thai cotton, which is soft, durable, and easier on the wallet than silk. Thai silk gained its reputation only after World War II, when technical innovations made it less expensive to produce.

People who visit Bangkok might brag about a custom-made suit that was completed in just a day or two, but the finished product often looks like the rush job that it was. If you want an excellent cut, give the tailor the time he needs, which could be up to a week at a reputable place.

Greyhound

MIXED CLOTHING | One of Bangkok's oldest local fashion labels started out primarily in menswear, but now sells casual yet chic streetwear for both genders. The original branch in Siam Center showcases the most current collections. ✉ *Siam Center, 979 Rama 1 Rd., 1st fl., Pathumwan* ☎ *02/610–7914* 🌐 *www.greyhound.co.th* [M] *BTS: Siam.*

Issue

MIXED CLOTHING | Collections from this hip local designer are inspired by the cultural influences of Thailand, from Buddhism to ancient royalty. ☒ *Siam Paragon, Rama I Rd., Pathumwan* ☎ *02/610–7862* ⊕ *www.issuethailand.com* Ⓜ *BTS: Siam.*

Platinum Fashion Mall

MIXED CLOTHING | Fashionistas will fall in love with this mall packed with endless rows of tiny shops selling clothing, shoes, and accessories at wholesale prices. If you buy more things at one shop, you'll likely get a discount—especially for the same model in different colors. The only downside is you probably won't be allowed to try anything on. ☒ *222 Phetchaburi Rd., Pathumwan* ⊹ *Across from Pratunam Market* ☎ ⊕ *www.platinumfashionmall.com* Ⓜ *BTS: Chidlom; Airport Rail Link: Ratchaprarop.*

Prayer Textile Gallery

WOMEN'S CLOTHING | Napajaree Suanduenchai studied fashion design in Germany, and more than two decades ago opened this business in her mother's former dress shop. She makes stunning items in naturally dyed silks and cottons and in antique fabrics from the farthest reaches of Thailand, Laos, and Cambodia. ☒ *197 Phayathai Rd., near Siam Sq., Pathumwan* ☎ *02/251–7549* ⊕ *www.facebook.com/PrayerTextileGallery* Ⓜ *BTS: National Stadium.*

Sretsis

WOMEN'S CLOTHING | Three Thai sisters, darlings of the local design scene who have gone international, created Sretsis, a feminine design label that has fashionistas around the world raving. ☒ *Central Embassy, 1031 Ploenchit Rd., 2nd fl., Pathumwan* ☎ *02/160–5874* ⊕ *www.sretsis.com* Ⓜ *BTS: Chidlom.*

MARKETS

Pratunam Market

MARKET | Hundreds of vendors selling inexpensive clothing jam the sidewalk each day here. The market is a popular destination for the Indian community and in the evening the surrounding Indian, Nepali, and Pakistani restaurants are bustling. ☒ *Phetchaburi and Ratchaprarop Rds., Ratchathewi* Ⓜ *BTS: Chidlom; Saen Saep Canal Boat: Pratunam.*

SHOPPING CENTERS

Central Chidlom

MALL | The flagship location of Thailand's largest department store chain has a quality selection of clothing, jewelry, sporting goods, housewares, and fabrics, including a Jim Thompson silk shop. An elevated walkway connects Central Chidlom with the even more upscale Central Embassy mall next door. ☒ *1027 Ploenchit Rd., Pathumwan* ⊹ *Connected to BTS Chidlom station by an elevated walkway.* ☎ *02/793–7777* ⊕ *www.central.co.th* Ⓜ *BTS: Chidlom.*

Central Embassy

MALL | Fashionistas will find much to explore at one of Bangkok's newer shopping malls; from high-end international brands to Thai designers like Boyy and Disaya. The Eathai section has street food nibbles and cooking ware displays, as well as Thai cooking classes at Issaya Cooking Studio. On Level 6 is Embassy Diplomat Screens, a state-of-the-art cinema house where staff bring snacks and beverages to your seat. ☒ *1031 Phloenchit Rd., Pathumwan* ☎ *02/160–59912* ⊕ *www.centralembassy.com* Ⓜ *BTS: Chidlom.*

CentralWorld

MALL | At more than 1 million square meters (nearly 11 million square feet), this megacenter claims to be Southeast Asia's biggest mall. It's packed with local and international retailers, as well as a multiplex cinema, a hotel, and many dining options. ☒ *Rama I Rd. and Ratchadamri Rd., Pathumwan* ☎ *02/021–9999* ⊕ *www.centralworld.co.th* Ⓜ *BTS: Chidlom.*

3

Bangkok PATHUMWAN

Gaysorn Village

MALL | This upscale shopping center outshines many of the others with its white marble-and-chrome fixtures. You'll find European and local labels and lauded restaurants such as Paste and Riedel Wine Bar & Cellar. ⊠ *999 Ploenchit Rd., Pathumwan* ✥ *At Ratchadamri Rd.* ☎ *02/656–1149* ⊕ *www.gaysornvillage. com* Ⓜ *BTS: Chidlom.*

MBK Center

MALL | At an impressive seven stories high, this is one of the busiest malls in the city. It's well-worn and not nearly as stylish as nearby Siam Center—the main attractions are stores selling cheap clothes, camera, cellphones, and electronics—but there are many other shops, as well as a movie theater and two food courts. ⊠ *444 Phayathai Rd., Pathumwan* ✥ *At Rama I Rd.* ☎ *02/620–9000 call center* ⊕ *www.mbk-center.co.th* Ⓜ *BTS: National Stadium.*

Pantip Plaza

MALL | This mall exists for the computer nerd in everyone. It houses an enormous number of shops selling computer hardware and software (some legal, most not). Shopping here can be overwhelming, but if you know what you're looking for, the bargains are worth it. ■ **TIP** ➔ **Remember that not all electronics will be compatible with what you have back home, so do your research.** ⊠ *604 Phetchaburi Rd., Ratchathewi* ☎ *02/254–9797* ⊕ *www. pantipplaza.com* Ⓜ *BTS: Ratchathewi.*

Siam Center

MALL | Siam Center has been the epicenter of Thai fashion since it opened in 1976, and has reinvented itself several times over since then. Bangkokians come here to check out the latest Thai labels, along with one-of-a-kind pieces of handmade clothing, shoes, and accessories. The shops ooze style, but be forewarned that the clothes are all made to Thai proportions, so they often run small compared to Western sizing. ⊠ *979*

Rama I Rd., Pathumwan ☎ *02/658–1000* ⊕ *www.siamcenter.co.th* Ⓜ *BTS: Siam.*

Siam Discovery

MALL | This seven-story mall is filled with shops selling funky international brands, with a heavy focus on fashion but also housewares and hobby items. ⊠ *989 Rama I Rd., Pathumwan* ✥ *At Phayathai Rd.* ☎ *02/658–1000* ⊕ *www.siamdiscovery.co.th* Ⓜ *BTS: Siam.*

Siam Paragon

MALL | This giant mall has 250 stores, including all the big international brands from Porsche to Chanel, plus a multiplex cinema and tons of restaurants. Oh, and there's an underwater marine park where you can dive with sharks. ⊠ *991/1 Rama 1 Rd., Pathumwan* ☎ *02/610–8000* ⊕ *www.siamparagon.co.th* Ⓜ *BTS: Siam.*

Spas

Anantara Spa

SPAS | A relaxing massage with warm oils is among the many treatments available at the Anantara Siam Bangkok. You can even arrange for a poolside massage. ⊠ *Anantara Siam Bangkok, 155 Ratchadamri Rd., Pathumwan* ☎ *02/126–8866* ⊕ *www.anantara.com/en/siam-bangkok/ spa* Ⓜ *BTS: Ratchadamri.*

COMO Shambhala Urban Escape

SPAS | There's a wide range of treatments at this ultimate urban escape, but it's particularly known for its detox programs. The COMO Shambhala Bath treatment starts with an invigorating salt scrub, followed by a luxurious soak, a relaxing massage, and a glass of fresh juice to finish. ⊠ *Metropolitan Hotel, 27 S. Sathorn Rd., Sathorn* ☎ *02/625–3355* ⊕ *www. comohotels.com/en/metropolitanbangkok/wellness* Ⓜ *MRT: Lumpini; BTS: Sala Daeng.*

Continued on page 119

BANGKOK STREET FOOD

by Robin Goldstein & Alexis Herschkowitsch

In Thailand a good rule of thumb is, the less you pay for food, the better it is. And the food offered by street vendors is very cheap and very good. At any hour, day or night, Thais crowd around sidewalk carts and stalls, slurping noodles or devouring fiery *som tam* (green papaya salad) all for just pennies.

The cooks at street stalls are Thailand's true culinary giants.

If you only eat at upscale restaurants geared to foreigners, you'll miss out on the chili, fish sauce, and bright herbal flavors that define Thai cuisine. Even if you're picky, consider trying simple noodle dishes and skewered meats.

A typical meal costs between B20 and B50 (you pay when you get your food), and most stalls have a few tables and chairs where you can eat.

Street food in Bangkok.

Vendors don't adhere to meal times, nor are different foods served for breakfast, lunch, or dinner, as Thais often eat multiple snacks throughout the day rather than full meals. It's OK to combine foods from more than one cart; vendors won't mind, especially if they're selling something like a curried stew that comes in a plastic bag with no utensils. Find a different stall that offers plates and cutlery, order rice, and add your curry to the mix. Enjoy!

SOM TAM

Thai chefs use contrasting flavors to create balance in their cuisine. The popular green papaya salad is a good example, with dried shrimp, tart lime, salty fish sauce, crunchy peanuts, and long thin slices of green papaya. Pair it with sticky rice for a refreshing treat on a hot day.

SOUR Lime adds a welcome tartness to salads and other dishes, counteracting sweetness.

SPICY Thais like it hot, sometimes using more than 10 fiery chili peppers per dish.

SALTY Instead of salt, Thais often use fish sauce and fermented shrimp paste, which have more nuanced flavors.

BITTER Roasted peanuts add a pleasant bitterness and crunch.

SWEET Palm sugar, a dark brown, natural, aromatic sweetener—will make you wonder why you've been using refined sugar all your life.

STAYING HEALTHY

Sanitary standards in Thailand are far higher than those in many developing countries. By taking a few precautions, you can safely enjoy this wonderful cuisine.

■ Avoid tap water. It's the bacteria in the water supply that causes most problems.

The water on the table at stalls and restaurants is almost always purified, but stick with bottled water to play it safe.

■ Lots of flies are never a good sign. Enough said.

■ Know your stomach. Freshly cooked, hot food is least likely to contain bacteria. Steer clear of raw

foods and fruits that cannot be peeled if you know you're sensitive.

■ Use common sense when selecting a street vendor or a restaurant. Crowds mean high turnover, which translates into fresher food.

Fruit from Chatusak Market, Bangkok.

WHAT SHOULD I ORDER?

Locals will probably be eating the cart's specialty, so if you're not sure what to order, don't be afraid to point. The following are a few common and delicious dishes you'll find in Bangkok.

Larb.

LARB Another refreshing and flavorful shredded salad, larb (pronounced lahb) consists of ground meat or fish, lime, fish sauce, and a generous helping of aromatic kaffir lime leaves.

PAD Noodles come in many varieties at street carts, and vendors add their own twists. Noodle soups with meat or innards, though traditionally Chinese or Vietnamese, are common in Bangkok, as are *pad khee mao* (drunken noodles) with vegetables, shellfish, or meat, wok-singed and served without broth. Another popular dish is *pad khee mao*—decadently big rice noodles with river prawns and basil.

Pad Thai.

TOM YUM This delicious and aromatic water-based soup—flavored with fish sauce, lemongrass, kaffir lime leaves, and vegetables—is a local favorite. *Tom yum goong,* with shrimp, is a popular variation.

YANG Thais love these marinated meat sticks, grilled over charcoal. Pork is usually the tastiest.

Tom yum.

WILL IT BE TOO SPICY?

Because most Thai cooks tone things down for foreigners, the biggest battle can sometimes be getting enough heat in your food. To be sure that your dish is spicy, ask for it *phet phet* (spicy); if you want it mild, request *mai phet* (less spicy). If you get a bite that's too spicy, water won't help—eat a bite of rice or something sweet to counteract the heat.

Food on sale at Damnoen Saduak floating market.

WHAT ARE ALL THE CONDIMENTS FOR?

At some street stalls, particularly soup and noodle shops, you'll be offered an array of seasonings and herbs to add to your dish: chilies marinated in salty fish sauce or soaking in oil; fresh herbs like mint, cilantro, and Thai basil; crunchy bits of toasted rice, peanuts, or fried onions; and lime wedges. Although it's a good idea to taste things you don't recognize so you don't over-flavor your meal, our advice is to pile it on!

Though it has a bad rap, the flavor enhancer MSG is sometimes used at street stalls and restaurants in Thailand. You can ask for food without it *(mai sai phong chu rat)* if it doesn't agree with you. You may also see MSG, a crystal that looks like white sugar, in a little jar on your table, along with sugar, chili paste, and fish sauce.

Two varieties of Thai basil.

YOU WANT ME TO EAT WHAT?

Pan-fried, seasoned insects such as ants, grasshoppers, and cockroaches, are popular snacks in Thailand. A plastic bag full of these crunchy delicacies will cost you about B20 or 50¢. To try your hand at insect-eating, start small. Little guys like ants are the most palatable, since they really just taste like whatever they've been flavored with (lime or chili, for example). Cockroaches have a higher squeamish factor: You have to pull the legs and the wings off the larger ones. And stay away from the silkworm cocoons, which do not taste any better than they sound.

At fruit stalls in Bangkok you may find the durian, a husk-covered fruit famous for its unpleasant smell. In fact the scent, which is a bit like spicy body odor, is so overpowering that some Thai hotels don't let you keep durians in your room. But don't judge the durian by its smell alone: Many love the fruit's pudding-like texture and intense tropical flavor, which is similar to passion fruit. Buy one at a fruit stand, ask the seller to cut it open, and taste its yellow flesh for yourself.

(above) Deep fried bugs (actual size).
(below) Durian.

Talking about Food

The first term you learn is "aroi," which means delicious. You'll no doubt use that one again and again, whether you're dining at food stalls or upscale restaurants. When someone asks "Aroi mai?" that's your cue to practice your Thai—most likely your answer will be a resounding "aroi mak" (It's very delicious).

Another useful word is "Kaw," which simply means "Could I have …?" However, the most important phrase to remember may be "Gin ped dai mai?" or "Can you eat spicy food?" Answer this one wrong and you might have a five-alarm fire in your mouth. You can answer with a basic "dai" (can), "mai dai" (cannot), or "dai nit noi" (a little). Most restaurants will tone down dishes for foreigners, but if you're visiting a food stall or if you're nervous, you can specify that you would like your food "mai ped" (not spicy), "ped nit noi khrup/kah" (a little spicy), or if you have very resilient taste buds, "ped mak" (very spicy). Don't be surprised if the latter request is met with some laughter—and if all Thai eyes are on you when you take your first bite. Remember, water won't put out the fire; you'll need to eat something sweet or oily, or drink beer or milk.

Essentials

Check bin khrup/kah: the check, please.

Gin jay: vegetarian.

Kaw eek noi khrup/kah: more, please!

Ped mai? Is it spicy?

Kaw glub baan khrup/kah: take away

Beverages

Thai iced tea (*cha yen*) is Thai black tea mixed with cinnamon, vanilla, star anise, often food coloring (for that very orange color), and sometimes other spices. It's usually served cold, but you might see a hot version being enjoyed at the end of a meal. It's very sweet. Use caution when buying from food stalls that are using a block of ice—though made with purified water, the ice is not always kept clean in transportation and storage.

plain water: nam plao

soda water: nam soda

tea: nam cha

iced coffee: ga-fare-yen

whisky: wis-gee

vodka: what gaa

a sweet drink brewed from lemongrass: nam takrai

How do you like it?

Pad king: stir-fried with ginger.

Pad ped: stir-fried hot and spicy.

Ping: grilled (use phao instead when referring to seafood).

Thom: boiled.

Tawd: deep fried.

Desserts

Kanom: dessert

Kanom krok: coconut pudding

Kao niao ma muang: mango with sticky rice

Kao larm: rice-based dessert cooked in coconut milk

Gluay bping: grilled bananas

Muay Thai, the Sport of Kings

Though it's often somewhat dismissed as a blood sport, Muay Thai is one of the world's oldest martial arts, and it was put to noble purposes long before it became a spectator sport. It's said to be more than 2,000 years old and has been practiced by kings and was used to defend the country. It's so important to Thai culture that until the 1920s Muay Thai instruction was part of the country's public school curriculum.

Techniques: Developed with the battlefield in mind, Muay Thai moves mimic the weapons of ancient combat. Punching combinations, similar to modern-day boxing, turn the fists into spears that jab relentlessly at an opponent. The roundhouse kick— delivered to the thigh, ribs, or head— turns the shinbone into a devastating striking surface. Elbow strikes to the face and strong knees to the abdomen mimic the motion of a battle-ax. Finally, strong front kicks, using the ball of the foot to jab at the abdomen, thigh, or face, mimic an array of weapons.

Rules: Professional bouts have five three-minute rounds, with a two-minute rest between. Fights are judged using a point system, with judges awarding rounds to each fighter, but not all rounds are given equal weight—later rounds are more important, as judges view fights as "marathons," with the winner being the fighter who's fared best through-out the match. The winner is determined by majority decision, or with a knockout or a technical knockout (when a fighter is conscious, but too injured to continue).

Rituals: The "dance" you see before each match is called the *ram muay* or *wai kru* (these terms are often used interchangeably, though the wai kru really refers to the homage paid to the *kru* or trainer). The ram muay serves to honor the fighter's supporters and his god, as well as to help him warm up, relax, and focus. Both fighters walk around the ring with one arm on the top rope to seal out bad spirits, pausing at each corner to say a short prayer. They then kneel in the center of the ring facing the direction of their birthplace and go through a set of specific movements. Fighters wear several good-luck charms, includ-ing armbands (*khruang rang*) and a headpiece (*mongkhon*). Live music accompanies each match, speeding up or slowing down according to the tempo of the fight.

New Lumpinee Boxing Stadium. This stadium hosts Muay Thai matches on Tuesday, Friday, and Saturday, start-ing at around 6:30 pm. Ticket prices are about B1,000–B2,000 ⊠ *6 Ramintra Rd., Anusawaree, Bang Khen* ✢ *about 10 km (6½ miles) south of Don Mueang airport* ☎ *02/252–8765* ⊕ *https://www.facebook.com/Lumpineeboxing-staduim* Ⓜ *MRT: Chatuchak Park, then taxi; BTS: Mo Chit, then taxi.*

Rajadamnern Stadium. Founded in 1945, art deco–style Rajadamnern Stadium presents Muay Thai bouts on Wednes-day and Thursday from 6:30 pm to 10 pm. Ringside seats for most matches cost about B2,000. ⊠ *8 Ratchadam-noen Nok Rd., Pom Prap Sattru Phai, Pom Prap Sattru Phai* ☎ *02/281–4205* ⊕ *rajadamnern.com.*

i.sawan Residential Spa and Club

SPAS | This spa's facilities are among the city's most cutting-edge, relaxing, and beautiful. The "residential spa cottages," luxurious suites clustered around a courtyard adjacent to the spa, have their own treatment spaces and seem worlds away from downtown Bangkok. Reasonably priced spa packages are available. ✉ *Grand Hyatt Erawan, 494 Ratchadamri Rd., Pathumwan* ☎ *02/254–1234* 🌐 *www.hyatt.com/corporate/spas/I-Sawan-Residential-Spa-and-Club/en/home.html* [M] *BTS: Ratchadamri.*

Sukhumvit

🍴 Restaurants

Sukhumvit is Bangkok's flashiest area for dining and going out. Consequently, many of the restaurants here have more style than substance, but there's very good food to be had, especially along the lanes of Sukhumvit between Soi 31 and Soi 65.

★ Appia

$$ | **ITALIAN** | Jarrett Wrisley, a food critic turned restaurateur, and Paolo Vitaletti, a five-star chef whose dad toiled in a storied Roman meat market, run this small cozy space for which reservations are highly advisable. The Italian menu is mostly devoted to Rome specialties. **Known for:** affordable Italian wine list; handmade pastas; slow-roasted meats like fresh-off-the-rotisserie porchetta. [$] *Average main: B400* ✉ *20/4 Sukhumvit Rd., Soi 31, Sukhumvit* ☎ *02/261–2056* 🌐 *www.appia-bangkok.com* 🕒 *No lunch Tues.–Sat.* [M] *BTS: Phrom Phong.*

Cabbages & Condoms

$$ | **THAI** | Established in the 1980s to raise funds for the Population and Community Development Association (PDA), a sex education/AIDS prevention organization, this restaurant serves traditional Thai dishes amid a quirky decor. The fairy lights and condom-decorated mannequins contrast with the traditional teakwood. **Known for:** outdoor seating available; free condoms instead of after-dinner mints; unconventional gift shop. [$] *Average main: B300* ✉ *6-10 Sukhumvit Rd., Soi 12, Sukhumvit* ☎ *02/229–4610* 🌐 *cabbagesandcondoms.co.th* [M] *MRT: Sukhumvit; BTS: Asok.*

The Commons Thonglor

$$ | **INTERNATIONAL** | It's easy to laze all afternoon at The Commons, a lofty community mall known for its gourmet food stands, restaurants, and comfortable open-air seating. You'll see groups dining on smorgasbords at single tables, with cuisines from Thai to Mexican, as well as dishes like fried chicken and waffles, artisanal sandwiches, and more—but plenty of people simply grab an iced coffee and hang out with their laptops. **Known for:** yoga studio and retail shops on second floor; good brunch and coffee at Roast; stands from popular Bangkok restaurants like Daniel Thaiger, Peppina, and Soul Food 55. [$] *Average main: B350* ✉ *335 Soi Thonglor 17, off Sukhumvit Soi 55, Thong Lor* ☎ *08/028–18339* 🌐 *www.thecommonsbkk.com/thonglor* 🕒 *Opening hrs of vendors vary* [M] *BTS: Thong Lor.*

Doo Rae

$$ | **KOREAN** | Many authentic Korean restaurants do business in Sukhumvit Plaza, but even with three stories of tables, there's often a wait day or night at Doo Rae. Go for the do-it-yourself barbecue grilling, with *bulgogi* (thin slices of beef in a tasty marinade) and fresh veggies, as well as sake or soju, a rice-based drink similar to vodka but with a lower alcohol content. **Known for:** substantial kimchi and tofu stews; location in a mall known as Bangkok's Korean Town; complimentary side dishes. [$] *Average main: B300* ✉ *212/15 Sukhumvit Plaza, at Soi 12, Sukhumvit* ☎ *02/653–3815* [M] *MRT: Sukhumvit; BTS: Asok.*

55 Pochana

$ | **THAI** | You wouldn't expect much by looking at this nondescript restaurant on Sukhumvit Road from the outside, but locals have been packing it night after night for years. The place, which started out as a late night khao tom rice soup eatery, has expanded to having one of the most extensive and tastiest Thai-Chinese menus in town. **Known for:** open late until 4:30 am; classic Thai dishes like tom yum soup; signature dishes like aw suan (oyster and egg soufflé) and dok krajon ("little flower" salad). [$] *Average main: B150* ✉ *1087–91 Sukhumvit Rd., Thong Lor* ✥ *100 meters (110 yds) east of the corner of Sukhumvit 55* ☎ *02/391–2021* 🌐 *www.facebook.com/55pochana* 🕒 *No lunch* [M] *BTS: Thong Lor.*

★ **Isao**

$$ | **SUSHI** | Bangkok has hundreds of Japanese restaurants, but only Isao has a line out the door almost every night, thanks to the most creative sushi rolls west of California. The owner studied under the chef at the revered Green Tea in Chicago, and the repeat clientele attests to the widespread enthusiasm for his culinary flights of fancy in sleek modern surrounds. **Known for:** reservations not accepted; reasonable prices; caterpillar-shaped sushi roll with shrimp and tempura. [$] *Average main: B400* ✉ *5 Sukhumvit, Soi 31, Sukhumvit* ☎ *09/561–54264, 09/566–14564* 🌐 *www.isaotaste.com* [M] *BTS: Phrom Phong.*

Je Ngor

$$ | **THAI** | Locals adore this Thai-Chinese eatery for various stir-fried seafood dishes, loaded with fried garlic, pepper, and fragrant curry, as well as reasonably priced lunch set menus. The decor is homey but attractive, with warm colors and lots of space, making the Sukhumvit location of this popular chain both comfy and convenient. **Known for:** traditional Thai desserts; special menu items like stir-fried rock lobster; hot pot soups. [$] *Average main: B250* ✉ *68/2 Sukhumvit, Soi 20, Sukhumvit* ☎ *02/258–8008* 🌐 *www.jengor-seafoods.com* [M] *BTS: Phrom Phong.*

Kuppa

$$ | **CAFÉ** | This light-and-airy space maintains the aura of its former life as a warehouse, but it's certainly more chic than shabby these days, with polished metal and blond wood adding a hip counterpoint to cement floors. Kuppa serves traditional Thai fare as well as many international dishes, and it has a dedicated following for its coffee, roasted on the premises. **Known for:** coffee roasted on-site; small portions; popular for weekend brunch. [$] *Average main: B350* ✉ *39 Sukhumvit Rd., Soi 16, Sukhumvit* ☎ *02/259–1954, 02/663–0450* 🌐 *www.kuppa.co.th* [M] *MRT: Sukhumvit; BTS: Asok.*

Le Dalat

$$ | **VIETNAMESE** | **FAMILY** | Classy Le Dalat is a favorite with Bangkok residents, serving royal Vietnamese cuisine in a former private home set among lovely gardens. The several intimate dining rooms have nostalgic design touches, such as vintage paintings and black-and-white photos, wicker seats with colorful pillows, and fine china tableware. **Known for:** reservations recommended; quiet, somewhat hidden location; seafood dishes like the Hanoi-style fried turmeric fish with dill. [$] *Average main: B260* ✉ *57 Sukhumvit Rd., Soi 23, Sukhumvit* ☎ *02/259–9593* 🌐 *www.ledalatbkk.com* [M] *MRT: Sukhumvit; BTS: Asok.*

★ **The Local**

$$ | **THAI** | The emphasis at this traditional Thai restaurant in a century-old house is on fresh seasonal ingredients and hard-to-find regional delicacies, with a regular menu but also a smaller one of specials that is consistently changing. The Local's decor, outdoor terrace, wood floors, and antiques and old photos

Dinner Cruises

Though they're definitely touristy, a dinner cruise on the Chao Phraya River is worth considering for the atmosphere. They're a great way to see the city at night, although the food is often not that great. You might even want to skip the dinner, just have drinks, and dine at a real Thai restaurant afterward. Two-hour cruises on modern boats or refurbished rice barges include a buffet or set-menu dinner, and often feature live music and sometimes a traditional dance show. Some operators also offer a less expensive lunch cruise, though the heat can make these not so pleasant. In general it's best to reserve a few days in advance.

Horizon. Operated from the Shangri-La Hotel, the buffet dinner cruise aboard the *Horizon*, with Thai and international cuisine, departs each evening at 7:30 pm. ⊠ *Shangri-La Hotel, 89 Soi Wat Suan Plu, Charoen Krung Rd., Bang Rak* ☏ *02/236–7777* ⊕ *www.shangri-la.com/bangkok/shangrila/dining/restaurants/horizon-cruise* ⊘ *No lunch* Ⓜ *BTS: Saphan Taksin.*

Manohra Dining Cruise. Beautifully restored antique rice barges depart from Anantara Riverside Bangkok at 5 pm, with Thai canapes by well-known Chef Phong. It's free for Anantara Riverside Bangkok guests. ⊠ *Anantara Bangkok Riverside Hotel, 257/1–3 Charoen Nakhon Rd., Thonburi* ☏ *02/476–0022* ⊕ *www.manohra-cruises.com* ☞ *Cruise is free for hotel guests.* Ⓜ *BTS: Saphan Taksin, then hotel boat.*

make for a pleasant setting. **Known for:** popular with tourists; separate vegetarian menu; tom yum martinis and dragon fruit mojitos. Ⓢ *Average main: B320* ⊠ *32-32/1 Sukhumvit Rd., Soi 23, Sukhumvit* ☏ *02/664–0664* ⊕ *www.thelocalthaicuisine.com* Ⓜ *MRT: Sukhumvit; BTS: Asok.*

Ministry of Crab
$$$$ | SEAFOOD | This branch of the Michelin-starred Sri Lankan restaurant, Ministry of Crab specializes in fresh, meaty crab flown in daily from that country. Crabs are prepared with your choice of sauce—garlic chili, baked, black pepper, or curry—and range in size from 500g "small" crabs to five-pound "crabzillas." Also on the menu are a variety of other crab dishes, including a creamy crab liver pate, fresh king prawns, clams, and oysters. **Known for:** signature black pepper sauce; crab liver pâté; fresh crab flown in from Sri Lanka. Ⓢ *Average main: 1,800* ⊠ *15/1 Sukhumvit Soi 31, Sukhumvit*

☏ *02/116–6220* ⊕ *www.ministryofcrab.com* ⊘ *Closed Mon.* Ⓜ *MRT: Sukhumvit, then taxi; BTS: Asoke, then taxi.*

My Choice
$$ | THAI | FAMILY | My Choice might be located a bit far off the main Sukhumvit drag, but it's very popular among Thais with a taste for their grandmothers' traditional recipes. Natural light, modern wood furniture, and leafy plants create a warm and inviting atmosphere, but when the weather is cool, diners prefer to sit outside. **Known for:** traditional recipes; popular for family dining; ped aob (whole roasted duck). Ⓢ *Average main: B250* ⊠ *19 Sukhumvit Rd., Soi 36, Sukhumvit* ☏ *02/258–6174, 02/259–9470* ⊕ *www.facebook.com/pages/My-Choice-Thai-Cuisine/1677636215845075?fref=ts* Ⓜ *BTS: Thong Lo.*

★ Peppina

$$$ | PIZZA | A top contender as Bangkok's best pizzeria, the warmly industrial-looking Peppina is booked solid most nights (although there are other locations). The attention to detail includes wood firing, pizza dough that's left to rise overnight, and fresh buffalo mozzarella and other ingredients imported from Italy. **Known for:** extensive drink list; inventive antipasti; gourmet pizza. *$ Average main: B450 ✉ 27/1 Sukhumvit, Soi 31, Sukhumvit ☎ 09/228–29861 ⊕ www.peppinabkk. com* Ⓜ *BTS: Asoke, then taxi.*

Sri Trat

$$ | THAI | In an attractive, 1970s vintage house decorated with old-school Thai touches, this is one of the only restaurants in the city focused on the cuisine of eastern Thailand, particularly Chanthaburi and Trat. Don't miss the *lon pu kai,* a creamy coconut-chili dip made with fresh chunks of mud crab and accompanied by fresh local herbs and vegetables. **Known for:** chili dips; crab-fried noodles; eastern Thai cooking. *$ Average main: 250 ✉ 90 Sukhumvit Soi 33, Sukhumvit ☎ 02/088–0968 ⊕ www.facebook.com/ sritrat* Ⓜ *MRT: Sukhumvit, then taxi; BTS: Asoke, then taxi.*

★ Supanniga Eating Room

$$ | THAI | Thanaruek Laoraowirodge, a successful restaurateur in New York City and Bangkok, has earned high praise for this cozy shophouse venue that specializes in regional dishes based on the recipes of his grandmother. The au courant cocktails go well with the eclectic menu, and Supanniga now has several other locations: in Bang Rak, Sathorn, and Tha Thien. **Known for:** street-food dishes like fried rice and noodles; charcoal-grilled meats; variations of nam prik (traditional spicy chili dip served with vegetables). *$ Average main: B240 ✉ 160/11 Sukhumvit, Soi 55, Thong Lor ✚ Between Thonglor Soi 6 and 8 ☎ 02/714–7508 ⊕ www.supannigaeatingroom.com* Ⓜ *BTS: Thong Lo.*

Hotels

★ Bangkok Marriott Hotel Sukhumvit

$ | HOTEL | This snazzy urban-design property in the area's tallest building brings five-star luxury to the Thong Lor area. **Pros:** great views; close to trendy Thong Lor restaurants and bars; nice outdoor pool. **Cons:** not in the heart of the city; horrible rush-hour traffic; away from tourist attractions. *$ Rooms from: B1,800 ✉ 2 Sukhumvit, Soi 57, Thong Lor ☎ 02/797–0000 ⊕ www.marriott.com/ hotels/travel/bkkms-bangkok-marriott-hotel-sukhumvit* ꭍ◯ℓ *No Meals* ⤷ *295 rooms and suites* Ⓜ *BTS: Thong Lor.*

The Davis Bangkok

$$$$ | HOTEL | The Davis has a main building and another one two doors down with a separate lobby and reception area but no matter where you end up, the rooms are comfortable and classy. **Pros:** individually decorated rooms; quiet location; beautiful pool area. **Cons:** separate buildings can be confusing; uninteresting view from rooms; not close to public transit. *$ Rooms from: B6,653 ✉ 80 Sukhumvit, Soi 24, Sukhumvit ☎ 02/260–8001 ⊕ www.davisbangkok. net* ꭍ◯ℓ *No Meals* ⤷ *247 rooms, 2 villas* Ⓜ *BTS: Phrom Phong.*

★ Indochinoise Residence

$$$$ | HOTEL | This colonial-style boutique hotel offers small and large suites, plus a few multibedroom residences, all in a style suggesting 1920s Shanghai. **Pros:** colonial-style property with period decor; rooftop pool; antiques-filled rooms. **Cons:** must book well in advance; expensive; congested area for traffic. *$ Rooms from: B6,100 ✉ 14/29 Sukhumvit, Soi 45, Sukhumvit ☎ 02/259–2871, 02/259–2872 ⊕ indochinise-residence.thailandhotels. site/th/* ꭍ◯ℓ *Free Breakfast* ⤷ *8 rooms* Ⓜ *BTS: Phrom Phong and Thong Lor.*

J. W. Marriott Hotel Bangkok

$$ | HOTEL | The J.W. Marriott's convenience to restaurants, businesses, and one of the city's biggest red-light districts will turn some travelers off and others on. **Pros:** many dining options; very friendly staff; nice gym. **Cons:** close to red-light district; not as nice as the Marriott in Thonburi; decor a bit uninspiring. [$] *Rooms from: B2,500* ✉ *4 Sukhumvit Rd., at Soi 2, Sukhumvit* ☎ *02/656–7700* 🌐 *www.marriott.com* 🛏 *441 rooms, 39 suites* [M] *BTS: Nana.*

The Landmark Bangkok

$$ | **HOTEL** | The generous use of polished wood in the reception area may suggest a grand European hotel, but The Landmark is surprisingly modern. **Pros:** good for business travelers; modern amenities; discount packages frequently available. **Cons:** some rooms noisy; may be too formal for families; close to red-light district. [$] *Rooms from: B3,600* ✉ *138 Sukhumvit Rd., Sukhumvit* ☎ *02/254–0404* 🌐 *www.landmarkbangkok.com* 🍴 *Free Breakfast* 🛏 *450 rooms* [M] *BTS: Nana.*

Pullman Bangkok Grande Sukhumvit

$$$ | **HOTEL** | A futuristic facade of soaring glass and odd angles sets the tone at this upscale lodging located conveniently in the heart of Sukhumvit. **Pros:** attentive service; centrally located; interesting exterior architecture. **Cons:** bathrooms lack privacy; many business travelers; design somewhat dated. [$] *Rooms from: B5,500* ✉ *30 Sukhumvit, Soi 21, Sukhumvit* ☎ *02/204–4000* 🌐 *www.pullmanbangkokgrandesukhumvit.com* 🍴 *No Meals* 🛏 *325 rooms* [M] *MRT: Sukhumvit; BTS: Asok.*

Sheraton Grande Sukhumvit

$$ | **HOTEL** | The Sheraton soars 33 floors above the noisy city streets, and the upper-floor suites get tons of natural light. **Pros:** impressive views from most rooms; near public transportation; high-quality live music lounge. **Cons:** somewhat impersonal due to size; huge; expensive for area. [$] *Rooms from: B2,000* ✉ *250 Sukhumvit Rd., Sukhumvit* ☎ *02/649–8888* 🌐 *www.sheratongrandesukhumvit.com* 🍴 *No Meals* 🛏 *420 rooms, 36 suites* [M] *MRT: Sukhumvit; BTS: Asok.*

The Westin Grande Sukhumvit

$$ | **HOTEL** | Fancy with sleek surfaces and neon lighting, the Westin is very convenient to Sukhumvit shopping and nightlife—it's just out the front door. **Pros:** comfortable beds; near Skytrain and subway; close to nightlife. **Cons:** overpriced compared to nearby options; on-site restaurants not great; dated design. [$] *Rooms from: B2,000* ✉ *259 Sukhumvit Rd., Sukhumvit* ☎ *02/207–8000* 🌐 *www.westingrandesukhumvit.com* 🍴 *No Meals* 🛏 *362 rooms, 31 suites* [M] *MRT: Sukhumvit; BTS: Asok.*

🍸 Nightlife

There's a great variety of bars and clubs around Sukhumvit. Lower Sukhumvit is where you'll find the Nana Plaza and Soi Cowboy red-light districts. Farther east, the neighborhoods of Thonglor and Ekkamai are *the* places for young Thais and foreigners to party, with lots of buzzy nightclubs and speakeasy-style cocktail bars.

BARS AND PUBS

Above Eleven

BARS | This rooftop bar on the 33nd floor of the Frasier Suites Sukhumvit offers sweeping views of the city in sophisticated surrounds. Order a pisco sour and some Japanese-Peruvian snacks, like ceviche and sushi, and enjoy the DJ's beats. ✉ *Frasier Suites Sukhumvit, 38/8 Sukhumvit, Soi 11, 33rd fl., Sukhumvit* ☎ *02/038–5111* 🌐 *www.aboveeleven.com* [M] *BTS: Nana.*

Craft Bangkok

BARS | Boutique beer lovers flock to this hip outdoor spot where, as you can guess from the name, all the brews are 100% craft. There are some U.S. favorites as well as Czech, Scandinavian, and Japanese options. There's another branch on Silom Road. ✉ *16 Sukhumvit, Soi 23, Sukhumvit* ✥ *About 200 meters*

(655 feet) up Soi 23 on right ☎ *02/258–0541* ⊕ *www.facebook.com/craftbkk* Ⓜ *MRT: Sukhumvit; BTS: Asok.*

FKA Black Amber

COCKTAIL LOUNGES | Hidden away in a small alley off Thonglor Soi 6, this bar established by Carson Quinn, one of Bangkok's top mixologists, and Scott Hess, a DJ of similar fame, offers an intimate ambience with wood paneling and subtle lighting in which to enjoy bespoke cocktails and an eclectic mix of tunes. ✉ *17-160 Thonglor Rd., Soi 6, Sukhumvit* ☎ *02/102–8617* ⊕ *www.facebook.com/FKA-Black-Amber-Social-Club-100550165569919* ⊗ *Closed Mon.* Ⓜ *BTS: Thong Lor.*

J. Boroski

COCKTAIL LOUNGES | There's no cocktail menu at this hidden speakeasy from legendary Bangkok mixologist Joseph Boroski: you simply tell the bartender what you're in the mood for and you'll get something special, made with dashes of rare ingredients. ✉ *Thonglor (Sukhumvit 55) Soi 9, Thong Lor* ⊹ *At the end of the alley on the right* ☎ *02/712–6025* ⊕ *www.sipslowly.com/jboroski-1* Ⓜ *BTS: Thong Lor.*

★ Octave

BARS | This downtown rooftop bar atop the Bangkok Marriott Hotel Sukhumvit is known for its 360-degree panoramas and for reasonable drink prices compared to other rooftop bars. ✉ *Bangkok Marriott Hotel Sukhumvit, 2 Sukhumvit, Soi 57, Thong Lor* ☎ *02/797–0000* ⊕ *https://modules.marriott.com* Ⓜ *BTS: Thong Lor.*

Oskar Bistro

BARS | On any night of the week, Oskar is full of a mixed Thai and foreign crowd enjoying good cocktails and wood-fired pizzas, along with more satisfying international bites. The electronic beats spill out onto the street and eclectic DJs are regularly on board. ✉ *24 Sukhumvit, Soi 11, Sukhumvit* ☎ *02/728–9441* ⊕ *www.oskar-bistro.com* Ⓜ *BTS: Nana.*

Royal Oak Pub

BARS | With many different beers on tap and in bottles, this very British pub tends to draw serious beer drinkers. There are also fun game nights on Wednesday and ladies' specials on Thursday. ✉ *595/10–11 Sukhumvit, Soi 33, Sukhumvit* ☎ *02/662–1652* ⊕ *www.facebook.com/royaloak.bkk/* Ⓜ *BTS: Phrom Phong.*

Tasting Room by Mikkeller

BARS | The craft-beer gypsy brewers from Denmark opened up shop in Bangkok at this hideaway in a residential garden home. Around 30 brews are on tap, many of them experimental and avant-garde specimens found only at the world's few Mikkeller branches. The garden is a fine spot to relax in, and there is also a bottle shop and a popular fine-dining restaurant. ✉ *26 Ekkamai, Soi 10, Yaek 2, Sukhumvit* ☎ *02/381–9891* ⊕ *www.facebook.com/tastingroombkk/* Ⓜ *BTS: Ekkamai.*

DANCE CLUBS

★ Beam

DANCE CLUBS | Beam is home to Asia's first "body kinetic" dance floor, shaking vibrations into dancer's feet during live techno and deep house gigs. The futuristic decor and throbbing lights fit perfectly with the progressive underground beats of DJs from Bangkok and abroad. ✉ *72 Courtyard, 72 Sukhumvit, Soi Thonglor (Soi 55), 1st fl., Thong Lor* ☎ *02/392–7750* ⊕ *www.beamclub.com* Ⓜ *BTS: Thong Lor.*

Glow

DANCE CLUBS | An underground dance club playing only cutting-edge electronic music, Glow lights up Sukhumvit with a revolving lineup of local and international DJs. You'll find a trendy mix of expats and locals here enjoying the top-notch sound system and an excellent vodka selection. ✉ *96/4–5 Sukhumvit Rd., Soi 23, Sukhumvit* ☎ *08/661–43355* ⊕ *www.facebook.com/GlowBkk* ⊗ *Closed Mon.* Ⓜ *MRT: Sukhumvit; BTS: Asok.*

★ Havana Social

DANCE CLUBS | The entrance to this secret salsa lair is a fake telephone booth in a dark unsuspecting alley across from the Frasier Suites Sukhumvit. Inside you'll find a diverse crowd shimmying to Afro-Cuban beats, sipping Cubra Libres on leather couches, and smoking in the cigar lounge, harking back to Havana before the revolution. ⊠ *1/1 Sukhumvit Rd., Soi 11, Sukhumvit ✛ Down the alley across from Frasier Suites Sukhumvit* ☎ *08/046–77409* ⊕ *www.facebook.com/havanasocialbkk* ♥ *Closed Mon.* Ⓜ *BTS: Nana.*

Sing Sing Theater

DANCE CLUBS | This stylish nightclub evokes 1930s Shanghai, with wrought-iron alcoves, spiral staircases, red lighting, and lanterns. DJs spin upbeat electronic music, beckoning some to squeeze onto the compact dance floor and others to lounge at tables and by the bar. ⊠ *45 Sukhumvit Rd., Soi 45, Sukhumvit* ☎ *02/322–51331* ⊕ *www.singsingbangkok.com* Ⓜ *BTS: Phrom Pong.*

Shopping

CLOTHING AND FABRICS

Raja's Fashions

Photographs here show former heads of state proudly modeling their new suits made by Raja Fashions. Raja has a reputation for tailoring some of the finest men's and women's fashions in the Sukhumvit area. ⊠ *160 Sukhumvit, Sukhumvit ✛ Between Soi 6 and 8* ☎ *02/253–8379* ⊕ *www.rajasfashions.com* Ⓜ *MRT: Sukhumvit; BTS: Nana.*

SHOPPING CENTERS

Emporium & EmQuartier (EM District)

MALL | This glitzy mall was renovated and expanded to include EmQuartier, a separate building across the BTS line from Emporium, together called EM District. There are exclusive high-end shops and fine dining throughout and the sixth floor full of beautiful silks, incense, and glassware, all reasonably priced. ⊠ *622 Sukhumvit Rd., Sukhumvit ✛ Between Sois 24 and 26* ☎ *02/269–1000* ⊕ *www.theemdistrict.com* Ⓜ *BTS: Phrom Phong; there's a dedicated walkway from the station to both sides of EM District.*

Terminal 21

MALL | Connected to the BTS Asok station via a broad walkway, the various levels at this upper-middle-class mall represent different parts of the world. There's a San Francisco section, for instance, complete with cable cars and a miniature Golden Gate Bridge, plus a London floor, an Istanbul, and many others. The food court on the top floor is one of Bangkok's best, and there's a multiplex cinema. There's another Terminal 21 branch on Rama III Road. ⊠ *88 Sukhumvit, Soi 19, Sukhumvit ✛ At Asok Rd.* ☎ *02/108–0888* ⊕ *www.terminal21.co.th/asok/* Ⓜ *BTS: Asok; a walkways links the mall with the BTS station.*

Spas

Health Land Spa

SPAS | This spa chain is known for its high-quality massages at reasonable prices, with a 120-minute traditional Thai massage costing B600. There are multiple locations around Bangkok, but the one at Asok is easy to get to by Skytrain or subway. Appointments book up fast, so call ahead. ⊠ *55/5 Sukhumvit Rd., Soi 21 (Soi Asoke), Sukhumvit ✛ Walk down Sukhumvit 19 and take your first right; from Sukhumvit 21 your first left.* ☎ *02/261–1110, 02/637–86771* ⊕ *www.healthlandspa.com* Ⓜ *MRT: Sukhumvit; BTS: Asok.*

Oasis Spa

SPAS | The treatments at Oasis Spa take place in a Thai-style house. Among the inventive options are a Thai coconut, loofah, and witch hazel scrub, and soothing aloe and lavender body wraps. A second branch at Sukhumvit, Soi 31, is just as lovely, and both offer free transportation from the BTS Phrom Phong station. ✉ *88 Sukhumvit, Soi 51, Sukhumvit* ☎ *02/262–2122* ⊕ *www.oasisspa.net* Ⓜ *BTS: Thong Lo.*

Yunomori Onsen & Spa

SPAS | Bangkok's first Japanese-style onsen (hot springs) uses real spring water—thousands of gallons of it—trucked up from the famed Raksa Warin Hot Springs in Ranong. You can immerse yourself in pools of different temperatures, from a toasty hot tub down to a cold plunge pool. There are first-class spa treatments, too. ✉ *A-Square 120/5, Sukhumvit, Soi 26, Sukhumvit* ⊹ *Take a taxi down Sukhumvit, Soi 26 to A-Square* ☎ *02/259–5778* ⊕ *www.yunomorionsen. com* Ⓜ *Skytrain: Phrom Phong.*

Silom, Sathorn, and Bang Rak

The Silom area, with a mix of tall office buildings and condos, residential streets, and entertainment areas, is Bangkok's busiest business district. Some of the city's finest hotels and restaurants are in this neighborhood, which retains some charm despite being so developed and layered in concrete. To the east is Sathorn, a district named for Sathorn Road, consisting of residences, embassies, markets, and a small but growing dining scene. Bang Rak is on the Chao Phraya River, and many of the hotels and bars here have wonderful views.

Sights

Baan Suan Phlu (M. R. Kukrit Heritage Home)

HISTORIC HOME | Former Prime Minister Kukrit Pramoj's house reflects his long, influential life. After founding Siam Rath newspaper in 1950 and writing several novels, he served as prime minister in 1975 and 1976. (Perhaps he practiced for that role 12 years earlier, when he

appeared with Marlon Brando as a fictional Southeast Asian prime minister in *The Ugly American*.) He died in 1995, and much of his living quarters—five interconnected teak houses—has been preserved. Throughout his life, Kukrit was dedicated to preserving Thai culture, and his house and grounds are monuments to a bygone era; the place is full of Thai and Khmer art and period furniture. The landscaped garden with its Khmer stonework is also a highlight. It took Pramoj 30 years to build the house, so it's no wonder that you can spend the better part of a day wandering around. ✉ *S. Sathorn Rd. 19, Soi Phra Pinit, Sathorn* ☎ *02/286–8185* 🎫 *B50* Ⓜ *BTS: Chong Nonsi, then taxi or walk.*

Lumphini Park

CITY PARK | Two lakes enhance this popular park, the oldest and largest in the center of the city. Expect to see children feeding bread to the turtles, aerobics and tai chi classes, and teenagers paddling boats. During the dry season (from December to February), the Bangkok Symphony Orchestra usually runs the free "Concert in the Park" series, which starts at 5:30 pm each Sunday. ✉ *Rama IV Rd., Pathumwan* ☎ *02/252–7006* Ⓜ *MRT: Silom; BTS: Sala Daeng.*

★ Queen Saovabha Memorial Institute

OTHER MUSEUM | **FAMILY** | The Thai Red Cross established this unusual and fascinating snake farm and toxicology research institute in 1923, and it is well worth a visit. Venom from cobras, pit vipers, and some of the other 56 types of deadly snakes found in Thailand is collected and used to make antidotes for snakebite victims. Venom extraction takes place on weekday mornings at 11. The snake handling show and photo op is at 2:30 on weekdays and 11 on weekends and holidays. ✉ *1871 Rama IV Rd., Pathumwan* ☎ *02/252–0161, 02/252–0167* ⊕ *www.saovabha.com/en/ snakefarm_service.asp* 🎫 *B200* Ⓜ *MRT: Silom; BTS: Sala Daeng.*

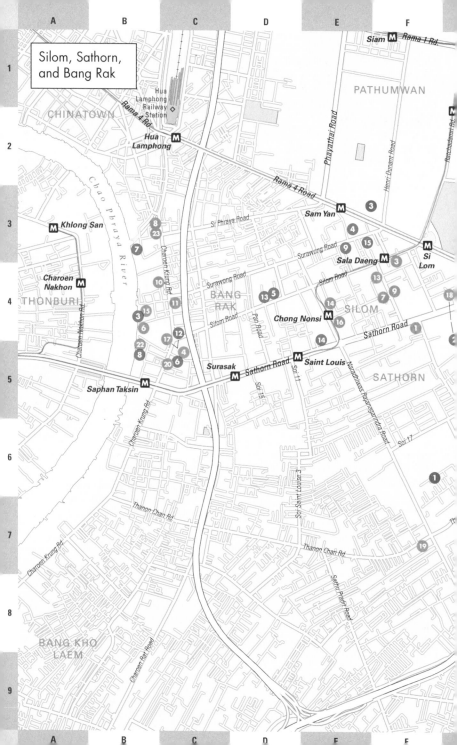

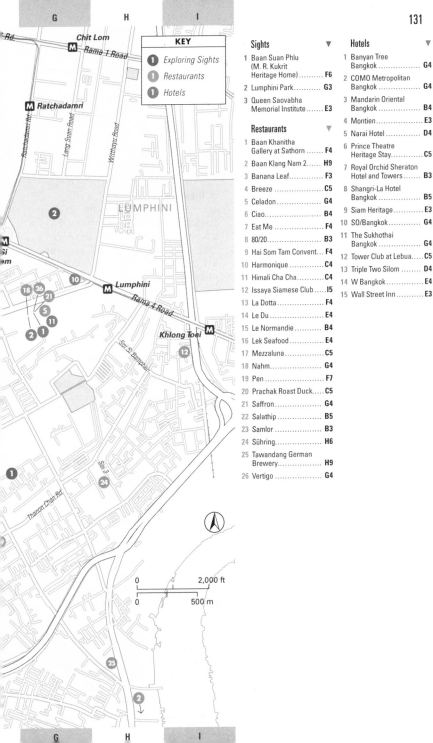

KEY

- Exploring Sights
- Restaurants
- Hotels

Sights ▼

Restaurants ▼

Hotels ▼

🍴 Restaurants

Around Silom, Sathorn, and Bang Rak are a wide selection of restaurants, many in hotels, on the upper floors of skyscrapers, or in lanes extending between Silom and Sathorn. You'll find everything from authentic, humble northeastern Thai food to elaborate, wallet-busting international cuisine. Bang Rak is the best neighborhood in the city for fine dining in restored century-old shophouses

Baan Khanitha Gallery at Sathorn

$$ | THAI | This restaurant in a converted house with a pleasant outdoor garden balances a casually upmarket feel with fairly authentic Thai cuisine oriented toward less adventurous palates. The basics are done well here, from *chu chee goong mae nam* (curried river prawns) to *khao yum* (southern Thai-style rice salad). **Known for:** local artwork; mango sticky rice; wide menu. $ *Average main: B300* ⌂ *69 S. Sathorn Rd., Silom* ☎ *02/675–4200* ⊕ *www.baan-khanitha.com* Ⓜ *BTS: Saint Louis; MRT: Lumpini.*

Baan Klang Nam 2

$$$ | THAI | If you cruise the Chao Phraya River at night, you might end up gazing upon the clapboard house this restaurant occupies, wishing you were among the crowd dining at this most romantic spot. Fresh Thai oysters, served raw with chili and herbs, are a big draw here. **Known for:** seafood dishes like steamed fish and spicy fried crab; white-teak traditional house; authentic Thai cuisine. $ *Average main: B400* ⌂ *762/7 Bangkok Sq., Rama III Rd., Yannawa* ✛ *South of Sathorn* ☎ *02/682–7180* ⊕ *www.facebook.com/bkn2restaurant* Ⓜ *BTS: Sala Daeng, then taxi.*

Banana Leaf

$$ | THAI | If you need to recuperate from Silom Road shopping, head up to the fourth floor of the Silom Complex at Banana Leaf for wonderful mid-priced eats. The mall atmosphere might turn off some, but friendly service and an extensive menu of Thai classics and seafood dishes make up for it. **Known for:** close to Skytrain station direct link; river prawns with glass noodles; good vegetarian options. $ *Average main: B250* ⌂ *Silom Complex, 191 Silom Rd., 4th fl., Silom* ✛ *Near BTS Sala Daeng's south exit* ☎ *02/231–3124* ⊕ *www.bananaleaf-thailand.com* Ⓜ *BTS: Sala Daeng; MRT: Silom.*

★ Breeze

$$$$ | ASIAN | Practically in the clouds at the State Tower, this ultrahip eatery has a futuristic design that may leave you feeling transported to 2060—especially at night on the outdoor Sky Bridge and in the dining room glowing purple neon. Pan-Asian cuisine creations culminate in chef Sam Pang's tasting menu priced at B4,500, but you can also order à la carte. **Known for:** high-profile guests; incredible views from the 51st and 52nd floors; luxurious flourishes like caviar selection. $ *Average main: B1,500* ⌂ *State Tower, 1055 Silom Rd., 52nd fl., Bang Rak* ☎ *02/624–9555* ⊕ *www.lebua.com/breeze* ☾ *No lunch* Ⓜ *BTS: Saphan Taksin.*

Celadon

$$$ | THAI | Lotus ponds reflect the city's beautiful evening lights at this romantic restaurant. The upmarket Thai food is good, with elegant touches that cater to locals as well as foreigners. **Known for:** seafood specialties like grilled river prawns; regional dishes like khao soi and southern-style yellow curry; several vegetarian options. $ *Average main: B550* ⌂ *The Sukhothai Bangkok, 13/3 S. Sathorn Rd., Sathorn* ☎ *02/344–8888* ⊕ *www.sukhothai.com/bangkok/en* Ⓜ *MRT: Lumpini.*

Ciao

$$$$ | ITALIAN | A riverside location with pleasant breezes and great views provides a relaxed setting for Ciao's classic Italian fare. From bruschetta to focaccia, everything on the menu is made with fine and fresh ingredients, meats and cheeses imported from Italy, and plenty

of attention to detail; top-notch wines also complement the elegant food and surroundings. **Known for:** oven-fired pizzas; great setting for romance; home-made pastas and risottos. $ *Average main: B1,500* ✉ *Mandarin Oriental, 48 Oriental Ave., Bang Rak* ☎ *02/659–9000* ⊕ *www.mandarinoriental.com* ⊗ *No lunch* Ⓜ *BTS: Saphan Taksin, then hotel shuttle boat.*

Eat Me
$$$$ | **INTERNATIONAL** | This Aussie establishment is both a high-end eatery and an art space where temporary exhibits from H Gallery provide quite a funky atmosphere. The international fusion menu is also reflected by a staff well mixed between foreigners and Thais, including mixologist Buntanes "Pop" Direkrittikul who's been generating buzz for his creative Thai-inspired cocktails using ingredients like toasted rice, shallots, and chili paste. **Known for:** premium Australian meats; young hip crowd; Thai-inspired cocktail tastings. $ *Average main: B800* ✉ *1/6 Soi Phiphat 2, Silom* ⊹ *Off Convent Rd.* ☎ *02/238–0931* ⊕ *www.eatmerestaurant.com* ⊗ *No lunch* Ⓜ *MRT: Silom; BTS: Sala Daeng.*

80/20
$$$$ | **THAI** | Founded by young chefs in a minimally restored old shophouse in Bang Rak, 80/20 earned its first Michelin star in record time. The kitchen team brings together rare Thai ingredients and European cooking techniques, along with head chef Andrew Martin's idea of *14-bite (B2,800) and 18-bite (B3,300) tasting menus.* **Known for:** trendy decor; tasting menus; fresh seafood. $ *Average main: 2,800* ✉ *1052-1054 Charoenkrung Soi 26, Bang Rak* ☎ *09/911–82200* ⊕ *www.8020bkk.com* Ⓜ *MRT: Hua Lampong; Chao Phraya River Express Boat: Si Phraya Pier.*

Hai Som Tam Convent
$ | **THAI** | A good sign of quality, this restaurant is packed with Thais sharing tables filled with northeastern favorites like grilled chicken, spicy papaya salad, and minced duck salad. The open-air dining area can be hot, it's often crowded and noisy, and the staff don't speak much English, so you'll need to pick and point from the menu—but that's part of the fun. **Known for:** cheap yet satisfying eats; properly spicy Thai food; no air-conditioning. $ *Average main: B80* ✉ *2/4-5 Convent Rd., Silom* ⊹ *Off Silom Rd.* ☎ *02/631–0216* ⊗ *Closed Sun.* ▭ *No credit cards* Ⓜ *MRT: Silom; BTS: Sala Daeng.*

Harmonique
$$ | **THAI** | This small house near the river is filled with Thai antiques and anatique chests scattered with bric-a-brac, which all gives the ambience of dining at a relative's house. The staff is very good at helping indecisive diners choose from the brief menu, and although the restaurant has become more touristy over the years, it also retains a loyal and regular local clientele. **Known for:** excellent curries; terrace and dining room seating; unusual Thai dishes like hoa mouk (fish curry in a banana leaf). $ *Average main: B250* ✉ *22 Charoen Krung Rd., Soi 34, Bang Rak* ☎ *02/237–8175* ⊕ *www.facebook.com/harmoniqueth* Ⓜ *BTS: Saphan Taksin; Chao Phraya Express Boat: Wat Muang Khae Pier.*

Himali Cha Cha
$$ | **INDIAN** | Cha Cha, who cooked for Indian Prime Minister Jawaharlal Nehru, died in 1996, but his recipes live on and are prepared with equal ability by his son Kovit. Typical Indian-themed decor and a long-standing menu of traditional dishes as well as intriguing daily specials make this restaurant an oldie but a goodie, with two other locations in Bangkok also available. **Known for:** garlic naan and cheese naan; famous tandoori chicken; northern Indian specialties. $ *Average main: B300* ✉ *1229/11 Charoen Krung Rd., Soi 47/1, Bang Rak* ☎ *02/235–1569, 02/630–6358* ⊕ *www.himalichacha.com* Ⓜ *BTS: Saphan Taksin.*

Issaya Siamese Club

$$$$ | THAI | An upscale and much-raved-about Thai restaurant, Issaya both surprises and charms with its delightfully laid-back atmosphere, set in a tropical garden peppered with colorful bean bags during dry season. The dining room is cozy with big couches and lots of antique touches, coupled with fun platings and garnishes and impeccable service. **Known for:** the beloved banana blossom and heart of palm salad; dishes inspired by celeb chef Ian Kittichai's childhood; good cocktails. $ *Average main: B800* ✉ *4 Soi Si Aksorn, Chua Ploeng Rd., Sathorn* ☎ *02/672–9040* ⊕ *www.issaya.com* Ⓜ *MRT: Khlong Toei, then taxi or walk.*

La Dotta

$$ | ITALIAN | Fresh pasta made with 100% Italian semolina and organic duck eggs is the signature at La Dotta, a Mediterranean-inspired dining room on Convent Road. Standouts include the wagyu bolognese with tagliatelle and bucatini all'amatriciana, topped with a sauce that is slow-cooked for four hours and served with dry-cured pork cheeks from Rome. **Known for:** fresh pasta; seafood; quality wine list. $ *Average main: 360* ✉ *10/15 Convent Road, Silom* ☎ *02/236–5558* ⊕ *www.ladotta.co* Ⓜ *BTS: Sala Daeng.*

Le Du

$$$$ | THAI | At this modern Michelin-starred Thai restaurant, helmed by chef Thitid "Ton" Tassanakajohn, you're likely to try something new in the 4-course and 6-course tasting menus (no à la carte)—maybe a crunchy ant larvae topping or a charcoal-grilled pork jowl curry. Sleek minimalist surroundings put the focus on the food and drink, and since the chef is also a sommelier, you can expect wine pairings that perfectly complement each course. **Known for:** fresh regional products including free-range chicken; creative Thai dishes like a deconstructed pad kra pao; young, trendy crowd. $ *Average main: B2,990* ✉ *399/3 Silom Rd., Soi 7, Bang Rak*

☎ *02/291–99969* ⊕ *www.ledubkk.com* ⊘ *Closed Sun.* Ⓜ *BTS: Chong Nonsi.*

★ Le Normandie

$$$$ | FRENCH | Atop the Mandarin Oriental, this legendary French restaurant excites with impressive views of the Chao Phraya and remarkable food. Chef Arnaud Dunand regularly imports high-quality ingredients from his home region of Savoy for dishes that taste classically of the old country yet with a haute personal touch—tasting menus are of good value compared to à la carte, with the five-course lunch priced at B2,450. **Known for:** formal dress code; French Alps–inspired cuisine like the signature roasted pigeon; winner of major culinary awards. $ *Average main: B2,700* ✉ *Mandarin Oriental, 48 Oriental Ave., Bang Rak* ☎ *02/659–9000* ⊕ *www. mandarinoriental.com/bangkok/chao-phraya-river/fine-dining* ⊘ *Closed Sun.* 🎩 *Jacket required* Ⓜ *BTS: Saphan Taksin, then hotel shuttle boat.*

★ Lek Seafood

$$ | THAI | This unassuming storefront beneath an overpass is the sort of establishment that brings international foodies flocking to Bangkok. The interior here is nothing special, with poor lighting and bluish walls, but you'll barely notice or care with the lively buzz of the local Thai clientele, expert preparations with balanced flavors, and reasonable prices compared to many other seafood joints. **Known for:** specialties like the curry crab and cockles; beloved by locals; no-frills dining. $ *Average main: B250* ✉ *89 Narathiwat Ratchanakharin Rd., Soi 3, Bang Rak* ✛ *Below BTS Chong Nonsi station* ☎ *09/664–59646* ⊘ *Closed Sun. No lunch* Ⓜ *BTS: Chong Nonsi.*

★ Mezzaluna

$$$$ | FUSION | Mezzaluna is a blockbuster restaurant for a couple of reasons: dramatic views of Bangkok from the soaring State Tower and a truly magical degustation menu from the French-trained chef Ryuki Kawasaki. The seven-course

menu features organic ingredients and deeply personal touches, such as the mind-blowing signature dish—buttery-soft Wagyu beef paired with sake, both from the chef's home in Japan. **Known for:** fine French ingredients like Brittany blue lobster and foie gras; excellent wine and sake pairings; award-winning cuisine. $ *Average main: B6,500* ⊠ *State Tower, 1055 Silom Rd., 65th fl., Bang Rak* ☎ *02/624–9555* ⊕ *www.lebua. com* ⊗ *Closed Mon. No lunch* 🍴 *smart casual* Ⓜ *BTS: Saphan Taksin.*

Nahm

$$$ | **THAI** | Started by master chef David Thompson, who won accolades for his Thai eatery in London, the distinguished Nahm changed hands to chef Pim Techamuanvivit in 2018. Her cuisine marries the traditionalist concept of Nahm—where Thompson turned heads with recipes from ancient cookbooks— with the labor-intensive approach of Techamuanvivit's first restaurant, San Francisco's Kin Khao, for an upscale yet authentic Thai experience. **Known for:** little-known regional dishes like the blue swimmer crab curry; carefully selected wines; à la carte options as well as a tasting menu. $ *Average main: B600* ⊠ *CO-MO Metropolitan Bangkok, 27 S. Sathorn Rd., Sathorn* ☎ *02/625–3333* ⊕ *www. comohotels.com/metropolitanbangkok/ dining/nahm* ⊗ *No lunch weekends* Ⓜ *MRT: Lumpini.*

★ Pen

$$$ | **THAI** | This restaurant has little in the way of atmosphere, but seafood aficionados still brave the traffic up to Yannawa in order to splurge. Pen is expensive by Thai restaurant standards, but it's still a bargain compared to most hotel restaurants for charcoal-grilled seafood and a range of classic Thai fare. **Known for:** no-frills dining; specialties like deep-fried parrotfish with shallots; local favorite. $ *Average main: B420* ⊠ *25 Chan Rd., Chong Nonsi, Yannawa* ⊹ *Just south of Silom* ☎ *02/287–2907,*

02/867061 ⊕ *penrestaurant.com* Ⓜ *BTS: Chong Nonsi, then taxi.*

Prachak Roast Duck

$ | **CHINESE** | This little place with bare walls and a tile floor is beloved by locals for its juicy *pet* (roast duck) and *moo daeng* (red pork). Getting here early is a good idea—by 6 pm there's often little duck left—and allow yourself time to find the entrance, which is easy to miss on the busy Charoen Krung road. **Known for:** open for over a century; popular with Thai families; wonton noodle soup. $ *Average main: B80* ⊠ *Bang Rak Market, 1415 Charoen Krung Rd., Bang Rak* ☎ *02/234–3755* ⊕ *www.prachakrestaurant.com* Ⓜ *BTS: Saphan Taksin.*

Saffron

$$$ | **THAI** | The menu at Saffron mixes creative modern Thai with classic dishes, and the food is just as exciting as the stunning views from the 52nd floor of the Banyan Tree Bangkok. Even if you don't come for dinner, stop by the adjoining bar on the balcony for a cocktail or some street food–inspired snacks—the comfy seating, cool breeze, and vistas are superb. **Known for:** lots of smaller bites available; traditional Thai favorites like banana blossom salad; rare ingredients like Tasmanian salmon in the signature yum pla salad. $ *Average main: B550* ⊠ *Banyan Tree Bangkok, 21/100 S. Sathorn Rd., Sathorn* ☎ *02/679–1200* ⊕ *www.saffronbanyantree.com* ⊗ *No lunch* 🍴 *Smart casual* Ⓜ *MRT: Lumphini.*

Salathip

$$$ | **THAI** | In Thai-style teak pavilions facing the Chao Phraya River, this restaurant has a setting that practically guarantees a romantic evening—book an outside table so you can enjoy the breeze. Although the food may not have as many chilies as locals would like, the Thai standards are represented on the menu, with à la carte and set menus of seven or eight Thai favorites starting at B1,680. **Known for:** seafood specialties like the Phuket lobster; stunning river views; traditional

Thai music. $ *Average main: B400* ✉ *Shangri-La Hotel, 89 Wat Suan Plu, Charoen Krung (New Rd.), Bang Rak* ☎ *02/236–7777* ⊕ *www.shangri-la.com/ bangkok/shangrila/dining/restaurants/sal-athip* ⊗ *No lunch* Ⓜ *BTS: Saphan Taksin.*

Samlor

$$$ | **THAI** | In this century-old corner building in Bang Rak, a small team of Thai chefs turn out *gub glam,* simple dishes that are traditionally meant to accompany an evening of drinking but the food more than stands up on its own. Signature dishes include fried chicken wings in a fish-sauce glaze and beef brisket braised in a soy ginger sauce and served with garlic rice and greens. **Known for:** top quality ingredients; large portions meant to be shared; amazing ice cream. $ *Average main: 550* ✉ *1076 Charoen Krung Rd., Bang Rak* ✛ *At the corner of Si Phraya Rd.* ☎ *06/421–01520* ⊕ *www. facebook.com/samlor.bkk* Ⓜ *BTS: Saphan Taksin, then taxi; Chao Phraya Express Boat: Si Phraya Pier.*

★ Sühring

$$$$ | **GERMAN** | This Michelin-starred restaurant from twin chefs Thomas and Matthew Sühring has evolved German cuisine past the stereotypes of schnitzel and sauerkraut. The brothers, who can be seen working together in a sleek open kitchen most nights, serve tasting menus inspired by their childhood in East Berlin—it's no wonder Sühring is one of Bangkok's trendiest restaurants. **Known for:** outstanding German wine list; multiple fine-dining awards; modern interpretations of German classics. $ *Average main: B3,000* ✉ *10 Yen Akat, Soi 3, Yannawa* ☎ *02/107–2777* ⊕ *restaurantsuhring.com* 🎩 *Smart casual* Ⓜ *MRT: Lumpini, then taxi.*

Tawandang German Brewery

$$ | **ECLECTIC** | From the outside, Tawandang looks like a big barrel representing the 40,000 liters of lager and other beers brewed here every month. With such an active brewery, you might think food

would be an afterthought, especially considering the cheesy entertainment such as comedy drag and Thai traditional dancing, but the kitchen actually turns out quite good Thai food, with some German and Chinese fare thrown in. **Known for:** fun crowd; Thailand's first microbrewery; good pub grub. $ *Average main: B380* ✉ *462/61 Rama III Rd., Yannawa* ☎ *02/678–1114* ⊕ *www.tawandang.co.th* ⊗ *No lunch* Ⓜ *BTS: Chong Nonsi, then taxi.*

Vertigo

$$$$ | **SEAFOOD** | You'll feel on top of the world at this classy 61st-floor space, one of the loftiest open-air restaurants in town. The international menu focuses on grilled seafood prepared with flair, and the service is friendly, but as with most of Bangkok's rooftop restaurants, you're paying for the sky-high setting, not the food—you might just prefer to come for a sunset drink to enjoy the stupendous views. **Known for:** good for romantic dates; à la carte and set menus available; frequent closures due to high winds. $ *Average main: B1,250* ✉ *Banyan Tree Bangkok, 21/100 S. Sathorn Rd., 61st fl., Sathorn* ☎ *02/679–1200* ⊕ *www. banyantree.com/en/bangkok* ⊗ *No lunch* 🎩 *Smart casual* Ⓜ *MRT: Lumphini; BTS: Sala Daeng.*

Hotels

Banyan Tree Bangkok

$$$ | **HOTEL** | After checking in on the ground floor, you'll soar up the elevators to your room at this 60-story hotel—the light-filled suites in the impossibly slender tower all have sweeping city views. **Pros:** feel on top of the world; wonderful views; cozy rooms. **Cons:** not near public transportation; long waits for elevator; expensive rates. $ *Rooms from: B5,500* ✉ *21/100 S. Sathorn Rd., Sathorn* ☎ *02/679–1200* ⊕ *www.banyantree.com/ en/thailand/bangkok* ⦿ *No Meals* ⇱ *327 rooms* Ⓜ *BTS: Lumpini.*

★ COMO Metropolitan Bangkok

$$$ | HOTEL | A modern aesthetic and a trendy focus on healthy living sets this hotel apart from the competition. **Pros:** high environmental and sustainability standards; free yoga classes and nice outdoor pool; excellent dining on-site. **Cons:** has declined in popularity; long walk from Sathorn Rd.; high prices. [$] *Rooms from: B5,400* ✉ *27 S. Sathorn, Sathorn* ☎ *02/625–3333* 🌐 *www.comohotels.com/metropolitanbangkok* 🍴 *Free Breakfast* 🛏 *160 rooms, 9 suites* [M] *MRT: Lumphini; BTS: Chong Nonsi.*

★ Mandarin Oriental Bangkok

$$$$ | HOTEL | With a rich history dating back to 1879, The Oriental is one of Bangkok's most prestigious hotels. **Pros:** butler service in all rooms; excellent staff; outstanding pool. **Cons:** can be very crowded; popular for private functions; pricey. [$] *Rooms from: B12,000* ✉ *48 Oriental Ave., Bang Rak* ☎ *02/659–9000* 🌐 *www.mandarinoriental.com/bangkok* 🍴 *No Meals* 🛏 *347 rooms, 35 suites* [M] *BTS: Saphan Taksin, then hotel shuttle boat.*

Montien

$$ | HOTEL | This hotel within stumbling distance of Patpong has been well maintained since it was built in 1970, playing up its old-fashioned aesthetic. **Pros:** tucked away from traffic on Surawong Road; regal decor; lots of space. **Cons:** popular with tour groups; not the most modern hotel; party clientele. [$] *Rooms from: B3,200* ✉ *54 Surawong Rd., Silom* ☎ *02/233–7060* 🌐 *montienbangkok.com* 🍴 *Free Breakfast* 🛏 *343 rooms* [M] *MRT: Silom; BTS: Sala Daeng.*

Narai Hotel

$$ | HOTEL | Dating back to 1968, this is one of Bangkok's older hotels, but it's well kept up and conveniently located by the business district on Silom Road. **Pros:** good value for proximity to business district; fun neighborhood; short walk to river. **Cons:** long walk to BTS; unexciting pool and decor; heavy traffic on Silom Road. [$] *Rooms from: B3,500* ✉ *222 Silom Rd., Silom* ☎ *02/237–0100* 🌐 *www.naraihotel.co.th* 🍴 *No Meals* 🛏 *475 rooms* [M] *BTS: Chong Nonsi.*

Prince Theatre Heritage Stay

$ | HOTEL | This four-suite hotel started life in 1917 as one of Bangkok's first cinema houses, and the art deco stained glass window and original theatre marquee have been preserved, along with an original 35mm projector and screen. **Pros:** not far from Saphan Taksin BTS and pier; cool history; excellent location for exploring Bang Rak. **Cons:** rooms tend to fill quickly; in a rather dark alley; traffic in the area can be congested. [$] *Rooms from: 1,400* ✉ *441/1 Charoeng Krung Rd., Sathorn* ☎ *06/259–12288, 02/090–2858* 🌐 *www.princeheritage.com* 🍴 *No Meals* 🛏 *4 suites* [M] *BTS: Saphan Taksin.*

Royal Orchid Sheraton Hotel and Towers

$$ | HOTEL | Of the luxury hotels along the riverfront, this 28-story palace is most popular with tour groups. **Pros:** good prices for a river hotel; nice river views; comfortable beds. **Cons:** tired decor; often busy with groups; far from public transportation unless you use boat shuttle. [$] *Rooms from: B3,393* ✉ *2 Charoen Krung Rd., Soi 30 (Captain Bush Lane), Bang Rak* ☎ *02/266–0123* 🌐 *www.royalorchidsheraton.com* 🍴 *Free Breakfast* 🛏 *726 rooms, 26 suites* [M] *BTS: Saphan Taksin; Chao Phraya Express Boat: Si Phraya Pier.*

★ Shangri-La Hotel Bangkok

$$$$ | HOTEL | One of Bangkok's most prestigious riverfront properties, the Shangri-La rivals even the more famous Mandarin Oriental. **Pros:** private balconies available; breathtaking lobby; gorgeous pool and terrace. **Cons:** slightly impersonal feel; older wing not as nice as newer area. [$] *Rooms from: B4,130* ✉ *89 Soi Wat Suan Plu, off Charoen Krung Rd., Bang Rak* ☎ *02/236–7777* 🌐 *www.shangri-la.com/bangkok* 🍴 *No Meals* 🛏 *802 rooms, 66 suites* [M] *BTS: Saphan Taksin.*

The view is spectacular from Bangkok's famous Sky Bar, in one of the city's tallest buildings.

Siam Heritage

$$ | **HOTEL** | The family that runs the Siam Heritage has created a classy boutique hotel with a purpose—to preserve and promote Thai heritage. **Pros:** cool Thai decor; reasonably priced; family run. **Cons:** rooms a bit small; not on river; very small pool. [$] *Rooms from: B2,000* ✉ *115/1 Surawong Rd., Bang Rak* ☎ *02/353–6166* 🌐 *www.thesiamheritage.com* 🍴 *Free Breakfast* 🛏 *73 rooms and suites* [M] *MRT: Silom; BTS: Sala Daeng.*

★ **SO/Bangkok**

$$$$ | **HOTEL** | An architectural gem, this elegant hotel is designed around the five elements of water, earth, wood, metal, and fire: the "earth" rooms, for example, resemble blue caves, and "water" rooms come with bathtubs overlooking the Bangkok skyline. **Pros:** fantastic location; superior service; free computers for in-room use. **Cons:** expensive; can get very busy; not all rooms have park views. [$] *Rooms from: B5,000* ✉ *2 N. Sathorn Rd., Sathorn* ☎ *262–40000* 🌐 *www.so-bangkok.com* 🍴 *No Meals* 🛏 *238 rooms* [M] *MRT: Lumpini.*

The Sukhothai Bangkok

$$$ | **HOTEL** | Spread over 6 landscaped acres on Sathorn Road, the Sukhothai has numerous courtyards that make the hustle and bustle of Bangkok seem worlds away. **Pros:** great on-site restaurants; beautiful decor in suites; spacious grounds. **Cons:** not all rooms have courtyard views; expensive rates; far walk to the main street. [$] *Rooms from: B5,600* ✉ *13/3 S. Sathorn Rd., Sathorn* ☎ *02/344–8888* 🌐 *www.sukhothai.com* 🍴 *Free Breakfast* 🛏 *210 rooms* [M] *MRT: Lumpini.*

★ **Tower Club at Lebua**

$$$ | **HOTEL** | With beautiful rooftop venues and abundant flair, the ultraluxurious Tower Club section of Lebua has spacious rooms with stunning upper-floor views and prices to match. **Pros:** spacious rooms; stunning panorama; use of Tower Lounge. **Cons:** popular with see-and-be-seen crowd; sky-high rates; long wait for the elevators. [$] *Rooms*

from: B4,180 ✉ *1055 Silom Rd., Silom* ☎ *02/624–9999* 🌐 *www.lebua.com/tower-club* 🍴 *No Meals* 🛏 *221 suites* [M] *BTS: Saphan Taksin.*

Triple Two Silom

$ | **HOTEL** | The trendy sister property of the adjacent Narai Hotel has spacious rooms with wood floors and modern fittings in deep brown, cream, black, and red. **Pros:** extra facilities at Narai; tasteful decor; friendly and helpful staff. **Cons:** not a great option for kids; some rooms can be noisy; heavy traffic on Silom Road. [$] *Rooms from: B1,430* ✉ *222 Silom Rd., Silom* ☎ *02/627–2222* 🌐 *www.tripletwosilom.com* 🍴 *No Meals* 🛏 *75 rooms* [M] *BTS: Chong Nonsi.*

W Bangkok

$$ | **HOTEL** | From gigantic sparkly Muay Thai boxing gloves on room beds to a swimming pool with an underwater sound system and twinkly LED lights, the high-flying W is loaded with snazzy design and high-tech touches. **Pros:** happening on-site bars and restaurants; 24-hour pool and fitness center; great central location. **Cons:** Woo Bar next to check-in area; views not great; often occupied with events. [$] *Rooms from: B3,402* ✉ *106 N. Sathorn Rd., Sathorn* ☎ *02/344–4000* 🌐 *www.whotels.com/bangkok* 🛏 *403 rooms* 🍴 *No Meals* [M] *MRT: Saint Louis.*

Wall Street Inn

$ | **HOTEL** | Most of the guests at this hotel on Surawong Road are from Japan, perhaps because of the many Japanese businesses in the immediate area, but its location near Lumpini Park, Patpong's night market, and Silom Road makes it an appealing option for anyone. **Pros:** traditional Thai massage available; happening location; very affordable deluxe rooms. **Cons:** proximity to nightlife can mean noise; boring room decor; standard rooms are windowless. [$] *Rooms from: B1,312* ✉ *Surawong Rd., 37/20–24 Soi Surawong Plaza, Silom* ☎ *02/233–4144, 02/233–4164* 🌐 *www.wallstreetinnhotel.com* 🍴 *Free Breakfast* 🛏 *75 rooms* [M] *MRT: Silom; BTS: Sala Daeng.*

Nightlife

Many of the best rooftop bars and upscale lounges are in Silom's high-rise towers and in fashionable spots along the Chao Phraya River. Here's where you'll also find the notorious Patpong red-light district and the Silom Soi 4 gay bars.

BARS AND PUBS

Distil

BARS | Thai A-listers have made Distil, on the 64th floor of one of Bangkok's tallest buildings, their stomping ground. A full-time sommelier is on hand to take care of your wine desires, and you can order a Hangovertini, created one floor down at the Sky Bar for the Hollywood film *Hangover II.* ✉ *Lebua at State Tower, 1055 Silom Rd., 64th fl., Bang Rak* ☎ *02/624–9555* 🌐 *www.lebua.com/distil* [M] *BTS: Saphan Taksin.*

Mahanakhon Bangkok Skybar

BARS | Perched on the 76th floor, this is the highest rooftop bar in the city, and with its gorgeous French-designer interiors, it never fails to impress. It's the perfect setting for a sophisticated cocktail with unparalleled views, and there's a cosmopolitan food menu ranging from Middle Eastern to Thai to French. ✉ *King Power Mahanakhon, 114 Narathiwas Rd., Sathorn* ☎ *02/677–722* 🌐 *www.mahanakhonbangkokskybar.com* [M] *BTS: Chong Nonsi.*

MIXO

BARS | The sophisticated rooftop bar adjoining the restaurant of the same name has marvelous skyline views and the finest perspective on vast Lumpini Park. It's the perfect spot to catch the sunset colors while downing a martini or glass of wine from the globe-trotting selection. ✉ *SO/Bangkok, 2 N. Sathorn Rd., Sathorn* ☎ *02/624–0000* 🌐 *www.so-bangkok.com/dining/mixo* [M] *BTS: Lumphini.*

★ Moon Bar

BARS | The views are staggering at the Banyan Tree Bangkok's 61st-floor alfresco bar, and the cost of cocktails is up there, too, but for the vistas alone it's worth the splurge. Come a bit before sunset—the bar opens at 5—to get the best view from the low-slung seating. If the weather is clear, you can stargaze using the bar's telescope. If the weather's bad at all, Moon Bar will be closed. ⊠ *Banyan Tree Bangkok, 21/100 S. Sathorn Rd., Sathorn* ☎ *02/679–1200* ⊕ *www.banyantree.com/en/thailand/bangkok/dining/moon-bar* Ⓜ *MRT: Lumpini.*

★ Sky Bar

BARS | There's nothing else quite like this bar on the 63rd floor of one of Bangkok's tallest buildings. Head toward the pyramidlike structure emitting eerie blue light at the far end of the restaurant and check out the head-spinning views. The place's most famous concoction, the Hangovertini, was made famous by the Hollywood film (*The Hangover II*) shot here. ⊠ *Lebua at State Tower, 1055 Silom Rd., 63rd fl., Bang Rak* ☎ *02/624–9555* ⊕ *www.lebua.com/sky-bar* Ⓜ *BTS: Saphan Taksin.*

★ Teens of Thailand

BARS | Hidden behind an old-fashioned Indian-style door in Chinatown, the gin bar Teens of Thailand has helped kick off a renaissance of trendy cocktail bars and art galleries in the area. Choose from a list of different gins and tonics for your perfect libation; otherwise the chalkboard cocktail specials change daily. ⊠ *76 Soi Nana, off Charoen Krung Rd., Bang Rak* ☎ *09/700–31173* ⊕ *www.facebook.com/teensofthailand* Ⓜ *MRT: Hua Lamphong.*

GAY BARS

Silom Soi 2 and Silom Soi 4 are the center of Bangkok's gay scene, with every establishment from restaurants to bars to clubs all catering to a gay clientele.

Balcony

BARS | Sometimes the party spills out onto the street at this bar that overlooks the crowds along Soi 4. Balcony has a friendly staff and one of the best happy hours on the soi. ⊠ *86–88 Silom, Soi 4, Bang Rak* ☎ *02/235–5891* ⊕ *www.balconypub.com* Ⓜ *MTR: Silom; BTS: Sala Daeng.*

DJ Station

BARS | A young crowd packs this snappy-looking bar to bask in the "fun, lust, and joy" (or so the website says). The B300 cover charge on weekends includes two drinks, while B150 on weekdays includes one. ⊠ *8/6–8 Silom, Soi 2, Silom* ☎ *02/266–4029* ⊕ *www.facebook.com/djstationbangkok* Ⓜ *MTR: Silom; BTS: Sala Daeng.*

Telephone

BARS | Bangkok's most venerable gay bar, the pub-style Telephone is hopping every night of the week. There are telephones on the table so you can chat up your neighbors, but very few people use them these days. ⊠ *114/1 Silom, Soi 4, Bang Rak* ☎ *02/234–3279* ⊕ *www.telephone-pub.com* Ⓜ *MRT: Silom; BTS: Sala Daeng.*

JAZZ BARS

Bamboo Bar

LIVE MUSIC | This legendary watering hole hosts international musicians playing easy-on-the-ears jazz. Expensive-looking animal print–upholstered furniture and dark wood create an upscale yet cozy space for listening to music and enjoying Thai-inspired cocktails. ⊠ *Mandarin Oriental, 48 Oriental Ave., Bang Rak* ☎ *02/659–9000* ⊕ *www.mandarinoriental.com/bangkok/chao-phraya-river/fine-dining/bars/the-bamboo-bar* Ⓜ *BTS: Saphan Taksin.*

Maggie Choo's

LIVE MUSIC | Hidden below street level next to the Novotel Bangkok Silom, Maggie Choo's is a Bangkok institution with nightly live performances

Bangkok's Contemporary Art Scene

In aging commercial pockets around Chinatown, abandoned shophouses tucked away in hidden back alleys are being reborn as cool spaces for urban art, documentary photography, and all kinds of eye candy.

JAM

JAM is a gallery, design office, bar, and restaurant, all rolled into one. It's stylish in a dive-bar sort of way, with a glass door and iron framing retaining the industrial feel of the space's former life as a factory. Art exhibitions, live music performances, and other events take place throughout the week. *www.facebook.com/JAMCAFEBKK/*

Speedy Grandma

Located in an old shophouse, this spot has a special focus on pop and urban artwork. Gallery owner Unchalee "Lee" Anantawat is a university art professor known for discovering and supporting local talent. The gallery only opens for events—check Facebook for updates. *www.facebook.com/SpeedyGrandma*

TCDC

Opened by the Thai government in 2005, the Thailand Creative Design Centre or TCDC, spotlights designers and entrepreneurs of diverse creative stripes. To get a full taste of what's happening around Silom and Bangrak, join one of the Centre's lively gallery crawls. *web.tcdc.or.th/en/Home*

MOCA

The Museum of Contemporary Art, or MOCA, houses six floors of Thai modern art and is Thailand's largest privately funded museum, with the works coming from the personal collection of billionaire mogul Boonchai Bencharongkul. *www.mocabangkok.com*

BACC

The Bangkok Arts & Culture Centre, or BACC, is the most well-known contemporary art gallery in the city, holding diverse exhibitions in a sprawling space. Be sure to stop by Icedea when you visit, to sample tasty ice cream treats that are fashioned into beautiful works of art. *www.bacc.or.th*

Kathmandu Photo Gallery

Housed in a vintage two-story building on Pan Road, a neighborhood favored by immigrants from the subcontinent, Kathmandu Photo Gallery (*www.facebook.com/kathmanduphotogallery*), founded by photographer Manit Sriwanichpoom, hosts exhibitions that tell moving, deeply personal stories from around the world.

of jazz and other smooth tunes. The surreal feeling of being transported back to 1930s Shanghai, with heavy vault doors and ladies in embroidered cheongsams dangling on swings, is only amplified by the stiff cocktails. ✉ *Novotel Bangkok Fenix Silom, 320 Silom Rd., Bang Rak* ☎ *02/206–9100* ⊕ *www.novotelbangkoksilom.com/bangkok-destination/bangkok-nightlife/maggie-choos-bangkok/*.

★ **Smalls**

LIVE MUSIC | The New York–born impresario behind the late Q Bar opened this unique establishment in a funky three-story corner building with spiral staircases that feels more Berlin or Paris than Bangkok. There's an open-air

3

Bangkok SILOM, SATHORN, AND BANG RAK

rooftop hangout and the second floor is sceney, but downstairs is the place to be to appreciate the French and Vietnamese antiques, the owner's impressive contemporary art collection, and the traditional absinthe spigots. Bartender Danny Yeung knows the classics but can improvise to taste. Jazz performances take place on the ground floor on Wednesdays and eclectic DJs spin on weekends. ⊠ *186/3 Suan Phlu, at Soi 1, Sathorn* ✛ *Down Suan Phlu from Sathorn intersection, on right* ☎ *08/966–65429* ⊕ *www.facebook.com/smallsbkk* ◷ *Closed Tues.* Ⓜ *MRT: Lumpini; BTS: Chong Nonsi.*

 Performing Arts

THEATER AND DANCE

Sala Rim Naam

THEATER | FAMILY | Across from the Mandarin Oriental, Sala Rim Naam stages a beautiful dance show nightly at 7:45, accompanied by a touristy dinner. ⊠ *Mandarin Oriental, 48 Oriental Ave.* ☎ *02/659–9000* ⊕ *www.mandarinoriental.com/bangkok* Ⓜ *BTS Saphan Taksin, then hotel shuttle boat.*

★ Silom Village

FOLK/TRADITIONAL DANCE | FAMILY | This block-size complex, open daily from 11 to 11:30, presents classical dance performances and has a restaurant that serves all the Thai favorites. It appeals largely to foreigners, but also draws some Thais, too. ⊠ *286 Silom Rd., Silom* ☎ *02/234–4448* ⊕ *www.silomvillage.co.th* Ⓜ *MRT: Silom; BTS: Sala Daeng.*

Shopping

CLOTHING AND FABRICS

Jim Thompson Thai Silk Company

FABRICS | The shops of the pioneering company are prime places to buy silk by the yard and as ready-made clothes. The prices are high, but so is the quality and design, and staff members are

knowledgeable. In addition to this Bang Rak shop there are numerous other locations throughout the city, including at the Mandarin Oriental, The Peninsula, CentralWorld, IconSiam, and many other shopping centers and five-star hotels. ⊠ *9 Surawong Rd., Bang Rak* ☎ *02/632–8100* ⊕ *www.jimthompson.com* Ⓜ *MRT: Silom; BTS: Sala Daeng.*

FOOD

Kad Kokoa

CHOCOLATE | Thai lawyers Nuttaya and Paniti Chunhasawatikul founded Kad Kokoa in 2018 and quickly earned respect. Their chocolate made with beans from a Chumphon cacao farm won a gold medal in Paris as a preeminent example of showcasing terroir. Along with plain chocolate, there is chocolate flavored with black pepper, salted tamarind, and shiso seeds. There's a cafe here serving chocolate-based drinks, cookies, brownies, truffles, and more. ⊠ *1076 Soi Narathiwat, Soi 17, Sathorn* ☎ *08/368–43921* ⊕ *kadkokoa.co* Ⓜ *BTS: Chong Nonsi.*

LEATHER

Chao Phya Bootery

LEATHER GOODS | You can get custom-made boots for around $200 here. The shop also stocks a large inventory of ready-made leather shoes, boots, and accessories. Liu's Bootery, farther southeast along Sukhumvit Road, is also recommended. ⊠ *141 Sukhumvit Rd., at Soi 11, Sukhumvit* ☎ *02/253–5400* ◷ *Closed Sun.* Ⓜ *BTS: Nana.*

Siam Leather Goods

LEATHER GOODS | This shop is a good stop for shoes and jackets, along with leather everything else, including pants, skirts, and purses, belts, and other accessories. ⊠ *River City Shopping Complex, 23 Soi Charoen Krung 24, Samphanthawong* ☎ *02/639–6301* ⊕ *www.siamleather.com* Ⓜ *BTS: Saphan Taksin; Chao Phraya Express Boat: Si Phraya Pier.*

MARKETS

Asiatique The Riverfront

MALL | In a prime spot by the Chao Phraya River, this complex of eateries, bars, and shops is in a group of renovated warehouses. The shopping focuses on local products, from clothes and handicrafts. You can get here via a free shuttle boat from the Saphan Taksin Pier next to the BTS station of the same name. ⊠ *2194 Charoen Krung Rd., Bang Rak* ☎ *02/108–4488, 02/246–0812* ⊕ *www.asiatiquethailand.com* Ⓜ *BTS: Saphan Taksin, then free shuttle boat from nearby pier.*

Patpong

MARKET | Bangkok's oldest red-light district, once frequented by U.S. troops stationed here during the Vietnam War, is these days also known for a night market with cheap electronics, ready-made dresses, T-shirts, sex toys, and fake designer goods. Be wary of pickpockets, as it gets very crowded. ⊠ *Silom Rd., Soi 2, Silom* Ⓜ *MRT: Silom; BTS: Sala Daeng.*

★ Soi Lalai Sap

MARKET | Silom Soi 5 was nicknamed Soi Lalai Sap, or "Melting Money Lane," because the shopping here is so good. The air-conditioned shops and sidewalk vendors sell a huge variety of inexpensive men's and women's clothes (including selections from up-and-coming Thai designers), handicrafts, and snacks. ⊠ *Silom Rd. Soi 5, Silom* Ⓜ *BTS: Sala Daeng; MRT: Silom.*

PORCELAIN, CERAMICS, AND CELADON

Thai Benjarong

CERAMICS | This massive ceramics shop has a huge inventory and makes dining sets, bowls, and vases to order. ⊠ *River City Shopping Complex, 23 Charoen Krung Rd. Soi 24, 3rd fl., Samphanthawong* ☎ *06/522–46464, 07/634–5103* ⊕ *www.thaibenjarong.com* Ⓜ *BTS: Saphan Taksin; Chao Phraya Boat Express: Si Phraya Pier.*

PRECIOUS METALS

Lin Silvercraft

HOUSEWARES | Among the knickknacks stacked floor to ceiling, this shop has some of the most finely crafted silver cutlery in town. ⊠ *9 Charoen Krung Rd., Bang Rak* ☎ *06/366–99636* ⊕ *www.linjewelers.com* Ⓜ *BTS: Saphan Taksin.*

Siam Bronze Factory

HOUSEWARES | This showroom near the Mandarin Oriental sells handmade items in bronze, brass, and stainless steel, including unique flatware. ⊠ *1250 Charoen Krung Rd., Bang Rak* ☎ *02/237–1534* ⊕ *siambronze.com* Ⓜ *BTS: Saphan Taksin.*

Spas

Away Spa

SPAS | The spa at W hotel has a variety of treatments to soothe you after long hours of travel or dealing with the chaos of Bangkok. The detoxifying Drain Away massage is sure to get rid of any body stress or sore muscles. ⊠ *W Bangkok, 106 N. Sathorn Rd., Silom, Silom* ☎ *02/344–4160* ⊕ *www.marriott.com/hotels/hotel-information/fitness-spa-services/bkkwb-w-bangkok/* Ⓜ *BTS: Chong Nonsi.*

The Oriental Spa

SPAS | A gentle massage in genteel surroundings is what you'll get at the spa in the Mandarian Oriental. Signature treatments run two hours and will leave you feeling exquisitely pampered. ⊠ *Mandarin Oriental, 48 Oriental Ave., Bang Rak* ☎ *02/659–9000* ⊕ *www.mandarinoriental.com/bangkok/chao-phraya-river/luxury-spa* Ⓜ *BTS: Saphan Taksin.*

Silom Bodyworks

SPAS | The decor is simple and rather old-fashioned, but the massages and other treatments are done well and reasonably priced—a 90-minute Thai massage with a hot compress is B500.

✉ *1035-1035/1 Silom 21, Silom Rd., Bang Rak* ☎ *02/234–5543* 🌐 *www.silombody-works.com* [M] *BTS: Saphan Taksin.*

Suvarnabhumi Airport

Airport hotels are convenient for flights that depart in the middle of the night.

Hotels

Novotel Suvarnabhumi Airport
$$$$ | **HOTEL** | This attractive hotel near Bangkok's main airport rents rooms in four-hour blocks, a boon during lengthy layovers. **Pros:** restaurants, spa, gym, and pool; no set check-in time; five minutes from airport via free shuttle service. **Cons:** big and impersonal; far from town; plane noise. [$] *Rooms from: B8,000* ✉ *999 Suvarnabhumi Airport Hotel Building Moo 1, Samut Prakan* ☎ *02/131–1111* 🌐 *www.novotelairportbkk.com* 🍴 *Free Breakfast* 🛏 *612 rooms* [M] *Airport Rail Link: Suvarnabhumi Airport.*

Chapter 4

AROUND
BANGKOK

4

Updated by
Duncan Forgan

 Sights
★★★★☆

 Restaurants
★★★☆☆

Hotels
★★★☆☆

 Shopping
★★★☆☆

 Nightlife
★☆☆☆☆

WELCOME TO AROUND BANGKOK

TOP REASONS TO GO

★ **Heading into the Wild:** A huge expanse of untouched jungle surrounds Kanchanaburi, a launchpad for trekking and river rafting.

★ **Floating Markets:** This area has more floating markets than anywhere else in Thailand. The most famous is at Damnoen Saduak, but less touristy options offer more breathing space.

★ **Seeing Old Siam:** Historic highlights outside Bangkok include Neolithic sites near Lopburi, the remains of a Khmer temple (Muang Singh Historical Park in Kanchanaburi), and Thailand's oldest seat of Buddhist learning in Nakhon Pathom.

★ **Bridge on the River Kwai:** For a glimpse of more recent history, visit the remnants of the ".Death Railway" in Kanchanaburi and walk across the bridge made famous by the movie *The Bridge on the River Kwai.*

★ **River Views in Ayutthaya:** This city, an easy day trip from Bangkok, combines great river views with an island full of fascinating temples.

1 **Muang Boran.** See replicas of Thailand's most important architectural sites.

2 **Damnoen Saduak.** Home to the most popular floating market in the region.

3 **Samut Songkhram.** A good base when exploring villages on the canal network.

4 **Nakhon Pathom.** A diverse city on Myanmar's doorstep.

5 **Phetchaburi.** These temples and royal summer palaces are best enjoyed on an overnight trip.

6 **Kanchanaburi.** The site of the famous Bridge on the River Kwai.

7 **Greater Kanchanaburi Province.** The main access point to the large national parks of western Thailand.

8 **Sangklaburi.** A diverse city on Myanmar's doorstep.

9 **Ayutthaya.** Once one of the country's most important cities.

10 **Bang Pa-In.** Famous for its 18th century Royal Palace and topiary gardens.

11 **Lopburi.** Best known for its monkey-infested temples.

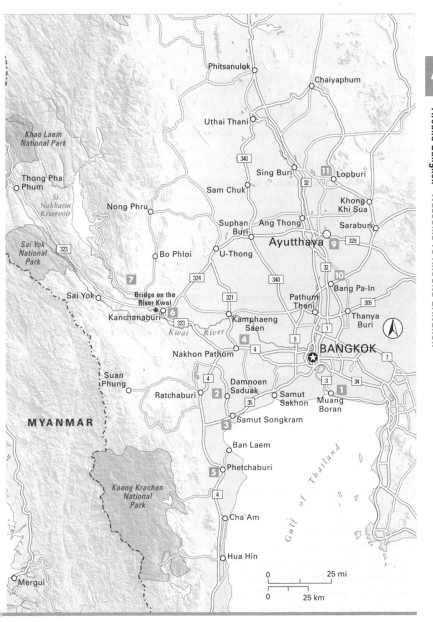

Escaping the congestion and chaos of Bangkok may seem complicated, but it's really quite simple. The surrounding provinces and cities offer myriad day trip opportunities, or an easy getaway for a few days. However you spend your time, you're sure to encounter amazing scenery, interesting culture, and unforgettable adventure.

Only 50 km (31 miles) west of Bangkok is Nakhon Pathom, which is a small haven for those seeking enlightenment. It has the tallest stupa in the world, Phra Pathom Chedi.

Travel a little farther west and you'll be in Kanchanaburi, with its mixture of tranquil scenery, war museums, and temples. Kanchanaburi is most known for the Bridge on the River Kwai, but there's plenty to keep you occupied. If you're an explorer at heart, this is a great starting-off point for visiting national parks and active adventures such as rafting and hiking.

If you're interested in seeing a traditional Thai floating market, visit Damnoen Saduak and Amphawa. At both you'll be surrounded by the colors and smells of a market while drifting in a small, wooden boat. Amphawa is a much more pleasant experience although it is only open on the weekends. Damnoen Saduak is open daily but is more crowded and touristy, with less interesting items for sale.

History buffs and Buddhists should travel a bit farther south to the enticing town of Phetchaburi for its wats and palaces.

Don't be frightened of the monkeys that roam the streets here.

Don't have time to travel the entire country? The peaceful grounds of Muang Boran, an outdoor park-museum, is shaped roughly like Thailand and displays replicas of important monuments from all parts of the country.

For seafood served Thai-style, head to Samut Songkhram, where you'll be able to eat your fill of clams and other fruit of the sea along the Gulf of Thailand.

If you have more time, check out Sangklaburi. Thai, Mon, Karen, and Bangladeshi communities flourish in this city near the Myanmar border. Many people who venture to Sangklaburi go on trekking tours and journey to the Three Pagodas Pass, which marks the international frontier.

MAJOR REGIONS

Visitors to Bangkok usually allow time for **day trips from Bangkok** to visit Thailand's most famous floating market (Damnoen Saduak) and Muang Boran, a huge park with replicas of the country's landmarks. To the west of Bangkok is Nakhon Pathom, location of Thailand's biggest stupa. **Phetchaburi**, to the southwest, has many interesting temples and a few royal summer palaces.

Kanchanaburi Province is home to the city of Kanchanaburi, two hours west of Bangkok, famous for its interesting and sometimes moving World War II historic sites, among them the Bridge on the River Kwai. If you're not in a hurry to get back to Bangkok, you can continue your exploration of Greater Kanchanaburi Province, a visually stunning area starring jungle-clad mountains and beautiful national parks with tumbling waterfalls.

Ayutthaya and its environs encompass an important historical journey that traces Thailand's progression to the modern era. Ayutthaya with its UNESCO World Heritage Site gets the most attention, drawing day-trippers from Bangkok. It's worth tacking on a visit to Lopburi. Its Khmer temples and French-influenced Phra Narai Ratchaniwet lend additional historical context to the museums and ransacked ruins found at Ayutthaya's historical park and the 18th-century Royal Palace in nearby Bang Pa-In.

Planning

When to Go

On weekends and national holidays, particularly during Songkran (Thai New Year) in mid-April, Kanchanaburi and Samut Songkhram's seafood restaurants are packed with Thais. In high season (from November to March) the floating market in Damnoen Saduak often seems to have more tourists than vendors. The waterfalls of Kanchanaburi Province are at their best during or just after the rainy season (from June to November). The fossil shells in Don Hoi Lod in Samut Songkhram are best seen in dry season or at low tide in rainy season. See the fireflies in Amphawa between May and October.

Planning Your Time

You can take in all the highlights north and west of Bangkok in about a week. Three or four days are enough to experience the top Kanchanaburi Province sights, starting with the serene River Kwai and the town of Kanchanaburi. From there you can take day trips to explore the waterfalls and other natural wonders. Historic Ayutthaya, a drive of little more than an hour from downtown Bangkok (depending on traffic), is an easy day trip. So, too, is Lopburi and the floating market at Damnoen Saduak.

Getting Here and Around

BUS
Most buses depart from Bangkok's Southern Bus Terminal. Tickets are sold on a first-come, first-served basis, but service is so frequent that it's seldom a problem finding an empty seat.

CAR
Distances from Bangkok are short enough to drive, though it's more relaxing to hire a car and driver.

TAXI AND SONGTHAEW
Taking one of Bangkok's air-conditioned taxis is a good way to access sights, particularly those in Nakhon Pathom, Samut Songkhram, and Muang Boran. Estimate around B500 per hour, with the final amount dependent upon your bargaining skills. Standard rates for trips outside Bangkok, implemented by the Ministry of Transport, are displayed in many, though not all, taxis and if available should be used as a starting point for any negotiations.

Health and Safety

The region is generally safe, and the towns mentioned in this hospitals, if you need one. Take normal precautions and keep valuables on your person at all times when traveling by bus or train. Too-good-to-be-true deals—particularly involving gems—are *always* a rip-off. On a more amusing note, the monkeys of Phetchaburi are cute but cunning, and may relieve you of your possessions, especially food.

Money Matters

Generally speaking, finding a bank or ATM isn't difficult, especially in towns. Most main bank branches close at 3:30 pm, with many smaller branches, often located in shopping malls and department stores, remaining open into the evening and on weekends. Remember that the farther out from civilization you travel, the fewer ATMs you'll find. Don't expect to withdraw money at a national park or in a tribal village. To be on the safe side, exchange the money you think you'll require before leaving Bangkok.

Restaurants

The areas around Bangkok allow you to sample both regional and ethnic foods. Kanchanaburi and Sangklaburi have Mon, Karen, Bangladeshi, and Burmese communities serving their own specialties. A must-try is *lahpet thoke,* a Burmese salad of nuts and fermented tea leaves. In Nakhon Pathom try the excellent rice-based dessert *khao lam.* Phetchaburi is famous for its desserts and for *khao chae,* chilled rice soaked in herb-infused water.

Hotels

An overnight stay is essential in Sangklaburi and highly recommended in Kanchanaburi and Phetchaburi. Stay in Damnoen Saduak the night before you visit the floating market to avoid an early-morning bus ride.

Luxury accommodations are available in and around most provincial towns. The best ones are usually located toward the outskirts of town. It's best to book ahead on weekends and national holidays in Kanchanaburi.

What It Costs in Baht			
$	$$	$$$	$$$$
RESTAURANTS			
under B200	B200–B300	B301–B400	over B400
HOTELS			
under B2,000	B2,000–B4,000	B4,001–B6,000	over B6,000

Tours

Asian Trails
It's easy to travel in the areas around Bangkok on your own, but this company organizes trips to the floating markets, as well as trekking trips, homestays, and bicycle tours. ⊠ *SG Tower, 161/1 Soi Mahadlek Luang 3, Rajdamri Rd., 9th fl., Pathumwan* ☎ *02/626–2000* ⊕ *www. asiantrails.travel* ⊠ *From B2,600.*

Diethelm Travel
Established in 1957 in Thailand, Diethelm Travel is one of the country's most respected tour operators. It is strong on every area of the country, including the sights and attractions near Bangkok. They can organize everything from a floating markets excursion to a river cruise to Ayutthaya. ⊠ *ITF Tower, 140/7 Silom Rd., 8th fl* ☎ *02/660–7000* ⊕ *www. diethelmtravel.com/Thailand* ⊠ *Call for pricing.*

Muang Boran

20 km (12 miles) southeast of Bangkok.

An easy and popular day trip from Bangkok, Muang Boran provides a captivating introduction to Thailand's architectural and cultural highlights via replicas and reconstructions.

GETTING HERE AND AROUND
BUS

The best bus choice from Bangkok to Muang Boran (two hours; B30) is the air-conditioned Bus 511, which leaves every half hour from Bangkok's Southern Bus Terminal; take it to the end of the line at Pak Nam. You can also catch this bus on Sukhumvit Road. Transfer to Songthaew 36 (B10), which goes to the entrance of Muang Boran.

CAR

Driving to Muang Boran requires engaging Bangkok's heavy and unpredictable traffic. Take the Samrong–Samut Prakan expressway and turn left at the Samut Prakan intersection onto Old Sukhumvit Road. Muang Boran is well signposted on the left at Km 33. The trip should take less than two hours.

TRAIN

The most convenient way to get to Muang Boran from Bangkok is to use the BTS Skytrain system. Get off at BTS Kheha station (E23) then take a free shuttle bus (weekend only) or taxi to Muang Boran. The ride from the station takes around 10 minutes.

Sights

Muang Boran (*Ancient City*)
MUSEUM VILLAGE | FAMILY | An outdoor museum with more than 100 replicas and reconstructions of Thailand's most important architectural sites, monuments, and palaces, this park is shaped like the country, and the attractions are placed roughly in their correct geographical position. A "traditional Thai village" on the grounds sells crafts, but the experience is surprisingly non-touristy. The park stretches over 320 acres, and takes about four hours to cover by car. Or you can rent a bicycle at the entrance for B50. Small outdoor cafés throughout the grounds serve decent Thai food. ⊠ *296/1 Sukhumvit Rd., Bangpoo, Samut Prakan*

☎ *02/202–68800* ⊕ *www.muangboran-museum.com/en* 🎫 *B700.*

Damnoen Saduak

109 km (68 miles) southwest of Bangkok.

The image of this frenetic market of floating vendors selling all sorts of raw and prepared food is so evocative that it has become an ad agency favorite. Though the market can feel touristy, a visit here is a memorable way to experience a Thai tradition.

GETTING HERE AND AROUND

Getting to Damnoen Saduak under your own steam can be tricky. It's probably best to join one of the tours offered at hotels and guesthouses.

Canary Travel Thailand
Kanchanaburi, Amphawa, and the floating market at Damnoen Saduak are among the destinations on sightseeing and package tours booked by this agency. Canary Travel does online and phone bookings, will arrange a pickup from your hotel in Bangkok, and offers several multiday stay packages. ⊠ *10 Tani Rd., Banglamphu, Taladyod, Pranakorn, Bangkok* ✚ *Khao San Rd.* ☎ *02/629–1687* ⊕ *www.canarytravelthailand.com* 🎫 *From B495.*

BUS

Buses to Damnoen Saduak (from two to three hours; B73) leave Bangkok's Southern Bus Terminal every 20 minutes starting at 5 am. From the station in Damnoen Saduak, walk or take a songthaew along the canal for 1½ km (1 mile) to the floating market. Buses also run from Nakhon Pathom and Samut Songkhram.

CAR

Take Route 4 (Phetkasem Road) and turn left at Km 80. Continue for 25 km (16 miles) along the Bang Phae–Damnoen Saduak Road. The drive from Samut Songkhram to Damnoen Saduak, along Route 325, is pleasant, particularly if you

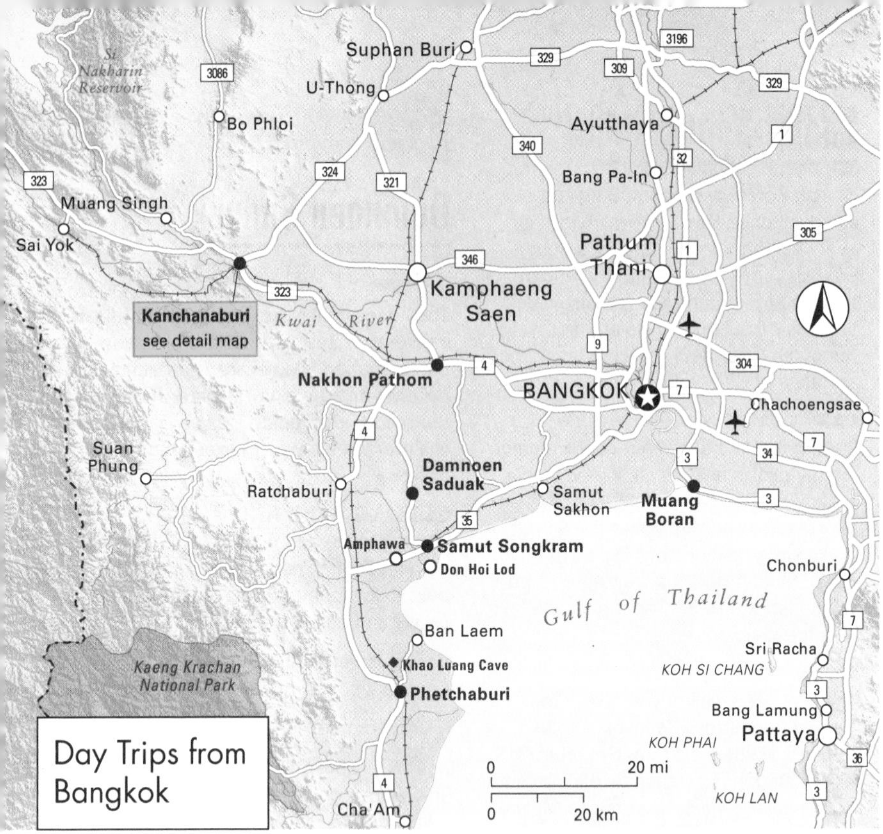

go via Amphawa. The entire trip takes two hours.

Sights

Damnoen Saduak Floating Market
MARKET | **FAMILY** | A colorful market of produce and other foods sold by vendors on small boats, Damnoen Saduak is an icon of Thai tourism. Often overrun with visitors, these days the market pays lip service to the authentic commercial life of this canal-strewn corner of Thailand. On the other hand, even though it feels like a theatrical production, this is one of the few opportunities to witness a fading Thai tradition. And some of the food—including noodle soup, seafood dishes, grilled meats, mango ice cream, coconut pancakes, and fried bananas—is extremely tasty. The best way to enjoy the market is to come early and hire a boat. The area only becomes more crowded as the day progresses and ever more tour groups arrive. ✥ *Off Rte. 325, 109 km (68 miles) southwest of Bangkok.*

Hotels

Maikaew Damnoen Resort
$ | **RESORT** | **FAMILY** | Just a 5-minute walk from the famous floating market, this classy resort feels removed from the mercantile frenzy farther down the canal. **Pros:** thoughtfully designed accommodations; peaceful vibe; helpful arranging tours. **Cons:** staff have limited English; not much else around; a/c can be noisy. [$] *Rooms from: 1,650* ✉ *333 Moo 9, Damnoen Saduak Floating Market, Damnoen Saduak* ☎ *032/245120, 081/527–9033* 🌐 *www.maikaew.com* 🍴 *Free Breakfast* 🛏 *65 rooms.*

Samut Songkhram

72 km (45 miles) south of Bangkok.

The provincial town of Samut Songkhram has little to recommend it, but the many nearby attractions make this an enjoyable day trip from Bangkok. There are terrific seafood restaurants along the waterfront at Don Hoi Lod. The area is also a good base for exploring some of the surrounding villages on the canal network, such as Amphawa, with its small floating market.

GETTING HERE AND AROUND

BUS

Frequent minivans leave from Bangkok's Victory Monument to Samut Songkhram (1 hour; B70). From there, you can hop in a songthaew near the market (B8) for the short ride to Amphawa. From Bangkok's Southern Bus Terminal board any bus bound for Damnoen Saduak and ask to get off at Amphawa (2 hours, B80).

CAR

Route 35, the main road south to Samut Songkhram (one hour), can be slow going if there's heavy traffic heading out from Bangkok. Add an extra half hour to all trip times for possible delays.

SONGTHAEW

In town there are frequent songthaews to Don Hoi Lod and Amphawa (10 minutes; up to B20).

Sights

Amphawa

TOWN | FAMILY | The charming village of Amphawa, 10 km (7 miles) by songthaew from Samut Songkhram, has a floating market similar to, but smaller than, the one in Damnoen Saduak. It is also touristy but less in-your-face about it with characterful cafés and boutiques, and because of this is often preferred. The market is open on Friday, Saturday, and Sunday from 12 to 8 pm. The food market in the street adjacent to the canal starts at around 1 pm. Popular firefly tours allow you to enjoy both the market and the beautiful insect-lighted trees. The bugs are best seen from May to October and in the waning moon. The hour-long tours usually run every half hour from 6 to 9 pm. You can arrange a tour directly with Mae Klong Market Pier (B800 for a boat) or through your hotel (around B70 per person). Unless you have private transportation, you'll have to spend the night in Amphawa, but there are some lovely options. The last bus back to Bangkok is in the early evening. ✉ *Amphawa* 🎟 *Free.*

Don Hoi Lod

TOWN | FAMILY | On weekends Thai families flock to the village of Don Hoi Lod, about 3 km (2 miles) south of Samut Songkhram, to feast on clams and other seafood dishes at tree-shaded restaurants and the local fresh market at the mouth of the Mae Khlong River. The village is named after a local clam with a tubular shell, the fossilized remains of which are found on the riverbanks. The best times to view the fossils are April and May, when the water is low. The rest of the year you can also see the fossils in the early morning and in the evening at low tide. ✉ *Samut Songkram* ✣ *Off Rte. 35.*

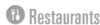

Restaurants

Kunpao

$$ | SEAFOOD | FAMILY | Among the last in a long row of seafood places in Don Hoi Lod, this restaurant on wooden stilts is usually packed with Thai families who come to enjoy the gentle breeze and seafood dishes. Try to get one of the few sit-on-the-floor tables directly above the water, and let your feet dangle down. **Known for:** busy on weekends and holidays; dishes made with fresh local seafood like fried sea bass, razor clams, and horseshoe-crab-egg spicy salad; children's playground. [$] *Average main: B250* ✉ *1/3 Moo 4, Tambon Bang Pakong, Amphoe Mueang, Samut Songkram*

☎ *034/723703, 08/1941–0376* 🌐 *www.thailandseafoods.com.*

Hotels

★ **House of Passion**

$$ | **B&B/INN** | This cozy boutique hotel is filled with character—rooms and suites feature four-poster beds, upcycled furniture, and wood floors, with some duplexes also available. **Pros:** romantic vibe good for couples; modern accommodation near floating market; swimming pool. **Cons:** not within walking distance of floating market; expensive weekend rates; mismatched furniture not everyone's taste. [$] *Rooms from: B2,500* ✉ *62 Moo 7, Bang Chang, Amphawa* ☎ *08/613–7838* 🛏 *24 rooms, 4 suites* 🍴 *Free Breakfast.*

Thanicha Resort

$ | **RESORT** | In an old wooden house close to the market, this boutique hotel by the main canal is a perfect weekend escape from Bangkok. **Pros:** right next to floating market; nice café and restaurant in front; free Wi-Fi in hotel. **Cons:** car park often full; busier and more expensive on weekends; only basic amenities. [$] *Rooms from: B1,590* ✉ *261 T. Ampawa A., Amphawa* ☎ *034/751942, 06/2324–2914* 🌐 *www.thanicha.com* 🛏 *25 rooms* 🍴 *Free Breakfast.*

Nakhon Pathom

56 km (35 miles) west of Bangkok.

Reputed to be Thailand's oldest city (it's thought to date from 150 BC), Nakhon Pathom was once the center of the Dvaravati kingdom, an affiliation of Mon city-states between the 6th and the 11th centuries. The region's first center of Buddhist learning, established about a millennium ago, it's home to the Buddhist monument Phra Pathom Chedi.

GETTING HERE AND AROUND

BUS

Frequent buses depart from Bangkok's Southern Bus Terminal for Nakhon Pathom (one hour; B40). More convenient are the regular minibuses from Victory Monument. These cost around B70.

CAR

Driving west from Bangkok, allow an hour to get to Nakhon Pathom on Route 4.

TRAIN

From Bangkok, trains run at regular intervals to Nakhon Pathom (1½ hours; from B50). Some of the Nakhon Pathom trains continue on to Phetchaburi (four hours; from B94) and points farther south. Trains to Kanchanaburi also stop in Nakhon Pathom.

Sights

Phra Pathom Chedi

RELIGIOUS BUILDING | The tallest stupa in the world, Phra Pathom Chedi tops out at 417 feet. Erected in the 6th century, the site's first chedi was destroyed in a Burmese attack in 1057. Surrounding the chedi is one of Thailand's most important temples, which contains the ashes of King Rama VI. The terraces around the temple complex are full of fascinating statuary, including Chinese figures, a large reclining Buddha, and an unusual Buddha seated in a chair. By walking around the inner circle surrounding the chedi, you can see novice monks in their classrooms through arched stone doorways. Traditional dances are sometimes performed in front of the temple, and during Loi Krathong, a festival in November that celebrates the end of the rainy season, a fair is set up in the adjacent park. ✉ *Khwa T. Phrapathom Chedi Rd., Nakhon Pathom* ✥ *Off Phetkasem Rd.* 🎫 *B60.*

Continued on page 160

THAI MARKETS

by Hana Borrowman

For an authentic Thai shopping experience, forget air-conditioned malls and head to the traditional markets, or *talaats*. Take a deep breath and prepare for an intoxicating medley of colors, sounds, smells, and tastes.

Entrepreneurs set up shop wherever there's an open space—roadsides, footbridges, and bustling waterways. You'll find all sorts of intriguing items: caramelized crickets and still-wriggling eels; "potency" potions made from pigs' feet; fierce-looking hand weapons like elegant samurai swords and knife-edged brass knuckles; temple offerings; plastic toys; and clothing.

Markets are an integral part of Thai life. Locals stop by for a meal from their favorite food vendor or to sit at a coffee stall, gossiping or discussing politics. Whole families take part: You might see an old woman bargaining with a customer at a hardware stall while her grandchild sleeps in a makeshift hammock strung up beneath the table.

Damnoen Saduak's floating market.

GREAT FINDS

Low prices make impulse buys almost irresistible. Here are a few things to keep your eyes out for while you shop.

Housewares. You'll find metal "monks' bowls" like those used for alms-collection, cushions, wicker baskets, carved tables, and ornate daybeds. Polished coconut-shell spoons and wooden salad servers are more practical if you're not up for shipping home your wares. Small wooden bowls and utensils start at around B150.

Memorabilia. Toy *tuk-tuks* (three-wheeled cabs) made from old tin cans, sequined elephants sewn onto cushion covers, satin Muay Thai boxer shorts, wooden frogs that croak—all make great and inexpensive souvenirs, and most Thai markets have them in droves.

Jewelry. Throughout the country, hill-tribe women sell beautiful silver and beaded jewelry. Silver bangles start at B250 and chunky silver rings with semiprecious stones like opal and mother-of-pearl are B350 and up. You'll also find "precious" gemstones and crystals, but you're better off making serious purchases at reputable shops in Bangkok.

Silk. Thailand is famous for its bright, beautiful silks. Raw Thai silk has a relatively coarse texture and a matte finish; it's good value, and wonderful for curtains and upholstery. You'll also find bolts of less expensive shimmering satins, and ready-made items like pajamas, purses, and scarves.

Prices vary enormously—depending on quality and weight—from B100 to upwards of B700 a meter. To test for authenticity, hold the fabric up to the light: If it's pure silk, the color changes, but fake silk shines a uniformly whitish tone. You can also ask for a swatch to burn—pure fibers crumble to ash, while synthetics curl or melt.

Clothes. Markets have tons of clothing: the ubiquitous Thai fisherman pants; factory seconds from The Gap; knockoff designer jeans; and, invariably, frilly underwear. But some of Thailand's edgiest designers are touting more modern apparel at markets as well. It's hard to say whether these up-and-comers are following catwalk trends or vice-versa. Bangkok fashion houses like **Sretsis** (feminine dresses; ⊕ www.sretsis.com) and **Greyhound** (casual, unisex urbanwear; ⊕ www.greyhound.co.th) are good places to scope out styles beforehand. Prices vary greatly—a cheaply made suit could cost as little as B1,000, while an expertly tailored, high-quality version might be B20,000 or more. But it's difficult to determine quality unless you're experienced.

FLOATING MARKETS

Sunday morning at Damnoen Saduak.

Floating markets date from Bangkok's "Venice of the East" era in the 19th century, when canal-side residents didn't have to go to market—the market came to them. Many waterways have been filled in to create roads, so there are only a handful of floating markets left. These survivors have a nostalgic appeal, with vendors in straw hats peddling produce, flowers, snacks, and crafts against a backdrop of stilt houses and riverbanks.

Thailand's original floating market in Damnoen Saduak (⇨ *above*) is very famous, but it's also crowded and overpriced. Still, you can get a taste of the old river life here, in addition to lots of touristy souvenirs. If you visit, try to stay nearby so that you can arrive near dawn; the market is open from 6 AM till noon, but by 9 it's usually swarming with sightseers.

The Amphawa Floating market near Samut Songkram, set on a leafy waterway dotted with temples and traditional Thai homes, is less crowded and more authentic.

LOGISTICS

Many hotels and guesthouses can arrange a longtail boat and an oarsman for you. You can also just head to the pier, though it's a good idea to ask your hotel what going rates are first. Private boats start at around B500 an hour, but oarsmen may try to charge much more. Haggle hard, and don't get in a boat before you've agreed on price and duration. If you join a group of locals in a boat, you'll often pay a set rate per person.

Longtail boat.

SHOPPING KNOW-HOW

Most markets begin to stir around dawn, and morning is the best time to visit—it's not too hot, and most Thais do their marketing early in the day, so you'll get to watch all the local action. Avoid rainy days: The scene loses a lot of its allure when everything's covered in plastic sheets.

Flower market in Bangkok.

SHOPPING TIPS

■ Check prices at less touristy spots—Chinatown, Pratunam Market, and MBK in Bangkok—to get a sense of cost.

■ Keep money and valuables like cell phones tucked away.

■ Avoid tuk-tuk drivers who offer you a shopping tour. They'll pressure you to drop a lot of cash at their friends' stalls.

■ Look for the One Tambon One Product (OTOP) government stamp on market goods. A tambon is a subdistrict—there are over 7,000 in the country, and one hand-made, locally sourced product is selected from each.

■ Steer clear of exotic animal products, such as lizard skins, ivory, tortoiseshell, and anything made of tiger. These products may come from endangered animals; if so, it's illegal to leave Thailand with them or bring them into the U.S. If not illegal, they may be counterfeit.

■ Only buy antiques at reputable shops; real Thai antiques cannot be exported without a license, which good shops provide. Most so-called antiques at markets are knockoffs.

■ Thai markets are full of counterfeits—DVDs, computer software, and designer clothes and accessories. In addition to being illegal, these items vary in quality, so examine the products and your conscience carefully before you buy.

Straw hats for sale.

HOW TO BARGAIN

Thais love theatrical bargaining, and it's customary to haggle over nearly everything. Here are some tips for getting a fair price. The most important thing is to have fun!

DO	DON'T
■ Decide about how much you're willing to pay before you start bargaining. ■ Let the vendor set the opening price. This is the standard etiquette; vendors who make you go first may be trying to take you for a ride. Vendors who don't speak English may type their price into a calculator, and you can respond in kind. ■ Come equipped with a few Thai phrases, such as "How much is this?" "A discount?" and "Expensive!" ■ Bargain quietly, and if possible, when the vendor is alone. Vendors are unlikely to give big discounts in front of an audience. ■ Be polite, no matter what. Confidence and charming persistence are winning tactics in Thailand—not hostility. ■ Honor your lowest bid if it's accepted. ■ Don't lose your temper or raise your voice. These are big no-no's in the land of smiles.	■ Don't hesitate to aim low. Your opening counteroffer should be around 50% or 60% of the vendor's price, and you can expect to settle for 10% to 30% off the initial price. If you're buying more than one item, shoot for a bigger discount. ■ Don't be afraid to walk away. Often the vendor will call you back with a lower price. ■ Don't get too caught up in negotiating. It's OK to back down if you really want something. ■ Don't bargain for food—prices are fixed.

Woman displaying Thai silk.

Phra Pathom Chedi National Museum

HISTORY MUSEUM | Next to Phra Pathom Chedi is the Phra Pathom Chedi National Museum, which contains Dvaravati artifacts such as images of the Buddha, stone carvings, and stuccos from the 6th to the 11th century. ⊠ *Khwa T. Phrapathom Chedi Rd., Nakhon Pathom* 🖾 *Free.*

Sanam Chandra Palace

CASTLE/PALACE | While still a prince, the future King Rama VI commissioned this palace, completed in 1911, that's notable architecturally for its French and British flourishes. The surrounding park, which includes ponds and broad lawns, is a lovely place to relax. English signs and translations provide information and guidance around the grounds. ✦ *Follow Petchkasem Rd. 2½ km (1½ miles) west from Phra Pathom Chedi* 🖾 *Free.*

Suan Sampran

GARDEN | **FAMILY** | Roses are just a part of this 50-acre complex where herbs, bananas, and various flowers, including orchids, flourish. Within the complex are traditional houses where guests can participate in activities such as garland and pottery making. ⊠ *Km 32, Pet Kasem Rd., Nakhon Pathom* ☏ *034/322588–93* ⊕ *www.suansampran.com* 🖾 *From B40 per activity.*

🍴 Restaurants

The road leading from Nakhon Pathom train station has several cafés, and a market where food stalls sell one-plate Thai meals. Similar dining options are at the entrance of the chedi. Keep an eye out for Nakhon Pathom specialties such as *khao lam* (sticky rice, palm sugar, and black beans grilled in hollowed-out bamboo sections) and sweet, pink-flesh pomelo (a large citrus fruit).

Phetchaburi

132 km (82 miles) south of Bangkok.

This bustling town with many wats once linked the old Thai capitals of Sukhothai and Ayutthaya with trade routes on the South China Sea and Indian Ocean. Phetchaburi is famous for *khao chae*, a chilled rice dish with various side dishes once favored by royals that has become a summer tradition in posh Bangkok hotels. You can find it around the day market on Phanit Charoen Road—look for people eating at stalls from small silver bowls—along with *khanom jeen thot man* (noodles with curried fish cake). The city was also a royal retreat during the reigns of Rama IV and Rama V (1851–1910) and has two palaces open to the public. Phetchaburi's wats are easily accessible on foot from the town center, particularly along Matayawong, Pongsuriya, and Phrasong roads.

■ **TIP→ Steer clear of the gangs of monkeys on the streets and around Khao Wang, especially if you have food in your hands.**

GETTING HERE AND AROUND
BIKE

A rental motorbike (from B150 per day) is a good way to get around the town and surrounding areas.

BUS

Air-conditioned buses run to/from Bangkok's Southern Bus Terminal with frequent departures (two hours; B120). Minivans leave from Victory Monument (two hours, B90) every 45 minutes from 5 am to 7:30 pm.

CAR

If you're driving, take Route 35, the main road south from Bangkok, then continue on Route 4 to Phetchaburi Province. The trip takes 90 minutes. On the way back to Bangkok, there are two alternatives. Follow signs to Samut Songkhram for the shorter trip along Route 35.

TRAIN

All trains to southern Thailand stop at Phetchaburi (three hours; from B84 to B358 depending on class). The train station is north of Phetchaburi on Rot Fai Road. You can hire motorbikes taxis or tuk-tuks from the train or bus station to get to sights or downtown.

 Sights

Khao Luang Cave

CAVE | Studded with stalactites, this cave overflows with images of the Buddha, among them a 10-meter-long reclining one. Some were put in place by kings Rama IV and Rama V. For a donation of B20 or so to pay for the electricity, a nun will light up the rear of the cave for you. It is about a kilometer's walk from the entrance, but a shuttle service is provided for B15. ■ **TIP→ The cave is best appreciated on a clear morning, between 9 and 10, when the sun shines in and reflects off the brass iconography.** ⊠ *Phetchaburi ✛ Off Rot Fai Rd., 5 km (3 miles) north of Phra Nakhon* ☎ ⧉ *Free*.

Phra Nakhon Khiri Historical Park (*Khao Wang*)

NATIONAL PARK | On a forested hillside at the edge of Phetchaburi, the park includes one of King Rama IV's palaces and a series of temples and shrines. Many of these are set high on the hilltop and have good views. Cable-car rides to the top and back are included in the admission price. Watch out for the monkeys, who are a major shoplifting hazard around the gift shops at the foot of the hill. ⊠ *Phetchaburi ✛ Off Phetkasem Rd., east of Rte. 4* ☎ *032/425600* ⊕ *www. finearts.go.th/pranakornkeereemuseum* ⧉ *B150*.

Phra Ram Ratchaniwet

HISTORIC HOME | Intended as a rainy-season retreat by King Rama V and started in 1910, the palace was eventually completed by King Rama VI in 1916. Phra Ram Ratchaniwet was modeled on a palace of Germany's Kaiser Wilhelm and consequently has a grand European-style design with art-nouveau flourishes. The dining room has ornate ceramic tiles. ⊠ *Ratchadamnoen Rd., Phetchaburi* ☎ *032/428083* ⧉ *B50*.

Wat Mahathat Worawihan

RELIGIOUS BUILDING | This 800-year-old Khmer-influenced structure on the western side of the Phetchaburi River is a royal temple located in a charming district with narrow lanes and wooden shophouses. It comprises five large prangs that are visible from all over town. It is notable for its fine stucco work, which is characteristic of the Phetchaburi school of art seen on many of its temples. ⊠ *Bandai-it and Damnoen Kasem Rds., Phetchaburi* ⧉ *Free*.

 Restaurants

Rabieng Rimnam Restaurant

$ | **THAI** | In a small wooden house by the river, this family-run restaurant attached to Rabieng Guesthouse serves many classic Thai dishes and a few Western ones for very reasonable prices. It opens early at 8 am but is one of just a few places in the area that stays open after sunset (until midnight daily). **Known for:** river views; friendly service; traditional Thai dishes like spicy banana-blossom salad and the stuffed chicken with pandanus leaves. ⓢ *Average main: B100* ⊠ *1 Shesrain Rd., Phetchaburi* ☎ *032/425707*.

 Hotels

Pimchanok Resort

$ | **B&B/INN** | This recent addition to the Phetchaburi lodging scene has everything you'd want from a wallet-friendly bed-and-breakfast, including spotless, modern rooms, comfortable beds, and warm, welcoming service from the friendly owners. **Pros:** modern lodging at a good price; quiet but convenient location; friendly owners supply personal touch. **Cons:** beds are on the soft side; lack of shade around the resort; access road is rather narrow. $ *Rooms from: 860* ⊠ *1/3 Moo 5, Tonmamuang, Phetchaburi* ☎ *91/1634999* ⊙| *No Meals* ↯ *5 rooms.*

Royal Diamond Hotel

$ | **HOTEL** | About 3 km (2 miles) north-west of town, the Royal Diamond is one of Phetchaburi's few choices for those seeking a hotel instead of a guest-house. **Pros:** rooms rather spacious; close to Phra Nakhon Khiri Historical Park; clean and comfortable. **Cons:** most rooms have no views; out of town; not modern. $ *Rooms from: B850* ⊠ *555 Moo 1, Phetkasem Rd., Ban Rai Som* ☎ *032/411061 up to 70* ⊕ *www.royaldiamondhotel.com* ↯ *54 rooms* ⊙| *Free Breakfast.*

White Monkey Guesthouse

$ | **B&B/INN** | One of the newer guest-houses in Petchaburi, White Monkey is simply decorated but cozy nonetheless. **Pros:** centrally located; modern facilities; free bikes for guests. **Cons:** limited occupancy; some rooms with shared bath; rooms accessible only by sets of stairs. $ *Rooms from: B900* ⊠ *78/7 Khlong Krachang Rd., Phetchaburi* ☎ *09/325–3885, 032/400187* ⊙| *No Meals* ↯ *12 rooms.*

Kanchanaburi

140 km (87 miles) west of Bangkok.

Most people come to Kanchanaburi, along the Mae Khlong and Kwai Yai rivers, because of its rather gruesome place in World War II history, though the scenic town has other attractions as well. Several museums and war cemeteries document the building of the Thailand-Burma Railway during World War II and the high cost paid in death and suffering. These attractions include the town's headline sight: the Bridge on the River Kwai.

GETTING HERE AND AROUND

BUS

Air-conditioned buses headed to Kanchanaburi leave from Bangkok's Southern Bus Terminal (two hours; B77 to B99) every 20 minutes from 5 am to 10:30 pm. Buses also leave hourly from 5 am to 4 pm from Bangkok's Mo Chit Northern Bus Terminal (three hours; B95 to B122). Frequent minivans depart from Victory Monument to Kanchanaburi (two hours; B120).

CAR

Allow two hours to reach Kanchanaburi along Route 4. The first half is on a busy truck route that continues to southern Thailand, but the second half is more pleasant, through agricultural land. The road to Kanchanaburi passes through Nakhon Pathom.

TAXI AND SONGTHAEW

In town, options for getting around include pedicabs and motorcycles with sidecars. Songthaews are better for longer forays out of town and can be flagged down. The few tuk-tuks and taxis are harder to find. The best option for striking out is to rent a motorbike (B150 per day) in town.

TRAIN

Two Kanchanaburi-bound trains (three hours; B100) leave every day from Bangkok Noi Railway Station, on the Thonburi side of the Chao Phraya River.

VISITOR AND TOUR INFORMATION

CONTACT Tourism Authority of Thailand. (*TAT*) ⊠ *325 Saengchuto Rd., Kanchanaburi* ☎ *034/511200* ⊕ *www.tourismthailand.org.*

Safarine

For guided adventure and cultural trips, this outfitter does a great job. ⊠ *117 soi Tha Makham, moo 2, Kanchanaburi* ⊕ *www.safarine.com.*

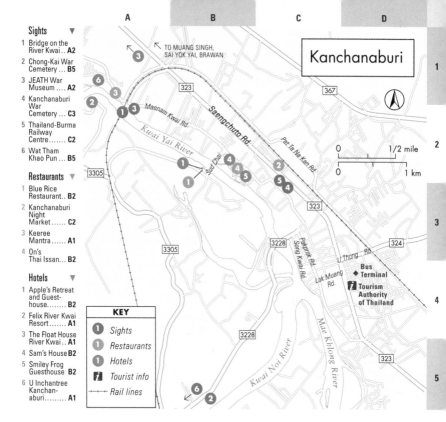

Sights ▼

1 Bridge on the River Kwai.. **A2**
2 Chong-Kai War Cemetery ... **B5**
3 JEATH War Museum **A2**
4 Kanchanaburi War Cemetery ... **C3**
5 Thailand-Burma Railway Centre....... **C2**
6 Wat Tham Khao Pun ... **B5**

Restaurants ▼

1 Blue Rice Restaurant.. **B2**
2 Kanchanaburi Night Market **C2**
3 Keeree Mantra **A1**
4 On's Thai Issan... **B2**

Hotels ▼

1 Apple's Retreat and Guest-house........ **B2**
2 Felix River Kwai Resort **A1**
3 The Float House River Kwai .. **A1**
4 Sam's House **B2**
5 Smiley Frog Guesthouse **B2**
6 U Inchantree Kanchan-aburi **A1**

KEY

1 Sights
1 Restaurants
1 Hotels
🛈 Tourist info
┼─── Rail lines

Kanchanaburi

TO MUANG SINGH, SAI YOK YAI, BRAWAN

Sights

★ Bridge on the River Kwai

HISTORIC SIGHT | Kanchanaburi is most famous as the location of this bridge, a section of the Thailand-Burma Railway immortalized in director David Lean's epic 1957 film *The Bridge on the River Kwai*. During World War II, the Japanese, with whom Thailand sided, forced about 16,000 prisoners of war and from 50,000 to 100,000 civilian slave laborers from neighboring countries to construct the railway, a supply route through the jungles of Thailand and Burma. Sure-footed visitors can walk across the bridge, whose arched portions are original. In December a big fair takes place with a sound-and-light show depicting the Allied bombing of the structure late in the war. Next to the bridge is a plaza with restaurants and souvenir shops.

✉ *Maenamkwai and New Zealand Rds., Kanchanaburi* 🎟 *Free.*

Chong-Kai War Cemetery

CEMETERY | The serene and simple resting place of many of the soldiers forced to work on the Thailand-Burma Railway has neatly organized rows of grave markers. On the grounds of a former hospital for prisoners of war, the cemetery is a little out of the way, and therefore rarely visited. To get here, hire a tuk-tuk or moto-taxi for about B60. ✉ *Kanchanaburi* ✛ *West side of river, 3 km (2 miles) from town* 🎟 *Free.*

JEATH War Museum

HISTORY MUSEUM | The letters in the first part of its name an acronym for Japan, England, America, Australia, Thailand, and Holland, this museum sits a little more than 2 km (1 mile) downriver from the Bridge on the River Kwai. The museum, founded in 1977 by a monk from the adjoining Wat Chaichumpol, is housed in a replica of the bamboo huts that were used to hold prisoners of war. On display are railway spikes, aerial photographs, newspaper clippings, and original sketches by ex-prisoners depicting their living conditions. ✉ *Wat Chaichumpol, Bantai* ☎ *034/515203* 🎟 *B40.*

Kanchanaburi War Cemetery

CEMETERY | Next to noisy Saengchuto Road, this cemetery has row upon row of neatly laid-out graves: 6,982 Australian, British, and Dutch prisoners of war are laid to rest here. The remains of the American POWs were returned to the United States during the Eisenhower administration. A remembrance ceremony is held every April 25th, Australia and New Zealand Army Corps Day. ✉ *Saengchuto Rd., Kanchanaburi* ✥ *Across from train station* 🎟 *Free.*

Thailand-Burma Railway Centre

HISTORY MUSEUM | A walk through the center's nine chronologically arranged galleries provides a good overview of the railway's history. Though small, the center is well designed and packed with informative displays. The second-floor coffee shop at the end of the exhibits has a view of the adjacent Kanchanaburi War Cemetery. ✉ *73 Jaokannun Rd., Kanchanaburi* ☎ *034/512721* 🌐 *www.tbrconline.com* 🎟 *B150.*

Wat Tham Khao Pun

CAVE | One of the Kanchanaburi area's best cave-temples, the wat displays Buddhist and Hindu statues and figurines amid stalagmites and stalactites. During World War II the Japanese used the cave complex as storerooms. A local may appear at the small shrine outside the cave and offer to direct you, but you can walk through the cave by yourself. Paying a donation to enter the cave is voluntary. ✉ *Kanchanaburi* ✥ *Rte. 3228, west side of river, 1½ km (1 mile) southwest of Chong-Kai War Cemetery* 🎟 *Free.*

🍴 Restaurants

Blue Rice Restaurant

$ | **THAI** | This quiet garden restaurant is decked out in wood with lots of local flourishes, from the thatched roof to the colorful woven tablecloths and settings. The signature dish, Massaman curry, is a righteous version of the classic—thick, mildly spiced, and made with heaps of palm sugar, it's a good balm for stomachs struggling with chili overdose. **Known for:** accommodations also available; authentic spicy dishes; cooking classes. [$] *Average main: B120* ✉ *153/4 Sutjai Bridge, Moo 4, Thamakhan Muang* ☎ *034/512017, 062/324–5879* 🌐 *www.applenoikanchanaburi.com/our-apples-restaurants/.*

Kanchanaburi Night Market

$ | **THAI** | For cheap eats, the market opens early in the evening with dozens of vendors selling Thai soups, rice dishes, satays, and other delights. The blended frozen fruit drinks are particularly good. **Known for:** cheap meals; good variety; lively local crowd. [$] *Average main: B40* ✉ *Saengchuto Rd., Kanchanaburi* ✥ *Next to train station* ☎ 💳 *No credit cards.*

Keeree Mantra

$$ | **THAI** | **FAMILY** | It's worth the effort to get to this excellent restaurant in the countryside, located just over the river Kwai Yai on the way to Sai Yok National Park. The food is just as enticing, with the authentic and uncompromising Thai flavors showcased in classics such as *tom yum* (hot, sour soup) and *hor mok* (steamed Thai fish custard) expertly rendered. **Known for:** authentic Thai flavors; stunning garden setting; steamed Thai fish. [$] *Average main: 200* ✉ *88/8 Moo 4, Sangchuto Road, Kanchanaburi* ☎ *34/540889* 🌐 *www.facebook.com/keereemantra.*

On's Thai Issan

$ | **THAI** | This is a great option for tasty vegan and vegetarian specialities from the northeast of Thailand, including curries that pack a fiery kick. The eponymous owner also offers cooking classes and it's clear from the punchy dishes that she has plenty of wisdom to pass on. **Known for:** Thai desserts; great option for vegetarians and vegans; actually spicy curries. [$] *Average main: 100* ✉ *268/1, Maenamkwai Road, Kanchanaburi* ☎ *87/3642264* 🌐 *www.facebook.com/OnsThaiIssan.*

Hotels

Apple's Retreat and Guesthouse

$ | **RESORT** | **FAMILY** | At this longtime favorite, in a tranquil orchard, you can experience the quieter side of Kanchanaburi life. **Pros:** tours and cooking classes available; can arrange pickup at the train or bus station; good restaurant. **Cons:** simple decor; can fill quickly in high season; long walk to attractions. [$] *Rooms from: B1200* ✉ *153/4 Moo 4, Thamakhan Muang, Kanchanaburi* ☎ *034/512017, 081/948–4646* 🌐 *www.applenoikanchanaburi.com* 🍴 *No Meals* 🛏 *16 rooms.*

Felix River Kwai Resort

$$ | **RESORT** | **FAMILY** | Kanchanaburi's first luxury hotel has faded somewhat, but it's still a good value. **Pros:** good for families; right by the famous bridge; wonderful tropical garden. **Cons:** aging decor; taxi required for trips to city center; inconsistent Wi-Fi. [$] *Rooms from: B3,450* ✉ *9/1 Moo 3, Tambon Thamakham* ☎ *034/551–00023, 02/634–4111 reservations center* 🌐 *www.felixriverkwai.co.th* 🛏 *255 rooms* 🍴 *Free Breakfast.*

The Float House River Kwai

$$ | **HOTEL** | It's all about nature at this splendid floating resort, near Sai Yok National Park. **Pros:** gorgeous location by the river; friendly Mon staff; romantic. **Cons:** rooms are relatively close together; long drive from Kanchanaburi city; limited dining options. [$] *Rooms from: 3500* ✉ *55, Wang Krachae, Tambon Thasaso* ☎ *84/725–8686* 🌐 *www.thefloathouseriverkwai.com* 🍴 *Free Breakfast* 🛏 *26 rooms.*

Sam's House

$ | **RESORT** | A popular launching pad for treks, Sam's House has air-conditioned rooms by the water that are nice, if a little cramped, as well as less expensive rooms set away from the river. **Pros:** well priced; some rooms have nice river views; can arrange tours. **Cons:** lots of mosquitoes; more expensive than other budget options; books up fast. [$] *Rooms from: B250* ✉ *14/2 River Kwai Rd., Kanchanaburi* ☎ *95/9316193* 💳 *No credit cards* 🛏 *31 rooms* 🍴 *No Meals.*

Smiley Frog Guesthouse

$ | **B&B/INN** | Popular with backpackers, the bungalow rooms here are spartan, though some face the river, and all are surrounded by gardens. **Pros:** nice garden with hammocks; budget-friendly; good location. **Cons:** not all rooms have private bath; not everyone will appreciate the backpacker vibe; some rooms need renovation. [$] *Rooms from: B100* ✉ *28 Soi China, at River Kwai Rd.,* ☎ *034/514579* 🛏 *55 rooms, 14 with shared bath* 🍴 *No Meals.*

U Inchantree Kanchanaburi

$ | **RESORT** | Rooms at this chic boutique hotel are in two-story buildings set around lush green courtyards, one of which is home to an inchan, the ancient tree which lends its name to the property. **Pros:** complimentary bicycles for guest use; riverside pool perfect for cooling down; quiet ambience. **Cons:** a bit removed from town; no bridge views; rooms are a little small. [$] *Rooms from: 1,399* ✉ *443, Mae Nam Kwai Road, Kanchanaburi* ☎ *34/521584* 🌐 *www.uhotelsresorts.com* 🍴 *Free Breakfast* 🛏 *50 rooms.*

Activities

TREKKING

Jungle treks of one to four days are possible all over the region. They typically include bamboo rafting, visits to Karen villages, sampling local food, and sometimes a cultural performance.

Good Times Travel

RAFTING | A reputable agency with a good track record, Good Times offers all the usual highlights, including national parks, rafting, caves, and Karen village stays. The agency's day trips and multiday excursions depart from Kanchanaburi or Bangkok; the price per person depends on the size of your group. ⊠ *63/1 River Kwai Rd., Kanchanaburi* ☎ *81/913–7758* ⊕ *www.good-times-travel.com* ✉ *From B2,850 per person (2 participants).*

Shopping

Blue sapphires from the Bo Phloi mines, 45 km (28 miles) north of Kanchanaburi Town, are for sale at many shops and stalls in the plaza near the bridge. The price is determined by the size and color of the stone, and, as usual, your bargaining skills. You'll do best when there are few tourists around and business is slow. Stick to stalls with licenses.

Greater Kanchanaburi Province

The third-largest province in Thailand, Kanchanaburi has scenic jungles, rivers, waterfalls, and mountains, especially near Sangklaburi, as you approach the Myanmar border. For centuries it was a favorite invasion route into Siam for the Burmese. Today it is home to Karen and Mon communities, whose villages can be visited.

GETTING HERE AND AROUND

The region is easily accessible by car. Roads 323 and 3199 take you to the main sights. It's also quite easy to travel around by public transportation, although package tours can be helpful if you have limited time. Reaching less-popular sights, such as Muang Singh Historical Park, is complicated if you don't have private transportation. Consider hiring a songthaew (around B750 for half a day). Public buses from Kanchanaburi leave the bus station, or from Saengchuto Road, close to the guesthouse area on River Kwai Road. There's also a private minibus office near the main bus station; minibuses go to many places in the province but are more expensive than public buses and fill up quickly. Sai Yok Noi National Park is accessible by train.

Sights

★ Erawan National Park

NATIONAL PARK | Some of Kanchanaburi Province's most spectacular scenery can be found in this park. The main attraction, Erawan Waterfall, has seven tiers; the topmost supposedly resembles the mythical three-headed elephant (Erawan) belonging to the Hindu god Indra. Getting to the top requires a steep 2-km (1-mile) hike. Comfortable footwear is essential for the two-hour trek, and don't forget to bring water. You can swim at each level of the waterfall (levels two through five are the most popular). The first tier has a small café, and there are several others near the visitor center. There are also eight-person bungalows costing from B800 to B5000—the ones nearest the waterfall are quieter. Five caves are among the massive park's other highlights. One of the caves, Ta Duang, has wall paintings, and another, Ruea, has prehistoric coffins. The caves are much farther away and are accessed via a different road. About 2 km (1 mile) from the park is Erawan Village; songthaews (B500 to B600) leave from its market

and travel to the park entrance and the caves. Erawan-bound Bus 8170 leaves Kanchanaburi's bus station every 50 minutes; the trip takes 90 minutes. ⊠ *Erawan National Park, Kanchanaburi* ☎ *034/574222, 034/574234* ⊕ *www.dnp. go.th* 🖃 *B300* ⊙ *Closed Aug. and Sept.*

★ Hellfire Pass

TRAIL | The museum at Hellfire Pass is a moving memorial to the Allied prisoners of war who built the River Kwai railway, tens of thousands of whom died in the process. Along with a film and exhibits, there's a 4½-km (3-mile) walk along a section of the railway, including the notorious Hellfire Pass, one of the most grueling sections to build. The pass got its name from the fire lanterns that flickered on the mountain walls as the men worked through the night. Many people do the walk in the early morning,

before the museum opens and before it gets too hot. Allow 2½ hours round-trip for the walk. Take plenty of water and snacks; there's a small shack near the museum that sells drinks, but not much food. The pass can be busy on weekends. Bus 8203 (two hours) makes the trip to the museum. The last bus back to Kanchanaburi is at 5 pm coming the other direction from Sangklaburi. The drive by car takes about an hour. ⊠ *Rte. 323, Km 66, Kanchanaburi* ☎ *034/919605* ⊕ *www.dva.gov.au/about-dva/publica-tions/commemorations-and-war-graves/ hellfire-pass-memorial* 🖃 *Free.*

Muang Singh Historical Park

HISTORIC SIGHT | The restored remains of this 13th- to 14th-century Khmer city, 45 km (28 miles) northwest of Kanchanaburi, range from mere foundations to a largely intact, well-preserved monument and building complex. There are also examples of Khmer statues and pottery and a prehistoric burial site. You can navigate the expansive grounds with the aid of taped commentary in English, Thai, or French, available at the park's entrance. Bicycle rentals cost around B20 per hour. If you don't want to make the 45-minute drive from Kanchanaburi, take the train to Tha Kilen Station (one hour; B15); the park is a 1-km (½-mile) walk west. There are lodgings and a small café on the grounds. ⊠ *Tha Kilen* ☎ *034/458-5052* 🖵 *B100.*

Sai Yok National Park

NATIONAL PARK | The national park's main attraction is **Sai Yok Yai waterfall,** which flows into the Kwai Noi River. The waterfall, an easy walk from the visitor center, is single tier and not nearly as spectacular as Erawan's. More unique are the **bat caves,** 2 km (1 mile) past the waterfall. They are the only place you can see the thumb-size Kitti's hog-nosed bat, the world's smallest mammal. Rent flashlights at the visitor center. Other caves worth visiting include Tham Wang Badan and Lawa Cave. This part of the park has several options for accommodations, all without electricity. The private raft houses on the Kwai Noi River are the more scenic choices. The accommodations near the waterfall have inexpensive restaurants that are more pleasant than the food stalls near the visitor center. Driving here from Bangkok or Kanchanaburi you'll pass **Sai Yok Noi waterfall,** also within the park's boundaries. Despite being taller than Sai Yok Yai, Sai Yok Noi has less water, but there's enough to swim in from June to November, when the area is often packed with Thai families on weekends. ⊠ *Park headquarters, Rte. 323, Km 97, Sai Yok* ☎ *034/686024* ⊕ *www.dnp.go.th* 🖵 *B300.*

Sangklaburi

203 km (126 miles) northwest of Kanchanaburi.

This sleepy town sits on a large lake created by the Khao Laem Dam. There was once a Mon village here, but when the dam was built in 1983 it was almost completely covered by water. (Some parts, including a temple, are still visible beneath the surface.) The Mon people were relocated to a village on the shore opposite Sangklaburi.

Due to its proximity to Myanmar's border, Sangklaburi is also home to Karen and Bangladeshi communities, whose residents you'll spot in the town's small night market. Jungle trekking and visits to Karen villages are popular activities for visitors.

GETTING HERE AND AROUND

BUS

Air-conditioned buses from Bangkok's Northern Bus Terminal leave for Sangklaburi four times a day (7 hours; B274). The last direct Bangkok-bound bus leaves Sangklaburi early in the afternoon. Air-conditioned buses from Kanchanaburi (three hours) leave hourly between 7:30 am and 4:30 pm. Guesthouses are accessible by motorcycle taxi (B10) or songthaew (B60) from the station.

CAR

The 2½- to 3-hour drive from Kanchanaburi, on well-paved Route 323, passes fields of pomelo, corn, and banana palms. Myanmar's mist-shrouded mountains are in the distance.

MOTORCYCLE TAXI

Motorcycle taxis (B10–B20) are the favored way to get around this sprawling provincial town. For longer trips, ask your hotel to arrange car transport or hire your own motorbike for around B200 a day.

Sights

Mon Village

TOWN | To make way for Khao Laem Dam, a village settled a half century ago by Mon people from Myanmar was relocated to the shore opposite Sangklaburi. The village has a temple with Indian and Burmese influences and a bronze-color pyramid chedi that's beautifully illuminated at night. A dry-goods market in the village sells Chinese and Burmese clothes and trinkets, with Mon dishes available at nearby food stalls. Get here by car or boat, or walk across Thailand's longest wooden bridge. ✉ *Sangkhla Buri.*

Restaurants

Six or seven guesthouses are on the lakeside road, all with views of the wooden bridge and the Mon village. They all have restaurants, and most offer Burmese and Mon food such as *hang lay curry* (a country dish made of whatever ingredients are on hand, but often including pork) and the coconut-milk-and-noodle dish *khao soi*. The temple's lights shimmer on the water at night. Other than watching this mesmerizing image, nightlife here consists of a karaoke bar and a noodle soup stall at the market that sells beer and local whiskey until the wee small hours.

Sangklaburi Night Market

$ | **THAI** | **FAMILY** | You'll find all the Thai classics at this typically lively night market, but what makes Sangklaburi's nightly open-air food fest different is the range of stalls selling interesting Karen, Mon, and Burmese dishes. Stroll around and see which direction your tastebuds take you. **Known for:** lively atmosphere; non-Thai dishes such as hang lay curry and tea leaf salad; lots of locals. [$] *Average main: 60* ✉ *Sangkhla Buri* 💳 *No credit cards.*

Hotels

P Guest House

$ | **B&B/INN** | The stone bungalows here sit in a stepped garden leading down to the lake. **Pros:** wooden deck for sunbathing and swimming; nice views; all rooms are very clean. **Cons:** front desk is not 24 hours; some rooms with shared bath; no air-conditioning in most rooms. [$] *Rooms from: B400* ✉ *81/2 Moo 1, Tambon Nongloo* ☎ *034/595061* 🌐 *www.p-guest-house.com* 🛏 *35 rooms* 🍴 *No Meals.*

Sripech Home

$ | **HOTEL** | There's a lot to love about this humble gem; ideally located near the Mon Bridge, the lodgings are within easy striking distance of all the top sights in Sangklaburi. **Pros:** close to Mon Bridge; cute sitting areas outside rooms; good value. **Cons:** no meals included; small rooms; very basic decor. [$] *Rooms from: 500* ✉ *100/3, Sam Prasob, Sangkhla Buri* ☎ *88/212–3456* 🍴 *No Meals* 🛏 *9 rooms* 💳 *No credit cards.*

Ayutthaya

72 km (45 miles) north of Bangkok.

Carefully preserved Ayutthaya, a UNESCO World Heritage Site, provides a fascinating snapshot of ancient Siam. Scattered ruins testify to the kingdom's brutal demise at the hands of the Burmese in 1767, while broad thoroughfares preserve a sense of its former greatness. Although the modern town is on the eastern bank of the Pa Sak, most of the temples are on an island. An exception is Wat Yai Chai Mongkol, a short tuk-tuk ride away. Ayutthaya is best appreciated in a historical context, and a visit to the Historical Study Center is a must for first-time visitors.

Certain sites are guaranteed to take your breath away—Wat Phra Si Sanphet, Wat Yai Chai Mongkol, Wat Phra Mahathat, and Wat Ratchaburana, to name a few.

Did You Know

Wat Phanan Choeng's central Buddha statue is surrounded by hundreds of small Buddha figures, which sit in niches along the temple walls. Each figure honors someone who has made a substantial donation to the temple.

Aside from the temples, Ayutthaya's friendly guesthouses, welcoming people, and floating restaurants make for a refreshing change from Bangkok.

Ayutthaya was named by King Ramatibodi after a mythical kingdom of the gods portrayed in the pages of the *Ramayana* legend. The city was completed in 1350 and became both a powerhouse of Southeast Asia and reputedly one of the region's most beautiful royal capitals. It was originally chosen as a capital for its eminently defensible position, lying on an island formed by a bend of the Chao Phraya River, where it meets the Pa Sak and Lopburi rivers. Early residents created the island by digging a curving canal along the northern perimeter, linking the Chao Phraya to the Lopburi River.

Ayutthaya quickly changed from being essentially a military base to an important center for the arts, medicine, and technology. Trade routes opened up following Siam's first treaty with a Western nation (Portugal, in 1516), and soon afterward the Dutch, English, Japanese, and, most influentially, the French, accelerated Ayutthaya's rise to importance in international relations under King Narai the Great. After Narai's death in 1688, the kingdom plunged into internal conflict and was laid waste by Burmese invading forces in 1767.

GETTING HERE AND AROUND
BUS
Regular buses to Ayutthaya (1½ hours) leave Bangkok's Mo Chit Northern Bus Terminal between 6 am and 7 pm. Tickets cost B50 for the 1½-hour trip. Minivans can be hailed at Bangkok's Victory Monument and cost B60 for the 1-hour ride.

CAR
Driving to Ayutthaya from Bangkok is an easy day trip once you're beyond the congestion of the big city. Follow the Sirat Expressway and then the Udon Ratthaya Expressway north to Route 32. Following this road will bring you to the outskirts of Bang Pa-In—a good opportunity to visit the Royal Palace before continuing to Ayutthaya.

TAXI AND TUK-TUK
All forms of local transport are available from samlors to songthaews, but the brightly colored tuk-tuks are most popular. Tuk-tuks can be hired for an hour for about B300 or the day for about B1,200 to B1,500 and make easier work of Ayutthaya's historical sites. Though the island site of the Old City is quite compact, don't be tempted to tour it on foot; hire a tuk-tuk (about B600 for an afternoon) or a three-wheel bicycle cab (about B500). You can also rent a bicycle for about B50 a day.

TRAIN
The Northeastern Line, which heads all the way up to Isan, has frequent service from Bangkok to Ayutthaya. Beginning at 4:30 am, trains depart about every 40 minutes from Bangkok's Hua Lamphong Station, arriving in Ayutthaya 90 minutes later.

MONEY MATTERS
ATMs and exchange services are abundant on Naresuan Road in Ayutthaya and in Lopburi on Ratchadamnoen Road.

TIMING
Ayutthaya can be visited on a day trip from Bangkok, but the city really warrants a longer stay. Besides the temple ruins there are many other attractions—such as boat tips on the Chao Praya River. Ayutthaya is an excellent base for exploring the surrounding region.

VISITOR AND TOUR INFORMATION
CONTACT Tourist Authority of Thailand (TAT). ⊠ *108/22 Moo 4, Si Sanphet Rd., Ayutthaya* ☎ *035/246–0767* ⊕ *www. tourismthailand.org.*

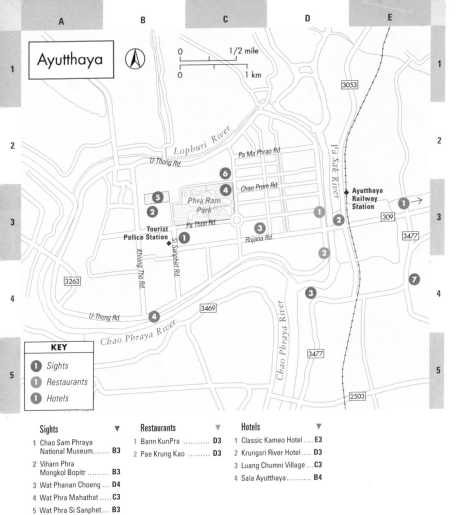

Ayutthaya

0   1/2 mile
0   1 km

Lopburi River

U-Thong Rd.

Pa Ma Phrao Rd.

Chao Prom Rd.

Phra Ram Park

Pa Thon Rd.

Tourist Police Station

Si Sanphet Rd.

Khlong Tho Rd.

Rojana Rd.

Pa Sak River

Ayutthaya Railway Station

309

3477

3053

3263

3469

U-Thong Rd.

Chao Phraya River

Chao Phraya River

3477

2503

KEY

● Sights
● Restaurants
● Hotels

Sights

Chao Sam Phraya National Museum

HISTORY MUSEUM | This museum on spacious grounds in the center of the Old City was opened by the king and queen of Thailand in 1961. Its many exhibits include Buddhist sculpture from the Dvaravati, Lopburi, Ayutthayan, and U-Thong periods. Also on display is a jewel-encrusted sword with which one Ayutthayan prince killed his brother in an elephant-back duel. ☒ *Rotchana Rd., Ayutthaya* ✛ *At Si San Phet Rd.* ☎ *035/241587* 💴 *B150*.

Viharn Phra Mongkol Bopitr

RELIGIOUS BUILDING | When this temple's roof collapsed in 1767, one of Thailand's biggest and most revered bronze Buddha images was revealed. It lay here uncovered for almost 200 years before a huge modern viharn was built in 1951. Historians have dated the image back to 1538. ☒ *Off Naresuan Rd., Ayutthaya* 💴 *Free*.

Wat Phanan Choeng

RELIGIOUS BUILDING | This bustling temple complex on the banks of the Lopburi River is an interesting diversion from the dormant ruins that dominate Ayutthaya. A short B3 ferry ride across the river sets the scene for its dramatic origins. The temple was built in 1324 (26 years before Ayutthaya's rise to power) by a U-Thong king in atonement for the death of his fiancée. Instead of bringing his bride, a Chinese princess, into the city himself, the king arranged an escort for her. Distraught at what she interpreted to be a lackluster welcome, the princess threw herself into the river (at the site of the current temple) and drowned. ☒ *Ayutthaya* ✛ *East of the Old City* 💴 *B20*.

★ Wat Phra Mahathat

RELIGIOUS BUILDING | Building began on this royal monastery in 1374 and was completed during the reign of King Ramesuan (1388–95). The tree-shaded, parklike grounds, a pleasant place to linger, contain what's left of the

monastery's 140-foot prang. The brick Khmer-style prang, which collapsed twice between 1610 and 1628, and again in the early 20th century, barely reflects its former glory. Partially in ruins, the prang is said to contain relics of the Lord Buddha. It and the beheaded Buddhas that remain in Wat Phra Mahathat are a result of the Burmese sacking of the temple in 1767. ☒ *Sois Naresuan and Chikun, Ayutthaya* 💴 *B50*.

Wat Phra Si Sanphet

RELIGIOUS BUILDING | The royal family worshipped at this wat, Ayutthaya's largest temple. The 14th-century structure lost its 50-foot Buddha in 1767, when the invading Burmese melted it down for its 374 pounds of gold. The trio of chedis survived and are the best existing examples of Ayutthaya architecture; enshrining the ashes of several kings, they stand as eternal memories of a golden age. If the design looks familiar, it's because Wat Phra Si Sanphet was the model for Wat Phra Keo at the Grand Palace in Bangkok. Beyond the monuments you can find a grassy field where the Royal Palace once stood. The foundation is all that remains of the palace that was home to 33 kings. ☒ *Naresuan Rd., Ayutthaya* 💴 *B50*.

Wat Ratchaburana

RELIGIOUS BUILDING | Across from Wat Phra Mahathat stands Wat Ratchaburana, whose Khmer-style prang dominates the skyline. King Borommaracha II (Chao Sam Phraya) built this temple in 1424 to commemorate the death of his two older brothers, whose duel for the throne ironically left him as king. Their relics, including their swords, were buried in a crypt under the prang's base, which was looted in 1957. Arrests were made, however, and the retrieved treasures can now be seen in the Chao Sam Phraya National Museum. ☒ *Sois Naresuan and Chikun, Ayutthaya* 💴 *B50*.

Wat Yai Chai Mongkol

RELIGIOUS BUILDING | King Naresuan constructed the enormous chedi at Wat Yai

Chai Mongkol, the largest in Ayutthaya, after defeating the Burmese crown prince during a battle atop elephants in 1593. A recent painting of the battle is one of the temple's highlights. The complex, parts of which date to 1357, was totally restored in 1982. Linger a while to pay your respects to the huge reclining Buddha, or climb to the top for a spectacular view. The site closes at 5 pm, but you can enter after that if the gates are left open, as they often are. The view at sunset is beautiful, and you'll completely escape the crowds. ✉ ✣ *Off Rte. 3477, 1 km (½ mile) south of Rte. 309* 🎟 *B20.*

🍴 Restaurants

Bann KunPra

$$ | **THAI** | Handsome locally fired floor tiles are among the original features of the century-old teak home this atmospheric old restaurant occupies. Step onto the riverside terrace and you could be in Venice—the waterway throbs with life, with tiny tugs pulling impossibly large barges loaded with rice, and a small jetty where guests get picked up for a dinner cruise. **Known for:** seafood dishes; attached guest rooms; nice views. [$] *Average main: B250* ✉ *48 Moo 3, Huarattanachai U-Thong Rd., Ayutthaya* ☎ *97/169–6939.*

Pae Krung Kao

$$ | **THAI** | An appealing mélange of local flora and traditional Thai decor greets patrons as they enter this charming bar and restaurant on the bank of the Pa Sak River. The visual delights continue in the low-ceilinged dining areas, which are packed with collectibles, from old bottles to timepieces, and half the restaurant sits on a pontoon floating on the water. **Known for:** traditional Thai food; opens early at 10 am; giant river prawns. [$] *Average main: B250* ✉ *4 Moo 2, U-Thong Rd., Ayutthaya* ☎ *035/241555.*

🛏 Hotels

A stay in Ayutthaya allows you to wander among the ruins at night, a romantic experience indeed. Most tourists leave Ayutthaya by 4 pm to head back to Bangkok, but those who remain are treated to a less hectic and more genuine version of Thai hospitality. This is particularly the case at the small-scale guesthouses along the waterfront, some in historic, beautifully restored timber-built homes. These lodgings often provide far better value than Ayutthaya's older, more established hotels, which look impressive from afar but often have rooms of questionable or no taste and lack a personal touch.

★ Classic Kameo Hotel

$$ | **HOTEL** | **FAMILY** | This hotel's contemporary fittings are in contrast to Ayutthaya's ancient vibes, but the rooms are clean and comfortable with firm beds and nice bathrooms. **Pros:** close to tourist sights; good facilities like hot tub, pool, and gym; modern design. **Cons:** on the expensive side; some rooms without nice views; not traditional like other Ayutthaya accommodations. [$] *Rooms from: B2000* ✉ *210–211, 148 Moo 5, Rojana Rd., Ayutthaya* ☎ *035/212535* 🌐 *www.kameocollection.com* 🛏 *208 rooms* 🍽 *Free Breakfast.*

Krungsri River Hotel

$ | **HOTEL** | A refreshingly cool and spacious marble-floor lobby distinguishes this luxury hotel. **Pros:** spacious suites; near the train station; river views. **Cons:** on the expensive side; dated decor in some rooms; not all rooms have views. [$] *Rooms from: B1,950* ✉ *27/2 Moo 11, Rojana Rd., Ayutthaya* ☎ *035/244333* 🌐 *www.krungsririver.com* 🛏 *206 rooms* 🍽 *Free Breakfast.*

Luang Chumni Village

$ | **HOTEL** | This warren of six snug teak rooms is one of the most popular lodgings in town, so booking well ahead is essential. **Pros:** tropical gardens; serene atmosphere; lots of polished teak. **Cons:**

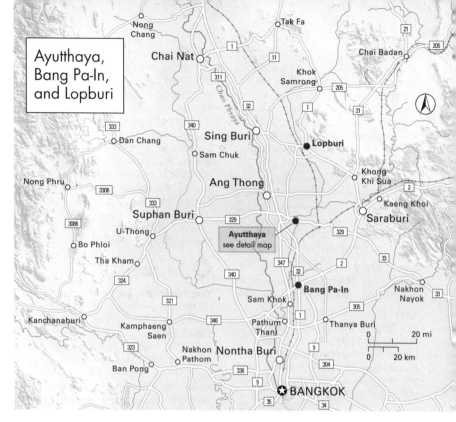

books up fast; some guests may miss an en suite bathroom; front desk not 24 hours. Ⓢ *Rooms from: B1000* ✉ *2/4 Rojana Rd., Ayutthaya* ☎ *035/322990* ⊕ *www. luangchumnivillage.com* ↝ *6 rooms* ⓄⅠ *Free Breakfast.*

★ **Sala Ayutthaya**

$$ | HOTEL | Just a short walk from the temples, this upbeat boutique hotel is another compelling reason to overnight in the ancient capital. **Pros:** riverside deck; outdoor pool; great location. **Cons:** some rooms lack river views; concrete in hallways can amplify sounds; rooms are a bit small. Ⓢ *Rooms from: 3315* ✉ *9/2 Moo 4, U-Thong Road, Pratu Chai* ☎ *35/242588* ⊕ *www.salahospitality.com* ⓄⅠ *No Meals* ↝ *26 rooms.*

Bang Pa-In

20 km (12 miles) south of Ayutthaya.

This village, a popular stopping point between Bangkok and Ayutthaya, is famous for its palace complex and lush grounds. The complex houses a Thai palace, a European-style temple, and a Chinese pagoda, all grouped around a lake and beautifully manicured grounds that encompass topiary animals and colorful flower gardens. Most visitors spend about two hours at the palace complex before heading for Ayutthaya, though if the weather's not too hot you might be tempted to linger longer on the banks of Bang Pa-In's calm lake.

GETTING HERE AND AROUND

BUS

Buses regularly leave from Bangkok's Northern Bus Terminal to Bang Pa-In Bus Station, less than half a mile from the palace. Fares are about B50 for an air-conditioned bus. From Ayutthaya, buses leave from the station on Naresuan Road.

CAR

Once you get out of Bangkok's labyrinthine roads, it's also easy to get to Bang Pa-In by car. Get on the northbound Route 32 and look out for signs. It's a 30-minute drive here from Ayutthaya.

SONGTHAEW

Songthaews travel regularly between the bus stations in Bang Pa-In and Ayutthaya.

TAXI

One-way taxi fares from Bangkok to Bang Pa-In should be about B800 (depending on your starting point), but be sure that the driver agrees to a fare before departing, or you may be charged more upon arrival.

TRAIN

Trains from Bangkok's Hua Lamphong Station take an hour to get to Bang Pa-In Station, where you can catch a tuk-tuk or songthaew to the palace. The train fares, which are generally less than B70, vary by class of travel.

Sights

Royal Palace

CASTLE/PALACE | Bang Pa-In's extravagant Royal Palace sits amid well-tended gardens. The original structure, built by King Prusat on the banks of the Pa Sak River, was used by the Ayutthaya kings until the Burmese invasion of 1767. After being neglected for 80 years, it was rebuilt during the reign of Rama IV and became the summer palace of King Rama V. King Rama V was interested in European architecture, and many influences are evident here. The most beautiful building,

however, is the Aisawan Thippaya, a Thai pavilion that seems to float on a small lake. China also fascinated the two rulers, and Phra Thinang Warophat Phiman, nicknamed the Peking Palace, is a replica of a Chinese imperial court palace. It was built from materials custom-made in China—a gift from Chinese Thais eager to win the king's favor. It contains a collection of exquisite jade and Ming porcelain. The Buddhist temple, Wat Nivet Thamaprawat, is built in British neo-Gothic style, with a fine steeple, buttresses, a belfry, and stained-glass windows. ⊠ Bang Pa-in ☎ 035/261044 ⊠ B100.

Shopping

Bang Sai Folk Arts and Craft Centre

CRAFTS | The center was set up by Queen Sirikit in 1982 to train farming families to make traditional crafts for extra income. Workers regularly demonstrate their technique, and a small souvenir shop provides the chance to buy the fruits of their labors. The center holds an annual fair at the end of January. ⊠ Bang Pa-in ✛ Off Rte. 3442, 24 km (14½ miles) south of Bang Pa-in ☎ 035/366252.

Lopburi

75 km (47 miles) north of Ayutthaya, 150 km (94 miles) north of Bangkok.

One of Thailand's oldest cities, Lopburi has been inhabited since the 4th century and had many rulers, leaving it with quite a strange mixture of Khmer, Thai, and Western architecture. It's somewhat off the beaten track for most tourists, and those who do come here are generally outnumbered by the city's monkey population. Some foreigners show up on their way to or from Ayutthaya, but few stay overnight. The rarity of foreigners may explain why locals are so friendly and eager to show you their town—and to practice their English. Samlors are available, but most of Lopburi's attractions are within easy walking distance of downtown and the train station.

The city was founded around the 4th century and in the 6th century its influence grew under the Dvaravati rulers, who dominated northern Thailand until the Khmers swept in from the east. From the beginning of the 10th century until the middle of the 13th, when the new Thai kingdom drove them out, the Khmers used Lopburi as their provincial capital. During the Sukhothai and early Ayutthaya periods, the city's importance declined until, in 1664, King Narai made it his second capital to escape the heat and humidity of Ayutthaya. He employed French architects to build his palace.

GETTING HERE AND AROUND
BUS
Buses to Lopburi leave Bangkok's Mo Chit Northern Bus Terminal (Mo Chit) about every 20 minutes between 6 am and 7 pm. Tickets for the three-hour journey start at around B120 for air-conditioned buses. Minivans leave regularly from Bangkok's Victory Monument. Lopburi is an hour and a half from Ayutthaya on the green Bus 607 from Ayutthaya's bus terminal. Lopburi's bus station is about 6 km (3½ miles) from town, making it necessary to take a tuk-tuk or songthaew into town.

CAR
If you're driving from Bangkok, take Route 1 (Phahonyothin) north via Salaburi or Route 32 via Ang Thong. The trip will take around two hours.

TRAIN
The northbound train line has frequent service from Bangkok. Three morning and two afternoon trains depart for the three-hour trip from Bangkok's Hua Lamphong Station. Trains back to Bangkok run in the early and late afternoon. Advance tickets aren't necessary. Fares for air-conditioned cars on the express train cost about B350. Lopburi's station is downtown near

Monkey Business

Lopburi has an unusually large monkey population. The monkeys cluster around the monuments, particularly Phra Prang Sam Yot. Each November the Lopburi Inn organizes a monkey banquet, in which a grand buffet is laid out for the monkeys and much of the town's population comes out to watch them feast.

the historic sites and lodgings on Na Phra Kan Road.

VISITOR AND TOUR INFORMATION
CONTACT Tourist Authority of Thailand (TAT). ✉ *28/9 Narai Maharach Rd., City Center* ☎ *036/770–0967* ⊕ *www.tourismthailand.org.*

 ## Sights

Phra Narai Ratchaniwet
CASTLE/PALACE | This palace's well-preserved buildings, completed between 1665 and 1677, have been converted into museums. Surrounding the buildings are castellated walls and triumphal archways grand enough to admit an entourage mounted on elephants. The most elaborate structure is the Dusit Mahaprasat Hall, built by King Narai to receive foreign ambassadors. The roof is gone, but you can spot the mixture of architectural styles: the square doors are Thai and the domed arches are Western. North of Phra Narai Ratchaniwet is the restored Wat Sao Thong Thong. ✉ *Ratchadamneon Rd., Lopburi* ☎ *036/411458* 🎟 *B150* 🕙 *Closed Mon. and Tues.*

Phra Prang Sam Yot
RELIGIOUS BUILDING | Lopburi's most famous landmark is this Khmer shrine whose three prangs symbolize the

sacred triad of Brahma, Vishnu, and Shiva. King Narai converted the shrine into a Buddhist temple, and a stucco image of the Buddha sits serenely before the central prang. The most memorable aspect of the monument is its hundreds of resident monkeys, including mothers and nursing babies, wizened old males, and aggressive youngsters. Hold tight to your possessions, as the monkeys steal everything from city maps to cameras. Most tourists wind up having a blast with the monkeys, though. Approach them and stand still for a minute, and you'll soon have monkeys all over your head, shoulders, and just about everywhere else—a perfect photo op. ✉ *Vichayen Rd., Lopburi* 🎟 *B30* 🕒 *Closed Mon. and Tues.*

Vichayen House

HISTORIC HOME | Built for King Louis XIV of France's personal representative, De Chaumont, Vichayen House was later occupied by King Narai's infamous Greek minister, Constantine Phaulkon, whose political schemes eventually resulted in the ouster of all Westerners from Thailand. When King Narai was dying in 1668, his army commander, Phra Phetracha, seized power and beheaded Phaulkon. ✉ *Vichayen Rd., Lopburi* 🎟 *B50* 🕒 *Closed Mon. and Tues.*

Wat Phra Si Rattana Mahathat

RELIGIOUS BUILDING | Built by the Khmers, this wat underwent so many restorations during the Sukhothai and Ayutthaya periods that it's difficult to discern the three original Khmer prangs—only the central one is intact. Several Sukhothai- and Ayutthaya-style chedis sit within the compound. ✉ *12, Ratchadamnoen 1 Alley, Lopburi* 🎟 *B50* 🕒 *Closed Mon. and Tues.*

🍴 Restaurants

Bualuang Restaurant

$$ | **THAI** | This large restaurant with white tablecloth seating inside and a pleasant garden outside is just the sort of local restaurant that you shouldn't miss. The menu is Thai-Chinese and you can feast on regional specialties and good seafood. **Known for:** helpful service; nice garden setting; seafood dishes like steamed blue crab and mussels hot pot. [$] *Average main: B250* ✉ *46/1 Moo 3, Lopburi* ☎ *036/413009, 036/422669* 🌐 *www.facebook.com/bualuang.1980.*

🛏 Hotels

Lopburi Inn Resort

$ | **RESORT** | This monkey-themed retreat is the best value in Lopburi, with stylish rooms decorated in a modern Thai style, a generous buffet breakfast, and a good range of facilities including a pleasant pool. **Pros:** gym; Wi-Fi access; pool. **Cons:** decor in rooms not modern; monkey theme on the tacky side; far from main sights. [$] *Rooms from: B1,000* ✉ *17/1–2 Ratchadamnoen Rd., Lopburi* ☎ *036/420777* 🍽 *Free Breakfast* 🛏 *100 rooms.*

Noom Guesthouse

$ | **B&B/INN** | The seven rooms at this comfortable city-center guesthouse are basically furnished but are more than adequate. **Pros:** close to attractions; central location; good restaurant. **Cons:** on-street parking; street noise can be heard in rooms; lack of decor. [$] *Rooms from: B250* ✉ *15/17 Phayakamjad Rd., City Center* ☎ *036/427693* 🌐 *www.facebook.com/Noom-Guesthouse-Restaurant-Lopburi-170752319694826* 🍽 *No Meals* 🛏 *7 rooms.*

THE GULF COAST BEACHES

Updated by
Duncan Forgan

◉ Sights	🍴 Restaurants	🛏 Hotels	🛍 Shopping	🍸 Nightlife
★★★★☆	★★★☆☆	★★★★☆	★☆☆☆☆	★★★★☆

WELCOME TO THE GULF COAST BEACHES

TOP REASONS TO GO

★ **Sunset at Hua Hin:** Take a stroll down the wide beaches at Hua Hin for unbeatable views of the setting sun—the same ones the king and queen of Thailand have enjoyed from their nearby palace.

★ **Relaxing Quick Getaway:** Bangkok weekenders flock to Cha-am to enjoy the sun, surf, seafood, and inexpensive accommodations. Of all the beaches a quick hop from Bangkok, this is by far the most laid-back.

★ **Island Diving:** A divers' heaven, the small island of Koh Tao has escaped the worst excesses of tourist development. Divers also flock to even tinier Koh Nang Yuan.

★ **Midnight Revelry:** Every month as many as 50,000 locals and visitors descend on the island of Koh Phangan for a late-night, full-moon beachfront bacchanal.

★ **Dramatic Koh Samui:** A drive around the dramatic coastline of Thailand's third-largest island takes you from one eye-popping view to another.

1 **Pattaya.** Buzzing coastal city with great water sports.

2 **Koh Samet.** Famous for its sugary white beaches.

3 **Chanthaburi.** Popular stop for its Gem Market and French architecture.

4 **Koh Chang.** Picturesque beaches verdant jungle.

5 **Cha-am.** An affordable beach getaway with sleepy charm.

6 **Hua Hin.** A small city with long beaches, busy markets, and summer guests including Thai Royals.

7 **Takiab Beach.** An escape from Hua Hin with luxury hotels and uncrowded beaches.

8 **Chumphon.** A gateway to the south with beaches and bird-watching.

9 **Surat Thani.** A great night market and a national park with a beautiful forest.

10 **Koh Samui.** Perfect beaches, turquoise waters, and idyllic weather.

11 **Koh Phangan.** Famous for its full moon parties and wellness scene.

12 **Koh Tao.** Known for excellent diving sites right off shore.

Andaman Sea

MERGUI ARCHIPELAGO

SURIN ISLANDS

SIMILAN ISLANDS

Phang Nga

Khao Lak

KOH PHUKET

Phuket

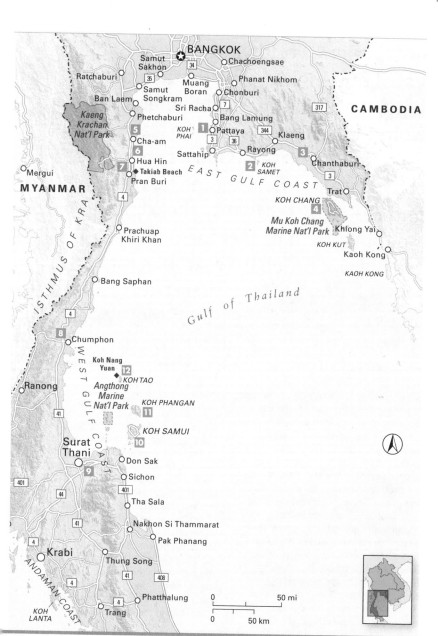

With its white sandy beaches, crystal-blue water, and laid-back lifestyle, the Gulf Coast captures the imaginations of travelers worldwide. East of Bangkok you'll find high-profile Pattaya, along with the islands of Koh Samet and Koh Chang, two longtime escape-from-Bangkok favorites. Popular spots near the capital to the west include Cha-am and Hua Hin, both near the top of a peninsula that stretches south to Malaysia. The island of Koh Samui is about halfway down this strip. On both sides of the gulf, the beaches only get prettier the farther south you go.

You don't have to travel far from Bangkok to find exhilarating beaches. The Eastern Gulf offers several close enough for a weekend getaway. Pattaya has a reputation as a full-on, often salacious party place. But city tourism leaders are trying to change that image and many resorts are secluded from the downtown bars and clubs. Farther southeast along the coastline, which extends to Thailand's border with Cambodia, are some swell beach resorts and even better islands. Two islands worth considering, as many Bangkok residents do, are tiny Koh Samet and Thailand's second-largest island, Koh Chang. The latter has seen considerable growth this decade, with classy resorts now achieving primacy over the modest budget bungalows of days past.

A bit south of Bangkok along the Western Gulf's narrow peninsula, which Thailand shares with Myanmar, lie Cha-am and Hua Hin. Cha-am has bigger resorts and more stand-alone ones; Hua Hin has both world-class resorts and less fancy accommodations. These two cities can fill up with escapees from the capital on weekends, but they're less busy during the week. Scores of beaches worth exploring can be found farther south. You can reach them all from Surat Thani, which is a one-hour flight or an 11-hour train ride from Bangkok. Northeast of Surat Thani in the Gulf is Koh Samui, popular in part because regular flights from Bangkok make it so easy to access.

MAJOR REGIONS

The Gulf Coast region southeast and southwest of Bangkok offers something for nearly everyone, from secluded spots in national marine parks to flashy resort towns whose bar scenes are bigger draws than their beaches. These destinations bordering the Gulf of Thailand, sometimes called the Gulf of Siam, include high-profile Koh Chang and Koh Samui.

The **Eastern Gulf** has long been a favorite escape from the heat and humidity of Bangkok. Its proximity to the capital means that weekend trips are possible, which in turn means that the area can be overrun with sunseekers during long or holiday weekends. Many visitors skip overdeveloped Pattaya, which is trying to shed its seedy image, and head farther east where splendid islands include Koh Samet, a longtime favorite of Bangkok residents. Chanthaburi and its Gem Market is a popular stop on the way to Koh Chang, farther east, which has experienced a considerable expansion in recent years.

South of Bangkok lies the **Western Gulf** coast, hundreds of miles of shoreline where resort towns are the exception rather than the rule. About three hours south of Bangkok are the laid-back beaches of Cha-am and Hua Hin. Bangkok residents have traveled to Hua Hin since the 1920s, when King Rama VII built a palace here. Where royalty goes, high society inevitably follows, but despite the attention the city received, Hua Hin was spared the pitfalls of rapid development. Directly to the south of Hua Hin, Takiab Beach is where well-off Thais go to avoid the well-off scene of Hua Hin while Chumphon is the gateway to the south, with trains and buses connecting here for Bangkok to the north and Surat Thani and Phuket to the south. As the former capital of an ancient Siamese kingdom,

Surat Thani developed its own artistic and architectural style. In modern times it has remained an important commercial and historic Thai city, and the province is home to one of the most pristine tropical forests in Thailand, Khao Sok National Park. Nevertheless, most travelers know Surat Thani as a departure point for the islands off its coast.

Though very developed, **Koh Samui,** the most popular destination on the Western Gulf, isn't too frenzied. The island's beaches are gorgeous, the weather's often perfect, and the mood is laid-back. After a few days exploring the island's many beaches and sights, travelers seeking more adventure take advantage of easy side trips, which include Koh Phangan, a short speedboat ride from Koh Samui that is famous for its beautiful beaches and full moon parties, or Koh Tao, a tiny island north of Koh Phangan that is a sought-after diving getaway.

Most towns along the gulf are either small fishing villages or culturally and historically significant towns like Surat Thani. Some touristy areas have grown up around the smaller villages, but they are considerably less developed than some of their counterparts in the other coastal areas. Thus, the allure of the Western Gulf is its charming towns, spectacular beaches, and not-yet-overgrown tourist destinations.

Planning

When to Go

The best time to visit the Gulf Coast is between December and March, when the seas are mostly calm and the skies generally clear. On the Eastern Gulf, Pattaya and Koh Samet are year-round destinations. Many places in Koh Chang and nearby islands used to close down during the rainy season but no more.

The big car ferries continue to run on a limited schedule during the rainy season, and most resorts and hotels stay open, offering cheaper rates. On the Western Gulf, Cha-am and Hua Hin are busy year-round. Flying to Koh Samui is still convenient in low season, and the island and its neighbors are beautiful even with cloudiness and rain.

Planning Your Time

Geographically disparate, the many beaches along the Gulf of Thailand would take nearly a month to survey. With Bangkok serving as the urban divider, most travelers choose either the gulf's east or west coast to explore, and then concentrate on one or—at most—a few places. This region is largely about relaxing and taking your time. Where you end up and how long you stay depend on what you're looking for. It only takes a day, for instance, to figure out what wild Pattaya is all about. But if this is your thing you could spend a fun week here. Ditto for genteel Koh Samet or developed, but not too hyper, Koh Chang. As with their east-coast counterparts, the west-coast beaches would take about two weeks to explore even superficially. Both Cha-am and Hua Hin, the closest of the major west-coast beaches to Bangkok, become very crowded on weekends and holidays; if you can arrange to visit at other times, you'll have a mellower experience. The farther south you go from Hua Hin, the less you need to worry about when you visit, except during major holidays or, in the case of Koh Phangan, the full moon party that takes place every four weeks.

Getting Here and Around

AIR
Relatively inexpensive flights depart daily from Bangkok for all the major beach destinations: Surat Thani, Trat, and Koh Samui. It's generally cheaper to fly to Surat Thani, mostly because the government owns the airport. There are some flights from Chiang Mai to the beaches. Thai Airways and Bangkok Airways have regular flights, as do the budget carriers AirAsia and Nok Air. All the airports in this region are small and much easier to deal with than Bangkok's Suvarnabhumi.

BOAT AND FERRY
Boats depart from the mainland to the islands from Chumphon and Surat Thani. High-speed catamarans, regular passenger ferries, and "slow boats," which are car ferries, make these trips. The main boat operators are Lomprayah, Seatran, Songserm, and Raja.

■ TIP→ **Don't take the chance of traveling on rickety or overcrowded boats. Because of lax safety standards, dangerously crowded boats are all too common. Ensure that life jackets are available and that the crew takes safety seriously. Responsible companies—and there are many—keep safety concerns front and center.**

CONTACTS Lomprayah. ☎ *06/3081 5000 Customer Care, 02/629–2569 in Bangkok, 077/953084 in Samui, 077/423761 on Koh Phangan* ⊕ *www.lomprayah.com.* **Raja Ferry.** ☎ *02/277–4488, 092/276–8211* ⊕ *www.rajaferryport.com.* **Seatran Ferry.** ☎ *077/950766* ⊕ *www.seatranferry.com.*

BUS
Buses travel regularly between Bangkok and all major destinations in southern Thailand. Bus service within the south is also good. Fleets of minivans also link Bangkok with most of the major destinations.

■ TIP→ **Public buses have a better reputation than private bus companies, on which travelers often report thefts from luggage compartments and other annoyances.**

CAR

Eastern Gulf resorts are fairly close to Bangkok, so driving is a possibility. The worst part is getting out of Bangkok. On the Western Gulf, it's a long, exhausting drive farther south to Chumphon, Surat Thani, or Krabi. It may be cheaper, safer, and more convenient to hire a car and driver. This is best done while in Bangkok; your hotel can make arrangements.

MOTORCYCLE AND SCOOTER

Scooters may seem like a fun way to explore the islands and beaches, but think twice before renting one. Every year hundreds of foreigners are killed or injured in accidents along the Gulf Coast. The consequences of even a minor snafu can be dire if you're only wearing shorts and flip-flops. If you've never driven a motorcycle before, this is not the time to learn.

SONGTHAEW, TAXI, AND TUK-TUK

Most areas of the south have everything from samlors (a 3-wheeled bicycle rickshaw) to tuk-tuks (motor rickshaws) to songthaews (a pickup turned into a shared taxi). "Metered" taxis can be found in the larger towns and on Samui. Drivers don't actually run the meters, however, and can be unscrupulous bargainers.

TRAIN

One daily train departs Bangkok's Hua Lamphong Station for Sri Racha and Pattaya; there's more frequent service to Hua Hin, Chumphon, and Surat Thani. In general, bus or minivan travel is a better way to go in southern Thailand.

Health and Safety

Malaria is very rare but not unheard of in Thailand's southeast. Health authorities have done a great job controlling mosquitoes in and around the southern resorts, but you'll still need a good supply of repellent.

Be careful at the beach, as the sun is stronger than you think. Wear a hat and plenty of sunscreen. Protective clothing while diving or snorkeling is a good idea, as accidentally brushing against or stepping on coral can be painful. Keep an eye out for sea urchins and even more dangerous creatures like jellyfish, especially during the monsoon season. If you are stung, seek medical attention immediately.

Strong undertows often develop during monsoon season, especially along the west coast. Pay attention to posted warnings and listen if locals tell you not to swim.

Condoms are available in southern Thailand; not all brands are equally reliable, so it may be simpler to bring any you'll need.

Take the same safety precautions you would in any other location. When traveling to isolated spots, let someone know where you are going and how long you expect to be away, and be aware of strangers you encounter along the way. Though rare, serious incidents involving tourists have taken place on the southern gulf islands, including murders and the suspicious deaths of several others.

Restaurants

Dining options in the beach regions vary from exclusive and expensive resort restaurants to wooden shacks that seem moments from toppling over. On the islands, beach-dining is an enduring highlight. Pattaya, Hua Hin, and Koh Samui have the widest range of restaurants, from fast-food chains to five-star restaurants.

Hotels

There's something for everyone in this region, from luxurious retreats to simple huts close to the beach. Many places

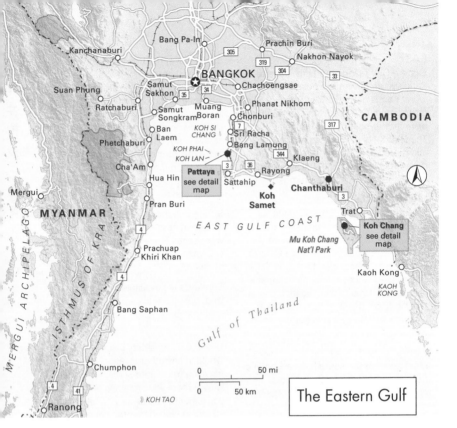

The Eastern Gulf

combine the two experiences by offering fancy bungalows. Rates fluctuate widely: in holiday periods they can more than double. Always double-check your rate when you book. In general, prices are lower than what you'd pay in Bangkok, but higher than in other parts of the country.

What It Costs in Baht			
$	$$	$$$	$$$$
RESTAURANTS			
under B200	B200–B300	B301–B400	over B400
HOTELS			
under B2,000	B2,000–B4,000	B4,001–B6,000	over B6,000

Pattaya

147 km (88 miles) southeast of Bangkok.

Pattaya's proponents boast that the city has finally emerged as a legitimate upscale beach destination. This is partly true: recent years have seen the opening of chic restaurants and more family-friendly attractions. Still, Pattaya remains a city as divided as ever between sand and sex—and the emphasis still falls clearly on the latter.

■ TIP→ **If you're averse to encountering live sex shows and smut shops at every turn, avoid Pattaya. Commercial sex is not just a reality here: it is the lifeblood of the city.**

Pattaya was not always like this. Until the end of the 1950s it was a fishing village with an unspoiled natural harbor.

Even after affluent Bangkok residents discovered the area, it remained small and tranquil. Then came the Vietnam War, with thousands of American soldiers stationed at nearby air and naval bases. They piled into Pattaya, and the resort grew with the unrestrained fervor of any boomtown. But the boom eventually went bust. Pattaya was nearly abandoned, but its proximity to Bangkok and the beauty of the natural harbor ensured that it didn't crumble completely.

In the late 1990s, after much talk and government planning, Pattaya started regaining popularity. Two expressways were finished, making the trip from Bangkok even easier. Now that Bangkok's international airport is located on the southeast side of the capital, it is even more convenient to visit Pattaya.

Curving Beach Road, with palm trees on the beach side and modern resort hotels on the other, traces the arc of Pattaya Bay in the heart of the city. Bars, clubs, and open-air cafés proliferate on the pedestrian streets by the old pier. South of here lies Jomtien, an agreeable, if somewhat overdeveloped, beach. The bay's northern part is Pattaya's quietest, most easygoing section. Pattaya's big water-sports industry caters to Jet Skiers, paragliders, and even water-skiers.

GETTING HERE AND AROUND
Buses to Pattaya leave from Bangkok's Eastern Bus Terminal on Sukhumvit at least every hour daily. The journey takes about an hour and a half, and fares are cheap—usually around B120. You can also drive from Bangkok, and many rental companies vie for your business. A number of taxi and limousine services are available, including Pattaya4leisure.

CONTACTS Pattaya4leisure. ⊕ *www. pattaya4leisure.com.*

SAFETY AND PRECAUTIONS
Pattaya is a city built on prostitution, and it has all the trappings that go with the seedy atmosphere generated by the sex trade. Street thefts do happen, and thefts from hotels are not unheard of. Take sensible precautions with valuables, always use hotel safes, and avoid late-night strolls down dark streets. Tourist police are on duty, and in recent years they've been joined by tourist police volunteers—expat residents acting as liaisons with the regular police units.

VISITOR AND TOUR INFORMATION
CONTACT Tourism Authority of Thailand.
✉ *609 Moo 10, Pratamnak Rd., Pattaya* ☎ *038/427667, 038/428750* ⊕ *www. tourismthailand.org.*

 ## Sights

Sanctuary of Truth
NOTABLE BUILDING | FAMILY | Wealthy businessman Lek Viriyaphant started building this massive teak structure in 1981, and it's still not finished. The aim of the sanctuary, whose intricate carvings blend modern and traditional styles, is to make a statement about the balance of different cultures. The waterfront setting north of Pattaya is pleasant. ✉ *206/2 Moo 5, Naklua Rd., Bang Lamung* ☎ *038/8225407* ⊠ *B500.*

 ## Beaches

Jomtien Beach
BEACH | Pattaya Beach's quieter neighbor to the south, Jomtien Beach is less gaudy, less crowded, and a bit less expensive. The white sand, cleaner water, and cordoned-off swimming areas are also draws. Shaded areas with deck chairs cover large sections of the beach, and vendors sell food and drink at inflated prices. Water sports play a dominant role here; you can rent Jet Skis, paragliders, and speedboats up and down the beach. Jomtien is home to a few

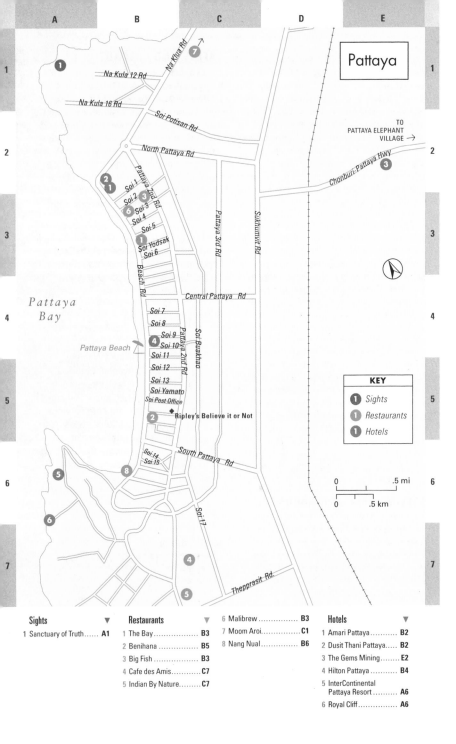

Pattaya

TO PATTAYA ELEPHANT VILLAGE →

Pattaya Bay

Pattaya Beach

Ripley's Believe it or Not

KEY

- ① Sights
- ① Restaurants
- ① Hotels

0 ————— .5 mi
0 ————— .5 km

Roads:
Na Khua Rd, Na Kula 12 Rd, Na Kula 16 Rd, Soi Potisan Rd, North Pattaya Rd, Chonburi-Pattaya Hwy, Pattaya 2nd Rd, Pattaya 3rd Rd, Sukhumvit Rd, Beach Rd, Central Pattaya Rd, Soi Buakhao, Soi Yodsak, South Pattaya Rd, Soi 17, Thepprasit Rd.

Soi 1, Soi 2, Soi 3, Soi 4, Soi 5, Soi 6, Soi 7, Soi 8, Soi 9, Soi 10, Soi 11, Soi 12, Soi 13, Soi Yamato, Soi Post Office, Soi 14, Soi 15

windsurfing schools. **Amenities:** food and drink. **Best for:** swimming; windsurfing. ✉ *Moo 12, Pattaya.*

Koh Lan

BEACH | From Pattaya Bay, shared speedboats take just 15 minutes to reach the island of Koh Lan. The beaches have white sand, and the water is cleaner than at Pattaya Beach. Koh Lan gets busy by midday, so arrive early if you want peace and quiet. The waters are crowded with speedboats and other motorized craft—and some speedboat operators are reckless, so be cautious when swimming. Food and drink vendors wander among the shaded deck chairs, although the prices are steep. Ferries leave South Pattaya Pier daily from 10 am to 6:30 pm. Private speedboats can be hired as well. **Amenities:** food and drink. **Best for:** swimming; nature lovers. ✉ *Koh Lan, Pattaya* 🎫 *Speedboats B300 per person (round-trip); private speedboats B2500 (round-trip); ferry B60 per person (round-trip).*

Pattaya Beach

BEACH | **FAMILY** | The city's namesake beach fronts slightly murky waters, but its sand is golden and fine, and safe swimming areas have been added in recent years. You can rent shaded deck chairs by the hour, and food vendors and trinket merchants wander up and down the beach. The bay is usually crowded with small boats, Jet Skis, and other diversions. Parallel to the shore, Pattaya Beach Road has a landscaped walkway that separates the beach from the restaurants, shopping malls, and resorts on the opposite side. **Amenities:** food and drink. **Best for:** walking. ✉ *Pattaya Beach Rd, Pattaya.*

🍴 Restaurants

Much of Pattaya feels like Little America, with McDonald's, Burger King, and KFC next to each other in the Royal Gardens Plaza mall, and other familiar names nearby. But Pattaya has access to just-picked produce and seafood fresh from the gulf, so you'll have no trouble finding worthwhile local cuisine. Fancier, if not necessarily better, restaurants can be a refuge from the noise and crowds at the simple beachside places.

The Bay

$$$ | **ASIAN** | This sleek, modern restaurant overlooking the Dusit Thani resort's expansive pool and shimmering Pattaya Bay offers an "international skewers" concept with a wide variety of Chinese, Thai, and Western takes on grilled meat, seafood, and vegetables on skewers. **Known for:** good seafood skewers; Pattaya Bay views; an all-inclusive Saturday night buffet. [$] *Average main: B400* ✉ *Dusit Thani Pattaya, 240/2 Pattaya Beach Rd., Pattaya* ☎ *038/425611* 🌐 *www.dusit.com.*

Benihana

$$$$ | **JAPANESE** | The concept—one familiar to western visitors, especially those from North America—is not exactly authentic to Japan or any country for that matter. But Benihana's take on Japanese-style teppanyaki has proved to be an enduring formula. **Known for:** good steaks; all the ingredients for an entertaining evening; nice sake selection. [$] *Average main: 600* ✉ *Avani Pattaya Resort, 281/2-4 M.10 Beach Rd., Pattaya* ☎ *38/412120* 🌐 *www.benihanathailand.com.*

Big Fish

$$$ | **SEAFOOD** | Pattaya's reputation as a top spot for sampling seafood is given fresh impetus at this lively restaurant. The venue is open daily for lunch, but it comes alive on weekend nights when gourmands flock to its seafood buffet, which is a kingly affair starring superfresh morsels served in an underwater-inspired space popping with eclectic artworks. **Known for:** an outstanding array of seafood; live music, which adds to the vibe; famous Sunday night buffet. [$] *Average main: 300* ✉ *390 Moo 9, Pattaya Sai 2*

Rd., Pattaya ☎ 038/930600 🌐 www.siamatsiam.com ⏲ No dinner Mon.–Thurs.

★ Cafe des Amis

$$$$ | **EUROPEAN** | Belying Pattaya's slightly unsophisticated reputation, this fine dining haven oozes Gallic class. Tucked away in a residential district between Pattaya and Jomtien, it's something of a romantic refuge. **Known for:** charming courtyard and al fresco dining area; some of the best steaks in town; a formidable wine selection. [$] *Average main: 450 ✉ 319/6 10 Thap Phraya Rd., Pattaya ☎ 08/40264989, 090/7729993 🌐 www.cafe-des-amis.com.*

Indian By Nature

$$$ | **INDIAN** | Regulars pack the room at this elegant Indian restaurant, which honors Pattaya's bountiful seafood supply with such dishes as a comforting fish curry and a crab masala special that's an absolute must when it's available. Service is attentive but never overbearing, living up to the awards this local favorite has earned since it opened in 2004. **Known for:** excellent dessert menu; a drink trolley devoted to gin; private dining for special occasions. [$] *Average main: B400 ✉ 306/64-68 Thapraya Rd., Pattaya ☎ 038/364656 🌐 www.indian-by-nature.com ⏲ No lunch.*

Malibrew

$$ | **INTERNATIONAL** | It's not all about the atmosphere at this lively venue: the kitchen is no slouch in the creativity department. Simplicity is key to your enjoyment, with choice cuts of meat and prime local produce getting top billing. **Known for:** excellent selection of international and local ales; eclectic musical entertainment; simple, but perfectly executed dishes. [$] *Average main: 300 ✉ A-One Hotel Pattaya, 499 Beach Rd., Pattaya ☎ 038/259588 🌐 www.facebook.com/malibrewpattaya/.*

Moom Aroi

$$$ | **SEAFOOD** | For a different side of Pattaya, head north of the city to this beautiful, romantic seafood restaurant that sits right on the waterfront. The almost exclusively Thai clientele enjoys hand-picked lobster, tiger prawns, crab, oysters, and fish amid shimmering pools, palm trees, and sweeping bay views. **Known for:** fresh seafood tanks; reasonable prices considering the quality of the food; point-and-smile ordering. [$] *Average main: B350 ✉ 83/4 Na Klua Rd., Pattaya ☎ 038/223252.*

Nang Nual

$$$ | **SEAFOOD** | At the southern end of Pattaya Beach Road is one of the city's best places for seafood. A huge array of freshly caught fish is laid out on blocks of ice at the entrance; point to what you want, explain how you'd like it cooked (most people prefer grilled), and ask for some fried rice on the side for a flawless meal. **Known for:** terrace dining overlooking the ocean; picture menus for indecisive diners; plump steaks for the non-seafood crowd. [$] *Average main: B350 ✉ 214–10 S. Pattaya Beach Rd., Pattaya ☎ 038/428177.*

🛏 Hotels

Only Bangkok beats Pattaya in number of hotel rooms. For seclusion, you'll have to stay at one of the high-end places.

★ Amari Pattaya

$$$ | **HOTEL** | Step into the modern, open-air lobby here, and you'll immediately be transported to a haven removed from Pattaya's hectic streets. **Pros:** prime beachside location; luxurious tower rooms; superb customer service. **Cons:** building looks imposing; not all rooms have great views; ongoing renovations. [$] *Rooms from: B4250 ✉ 240 Pattaya Beach Rd., Pattaya ☎ 038/418418 🌐 www.amari.com/pattaya 🛏 297 rooms 🍴 Free Breakfast.*

Dusit Thani Pattaya

$$ | RESORT | At the northern end of Pattaya Beach, this sprawling hotel has superb bay views and several pools, including one with a swim-up bar. **Pros:** immaculate grounds; calm amid Pattaya's chaos; many rooms have private balconies with great views. **Cons:** can feel large and impersonal; rudimentary service; a short songthaew ride from Pattaya's main attractions. $ *Rooms from: B4,000 ⊠ 240/2 Pattaya Beach Rd., Pattaya* ☎ *038/425611* ⊕ *www.dusit.com* ◉| *Free Breakfast* ↪ *457 rooms.*

The Gems Mining

$$ | HOTEL | Despite a somewhat odd African theme, Gem's Mining is one of Pattaya's classiest new luxury properties. **Pros:** gorgeous landscaping; 1 bedrooms and up have private pools; friendly and helpful staff. **Cons:** unimaginative breakfast buffet; no communal pool area; African theme feels a bit clumsy. $ *Rooms from: 3800 ⊠ 888 Moo 1 Nongprue Banglamung, Pattaya* ☎ *038/222222* ⊕ *www.thegemspattaya.com* ◉| *Free Breakfast.*

Hilton Pattaya

$$ | HOTEL | In the middle of the beach yet convenient to much of Pattaya—especially the shopping mall it looms over—the Hilton serves up no-fuss luxury. **Pros:** bay-facing business suites; central location; outstanding restaurants. **Cons:** unimaginative room decor; beginning to show its age; noise from nearby bars. $ *Rooms from: B4,000 ⊠ 333/101 Moo 9, Nong Prue, Banglamung, Pattaya Beach Rd., Pattaya* ☎ *038/253000* ⊕ *www.hilton.com* ◉| *Free Breakfast* ↪ *304 rooms.*

★ InterContinental Pattaya Resort

$$$ | HOTEL | Located on a green, forested headland overlooking Koh Lan, this is one of Pattaya's most enticing properties. **Pros:** the region's most luxurious spa; unbeatable setting; three lagoon-like swimming pools. **Cons:** slightly removed from the action; breakfast buffet not the most expansive; beach manmade, with steps leading down to the water. $ *Rooms from: B4500 ⊠ 437 Phra Tamnak Rd., 1½ km (1 mile) south of town, Pattaya* ☎ *038/259888* ⊕ *www.pattaya.intercontinental.com* ↪ *156 rooms* ◉| *Free Breakfast.*

Royal Cliff

$$ | RESORT | FAMILY | High on a bluff about 1½ km (1 mile) south of town, this four-hotel ensemble, a Thai institution, is known far and wide for its gulf views, setting, and staggering size. **Pros:** attractive Thai decor; several picturesque pools; beautiful views. **Cons:** out-of-town location; so-so dining; tricky to get to beach. $ *Rooms from: B3000 ⊠ 353 Phra Tamnak Rd., Pattaya* ☎ *038/250421* ⊕ *www.royalcliff.com* ↪ *1128 rooms* ◉| *Free Breakfast.*

Nightlife

Nightlife in Pattaya centers on the sex trade. Scattered throughout town (though mostly concentrated on Sai Song) are hundreds of beer bars—low-key places whose hostesses merely want to keep customers buying drinks. Raunchier go-go bars are mostly found on the southern end of town. Pattaya's, and perhaps Thailand's, most shockingly in-your-face red-light district is on Soi 6, about a block in from the beach. Whether you find it intriguing or beyond the pale, the street is a sight to behold, with hundreds of prostitutes lined up shoulder-to-shoulder at all hours, spilling out of bars and storefronts and catcalling to every male passerby. Gay bars are in the sois between Pattaya Beach Road and Pattaya 2 Road called Pattayaland.

■ **TIP→ Generally, the only bars in town that are somewhat removed from the commercial sex trade are in pricey hotels.**

Hot Tuna
LIVE MUSIC | There's more to Pattaya's infamous Walking Street than go-go bars. This live music perennial serves to mix things up courtesy of a well-drilled regular band that pumps out everything from rock classics to Thai hits. ⊠ *Pattaya Walking Street, Pattaya* ⊕ *www.facebook.com/pages/Hot%20Tuna%20Bar/201010653264553/.*

Latitude
COCKTAIL LOUNGES | At this hotel bar you'll get a great view of the sunset over the Gulf of Thailand—through plate-glass windows or, better yet, alfresco—while sipping wines or well-crafted cocktails, perhaps accompanied by tapas. There's a small library adjacent to the wine bar. ⊠ *InterContinental Pattaya Resort, 437 Phra Tamnak Rd., Pattaya* ☎ *038/259888* ⊕ *www.pattaya.intercontinental.com.*

Mulligan's Pub and Restaurant
Antique Irish liquor posters adorn the walls of this pub that's as authentically Irish as it gets in Pattaya. Sports play a central role, with large flat-screen TVs showing all manner of events. The staff is friendly and well trained. ⊠ *Central Festival Pattaya Beach, 333/99 Moo 9 Beach Rd., Pattaya* ☎ *038/043388* ⊕ *www.facebook.com/MulliganPattaya/.*

Tiffany
CABARET | This world-renowned, award-winning extravaganza has been entertaining curious locals and ecstatic travelers for more than 40 years now. It's famous throughout Southeast Asia for being one of the first cabaret shows to feature transgender performers—setting the stage for similar performances throughout Thailand. ⊠ *464 Moo 9, Pattaya 2 Rd., Pattaya* ☎ *038/421700* ⊕ *www.tiffany-show.co.th.*

Activities

Pattaya Beach is the spot for water sports. Water-skiing starts at B1,500 for 30 minutes, Jet Skiing costs B1,000 for 30 minutes, and parasailing runs B500 for 15 minutes. Big inflatable bananas, yet another thing to dodge when you're in the water, hold five people and are towed behind a speedboat. They go for B1,000 or more for 30 minutes. For windsurfing, head to Jomtien Beach.

■ **TIP →** Beware of a common scam among shady Jet Ski vendors who try to charge for preexisting damage. Before heading out, inspect the equipment and take pictures of any dings, dents, or scratches.

Koh Samet

30 minutes by passenger ferry from Ban Phe, which is 223 km (139 miles) southeast of Bangkok.

Koh Samet's beautiful beaches are a hit with Thais and Bangkok expats, especially on weekends. Although newer resort areas beckon, Koh Samet remains popular with laid-back travelers who just want to sunbathe and read on the beach. There are no high-rises, and just one road stretching down the length of the island.

GETTING HERE AND AROUND
Koh Samet is a 30-minute passenger ferry ride—costing between B100 and B200 depending on the destination—from one of three piers in the small village of Ban Phe, a 90-minute minibus ride east of Pattaya, and a 2.5-hour ride from Bangkok. Ferries to Koh Samet dock at Na Duan on the north shore and An Vong Duan on the eastern shore. The islands' beaches are an easy songthaew ride from either village.

Sights

Koh Samet National Park
NATIONAL PARK | The government has been unable—or unwilling—to control development on some parts of Koh Samet despite its protected status as a national marine park, but its fine sand and smooth water is still serene and

beautiful in many places. Development is greatest in the main village and northern beaches. Other irritants involve Jet Skis, which can be heard roaring away in some places. Trash is also an increasingly vexing issue. All the beaches have licensed ladies offering one- and two-hour Thai massages, which generally cost B300 an hour, not including tip. ✈ *30-min ferry ride from Ban Phe* 🚢 *B200.*

Beaches

Ao Kiu

BEACH | On the southern end of Koh Samet, this beautiful and secluded beach has crystal-blue waters and fine white sand that lend the strand a picture-postcard feel. If you're looking to relax, Ao Kiu is an ideal choice. **Amenities:** food and drink. **Best for:** solitude. ✉ *Koh Samet.*

Ao Vong Duan

BEACH | This beautiful shoreline of a half-moon bay is packed with resorts and restaurants, so food and drink are never far away. Ao Vong Duan is the epicenter of water sports on Koh Samet, with Jet Skis and speedboats operating from the beach. The white sands and crystal-blue waters make the beach worth a visit, and the beaches of Ao Cho to the north and Ao Thian to the south are an enjoyable five-minute stroll away. **Amenities:** food and drink; water sports. **Best for:** sunrise; walking. ✉ *Koh Samet.*

Haad Sai Kaew

BEACH | This beach on Koh Samet's northeastern edge is the island's longest and busiest one. The sand is white and the water is clear, though in the rainy season the sea does get a little rough. A few boats operate from the beach, but Haad Sai Kaew is a better place to relax than the crowded beaches of Pattaya. All manner of food and drink is available from the nearby resorts and restaurants. **Amenities:** food and drink; water sports. **Best for:** partiers. ✉ *Beach Rd., Koh Samet.*

Ao Prao

BEACH | **FAMILY** | This crescent-shaped stretch of sand is the only real beach on the western side of the island, and it's a beauty. Quieter than the beaches in the island's northeast, it's a hit with couples who come for candlelit dinners on the sand, a real highlight for many. **Amenities:** food and drink; water sports. **Best for:** sunset. ✉ *Koh Samet.*

Hotels

The island has many bungalows and cottages with electricity. Most of the resorts have good restaurants, but you'll have a more memorable experience if you try some of the seafood and spicy salad sold by the vendors who patrol the beaches each afternoon.

Paradee Resort

$$$$ | **RESORT** | For serious luxury away from the fray, head to this resort at the island's far southern reaches. **Pros:** private pools; beautiful grounds; more secluded than most Samet resorts. **Cons:** may feel isolated; very pricey; not good for families. 💲 *Rooms from: B9000* ✉ *76 Moo 4, Rayong* ☎ *038/644–2846* ⊕ *www.samedresorts.com/paradee/* ⊠ *No Meals* 🛏 *40 bungalows.*

Samed Cliff Resort

$ | **RESORT** | This resort's bungalows are simply furnished, but they're clean and comfortable and have the requisite amenities, including hot water and air-conditioning. **Pros:** white sand; beachside dining and grills; on scenic stretch of beach. **Cons:** few creature comforts; rooms are dated; busy at night. 💲 *Rooms from: B1,800* ✉ *Noi Na Beach, Koh Samet* ☎ *086/578–0300* ⊕ *www.facebook.com/samedcliff* ⊠ *No Meals* 🛏 *38 bungalows.*

Continued on page 200

Thailand's Beaches

Thailand is a beach-lover's paradise, with nearly 2,000 miles of coastline divided between two stunning shores. Whether you're looking for an exclusive resort, a tranquil beach town, an island with great rock-climbing, or a secluded cove, you can find the right atmosphere on the Andaman or the Gulf coast.

by Martin Young

With so many beaches to choose from, deciding where to go can be overwhelming. What time of year you're traveling helps narrow things down, since the two coasts have different monsoon seasons.

In general, the Andaman Coast has bigger waves and better water clarity, although the Gulf Coast has some great snorkeling and diving spots too, particularly around the islands. On both coasts there are windy spots ideal for wind- and kitesurfing, and peaceful bays that beckon swimmers and sunbathers.

Sea temperature averages near a luxurious 80 degrees on both coasts, and almost all beaches are sandy; Andaman beaches tend to have more powdery sand, while Gulf sand is a bit grainier. Developed beaches on both coasts offer tons of activities like sailing, fishing, and rock climbing.

Ao Nang beach, Krabi.

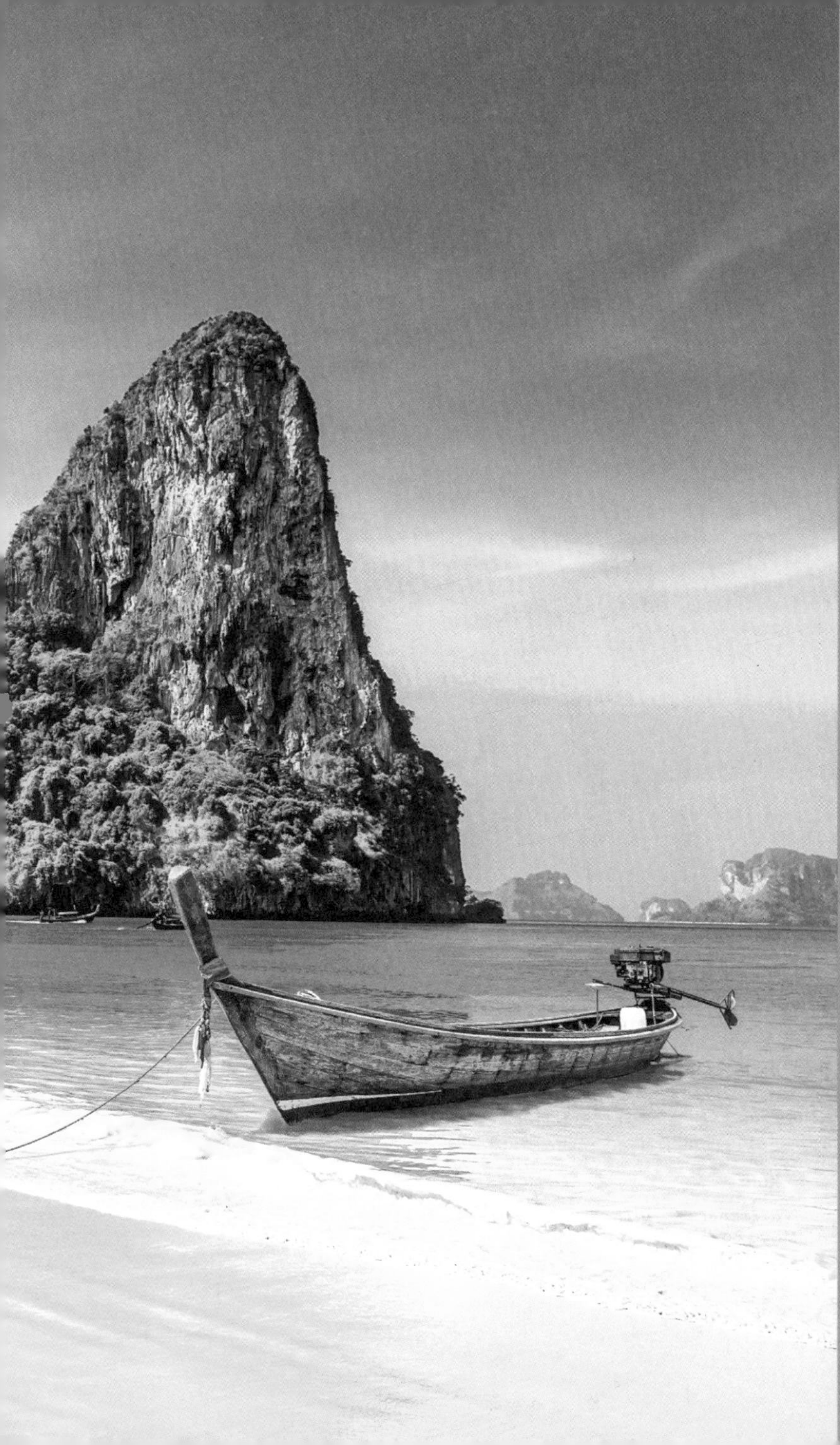

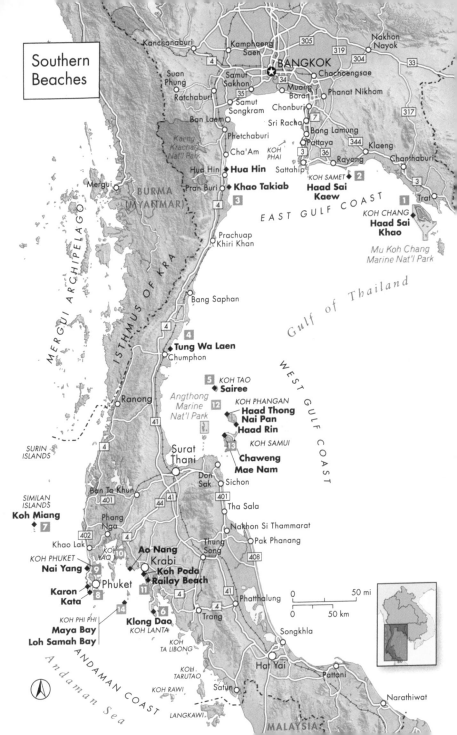

TOP SPOTS

(left) Kata beach, Phuket (right) Maya Bay, famous from the Hollywood film *The Beach*.

1 On mountainous **Koh Chang**, hillside meets powdery white sand and calm, clear water at **Haad Sai Khao**.

2 **Koh Samet** is famous for its sugary beaches and crystal-clear water; there's room for everyone on **Haad Sai Kaew**, the island's longest beach.

3 Water sports enthusiasts like **Hua Hin's** wide, sandy beach. Just south, **Khao Takiab's** longer, wider beach is more popular with locals, but gets busy on weekends and holidays.

4 Kitesurfers love long, quiet **Tung Wa Laen** beach for its winds and shallow water.

5 **Koh Tao's** most developed beach, **Sairee**, is the place to learn to dive and has gorgeous sunsets.

6 Laid-back **Klong Dao** on **Koh Lanta** has long expanses of palm-fringed white sand and azure water.

7 The clear water around the nine **Similan Islands** is Thailand's best underwater playground. **Koh Miang** has some basic bungalows and tranquil white-sand beaches.

8 On **Phuket**, neighboring beaches **Karon** and **Kata** have killer sunsets, great waves, and plenty of daytime and nighttime activities.

9 **Nai Yang**, a tranquil, curving beach on northern **Phuket**, is a pretty place to relax.

10 **Ao Nang** has a nice strip of shops and restaurants and stunning views of the islands in Phanga Bay from its beach. Boats to **Koh Poda**—a small island with white coral sand, hidden coves, and jaw-dropping views—leave from here.

11 **Railay Beach** peninsula has limestone cliffs, knockout views, and crystal-clear water.

12 Backpackers flock to **Haad Rin** for **Koh Phangan's** famous full-moon parties. To get away from the crowds, head north to **Haad Thong Nai Pan**, a beautiful horseshoe bay on **Phangan's** more remote east coast.

13 **Chaweng**, Koh Samui's busiest beach, has gently sloping white sand, clear water, and vibrant nightlife. On the north coast, less developed **Mae Nam** beach is a natural beauty.

14 On **Koh Phi Phi**, breathtaking **Maya Bay**, closes periodically as it gets very crowded; small but beautiful **Loh Samah Bay** on the other side of the island is less hectic.

KEY	
	Diving
	Fishing
	Kayaking
	Land Sports
	Sailing
	Snorkeling
	Surfing

BEACH FINDER

KEY: ○ = Available ● = Exceptional

BEACH	NATURAL BEAUTY	DESERTED	PARTY SCENE	THAI CULTURE	RESORTS	BUNGALOWS	GOLF	SNORKELING/ DIVING	SURFING	KITEBOARDING/ WINDSURFING	ACCESSIBILITY
EASTERN GULF											
Pattaya	○		●		○	○		○	○	●	●
Koh Samet	●	●		○		○					○
Koh Chang	○		○		○	●		●			○
Koh Si Chang	○	○		○		○					○
WESTERN GULF											
Cha-am	○	○		●	○			○	○		●
Hua Hin	●		○		○	○		○	○	○	●
Takiab Beach	○			○	○	○		●	○	●	●
Koh Samui	●		○	○	●	○	○	○	○		○
Koh Phangan	●		○			●		○			○
Koh Tao	●	○				●		●	○		○
KOH PHUKET											
Mai Khao Beach	○	●		○	○	●	○	○			●
Nai Yang Beach	○	●		○	○	○	○				●
Nai Thon & Layan Beaches	○	●			○	○	○				○
Bang Thao Beach	○	●		○	○	○	○			●	○
Pansea, Surin & Laem Beaches	○	○			○	○	○				○
Kamala Beach	●	○			○	○		○			○
Patong	●		●		●	●	○	○		○	●
Karon Beach	●	○			●	●	○	○			○
Kata Beach	○		●		●	●	○	○	●	○	○
Nai Harn	○	●		●	○	○	○				○
Chalong		●		●			○				○
ANDAMAN COAST											
Phang Nga Bay	●		●					●			
Koh Yao	○	●		○	○	○		●			○
Khao Lak	●		○	○	○	○	○	●			○
Similan Islands	●	○		○		○		●			
Surin Islands	●	○		○		○		●			
Ao Nang	○		●		○	●		●	○		○
Nang Cape/Railay Beach	●	○	●	○	●	●		●			
Koh Phi Phi	●	○	●		●	●		●			
Koh Lanta	○	○	○		●	●	○	○			●

KEY: ○ = Available ● = Exceptional

GOOD TO KNOW

WHAT SHOULD I WEAR?

On most beaches, bikinis, Speedos, and other swimwear are all perfectly OK. But wear *something*—going topless or nude is generally not acceptable. Women should exercise some caution on remote beaches where skimpy attire might attract unwanted attention from locals.

Once you leave the beach, throw on a cover up or a sarong. Unbuttoned shirts are fine, but sitting at a restaurant or walking through town in only your bathing suit is tacky, though you'll see other travelers doing it. Some areas have a Muslim majority, and too much exposed skin is frowned upon.

Beachside dining on Khao Lak.

WHAT TO EXPECT

Eating & Drinking: most popular beaches have a number of bars and restaurants.

Restrooms: few beaches have public facilities, so buy a drink at a restaurant and use theirs.

Rentals & Guides: You can arrange rentals and guides once you arrive. A dive trip costs B2,000 to B3,000 per person; snorkeling gear starts at about B300 a day; a surfboard or a board and kite is B1,000 to B1,500 a day; and a jet-ski rental runs around B500 for 15 minutes.

Hawkers: Vendors selling fruit, drinks, sarongs, and souvenirs can become a nuisance, but a firm "No, thank you" and a smile is the only required response.

Beach chairs: The chairs you'll see at many beaches are for rent; if you plop down in one, someone will usually appear to collect your baht.

WHAT TO WATCH OUT FOR

■ **The tropical sun.** Wear strong sunscreen. Drink lots of water. Enough said.

■ **Undertows** are a danger, and most beaces lack lifeguards.

■ **Jellyfish** are a problem at certain times of year, usually before the rainy season. If you are stung, apply vinegar to the sting—beachside restaurants will probably have some. ("Jellyfish sting" in Thai is *maeng ga-proon fai*, but the locals will probably understand your sign language.)

■ **Nefarious characters,** including prostitutes and drug dealers, may approach you, particularly in Patong and Pattaya. As with hawkers, a firm "No, thank you" should send them on their way.

BEACH VOCABULARY

Here are a few words help you decipher Thai beach names.

Ao means "bay."
Haad means "beach."
Koh means "island."
Talay means "sea."

Vongdeuan Resort

$$ | **RESORT** | This resort has the best bungalows on Ao Vong Duan Beach and is near much of the island's activity. **Pros:** fun atmosphere; reasonable bungalow rates; near all the action. **Cons:** not everything has air-conditioning; could use sprucing up; noisy from nearby boats. *[$] Rooms from: B2100 ✉ 22/2 Moo 4, Koh Samet ☎ 038/651777, 095/535–7555 🌐 www.vrsamed.com 🍴 No Meals 🛏 45 bungalows.*

Chanthaburi

100 km (62 miles) east of Rayong, 180 km (108 miles) east of Pattaya.

Chanthaburi has played a big role in Thai history. It was here that the man who would become King Taksin gathered and prepared his troops to retake Ayutthaya from the Burmese after they sacked the capital of Siam in 1767. The King Taksin Shrine, shaped like a house-sized helmet from that era, is on the north end of town. The French occupied the city from 1893 to 1905, and you can spot some architecture from that era along the river. Gems and jewelry form an important part of the town's modern economy, and you will see plenty of evidence of the gem trade in and around town. Most visitors stop here on the way to Koh Chang, attracted by either gem shopping or the fruit season (Chanthaburi is famed for its bounty of fruits like durian, mangosteen, and rambutan) in May and June.

GETTING HERE AND AROUND

Buses make the 90-minute journey from Rayong and Ban Phe. There's also a bus from Bangkok's Eastern Bus Terminal that takes from four to five hours.

Sights

Cathedral of Immaculate Conception

CHURCH | Chanthaburi's French influence is evident in its dual-spired Catholic cathedral, across the river from the center of town. Christian Vietnamese who migrated to the area erected the first church on this site in 1711, and the cathedral has been rebuilt four times since. The present Gothic-inspired structure was completed in the early 1900s, when the city was under French control. The best time to visit is during the morning market, when local foods, fruits, and desserts are sold on the grounds. *✉ 110 Moo 5, Chanthanimit Rd., Chanthaburi ✥ Past eastern end of Sichan Rd., take footbridge across Chanthaburi River 🎟 Free.*

Gem Market

MARKET | Chanthaburi's gem mines are mostly closed, but the Gem Market, which still operates in the center of town, attracts traders. You can often see them sorting through rubies and sapphires and making deals worth hundreds of thousands of baht. The market, an assortment of tables and stalls, takes place on Friday and Saturday along Sichan Road and various alleys off and near it. *✉ Sichan Rd., Chanthaburi 🎟 Free.*

Koh Chang

1 hour by ferry from Laem Ngop, which is 15 km (9 miles) southwest of Trat; Trat is 400 km (250 miles) southeast of Bangkok.

Koh Chang, or Elephant Island, is the largest and most developed of the 52-island archipelago that became Mu Koh Chang National Park in 1982. Most of the 30-km-long (18-mile-long) island is mountainous—there are only a few small beaches and only nine villages. Beautiful, albeit somewhat inaccessible, rain forest covers a large portion of this little paradise, making it ideal for those wanting more than just sun and sand. But the island is also a good bet for seaside relaxation: the beaches are picturesque and lack the overheated party scene of

Pattaya. As the tourism industry grows on Koh Chang, mid-level resorts are becoming more common than expensive upscale establishments. Resorts are also being built on some of the other islands in the national park, including Koh Mak and Koh Kood, which is home to stunning Soneva Kiri, one of Thailand's most spectacular properties.

■ TIP→ **Every beach on Koh Chang seems to have something being built or renovated, so before you book your hotel, make sure there is no major construction project going on nearby.**

GETTING HERE AND AROUND

To get to Koh Chang you must first get to Trat, 96 km (60 miles) southeast of Chanthaburi. The easiest way is to take one of Bangkok Airways' flights. It's a short (15-minute) ride from the airport to the ferry pier. There are also air-conditioned buses from Bangkok's Eastern and Northern bus terminals; the trip takes a bit more than five hours and costs about B270.

BOAT

Take a ferry from one of three piers in Trat (Laem Ngop, Center Point, or Ao Thammachat) to one of two piers on Koh Chang. The trip takes a little more than 30 minutes, and the fare is roughly B140 round-trip.

SONGTHAEW

Once you're on the island, songthaews (shared converted pickup taxis) are the easiest way to get around. They cost between B30 and B50 per ride, or more if you venture toward the eastern part of the island.

SAFETY AND PRECAUTIONS

Koh Chang is becoming a bustling resort island, and though the crime rate is still very low, thieves do strike. Keep your valuables secured and use hotel safes.

During monsoon season, from June to October, take particular care when swimming. Currents can be deceptive,

creating dangerous riptides that make swimming dangerous. Warning signs have been installed, but the beaches still lack lifeguards.

VISITOR AND TOUR INFORMATION
CONTACT Tourism Authority of Thailand.
✉ *100 Moo 1, Trat* ✛ *Near Laem Ngop pier* ☎ *039/597259.*

 ## Sights

Mu Koh Chang National Park
ISLAND | This 52-island marine national park covers all of Koh Chang. It's mostly mountainous, and there are only a few beaches, the best of them along the western shore of the island. Haad Sai Khao (White Sand Beach) is the farthest north and the most developed. A few miles south is the more serene Haad Khlong Phrao, a long, curving stretch of pale golden sand. Nearby Haad Kai Bae is a mix of sand and pebbles. Still farther south is Haad Ta Nam (Lonely Beach), which is perhaps the most picturesque of all. But it's also the smallest one and therefore more crowded. In the southwest corner of the island is the fishing village Bang Bao, with restaurants, dive shops, and cheap bungalows. The east coast is beautiful, but it's mostly rugged rain forest, and beaches are in short supply. ✉ *Koh Chang* ✛ *Take Koh Chang Ferry (30 mins) from Trat.*

 ## Beaches

Haad Kai Bae
BEACH | Its mix of pebbles and sand makes Kai Bae less popular than nearby strands, but this beach provides the best, and safest, swimming on Koh Chang. Quiet and relaxed, still enjoying a sleepy feel, Kai Bae has only a few restaurants and resorts. **Amenities:** food and drink. **Best for:** solitude; swimming. ✉ *Haad Kai Bae, Koh Chang.*

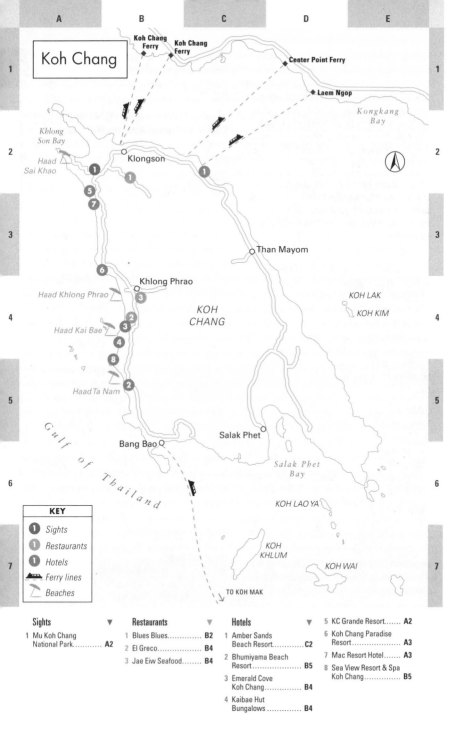

Koh Chang

Sights ▼

1 Mu Koh Chang
   National Park............ **A2**

Restaurants ▼

1 Blues Blues............... **B2**
2 El Greco.................. **B4**
3 Jae Eiw Seafood........ **B4**

Hotels ▼

1 Amber Sands
   Beach Resort............ **C2**
2 Bhumiyama Beach
   Resort.................... **B5**
3 Emerald Cove
   Koh Chang............... **B4**
4 Kaibae Hut
   Bungalows.............. **B4**
5 KC Grande Resort....... **A2**
6 Koh Chang Paradise
   Resort.................... **A3**
7 Mac Resort Hotel....... **A3**
8 Sea View Resort & Spa
   Koh Chang.............. **B5**

KEY

1 Sights
1 Restaurants
1 Hotels
Ferry lines
Beaches

Haad Khlong Phrao

BEACH | Khlong Phrao is an arc of golden sand leading down to placid waters. Scattered around the beach are a few high-end resorts and restaurants. The shallow waters discourage boaters, but also don't invite much swimming. **Amenities:** food and drink. **Best for:** walking. ✉ *Haad Khlong Phrao, Koh Chang.*

Haad Sai Khao

BEACH | With numerous resorts and some great restaurants, Koh Chang's busiest beach is ideal for those seeking a bustling atmosphere. The beach remains free from deck chair vendors, but a few hawkers wander through during the day. Especially during the rainy season, between June and October, severe riptides can occur, and swimming can be unsafe for extended periods. **Amenities:** food and drink. **Best for:** partiers. ✉ *Haad Sai Khao, Koh Chang.*

Haad Ta Nam (*Lonely Beach*)

BEACH | Koh Chang's hangout for the backpacker set has murky, sometimes rough water that's not ideal for swimming, but the vibe is cool. Though the beach itself is strewn with rocks, the hammock-lined bars draw patrons seeking a bit of spiritual enlightenment, cheap drinks, or both. Despite its name, beautiful Lonely Beach can get crowded. **Amenities:** food and drink. **Best for:** partiers. ✉ *Haad Ta Nam, Koh Chang.*

🍴 Restaurants

Blues Blues

$ | **THAI** | Hidden in plain sight on the way to an elephant camp and waterfall is this family-run Thai restaurant that brings a love of food, art (one of the owners is a multimedia artist and the decor reflects this), and music together under one canopy. Keep it classic with curries, stir-fries, or stuffed omelets—all fairly priced and full of flavor. **Known for:** simple yet satisfying local dishes; open-air dining; unique decor. [$] *Average main: B100* ✉ *Klong Son, Koh Chang* ☎ *087/144–6412.*

El Greco

$$$ | **GREEK** | El Greco brings a taste of the Ionian to the tropics. The emphasis is on prime ingredients perfectly cooked: a simple creed that is executed via offerings such as shrimp saganaki (shrimp with feta, fresh oregano, tomatoes, and olive oil) and giant souvlaki platters **Known for:** great for sharing; delicious dips; king-sized platters. [$] *Average main: 400* ✉ *24/7 Moo 4, Klong Prao, Koh Chang* ☎ *086/843–8417* 🌐 *www.elgreco-kohchang.com.*

Jae Eiw Seafood

$$ | **THAI** | **FAMILY** | Rated by many Thais as being among the best seafood restaurants in the entire province, this humble venue has serious credentials. The kitchen backs up its rep courtesy of perfectly cooked Thai-style seafood. **Known for:** popular with the locals; seriously good seafood; English-language menu. [$] *Average main: 250* ✉ *10/10/1 Moo 4, Klong Prao, Klongsan* ☎ *081/982–3954.*

🛏 Hotels

Amber Sands Beach Resort

$$ | **RESORT** | Located on the unfashionable east coast of the island, this is the perfect getaway for those who like a bit of seclusion along with their beach vacation. **Pros:** friendly welcome; bungalows right on the beach; peace and quiet. **Cons:** beach is not the island's prettiest; swimming pool is quite small; not much around. [$] *Rooms from: 2,000* ✉ *51/6 Moo 2, Dan Kao, Koh Chang* ☎ *39/586177* 🌐 *www.ambersands-beachresort.com* 🍽 *No Meals* 🔑 *8 rooms.*

Bhumiyama Beach Resort

$$ | **RESORT** | These two-story bungalows set in a tropical garden have a modern look and a luxurious feel, with white walls and much polished wood. **Pros:** next to Lonely Beach; good deal;

interesting decor. **Cons:** some rooms lack sea views; slightly claustrophobic feel; breakfast is very basic. [$] *Rooms from: B3271* ✉ *Lonely Beach, 99/1 Moo 4, Koh Chang* ☎ *02/236–5064* 🌐 *www.bhumiyama.com* 🛏 *43 rooms* 🍴 *Free Breakfast.*

★ Emerald Cove Koh Chang
$$$ | **RESORT** | One of Koh Chang's top hotels lives up to its five-star reputation with spacious and tastefully decorated rooms with hardwood floors and private balconies. **Pros:** plenty of sun beds; classy accommodations; high level of service. **Cons:** a little isolated; unexciting dining; beach is on the small side. [$] *Rooms from: B4699* ✉ *88/8 Moo 4, Tambol, Haad Khlong Phrao, Koh Chang* ☎ *039/552000, 089/536–2000 in Bangkok* 🌐 *www.emeraldcovekohchang.com* 🍴 *Free Breakfast* 🛏 *165 rooms.*

Kaibae Hut Bungalows
$ | **RESORT** | There are many strings of bungalows on Kai Bae Beach, but this property is the most established and reliable. **Pros:** stable Wi-Fi; attentive staff; central location. **Cons:** some bungalows could use upgrading (and don't have a/c); beach is far from some rooms; nearby bar can be noisy at night. [$] *Rooms from: B1300* ✉ *Kai Bae Beach, 10/3 Moo 4, Koh Chang* ☎ *81/862–8426* 🛏 *54 rooms* 🍴 *Free Breakfast.*

KC Grande Resort
$$ | **RESORT** | The bungalows here range from fan-cooled huts to spacious, amenities-laden suites; some of the best accommodations are right on the beach. **Pros:** lots of variety at breakfast; beautiful location; bungalows feel very private. **Cons:** least expensive rooms not so desirable; atmosphere may feel stuffy; could use an upgrade in some areas. [$] *Rooms from: B2500* ✉ *White Sand Beach, 1/1 Moo 4, Koh Chang* ☎ *039/552111* 🌐 *www.kckohchang.com* 🛏 *61 bungalows* 🍴 *No Meals.*

Koh Chang Paradise Resort
$$ | **RESORT** | With all the amenities of a big-city hotel, these spacious bungalows have private porches for enjoying the breeze. **Pros:** fire show a few nights a week; swim-up bar; lovely beachside location. **Cons:** subpar food; not luxurious; superior bungalows suffer from street noise. [$] *Rooms from: B3,000* ✉ *39/4 Moo 4, Haad Khlong Phrao, Koh Chang* ☎ *039/551100* 🌐 *www.kohchangparadise.com* 🍴 *No Meals* 🛏 *69 bungalows.*

Mac Resort Hotel
$ | **RESORT** | An ocean-view room with a hot tub and private balcony—or if not that, a poolside beachfront bungalow—is the way to go at the Mac. This is a friendly place, and there's a nightly barbecue on the beach. **Pros:** wide range of accommodations; reasonable rates; generally cool guests. **Cons:** noise from nearby nightclub; not fancy; food is unremarkable. [$] *Rooms from: B1000* ✉ *Sai Khao Beach, 7/3 Moo 4, Koh Chang* ☎ *39/551124* 🌐 *macresortkohchang.com* 🛏 *25 rooms* 🍴 *Free Breakfast.*

Sea View Resort & Spa Koh Chang
$$ | **RESORT** | At the far end of the beach, this resort is quieter than most at Kai Bae. Choose between bungalows a stone's throw from the surf or rooms in a building looming over the strand. **Pros:** breakfast comes with beautiful views; private beach access; well-manicured grounds. **Cons:** limited food options; removed from action; steep hill setting. [$] *Rooms from: B3000* ✉ *63 Moo 4, Koh Chang* ☎ *039/552888* 🌐 *www.seaviewkohchang.com* 🛏 *76 rooms* 🍴 *Free Breakfast.*

Activities

HIKING AND TREKKING

Hiking trips, particularly to some of the island's waterfalls, are popular. It's a good idea to hire a guide if you plan to venture farther than one of the well-traveled

Koh Mak, an island just south of Koh Chang, is known for its spectacular sunsets.

routes, as good maps of the mostly jungle terrain are hard to come by.

Tan Trekking
HIKING & WALKING | FAMILY | Thailand's third-largest island (after Phuket and Koh Samui), Koh Chang is ripe for exploration. The fact that its jungle-clad interior is barely bisected by paved roads makes it even more appealing as a hiking destination. The man to call to uncover the island's trekking manna is Khun Tan, who has an intimate knowledge of trails that take in lofty peaks, hidden waterfalls, and deep, dense undergrowth. Just be aware that Mr. Tan doesn't have a website. ✉ *Koh Chang* ☎ *089/645–2019, 089/832–2531* 💲 *Treks from B600 per person, depending on the route.*

SCUBA DIVING AND SNORKELING
Scuba diving, including PADI-certified courses, is readily available. Divers report that the fish are smaller than in other parts of Thailand, but the coral is better. Prices run from B3,500 for an introductory dive to more than B20,000 for dive-master certification. Snorkeling off a boat costs as little as B900 a day. Snorkelers usually just tag along on dive boats, but boat snorkeling excursions also take place.

BB Divers
DIVING & SNORKELING | One of the oldest dive schools on the island, BB has been taking budding divers below the waters since 2003. The school offers all PADI courses, daily fun dives, and snorkeling in a relaxed atmosphere. ✉ *Bang Bao 16/2, Koh Chang* ☎ *96/841–5951* ⊕ *www.bbdivers-koh-chang.com* 💲 *Diving trips from B3500, snorkeling trips from B1000.*

Chang Diving Center
DIVING & SNORKELING | Snorkeling trips in the shallow parts of this company's dive sites are offered here, along with scuba courses that cover all sorts of skill sets and special interests. ✉ *Klong Praw Beach, 21/17 Moo 4* ☎ *89/401–3927* ⊕ *www.changdiving.com* 💲 *Fun dives from B2990, snorkeling trips from B999.*

Scuba Dawgs
DIVING & SNORKELING | Experienced divers are encouraged to book a shipwreck trip with this courteous and professional company. They also organize daily snorkeling trips and host a wide array of educational classes, from refresher courses to advanced open-water techniques. ✉ *114/1 Bang Bao Pier Tambon,* ☎ *080/038–5166* 🌐 *www.scuba-dawgs.com* 🎫 *Single dives from B3000; Snorkeling from B1000.*

Cha-am

163 km (101 miles) south of Bangkok, 40 km (25 miles) from Petchaburi.

It may not be the most picturesque seaside town, but Cha-am does offer an authentic Thai-style beach experience. The pier at the north end of Cha-am Beach is the center of this small quiet town. Its main street, Ruamchit Beach Road, passes by a tree-lined strip of beach on one side and restaurants, bars, guesthouses, and hotels on the other. Fresh seafood is available at small cafés along this road, where there are also stalls selling trays of deep-fried squid, shrimp, and tiny crab for around B25. Cha-am retains its sleepy charm, and those searching for peace and quiet may find their niche here.

GETTING HERE AND AROUND

Buses leave Bangkok's Southern Bus Terminal every 30 minutes between 5 am and 10 pm; the 3-hour trip costs around B160. Once you're here, tuk-tuks are the best way to get around.

VISITOR AND TOUR INFORMATION

CONTACT Tourism Authority of Thailand. ✉ *Petchkasem Rd., Cha-am* ☎ *032/471005, 032/471502* 🌐 *www.tourismthailand.org.*

Beaches

Cha-am Beach
BEACH | At Cha-am's broad town beach you can often see Bangkok families gathered at umbrella-covered tables for all-day meals, stocking up on fresh fruit and seafood and cold beer from wandering vendors. The beach's sand, though, is fairly dark and dirty. Most visitors head to one of the all-inclusive resorts farther away, where the sand is prettier and the water better for swimming. **Amenities:** food and drink; parking; toilets. **Best for:** walking. ✉ *Ruamchit Beach Rd., Cha-am.*

Restaurants

DiDiNE
$$ | **FRENCH** | Welcome to the best-value French restaurant in Thailand. At Didine the emphasis is not on fancy plating or any of the familiar gallic niceties but rather on delivering great-tasting dishes at extraordinary prices. **Known for:** big portions; great value; pizza and pasta. [$] *Average main: 210* ✉ *Chaolay 3/1, Cha-am* ☎ *87/189–3864* 🌐 *www.didine.chaam.com* 🕒 *No lunch.*

Hotels

Regent Cha-am
$$ | **RESORT** | Taking a swim couldn't be easier than at this resort with its impressive two pools amid dozens of bungalows facing the beach. **Pros:** solid food options; pretty layout; fun nightlife. **Cons:** remote location; unpredictable availability; lack of air-conditioning. [$] *Rooms from: B2,900* ✉ *849/21 Cha-am Beach, Cha-am* ☎ *032/451240* 🌐 *www.regent-chaam.com* 🛏 *660 rooms* 🍴 *Free Breakfast.*

SO Sofitel Hua Hin
$$ | **RESORT** | The resort, formerly the Hotel De La Paix, has preserved the design flair that characterized its previous guise while adding other flamboyant touches that enhance the property's

strong air of fabulousity, a trait under-scored by regular DJ parties on the beach. **Pros:** showpiece spa; bespoke beach cocktails; whimsical touches abound. **Cons:** a long way from the action; too flamboyant for some; not great for families. $ *Rooms from: 3,000* ✉ *115 Moo 7 Tambol Bangkao, Cha-am* ☎ *032/709555* ⊕ *www.accorhotels.com* ❢⃝*No Meals* ↪ *77 rooms.*

Hua Hin

26 km (16 miles) from Cha-am, 189 km (118 miles) south of Bangkok.

The golden sands near the small seaside city of Hua Hin have long attracted Bangkok's rich and famous. The most renowned advocates of the destination are members of Thailand's royal family. King Bhumibol Adulyadej, the country's beloved former monarch, used Klai Kang-wol Palace north of Hua Hin town as his primary summer residence. The palace was completed in 1928 by King Rama VII, who gave it the name Klai Kangwol, which means "Far From Worries."

Hua Hin is a year-round destination. Weekends and Thai public holidays are times to avoid, when the Bangkok set floods the city—prices rise and the streets become noticeably busier.

GETTING HERE AND AROUND
The bus is the most convenient way to get here from Bangkok. Buses depart hourly from the Southern Bus Terminal; the trip takes three hours and costs about B175. Minivans (B200) head here from Bangkok's Victory Monument and are faster than buses, though some operators try to squeeze in too many passengers. Train is a good option for those who don't mind a slower journey. Trains depart Bangkok at 8:05 and 9:20 am, then roughly every hour from 1:00 pm to 7:30 pm, and again at 10:50. The journey typically takes between four and five hours.

BUS CONTACT Hua Hin. ✉ *1991/20 Phet Kasem Rd., Hua Hin.*

SAFETY AND PRECAUTIONS
Hua Hin has witnessed an expat boom in recent years, and along with high-rise condos has come an inevitable influx of less desirable elements. Pickpockets sometimes operate in town, and some hotel-room theft has occurred. These incidents are few and far between, however.

Overall the town is safe, as you would expect for a place that hosts Thai royalty, and the police are in full evidence day and night. Always engage a registered tuk-tuk driver (easy to spot because they will display their credentials) if you are going some distance.

 Sights

Chatchai Street Market
MARKET | This long-established market is a favorite with locals and tourists. Residents come during the day to purchase meats, seafood, and produce; after 5 pm you'll find everything from jewelry and clothing to toys and artworks. The evening market also has interesting eats, including Thai *kanom* (sweets), exotic fruits, barbecued meats, and traditional Thai dishes. ✉ *Dechanuchit St., Hua Hin.*

Khao Sam Roi Yod National Park
NATIONAL PARK | You'll pass rice fields, sugar palms, pineapple plantations, and crab farms as you make your way to this park south of Hua Hin, the gloriously named "300 Peaks." It has two main trails and is a great place to spot wildlife, especially monitor lizards and barking deer. With a little luck you might even see the adorable dusky langur, a monkey known for the white circles around its eyes. About a kilometer (½ mile) from the park's headquarters is Khao Daeng Hill, which is worth a hike up to the viewpoint, especially at sunrise. Another 16 km (10 miles) from the headquarters is Haad Laem Sala, a white-sand beach. Near the beach is Phraya Nakhon Cave,

once visited by King Rama V. The cave has an opening in its roof where sunlight shines through for a beautiful effect. If you don't have a car or haven't hired one, you'll have to take a bus to Pranburi, which is a 30-kilometer journey from Hua Hin. From here you take a songthaew to the park. ✉ *Hua Hin* ✣ *About 63 km (39 miles) south of Hua Hin* ☎ *32/821568* 🌐 *www.dnp.go.th* 🎫 *B200.*

Beaches

Hua Hin Beach

BEACH | Hua Hin's namesake beach is the nicest of those along this part of the coast, but it's also the most popular. Though not as stunning as other Thai beaches, it's a wide, 7-km-long (4½-mile-long) boulevard of golden sand. Vendors hawk food and drink nonstop, but you can escape this parade by booking a relaxing beach massage or taking a horseback ride to less populated areas. Water sports can be arranged at various points. It can get rough and the sea isn't clear, but you can definitely swim here. **Amenities:** food and drink; water sports. **Best for:** walking. ✉ *Hua Hin* ✣ *Off Petchkasem Rd.*

Restaurants

★ Koti

$$ | **SEAFOOD** | A longtime local favorite for Thai-style seafood, Koti has a no-nonsense decor and a packed dining room that attests to the flavor of dishes like *hor mok talay* (steamed seafood curry). The large menu includes such crowd-pleasers as fried fish with garlic and pepper. **Known for:** open kitchen; prime night market location; bustling atmosphere. [$] *Average main: B200* ✉ *61/1 Dechanuchit Rd., Hua Hin* ☎ *32/511252.*

★ Ogen

$$$ | **MIDDLE EASTERN** | This Israeli-run joint brings a mouthwatering taste of the Levant to Thailand's most venerable beach enclave. While the smoky aroma of meat, fish, and kebabs grilling over charcoal make this a heaven for carnivores, vegans are equally well-fed with a selection of salads, dips, and righteous falafel and hummus plates. **Known for:** attentive, friendly service; generous portions; both vegetarian- and vegan-friendly. [$] *Average main: 350* ✉ *250/131 Petchkasem Rd., Soi 94, Hua Hin* ✣ *Opposite Hotel Narawan* ☎ *092/260–0376* 🌐 *www.facebook.com/OgenHuaHin.restaurant/.*

Orchids Restaurant

$$ | **FRENCH FUSION** | The chefs at this Thai-French restaurant acknowledge its Asian influences while relying mainly on French technique. Prawns might come, for instance, Thai-style in a curry with fresh coriander in coconut milk or with echoes of France in a vermouth sauce. **Known for:** understated decor with traditional Thai flourishes; locally grown organic vegetables; steak and seafood. [$] *Average main: B250* ✉ *Fulay Hotel, 110/1 Naresdamri Rd., Hua Hin* ☎ *032/513670* 🌐 *www.fulayhuahin.com.*

Saeng Thai

$$ | **SEAFOOD** | Popular with Thais (always a good sign), Saeng Thai serves everything from grilled prawns with bean noodles to fried grouper with chili and tamarind juice. Now in a new larger location that's a step up from its original ramshackle setting. **Known for:** private air-conditioned rooms; eclectic seafood dishes; huge prawns. [$] *Average main: B250* ✉ *8/3 Naebkehardt Rd., Hua Hin* ☎ *032/530343.*

Hotels

Anantara Hua Hin Resort

$$ | **RESORT** | Surrounded by a 10-foot-tall terra-cotta wall, this luxurious beach resort looks like an ancient Thai village. **Pros:** Thai sense of place; inspiring setting; many activities. **Cons:** expensive rates; verges on stuffy; service can be inconsistent. [$] *Rooms from: B4,000* ✉ *43/1 Phetkasem Beach Rd., Hua Hin*

☎ *032/520250* 🌐 *www.anantara.com* 🍴 *Free Breakfast* 🛏 *187 rooms.*

Blue Lotus
$$$ | **RESORT** | Formerly an Evason property, this boutique resort is located on a quiet beach in Pranburi, about 20 minutes south of Hua Hin. It offers newly renovated guest rooms and pool villas offering light designs to create a natural ambience. **Pros:** great beachside pool; lots of activities; classy and comfortable accommodations. **Cons:** too quiet for some; out of the way location; not-so-great beach. [$] *Rooms from: B4500* ✉ *9/22 Moo 5 Paknampran, Pran Buri* ☎ *032/632111* 🌐 *www.bluelotushuahin.com* 🍴 *Free Breakfast* 🛏 *64 rooms.*

★ **Centara Grand Beach Resort and Villas**
$$ | **HOTEL** | Even if you don't stay at this local landmark, its old-world charm makes it worth a visit. **Pros:** fantastic ocean views on the second floor; tricked-out topiaries; cool atmosphere. **Cons:** can be too quiet for some; pricey; service is slipping a little. [$] *Rooms from: B3500* ✉ *1 Damnernkasem Rd., Hua Hin* ☎ *032/512021* 🌐 *www.centarahotelsresorts.com* 🛏 *251 rooms* 🍴 *No Meals.*

★ **Chiva-Som**
$$$$ | **HOTEL** | One of the best spa resorts in the region—and possibly the world—Chiva-Som has tasteful and comfortable rooms accented with natural woods. **Pros:** unique spa program; great variety of activities and services; high level of service. **Cons:** three-night minimum; expensive rates; not for partiers. [$] *Rooms from: B29000* ✉ *73/4 Petchkasem Rd.,* ☎ *032/536536* 🌐 *www.chivasom.com* 🛏 *57 rooms* 🍴 *No Meals.*

Fulay Guesthouse
$ | **B&B/INN** | On a pier that juts out over the water, this guesthouse is unlike any other in Hua Hin. The Cape Cod–blue planks of the pier match the color of the trim around the whitewashed walls. **Pros:** sounds of the sea everywhere; hard to beat the price; cool location. **Cons:** some rooms lack air-conditioning; questionable decor; thin walls. [$] *Rooms from: B900* ✉ *110/1 Naresdamri Rd., Hua Hin* ☎ *032/513145* 🌐 *www.fulayhuahin.net* 🛏 *20 rooms* 🍴 *Free Breakfast.*

Hilton Hua Hin Resort and Spa
$$$ | **HOTEL** | In the liveliest part of town, the Hilton is perfect for fun-and-sun enthusiasts who want to be close to the action. **Pros:** high-tech touches; central location; rooms with great views. **Cons:** too much foot traffic; narrow road leading to the hotel; slightly generic decor. [$] *Rooms from: B4200* ✉ *33 Naresdamri Rd., Hua Hin* ☎ *032/538999* 🌐 *www.hilton.com* 🛏 *296 rooms* 🍴 *Free Breakfast.*

Hua Hin Marriott Resort & Spa
$$$ | **RESORT** | **FAMILY** | A massive lobby area makes a striking first impression while guest rooms are as opulent as one might expect, with many offering direct access to a pool that loops around the verdant tropical grounds and joins with the bigger, lagoon-style, family pool. **Pros:** fantastic pool; lively feel when busy; kid's club great for families. **Cons:** breakfast buffet can be crowded; rooms a little small; lots of kids around. [$] *Rooms from: 4,500* ✉ *107/1 Petchkasem Rd., Hua Hin* ☎ *032/904666* 🌐 *www.marriott.com* 🍴 *No Meals* 🛏 *322 rooms.*

★ **InterContinental Hua Hin Resort**
$$ | **RESORT** | **FAMILY** | This stunning resort packs a lot into its relatively demure dimensions. **Pros:** on a particularly nice stretch of beach; top-notch food and beverage outlets; elevated standards for great value. **Cons:** service can be slightly confused; one wing (beachside) is superior to the other; small parking area. [$] *Rooms from: 3,857* ✉ *33/33 Petchkasem Rd., Hua Hin* ☎ *032/616999* 🌐 *www.ihg.com* 🍴 *No Meals* 🛏 *159 rooms.*

Movenpick Asara Resort & Spa
$$$ | **RESORT** | There's a real sense of place at this tropical retreat, which eschews

contemporary decor for an old-world Southeast Asian feel that maximizes water features, lush foliage, and Thai-style design. **Pros:** lush tropical grounds; great pools; daily chocolate buffet at 3 pm. **Cons:** breakfast selection just adequate; not much around the resort; villas could use a little more design flair. [$] *Rooms from: 4,000* ✉ *53 Hua Hin 5 Alley, Hua Hin* ☎ *032/520–777* 🌐 *www.movenpick.com* 🍴 *Free Breakfast* 🛏 *96 rooms.*

Sirin Hotel

$ | HOTEL | About a block from the beach, this hotel has huge, comfortable rooms with extra-large beds and plenty of light streaming in through the wide windows. **Pros:** good value; large rooms with lots of natural light; central location. **Cons:** breakfast is a bore; rooms need some renovation; weak and lukewarm shower. [$] *Rooms from: B1500* ✉ *6/3 Damnernkasem Rd., Hua Hin* ☎ *032/511150* 🌐 *www.sirinhuahin.com* 🍴 *Free Breakfast* 🛏 *25 rooms.*

Nightlife

Hua Hin Brewing Company

BARS | Local bands energetically perform Thai and Western pop-rock music here nightly. Although this isn't a true brewpub (the beers are made in Bangkok), the selection is good, and you can try a sampler of three tasty beers. The outdoor patio offers a full multicultural dining menu and is a prime spot to people-watch. ✉ *Hilton Hua Hin Resort & Spa, 33 Naresdamri Rd., Hua Hin* ☎ *032/512888* 🌐 *www3.hilton.com.*

Activities

GOLF

Hua Hin Golf Tours

GOLF | This company can arrange play at any of the area's 10 or so courses, and no surcharge is added to the greens fee. You can rent clubs, and free transportation is provided. Packages that include accommodations are available. ✉ *2/136 Naebkehardt Rd., Hua Hin* ☎ *032/530119* 🌐 *www.huahingolf.com.*

Royal Hua Hin Golf Course

GOLF | This course, the area's oldest, sits across the tracks from the quaint wooden Hua Hin Railway Station. Though it shows its age in some spots, Royal Hua Hin has a great layout, and the setting is incomparable. There's a lounge for refreshments. ✉ *Hua Hin* ✣ *Off Prapokklao Rd.* ☎ *032/512475* 🌐 *www.santiburi.com/huahin/* 🎫 *B2,500, includes caddie* ⛳ *18 holes, 6678 yards, par 72.*

Takiab Beach

4 km (2½ miles) south of Hua Hin.

Directly to the south of Hua Hin, Khao Takiab is a good alternative for people who wish to avoid Hua Hin's busier scene. Takiab is favored by well-off Thais who prefer Takiab's exclusivity to Hua Hin's touristy atmosphere, and you can find many upscale condos and small luxury hotels here. The beach itself is wide and long, but the water is a little murky and not very suitable for swimming.

GETTING HERE AND AROUND

To get to Takiab, flag down a songthaew (B20) on Petchkasem Road in Hua Hin. You can also hire a horse and trot down the coast.

Beaches

Khao Takiab Beach

BEACH | Sunbathing is the ideal activity at Khao Takiab, especially during low tide, when the golden, sandy strand is flat and dry. Jet Skiing, banana boat rides, and other water-sports activities are available here, all the more enjoyable than in Hua Hin because the beach and water are less crowded. A granite headland also named Khao Takiab separates the beach's northern and southern sections. On the headland's northern side, there's a tall standing image of the Buddha. You can hike to the top of the hill, where you'll find a small Buddhist monastery and several restaurants with excellent views. **Amenities:** food and drink; water sports. **Best for:** walking. ✉ *Nong Kae* ✥ *South of Hua Hin Beach.*

🍴 Restaurants

Sopa Seafood

$$ | **SEAFOOD** | **FAMILY** | The Hua Hin area, including Takiab, is famed for its fresh seafood, and there are literally dozens of great places to sample its marine bounty cooked Thai-style in an array of stir-fries, soups, and spicy salads. Among these venues, Sopa gets consistently good reviews, and the very reasonable prices add to its cache among the discerning local audience. **Known for:** popular with the locals; good value for money; crabmeat with yellow curry. [$] *Average main: 250* ✉ *Soi Ta-Kiab Bay 5, Hua Hin* ☎ *081/880–7112.*

🛏 Hotels

Chom View Hotel

$$ | **HOTEL** | **FAMILY** | This serene hotel is on the beach but with easy access to the rest of Hua Hin. The accommodations range from clean and simple standard rooms to expansive sea-view duplexes. **Pros:** pleasing modern decor; family-friendly; steps away from the sea. **Cons:** unreliable Wi-Fi; can feel isolated; sad breakfast spread. [$] *Rooms from: B2300* ✉ *93 Soi Huatanon 23, Nongkae, Hua Hin* ✥ *Off Petkasem Rd.* ☎ *032/655–2925* 🌐 *www.chomviewhotel.com* 🍽 *Free Breakfast* 🛏 *134 rooms.*

Holiday Inn Resort Vana Nava Hua Hin

$$ | **HOTEL** | **FAMILY** | Families with kids will love this Holiday Inn, which is located just north of Takiab Beach on the way to Hua Hin, especially since it's attached to the Vana Nava water park, which—with its array of fun slides—counts among the best in Thailand. **Pros:** excellent kids' club; waterpark makes a giant splash; superb ocean views from rooms. **Cons:** slightly imposing architecture; not much within walking distance; breakfast buffet can get crowded. [$] *Rooms from: 3,000* ✉ *129/129 Petchkasem Rd., Nong Kae* ☎ *32/809999* 🌐 *www.ihg.com* 🍽 *No Meals* 🛏 *300 rooms.*

Chumphon

465 km (240 miles) south of Bangkok, 270 km (131 miles) south of Hua Hin.

Chumphon is regarded as the gateway to the south, primarily because trains and buses usually connect here to Bangkok to the north, to Surat Thani and Phuket to the south, and to Ranong to the southwest. Ferries to Koh Tao dock at Pak Nam at the mouth of the Chumphon River, 11 km (7 miles) southeast of town. Most of the city's boat services run a free shuttle to the docks.

GETTING HERE AND AROUND

Buses leave regularly from Bangkok's Southern Terminal. The journey takes between six and nine hours; most buses leave at night, so you'll arrive early in the morning, and tickets are between B300 and B600. Though buses are cheaper and more reliable, the *Southern Line* train from Bangkok's Hualamphong Station stops here. In Chumphon proper, tuk-tuks are a ubiquitous and easy way to get around.

SAFETY AND PRECAUTIONS

Theft sometimes occurs on overnight private buses traveling between Bangkok and Chumphon. Never leave valuables in luggage that's out of view.

Beaches

Thung Wua Laen Beach

BEACH | Small islands that make up one of the world's strangest bird sanctuaries dot the horizon of this excellent 3-km (2-mile) stretch of curving white-yellow sand. Vast flocks of swifts breed on the islands, and their nests are harvested—not without controversy—for the bird's-nest soup served in Chinese restaurants throughout Southeast Asia. It's such a lucrative business that the concessionaires patrol their properties with armed guards. But all is calm and serene on the beach, which is just north of Chumphon. To get here, catch a songthaew on the street across from the bus station. **Amenities:** food and drink. **Best for:** solitude. ☒ *Chumphon.*

Hotels

Morakot Twin

$ | **HOTEL** | Lodging options are few in Chumphon, but this centrally located hotel has comfortable rooms and provides a reasonable level of service. **Pros:** newly renovated rooms; inexpensive; centrally located. **Cons:** few amenities; some rooms lack air-conditioning; breakfast is basic. ⓢ *Rooms from: B990* ☒ *102–112 Taweesinka Rd., Chumphon* ☏ *077/502999, 086/478–6377* ⊕ *www.morakothotel.com* ⇆ *130 rooms* ❍l *Free Breakfast.*

Talay Sai

$ | **HOTEL** | **FAMILY** | Unassuming yet comfortable, this is one of the best options on Thung Wua Laen Beach. **Pros:** attractive balconies in some rooms; friendly welcome; great seafood restaurant. **Cons:** occasional noise from the beach; concrete building is not beautiful; electric wires block the sea view. ⓢ *Rooms from: 800* ☒ *543 Moo. 8 Saplee Pathiu, Chumphon* ☏ *077/622789* ⊕ *www.talaysai-hotel.com* ❍l *No Meals* ⇆ *12 rooms.*

Surat Thani

193 km (120 miles) south of Chumphon, 685 km (425 miles) south of Bangkok.

Though not particularly charismatic, Surat Thani has a few culturally interesting sights that make it a good destination for those easily bored by the beach, and the mountains and greenery of Khao Sok National Park are a few hours away by bus. There are also some good restaurants and a handsome hotel. Boats to Koh Samui leave from Donsak Pier, about 70 km west of Surat Thani (the pier is often called "Surat Thani Donsak Pier," which can be confusing).

GETTING HERE AND AROUND

Both buses and trains from Bangkok go to Surat Thani, but flying is the most efficient way to arrive. Bus trips from Bangkok's Southern Bus Terminal take about 10 hours and cost from B400 to B800. There's also an overnight train here from Bangkok's Hua Lamphong Station. Thai Air Asia, Nok Air, and Thai Lion Air often have low fares; flights take only 1 hour 15 minutes and can be as cheap as B1300.

VISITOR AND TOUR INFORMATION

CONTACT Tourism Authority of Thailand. ☒ *5 Talat Mai Rd., Surat Thani* ☏ *077/288817* ⊕ *www.tourismthailand.org.*

Sights

San Chao Night Market

MARKET | **FAMILY** | Every night the sleepy downtown turns into an electrifying street fair centered around the San Chao Night Market, which is illuminated by the lights of numerous food stalls and shop carts. The market is popular with tourists and locals, especially for the tasty seafood meals on offer. ☒ *Surat Thani* ✛ *Alley off Na Muang Rd.*

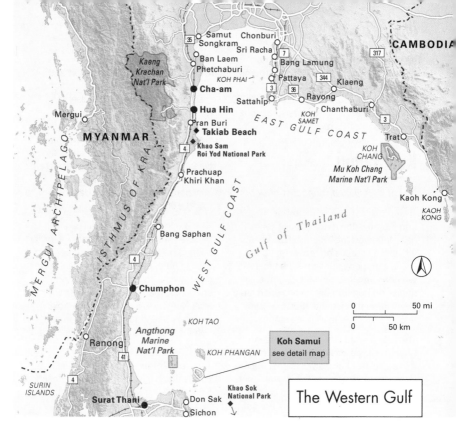

Koh Samui
see detail map

The Western Gulf

Khao Sok National Park

NATIONAL PARK | A landscape of tall mountains, lush greenery, and small streams, this 161,000-acre park contains the most beautiful forest in Thailand. The diverse and rare wildlife that thrives here includes gaurs, bantengs, sambar deer, bears, Malayan tapirs, macaques, gibbons, mouse deer, and porcupines. Khao Sok is also one of the few places to see a rafflesia, the world's largest flower, and rare bird species such as hornbills live here. Hiking, boat rides, and night safaris are some of the activities that take place in the park. Rain is frequent in Khao Sok, as the weather is influenced by monsoon winds from both the northeast and west—the best and driest time to visit is between December and April. Both the national park and some private resorts offer various types of lodging.

Only very basic accommodations can be found in the park. But there is additional private accommodation outside the park, some of it very comfortable indeed. The bus ride (B120) from the station in Surat Thani to the park takes about 2½ hours. Minivans (B200) leave from the center of town and take around 2 hours. The TAT office in Surat Thani has information about the park. ⊠ *Moo 6 Phanom, Surat Thani* ✛ *190 km west of Surat Thani* ☎ *077/395154* ⊕ *www.dnp.go.th* ⊠ *B300.*

Hotels

Wang Tai Hotel

$ | HOTEL | This modern high-rise offers everything you need for a Surat Thani stopover as you prepare for your onward journey. **Pros:** great views; handy location;

tasty food. **Cons:** far from city center; doesn't feel particularly Thai; the rooms are tatty. $ *Rooms from: B1250* ✉ *1 Talad Mai Rd., Surat Thani* ☎ *077/283020, 077/281007* ⊕ *www.wangtaisurat.com* ⇌ *230 rooms* ⚏ *Free Breakfast.*

Koh Samui

20 km (12 miles) by boat east of Don Sak.

Koh Samui is the most popular tourist destination on the Western Gulf coast, which isn't surprising, considering the island's gorgeous beaches, near-perfect weather, and sparkling blue, almost turquoise, water. Koh Samui has seen rapid development since the 1990s, and you'll encounter hotels in all price ranges.

The island is less than half the size of Phuket, so you could easily drive around it in a day. But Koh Samui is best appreciated by those who take a slower, more casual approach. Most people come for the sun and sea, so they head straight to their hotel and rarely venture beyond its beach. But it's worth exploring beyond your lodging. Every beach has its own character, and you might find the perfect one for you.

One beach many visitors find to their liking is Chawaeng. On Koh Samui's east coast, this stretch of glistening white sand is divided into two main sections—Chawaeng Yai (*yai* means "big") and Chawaeng Noi (*noi* means "little"). You'll find the greatest variety of hotels, restaurants, and bars here. Despite the crowds, Chawaeng is very laid-back. A rocky headland separates Chawaeng from Lamai Beach, whose clear water and long stretches of sand were the first location on the island to attract developers. More budget accommodations are available here than in Chawaeng, and there are some happening nightclubs.

On the west coast of Koh Samui, Na Thon is the island's primary port and the spot where ferries arrive from the mainland. It's home to the island's governmental offices, including the Tourism Authority of Thailand, and there are banks, foreign-exchange booths, travel agents, shops, restaurants, and cafés by the ferry pier. A few places rent rooms, but there's really no reason to stay here—nicer accommodations can be found a short songthaew ride away.

To the north and east of Na Thon lie a few beaches worthy of exploration. Laem Yai, 5 km (3 miles) north, has great seafood. East of here, a small headland separates two low-key communities on the northern shore, Mae Nam and Bophut Beach. Mae Nam is also the departure point for boats bound for Koh Phangan and Koh Tao *(see Side Trips from Koh Samui, below).*

Just south of the Samui's northeastern tip you'll find sandy Choengmon Beach, a good area for swimming that's not overdeveloped.

GETTING HERE AND AROUND
AIR
Bangkok Airways offers multiple daily flights from Bangkok. The hour-long flight is a bit pricier than other flights within Thailand, mainly because the airport is owned by Bangkok Airways and not, as in most cases in Thailand, by the government.

BOAT
From Surat Thani's Donsak Pier, ferries leave regularly for Koh Samui's Na Thon Pier on the west coast; the trip takes roughly an hour in a high-speed catamaran. Tour operators in Surat Thani and Koh Samui have information on the ferry schedules, or you can also just head to the pier. Expect to pay around B250 for the trip.

CAR AND TAXI

Koh Samui is a delight to explore, and it's one of the few destinations in Thailand where having a car can come in really handy. A drive along the coastal road will provide one beautiful view after another; the interior of the island is also scenic. Budget and Hertz have counters at the Koh Samui airport, and National has its counter in downtown Koh Samui. Drive Car Rental has a counter near the airport, and the company will deliver your car to you when you land. TA Car Rental is a reputable local company based on Samui.

Taxis don't always meet incoming flights at the airport in Koh Samui, but they can easily be called.

CONTACTS T A Car Rental. ⊠ *59/8 Moo 5, Tambon Bophut, Choeng Mon Beach* ☎ *077/245129.* **Drive Car Rental.** ⊠ *USM Airport, Koh Samui* ☎ *084/700–4388.*

SAFETY AND PRECAUTIONS

Samui is a safe place. Crime rarely affects visitors, but there are the odd reports of thefts from hotel rooms and late-night robberies. Take sensible precautions, though, and your risk will be minimal.

The greatest safety issue for visitors involves ones with no experience who rent motorcycles and don't wear helmets. Additionally, some roads are hazardous, and there are reckless drivers who take advantage of lax law enforcement.

VISITOR INFORMATION
CONTACTS Tourism Authority of Thailand. ⊠ *370 Moo 3, Tambon Ang Thong, Koh Samui* ☎ *077/420504* ⊕ *www.tourismthailand.org.*

 Sights

Coral Buddha
PUBLIC ART | About 4 km (2½ miles) from Lamai, at the small Chinese fishing village of Baan Hua Thanon, the road that forks inland toward Na Thon leads to the

Coral Buddha, a small temple complex built on a natural rock formation carved by years of erosion. One of Samui's most serene and least touristy spots, the Coral Buddha provides a glimpse of a more fundamental, traditional world of Buddhism less apparent at brasher, more high-profile destinations. ⊠ *Ban Hua Thanon.*

Wat Phra Yai
TEMPLE | Off the northeastern tip of Koh Samui is Koh Fan (not to be confused with Koh Fan Noi), a little island with a huge Buddha. Indeed, the statue is better known as the "big Buddha." The island is best visited at sunset, when the light off the water shows it at its best. ⊠ *Koh Samui.*

Mu Koh Angthong National Marine Park
NATIONAL PARK | This archipelago of 42 islands covers some 102 square km (40 square miles) and lies 35 km (22 miles) northwest of Koh Samui. It's around 45 minutes there by speedboat from Koh Samui. The seven main islands are Wua Talap Island (which houses the national park's headquarters), Phaluai Island, Mae Koh Island, Sam Sao Island, Hin Dap Island, Nai Phut Island, and Phai Luak Island. The islands contain limestone mountains, strangely shaped caves, emerald-green lakes and ponds. Most tourists visit on a one-day trip, which can be arranged from Koh Samui. Numerous operators offer trips. Recommended outfits include Samui Explorer. Prices vary depending on the tour (some offer kayaking around several islands, and others take you out on small speedboats for snorkeling or cave tours). The park is open year-round, although the seas can be rough and the water less clear during the monsoon season, between October and December. ⊠ *Koh Samui* ⊕ *www.dnp.go.th* 💲 *B300.*

Na Muang
WATERFALL | On the inland road to Na Thon lies the village of Baan Thurian, famous for its durian trees. A track climbs up

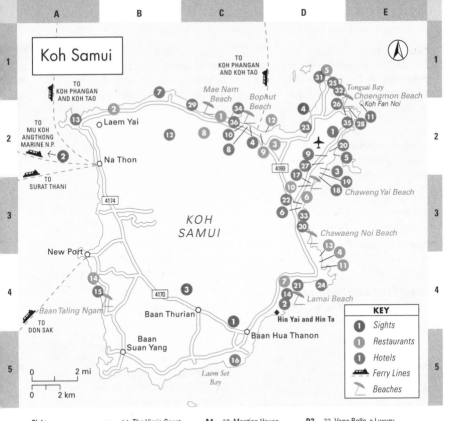

Koh Samui

KEY
- Sights
- Restaurants
- Hotels
- Ferry Lines
- Beaches

into jungle-clad hills to the island's best waterfall, Na Muang. The 105-foot falls are spectacular—especially just after the rainy season—as they tumble from a limestone cliff into a small pool. You are cooled by the spray and warmed by the sun. For a thrill, swim through the curtain of falling water; you can sit on a ledge at the back to catch your breath. ⊠ *Koh Samui.*

 Beaches

Bophut Beach

BEACH | Quaint and romantic Bophut has a devoted following of return visitors who enjoy its quiet vibe. This north-shore beach is narrow, but more than wide enough for sunbathing. The water is like glass, making it good for swimming, though it's deep enough to be unsuitable for young children. Bophut has a bit of nightlife. Central Bophut, known to everyone as Fisherman's Village, has a beachside strip of old houses that have been converted into restaurants, bars, and boutiques. **Amenities:** food and drink. **Best for:** swimming. ⊠ *Tambon Bophut.*

Chawaeng Noi Beach

BEACH | The smaller and less developed of the east-coast beaches adjoining Chawaeng town, Chawaeng Noi lacks the charms and spectacular golden curve of its bigger brother, Chawaeng Yai. It's quieter and more relaxed, though, and there are nearby resorts where you can grab a snack. **Amenities:** food and drink; water sports. **Best for:** solitude. ⊠ *Chaweng Noi Beach.*

Chawaeng Yai Beach

BEACH | Travelers in search of sun and fun flock here, especially during high season. The northern half of this beautiful east-coast beach is a hit with backpackers because it's lined with budget lodgings. The southern half, more popular with the package tourists, has more in the way of high-end resorts. Chawaeng Yai is a great swimming beach. The fine sand is brilliant white, and the waters are clear and usually calm. During the day, tourists pack in and the water buzzes with Jet Skis and banana boats. At night the streets come alive as shops, bars, and restaurants vie for your vacation allowance. **Amenities:** food and drink; water sports. **Best for:** swimming. ⊠ *Chaweng Noi Beach.*

Choengmon Beach

BEACH | A mellow spot on Samui's northeastern coast, this beach is blessed with crystal-clear water. Choengmon was once pitched as the island's next big thing. There's hardly a boom, but a few guesthouses, a handful of luxury resorts, and some restaurants are scattered along the wide shore. The sand is firm and strewn with pebbles and shells, but the beach is adequate for sunbathing. A few of its food options are right on the beach. **Amenities:** food and drink; water sports. **Best for:** swimming. ⊠ *Choeng Mon Beach.*

Lamai Beach

BEACH | Popular Lamai lacks the glistening white sand of Chawaeng Beach, but its water is clear and the beach is ideal for swimming. The steeply shelved shoreline might be too much for kids, though. Numerous bars and restaurants which line the beach underscore that Lamai has a strong nightlife slant. Almost every visitor to Koh Samui makes a pilgrimage to the point marking the southern end of Lamai Beach to see two rocks, named *Hin Yai* (Grandmother Rock) and *Hin Ta* (Grandfather Rock). Erosion has shaped the rocks to resemble weathered and wrinkled private parts. It's nature at its most whimsical. Laem Set Bay, a small rocky cape on the southeastern tip of the island, is just south of Lamai. It's a good 3 km (2 miles) off the main road, so it's hard to reach without your own car. Head here to escape the hustle and bustle of the tourist areas. **Amenities:** food and drink; water sports. **Best for:** partiers; swimming. ⊠ *Ban Lamai.*

Koh Samui's accessibility and beautiful beaches make it a popular destination year-round.

Mae Nam Beach

BEACH | The long, curving beach at Mae Nam has coarse, golden sand shaded by tall coconut trees. It's one of the island's more unspoiled beaches—inexpensive guesthouses and a few luxurious resorts share the 5-km (3-mile) strand. Quiet both day and night, this north-shore beach has little nightlife and only a scattering of restaurants. The shallow waters are suitable for swimming, and several water-sports companies operate in the area. **Amenities:** food and drink; water sports. **Best for:** swimming. ✉ *Mae Nam Beach.*

🍴 Restaurants

CHAWAENG

The Hungry Wolf

$$ | **EUROPEAN** | A pair of fine-dining vets from Poland are behind this cutting-edge café, which leans heavily on crowd-pleasing Western food made with quality ingredients. They were at first known for their beef-tongue burgers, which were a tough sell to a casual beach crowd, but a gourmet Wagyu option is now the attention-grabber. **Known for:** wide vegan menu; homemade pizza, bread, and pasta; high-end techniques without the pretense. [$] *Average main: B300* ✉ *17/46 Moo 3, Koh Samui* ☎ *094/408–2243* 🌐 *thehungrywolf.xyz.*

The Page

$$$$ | **THAI** | Stick to the fun and interesting cocktails at the Library's popular restaurant—it claims to make 101 different kinds—and after a few sips you'll feel as hip as the surroundings. The menu is mostly Thai, featuring contemporary takes on traditional favorites like prawns with garlic and pepper, and sea bass with chili and basil. **Known for:** Wagyu beef; smartly designed surroundings; "tea by the sea" afternoon service. [$] *Average main: B500* ✉ *14/1 Moo 2, Chaweng Noi Beach* ☎ *077/422767* 🌐 *www.thelibrarysamui.com/the-page/.*

Tarua Samui Seafood

$$$ | **SEAFOOD** | The view is definitely what you come here for—high up on a mountain, the restaurant juts out above

the beach and the turquoise ocean—but the food is also memorable. Check the seafood tank as you walk in; you might spy something you can't resist. **Known for:** plump grilled prawns with garlic or curry; seafood you hand-select; Thai-Chinese techniques. $ Average main: B350 ⊠ 210/9 Moo 4, Chaweng Noi Beach ☎ 077/960635, 077/448495.

Vikasa Life Cafe
$$ | VEGETARIAN | Organic vegetables take center stage at this collaboration between a couple of acclaimed chefs from Paris and Berlin. Begin your day with a freshly packed jar of chia pudding, a superfood bowl, or a chili-spiked Thai Greens smoothie, and come back later for an encyclopedic array of clean eats. **Known for:** LA-caliber light dishes; dawn-to-dusk deliciousness; rarely seen raw food. $ Average main: B300 ⊠ 211 Bontji Moo 4, Koh Samui ☎ 077/422232 ⊕ www.vikasayoga.com/the-place/life-cafe/.

LAMAI
The Cliff
$$$$ | MEDITERRANEAN | Halfway along the road from Chawaeng to Lamai, the Cliff perches on a big boulder overlooking the sea. You can have lunch or dinner inside a spartan dining room or out on a scenic terrace. **Known for:** locally caught seafood; reservation-worthy views; cooler-than-thou cocktails and solid wine selection. $ Average main: B500 ⊠ 124/2 Samui Ring Rd., Lamai Beach ☎ 099/434–1529 ⊕ www.thecliffsamui.com.

Kob Thai Restaurant
$$ | THAI | Everything on the menu at this well-run Lamai restaurant is excellent. The venue doesn't reinvent the wheel. **Known for:** authentic Thai food; prideful service; a serene tropical setting. $ Average main: B200 ⊠ 101/18 Moo 3, Koh Samui ☎ 082/534–9325 ⊕ www.facebook.com/KobThaiRestaurant.

BAAN TALING NGAM
The Virgin Coast
$$$ | SEAFOOD | Top-notch Thai cuisine and a relaxing tropical setting await guests at this beachfront restaurant, which offers laid-back charm, superlative service, and high-quality cooking. **Known for:** friendly, attentive staff; killer ocean views; locally sourced ingredients. $ Average main: B350 ⊠ Ban Taling Ngam ☎ 089/499–6334 ⊕ www.facebook.com/The-Virgin-Coast-Samui-415348348619031/.

MAE NAM
Angela's at Moonhut
$ | CAFÉ | This beachfront diner serves salads and sandwiches, both traditional and inventive. Among the latter, the "Hot Bandana" is a tasty vegetarian sandwich baked inside a bread bowl and served wrapped in a bandana. **Known for:** a ridiculous amount of bread and baked goods; British standards like bangers and mash; imported meat and cheese. $ Average main: B100 ⊠ Moon Hut Bungalows, 67/2 Moo1 Maenam, Mae Nam Beach ☎ 077/427396 ⊕ www.facebook.com/AngelasatMoonhut/.

★ Bang Po Seafood
$$ | SEAFOOD | Mere feet from lapping waves, this perennial favorite serves the freshest seafood at reasonable prices. The purple baby-octopus soup and the sour curry with local turmeric and fish are two great options. **Known for:** a sea urchin salad that doesn't break the bank; sandy beach setting; truly authentic tom yum. $ Average main: B200 ⊠ 56/4 Moo 6, Mae Nam Beach ☎ 077/420010.

Ko Seng
$$ | SEAFOOD | This two-story seafood restaurant has been feeding Mae Nam residents for decades. The menu changes daily depending on the day's catch. **Known for:** house-grown organic vegetables; low prices; rotating catch-of-the-day specials. $ Average main: B250 ⊠ 95 Soi Kohseng, Mae Nam Beach

☎ *089/874–3516* 🌐 *www.facebook.com/kosengsamui/.*

BOPHUT

Chez Francois

$$$$ | FRENCH | Chef/owner Francois Porte holds fort at this bijou fine dining option in Bophut. While the prices seem lofty by Samui standards, they are actually very reasonable considering the caliber of the culinary offerings. **Known for:** divine desserts; fine French cuisine; intimate atmosphere. [$] *Average main: 760* ✉ *33/2 Moo 1, Fisherman's Village, Tambon Bophut* ☎ *096/071–1800* 🌐 *www.chez-francoissamui.com* 🕒 *Closed Sun. and Mon. No lunch.*

★ 2 Fishes

$$$$ | ITALIAN | One of the most creative restaurants on Samui fuses culinary sophistication with a welcoming, casual atmosphere in keeping with its surroundings. Chefs perform alchemy from the venue's open-counter kitchen, providing dishes such as linguine with prawns, clams, mussels, and chilies in a white wine and tomato sauce; and king prawns with garlic, chili, and lemon. **Known for:** culinary sophistication; open kitchen is a nice touch; excellent fish of the day. [$] *Average main: 500* ✉ *79/5 Moo 1, Fisherman's Village, Tambon Bophut* ☎ *099/281–9973* 🌐 *www.2fishessamui.com* 🕒 *Closed Mon. No lunch.*

CHOENGMON

Dining on the Rocks

$$$$ | INTERNATIONAL | Arranged on several terraces, the tables here all have panoramic sea views; arrive before sunset to get the full effect. In addition to à la carte entrées and apps like iced tom yum gazpacho with oysters, this Six Senses' staple offers a wide range of revelatory set menus, including one for vegetarians. **Known for:** the island's most ambitious tasting menus; thoughtful vegan and vegetarian options; progressive wine pairings. [$] *Average main: B700* ✉ *Six Senses Samui, 9/10 Moo 5, Baan Plai Laem, Tambon Bophut* ☎ *077/245678* 🌐 *www.sixsenses.com/resorts/samui/dining.*

Long Dtai

$$$$ | THAI | Australian chef David Thompson is a legend of Thai cuisine, having helped raise its profile internationally at Nahm, his legendary venture in Bangkok. This, his debut on Koh Samui, is a more casual affair. **Known for:** very reasonable prices; a southern sojurn by a master of Thai cuisine; uncompromising spicy flavors. [$] *Average main: 620* ✉ *Cape Fahn Hotel, 24/269 Moo 5, Choeng Mon Beach* ☎ *077/602–3012* 🌐 *www.longdtai.com* 🕒 *Closed Tues. and Wed.*

Hotels

CHAWAENG

Amari Koh Samui

$$$ | RESORT | FAMILY | This luxurious resort faces a beach where the water's too shallow for swimming—which can be an advantage, as it keeps the crowds away. **Pros:** on the beach; local touches to the rooms; lovely views. **Cons:** overrun with raucous families; inconsistent service; garden wing can't compete with the beach one. [$] *Rooms from: B4400* ✉ *14/3 Chaweng Beach, Chaweng Noi Beach* ☎ *077/300–3069, 077/915250* 🌐 *www.amari.com/koh-samui/* 🛏 *187 rooms* 🍴 *Free Breakfast.*

Anantara Lawana Koh Samui Resort

$$$ | RESORT | FAMILY | Hidden away at the quiet northern end of Chaweng, this refuge stands apart while remaining close to the action. **Pros:** gorgeous pool villas; convenient location, yet removed from the crowds; four-poster beds provide added class. **Cons:** not the most extensive breakfast; beach can be rocky at low tide; some might find it too quiet. [$] *Rooms from: 6,000* ✉ *92/1 Moo 2, Bophut, North Chaweng Beach* ☎ *077/960333* 🌐 *www.anantara.com* 🍴 *Free Breakfast* 🛏 *122 rooms.*

Baan Talay Resort

$$ | **RESORT** | **FAMILY** | Bungalows huddled around a shimmering pool are the focal point at Baan Talay, but the real reasons to stay here are the few rooms just a stone's throw from the beach. **Pros:** clean and comfortable rooms; close to beach; quieter side of Chaweng. **Cons:** noise from nearby road; outdated decor; forgettable breakfast. [$] *Rooms from: B2500* ✉ *17/36 Moo 3 Chawaeng Beach Rd., Chaweng Noi Beach* ☎ *077/413555* 🌐 *www.baantalay.com* 🛏 *54 rooms* 🍴 *Free Breakfast.*

The Briza

$$ | **RESORT** | **FAMILY** | Rather than attempt yet another iteration of Thai design, this resort opted for what can best be described as a fusion of Indian and Chinese styles for its villas. **Pros:** deck chairs double as massage beds; unique style; luxurious, secluded, and exclusive. **Cons:** slightly jumbled architectural ethos; villa terraces on the small side; breakfast is a bore. [$] *Rooms from: B2000* ✉ *173/22 Moo 2, Chawaeng Beach, Koh Samui* ☎ *077/231997* 🌐 *www.thebriza.com* 🛏 *57 villas* 🍴 *Free Breakfast.*

The Library

$$$ | **RESORT** | This place is worth a visit for its amusingly hip decor alone; check out the white figures reading books on the lawn, inviting you to lounge as well. **Pros:** cool, young crowd; very stylish; 20 private spaces. **Cons:** not suited to families; not ideal if you're looking for quiet; some of the fusion food here shouldn't have been fused. [$] *Rooms from: B4500* ✉ *14/1 Moo 2 Chawaeng Beach, Chaweng Noi Beach* ☎ *077/422767* 🌐 *www.thelibrary.co.th* 🛏 *26 rooms* 🍴 *Free Breakfast.*

Montien House

$$ | **RESORT** | **FAMILY** | Two rows of charming bungalows line the path leading to the beach at this comfortable little resort. **Pros:** close to Chaweng without the chaos; cute rooms; attentive staff and management. **Cons:** lacks creature comforts; not much pizzazz; average food. [$] *Rooms from: B2500* ✉ *5 Moo 2, Chaweng Noi Beach* ☎ *077/422169* 🌐 *www.montienhouse.com* 🛏 *60 rooms* 🍴 *Free Breakfast.*

Muang Samui Spa Resort

$$$ | **RESORT** | At this tranquil resort, a meandering garden path with small bridges and stepping-stones crosses a flowing, fish-filled stream. **Pros:** Thai cooking classes; well-kept grounds; different sense of style. **Cons:** expensive; feels sprawling; some rooms in need of renovation. [$] *Rooms from: B6000* ✉ *13/1 Moo 2, Chaweng Noi Beach* ☎ *077/429700* 🌐 *www.muangsamui.com* 🛏 *53 suites* 🍴 *Free Breakfast.*

Nora Beach Resort and Spa

$$ | **RESORT** | A big plus of this hotel is that about two dozen rooms have sea views and many overlook the pool, so you're almost guaranteed an aquatic perspective. **Pros:** brisk Wi-Fi; comfortable surroundings; spacious bathrooms. **Cons:** not cheap; unexciting furnishings; lack of sun beds. [$] *Rooms from: B2000* ✉ *222 Moo 2 Chawaeng Beach, North Chaweng Beach* ☎ *077/413999, 077/429400* 🌐 *www.norabeachresort.com* 🛏 *113 rooms* 🍴 *Free Breakfast.*

Poppies

$$$ | **RESORT** | Dozens of cheerful employees are on hand to attend to your every need at this romantic beachfront resort on the quiet southern end of Chawaeng Beach. **Pros:** restaurant is as remarkable as the resort itself; snappy service; immediate area not too crazy. **Cons:** not cheap; a little staid; long walk from busiest stretch of Chaweng Beach. [$] *Rooms from: B4,500* ✉ *28/1 Moo 3, South Chaweng Beach* ☎ *077/422419* 🌐 *www.poppiessamui.com* 🍴 *Free Breakfast* 🛏 *24 cottages.*

Sala Samui Chaweng Beach

$$ | **RESORT** | Thai hospitality brand Sala has forged a reputation for creating properties bursting with both substance and

style, and this, the firm's second opening on Koh Samui, showcases its trademark flair. **Pros:** superb spa showcasing Thai beauty products; great tropical cocktails to tickle your palate; crisp, contemporary design. **Cons:** punchy prices for drinks; garden block not as desirable as beachfront; beachfront pool not great for laps. [$] *Rooms from: 3,000* ✉ *99/10 Moo 2, Chaweng Beach, Central Chaweng* ☎ *077/905888* 🌐 *www.salahospitality.com* 🍴 *Free Breakfast* 🛏 *82 rooms.*

Sheraton Samui Resort

$$$ | **RESORT** | A landscaped terrace leads down to a private beach at this resort on the less crowded southern end of Chawaeng Noi. If you want to do more than catch rays, this is the place for you—the Sheraton offers every kind of beach activity imaginable. **Pros:** lots of beach activities; great views from pool terrace; good beachside restaurant. **Cons:** downhill walk to beach; may be too quiet for some people; no elevator. [$] *Rooms from: B4500* ✉ *86 Moo 3, Chawaeng Noi Beach, Chaweng Noi Beach* ☎ *077/422020* 🌐 *www.sheratonsamui.com* 🛏 *141 rooms* 🍴 *Free Breakfast.*

Vana Belle, a Luxury Collection Resort, Koh Samui

$$$$ | **RESORT** | Spend your days flitting between a spacious beach villa, a magical pool area (which even has its own secluded waterfall), and the beach itself with its crystal blue waters. **Pros:** wonderful pool area; gracious Thai service at its best; premium Panpuri toiletries. **Cons:** some misses on the breakfast menu; not much within walking distance; not much atmosphere at restaurant. [$] *Rooms from: 8,000* ✉ *9/99 Moo 3, Chaweng Noi Beach, Chaweng Noi Beach* ☎ *077/915555* 🌐 *www.marriott.com* 🍴 *Free Breakfast* 🛏 *79 rooms.*

LAMAI

Aloha Resort

$$ | **RESORT** | **FAMILY** | All the rooms at this oceanfront resort have private terraces or balconies that face in the general direction of the beach. **Pros:** family-friendly; can accommodate larger groups; reasonable price. **Cons:** outdated decor; some rooms defiitely not as nice; small beach. [$] *Rooms from: B3,000* ✉ *128 Moo 3 Lamai Beach, Ban Lamai* ☎ *077/424014* 🌐 *www.alohasamui.com* 🛏 *74 rooms* 🍴 *Free Breakfast.*

The Hive

$$ | **RESORT** | Formerly the Lamai Wanta, this resort has emerged refreshed and renovated under its new name. **Pros:** well-kept grounds; Insta-worthy pool; beautiful beach. **Cons:** breakfast gets boring quick; blah decor; pesky geckos. [$] *Rooms from: B2600* ✉ *124/264 Moo 3, T. Maret Lamai Beach, Ban Lamai* ☎ *077/424550* 🌐 *www.lamaiwanta.com* 🛏 *50 rooms* 🍴 *Free Breakfast.*

Kamalaya Koh Samui

$$$ | **RESORT** | In our stressful world respite is often necessary, and this well-regarded wellness and spa resort on the paradise island of Koh Samui provides it. **Pros:** excellent fitness facilities; peaceful environment; healthy, tasty cuisine. **Cons:** kids aren't welcome; no TVs; too quiet for some. [$] *Rooms from: 4,300* ✉ *102/9 Laem-Set Rd., Laem Set* ☎ *077/429800* 🌐 *www.kamalaya.com* 🍴 *No Meals* 🛏 *75 rooms.*

Pavilion

$$ | **RESORT** | This amiable place offers a little respite from the downtown hustle and bustle. **Pros:** convenient beach location without the chaos; near reputable bars and restaurants; hot tubs in some rooms. **Cons:** not the most modern hotel; can get expensive; common areas aren't as nice as the rooms. [$] *Rooms from: B3125* ✉ *124/24 Lamai Beach, Ban Lamai* ☎ *077/424030* 🌐 *www.pavilionsamui.com* 🛏 *70 rooms* 🍴 *Free Breakfast.*

Renaissance Koh Samui Resort & Spa

$$$ | **RESORT** | At the far northern end of Lamai, the Renaissance sits on its own secluded beach—two small beaches to

be exact. **Pros:** the epitome of a private getaway; sprawling grounds; high-end feel. **Cons:** pricey; isolated location; road to hotel is rough. [$] *Rooms from: B4,700* ✉ *208/1 Moo 4, T. Maret, Lamai Beach* ☎ *077/429300* 🌐 *www.marriott.com* 🍴 *Free Breakfast* 🛏 *78 rooms.*

BAAN TALING NGAM

InterContinental Koh Samui Resort
$$$ | **RESORT** | Most of the rooms at this outstanding resort are built into a 200-foot cliff, and the beachside villas are even more amazing. **Pros:** perfect jumping-off point for Marine Park; beautiful views; plenty of activities. **Cons:** somewhat isolated; can't lounge on narrow beach; not quite five-star service. [$] *Rooms from: B5000* ✉ *295 Moo 3 Taling Ngam Beach, Ban Taling Ngam* ☎ *02/656–0400* 🌐 *samui.intercontinental.com* 🛏 *70 rooms* 🍴 *Free Breakfast.*

MAE NAM AND LAEM YAI

Belmond Napasai
$$$ | **RESORT** | If you book a beachfront room here you can enjoy views of both the sky *and* sea from your outdoor terrace, room, or bathtub. **Pros:** stable Wi-Fi speed; great views; superb staff. **Cons:** some rooms starting to show their age; pricey; food and drinks not as good as some other resorts. [$] *Rooms from: B5500* ✉ *65/10 Baan Tai, Mae Nam Beach* ☎ *077/429200* 🌐 *www.belmond.com* 🛏 *69 rooms* 🍴 *Free Breakfast.*

The Florist Resort
$$ | **RESORT** | This guesthouse is tiny but in a cute and cozy way. **Pros:** seafront room has perfect view of Koh Phangan; good bang for your buck; easy beach access. **Cons:** staff not so attentive; lacks the comfort of some megachains; old wing has aging furniture and slightly musty smell. [$] *Rooms from: B2600* ✉ *190 Moo 1, Tambon Maenam, Mae Nam Beach* ☎ *086/313–7725* 🌐 *www.floristresort.com* 🛏 *32 rooms* 🍴 *Free Breakfast.*

★ **Four Seasons Koh Samui**
$$$$ | **RESORT** | This is easily one of the most spectacular hotels in the world. **Pros:** excellent food on-site; ultimate luxury and relaxation; cool room design. **Cons:** golf carts necessary to get around; rates might break the bank; can feel isolated. [$] *Rooms from: B16000* ✉ *219 Moo 5, Angthong, Laem Yai* ☎ *077/243000* 🌐 *www.fourseasons.com* 🛏 *74 villas* 🍴 *No Meals.*

★ **Santiburi Resort and Spa**
$$$$ | **RESORT** | The villas on this beachfront estate have the feel of a billionaire's holiday hideaway; accordingly, this is one of the most expensive lodgings on the island. **Pros:** fantastic Thai food; on a private beach; elegant rooms. **Cons:** decor beginning to look dated; not ideal for families; some villas are more private than others. [$] *Rooms from: B23500* ✉ *12/12 Samui Ring Rd., Mae Nam Beach* ☎ *077/425031* 🌐 *www.santiburis-amui.com* 🛏 *71 suites* 🍴 *Free Breakfast.*

W Retreat Koh Samui
$$$$ | **RESORT** | Oozing flashy flair, the W Retreat Koh Samui is most definitely a place to see and be seen. **Pros:** pool villas are real tropical party pads; free ice cream helps the cooling process; Woo Bar offers the ultimate in IG opportunities. **Cons:** perhaps tries too hard; not much around the resort; ubiquitous dance beats not for everyone. [$] *Rooms from: 12,000* ✉ *4/1 Moo1, Tambol Maenam, Mae Nam Beach* ☎ *077/915999* 🌐 *www.marriott.com* 🍴 *Free Breakfast* 🛏 *74 rooms.*

BOPHUT

Anantara Bophut Resort and Spa
$$$ | **RESORT** | **FAMILY** | Anantara captures the essence of Samui: coconut trees dot the grounds, monkey statues and sculptures decorate the interior, and, of course, there's a beautiful beach. **Pros:** prime vantage points; pretty place; decent dining. **Cons:** cleanliness is inconsistent; not for young party crowd; feels

quite big. [$] *Rooms from: B4500* ✉ *99/9 Bophut Bay, Bophut Beach, Koh Samui* ☎ *077/428300* 🌐 *www.anantara.com* 🍴 *Free Breakfast* 🛏 *106 rooms.*

Bo Phut Resort and Spa

$$ | **RESORT** | Not every beach hotel that claims to be a "resort and spa" measures up, which is why the massages, scrubs, and herbal steam therapies here are such a pleasant surprise and make this a resort worth visiting. **Pros:** rather calm atmosphere; spectacular spa; nice restaurant. **Cons:** not the most happening location; a bit overpriced; sand around here is rough. [$] *Rooms from: B4,000* ✉ *12/12 Moo 1, Tambon Bophut* ☎ *077/430212, 077/430201, 077/245777* 🌐 *www.bophutresort.com* 🍴 *Free Breakfast* 🛏 *61 rooms.*

Cactus Bungalows

$ | **RESORT** | This laid-back place caters mostly to the budget backpacker crowd. **Pros:** peace and quiet; interesting decor; good vibes. **Cons:** not luxurious; some rooms lack air-conditioning; poorly maintained. [$] *Rooms from: B800* ✉ *175/7 Moo 1, Tambon Bophut* ☎ *077/245565* 🌐 *www.cactus-bungalow.com* 🛏 *14 rooms* 🍴 *Free Breakfast.*

Punnpreeda

$ | **RESORT** | Although it doesn't quite achieve the effortless cool it's striving for, Punnpreeda is still a fine place to stay. **Pros:** near the Big Buddha and Wat Plai Laem; fun atmosphere; convenient shuttle. **Cons:** a taxi ride away from Koh Samui's main drag; not ideal for families; trying a little too hard. [$] *Rooms from: B1302* ✉ *199 Moo 1, Bang Rak Beach, Tambon Bophut* ☎ *077/950558, 094/979–1664* 🌐 *www.punnpreeda.com* 🍴 *Free Breakfast* 🛏 *25 rooms.*

Zazen

$$ | **RESORT** | Minimalist Japanese style makes this hotel a refreshing change of pace, especially if you've been in Thailand for a while. **Pros:** on a nice stretch of sand; first-rate spa; great atmosphere. **Cons:** beach itself is small; not a party destination; expensive. [$] *Rooms from: B4,000* ✉ *177 Moo 1, Tambon Bophut* ☎ *077/425177* 🌐 *www.samuizazen.com* 🍴 *Free Breakfast* 🛏 *35 rooms.*

CHOENGMON

Absolute Sanctuary

$$$ | **RESORT** | If you're on vacation to detox, this is the spot—and if you aren't, well, it probably isn't. **Pros:** terrific massage treatments; prime yoga facilities; unique concept. **Cons:** doesn't quite live up to its star rating; no fun if you're not detoxing; lacks the luxe feel of other properties. [$] *Rooms from: B4300* ✉ *88 Moo 5, Tambol, Tambon Bophut* ☎ *077/601190* 🌐 *www.absolutesanctuary.com* 🛏 *38 rooms* 🍴 *Free Breakfast.*

Cape Fahn Hotel

$$$$ | **RESORT** | The very image of an idyllic tropical island escape, Cape Fahn offers 22 gorgeous pool villas, two excellent restaurants (one, Long Dtai, by celebrity chef David Thompson), and a spa on a private island. **Pros:** elegant spa with invigorating Thai treatments; uninterrupted Gulf views; perfectly proportioned private pools. **Cons:** gym is rather small; resort dining can be pricey without a dining package; you are confined to the resort. [$] *Rooms from: 15,000* ✉ *24/269, Bo-Phut, Choeng Mon Beach* ☎ *077/602301* 🌐 *www.capefahnhotel.com* 🍴 *Free Breakfast* 🛏 *22 rooms.*

The Ritz-Carlton, Koh Samui

$$$$ | **RESORT** | The biggest property on Koh Samui in terms of area, the Ritz-Carlton revels in all that space. **Pros:** beautiful main infinity pool; the steaks at The Ranch at Shook; grandstand views from resort's highest points. **Cons:** villa design a little cookie-cutter; resort can feel sprawling; golf carts can take a while to arrive. [$] *Rooms from: 9,000* ✉ *9/123, Plai Laem Beach, Choeng Mon Beach* ☎ *077/915777* 🌐 *www.ritzcarlton.com* 🍴 *Free Breakfast* 🛏 *175 rooms.*

Sala Samui Choengmon Beach

$$$$ | **RESORT** | Bright, nearly all-white rooms open onto private courtyards on one side and curtain-enclosed bathrooms on the other. **Pros:** nice pool; lots of privacy; good dining options. **Cons:** beach views aren't the best; could use some improvements considering the cost; water is cloudy and for wading, not swimming. $ *Rooms from: B10800* ✉ *10/9 Moo 5, Baan Plai Laem, Tambon Bophut* ☎ *077/245888* ⊕ *www.salahospitality.com/samui/* ⤴ *69 rooms* ⦿ *Free Breakfast.*

Samui Honey Cottages

$ | **RESORT** | The cottages at this small resort on one of the island's quieter beaches have glass sliding doors and peaked roofs, and bathrooms have showers with glass ceilings. **Pros:** free kayaks; well located; welcoming staff. **Cons:** no real nightlife nearby; not that special; simple breakfast. $ *Rooms from: B800* ✉ *24/34 Moo 5, Choeng Mon Beach* ☎ *083/646–4188* ⊕ *www.samuihoney. com* ⤴ *20 rooms* ⦿ *Free Breakfast.*

★ Six Senses Samui

$$$$ | **RESORT** | From the moment that you're introduced to your private butler, you'll realize that this is not just another high-end resort—you're about to embark on an amazing experience. **Pros:** 30-meter infinity pool on the cliff; butler service; excellent restaurant. **Cons:** sprawling property difficult to navigate; expensive; location can feel isolated. $ *Rooms from: B10500* ✉ *9/10 Moo 5, Baan Plai Laem, Tambon Bophut* ☎ *077/245678* ⊕ *www.sixsenses.com* ⤴ *66 villas* ⦿ *Free Breakfast.*

Tongsai Bay

$$$ | **RESORT** | The owners of this splendid all-suites resort managed to build it without sacrificing even one of the tropical trees that give the place a refreshing sense of utter seclusion. **Pros:** romantic setting; beautiful exterior and interior; luxurious bungalows. **Cons:** staff could be more attentive; beach so-so for lounging;

lots of walking and stairs if you have mobility issues. $ *Rooms from: B4500* ✉ *84 Tongsai Bay, Choeng Mon Beach* ☎ *077/913750* ⊕ *www.tongsaibay.co.th* ⤴ *83 suites* ⦿ *Free Breakfast.*

White House Beach Resort and Spa

$$ | **RESORT** | Step back in time as you pass under the Khmer-style stone facade and enter the classic lobby, which is filled with giant Chinese vases, Persian carpets, and classic Lanna art. **Pros:** gardens are lush and lovely; quiet location on beach; old-world opulence. **Cons:** could be cleaner; some rooms need renovating; moldy smell in some rooms. $ *Rooms from: B2000* ✉ *59/3 Moo 5, Choeng Mon Beach* ☎ *077/332648* ⊕ *www.samuithewhitehouse.com* ⤴ *43 rooms* ⦿ *Free Breakfast.*

Nightlife

You'll find the most nighttime action in central Lamai and on Chawaeng's Soi Green Mango—a looping street chock-ablock with beer bars and nightclubs of all sizes.

Ark Bar

BARS | One of Samui's original nightlife venues on the beach, the Ark throws a free barbecue every Wednesday around sunset. ✉ *159/75 Moo 2, Chaweng Noi Beach* ☎ *077/961333* ⊕ *www.ark-bar. com.*

★ Coco Tam's

BARS | The place to be in Fisherman's Village, Coco Tam's is reliably packed on a nightly basis. The formula is simple, but effective with ample beach seating available in the shape of beanbags and giant cushions. Attentive staff roam the sand dishing out reasonably priced cocktails and decent bar fare including pizzas by Peppina: a big noise in Bangkok's pie game. ✉ *62/1 Moo 1, Tambon Bophut* ☎ *091/915–5664* ⊕ *www.facebook.com/ CoCoTams/.*

Islander Pub & Restaurant

PUBS | The many large-screen TVs at this popular place broadcast Thai, Australian, and Malaysian programs—lots of sports—and there are pool competitions and quiz nights. ⊠ *166/79 Chaweng Beach Rd., Central Chaweng* ☎ *077/230836.*

Activities

Canopy Adventures

ZIP LINING | For a bird's-eye view of the jungle, zipline through the air on 330 yards of wire strung among six tree houses. This outfit also arranges fun expeditions to waterfalls and will pick you up at your hotel. ⊠ *Koh Samui* ☎ *077/300340, 087/046–7307* ⊕ *www.canopyadventuresthailand.com* ⊠ *From B2950.*

Santiburi Samui Country Club

GOLF | The Santiburi Resort has a driving range and a beautiful 18-hole course that incorporates the natural terrain of the Samui mountains to create a challenging multilevel golfing experience. You can play 9 holes for half the full-course greens fee. ⊠ *Koh Samui* ☎ *077/421700* ⊕ *www.santiburigolfsamui.com* ⊠ *B5,600 (B3,350 for early-bird tee time before 7 am)* ⅃ *18 holes, 6930 yards, par 72.*

Side Trips from Koh Samui

Koh Phangan

12 km (7 miles) by boat north of Koh Samui.

As Koh Samui developed into an international hot spot, travelers looking for a more laid-back scene headed for Koh Phangan. Decades ago, the few wanderers who arrived here stayed in fishermen's houses or slung hammocks on the beach. Investors bought up beach property with plans for sprawling resorts, but before commercial development marred too much of the island, the allure of Koh Tao's crystalline waters starting drawing away a lot of the attention.

Samui is an obvious yardstick. The two islands are a mere twenty minutes apart by speedboat and share similar paradisiacal qualities. Koh Phangan has traditionally acted as an overspill for alternative types turned off by Samui's commercialism. The bigger island remains the Gulf's tourism heavyweight, but it is hard to argue that over-development hasn't robbed it of some of its charms.

Koh Phangan appears to be managing its evolution in a more considered way. The island is definitely going upscale. Existing backpacker haunts and low-rise resorts are being complemented by a growing selection of high-end bolt-holes and private villas. Even so, there's plenty of scope for backpackers looking for beautiful beaches with budget accommodations, and hippies (old-school and nouveau) searching for chilled-out beaches and alternative retreats.

Haad Rin has many good restaurants and bars. It's densely built up, and not very quiet, but full of fun. The town is sandwiched between the beaches of Haad Rin West and Haad Rin East.

While Haad Rin boomed as a result of its world-famous full moon party, most of Koh Phangan's smaller beaches continued to develop, but at a much slower pace.

Close to Haad Rin are Haad Sarikantang, Haad Yuan, and Haad Thien: good choices for those interested in going to the full moon party, but who want to stay on a nicer, more relaxing beach.

If you aren't here for the full moon party, head up the east coast to quieter Haad Thong Nai Pan, or even farther afield.

Koh Phangan's beaches are popular with travelers looking for a tranquil getaway.

One of the island's most remote beaches—and the most beautiful—is Haad Kuat (better known as Bottle Beach), which has gorgeous white sand and simple accommodations. Haad Salad and Haad Yao, on the northwest coast, are more convenient, yet sufficiently idyllic, options.

GETTING HERE AND AROUND

The best way to get here is by ferry or high-speed catamaran from Koh Samui, or from Surat Thani via Koh Samui. Boats depart hourly from Surat Thani's Donsak Pier for Na Thon Pier on Koh Samui; the price includes the hour-long bus ride from Surat Thani's airport to the pier. After the 2½-hour voyage to Samui, passengers must disembark and catch a second boat to Koh Phangan's Thong Sala Pier, a 30-minute journey. Seatran boats depart from Koh Samui for Koh Phangan daily at 8 am and 1:30 pm. Return travel from Koh Phangan to Koh Samui is at 10:30 am and 4:30 pm.

If you take a Songserm ferry instead, you won't have to switch boats on Samui;

however, Songserm makes the Surat Thani–Koh Samui–Koh Phangan run only once a day, leaving Surat Thani at 8 am and returning from Koh Phangan at 12:30 pm.

There are a number of ways to travel between Koh Phangan and either Koh Samui or Koh Tao—Lomphrayah and Seatran boats are the best options. Boats to and from Koh Tao take from 2 to 2½ hours.

Road improvements mean that most beaches are accessible via songthaew. You can also beach-hop via boat. Be careful if you opt to travel around Koh Phangan on a motorcycle: accidents involving motorcycles are a far too regular occurrence.

SAFETY AND PRECAUTIONS

Koh Phangan has become famous for its full moon parties and for numerous other parties associated with the moon's waxing and waning. These events attract as many as 50,000 revelers (although those numbers may never be repeated) and the criminal element knows this. Break-ins are a problem. Thieves assume you're out partying, so don't leave valuables in your room.

The biggest problem is drugs, which are treated very seriously by Thai authorities. There are all-too-frequent stories of travelers who have been arrested, either for purchasing or consuming, so expect harsh treatment if you're caught.

TIMING

The Full Moon Party, probably the biggest draw to the island, happens 12 times a year on Haad Rin East. If you want some peace and quiet, consult your lunar calendar. At other times the island is a tranquil place.

Beaches

★ **Haad Kuat** (*Bottle Beach*)

BEACH | With a quarter mile of fine white sand, this isolated beach on the island's north coast is a sunbather's paradise. The vibe is decidedly young and funky, and there are several places to grab a decent meal. Get here by longtail boat from Chaloklum pier (B250 per person) or Thong Nai Pan. Another option is to hike the track that starts at the end of the paved road at Haad Khom. The route over the mountain takes around 90 minutes and is one of the island's best activities. Haad Kuat might be more difficult to reach than other beaches, but it's one of Koh Phangan's best and definitely worth the effort. **Amenities:** food and drink; water sports. **Best for:** solitude, swimming, walking. ⊠ *Haad Kuat, Haad Rin.*

Haad Rin

BEACH | If you are looking for the party, then head to Haad Rin. The beach is divided into two parts, Haad Rin West and Haad Rin East, each with its own personality. Haad Rin West has swimmable water, but you needn't settle for this beach when Haad Rin East is only a short walk away. Beautiful Haad Rin East is lined with bungalows and bars fronting pristine waters. Every four weeks, Haad Rin East gets seriously crowded when throngs of young people gather on the beach for an all-night full moon party. **Amenities:** food and drink. **Best for:** partiers; swimming. ⊠ *Haad Rin, Koh Phangan.*

Haad Sarikantang

BEACH | Just south of Haad Rin, this smaller strand is close to the party yet relatively peaceful. Also known as Leela Beach, Haad Sarikantang has picturesque palms, fine white sand, and clear blue water. Resorts and restaurants surround the beach. **Amenities:** food and drink. **Best for:** swimming. ⊠ *Haad Sarikantang, Haad Rin.*

Haad Thien

BEACH | A small strip north of the party beaches at Haad Rin, this is an ideal choice for those seeking relaxation and smaller crowds. The sand is a fine yellow and the waters are shallow and clear. A few resort hotels and several good restaurants do business on the waterfront or near the beach. **Amenities:** food and drink; water sports. **Best for:** swimming. ⊠ *Haad Thien, Haad Rin.*

Haad Thong Nai Pan

BEACH | On a horseshoe bay at the island's northern end, Haad Thong Nai Pan is split into two. The northern part is the most beautiful, with stunning golden sands set around crystal-blue waters. The seas are usually calm, but swimming can be rough when the monsoon rains sweep in. Guesthouses and mid-range resorts surround the beach. Food and drink are available from the nearby restaurants. **Amenities:** food and drink; water sports. **Best for:** swimming. ⊠ *Haad Thong Nai Pan, Haad Rin.*

Haad Yuan

BEACH | A 10-minute boat ride from Haad Rin, small beautiful Haad Yuan is worlds away. Extremely quiet most of the time, the beach is wide and clean, with fine sand and crystal-blue waters. The rocky outcrop at one end makes a fine photo backdrop. The swimming is good here, but the water occasionally gets rough. **Amenities:** food and drink. **Best for:** solitude; swimming; walking. ⊠ *Haad Yuan, Haad Rin.*

Restaurants

Previously, dining options on Koh Phangan weren't overly exciting. Staples like fried rice and watered-down Thai curries took care of the daily basics at the guesthouse while post-party blowouts were limited to a small coterie of higher-end options. While the island's loved-up vibe remains, its culinary appeal has evolved since that utilitarian era. These days, gourmands can sample everything from kleftiko lamb and aromatic Persian kebabs to handmade Italian pasta and expansive charcuterie platters.

HAAD RIN
Rimini

$$ | **ITALIAN** | Lovers of Italian food are particularly well-served on the island, with several stellar options. One of the most memorable is where chef-proprietor Alessandro Paterno presides (usually with cigarette fixed to mouth) over a daily-changing selection of fish and seafood creations. **Known for:** the giant octopus salad; fresh seafood; family-run and friendly. Ⓢ *Average main: 250* ⊠ *Chaloklum, Haad Rin* ☏ *086/758–1405* ⊕ *www.facebook.com/RistoranteRimini-Bungalow* ⊙ *Closed Mon. No lunch* ▭ *No credit cards.*

Satipot

$$$ | **PERSIAN** | Sati Pot lays a strong claim to be Thailand's finest Persian restaurant. Such is its reputation that it is often necessary to make a booking for a table. **Known for:** cuisine that is unique in Thailand; cool, casual vibe; giant portions. Ⓢ *Average main: 350* ⊠ *Hin Kong Beach, Haad Rin* ☏ *092/404–4613* ⊕ *www.face-book.com/SatiPotKohPhangan/* ⊙ *Closed Wed. No lunch.*

Hotels

HAAD RIN
House of Sanskara

$ | **RESORT** | These simple wooden huts directly on the beach at the "quieter" northern end of Haad Rin East are the best deal in the area—for the best location. **Pros:** good deal; extremely low-key vibe; can arrange transportation. **Cons:** not near the action; breakfast available at restaurant but not included in rates; some rooms lack air-conditioning. Ⓢ *Rooms from: B700* ⊠ *134 Moo 6, Haad Rin East, Haad Rin* ☏ *077/375160* ⊕ *www.houseofsanskara.com* ⊋ *40 rooms* ⦶ *No Meals.*

Phangan Bayshore Resort

$ | **RESORT** | On Haad Rin East near the action but away from the crowds, this was one of the island's original resorts. **Pros:** spacious layout; close to the party; good value. **Cons:** modern huts lack personality; some rooms need renovation; food is unremarkable. Ⓢ *Rooms from: B1,500* ⊠ *141 Moo 6, Haad Rin, Haad Rin* ☏ *077/375227* ⊕ *www.phanganbayshore.com* ⦶ *Free Breakfast* ⊋ *71 rooms.*

Sarikantang Resort & Spa

$ | **RESORT** | On Haad Sarikantang, this small resort is a short walk from the festive atmosphere at Haad Rin. The nicer accommodations have outdoor showers and baths, hot water, air-conditioning, and hammocks, while some of the wooden bungalows have only the most basic amenities. **Pros:** picture-perfect location; ample ocean views; friendly staff. **Cons:** least expensive rooms not comfortable; could be more central; beach is private but rocky. Ⓢ *Rooms from: B1,800* ⊠ *129/3 Leela Beach, Haad Rin* ☏ *077/375055, 086/789–9541* ⊕ *www.sarikantang.com* ⦶ *Free Breakfast* ⊋ *47 rooms.*

HAAD THONG NAI PAN

★ **Anantara Rasananda Koh Phangan Villas**

$$$$ | **RESORT** | Villas and suites at this upscale hideaway, which deserves its reputation as the most luxurious bolt-hole on the island, all have their own private plunge pools, while the signature spa built into the mountainside is the perfect place for pampering. **Pros:** ultimate in barefoot luxury; swim-up bar in main pool; genuinely creative cuisine. **Cons:** parking is a little meager; an expensive treat; some suites could stand a refresh. $ Rooms from: 7,000 ✉ 5/5 Moo 5 Thong Nai Pan Noi Beach, Haad Rin ☎ 077/956660 ⊕ www.anantara.com ⦿ Free Breakfast ⤣ 64 rooms.

Longtail Beach Resort

$ | **RESORT** | **FAMILY** | The bungalows and restaurant at this well-landscaped resort in northern Koh Phangan are built of wood, thatch, and bamboo in traditional southern Thai style. **Pros:** local touches to the rooms and resort; close to the beach; inexpensive. **Cons:** full of families; small pool; few amenities. $ Rooms from: B1250 ✉ 2/5 Moo 5, Thong Nai Pan Yai Beach, Haad Rin ☎ 77/445018 ⊕ www.longtailbeachresort.com ⤣ 22 bungalows ⦿ No Meals.

Panviman Resort

$$ | **RESORT** | **FAMILY** | The big attractions at this cheerful resort on Koh Phangan's northern coast are its two restaurants: one is a circular dining area that's open to the ocean breezes; the other is a seaside terrace. **Pros:** gorgeous, well-maintained grounds; good for families; shuttle service back to Bangkok. **Cons:** not near interesting nightlife; high rates; fairly remote. $ Rooms from: B2500 ✉ 22/1 Moo 5, Thong Nai Pan Noi Bay, Haad Rin ☎ 077/445–1019, 02/459–47057 ⊕ www.panvimanresortkohphangan.com ⦿ Free Breakfast ⤣ 104 rooms.

HAAD KUAT

Smile Bungalows

$ | **RESORT** | Of the guesthouses on northern Koh Phangan's Haad Kuat (Bottle Beach), this one on the beach's western end is the best, though it lacks most amenities besides a restaurant. **Pros:** white sand and turquoise waters; duplexes have dramatic views; personable staff. **Cons:** lacks amenities; no air-conditioning; hard to get here. $ Rooms from: B550 ✉ Bottle Beach, Haad Rin ☎ 092/656–6567 ⦿ No Meals ⤣ 25 rooms ⊟ No credit cards.

HAAD SALAD

Cookies Salad

$ | **RESORT** | **FAMILY** | Cascading down a jungle-clad hillside at the southern end of Haad Salad, Cookies Salad offers something for everyone. **Pros:** kayaks for hire; great value for money; excellent coffee in the restaurant. **Cons:** accommodations are quite close together; steep climb out of the resort; limited dining options nearby. $ Rooms from: 800 ✉ 61/8 Moo 8, Haad Salad, Haad Rin ☎ 077/349125, 083/181–7125 ⊕ www.cookies-phangan.com ⦿ Free Breakfast ⤣ 27 rooms.

THONG SALA

Baan Manali

$ | **RESORT** | **FAMILY** | Although Thong Sala (the island's main town) is often overlooked as in favor of other beaches there's plenty to like about the unassuming stretches of sand nearest to the "big city" and this lovely property is one of the best places to stay, with secluded bungalows, a fine restaurant, and a swimming pool. **Pros:** great value; close to the shops and restaurants of Thong Sala; a stone's throw from the ferry port. **Cons:** can get windy in the afternoon; not the most beautiful beach on the island; bungalows are a little small. $ Rooms from: 800 ✉ 210/20 Moo 1, Ao Nai Wok, Haad Rin ☎ 077/377917 ⊕ www.baan-manali.com ⦿ No Meals ⤣ 15 rooms.

Divers travel between Koh Tao's islands by longtail boats.

Nightlife

Haad Rin East is lined with bars and clubs—music pumps and drinks pour from dusk until dawn, seven days a week, 365 days a year. All this culminates in a huge beach party with tens of thousands of revelers every full moon (or the night after, if the full moon lands on a major Buddhist holiday). Check out *www.fullmoonparty-thailand.com* for details.

Koh Tao

47 km (29 miles) by boat north of Koh Phangan.

In just a few decades, the tiny island of Koh Tao has evolved from a sleepy backwater to a sought-after diving getaway, with lodgings that range from basic bungalows to luxurious resorts. The peace and quiet has disappeared from the main beaches, with a strong, backpacker-oriented, party scene in the island's two main areas. Along with cheap drinks, the bars, pubs, and clubs in each offer all manner of pub crawls and late-night shenanigans. This said, the primary reason to come here remains the underwater world. Koh Tao is an excellent place to get your scuba certification. Many operators don't have pools, so the initial dives must be done in the shallow, crystal-clear ocean water. Advanced divers will appreciate the great visibility, decent amount of coral, and exotic and plentiful marine life.

GETTING HERE AND AROUND

Getting to Koh Tao is easy—it's on the scheduled ferry routes out of Koh Phangan and Koh Samui, and several boats a day make the trip from Donsak and Chumpon on the mainland.

Lomprayah Catamaran has 1¾-hour trips between Koh Samui and Koh Tao.

CONTACTS Lomprayah High Speed Catamaran. ✉ *Koh Phangan* ⊕ *www.lomprayah.com.*

Diving and Snorkeling Responsibly

Decades of visitors scuba diving on Thailand's islands and reefs have had far greater negative effects on marine life than any tsunami. All divers need to be aware of, and consequently minimize, their impact on the environment.

Touch nothing, stand only on sand: As fascinating as something you see may be, resist the urge to handle it, and never stand on anything that isn't sand. Coral is extremely fragile, urchins are as painful as they look, and although sharks may be no threat to divers, you can appreciate the foolishness of grabbing one's tail. Other dangers to both you and the environment are less obvious: eels live within holes in rocks and reef; turtles are reptiles that require air to breathe, and even some dive instructors are guilty of "hitching a ride" on them, causing the turtles to expend precious air. Furthermore, don't feed fish human food.

Secure diving equipment, maintain level buoyancy: Divers should make sure equipment is securely fastened or stored, so that no items are lost or scrape against coral. Divers should also maintain level buoyancy to prevent inadvertent brushes with coral, as well as to save air. Snorkelers who need to remove their masks should pull them down around their necks rather than up on their foreheads. Masks can fall off and quickly sink, and a mask on the forehead is considered a symbol of distress.

Check your pockets, no butts: Minimize underwater pollution when snorkeling by checking your pockets before jumping into the water. Conscientious divers can clip a stuff sack to their BCDs to pocket random trash they encounter. Lastly, if you smoke, don't flick cigarette butts into the water.

Protect yourself and nature: Sunscreen is a must anytime you are exposed to Thailand's tropical sun. Snorkeling unprotected is a guaranteed skin disaster (and painful obstacle to the rest of your holiday); however, sunblock, when dissolving into the water from hundreds of visitors each day, is bound to take its toll on the marine environment. You can limit the amount of sunscreen you must slather on by covering your back with a Lycra rash guard or a short- or long-sleeved shirt while snorkeling.

Follow the credo, "Leave only footprints, take only memories." Try to minimize your impact on this ecosystem in which you are only a visitor.

Sights

Koh Nang Yuan

ISLAND | The three small islands of Koh Nang Yuan lie close to Koh Tao. At high tide the islands, separated by shallow, translucent water, look like the endpoints of an obtuse triangle. At low tide the receding water exposes two narrow sandbars that connect the outer islands, which contain bungalows for overnight stays, to the central island, which has a lodge, a restaurant and beach bar, and a coffee shop. The islands are privately owned by the Nangyuan Island Dive Resort, and all visitors who wish to set foot on Koh Nang Yuan must shell out a small fee. Although many visitors opt to pay, others simply dock offshore to snorkel and dive the gorgeous waters surrounding the islands. To get here from Koh Tao, you can kayak from Sairee Beach or hire a longtail boat (B200 round-trip from Sairee) to ferry you here. The trip takes about 15 minutes—it works best to arrange your return with the same operator. While you are visiting, be sure to slip up to the viewpoint on the southern island to snap photos guaranteed to make your friends back home jealous. ■ **TIP➔ The islands are busy throughout the day; it's best to visit early in the morning or late in the afternoon.** ⊠ *Koh Tao ✛ 15-min longtail ride from Koh Tao* ⊕ *www.nangyuan.com* ⊠ *B100.*

Beaches

Chalok Baan Kao Beach

BEACH | A peaceful strand on Koh Tao's southern shore, Chalok Baan Kao has a relaxed, friendly vibe. The beach itself lacks the crystal-blue water and golden sands of other beaches in the region, but it's reasonably good for swimming. Budget accommodations surround the beach. **Amenities:** food and drink. **Best for:** solitude; swimming. ⊠ *Koh Tao.*

Sairee Beach

BEACH | Palm trees at crescent-shaped Sairee, Koh Tao's most popular beach, arch over the aquamarine water as if yearning to sip from the sea. Along the thin sliver of golden sand sit rustic, traditional wooden beach huts with bohemian youths lounging in hammocks, novice divers practicing in seaside pools, and European students sampling cocktails at basic beach bars. On the far northern end of the beach, a few resorts nestle amid manicured landscapes. Sairee faces west, making it great for watching the sunset and for kayaking to Koh Nang Yuan. **Amenities:** food and drink; water sports. **Best for:** partiers; sunset. ⊠ *Koh Tao.*

Restaurants

Gambero Rosso Andrea

$$ | ITALIAN | Beachfront trattorias don't come more inviting than this one. Pizza is the specialty of the house, and pies come in various thin-crusted, wood-fired guises. **Known for:** reasonable wine selection; authentic wood-fired pizza; beachside vibes. $ *Average main: 250* ⊠ *21/1 Moo 2, Koh Tao* ☎ *098/468–6030* ⊕ *www.facebook.com/TonyAndreaAoi.*

The Gallery

$$ | THAI | Combining fine dining and photography, this restaurant–gallery serves delicate interpretations of southern Thai classics—fish dishes, curries, grilled seafood, and the like. The service is first-rate, the atmosphere relaxed and romantic. **Known for:** lavish wine list; fine art meets fine dining; "Trust the chef" prix-fixe menu. $ *Average main: B300* ⊠ *10/29 Moo 1, Sairee Village, Koh Tao* ☎ *077/456547* ⊕ *www.thegallerykohtao. com.*

🛏 Hotels

Ban's Diving Resort

$ | RESORT | Ban's is set up for diving, so this is an ideal place to do your scuba certification, but it's a fine place to lay your head even if you don't plan to dive. **Pros:** lively scene; heaven for scuba divers; great value rooms. **Cons:** older wing needs some love; beach can be crowded and noisy; hillside wing far from beach. $ *Rooms from: 800* ⊠ *Haad Sairee, Sairee Beach* ☎ *092/447–2200* ⊕ *www. bansdivingresortkohtao.com* ℡ *Free Breakfast* ⇄ *29 rooms.*

Chintakiri Resort

$$ | RESORT | Set against a mountain backdrop and surrounded by a lush garden, this resort close to Sairee Beach has 19 wooden bungalows with spectacular views of the turquoise ocean. **Pros:** small pool; eco-friendly; spectacular views.

Cons: difficult for anyone with mobility issues; breakfast is basic; long uphill access to the resort. $ *Rooms from: B2,900* ⊠ *19/59–77 Moo 3, Chalok Baan Kao, Koh Tao* ☎ *077/456391* ⊕ *www.chintakiriresort.com* ❄ *Free Breakfast* ⇗ *19 bungalows.*

★ Charm Churee Villa

$$ | **RESORT** | Whether you opt to stay in one of the uniquely designed tropical villas, a deluxe room, or a basic bungalow, you'll enjoy a tiny corner of heaven on the private beach at Jansom Bay. Rooms and thatch-roof villas are built into the landscape, constructed on or around massive boulders and trees, and situated to maximize exposure to the magnificent views of Sairee Beach. **Pros:** private beach; snorkeling can be spectacular; sweeping views. **Cons:** staff is very lax; feels spread out; isolated. $ *Rooms from: B2500* ⊠ *30/1 Moo 2, Jansom Bay, Koh Tao* ☎ *077/456–3934, 097/921–6048* ⊕ *www.charmchureevilla.com* ❄ *Free Breakfast* ⇗ *40 rooms.*

Koh Tao Cabana

$$$ | **RESORT** | On the far northern end of Sairee Beach, this is one of Koh Tao's few boutique resorts. **Pros:** locally sourced ingredients at restaurant; attractive, stylish decor; on a beautiful beach. **Cons:** some rooms lack easy beach access; so-so food; poor Wi-Fi. $ *Rooms from: B4500* ⊠ *16 Moo 1, Baan Haad Sai Ree, Sairee Beach* ☎ *02/621–7890, 089/698–2266* ⊕ *www.kohtaocabana.com* ⇗ *33 villas* ❄ *Free Breakfast.*

Koh Tao Coral Grand Resort

$ | **RESORT** | On the quieter northern end of Sairee Beach, this resort is a good place to get your scuba certification. **Pros:** strong dive program; lush, peaceful surroundings; lots of amenities. **Cons:** some foot traffic; some guests report bugs and geckos in rooms; not a lot happening around here. $ *Rooms from: B1,400* ⊠ *15/4 Moo 1, Sairee Beach* ☎ *02/939–4896* ⊕ *www.kohtaocoral.com* ❄ *Free Breakfast* ⇗ *42 rooms.*

★ The Place Luxury Boutique Villas

$$$ | **RESORT** | A total escape that provides serious pampering, this resort nestles on the hillside above Sairee Beach. **Pros:** stunning views out to sea; private infinity pool with each villa; award-winning accommodations. **Cons:** may be too isolated for some; a bit of a hike up to the highest villas; breakfast not included. $ *Rooms from: B4500* ⊠ *15/4 Moo 2, Sairee Beach, Koh Tao* ☎ *087/887–5066* ⊕ *www.theplacekohtao.com* ❄ *No Meals* ⇗ *9 villas.*

Chapter 6

PHUKET AND THE ANDAMAN COAST

6

Updated by
Amy Bensema

⦿ Sights	🍴 Restaurants	🛏 Hotels	🛍 Shopping	🎭 Nightlife
★★★★☆	★★★☆☆	★★★★☆	★☆☆☆☆	★★★☆☆

WELCOME TO
PHUKET AND THE ANDAMAN COAST

TOP REASONS TO GO

★ **Sunsets at Railay Beach:** Unforgettable sunsets framed by limestone karsts.

★ **Kayaking Phang Nga Bay:** Phang Nga Bay's maze of islands is ideal for gliding alongside towering cliffs and exploring caves.

★ **Discovering Koh Lanta:** A laid-back destination with long sandy beaches, plenty of beach bars, art galleries, and breathtaking sunsets.

★ **Snorkeling at Koh Similan:** This gorgeous national park has some of the best visibility and incredible marine life.

★ **Exploring Koh Phi Phi:** Make day trips aboard a longtail boat to discover the true beauty of Koh Phi Phi. Quieter Loh Samah Bay is magical.

★ **Walking Old Phuket Town:** Admire Sin-Portuguese architecture, century-old shophouses, sample authentic Phuketian cuisine, and discover the unique atmosphere of the Old Town.

1 Phuket Town. A town steeped in local culture.

2 Khao Phra Taew National Park. The last virgin rain forest in Phuket.

3 Mai Khao Beach. A prime destination for snorkeling, diving, and spotting sea turtles.

4 Nai Yang Beach. A quiet beach perfect for doing not much.

5 Nai Thon and Layan Beaches. Two tranquil beaches with tropical rain forest.

6 Bang Thao Beach. An upscale resort area with one of the longest beaches in Phuket.

7 Pansea, Surin, and Laem Sing. Three stunning white sand beaches with crystal clear waters.

8 Kamala Beach. A beautiful long beach with clear waters, beachfront cafes, and hip bistros.

9 Patong. Overdeveloped and crowded, but a nice beach and lively nightlife.

10 Karon Beach. Popular with families for its choice of restaurants, bars, and nightlife activities.

11 Kata Beach. Chill surfer beaches.

12 Nai Harn. Famous for viewpoints such as Promthep Cape and Black Rock Viewpoint.

13 Cape Yamu. An isolated cape with excellent views of Phang Nga Bay.

14 Chalong. Access to snorkeling, diving, and day trips to the surrounding islands.

15 Phang Nga Bay National Marine Park. Vertical cliffs and day-trippers from Phuket.

16 Khao Lak. Peaceful with a National Park, waterfalls, and uncrowded beaches.

17 Koh Yao. A pair of unspoiled islands with pristine beaches.

18 Similan Islands. Rare marine life, excellent diving, and amazing unspoiled beaches.

19 Surin Islands. Islands popular with divers, snorkelers, and fishermen.

20 Krabi. A friendly town and gateway to the nearby islands.

21 Ao Nang. A convenient base for exploring nearby islands and beaches.

22 Nang Cape. Beaches surrounded by limestone cliffs.

23 Koh Lanta. Beautiful beaches, a laid-back vibe, and a charming Old Town.

24 Koh Phi Phi. Overdeveloped, but with stunning beaches and landscapes.

EATING AND DRINKING WELL IN SOUTHERN THAILAND

Get ready for the south's distinctive flavors. Turmeric, peanuts, bird's-eye chili, and coconut milk are a few ingredients that play larger roles here than they do in the north. And, of course, there's no shortage of delectable fresh seafood.

Southern Thailand has a larger Muslim population than the rest of the country, and you'll find this halal diversity in southern cuisine, which was historically influenced by ethnic Malays living farther south. But in Phuket, where much of the population is descended from Chinese immigrants, you'll also discover similarities with the Hokkien cuisine found in Penang. Regardless of origin, spiciness is a defining characteristic of all southern food, though as in other regions, restaurants that cater to tourists sometimes tone down the chilies (if you really want to eat as the locals do, then order *Thai phet*—Thai spicy). A meal in the south is all about the experience. Don't be afraid to sit down on plastic stools with the locals. It's hard to beat a frosty Singha beer and fresh crab married with a complex curry paste and coconut cream, just steps from the edge of the Andaman Sea.

SEAFOOD

In the Andaman Coast it's all about abundant seafood varieties. Beachside shacks serve all sorts of aquatic treats, from octopus to crab—and foodies will absolutely love the prices. Imagine a heaping plate of fresh, grilled sea bass for just a few dollars; that same dish stateside would have a couple of more zeros attached to it.

GAENG MASSAMAN

A Muslim dish by origin (its name is derived from Musulman, an older version of the word "Muslim"), Massaman curry has a distinct flavor that's somewhat reminiscent of Malay and Indian cuisine. It's not usually a spicy dish, but star anise and cinnamon add a big burst of flavor and peanuts an even bigger crunch. Usually made with beef, coconut milk softens everything, and the result is a soupy and comforting curry.

GAENG SOM

Known as sour curry, this local favorite is usually spicy as well as tart. It's made with fish sauce instead of coconut milk, and the flavor can take some getting used to. It's typically made with fish (*gaeng som pla*) and green vegetables, such as cabbage and beans. Sour curry is runnier than coconut-milk curries—more like a sauce—and tends to acquire a greenish hue from all the vegetables it contains.

KHAO MOK KAI

This simple but delicious chicken-and-rice dish is a Thai version of Indian chicken *biryani,* which means "fried" or "roasted." Chicken—which is usually on the bone—lies under a fragrant mound of rice, which owes its bright yellow color to a liberal amount of

turmeric. Though turmeric often shows up in Indian cuisine, this is one of its few cameos in southern Thailand food. Deep-fried shallots add another element of textural complexity.

BOO PAHT PONG KAREE

Curry-powder crab is not a traditional, soupy curry: instead whole crab is fried in a mixture of curry powder and other spices. The piquant curry is a perfect counterpoint to the sweet crabmeat. Coconut milk is often used to moisten the mix and moderate the spiciness. You'll find other kinds of seafood prepared this way in the south, but crab is particularly tasty.

PLA

Whole fish such as *garoupa* (grouper) is often on the menu in the south, and is so much more flavorful than fillets. Garlic and chilies are common seasonings, and the skin is usually cooked until it's deliciously crispy. It may be spicy, but whole fish is definitely a treat you don't get to enjoy too often stateside. You can also find steamed versions and less spicy seasonings like ginger.

The swoon-worthy treasures of the Andaman Coast include spectacular giant limestones karsts, secluded islands with crystal waters, and miles of unspoiled beaches. The beauty of this stretch along the Andaman Sea is legendary, but it's far from undiscovered. Phuket Island is Thailand's largest island and Phuket Town has consistently been voted as one of the world's favorite tourist destinations, both for budget travelers and those seeking sumptuous luxury. Though it has its share of overdevelopment issues, the island has many beautiful beaches and a dazzling array of restaurants, hotels, activities, and nightlife.

Phuket is the busy hub of the southwestern coast, with daily flights from Bangkok and around the world landing in its airport, and boats to scenic but often packed Ko Phi Phi, Krabi, and the dreamy Similan and Surin islands departing daily from its docks. Beyond Phuket, the secrets of this magical coastline begin to reveal itself. Krabi has powdery white sand and magnificent limestone cliffs shooting straight up out of emerald waters that have become popular with all levels of rock-climbing enthusiasts. Railay Beach is especially sought out by adventurers who enjoy acrobatics and climbing. Nearby the Phang Nga National Park attracts nature lovers because of its world-renowned postcard-perfect locations, such as Koh Phing Kan, also known as James Bond Island. Ko Phi Phi is a prime destination for snorkeling and diving (you may actually see more divers than fish in some waters as it gets incredibly busy in high season), along with being a mainstay of the easygoing backpacker tourist circuit. Koh Lanta has developed its own scene and attracts visitors who like fewer crowds and more offbeat individuality—as reflected in some of its quirky shops and restaurants; it combines lovely beaches with colorful villages where you will meet interesting locals and expats who differ from those in other parts of the Andaman Coast. Ao Nang has become very popular over the years, and numerous resorts have sprung up near its popular beaches and shops to cater to all tastes and budgets.

A note of caution: don't take chances getting on rickety or overcrowded boats, and when you do get on a boat, make sure that life jackets are available and that the crew takes safety seriously.

MAJOR REGIONS

Phuket Island is the attractive hub of the Andaman coast, and Phuket Town is in the center of the island. It's a culturally interesting place, with its Old Chinese quarter and one of the island's revered landmarks, the Big Buddha. Khao Phra Taew National Park in the north of the island is worth a visit for Tonsai Waterfall and a wander through a real tropical rain forest. On the northwest coast of Phuket, Mai Khao Beach, part of Sirinat National Park, is mostly undeveloped and a haven for leatherback turtles. Mai Khao connects to Nai Yang Beach to its south to form Phuket's longest stretch of sand. Nai Yang is quieter than most of Phuket's beaches, with just a small string of beachside restaurants and bars. Nai Thon and Layan beaches exude a calm vibe attracting more wildlife than nightlife. Bang Thao Beach, once the site of a tin mine, attracts an affluent clientele with its upscale accommodations, eateries, and golf courses. The picturesque beaches of Pansea, Surin, and Laem Sing are where Phuket's wealthy set call home and you can also find high-end resorts. Kamala Beach is a good base for exploring the island and its affordable accommodation options attract a laid-back, long-term visitor.

About 8 miles west of Phuket Town, Patong is a thriving, beach-resort

community with a lively nightlife scene, shopping, good Thai food, and water sports making it a hot spot for weekending Bangkokians and international tourists. Just south of Patong, Karon Beach caters to Patong's spillover. Farther southwest of Phuket Town, Kata Beach offers stunning white-sand beaches with turquoise waters that are a big draw for surfers. Less busy Nai Harn is a local hot spot but visitors throng here at sunset for the views from Phromthep Cape. The isolated headland at Cape Yamu, on Phuket's east side, hosts some of the island's most exclusive properties. Just 7 miles south of Phuket Town, Chalong is a working port and a good spot for chartering boats and booking diving or snorkeling trips to nearby islands. You'll also find Wat Chalong, the largest and most famous of Phuket's Buddhist temples.

The Andaman Coast stretches from Ranong Province, bordering Myanmar (Burma) to the north, to Satun Province, flanking Malaysia to the south. Along this shore are hundreds of islands and thousands of beaches. Because of their proximity to Phuket, Phang Nga and Krabi provinces are the two most appealing destinations on the Andaman Coast. Phang Nga Bay National Marine Park is Phang Nga's most heralded attraction, drawing thousands of day-trippers from Phuket. There are dozens of little islands to explore, as well as offshore caves and startling karst formations rising out of the sea. Most visitors make an obligatory stop at Phing Kan Island, made famous by the James Bond movie *The Man with the Golden Gun*. Khao Lak's Khao Lak Lamru National Park attracts nature lovers, while the beaches along this coast draw beachgoers who want a vibe more tranquil than Phuket has to offer. Travelers looking for even greater seclusion head to the Koh Yao Islands, which have cultural tours and homestays that provide insight into southern Thai lifestyles. The Similan Islands and Surin Islands national parks are well-known to scuba divers for their crystalline waters and abundant marine life. There is no commercial lodging available in either park but pre-Covid you could camp or stay in a national park bungalow on either of the islands; check to see if this becomes possible again. Many divers opt to stay on live-aboard ships departing from Phuket or Khao Lak.

Krabi lies to the east of Phuket. Its capital, Krabi Town, sits on the northeastern shore of Phuket Bay. Once a favorite harbor for smugglers bringing in alcohol and tobacco from Malaysia, the town has been transformed into a gateway to the nearby islands. Ao Nang, a short distance from Krabi Town, has evolved into a busy beach town. Ao Nang and nearby Nopphrat Thara exist simply to cater to tourists, with restaurants and shopping for every taste. Ao Nang is a more convenient base of operations than Krabi Town for exploring nearby islands and beaches. Longtail boats and ferries depart from Ao Nang for Nang Cape, Koh Lanta, Koh Phi Phi, and the multitude of smaller islands in eastern Phang Nga Bay.

Planning

When to Go

The peak season on the Andaman Coast is November through April. The monsoon season is May through October, during which high seas can make boat travel unwise and beaches unsafe for swimming (a number of tourist deaths are registered each year in the treacherous monsoon waters) though hotel prices are considerably lower.

Planning Your Time

Whether you want to relax or find fun new adventures and activities, there are almost endless possibilities around Phuket and the Andaman Coast. Children and families will find plenty to do and see, as will singles and couples. There is an excellent tourism infrastructure to help you plan.

Getting Here and Around

AIR

There are daily, relatively inexpensive flights from Bangkok to the major beach destinations in the south: Phuket and Krabi, though air travel to Koh Samui is pricey (try Surat Thai on the mainland instead). There are also some flights from Chiang Mai to the beaches, including on Thai Smile, Bangkok Airways, and Air Asia. If you're flexible with your dates, you can find some extremely cheap fares. Keep in mind that planes fill up fast during the high season, and the lowest fares are mostly available if booked weeks or months in advance.

All the airports in this region are small and much easier to deal with than Bangkok's Suvarnabhumi, though Phuket can get busy with its growing number of international destinations.

BUS

Buses travel regularly between Bangkok and all major destinations on the Andaman Coast. There's also good bus service within the south. Many Bangkok travel agents charge three times the price for bus tickets, and organize a long, exhausting, and convoluted trip with various stops to the main bus stations. It's best to visit the bus station under your own steam and buy your ticket either in advance or on the day; you will save both time and money. Buses leave from Bangkok's Southern Bus Terminal, generally in the late afternoon and evening. The trip to Phuket takes from 12 to 14 hours, depending on the bus and road conditions. You'll need to go to either a travel agent or to the bus station to check exact times and purchase tickets in advance, especially for VIP buses. Costs run from B500 for a large 32-seat air-conditioned bus to around B1,000 for a 24-seat air-conditioned VIP bus. Most long-haul VIP buses travel overnight, but day trips are recommended, as Thailand's highways grow even more dangerous at night. There are buses from Phuket to almost every major destination in southern Thailand. This includes, but is not limited to: Surat Thani, Krabi, Trang, Hat Yai, Satun, Phang Nga, and the ferry crossing to Koh Samui. You can check departure times at your hotel or the centrally located bus station just east of Montri Road, two blocks north of Phang Nga Road in Phuket Town.

■ TIP → **Private buses are less reputable than public buses.**

CAR

You can take Highway 4 from Thonburi in Bangkok all the way to the bridge at the north end of Phuket Island, where it turns into Highway 402. It's a long, exhausting, and not particularly recommended, drive, but once you're out of the capital all you have to do is follow the compass due south. For the scenic route, follow Highway 4 to Chumphon, where it jogs west and south and follows the Andaman Sea coast to Phuket Island. Phuket Town is 862 km (517 miles) from Bangkok; bus companies make the trip in 13 to 15 hours.

(See Car Travel in Travel Smart.)

MOTORCYCLE

Cheap and readily available, scooters are probably the easiest hassle-free (park anywhere) way to get around and discover all sites and beaches, but think twice before renting one. Accidents are not uncommon on Phuket, Koh Lanta, or in Krabi, as the Thais tend to speed, many tourists drink and drive, and helmets are often shunned. If you've never driven a motorcycle before, this is not the time or place to learn. A somewhat safer, if expensive option could be to hire a tuk-tuk.

SONGTHAEW, TAXI, AND TUK-TUK

Most areas of the south have a variety of motorized taxi services from samlors to tuk-tuks to songthaews. Some "metered" taxis can be found in most of the region now, but they usually don't run their meters, preferring to set a price at the start of the trip. Alternatively, popular Southeast Asian taxi app Grab (a local version of Uber) has arrived locally. It makes it much easier to book a vehicle, though the prices may not be much cheaper.

TRAIN TRAVEL

Bangkok is connected to Sri Racha and Pattaya via one daily train; there are more frequent trains to Hua Hin, Chumphon, and Surat Thani. There are regular express trains to Surat Thani, the closest station to Phuket (albeit still a distance away), which leave Bangkok's Hua Lamphong Station. From Surat Thani you can take a bus to Phuket. Express trains from Bangkok's Hua Lamphong railway station stop at Surat Thani on their way south. The journey takes 12 hours or so; if you leave Bangkok at 3 pm, you'll arrive at a dark train station in Surat Thani at around 3 am.

(See Train Travel in Travel Smart.)

Bus services or flights, though, are generally considered to be a far better way to get to the Andaman Coast.

Health and Safety

Malaria and dengue fever are rare but not unheard of in Thailand's southwest. Health authorities have done a great job controlling mosquitoes in the more urban areas, but you'll still need a good supply of repellent. Wear long-sleeve shirts and long pants at dusk to reduce the chances of dengue.

As with any developed resort locations, the dangers and annoyances usually involve petty theft. Phuket has its fair share of crime, usually items being stolen from hotel rooms or pickpockets operating in the entertainment areas. Especially watch out for motorcycle "snatch" theives, and ensure that your valuables are secured at all times. Brawls caused by too much liquor and sun can also be a problem. There are many bars and pubs here, and people tend to over-indulge. The police do patrol tourist areas, but violence does occasionally break out.

Be careful at the beach, as the sun is stronger than you think. Wear a hat, plenty of sunscreen, and anti-UV cloth-ing. Protective footwear while diving or snorkeling is a good idea, as accidentally stepping on coral or sea urchins can be painful. Keep an eye out for dangerous creatures like jellyfish, especially during the monsoon season. If you are stung, seek medical attention immediately.

Strong undertows often develop during monsoon season, especially along the west coast. Pay attention to posted warnings, only swim in designated areas where marked, and listen if locals tell you not to swim.

Money Matters

Banks and ATMs are everywhere, and can always be found outside the numerous 7-Eleven and Family Mart convenience stores, but it's still always a good idea to carry some extra cash. There have also been cases of stand-alone ATMs being hacked, so try to use ones directly attached to banks where possible. Remote islands do not widely accept credit cards but have many eager currency exchangers. Some places add a small service charge, typically 3%, when you pay with a credit card.

Restaurants

Restaurants of all sorts are available in the beach regions, from exclusive (and usually expensive) resort eateries to wooden shacks that seem like they're about to fall over, though a govern-ment-mandated beach cleanup project in Phuket led to many disappearing. On Koh Lanta food stalls pop up just before dusk on the beaches, where in the daytime there's only sand and sunbathers. Phuket has the widest range of restaurants, from the fast-food giants of America (with some Thai adaptations on their menus) to beach huts to five-star Western-style res-taurants, while Khao Lak in Phang Nga and Ao Nang in Krabi also has a great many dining spots to choose from.

Hotels

Hotel prices in beach areas are generally lower than what you'd pay in Bangkok (Phuket excluded) but higher than in oth-er parts of the country. There are budget bungalows and guesthouses every-where, though if you haven't booked ahead in high season you may end up in a questionable room with just a humble fan. At the other end of the spectrum are upscale resorts that run more than $1,000-plus a night—though they are some of the most luxurious resorts in the world.

Many places combine the two experi-ences by offering pricey luxury bunga-lows. Rates fluctuate widely—in holiday periods they can be more than double. Always double-check your rate when you book.

What It Costs in Baht			
$	$$	$$$	$$$$
RESTAURANTS			
under B200	B200–B300	B301–B400	over B400
HOTELS			
under B2,000	B2,000–B4,000	B4,001–B6,000	over B6,000

Phuket Town

862 km (539 miles) south of Bangkok.

Increasingly popular with tourists, Phuket Town, the provincial capital, is one of the more culturally interesting places on the island to spend a day. About one-third of the island's population lives here, and the town is an intriguing mix of old Sino-Colonial architecture and the influences of the ethnic Chinese, Malays, and Thais that inhabit it. The old shophouses around Thalang Road make it especially good for a stroll, filled as they are with a variety of antiques shops, art studios, and trendy cafés.

Besides Thalang, the major thoroughfares are Ratsada, Phuket, Dibuk, and Ranong roads. Ratsada connects Phuket Road to Ranong Road, where there's an aromatic local market filled with fruits, vegetables, spices, and meats, though it's at the weekly Sunday Walking Street, when Thalang Road is closed to traffic and fills with food stalls, handicraft sellers, and musical performers, that the area really comes alive.

GETTING HERE AND AROUND

Phuket Town is in the southeast of the island. Taxis, tuk-tuks, motorcycles, and local buses will take you from here to the west-coast beaches and to the airport. Expect to pay approximately B500 to travel from the town to the airport or Patong via taxi—a little more to most other southern and northern beaches. The price will depend on your negotiation techniques. The best place to pick up transport is at the bus station in the center of town. Ranong Road also has a songthaew terminal, where minibuses depart for the most popular beaches every half hour. The fare is B30 to B100.

VISITOR INFORMATION AND TOURS

As the saying goes, you can't throw a stone in Phuket without hitting a tour operator. Nearly all of them are selling the same package tours and renting the same cars and motorcycles, so feel free to comparison shop and haggle over prices. Common half-day sightseeing tours include visits to Wat Chalong, Rawai Beach, Phromthep Cape, and Khao Rang.

In general, be wary of what tour operators tell you; they are in business to sell you a trip to the beach, not to tell you how to get there on your own. If you feel you have been ripped off, note the offender's name and other info and report him to the local Tourism Authority of Thailand (TAT) office. Also let the manager at your hotel know, so he or she can steer other tourists clear.

Dive Asia
Based on Kata Beach, Dive Asia is a PADI-certified instructor and operator that's been in business for more than two decades. They do a multitude of day trips to different dive sites and snorkeling spots. ✉ *Kata Beach* ☎ *076/330598* ⊕ *www.diveasia.com* ✉ *From B3,400.*

John Gray's Sea Canoe
This company is known internationally for ecotourism trips, including awesome canoeing through Phang Nga Bay. Look for their flyers at travel agencies. Various tours are offered, from day trips to longer overnight stays. ✉ *Phuket* ☎ *076/254505* ⊕ *www.johngray-seacanoe.com* ✉ *From B3,950.*

Thailand Divers
Day trips by boat, snorkeling, and a broad range of diving courses are offered by this well-organized, friendly, and highly professional agency. ✉ *Patong* ☎ ⊕ *www.thailand-divers.com* ✉ *From B2,000.*

Tourism Authority of Thailand
The efficient Tourism Authority of Thailand in Phuket Town provides up-to-date maps, and brochures, as well as thorough information about local excursions. ✉ *Phuket* ☎ *076/212213* ⊕ *www.tourismthailand.org.*

Sights

★ Big Buddha

VIEWPOINT | This huge, white marble Buddha on top of the Nakkerd Hills between Chalong and Katais is one of the island's most revered landmarks. It's 45 meters high, and the site offers the best 360-degree views of the island. Take the road from Phuket's main artery—it's a must-visit island destination. ✉ *Phuket.*

Khao Rang

VIEWPOINT | If you want to get your bearings, there's a fine view of Phuket Town, the island's interior, and even the 45-meter-high Big Buddha from atop Khao Rang, a hill north of town. From the town's center, take either Ranong or Thalang Road west and turn north on Khaw Sim Bee Road. Follow the winding, ascending, forested road. There are a few restaurants and a picnic area once you reach the top, where you can relax after soaking in the vista from the large viewing platform next to a tower (which you can't ascend). ✉ *Northwest, Phuket.*

Siam Niramit

MUSEUM VILLAGE | **FAMILY** | This huge entertainment park contains a cultural village, complete with boats, games, and traditional crafts, and an indoor theater where Thai history is told through dance, performance, and song. The main show starts nightly at 8:30 pm, but come early to wander among the stalls. ☎ *076/335000* 🌐 *www.siamniramit.com* 🎫 *Tickets from B1,500.*

Thalang National Museum

HISTORY MUSEUM | **FAMILY** | The National Museum, opposite the Heroine's Monument, has an engaging exhibition of the island's culture and history, including its encounter with the Burmese and their defeat by the island's two heroines. The building itself gives a glimpse into local culture, with its attractive architecture and design. The halls each show a different period of local and wider Thai history. ✉ *Srisoonthorn, Phuket*

Than Bokkharani

Between Krabi and Phang Nga is this forested park, which has several emerald-green ponds surrounded by tropical foliage, including wild gardenia and apocynaceae. The pools are filled with refreshing cool water, fed by a mountain spring 4 km (2½ miles) away. The largest pond is 130 feet by 100 feet, deep and suitable for swimming. The pools are best visited in the dry season, as they get quite murky when it rains. From Krabi: take Hwy. 4 to Ao Luek, then turn onto Rte. 4039.

✣ *12 km (7 miles) north of Phuket Town* ☎ *076/311426* 🎫 *B100.*

Restaurants

Bookhemian

$ | **THAI** | This bohemian-chic café in Phuket's Old Town is part of a new wave of trendy global enterprises that focuses on excellent coffee and baked goods. It's also home to a design bookshop, as well as an exhibition arts space, and there's an upstairs film room, where indie flicks are played from time to time. **Known for:** artsy clientele; homemade brownies and freshly ground coffee; collection of design books. [$] *Average main: B115* ✉ *61 Thalang Rd., Phuket* ☎ *98/090–0657.*

Campus Coffee Roaster

$ | **CAFÉ** | Championship baristas pull specialty coffee drinks and serve homemade cakes and pastries at this bright little spot in the heart of Phuket Old Town. They also sell freshly roasted coffee beans and coffee accessories. **Known for:** great desserts; bright, modern space; great coffee. [$] *Average main: 80* ✉ *6*

Krabi Road, Tambon Talat Nuea, Phuket ☎ 092/218–9292 🌐 www.facebook.com/campuscoffeeroaster 💳 No credit cards.

Chino Café Gallery

$ | **CAFÉ** | The scent of freshly ground espresso greets you as you enter this lovely café next to one end of the weekly Sunday Walking Street. In addition to light meals, coffee, and desserts there are souvenirs made with natural materials, notebooks, and postcards. **Known for:** near Sunday Walking Street; natural wood decor; handmade souvenirs. [$] *Average main: B115 ✉ 4 Thalang Rd., Taladyai Muang, Phuket ☎ 081/979–6190.*

Khun Jeed Yod Pak

$ | **THAI** | The decor is simple but locals love this spot for the *radna*—a noodle dish served with pork or chicken and a thick gravy—as well as the grilled pork or chicken satay, radish cakes, and varieties of fried rice. It's so popular that there's often a line for a table. **Known for:** local vibe; chicken satay; busy at lunch time. [$] *Average main: 195 ✉ 31 Phang Nga Road, Tambon Talat Yai, Mueang Phuket, Phuket 🌐 www.facebook.com/khunjeedyodpak1 🕒 Closed Wed. 💳 No credit cards.*

Kopi de Phuket

$ | **CAFÉ** | For a good cup of coffee, try this artsy store, which sells funky designer souvenirs and serves traditional Thai food and international snacks, sandwiches, desserts, and shakes. It opens daily at 9:30 am. **Known for:** baked garlic butter prawns; southern Thai snacks; designer souvenirs. [$] *Average main: B150 ✉ Phuket Rd., Phuket ☎ 076/212225 🌐 www.kopidephuket.com.*

★ **Kopitiam by Wilai**

$ | **THAI** | The walls of this unique restaurant–café in the heart of the architecturally quaint Sino-Colonial Old Town are lined with vintage black-and-white images of Phuket, which pretty much reflect the kind of food served here—old-school Thai-Chinese fare. Signature dishes are inspired by family recipes, and include *bak kut teh* (a pungent shiitake-mushroom-and-pork soup), *mee sua pad* (noodles with seafood and spices), and the crispy noodle and egg salad. **Known for:** interesting flavors of iced tea; traditional treats; old-world charm. [$] *Average main: B160 ✉ 18 Thalang Rd., Phuket ☎ 083/606–9776 🕒 Closed Sun.*

★ **Raya Restaurant**

$ | **THAI** | In the heart of Phuket Old Town, this beloved restaurant is in a historical Sino-Thai mansion, built in the early 20th century by a rich tin-mining family. Authentic Phuket dishes are the specialty here; try the yellow crab curry with rice noodles or the whole red snapper with roasted garlic. **Known for:** family antiques; yellow crab curry; historic surroundings. [$] *Average main: B160 ✉ 48/1 New Debuk Rd., Phuket ☎ 076/218155.*

Tu Kab Khao

$$ | **THAI** | Located in one of the Old Town's most impressive mansions, this stylish eatery pays homage to classic home-cooked Phuket dishes—hence the name, which translates as "food cupboard." Pay attention to your dining neighbors, as the local cusine draws Thai celebrities from as far away as Bangkok. **Known for:** stylish decor; celebrity guests; Phuket specialties. [$] *Average main: B200 ✉ 8 Phangnga Rd., Phuket ☎ 076/608888.*

Tunk Ka Cafe

$ | **THAI** | Nestled in a jungle setting atop the biggest hill in Phuket Town, Tunk Ka serves Thai food made from fresh local ingredients and the views are marvelous, especially at sunset, which more than justify the tuk-tuk drive up. The Ruby Red dessert (red water chestnut in coconut cream with lashes of young coconut and jackfruit) will satisfy even the most demanding sweet tooth. **Known for:** romantic setting; Old Town views; Ruby Red dessert. [$] *Average main: B180 ✉ Phuket ✣ Top of Rang Hill ☎ 076/211500, 082/412–2131.*

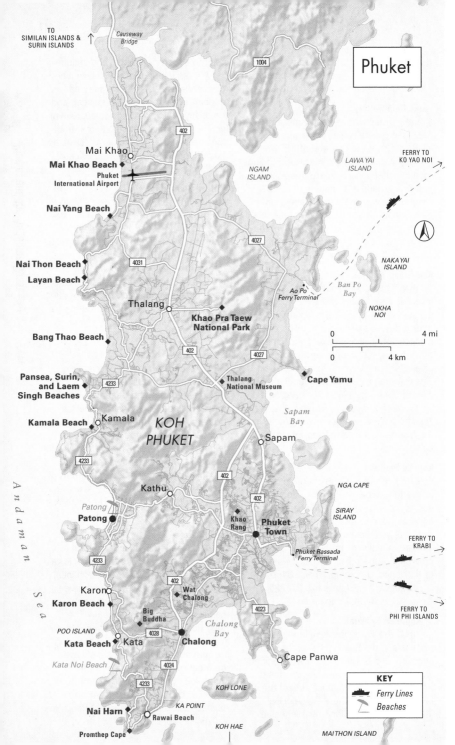

Hotels

Casa Blanca

$$ | **B&B/INN** | One of the best among a string of boutique bed-and-breakfasts in the charming Sino-Colonial Old Town, Casa Blanca is comprised of 17 tasteful rooms with either garden courtyard views or a small balcony looking out onto the street. **Pros:** historic building with lots of charm; good location; swimming pool. **Cons:** hot water access erratic; breakfast not included; far from the beach. [$] *Rooms from: B2,000* ✉ *26 Phuket Rd., Talat Yai, Phuket* ☎ *076/219019* 🌐 *www.casablancaphuket.com* 🍴 *No Meals* 🛏 *17 rooms.*

Metropole

$ | **HOTEL** | The grand old Metropole—the town's first luxury hotel—has a shuttle service to the closest beaches, so you can stay in town and commute to the sea. **Pros:** reasonable rates; shuttle service to beaches; decent food. **Cons:** a little run-down; busy with large tour groups; impersonal. [$] *Rooms from: B1,000* ✉ *1 Montri Rd., Phuket* ☎ *076/215050, 076/214020* 🌐 *www.metropolephuket.com* 🍴 *No Meals* 🛏 *26 rooms.*

Pearl Hotel

$ | **HOTEL** | For a less expensive option, this is a comfortable, convenient hotel in the center of Phuket Town, though it's a little tired around the edges. **Pros:** great live music; convenient location; shuttle service. **Cons:** basic; needs renovation; can be noisy. [$] *Rooms from: B1,300* ✉ *42 Montri Rd., Phuket* ☎ *076/211044* 🌐 *www.pearlhotel.co.th* 🍴 *No Meals* 🛏 *212 rooms.*

Royal Phuket City Hotel

$$ | **HOTEL** | This is arguably Phuket Town's best address, with rooms that are spacious and contemporary. **Pros:** conference center; large rooms; good gym. **Cons:** in-room Wi-Fi is extra; some rooms lack views; a little short on personality. [$] *Rooms from: B2,300* ✉ *154 Phang Nga Rd., Phuket, Phuket* ☎ *076/233333* 🌐 *www.royalphuketcity.com* 🍴 *No Meals* 🛏 *251 rooms.*

Sino House

$$ | **HOTEL** | This addition to Phuket Town provides a pleasant option from the larger, often less charming hotels in the area. **Pros:** nice decor; central; spa discounts for guests. **Cons:** noisy air-conditioning; poor English; dull views. [$] *Rooms from: B2,000* ✉ *1 Montree Rd., Talad Yai, Phuket* ☎ *076/232494 up to 95* 🌐 *www.sinohousephuket.com* 🛏 *57 rooms* 🍴 *No Meals.*

Thalang 37 Guesthouse

$ | **B&B/INN** | This inexpensive guesthouse in a lovely building is becoming ever more popular with backpackers, offering both basic fan-cooled rooms and some air-conditioned ones in an old building. **Pros:** inexpensive; good views from roof; convenenient location in Old Town. **Cons:** street-side rooms can be noisy; not all rooms have a/c; clean but a little worn. [$] *Rooms from: B600* ✉ *37 Thalang Rd., Phuket* ☎ *076/214225* 🌐 *www.thalangguesthouse.com* 🛏 *13 rooms* 🍴 *No Meals.*

Nightlife

★ **Z1mplex**

COCKTAIL LOUNGES | Designed to look like a science laboratory and serving cocktails with names like Parallel Universe and Nebula Jellyfish that look like gorgeous science experiments and taste out of this world, Z1mplex is surely one of Thailand's coolest cocktail bars. It's located on the quiet end of Phang Nga Road in Phuket Town, and is open from 8 pm to midnight. ✉ *156/48 Phangnga Rd, Phuket* ☎ *84/003-6664.*

Khao Pra Taew National Park

19 km (12 miles) north of Phuket Town.

In the north of the island, Khao Pra Taew is the last virgin rain forest in Phuket and is home to populations of several endangered animals, as well as two easily accessible waterfalls. The standard foreigner's fee to enter the park is B200 (Thais pay B40). To access Tonsai Waterfall on the other side of the park, follow the signs and turn east off Highway 402. Here you can find two trails (600 meters and 2 km [1 mile]), through rich, tropical, evergreen forest. Expect lots of rain in the monsoon season. Gibbons, civets, macaques, mouse deer, wild boar, lemurs, and loris live in the park, but they're not easy to spot. Both entrances to the park have bathrooms, parking lots, and food stalls. If you plan to visit both waterfalls, make sure you get entrance tickets at your first stop—they're good for both sites.

The Gibbon Center, inside the park, works to rehabilitate these small apes who were poached from jungles around Thailand and kept as pets or zoo and bar amusements. As a branch of the Wild Animal Rescue Foundation of Thailand, the center aims to release the gibbons back into their natural habitat. Things to know are that you can't see the animals (though you can hear them) and the center, which sits near the parking lot at Bang Pae, receives none of your entrance fee.

GETTING HERE AND AROUND

You can take a taxi, tuk-tuk, or motorcycle here from any of the island's beaches or from Phuket Town. The cost depends on distance—a taxi from Phuket Town would be about B400, a tuk-tuk a little more. If you're driving, take Highway 4027, watch the signs, and turn west toward Bang Pae Waterfall.

Mai Khao Beach

37 km (23 miles) northwest of Phuket Town.

On the northwest coast of Phuket, this 11-km-long beach is part of the Sirinat National Park and is relatively undeveloped, although there are a few resorts and Phuket International Airport isn't far away. The sand here isn't as white and powdery as other Phuket beaches, and as a result, it's usually very quiet.

Beaches

Mai Khao Beach

BEACH | This is Phuket's northernmost beach and it's still a haven for leatherback turtles that lay their eggs here between November and February. The J. W. Marriott here has a beach club if you're looking for a bite to eat and the next-door Sirinath Marine National Park is worth a visit to learn about the turtles. Mai Khao connects with Nai Yang Beach to form Phuket's longest stretch of sand, and is ideal for long walks or a jog. It's dangerous to swim during the monsoons. **Amenities:** food and drink. **Best for:** solitude; sunset; walking. ✉ *Phuket.*

Hotels

Baan Ar-Jor

$$$ | **HOUSE** | A stay in this gorgeous heritage home, lovingly decorated with family heirlooms and and artifacts from the Peranakan period, will give you a taste of Phuket as it was in the 1930s. **Pros:** historic decor; great restaurant; comfortable beds. **Cons:** rooms on the small side; a wonderful experience but not luxe; remote location. [$] *Rooms from: 4,500* ✉ *102 Thepkrasatree Rd, Mai Khao, Mueang Phuket, Thalang* ☎ *062/459–8889* 🌐 *www.baanarjor.com* 🍴 *Free Breakfast* 🛏 *7 rooms, 1 suite.*

★ J. W. Marriott Resort & Spa
$$$ | **RESORT** | Far from the crowds, this
secluded resort is on a vast stretch of
sand and has spotlessly clean, luxurious
rooms with impeccable classic Thai
design. **Pros:** Thai-style rooms; long and
quiet beach; a wide range of ameni-
ties. **Cons:** surf sometimes too rough
for swimming; may be too isolated for
some; not much else around. $ *Rooms
from: B4,400 ⊠ 231 Moo 3, Mai Khao,
Phuket ☎ 076/338000 ⊕ www.marriott.
com/HKTJW ⌁ 265 rooms* ⦿ No Meals.

Nai Yang Beach

*34 km (20 miles) northwest of Phuket
Town.*

This relatively small, laid-back beach is
popular with locals and the expat crowd.
The fact that part of the beach is inside
Sirinath National Park means that it's
somewhat shielded from the over-de-
velopment juggernaut, though there is a
nice selection of places to stay.

GETTING HERE AND AROUND
Nai Yang Beach is accessible from High-
way 4027, the main road running through
the island. Taxis, tuk-tuks, and motorcy-
cles will take you to and from other parts
of the island.

■ TIP→ **Transport is often difficult to find on
the road through Nai Yang Beach.**

Your hotel may be able to help arrange
transportation.

Beaches

Nai Yang Beach
BEACH | Nai Yang Beach is really a contin-
uation south of Mai Khao, making a long
stretch of sand good for a jog or swim-
ming in the dry season. Casuarina trees
line the gently curving shore offering
shade. It's a far quieter beach than most,
with a strip of trees and a small string
of beachside restaurants and bars, tour

guides, tailors, and shops. Fishing boats
anchor nearby, making for picture-perfect
sunrises and sunsets. **Amenities:** food
and drink. **Best for:** snorkeling; sunrise;
sunset; swimming. ⊠ *Nai Yang Beach
Rd., Phuket* ✢ *Near airport.*

Restaurants

You can find tasty, fresh seafood at Nai
Yang's beachside restaurants.

Hotels

★ The Slate
$$$ | **HOTEL** | **FAMILY** | Phuket's tin-mining
history is the inspiration at The Slate, and
the resort features interesting collectibles from the Na-Rarong family mines,
with a decor that blends funky postin-
dustrial concrete with a hint of Thai rustic
luxury. **Pros:** good spa; great breakfast;
unique decor. **Cons:** some rooms affected
by noise from nearby beach bar; staff
can be unhelpful; lots of mosquitoes.
$ *Rooms from: B4,300 ⊠ Nai Yang Beach
and National Park, 116 Moo 1, Phuket
☎ 076/327006, 076/327015 ⊕ www.
theslatephuket.com ⌁ 177 rooms* ⦿ No
Meals.

Nai Thon and Layan Beaches

*30 km (18½ miles) northwest of Phuket
Town.*

Being one of smallest beaches on the
island, this spot exudes a calm and
relaxed vibe. The lush, tropical rain forest
acts as a natural barrier too—mainly
keeping many visitors away! If you
make it here, you can easily feel alone
when wandering along the wide, sandy
expanse. There is a smattering of beach
resorts, but they're totally unobtrusive as
you stroll along the palm-fringed beaches
in the warm, azure water.

GETTING HERE AND AROUND

Nai Thon and Layan beaches are easily accessible from all parts of Phuket Island. Taxis, tuk-tuks, and motorcycles will gladly ferry you to and from these quiet beaches.

Beaches

Nai Thon and Layan Beaches

BEACH | A few miles north of Bang Thao Bay, follow a smaller highway off the main routes (4030 and 4031) along a scenic coastline reminiscent of California's Pacific Coast Highway. These beaches are good for swimming and snorkeling in the dry season. Layan is a wildlife hot spot, as the lake behind the beach attracts lots of wildfowl. Nai Thon is 1 km long and still has few accommodations. **Amenities:** food and drink. **Best for:** snorkeling; swimming; walking. ✉ *Phuket.*

Hotels

The Pavilions Phuket

$$$$ | **RESORT** | At the Pavilions, each of the private villas has a pool and a small kitchen, plus you can have meals delivered to your room, and spa treatments, too, so you never have to see other guests if you don't want to. **Pros:** fabulous views from the bar; real sense of privacy; ideal honeymoon retreat. **Cons:** no children under 14; a bit isolated; the beach is a bit far. [$] *Rooms from: B9,000* ✉ *31/1 Moo 6, Cherngtalay, Thalang* ☎ *076/317600, 091/621–4841 in Bangkok* 🌐 *www.pavilions-resorts.com* 🛏 *30 villas* 🍴 *Free Breakfast.*

Trisara

$$$$ | **RESORT** | Opulence is the standard at the Trisara resort; rooms feature a variety of Thai wooden art pieces, silk throw pillows on the divans, and 32-inch plasma TVs hidden in the walls. **Pros:** golf course; beautiful Thai decor; subtle and professional service. **Cons:** pricey; often fully booked. [$] *Rooms from: B21,000* ✉ *60/1 Moo 6, Srisoonthorn Rd., Cherngtalay, Phuket* ☎ *076/310100, 076/310355* 🌐 *www.trisara.com* 🍴 *Free Breakfast* 🛏 *42 rooms.*

Bang Thao Beach

22 km (14 miles) northwest of Phuket Town.

A favorite of those seeking a more relaxed pace than the hectic and developed Phuket beaches, Bang Thao Beach (a resort area collectively called Laguna Phuket) has shallow water and a number of upmarket resorts and luxury villas along its 4-mile stretch of sand.

GETTING HERE AND AROUND

Bang Thao Beach is accessible from Highway 4027. Taxis, tuk-tuks, and motorcycles can all take you to and from the beach. It can be difficult to find transportation leaving the beach but if you wait on the beach road a taxi or another form of transport will materialize eventually, or you can use the Grab app to call a taxi. There's a free shuttle service that takes you between the resorts along the shore.

Beaches

Bang Thao Beach

BEACH | The beach itself is a long stretch (4 miles) of white sand, with vendors offering a variety of sports equipment rentals, inexpensive seafood, beach massages, and cocktails. The beach is good for swimming in the hot season, the lagoon for kayaking anytime. The atmosphere is relaxed, making this a beach well suited to young families. **Amenities:** food and drink; showers; toilets; water sports. **Best for:** sunset; swimming; walking. ✉ *Soi Ao Bangtao, Cherng Talay, Bang Thao Beach.*

🍴 Restaurants

Catch Beach Club
$$$$ | **FUSION** | Although now just one among many superb venues, Catch remains the standard-bearer for beach clubs on the island. In its former location on Surin Beach, this gleaming white, St. Tropez–style lounge drew Phuket's rich—and occasionally famous—with its DJ beats, imported Champagne and fine-dining tapas. **Known for:** DJ tunes; wood-fired pizza; popular Sunday brunch. [$] *Average main: B500* ✉ *12/88 Moo 2, Cherng Talay, Bang Thao Beach* ☎ *65/348–2017* 🌐 *www.catchbeachclub.com.*

Seafood
$ | **SEAFOOD** | The friendly ladies at this popular street-side shanty serve made-to-order noodles and stir-fries with seafood. Every meal comes with a complimentary bowl of aromatic cardamom soup, which is delicious and known to aid digestion. **Known for:** authentic flavors; free cardamom soup; everything made-to-order. [$] *Average main: B100* ✉ *Phuket* ✣ *About 5 km (3 miles) east of resort. Look for small sign on left side of road that reads "Seafood." If you reach mosque, you've gone too far* ☎.

🛏 Hotels

Andaman Bangtao Bay Resort
$ | **RESORT** | **FAMILY** | It's not opulent, but this small, friendly, and wonderfully situated resort offers comfortable rooms only 20 meters from the beach, with nice en suite bathrooms, air-conditioning, satellite TV, and beachfront patios. **Pros:** good restaurant; peaceful location; friendly service. **Cons:** pool very small; beach is not that great; a little pricey for what you get. [$] *Rooms from: B1,900* ✉ *82/9 Moo 3, Cherngtalay, Bang Thao Beach* ☎ *076/314214, 081/599–7889, 084/734-5230* 🌐 *www.andamanbangtaobayresort.com* 🍴 *Free Breakfast* 🛏 *8 rooms.*

Angsana Laguna Phuket
$$$ | **RESORT** | **FAMILY** | Set on Bang Thao Beach, this resort is stylish and contemporary with tastefully decorated rooms and suites that all have either garden, lagoon, pool, or ocean views. **Pros:** tranquil setting; there is a free shuttle bus/boat around the property; great spa. **Cons:** some accommodations are far from the beach; loud music from the on-site beach club; resort is huge. [$] *Rooms from: 5,000* ✉ *10 Moo 4, Srisoonthorn Road Cherngtalay, Thalang* ☎ *076/324101* 🌐 *www.angsana.com/en/thailand/laguna-phuket* 🍴 *Free Breakfast* 🛏 *371 rooms.*

★ **Banyan Tree Phuket**
$$$$ | **RESORT** | **FAMILY** | Of the quintet of resorts on Laguna Beach, this is the most exclusive—and expensive. **Pros:** peaceful setting; great spa; children's programs. **Cons:** pricey; not much else nearby; resort is huge. [$] *Rooms from: B12,000* ✉ *33 Moo 4, Srisoonthorn Rd., Cherngtalay, Amphur Talang, Phuket* ☎ *076/372400* 🌐 *www.banyantree.com* 🛏 *123 villas* 🍴 *Free Breakfast.*

Sunwing Bangtao Beach
$$ | **RESORT** | **FAMILY** | This resort really caters to families, with well-organized daily activities of kids of all ages and babysitting services, as well as two pools, and a beachfront location. **Pros:** safe, fun environment for kids; two restaurants have varied, interesting menus; resort shop sells all the essentials. **Cons:** somewhat remote from shops or restaurants; there are a lot of kids running around; poolside can be chaotic. [$] *Rooms from: B3,500* ✉ *22 Moo 2, Chueng Thalay, Phuket* ☎ *076/314263 up to 65* 🌐 *www.sunwingphuket.com* 🛏 *283 rooms* 🍴 *Free Breakfast.*

Pansea, Surin, and Laem Singh Beaches

21 km (12 miles) northwest of Phuket Town.

Located on Phuket's west coast, many of the island's rich set have houses here (it's known locally as Millionaires' Mile), nestled among high-end resorts. The sand is white, the water is clear, and it's remained pretty quiet here. There are just a few very local, rustic Thai eateries, and lots of serenity.

GETTING HERE AND AROUND

Pansea and Surin beaches are accessible from Highway 4027. Taxis, tuk-tuks, and motorcycles can all take you to and from the beach. A taxi to or from Phuket Town should cost approximately B550 to B700; expect to pay a little more for a tuk-tuk. Laem Singh is only reachable by boat.

 Beaches

Laem Singh Beach

BEACH | Lovely little Laem Singh beach has become more off the beaten path since road access was cut off when the adjacent land was sold to a property developer in 2017. These days it's only accessible by water: You can hire one of the small orange boats from Surin Beach for just B100 per person. There are no facilities on Laem Singh, so bring refreshments. **Amenities:** none. **Best for:** solitude; swimming. ⊠ *Laem Sing Beach.*

Pansea Beach

BEACH | FAMILY | On Phuket's west coast just north of Surin Beach, this small, secluded stretch of sand is backed by coconut trees and a variety of exotic flora and fauna. At the southern end of the beach is a small shack serving drinks and snacks, and there are loungers for hire. **Amenities:** food and drink. **Best for:** snorkeling; sunrise; sunset. ⊠ *Pansea Beach, Surin Beach.*

Surin Beach

BEACH | This long stretch of sandy beach has some grassy areas shaded by pine trees—great spots to take refuge from the midday sun. The beach is generally quiet but it does get busy on weekends, as it's popular with local Thais and expats. The area is best avoided during the rainy season, as the seas can get rough and there are strong, dangerous currents. Refreshments can be bought from local vendors working the beach. **Amenities:** food and drink; toilets. **Best for:** snorkeling; swimming; walking. ⊠ *Surin Beach, Choeng Thale, Thalang* ⊹ *Go through Kamala and continue past Laem Singh Beach. Take sharp left turn down to beach when you reach the three-way junction. It's a 25-min drive north from Patong.*

 Hotels

★ Amanpuri Resort

$$$$ | RESORT | You'd be hard-pressed to find a more sparklingly dignified hotel in Thailand—nor one quite as expensive. **Pros:** private beach; so much luxury; great sunsets. **Cons:** too isolated for some; expensive; service can be apathetic at times. Ⓢ *Rooms from: B35124* ⊠ *Pansea Beach, Cherngtalay, Thalang, Phuket* ☎ *076/324333* ⊕ *www.amanpuri.com* ⦿ *All-Inclusive* ⤵ *71 villas.*

Surin Bay Inn

$ | B&B/INN | It's just a few minutes walk from the beach but it means the prices at this small, friendly hotel are quite reasonable, and some rooms have balconies overlooking the street along the beach. **Pros:** particularly helpful staff; nice restaurant; great rooms for moderate price. **Cons:** no elevator; not on beach; only top-floor rooms have good views. Ⓢ *Rooms from: B1,100* ⊠ *106/11 Surin Beach, Surin Beach* ☎ *081/894–1162* ⦿ *Free Breakfast* ⤵ *12 rooms.*

The Surin Phuket
$$$$ | RESORT | Almost completely concealed by a grove of coconut palms, this resort has more than 100 thatched-roof cottages—each with its own sundeck—overlooking a quiet beach. **Pros:** private beach; great location; fab pool area. **Cons:** long walk (uphill) from the beach to top villas; layout a little confusing; isolated. [$] *Rooms from: B6,200* ✉ *118 Moo 3, Cherngtalay, Phuket* ☎ *076/621580 up to 82* 🌐 *www.thesurinphuket.com* 🛏 *103 chalets* 🍴 *Free Breakfast.*

Kamala Beach

18 km (11 miles) west of Phuket Town.

Kamala Beach is quieter and less touristy than its neighbor, Patong, and is a good, fairly central base. There are a few reasonably priced accommodations that attract longer-stay visitors, and a small entertainment complex has a few bars and eateries, but overall the area is calm and quiet compared to the more developed beaches on the island. A few of the European dance clubs are here but they're far from the residential areas.

GETTING HERE AND AROUND

A taxi from Phuket Town or Patong Beach will cost about B500.

Beaches

Kamala Beach
BEACH | Kamala Beach is unremarkable but endearing, particularly to pensioners who return here year after year for the beach's more reserved ambience. Kamala can get cramped during the day and offers numerous accommodation and dining options, but if you're staying, don't expect a lively nightlife. **Amenities:** food and drink; water sports. **Best for:** swimming. ✉ *Phuket.*

Hotels

Hyatt Regency Phuket Resort
$$$ | RESORT | FAMILY | On the tropical hillside at Kamala Bay, these spacious, contemporary rooms and suites all have private balconies with spectacular sea views. **Pros:** large rooms and suites; children's activities; modern decor. **Cons:** not that close to the shops in Kamala; remote location; not on the beach. [$] *Rooms from: 5,000* ✉ *16/12 Moo 6 Kamala, Amphur Kathu, Kamala Beach* ☎ *076/231234* 🌐 *www.hyatt.com/en-US/hotel/thailand/hyatt-regency-phuket-resort/phuhr?src=corp_lclb_gmb_seo_phuhr* 🍴 *Free Breakfast* 🛏 *201 rooms.*

★ **Keemala**
$$$$ | RESORT | The unique-looking thatched tree houses of this luxurious resort are tucked into the slopes of a serene jungle valley close to the shores of Kamala Beach. **Pros:** unique lodgings; innovative theme; health-focused cuisine. **Cons:** steep inclines to walk; not on the beach; too quirky for some. [$] *Rooms from: B26,000* ✉ *10/88 Moo 6, Nakasud Rd., Kamala Beach* ☎ *076/358777* 🌐 *keemala.com* 🛏 *38 rooms* 🍴 *Free Breakfast.*

PapaCrab Boutique Guesthouse
$ | B&B/INN | This small, friendly, family-run boutique guesthouse is in a quiet spot near town, on the quieter south end of Kamala Beach. **Pros:** just off the beach; excellent price for what is offered; good service. **Cons:** patchy Wi-Fi; not great views; rooms are on the small side. [$] *Rooms from: B950* ✉ *93/5 Moo 3, Kamala Beach* ☎ *084/744–0482* 🌐 *phuketpapacrab.com* 🍴 *No Meals* 🛏 *10 rooms.*

Patong

13 km (8 miles) west of Phuket Town.

You'd hardly believe it today, but Patong was once the island's most remote beach, completely cut off by the surrounding mountains and only accessible by boat. Today it's a thriving, thronged, beach-resort community frequented mainly by international visitors. Though overdeveloped, its convenience and compact size makes Patong a great place for new visitors to Thailand looking for a nice beach with characteristic Thai experiences, like Muay Thai (Thai boxing), street shopping, and authentic Thai food, as well as familiar facilities, like Starbucks, sushi bars, shopping malls, and chain hotels.

The lively nightlife scene remains a big draw for many tourists, but the sheer variety of restaurants, hotels, and entertainment on offer ensures Patong's popularity with a wide variety of visitors.

GETTING HERE AND AROUND

Every street, hotel, and shop in Patong seems to have a ready team of taxis, tuk-tuks, and motorcycles whose drivers are all more than happy to ferry you around. Just pick your vehicle of choice and bargain hard. Tuk-tuks to Phuket Town should cost approximately B500; to Karon will be B400; and to Kamala will cost around B300. It can be a little frustrating to get to the beach during morning rush hour, because the road from Phuket Town is often congested.

 Beaches

Patong Beach

BEACH | Once cluttered with beach umbrellas, Patong Beach now has some room for both sunbathing and playing soccer or Frisbee on the beach. Every conceivable beach activity from wakeboarding to Jet Skiing to parasailing is available. Patong became so popular because of its picture-perfect paradisical nature, and now its popularity has caused some degradation of the environment, particularly noticeable when the monsoon rains wash the grime off the street and onto the beach. **Amenities:** food and drink; showers; toilets; water sports. **Best for:** partiers; sunset; swimming; walking. ⊠ *Thaweewong Rd., Phuket.*

 Restaurants

Acqua Restaurant

$$$$ | **ITALIAN** | For a change of pace from Thai food, head to this Italian restaurant specializing in seafood and Sicilian specialities. Dishes are presented with flair and the busy dining room is a lively backdrop. **Known for:** good wine selection; bustling atmosphere; well-executed seafood. Ⓢ *Average main: 700* ⊠ *324/15 Prabaramee Road, Patong Kalim, Patong* ☎ *076/618127, 087/270–5929* ⊕ *www. acquarestaurantphuket.com.*

Baan Rim Pa

$$$$ | **THAI** | Just about 2 km north of Patong and perched over the water, the magnificent Baan Rim Pa Thai restaurant is laid out over several levels to showcase the stunning panoramic views of the Andaman Sea. Elegant teak and silk decor, a piano and cocktail bar, and excellent Thai food make this one of Phuket's premier dining establishments. **Known for:** extensive wine cellar; cliff-side dining; sunset views. Ⓢ *Average main: B1,450* ⊠ *249/4 Pa Tong, Kalim Beach, Patong* ☎ *092/274–9095* ⊕ *www.baanrimpa.com.*

Sam's Steaks & Grill

$$$$ | **STEAKHOUSE** | This stylish restaurant in the Holiday Inn Resort serves prime cuts of imported beef prepared with notable French flair and elegantly presented. The atmosphere is peaceful, away from the crowds on Patong's busy streets. **Known for:** romantic evenings; quality meat; sophisticated atmosphere. Ⓢ *Average main: B950* ⊠ *52 Thaweewong Rd., Patong* ☎ *076/370200.*

Hotels

Four Points by Sheraton Phuket Patong Beach Resort

$$$ | **RESORT** | **FAMILY** | Located across from Patong Beach, this stylish and contemporary resort has a bit of everything, including five restaurants, a bar, a kids club, a playground, a swimming pool, and more. **Pros:** great for families; great location; vast pool. **Cons:** decor is rather generic in feel; fills up fast; lots of kids. $ Rooms from: 5,000 ⊠ 198/8-9 Thaweewong Rd, Patong ☎ 076/645999 ⊕ www.marriott.com/hotels/travel/hktfp-four-points-phuket-patong-beach-resort ❚⊙❙ Free Breakfast ⥂ 600 rooms and suites.

FunDee Boutique Hotel

$ | **HOTEL** | In the heart of Patong and close to all the action, the FunDee is a good budget option for this bustling area. **Pros:** friendly service; central but quiet location; reliable Wi-Fi. **Cons:** only one elevator; bit of a trek to the beach (10 minutes); no views. $ Rooms from: B600 ⊠ 232/3-4 Phung Muang Sai Gor Rd., Patong Kathu, Patong ☎ 076/366780 ⊕ www.fundee.co.th ⥂ 36 rooms ❚⊙❙ No Meals.

Holiday Inn Resort Phuket

$$ | **RESORT** | **FAMILY** | This stylish, modern hotel exudes the kind of sophistication that most people would never imagine possible from a Holiday Inn or from Patong in general. **Pros:** central location; next to beach; children's programs. **Cons:** large complex; central location also means it can be noisy; family atmosphere not ideal for everyone. $ Rooms from: B3,400 ⊠ 52 Thaweewong Rd., Patong Beach, Patong ☎ 076/349991 up to 92, 076/370200 ⊕ www.phuket.holidayinnresorts.com ❚⊙❙ Free Breakfast ⥂ 405 rooms.

Impiana Resort Patong

$$ | **RESORT** | This hotel's chief attraction is its unbeatable location, right in the middle of the city yet facing the beach. **Pros:** good restaurant and bar; best location

in Patong; beachfront spa. **Cons:** busy beach road traffic; not all rooms have a view; beach fills up. $ Rooms from: B3,500 ⊠ 41 Taweewong Rd., Patong ☎ 076/340138 ⊕ phukethotels.impiana.com.my ⥂ 68 rooms ❚⊙❙ No Meals.

Red Planet Phuket Hotel

$ | **HOTEL** | This convenient, practical budget option has a great location, well-trained staff, and immaculate rooms. **Pros:** immaculate; good value; lots of breakfast options. **Cons:** no pool; small rooms; no direct beach access. $ Rooms from: B700 ⊠ 56 Raj, Uthit 200 Pee Rd., Karon Beach ✛ Opposite Patong Post Office ☎ 26/135888 ⊕ www.redplanethotels.com ⥂ 60 rooms ❚⊙❙ Free Breakfast.

★ Rosewood Phuket

$$$$ | **RESORT** | **FAMILY** | On an island filled with luxury resorts, the Rosewood sets itself apart, literally, with its 600-meter secluded beach and expansive private pavilions and villas, instead of standard rooms or suites. **Pros:** only villas and pavilions; private beach; luxury spa. **Cons:** few local restaurants; long walk to town; pricey. $ Rooms from: B25,500 ⊠ 88/28 Muen-Ngern Rd, Patong ☎ 076/356888 ⊕ rosewoodhotels.com/en/phuket ❚⊙❙ Free Breakfast ⥂ 71 villas.

 Nightlife

Bangla Road, the main walking street, is vivid and exciting but more like a carnival than anything sleazy. Children pose for photos with flamboyant and friendly ladyboys; honeymooning couples people-watch from the beer bars along the traffic-free promenade, and everyone else simply strolls the strip, some stopping to dance or play Connect Four, Jenga, or a curiously popular nail-hammering game with friendly Thai hostesses.

There are regularly scheduled Muay Thai fights at the arena on the corner of Bangla and Rat-U-Thit Songroipee roads.

The Boat Bar Disco & Cabaret

DANCE CLUBS | With numerous male staff, two dance performances every night, and live DJ sessions, this gay-friendly bar attracts huge crowds for fun, late-night parties. ✉ *Paradise Complex, 125/20 Rat-U-Thit Rd., Patong* ☎ *076/342206* 🌐 *www.facebook.com/Boatbar.*

Illuzion

DANCE CLUBS | If you're looking for a large-scale party, this massive club has it all, including international DJs and live music, with a capacity to hold a crowd of over 5,000. A state-of-the-art sound system and lively atmosphere ensure a great night out in Patong. ✉ *31 Bangla Road, Patong* ☎ *076/683030* 🌐 *www.illuzionphuket.com.*

Simon Cabaret

CABARET | This is Patong's most sensational drag show, with beautiful costumes and fabulous choreography. There are two shows nightly, at 7:30 and 9:30. ✉ *8 Sirirach Rd., Patong* ☎ *076/342011* 🌐 *www.phuket-simoncabaret.com.*

Thaweewong Road

LIVE MUSIC | Patong has a reputation for its happening nightlife, and the seedy side of it is easily avoidable. Some of the more tasteful nightlife venues are found along **Thaweewong Road**, including live music bars, expat pubs, and folks picking up a to-go drink from 7-Eleven and sitting on the beach. ✉ *Thaweewong Rd., Patong.*

Karon Beach

20 km (12 miles) southwest of Phuket Town.

Just south of the loud, brash Patong, Karon Beach and its smaller northern counterpart, Karon Noi, are much more laid-back and family-friendly. Hotels, restaurants, tailors, dive operators, and gift shops line the main beach strip, catering to tourists around the clock. What some don't know is that the Karon area is home to a small community of local artists, who live and work in a cluster of huts and galleries.

GETTING HERE AND AROUND

Taxis, tuk-tuks, and motorcycles take you to and from Karon Beach. A taxi costs about B400 for the 5-km (3-mile) ride to Patong; a tuk-tuk is about B300.

Sights

Karon Beach

BEACH | A long stretch of white sand and good dry-season swimming are the big appeal here, though the beach is more open than most in Phuket, and there's very little shade. **Amenities:** food and drink; showers; water sports. **Best for:** snorkeling; sunset; swimming; walking. ✉ *Karon Beach.*

Restaurants

El Gaucho Steakhouse

$$$$ | **BRAZILIAN** | Churrasco (Brazilian grilled meat) is the specialty at the Mövenpick resort's restaurant, with a terrace overlooking Karon Beach and sunset views that make dining here delightful. The space is large but still manages to be atmospheric, with discreet background music and friendly staff. **Known for:** efficient staff; Brazilian barbecue; beach views. [$] *Average main: B900* ✉ *Karon Beach Sq., Movenpick Resort, 509 Patak Rd., Karon Beach* 🌐 *www.moevenpick-hotels.com/en/asia/thailand/phuket/resort-phuket-karon-beach/restaurants/restaurants/el-gaucho/.*

★ **On the Rock**

$$$ | **ECLECTIC** | Built on a rock overlooking Karon Beach, this restaurant has great views of the water. Seafood is the specialty, but well-made Italian and traditional Thai dishes are also on the menu. **Known for:** beachside tables; local seafood; good Italian food. [$] *Average main: B350* ✉ *47 Karon Rd., Marina Cottage*

A Festival for Health and Purity

The annual Vegetarian Festival in Phuket, held in late September or early October, is the biggest fete in town. According to local legend, it started in 1825 when a traveling Chinese opera group fell ill in the mining village of Kathu. The Taoist group feared that their illnesses were the result of their failure to pay proper respects to the nine Emperor Gods. After sticking to a strict vegetarian diet to honor these gods, they quickly recovered. This made quite an impression on the local villagers, and the island has celebrated a nine-day festival for good health ever since. Along with detoxing the body, the festival is meant to renew the soul—not killing animals for food is supposed to calm and purify the spirit.

The festival involves numerous temple ceremonies, parades, and fireworks. But what most fascinates visitors are the tests of faith, including fire walking and climbing ladders made of sharp blades, and the grisly body-piercing rituals. Some devotees become mediums for warrior spirits, known as *mah song*, going into trances and mutilating their bodies to ward off demons and bring the whole community good luck. These mediums pierce their bodies (tongues and cheeks are popular choices) with all sorts of things from swords to bicycle spokes. Supposedly, the presence of the spirits within them keeps them from feeling any pain.

The events are centered on the island's 40 or so Chinese shrines and temples. Processions are held daily from morning until midafternoon, all finishing at the seaside Kiew Teng Heng temple on the Saphan Hin Peninsula. The Tourism Authority of Thailand office in Phuket Town can provide a list of all activities and their locations, as does local newspaper *The Phuket News*. Note that you might want to bring earplugs—it's believed that the louder the fireworks, the more evil spirits they'll scare away.

Hotel, Karon Beach ✥ South end of Karon Beach ☎ 076/330625, 076/330493 up to 95 🌐 www.marinaphuket.com/restaurants.html.

Hotels

Fantasy Hill Bungalows

$ | **B&B/INN** | On a hill between the two beach areas of Kata and Karon, these well-situated accommodations are a great value. **Pros:** good location; garden courtyard; balconies. **Cons:** not all rooms have air-conditioning; few amenities; breakfast is extra. *[$] Rooms from: B400 ✉ 8/1 Karon Rd., Karon Beach ☎ 076/330106 ✉ fantasyhill@hotmail.com 🛏 18 rooms, 6 bungalows 🍴 No Meals.*

In On the Beach

$ | **HOTEL** | This hotel way at the north end of Karon is literally on the beach, with great sea views from many of the rooms, which are decorated in a modern, functional style. **Pros:** nice swimming pool; beach location; quiet. **Cons:** ground-floor rooms lack some privacy; slightly removed from center of town; noisy air-conditioning. *[$] Rooms from: B1,750 ✉ Moo 1, Patak Rd., Karon Beach ☎ 076/398220 up to 24 🌐 www.karon-inonthebeach.com 💳 No credit cards 🛏 30 rooms 🍴 Free Breakfast.*

Le Meridien

$$ | RESORT | FAMILY | Between Patong and Karon Beach, this sprawling resort has more bars, cafés, and restaurants than in many small towns, while the range of outdoor diversions—everything from tennis to water skiing—means you never have to leave the property. **Pros:** private beach; large swimming pool; excellent activities. **Cons:** not all rooms have a view; too big for some. $ *Rooms from: B3,750* ✉ *29 Soi Karon Nui, Tambon Karon, Amphur Muang, Karon Beach* ☎ *076/370100* ⊕ *www.lemeridienphuket-beachresort.com* ▤ *No credit cards* 🛏 *470 rooms* ○ *No Meals.*

Marina Phuket Resort

$$$$ | RESORT | This surprisingly quiet option has luxury cottages that stretch over the lush hillside that separates Karon from Kata Beach—those higher on the hill are the quietest. **Pros:** good location; private beach and nice pool; free airport shuttle. **Cons:** difference in amenities between rooms; pool closes after sunset; no hotel loungers on beach. $ *Rooms from: B7,500* ✉ *47 Karon Rd., Karon Beach* ☎ *076/330493 to 95, 076/330625* ⊕ *www.marinaphuket.com* 🛏 *89 rooms* ○ *Free Breakfast.*

Movenpick Resort and Spa

$$$ | RESORT | FAMILY | This resort takes great pride in its service levels, with polite, knowledgeable, and informative staff. **Pros:** beachfront location; so many facilities; close to Karon Town. **Cons:** slight package-tour feel; same spaces could use an upgrade; very complex. $ *Rooms from: B4,500* ✉ *509 Patak Rd., Karon Beach, Karon Beach* ☎ *076/396139* ⊕ *www.moevenpick-hotels.com* 🛏 *175 rooms, 159 suites* ○ *Free Breakfast.*

Phuket Orchid Resort

$ | RESORT | FAMILY | Though this resort is slightly inland, the beach is a short walk away and the lack of a beachfront brings the rates down considerably (though this also makes it very popular). **Pros:** great pool; interesting design influences including Khmer and Chinese; budget-friendly. **Cons:** only partly renovated; not on beach; make sure to ask for a no-smoking room. $ *Rooms from: B1,500* ✉ *34 Luang Pohchuan Rd., Karon Muang, Karon Beach* ☎ *076/396519* ⊕ *www.katagroup.com* ○ *No Meals* 🛏 *525 rooms.*

 ## Activities

Dino Park Mini Golf

MINIATURE GOLF | FAMILY | These Flint-stones-style buildings along the road in central Karon village belong to Dino Park Mini Golf, with a dinosaur-themed bar and restaurant and 18 holes of miniature golf, featuring a swamp, a lava cave, and a whole lot of dinosaurs. ✉ *Karon Beach* ☎ *076/330625* ⊕ *www.dinopark.com* 🎫 *B240.*

 ## Shopping

Karon is a hub for local artists with art galleries selling unique paintings, jewelry made with Thai silver, woven sandals from the Northern tribes, small wooden elephants and frog carvings, and hand-made bags. There's a market at the Karon Temple on Tuesdays where you can find lots of handicrafts, and a large bazaar on the Karon Beach Road, as well.

Kata Beach

22 km (13 miles) southwest of Phuket Town.

Popular for its stunning white-sand beach with warm, crystal clear waters, Kata is one of the most photographed beaches in Thailand. There's plenty to see and do here besides relaxing and taking in the beautiful landscape. Surfing is one of the main draws to Kata, coinciding with "low season" from May to October, so there's pretty much always a lively restaurant and nightlife scene. This is Phuket's main family destination, in part because it's laid-back but also because it doesn't have the hard-core element of Patong, plus there's a greater variety of restaurants and shopping than nearby Karon.

GETTING HERE AND AROUND

Taxis, tuk-tuks, and motorcycles all vie for your attention to take you to and from Kata Beach. Expect to pay B500 into Phuket Town or B400 into Patong by taxi, and about B50 more for a tuk-tuk.

Beaches

Kata Beach is essentially two sections: Kata Yai is the main beach, located near the main shopping street of Thai Na. The southern, more secluded part, is Kata Noi. Kata Noi is generally very quiet although taken up with the long and expensive Katathani Phuket Beach Resort. Navigating Kata is easy—just follow the beach road from north to south.

Kata Yai Beach

BEACH | Of the popular beaches on the west coast of Phuket, Kata Yai, in central Kata, has the calmest waters, and a shaded sidewalk runs the length of the beach. Club Med dominates a large hunk of the beachfront, keeping the development frenzy to the southern end. There's also a committed group of regulars here who surf the small local breaks. This is one of the calmer beach scenes in Phuket, and so is especially good for families. **Amenities:** food and drink; water sports. **Best for:** sunset; surfing; swimming; windsurfing. ✉ *Pakbang Rd., Laem Sai, Kata Beach.*

Hotels

The Boathouse Phuket

$$$$ | RESORT | This landmark resort—one of Phuket's oldest—has long been one of the most sought-after places to stay. **Pros:** cooking classes available; spacious, modern rooms; right on Kata Beach. **Cons:** limited parking; not all rooms have beach views; swimming pool area a bit on the small side. [$] *Rooms from: B8,700* ✉ *182 Koktanode Rd., Kata Beach* ☎ *076/330015* 🌐 *www.boathousephuket.com* 🍴 *Free Breakfast* 🛏 *45 rooms.*

Katathani Phuket Beach Resort

$$ | RESORT | FAMILY | This long, sprawling lodge fronts most of the Kata Noi Beach, which tends to keep nonguests away and leave nearly 1 km (½ mile) of smooth sand delightfully peaceful. **Pros:** spacious, well-kept grounds; many pools, including ones for kids; fabulous views. **Cons:** in-room Wi-Fi extra charge; the food is average; large and rather impersonal touch. [$] *Rooms from: B3,400* ✉ *14 Kata Noi Rd., Karon, Muang, Phuket, Kata Beach* ☎ *076/330124 up to 26* 🌐 *www.katathani.com* 🛏 *479 rooms* 🍴 *Free Breakfast.*

Sawasdee Village

$$ | RESORT | A few minutes' walk from Kata Beach, this resort comprises a spacious garden with four large swimming pools, lush greenery, beautiful stone-carved fountains, and a complex of villas and rooms designed and decorated in a Thai–Moroccan style. **Pros:** good dining; attentive staff. **Cons:** mosquitoes; 10 minutes from Kata Beach; rooms on the small side. [$] *Rooms from: B4,000* ✉ *38 Katekwan Rd., Kata Beach* ☎ *076/330870 up to 71* 🌐 *www.phuketsawasdee.com* 🛏 *40 rooms* 🍴 *Free Breakfast.*

Nai Harn

18 km (11 miles) southwest of Phuket Town.

South of Kata Beach the road cuts inland across the hills then drops into yet another beautiful bay, Nai Harn. Less busy than other nearby beaches, though popular among locals and expats, Nai Harn has a small but interesting choice of accommodations and nearby attractions, such as Nai Harn Lake and viewpoints such as the Promthep Cape, as well as simple but authentic restaurants. Over at Rawai

Beach, the pier is a pleasant place for an early-evening walk.

GETTING HERE AND AROUND

This is the southernmost beach on Phuket. You can get here from Phuket Town or along the coastal road through Kata, Karon, and Patong. Taxis, tuk-tuks, and motorcycles will all take you to and from Nai Harn; a taxi to or from Phuket Town should be about B550, and it costs B1,000 to get to the airport.

Sights

Promthep Cape

VIEWPOINT | From the top of the cliff at Promthep Cape, the southernmost point on Phuket, you're treated to a fantastic, panoramic view of Nai Harn Bay, the coastline, and a few outlying islands. At sunset you can share the view with swarms of others who pour forth from tour buses to view the same sight. If you're driving, arrive early so you get a parking spot. There's a lighthouse atop the point, as well as a collection of elephant statues where locals go to pray for good fortune. ✉ *Nai Harn.*

Restaurants

Promthep Cape Restaurant

$ | **THAI** | Although it doesn't look like much from the Promthep Cape parking lot, views from the tables out back are hard to beat. The restaurant serves Thai food, specializing in fresh seafood, and some Western fare. **Known for:** fresh seafood; secluded setting; proximity to lighthouse. [$] *Average main: B180* ✉ *94/6 Moo 6, Rawai Beach, Nai Harn* ☎ *076/288656, 076/288084* 🌐 *www.phuketdir.com/phromthepcaperest* 💳 *No credit cards.*

Hotels

The Nai Harn

$$$$ | **HOTEL** | Once known as the Royal Phuket Yacht Club, this long-standing resort has been through several incarnations and once welcomed celebrity guests such as Roger Moore and Prince Albert of Monaco. **Pros:** on a lovely beach; modern Thai furnishings; great views. **Cons:** no direct access to beach; isolated location; long way from airport. [$] *Rooms from: B7,000* ✉ *Nai Harn Beach, Phuket 23/3 Moo 1, Vises Rd., Nai Harn* ☎ *076/380200* 🌐 *www.thenaiharn.com* 🍴 *No Meals* 🛏 *64 rooms, 25 suites* 💳 *No credit cards.*

Roost Glamping

$$ | **RESORT** | **FAMILY** | Surrounded by landscaped gardens, this eco-friendly boutique retreat has an infinity pool and tents with either queen or single beds, a choice of air-conditioning or fan, and free Wi-Fi. **Pros:** clean facilities; stunning location; tents are basic but comfy. **Cons:** limited dining options; remote; shared bathrooms. [$] *Rooms from: 2,000* ✉ *87/70 Rawai, Nai Harn* ☎ *076/602133* 🌐 *www.roostglamping.com* 🍴 *No Meals* 🛏 *22 rooms.*

Wyndham Grand Nai Harn Beach Phuket

$$ | **RESORT** | Set near a lagoon among well-maintained gardens, this modern resort is just a short walk from Nai Harn beach. **Pros:** many rooms have direct pool access; modern decor; great service and staff. **Cons:** family atmosphere not for everyone; small rooms; not on the beach. [$] *Rooms from: 4,000* ✉ *15/328 Soi Naya, Nai Harn* ☎ *076/606255* 🌐 *www.wyndhamhotels.com/wyndham-grand/phuket-thailand/wyndham-grand-nai-harn-beach-phuket/overview* 🍴 *Free Breakfast* 🛏 *353 rooms and suites.*

Cape Yamu

21km (13 miles) east of Phuket Town.

The headland at Yamu is an isolated part of Phuket and, because of the isolation, is quiet and exclusive. There is no beach here, but the rocky point hosts some of Phuket's most exclusive villas and properties. Boats at the jetty are available to take travelers off to beach spots on Phuket and nearby islands.

GETTING HERE AND AROUND

This is an isolated cape on Phuket's eastern side. You can get here from Phuket Town or along the main arterial roads from Phuket Airport or any of Phuket's main destinations. Taxis are the best choice to get here, but minivans serve the destination from the airport; a taxi to or from Phuket Town should be about B700; from Patong it will cost about B800, and it costs B800 to get to the airport.

 ## Restaurants

★ Taste at Cape Yamu

$$$$ | **INTERNATIONAL** | At the top of the cape, overlooking the isolated bay, Taste is one of Phuket's finest restaurants, with a romantic al fresco setting. Chef Martin and his team pride themselves on preparing classic international dishes with a local twist, like the soft-shell crab burger, lamb tenderloin, and Thai twice-cooked pork cheek. **Known for:** delicious food; hilltop location; open-air dining. $ *Average main: B750* ✉ *224, Moo 7, Pa Klok, Laem Yamu, Thalang* ✛ *Atop the farthest part of the cape, just outside the Point Yamu hotel* ☎ *087/886-6401* ⊕ *www. tastebargrill.com.*

 ## Hotels

★ COMO Point Yamu

$$$$ | **HOTEL** | **FAMILY** | From the moment you enter the vast, open lobby, it's obvious that a great deal of care has gone into every aspect of this stunningly situated, modern hotel. **Pros:** playful minimalist design; luxury rooms, most with plunge pools; service levels are extraordinary. **Cons:** isolated; no direct beach access; expensive airport transfers. $ *Rooms from: B10,500* ✉ *225 Moo 7, Paklok, Talang, Thalang* ☎ *076/360100* ⊕ *www.*

comohotels.com ❙◯❙ *Free Breakfast* ⤵ *106 rooms.*

★ Thanyapura Sports & Health Resort

$$ | **HOTEL** | Travelers looking for an active, health-conscious getaway love Thanyapura for the personalized programs involving fitness and nutrition (professional and Olympic athletes often come here). **Pros:** excellent spa; highly professional staff; unbeatable sports facilities, including an Olympic-size pool. **Cons:** very quiet in the evenings; remote location; a bit of a mishmash between hotel and sports resort. $ *Rooms from: B3,250* ✉ *120/1 Moo 7 Thepkasattri Rd., Thepkasattri, Thalang* ☎ *076/336000* ⊕ *www.thanyapura.com* ❙◯❙ *Free Breakfast* ⤵ *115 rooms.*

Chalong

11 km (7 miles) south of Phuket Town.

Most people come to horseshoe-shaped Chalong Bay for its proximity to Wat Chalong and because it's a good jumping-off point for the surrounding islands. From here you can easily catch ferries or longtail boats or book one-day or half-day trips to Koh Hae, Koh Lone, and other nearby islands for snorkeling, diving, parasailing, and other activities. That said, the waters in the bay are usually calm, as the entrance is guarded by the twin isles of Koh Lone and Koh Hae.

GETTING HERE AND AROUND

Chalong Bay is an easy 11-km (7-mile) ride from Phuket Town. Taxis, tuk-tuks, and motorcycles will all take you here.

 ## Sights

Chalong Bay Distillery & Bar

DISTILLERY | Phuket's first and only rum and gin distillery is set in a sugarcane garden and offers distillery tours, cocktail workshops, and a variety of weekly events. Traditional French production methods are used to distill the gin and rum, and bottles are available for purchase. The onsite SUAY x Chalong Bay restaurant serves international cuisine and Thai-fusion dishes curated by local celebrity chef Tammasak 'Noi' Chootong. ✉ *Soi 2, Chalong* ☎ *093/575–1119* 🌐 *www.chalongbayrum.com/en/home* ✍ *Reservations are recommended.*

Wat Chalong

RELIGIOUS BUILDING | Notable for its steeple-shaped roof, Wat Chalong is the largest and most famous of Phuket's Buddhist temples. Inside are the gilt statues of two revered monks who helped quell an 1876 Chinese rebellion. They're wrapped in brilliant saffron robes. It's generally open during daylight hours, and you can show up at 5 pm to see the resident monks pray. It's also home to the annual Chalong Temple Fair, held every February. ✉ *Chaofa Rd. (West), Chalong.*

Restaurants

Kan Eang at Pier

$$ | **SEAFOOD** | Get a seat at a palm-shaded table next to the seawall, order some delicious grilled fish, and enjoy—though be sure that your waiter understands whether you want yours served *phet* (spicy hot) or *mai phet* (not spicy). Succulent and sweet crabs should be a part of any meal here. **Known for:** casual atmosphere; fresh seafood; ocean views. [$] *Average main: B200* ✉ *44/1 Viset Rd., Chalong* ☎ *076/381212* 💳 *No credit cards.*

Hotels

★ **Sri Panwa**

$$$$ | **RESORT** | On a lush headland near Cape Panwa this beautifully designed resort has a cool, contemporary vibe that makes it popular with visiting celebrities seeking luxury and seclusion. **Pros:** stunning views; exceptional service; rooftop bars. **Cons:** it's on a steep hill; not much else in the area; no families in the Pool Suites. [$] *Rooms from: B28,000* ✉ *88 Moo 8, Sakdidej Rd., Vichit, Muang, Chalong* ☎ *076/371000* 🌐 *www.sripanwa.com* 🍴 *No Meals* 🛏 *52 villas.*

Villa Zolitude Resort & Spa

$$$$ | **RESORT** | Nestled on the forested mountainside, this resort has stunning panoramic views and luxurious features like private pool villas. **Pros:** luxurious natural escape; great spa; excellent service. **Cons:** limited food options; sloping grounds problematic for those with mobility issues; remote location. [$] *Rooms from: 10,000* ✉ *53/25 Moo 5 Soi Bann Nai Trok, Chaofa Nok Rd, Chalong* ☎ *076/521333* 🌐 *www.villazolitude.com* 🍴 *No Meals* 🛏 *45 villas.*

Phang Nga Bay National Marine Park

100 km (62 miles) north of Phuket, 93 km (56 miles) northwest of Krabi.

The looming limestone karsts are the most spectacular feature of Phang Nga Bay, rising from the sea in secluded, crystal-clear bays. They have been made famous in movies and a thousand picture postcards. The only way to visit is by boat. Tours (B1,000 to B3,000) can be arranged through your hotel or resort if you're staying in the area.

There are several key sights around Phang Nga Bay. The island of Koh Panyi has a Muslim fishing village consisting of houses built on stilts. Koh Phing Kan, now known locally as James Bond Island, is a popular tour destination. The island of Koh Tapu resembles a nail driven into the sea, while Kao Kien has overhanging cliffs covered with primitive paintings of elephants, fish, and crabs. Many are thought to be at least 3,500 years old.

GETTING HERE AND AROUND

Many travel agencies in Phuket offer half-day tours of the area, and this is the way most travelers see the park. Another option is to take a bus heading

north from Phuket Town (B120) to one of two inlets near the town of Phang Nga, where you can hire a longtail boat and explore at your own pace, but unless you speak Thai or are intrepid, this is likely to be more of a hassle than it's worth. At the western inlet, you can rent a boat for about B1,800 for two hours. The second inlet sees fewer foreign tourists, so the prices are better—about B1,200 for three hours. The bay can also be explored via tour boat, speedboat, or sea canoe. Most tourists don't arrive from Phuket until 11 am, so if you get into the bay earlier, you can explore it in solitude. To get an early start, you may want to stay overnight in the area. Be sure to take time to appreciate the sunsets, which are particularly beautiful on the island of **Koh Mak.**

Sights

James Bond Island

ISLAND | Known familiarly as "James Bond island" because the 1974 film *The Man with the Golden Gun* was filmed here, Koh Phing Kan has fallen victim to greedy tour operators and merchants and become overrun with tourists, though it's still stunningly beautiful. Visiting the island (with a stopover often not longer than half an hour) usually involves a day trip that combines this with several other stops and lunch. ✉ *Phang Nga.*

Koh Panyi

ISLAND | The island of Koh Panyi has a Muslim fishing village with houses built on stilts. The whole village backs onto a looming limestone cliff, giving it some protection from nature. The village is an interesting study in marine sustainability, but it does have the feel of a tourist trap—quirky floating soccer pitch aside. Restaurants here are expensive, tripling their prices for tourists. ✉ *Phang Nga.*

Tham Lot Cave

CAVE | Tham Lot is a large, limestone cave with an an opening to the sea large enough for boats to pass through. It can be explored by canoe or an inflatable boat, to see the impressive stalactites and stalagmites, some as long as 100 meters. No guide required. ✉ *Tarnboke Koranee National Park, Ao Luk District, Phang Nga.*

★ **Wat Tham Cave**

CAVE | Wat Tham Suwan Khuha, also known as the The Buddha Cave, is an impressively large cavern filled with a broad and beautiful variety of Buddha statues. It's mostly known for its giant gold statue of a reclining Buddha, before which a stage is set so visitors can light incense and pray under his gaze. There are an abundance of gray monkeys around here, so if you want to interact, have some peanuts, bananas, or coconut handy but be warned they can be very grabby. There are several tourist stalls around selling snacks and other items such as jewelry and souvenirs. ✉ *6 miles outside Phang Nga, Phang Nga.*

Hotels

★ **Aleenta Phuket Resort & Spa**

$$$$ | **RESORT** | Stylish design, a romantic atmosphere, and a beautiful beach are all part of the package at the Aleenta. **Pros:** quiet location; great sunset views from some suites; stylish, spacious interiors. **Cons:** remote location; not all rooms have sea views; fills up early in high season. [$] *Rooms from: B6,300* ✉ *33 Moo 5, Khokkloy, Phang Nga, Phang Nga* ☎ *066/251–48112* 🌐 *www.aleenta.com* 🍴 *Free Breakfast* 🛏 *15 suites.*

Ao Phang Nga National Park

$ | **B&B/INN** | If you want to get really close to nature, the campgrounds at Ao Phang Nga rent tents and have a few simple one- to three-bedroom bungalows. **Pros:** decent service; lots of restaurants nearby; good base for exploring the area. **Cons:** lack of amenities; some rooms are basic; often booked up.

0 ____ 10 mi
0 ____ 10 km

$ *Rooms from: B100* ✉ *80 Ban Tha Dan, Koh Panyi, Phang Nga* ☎ *025/620760 for reservations* ⦿| *No Meals* ⤴ *15 bungalows* ▭ *No credit cards.*

Baba Ecolodge

$$$$ | **RESORT** | **FAMILY** | Sprawling along the shoreline of a sheltered bay, this eco-resort has the atmosphere of a luxurious desert island, with its own stunning 10-km (6-mile) beach. **Pros:** wonderful beach; yoga classes; helpful, friendly staff. **Cons:** limited dining options; remote; no air-conditioning. $ *Rooms from: B5,000* ✉ *131 Moo 2, Ko Phra Thong* ☎ *081/892–2208* ⊕ *www.baba-lodge.com* ⦿| *Free Breakfast* ⤴ *27 villas.*

Koh Yao

30 mins by boat from Bangrong Pier, Phuket, or 45 mins by boat from Chaofa Pier, Krabi.

Koh Yao Yai and Koh Yao Noi are the two islands in the center of Phang Nga Bay—"yai" is "large" and "noi" is "little." Both are quiet, peaceful places, fringed with sandy beaches and clear water. Koh Yao Noi is the more developed of the pair, but it's still a world away from the development onslaught on Phuket and other parts of the Andaman Coast.

A visit to Koh Yao will allow you to experience the local culture and customs while exploring the beauty of the islands (kayaks and mountain bikes are popular transportation options). There are also lots of opportunities for kayaking, snorkeling, and diving. The Ecotourism Club provides homestays if you want the full experience of the islands; otherwise, most resorts provide day tours or information for self-guided exploration.

GETTING HERE AND AROUND

Public ferry is the easiest, most scenic, and cheapest way to get to and from Koh Yao Noi. Most of the tourist developments can be found on Koh Yao Noi. Ferries from Bang Rong Pier to the north of Phuket leave regularly throughout the day and cost B150 per person. You can also travel from Chaofa Pier in Krabi for B160.

Sights

Koh Yao Noi Ecotourism Club

BOAT TOURS | Most inhabitants of the islands still make their living by traditional means such as fishing, rubber tapping, and batik painting. Considering their size and proximity to Phuket and Krabi, it's surprising how little development these islands have seen. During the 1990s many tourists began to discover the islands and the impact was negative. To reduce the impact on the land and their culture, the villagers residing on Koh Yao organized the Koh Yao Noi Ecotourism Club to regulate growth on the islands. They've certainly been successful—they even picked up an award for tourism development sponsored by Conservation International. ✉ *Phuket.*

Hotels

Koh Yao Homestay

$$$$ | **B&B/INN** | Organized by a community of Koh Yao residents, locals invite visitors to stay in their homes, share meals with them (consisting primarily of fish caught by village fishermen), and learn about about local customs like rubber-tapping, batik-dying, fishing, rice-farming, coconut-harvesting, and other traditional trades. **Pros:** up-close cultural experience; well organized; friendly locals. **Cons:** most lodgings are pretty basic; no alcohol permitted; not much choice with food options. [$] *Rooms from: B6,500* ✉ *Baan Laem Sai, Koh Yao Noi, Phang Nga* ☎ *089/970–3384* 🌐 *www.kohyao-homestay.com* 🍴 *All-Inclusive* 🛏 *10 rooms* 💳 *No credit cards.*

★ **Koyao Island Resort**

$$$$ | **RESORT** | The open-air bungalows at Koyao Island Resort allow you to admire the surroundings from your own luxury accommodations; you can even throw open the doors and watch the sunrise from your bed. **Pros:** many activities; captivating views of nearby islands; attentive service. **Cons:** beach itself could be better; open air can make you more mosquito accessible; not family oriented. [$] *Rooms from: B6,500* ✉ *24/2 Koh Yao Noi, Phang Nga* ☎ *076/597474 up to 76* 🌐 *www.koyao.com* 💳 *No credit cards* 🛏 *15 villas* 🍴 *Free Breakfast.*

Khao Lak

80 km (50 miles) north of Phuket.

Looking for a low-key spot for your Phuket holiday? Khao Lak has all the amenities you might want, but without the overdevelopment that is found along much of the Andaman coastline.

GETTING HERE AND AROUND

VIP and first-class buses leave for Khao Lak from Bangkok's Southern Bus Terminal each evening around 6 or 7 pm. The journey takes at least 12 hours. There's also regular bus service here from other beach areas. The journey to Phuket takes about two hours and costs around B200 (by taxi expect to pay anywhere between B1,600 and B2,000). There's no direct bus from Phuket to Khao Lak, but you can take a local bus bound for Ranong, Surat Thani, or Kuraburi and ask to get dropped off in Khao Lak.

The usual array of motorcycles, songthaews, and taxis will shuttle you around the area.

Sights

Khao Lak Beach

BEACH | The beaches of Khao Lak, fringed by palm and casuarina trees and with sand as soft as powder, are south of the national park. Most resorts and dive operators purporting to hail from Khao Lak actually line the coasts of Nang Thong, Bang Niang, Khuk Khak, and Bang Sak beaches to the north. There are a few local vendors selling drinks and snacks, and most beaches here have access to a few restaurants. From November to May, the ocean is calm and clear. During the green season, from June to October, the waves are rough and it can be dangerous to swim. **Amenities:** food and drink; showers; toilets; water sports. **Best for:** sunset; surfing; swimming; walking. ✉ *Thanon Phet Kasem, Khao Lak.*

Khao Lak Lamru National Marine Park

NATIONAL PARK | Stretching from the sea to the mountains, Khao Lak Lamru National Marine Park covers more than 325 square km (125 square miles). There's a secluded sandy beach, several waterfalls with swimmable pools, and an abundance of pristine tropical evergreen forest. Wildlife includes wild pigs, barking deer, macaques, and reticulated pythons. Walking trails lead to waterfalls with swimmable pools. Three rudimentary cabins are available for overnight stays, as are tent rentals for visitors who do not have their own. The park headquarters, on the road from Khao Lak Beach to Khao Lak town, provides information about exploring or staying in the park. ☎ *025/794842, 025/578–0529 National Park Division in Bangkok* 🌐 *www.dnp.go.th.*

Restaurants

Garang Artisan Ice Cream

$ | **ICE CREAM** | **FAMILY** | Although this sleek café sells delicious baked goods like orange cinnamon rolls and croissants, it's the ice cream, made on-site in a variety of unique and delicious flavors, that really draws the crowd. Try the Tom Yum Kung ice cream for a real taste of Thailand or more traditional with Almond Espresso. **Known for:** fresh pastries, too; casual seating area; unique flavors. [$] *Average main: 150* ✉ *7 Bang Muang, Takua Pa, Khao Lak* ☎ *098/324–5629* 🌐 *www.garangicecream.com* 🕒 *Closed Tues.*

Hill Tribes Restaurant

$ | **THAI** | The chefs at this bamboo-patio restaurant specialize in seafood and fish dishes made according to traditional recipes from the northern hill tribes, like tempura of banana flowers, a sizzling seafood hot plate, or the prawns fried with herbs in a red-whisky sauce. The dessert of sticky rice with coconut cream and ripe mango is just wonderful. **Known for:** northern Thai cuisine; mango sticky rice; colorful hill tribe pillows and decor. [$] *Average main: B145* ✉ *13/22 Phetchkasem Rd., Bangniang, Khao Lak* ☎ *086/283–0933* 🌐 *www.hilltribe-restaurant.com.*

Karkinos Khao Lak

$$ | **ITALIAN** | For a remarkably pleasant meal of pizza and pasta taking in the sea views, it's hard to do better than this rustic beach club and restaurant with an open-air design. The seafood is sustainably caught by local fishermen. **Known for:** good pizza; good cocktails; the views. [$] *Average main: 300* ✉ *45 (1) Moo 2 Kukkak, Takua Pa, Khao Lak* ☎ *076/584447* 🌐 *www.karkinoskhaolak.com* 🕒 *Closed Mon.*

Smile

$$ | **THAI** | **FAMILY** | There are plenty of delicious Thai curries to choose from, as well as some French-influenced salads and stir-fries at this casual restaurant.

An added bonus are the vegetarian and vegan options, as well as options for diners with other food sensitivities. **Known for:** Thai curries; gets busy at lunch; vegan options. $ *Average main: B200* ✉ *29/31 Phetkasem Rd., Phangnga, Phang Nga* ☎ *083/391–2600.*

Smoh Ruer Restaurant

$ | **THAI** | A few minutes' tuk-tuk ride north from the busy part of town, Smoh Ruer prepares top-notch food in the local Khao Lak style. Dishes include a spicy wild-boar red curry, perfectly cooked prawns fried in sesame oil on a bed of rice noodles and celery, and the mellow egg-fried morning glory in oyster sauce. **Known for:** relaxed atmosphere; wild-boar red curry; more interesting menu than the typical spot. $ *Average main: B160* ✉ *12/2 Moo 6, T. Khukkak, Khao Lak* ☎ *089/288–9889, 089/875–9018.*

 # Hotels

Baan Krating

$ | **RESORT** | On a cliff above a beach, this boutique resort boasts a beautiful view and a path down to the shore that travels within Khao Lak Lamru National Marine Park. **Pros:** clean rooms; relaxed atmosphere; captivating views. **Cons:** slightly worn decor; spartan accommodations; a bit of a trek to beach. $ *Rooms from: B1,100* ✉ *28 Khao Lak, Takuapa, Phang Nga* ☎ *076/485188 up to 89* ⊕ *www.baankrating.com* ⌁ *24 cottages* ♦ *No Meals.*

Centara Seaview Resort Khao Lak

$ | **RESORT** | **FAMILY** | Octagonal villas with high ceilings, four-poster beds, and whirlpool tubs epitomize the luxury available to guests at this resort on a small private stretch of sand. **Pros:** friendly staff; great pool; luxurious feel. **Cons:** somewhat costly; not the best views; beach isn't the best around. $ *Rooms from: B1,700* ✉ *18/1 Moo 7, Petchkasem Rd., Khuk Khak* ☎ *076/429800* ⊕ *www.*

centarahotelsresorts.com ⌁ *197 rooms* ♦ *Free Breakfast.*

Green Beach Resort

$ | **RESORT** | You can choose from standard bungalows or sea-view bungalows at this budget-friendly option. **Pros:** beachfront; inexpensive; outdoor showers in deluxe rooms. **Cons:** interior decor nothing special; bland feeling; slightly tacky exterior. $ *Rooms from: B1,600* ✉ *13/51 Moo 7, Haad Nangtong, Khuk Khak* ☎ *076/420046* ⊕ *www.khaolakgreen-beachresort.com* ⊘ *Closed May–Nov.* ♦ *No Meals* ⌁ *40 bungalows* ⊟ *No credit cards.*

★ La Flora Khao Lak

$$$ | **RESORT** | This lovely boutique resort has modern rooms with local Southern Thai elements, and most have balconies or daybeds; villas have more features, including private outdoor rain showers. **Pros:** great villas; lovely beach with deep waters; tasteful, spacious rooms. **Cons:** service can be inconsistent; grounds could use some sprucing up; families may find it a little isolated. $ *Rooms from: B4,400* ✉ *59/1 Moo 5, Khuk Khak, Phang Nga* ☎ *076/428000, 026/798828* ⊕ *www.lafloraresort.com* ♦ *Free Breakfast* ⌁ *125 rooms, 13 villas.*

Mukdara Beach Villa & Spa Resort

$$ | **RESORT** | This sumptuous resort has been designed in classical Thai style, with a great deal of emphasis on wood and traditional craftsmanship. **Pros:** villas on beach; tasteful Thai furnishings; luxurious. **Cons:** large resort, so not intimate; Internet can be slow; layout of some rooms is odd. $ *Rooms from: B2,800* ✉ *26/14 Moo 7* ☎ *076/429999* ⊕ *www.mukdarabeach.com* ⌁ *141 rooms* ♦ *Free Breakfast.*

Nang Thong Bay Resort

$ | **RESORT** | The majority of rooms here are surprisingly inexpensive cottages that face the beach and are surrounded by well-maintained gardens. **Pros:** good value; well located; great pool. **Cons:**

Tropical forest meets powdery white sand on the Similan Islands.

restaurant is nothing special; some rooms away from the beach; service can be off. [$] *Rooms from: B1,000* ✉ *13/5 Moo 7, Thanon Khuk Khak, Takuapa, Phang Nga* ☎ *076/485088 up to 89* 🌐 *www.nangthong.com* 💳 *No credit cards* 🛏 *82 rooms* 🍴 *Free Breakfast.*

Pullman Khao Lak Resort

$$$ | RESORT | FAMILY | This is a stunning resort with scenic vantage points, and a unique design infused with Sino-Portuguese heritage. **Pros:** beautiful beach; good restaurant; near Khao Sak National Park. **Cons:** service is hit and miss; suites not that spacious; remote. [$] *Rooms from: 5,000* ✉ *46/109, Moo 2, Soi 46 Laem Son Takua Pa, Khao Lak* ☎ *076/592233* 🌐 *www.pullmankhaolakresort.com* 🍴 *Free Breakfast* 🛏 *253 rooms and pool villas.*

The Sarojin

$$$$ | RESORT | This secluded luxury beach resort's smaller size makes it intimate and exclusive. **Pros:** intimate and exclusive; unique design; cooking classes. **Cons:** some rooms a bit worn; price a bit higher than at comparable resorts; staff can be aloof. [$] *Rooms from: B7,150* ✉ *60 Moo 2, Khuk Khak, Takuapa, Phang Nga* ☎ *076/427900 up to 07* 🌐 *www.sarojin.com* 🍴 *Free Breakfast* 🛏 *56 rooms.*

Similan Islands

70 km (45 miles) or 1½ hours by boat from Thaplamu Pier.

The diving around the Similan Islands is world-class, with visibility of up to 120 feet; abundant blue, green, and purple coral; and rare marine life, such as the whale shark, the world's largest fish. In addition to sparkling, crystal-clear water, the Similan Islands also have ultrafine, powdery white-sand beaches and lush tropical forests.

The archipelago consists of the nine Similan Islands, as well as Koh Tachai and Koh Bon, which are farther north. Pre-Covid, the National Park Service allowed visitors to stay on the beaches of Koh Miang (Island 4) and Koh Similan (Island 8). If you plan to dive, contact a dive operator in Phuket or Khao Lak; there are no dive shops on the islands, though snorkeling gear is available for rent from the ranger stations.

GETTING HERE AND AROUND

BOAT

Speedboats to Similan National Park leave from Thap Lamu Pier in the Tai Muang District just south of Khao Lak Beach at 8:30 am when the park is open to the public (November to May). Once you reach Koh Similan, motorboats will take you to other islands for between B250 and B600, depending on distance.

You can also take a private tour boat from Thap Lamu Pier for around B2,000 per person. The tour boat departs from Thap Lamu at 8 am daily and returns at 2 pm. Direct tickets, booked through the national parks, cost B2,000; however, private tours are a better value.

Surin Islands

60 km (37 miles) or 2 hrs by boat from Kuraburi Pier.

Sixty kilometers (37 miles) off the west coast of Phang Nga, the five Surin Islands (also known as Mu Koh Surin National Marine Park) are a remote island paradise practically unknown other than to adventurous scuba divers and local Thais. The visibility and diversity of marine life is spectacular, and this is arguably the most unspoiled Thai island retreat, owing to national park status (which meant a stop to development), its remote location, and low number of visitors. Note that the park is normally closed during the rainy season (June to November).

If you get tired of sun and sea, there are several hiking trails that lead to waterfalls and a community of Moken, sometimes called sea gypsies, living here, who sell artisanal crafts.

GETTING HERE AND AROUND

Khuraburi Pier, north of Khao Lak Beach, is the departure point for boats to the Surin Islands and can be reached by any bus going to or from Ranong (about B200 from Phuket or Krabi). Songthaews will take you to the pier, approximately 9 km (5½ miles) out of town. Expect to pay B1,000 and up for boat trips to the various islands. Negotiating prices is not really an option here. An easier option is to book a trip through your resort. They will arrange your transportation to Khuraburi and your boat ticket.

🛏 Hotels

Koh Surin Nua

$$ | **RESORT** | There are 10 recently built, comfortable, fan-cooled, wooden huts on Koh Surin Nua (B2,000), and tent camping is allowed at a site that has decent facilities, including toilets and showers. **Pros:** tranquil; paradise setting; amazing underwater life. **Cons:** hard to get to; pretty bare facilities; isolated. [$] *Rooms from: B2,000* ☎ *02/562–0760 inquiries and bungalow reservations, 076/491378* 🌐 *www.dnp.go.th* 🍴 *No Meals* 🛏 *10 bungalows.*

Krabi

814 km (506 miles) south of Bangkok, 180 km (117 miles) southeast of Phuket, 43 km (27 miles) by boat east of Koh Phi Phi.

As a major travel hub in southern Thailand, travelers used to breeze through without stopping to enjoy the atmosphere. These days, Krabi is increasingly a destination in itself, with more international flights added to the province's airport. There are a few good restaurants in Krabi Town, mostly seafood spots, though Ao Nang has a better variety, and there's a fun night market for great street food, clothes, and souvenirs.

GETTING HERE AND AROUND
AIR

Flying is the easiest way to get here from Bangkok. Thai Airways, Bangkok Airways, and Air Asia all have daily flights to Krabi International Airport. One-way prices from Bangkok range from B1,000 to B3,500; the flight takes about an hour.

The airport is a 20-minute ride from Krabi Town, and there are taxis (B400) and minibuses (B150) waiting outside the airport. These vehicles can also take you to other nearby (and not-so-nearby) beach areas. Minivans don't leave until they're full, which can happen quickly or after a long wait. Your best bet is to check in with the minivans first to make sure you get a seat if one is about to depart—if not, you can opt for a taxi. Another, more recent transport addition, is the regular bus service to and from Krabi Town. The bus departs hourly (B100) from 6 am and runs throughout the day until 10 pm.

BUS AND SONGTHAEW

Buses from Bangkok to Krabi leave from Bangkok's Southern Bus Terminal and take at least 12 hours. VIP and first-class buses leave once every evening around 6 or 7 pm. Public buses leave Krabi for Bangkok at 8 am and 4 and 5:30 pm. First-class buses travel between Phuket and Krabi (a three-hour journey) every hour. Getting around town or to Ao Nang is best done by songthaew. You can find songthaews at the corner of Maharat Soi 4 and Pruksa Uthit Road.

Bus and boat combination tickets are available from Krabi to Koh Samui and Koh Phangan.

There are a few bus terminals in Krabi, but if you don't arrive at the pier, songthaews can take you there; if you've purchased a combination ticket, this transfer is included.

CAR

The airport has Avis, National, and Budget rental counters. Prices start at about B1,500 per day; for a little more, you can also rent a four-wheel-drive jeep in town.

VISITOR INFORMATION

Krabi has its own small Tourism Authority of Thailand (TAT) offices, where you can pick up maps and brochures, as well as information about local excursions. Tour operators and your hotel's tour desk are also good sources of information.

CONTACTS Krabi Tourist Information Center. ☒ *Uttarakit Rd., Krabi* ☎ *075/622163.*

 # Sights

Wat Tham Sua

RELIGIOUS BUILDING | Just 3 km (2 miles, or 10 minutes' drive) from Krabi Town is Wat Tham Sua, with its giant Buddha statue and scenic surrounding landscapes. Built in 1976 as a monastery and meditation retreat, Wat Tham Sua is both respected by the local population and popular with tourists. Locals come to participate in Buddhist rituals, while most tourists come to climb the 1,277 steps to panoramic views of the cliffs, Krabi Town, Krabi River, and the Panom Benja mountain range. There's also a cave with many chambers, which can be fun to explore, though it's not terribly attractive. A really large tree grows outside the entrance. The wat is between Krabi Town and the airport. ☒ *Tambon Muang Chum, Krabi* ⊹ *4 km (2½ miles) after Wachiralongkorn Dam.*

 # Restaurants

Bistro Monaco

$$ | EUROPEAN | FAMILY | If you find yourself craving European dishes like pizza, schnitzel, and hearty sausages, this is one of the best places in town. The portions are large, the atmosphere is casual, and the prices are affordable. **Known for:** friendly waitstaff; comfort food; known as best pizza in Krabi Town. *[$] Average main: 250 ✉ Klong Ka 238, Krabi ☎ 096/673–1138 🌐 www.facebook.com/abisserlwoasgehtimmer ⏲ Closed Sun. and Mon.*

Carnivore Steak and Grill

$$ | **INTERNATIONAL** | As the name suggests, this is the place to come for high-quality imported cuts served with delicious sauces and sides, though the seafood is top quality, too. Fresh lobster bisque, perfectly grilled tuna steak, and white snapper in butter-and-garlic cream sauce are all good non-meat options. **Known for:** smart service; lively atmosphere; imported steaks. *[$] Average main: B230 ✉ 127 Moo 3, Krabi ☎ 075/661061 🌐 www.carnivore-thailand.com ⏲ No lunch.*

★ Chao Fa Pier Street Food Stalls

$ | **THAI** | Looking for delicious local food at a low price: This strip of street-side food stalls serves everything from simple fried rice and papaya salad to more sophisticated southern delicacies such as *kanom jeen* (rice noodles topped with whatever sauces and vegetables you want). Open from nightfall until midnight, the stalls provide an excellent opportunity to discover some exotic and enjoyable Thai foods. **Known for:** fun atmosphere; southern delicacies; a real highlight of Krabi Town. *[$] Average main: B60 ✉ Chao Fa Pier, Khong Kha Rd., Krabi 💳 No credit cards ⏲ No lunch.*

Frog and Catfish

$ | **SEAFOOD** | Over in the small village of Din Daeang Noi, this is the place to try delicious regional specialties that are not easy to find elsewhere. The seafood is excellent—try the fresh crab spring rolls—as are the curries. **Known for:** knowledgeable and friendly owner; out-of-the-way location; fantastic seafood. *[$] Average main: B175 ✉ 76 Moo 6, Din Daeng Noi ☎ 084/773–0301 🌐 www.frogandcatfishkrabi.com 💳 No credit cards.*

★ Marina Villa

$$ | **SEAFOOD** | This long-standing restaurant (it opened in 2011) is in a picturesque marina on the banks of Krabi River and specializes in thoughtfully presented Thai seafood dishes. The space itself is modern and dimly lighted with blues and greens, but weather permitting, tables by the river are the way to go. **Known for:** mussels with garlic; upscale crowd; riverside location. *[$] Average main: B300 ✉ Krabi Marina, Krabi ✥ Next to yacht club ☎ 075/611635, 086/276–8556 💳 No credit cards.*

Relax Coffee and Restaurant

$ | **CAFÉ** | The extensive menu at this street-side café includes breakfast platters, sandwiches served on freshly baked bread, Thai dishes, and, not surprisingly, a huge variety of coffee drinks, like raspberry latte frappés. It's in the heart of the hotel district and caters mainly to foreigners. **Known for:** fresh bread; breakfast platters; interesting coffee options. *[$] Average main: B100 ✉ 7/4 Chaofa Rd., Krabi ☎ 075/611570 💳 No credit cards ⏲ Closed 2nd and 4th Fri. of each month.*

🛏 Hotels

City Hotel

$ | **HOTEL** | This popular budget property is one of the largest (and oldest) hotels in Krabi—rooms in the new wing are more modern. **Pros:** budget-friendly; free Wi-Fi; central location. **Cons:** old wing needs renovation; only rooms in the new wing worth staying in; basic. *[$] Rooms from: B850 ✉ 15/2-4 Soi 10 Maharat Rd., Krabi ☎ 075/621280 to 1 💳 No credit cards ⏲ www.citykrabi.com 🛏 124 rooms 🍴 No Meals.*

Hometel

$ | **HOTEL** | A solid budget choice, this family-run hotel is a great base for those using Krabi as a stepping-stone to the islands beyond. **Pros:** good restaurant; central; speedy, free Wi-Fi. **Cons:** not enough natural light in the rooms; book well in advance; some rooms are small. [$] *Rooms from: B500* ✉ *7 Maharaj Rd., Soi 10, Pak Nam, Krabi* ☎ *075/622301* 💳 *No credit cards* 🛏 *10 rooms* 🍴 *No Meals.*

Krabi River Hotel

$ | **HOTEL** | It's pretty basic, but the Krabi River Hotel, on the banks of Khlong Krabi Yai, is a good budget option with pleasant views. **Pros:** pleasant riverside location; free Wi-Fi; some rooms have nice views. **Cons:** decor is borderline tacky; rooms at the back are small and have no views; off the main drag. [$] *Rooms from: B600* ✉ *73/1 Kongkha Rd., Krabi* ☎ *075/612321* 💳 *No credit cards* 🛏 *20 rooms* 🍴 *No Meals.*

Ao Nang

20 km (12 miles) from Krabi Town.

During the day, the stretch of white sand beach here is crowded with people lazing on recliners, sipping coconuts, and taking dips in the warm, clear waters. In the heart of town the beach is referred to as Ao Nang Beach but farther down toward the Nopparat Thara National Park it's called Nopparat Thara Beach.

In the evening storefronts light up the sidewalks and the open-air restaurants fill with diners and people relaxing with a beer and watching the world go by. If you're looking for a more romantic atmosphere, you can head to the half dozen seafood restaurants on the pier between Ao Nang and Noppharat Thara beaches.

For even better beaches and azure sparkling oceans, take one of the many longtail boats that depart from Ao Nang during the day for Hong, Poda, Gai, Lanta, the Phi Phi Islands, and nearby Railay Beach.

GETTING HERE AND AROUND

Buses from Bangkok headed to Krabi stop here. If you fly into Krabi, it takes about 45 minutes to Ao Nang in a taxi. Songthaews travel between Ao Nang and Krabi Town regularly. The fare shouldn't be more than B80; you can find them on the main road, displaying Krabi–Ao Nang signs. A taxi from the airport will cost you considerably more—usually the minimum fare is B650.

Beaches

Ao Nang Beach

BEACH | **FAMILY** | Fringed by palm trees, this long stretch of soft white sand is the main beach in town. There's a long, winding promenade stretching from one end of the beach to the other. Ao Nang Beach is the jumping-off point for longtail boats to Railay and Tonsai beaches, and to the limestone islands of Ko Hong, Ko Poda, and Ko Gai. **Amenities:** food and drink; parking (fee); toilets. **Best for:** solitude; sunset; surfing; swimming; walking. ✉ *Ao Nang.*

Klong Muang

BEACH | West of Ao Nang on the mainland, the beaches of Klong Muang and Tubkaak are beautiful stretches of sand with amazing views of the limestone karst islands on the horizon. These beaches are largely occupied by upmarket resorts such as the Sheraton and The Tubkaak, though, and none of the amenities come free. **Amenities:** food and drink; toilet; water sports. **Best for:** solitude; sunset; walking. ✉ *Krabi.*

Laem Son Beach

BEACH | On the western edge of Noppharat Thara National Park, Laem Son Beach is a long stretch of sand with a few vendors selling Thai specialities. There are a few inexpensive beachside bungalows to stay at, too. **Amenities:** food and drink; parking (free). **Best for:** solitude; sunset; swimming. ✉ *Krabi.*

Noppharat Thara Beach

BEACH | Noppharat Thara Beach, part of Noppharat Thara National Park, is a 15-minute walk from central Ao Nang. After the renovated walking path was extended from Ao Nang in 2004, a mish-mash of development followed (even though it's supposedly part of the national park). The beach is still pleasant but many of the trees have been uprooted to make way for resorts. **Amenities:** food and drink. **Best for:** swimming; walking. ✉ *96 Moo 3, Nopphara Thara, Krabi.*

🍴 Restaurants

Ao Nang Cuisine

$ | **THAI** | The chicken satay, an otherwise ordinary dish of chicken skewers served with a side of spicy peanut sauce, is especially skillfully prepared at this traditional restaurant. More elaborate Thai dishes are available as well. **Known for:** large portions; excellent chicken satay; excellent value. [$] *Average main: B100* ✉ *245/4 Liab Chai Haad Rd., Krabi* ☎ *075/695399.*

Cafe'de Rimlay

$ | **THAI** | Right on the beach, this open-air café is popular for its boho chic vibe, unique decor, and excellent food. The menu features freshly brewed Italian coffee, classic Thai dishes such as green curry with jumbo prawns, international fare such as pasta and pizza, and a wide range of imported and local beers, as well as tropical cocktails. **Known for:** delicious cocktails; very good Thai food; homemade cakes. [$] *Average main: 150* ✉ *80 Moo 4, Ao Nang* ☎ *093/554–7444* 🌐 *www.facebook.com/cafederimlay* 💳 *No credit cards.*

Kodam Kitchen

$ | **THAI** | **FAMILY** | There's not much to this casual restaurant, but their renditions of Thai dishes are very tasty and come at great prices. Seafood options are recommend, including the signature Pineapple Fried Rice with Shrimp or any of the spicy curries. **Known for:** authentic Southern Thai cuisine; relaxed setting; friendly service. [$] *Average main: 150* ✉ *55/7 Moo 3, Ao Nang* ☎ *062/723–1234* 🌐 *www.facebook.com/kodamkitchen2020* 💳 *No credit cards.*

Krua Thara

$ | **SEAFOOD** | There are two positive signs at this restaurant before you even try the food—locals hanging out, and the fish and seafood that will end up on your plate are on display in tanks in all their variety. You'll find every kind of fresh catch prepared using lots of local herbs and spices at this friendly, colorful place. **Known for:** friendly atmosphere; popular with locals; well-prepared seafood. [$] *Average main: B115* ✉ *82 Moo 5, Nopparat Thara Rd., Krabi* ☎ *075/637361* 💳 *No credit cards.*

Lae Lay Grill

$$ | **SEAFOOD** | The seafood here is perfectly cooked and artfully presented, but what makes Lae Lay Grill extra-special is the location. The restaurant is on a terrace on a hill overlooking Ao Nang and the sea, which makes it a highly romantic spot from sunset on, but also lovely during the day. **Known for:** seafood dishes; hillside location; van pickup from your hotel. [$] *Average main: B200* ✉ *89 Moo 3, Ao Nang* ☎ *075/661588* 🌐 *www.laelaygrill.com.*

Sister Mon Thai Food & Seafood

$ | **THAI** | **FAMILY** | The menu at this simple Thai restaurant is encyclopedic, but the speciality is Tom Yam Pla, a spicy fish soup. The open-air setting is pleasant and the charming owner is happy to chat—he speaks a variety of languages. **Known for:** friendly atmosphere; ample portions; huge menu. [$] *Average main: 80* ✉ *415 Moo 2, Ao Nang* ☎ *093/446–3668* 💳 *No credit cards.*

Yesterday Bar & Cafe

$$ | **INTERNATIONAL** | In the heart of the action, this bar–cafe is the kind of place you just want to keep coming back to.

The menu is a mix of Thai classics and Tex-Mex favorites and there's live music most nights. **Known for:** chicken burritos; chill crowd; good drinks. [$] *Average main: 200* ✉ *246/17 Moo 2, Ao Nang* ☎ *095/426–2093* 🌐 *www.facebook.com/yesterdaybaraonang* 💳 *No credit cards.*

Hotels

Alisea Boutique Hotel

$ | **HOTEL** | Whitewashed walls and red, ceramic-tile floors give a Moroccan feel to this design at Alisea. **Pros:** good facilities for the price; polite, helpful staff; free shuttle and access to Andaman Beach club. **Cons:** only some room rates have free breakfast; staff can be apathetic; whitewash needs to be reapplied. [$] *Rooms from: B1,750* ✉ *125 Moo 3, Ao Nang* ☎ *075/638000, 02/801–0760 in Bangkok* 🌐 *www.alisthailand.com* 🍴 *No Meals* 🛏 *34 rooms.*

Anyavee Ao Nang Bay Resort

$ | **RESORT** | This small resort overlooking the hills and the water is a made up of cluster of four-story buildings in Thai design, including northern-style peaked roofs. **Pros:** good selection of facilities; pool and pool bar; great location for nature lovers. **Cons:** a bit removed from beach; limited dining options nearby; exterior needs some renovation. [$] *Rooms from: B1,900* ✉ *31/3 Liab Chai Haad Rd., Ao Nang* ☎ *075/661400* 🌐 *www.anyavee.com* 🛏 *71 rooms* 🍴 *Free Breakfast.*

★ **Banyan Tree Krabi**

$$$$ | **RESORT** | On the beach with a rolling garden, the Banyan Tree is a luxurious sanctuary. **Pros:** stunning beachfront location; large garden; spacious suites and villas. **Cons:** ants; remote location; breakfast a bit mediocre. [$] *Rooms from: 15,000* ✉ *279 Tambon Nongtalay, Amphoe Muang, Krabi* ☎ *075/811888* 🌐 *www.banyantree.com/en/thailand/krabi* 🍴 *Free Breakfast* 🛏 *72 suites.*

Centra by Centara Phu Phano Resort Krabi

$$ | **RESORT** | **FAMILY** | About a 10-minute walk to Ao Nang Beach, this sleekly designed resort has rooms and suites that look out over the swimming pool or the limestone cliffs. **Pros:** tasteful decor; delightful staff; great hot water. **Cons:** road to the resort is not well lit at night; the restaurant is mediocre; can be noisy. [$] *Rooms from: 3,000* ✉ *879 Moo 2, Soi Ao Nang 11, Ao Nang* ☎ *075/607888* 🌐 *www.centarahotelsresorts.com/centra/cpp* 🍴 *Free Breakfast* 🛏 *158 rooms.*

The Cliff

$ | **RESORT** | You'll get a great view of the cliff that inspired the hotel's name as soon as you step into the lobby, but then your attention will quickly shift to burned bricks, charred wooden tiles, and natural wooden beams that create an atmosphere reminiscent of Siam's ancient Srivijaya period. **Pros:** atmospheric design; stunning location; good Wi-Fi connection. **Cons:** not on beach; could use some updating; some rooms are stuffy. [$] *Rooms from: B1,750* ✉ *85/2 Liab Chai Haad Rd., Ao Nang* ☎ *075/638117 up to 18* 🌐 *www.thecliffkrabi.com* 🛏 *21 rooms* 🍴 *No Meals.*

Dusit Thani Krabi Beach Resort

$$$ | **RESORT** | **FAMILY** | This modern resort is spread around an expansive mangrove forest, directly on the beach: the contemporary and colorful standard rooms overlook the forest, while the six suites have views of the sea. **Pros:** two large pools; lots of activities; great for families; beachfront location. **Cons:** a little in need of refreshing; location may disappoint beach purists—water isn't crystal clear; lacks local character. [$] *Rooms from: B5,000* ✉ *155 Klong Muang Beach, Nongtalay, Krabi* ☎ *075/628000* 🍴 *Free Breakfast* 🛏 *252 rooms.*

J Mansion

$ | **HOTEL** | The primary reason to stay here is to save money for day trips and nightlife, and the view is a nice bonus. **Pros:**

large rooms; good views from top floor; friendly staff. **Cons:** slow Internet; not all rooms have a/c; very basic. $ *Rooms from: B1,000* ✉ *23/3 Moo 2, Ao Nang* ☎ *075/695128* ⊕ *www.jmansionaonang. com/accommodation.htm* ⟿ *21 rooms* ⦿ *No Meals.*

Krabi Resort

$$ | RESORT | These are the only beach-front bungalows in Ao Nang Town and they have the best swimming as well as a seaside park with plenty of benches positioned for gazing at the sea. **Pros:** lots of facilities for the price; great location; large rooms. **Cons:** decor doesn't feel very local; breakfast buffet can be bland; pools often filled with kids. $ *Rooms from: B2,400* ✉ *232 Liab Chai Haad Rd., Ao Nang* ☎ *075/637030 up to 35, 02/208–9165 in Bangkok* ⊕ *www.krabiresort.net* ⟿ *132 rooms* ⦿ *No Meals.*

Phra Nang Inn

$ | B&B/INN | This longstanding resort on the Ao Nang beachfront has tastefully decorated rooms, an on-site spa, two swimming pools, a beach bar, and a restaurant. **Pros:** central location; airport shuttle available; great pool area. **Cons:** slow Internet; staff can be aloof; some room decor a bit dated. $ *Rooms from: B1,400* ✉ *119 Moo 2, Ao Nang* ☎ *075/637135* ⊕ *www.vacationvillage. co.th/phrananginn* ⦿ *Free Breakfast* ⟿ *74 rooms.*

The Small, Krabi

$$ | HOTEL | This sleek boutique hotel is in one of the busier parts of Ao Nang, offering proximity to shopping, dining, and drinking, plus swimming at the Nopphartthara and Ao Nang beaches on either side. **Pros:** great location; cleanliness and attention to detail; short walk to beach. **Cons:** having a TV in the bathroom is not to everyone's taste; no big pool; not a tranquil getaway. $ *Rooms from: B2,000* ✉ *167 Moo 3, Tambon, Amphur Muang, Ao Nang* ☎ *086/341–1704* ⊕ *www.thesmallhotelgroup.com/krabi/* ⦿ *No Meals* ⟿ *38 rooms.*

Srisuksant Resort

$$ | HOTEL | FAMILY | On the eastern end of Noppharat Thara, Srisuksant is a short walk from Ao Nang's shops and directly across from the beach. **Pros:** friendly staff; nice pools; well set up for kids and families. **Cons:** staff speak limited English; not all rooms have views; a little overwhelming for couples without kids. $ *Rooms from: B2,000* ✉ *145 Noppharat, Thara Beach, Ao Nang* ☎ *075/638002 up to 04* ⊕ *www.srisuksantresort.com* ▭ *No credit cards* ⟿ *66 rooms* ⦿ *Free Breakfast.*

The Tubkaak Krabi Boutique Resort

$$$$ | RESORT | This intimate resort is on a calm, lovely beach and the rooms have spectacular views of the Hong Islands. **Pros:** beach location; great pool area; relaxed environment. **Cons:** location is remote; lots of stairs; rooms are small. $ *Rooms from: B7,500* ✉ *123 Moo 3, Nongtalay, Ao Nang* ☎ *075/628456* ⊕ *www.tubkaakresort.com* ⦿ *Free Breakfast* ⟿ *46 rooms.*

 Nightlife

The Last Fisherman

BARS | At the end of Ao Nang Beach, this is the perfect spot for a sundowner beverage, though it's open for lunch and dinner, too, serving surf-and-turf, salads, and good desserts. ✉ *266 Moo 2, Ao Nang* ☎ *075/637968.*

Nang Cape/Railay Beach

15 mins by longtail boat east of Ao Nang.

The talcum-powder soft sand and crystal-line waters of the four areas (Tonsai, Phra Nang, East Railay, and West Railay) that collectively make up Railay are surrounded by impressive verdant, vertical cliffs. They're all connected by walking paths but each has its own distinct personality.

Tonsai Beach, with a pebble-strewn shore and shallow, rocky water, caters to budget travelers and rock climbers. West Railay has powdery white sand, shallow but swimmable water, gorgeous sunset views, and many kayaks for hire. Phra Nang Beach, one of the nicest beaches in all Krabi, is ideal for swimming, sunbathing, and rock-climbing. East Railay is a mangrove-lined shore unsuitable for beach or water activities but has a wide range of accommodations, restaurants, and bars.

GETTING HERE AND AROUND

Longtails will ferry you here from Ao Nang. Prices vary depending on time of day and which beach you're headed to, but expect to pay around B100 or B120 each way. Prices can rise dramatically in the evening, so leave early to save money.

🍴 Restaurants

There are plenty of bars and restaurants along each of the beaches. Most restaurants serve pretty standard Thai and Western fare, but as you move away from the beach, the options are less expensive and the places are more atmospheric.

🛏 Hotels

Bhu Nga Thani Resort and Spa
$$ | **RESORT** | This resort in East Railay has a lovely infinity pool and a popular spa. **Pros:** resort arranges excursions; most rooms have ocean views; bars and restaurants nearby. **Cons:** not on a swimming beach; 10-minute walk from boat drop; decor could use some updating. [$] *Rooms from: B4,000* ✉ *479 Moo 2, East Railay, Railay Beach* ☎ *075/819451 up to 04* 🌐 *www.bhungathani.com* 🛏 *60 rooms* 🍴 *No Meals.*

Koh Jum Lodge
$$$ | **B&B/INN** | On the island of Koh Jum, in Phang Nga Bay between Krabi, Phi Phi, and Koh Lanta, Koh Jum Lodge has rooms in 20 wooden cottages designed in traditional Thai architectural style, on the grounds of a coconut palm plantation in a tropical garden setting. **Pros:** stunning sunset over the Phi Phi Islands; traditional Thai design; helpful management and staff. **Cons:** difficult to access in off-peak season; a bit isolated from resort towns; food and drinks pricey. [$] *Rooms from: B4,500* ✉ *286 Moo 3, Koh Jum, Railay Beach* ☎ *075/618275, 089/921–1621* 🌐 *www.kohjumlodge.com* 💳 *No credit cards* 🛏 *20 bungalows* 🍴 *No Meals.*

Railay Bay Resort and Spa
$$ | **RESORT** | In the center of West Railay, the basic cottages and rooms in a row of modern two-story buildings here are perfectly comfortable, but the added bonuses are great Thai food and a beachside patio and bar from which you can watch the sunset. **Pros:** good food; great views; central location. **Cons:** sometimes patchy Wi-Fi; pricey spa; staff may not speak great English. [$] *Rooms from: B3,500* ✉ *145 Moo 2, West Railay, Railay Beach* ☎ *075/622998 up to 99* 🌐 *www.railaybayresort.com* 💳 *No credit cards* 🛏 *150 rooms* 🍴 *Free Breakfast.*

Railay Garden View Resort
$ | **B&B/INN** | Among the best of the less expensive options on Railay, this place has clean bungalows in a garden setting, and a great location near the beach. **Pros:** free Wi-Fi; good restaurant; complimentary breakfast. **Cons:** no sea view; not so many amenities; noise from longtail boats can get tiring. [$] *Rooms from: B750* ✉ *147 Moo 5, Railay East, Railay Beach* ☎ *088/765–0484, 084/295–1112* 🌐 *www.railaygardenview.com/en/* 🍴 *Free Breakfast* 🛏 *10 rooms.*

Railay Phutawan Resort
$$ | **RESORT** | From practically everywhere you stand at this resort, you can enjoy overwhelming vistas of the bay and gorgeous limestone cliffs. **Pros:** good food; budget-friendly; stunning views. **Cons:** other than the pool, not a lot of facilities; property is spread out; an uphill

trek to get there. $ *Rooms from: B2,000* ✉ *Moo 1, Railay East, Railay Beach* ☎ *097/285–9839* 🌐 *www.railayphutawan.com* 🍴 *Free Breakfast* 🛏 *20 bungalows.*

Railay Princess Resort and Spa

$ | **HOTEL** | Thai-style lamps and silk throw pillows on the beds and sofas are colorful touches at this quiet retreat midway between East and West Railay beaches. **Pros:** quiet location; good value; tasteful details. **Cons:** not on beach; watch out for hidden charges like lost room keys, or towels getting stained; furniture is a bit worn. $ *Rooms from: B1,900* ✉ *145/1 Moo 2, West Railay, Railay Beach* ☎ *075/819401 up to 03, 075/819407 up to 09* 🌐 *www.krabi-railayprincess.com* 🛏 *59 rooms* 🍴 *Free Breakfast.*

★ **Railei Beach Club**

$$ | **HOUSE** | **FAMILY** | The 24 houses that make up this "beach club" are unique in design and sleep between two and eight people, and most have large decks and kitchens. **Pros:** you can arrange for someone to do your grocery shopping; great choice of accommodations and prices; good location. **Cons:** some staff can be aloof; fills up early in high season; bring your own beach towels. $ *Rooms from: B2,000* ✉ *200 Moo 2, Railay West* ☎ *075/622582, 086/685–9359* 🌐 *www.raileibeachclub.com* 🛏 *24 houses* 🍴 *No Meals.*

Rayavadee Resort

$$$$ | **RESORT** | Scattered across 26 landscaped acres, this magnificent resort is set in coconut groves with white-sand beaches on three sides. **Pros:** plenty of facilities; great dining variety; intricate room design. **Cons:** beach very busy during the day; notably nonecological use of wood; during low tide boat access is challenging. $ *Rooms from: B12,000* ✉ *214 Moo 2, Tambol Ao Nang, Krabi* ☎ *075/620740 up to 43* 🌐 *www.rayavadee.com* 🍴 *Free Breakfast* 🛏 *103 rooms* 💳 *No credit cards.*

Activities

Many outdoor enthusiasts come to Railay for the rock climbing but kayaking tours are also popular. You can go with a guide or rent your own from stands on the beach.

ROCK CLIMBING

The mostly vertical cliffs rising up out of the sea around Railay are a dream come true for hard-core climbers and today anyone daring enough can learn to scale the face of a rock in one of the most beautiful destinations in the world. There are 500 to 600 established climbing routes. Notable feats include the Tonsai Beach overhang and Thaiwand Wall, where climbers must use lanterns to pass through a cave and then rappel down from the top. Beginners can learn some skills with half-day or full-day courses for fixed rates of B1,200 or B2,000, respectively. Most climbing organizations are found on East Railay, and they're all pretty much the same, though we list a few notable ones below. There are also boat trips out to the lagoon, where you can free climb the rocks—when you fall you just land in the water.

King Climbers

ROCK CLIMBING | All the guides here are accredited by the ACGA and have a minimum of five years' climbing experience. ✉ *East Railay, Railay Beach* ☎ *075/637125* 🌐 *www.railay.com.*

Tex Rock Climbing

ROCK CLIMBING | Half-day to three-day climbing courses can be arranged here. ✉ *East Railay, Railay Beach* ☎ *075/631509.*

Koh Lanta

70 km (42 miles) south of Krabi Town.

With its long beaches, crystal-clear water, and laid-back natural environment, Koh Lanta is one of Thailand's most appealing island districts. It's made up of the major islands of Ko Lanta Yai (the largest of the islands), Ko Lanta Nai, and Ko Klang, as well as many much smaller islands.

Although the area became popular on the tourist circuit in the early 2000s, it remains relatively quiet. There are hundreds of budget bungalows and several upmarket resorts along the west coast of Lanta Yai (Lanta Noi's coast is less suitable for development); however, as one of the largest islands in Thailand, Lanta was able to absorb the explosion in popularity and therefore remains relatively uncluttered when compared to Krabi Town 70 km (44 miles) away.

Most smaller resorts are closed during the low season (May through October), but the crossover months of May and October can be a good time to visit. The weather is still generally good but the rates are lower and the beaches are less crowded.

GETTING HERE AND AROUND

Krabi's airport is about two hours from Koh Lanta by taxi (B2,300 to B3,000) or minibus (B350). Minibuses depart from Krabi Town and Ao Nang, not the airport. There's no direct bus service from Bangkok to Koh Lanta; you'll have to take the bus to Trang or Krabi and then continue on in a minivan (songthaews will take you from the bus station to the minivans bound for Koh Lanta). There are two short (15 minutes) Ro-Ro ferry crossings between the mainland and Lanta catering specifically to those coming by car or bus. There's one direct passenger ferry every morning from Krabi at 11:30 am; it costs B400. A bridge built in 2016 now

connects Koh Lanta Yai and Lanta Noi, but a ferry is still required to reach the Krabi mainland.

One main road runs along the island that will take you to all major resorts. Pickup trucks masquerading as taxis and motorcycles with sidecars will take you wherever you want to go. Negotiate hard for good fares; prices start at about B60 for a short ride of 1 km (½ mile).

Beaches

Klong Dao Beach and Phra Ae Beach, both on Lanta Yai's west coast, are the most developed. If you head south, you'll reach calmer Klong Nin Beach and southern Lanta's quiet, scenic coves. Southern Lanta has several widely dispersed small coves and beaches ending at Klong Chak National Park. Immediately south of Klong Nin the road suddenly becomes well paved (much smoother than the road from Long Beach to Klong Nin), making the southern beaches accessible by road as well as by taxi boat. The nicest of the southern beaches is Bakantiang Beach, a beautiful one to visit on the way to the national park.

★ Bakantiang (Kantiang) Beach

BEACH | The last beach before the national park on the southern tip of Koh Lanta, crescent-shaped Kantiang Beach is small but truly stunning. The fine white sands are favored by those who want to get away from the busier beaches. The village that backs the sand is the friendliest on the island, and there are a few food stalls and roadside cafés that serve some of the tastiest food on Koh Lanta. **Amenities:** food and drink; showers; toilets. **Best for:** snorkeling; sunset; swimming. ⊹ *Last stop on main road heading south, before national park.*

Klong Dao Beach

BEACH | FAMILY | Klong Dao Beach is a 2-km-long (1-mile) beach on the northern coast of Lanta Yai. Most resorts along

Klong Dao are larger facilities catering to families and couples looking for a quiet environment. The water is shallow but swimmable, and at low tide the firm, exposed sand is ideal for long jogs on the beach. **Amenities:** food and drink; toilets. **Best for:** sunset; swimming; walking. ✢ *To right of Lanta's main road, first beach after port town Saladan.*

Klong Nin Beach

BEACH | Klong Nin Beach, approximately 30 minutes south of Phra Ae Beach (aka Long Beach) by car or boat, is one of the larger, nicer beaches toward the southern end of Lanta Yai. Klong Nin is less developed and more tranquil than Phra Ae Beach. A typical day on Klong Nin can be a long walk on the silky soft sand interrupted by occasional dips in the sea, a spectacular sunset, a seaside massage, and a candlelight barbecue beneath a canopy of stars. Central Klong Nin is the best for swimming, as rocks punctuate the rest of the shoreline. Kayaks are available from some resorts, and longtail boat taxis are for hire along the sea. Most resorts here rent motorbikes, as the road to the south is much smoother than the road from Phra Ae Beach. **Amenities:** food and drink; toilets. **Best for:** solitude; sunset; swimming; walking. ✢ *To right of Lanta's main road from Saladan, after intersection for Old Town and Southern Lanta.*

Phra Ae Beach (*Long Beach*)

BEACH | Long and wide, Phra Ae Beach is Lanta Yai's main tourist destination. The sand is soft and fine, perfect for both sunbathing and long walks. The water is less shallow than at other Lanta beaches, and therefore more suitable for swimming. Nevertheless, kayaks, catamarans, and other water activities, while available, are not as ubiquitous as on other islands. Although most lodging consists of simple budget resorts, the beachfront does have several three- and four-star accommodations. Along the beach and on the main road are many restaurants, bars, cafés, and dive operators. **Amenities:** food and drink; showers; toilets; water sports. **Best for:** sunset; swimming; walking. ✢ *Second beach to right of Lanta's main road from port town Saladan.*

🍴 Restaurants

KLONG DAO

Black Coral Restaurant & Bar

$$ | **INTERNATIONAL** | There are plenty of restaurants along the beach, serving international dishes and Thai classics, but this one is a step above. The seafood here is superb, especially the barracuda fillet. **Known for:** exceptional seafood; friendly service; great sea views. [$] *Average main: 200* ✉ *117 Moo #, Koh Lanta* ☎ *085/691–2146* 🌐 *blackcoral-lanta.com* 💳 *No credit cards.*

Fat Monkey (Ling Uan)

$$ | **EUROPEAN** | There are two kitchens, and two cuisines—Thai and Western—but the Fat Monkey is best known and loved for its large, juicy burgers. It's a pleasant place for a meal, with a pretty garden. **Known for:** chill atmosphere; juicy burgers; ice-cream cocktails. [$] *Average main: B200* ✉ *Klong Dao Rd., Saladan* ✢ *Center of Klong Dao Beach* ☎ *087/886–5017* 🕓 *Closed Mon.*

★ **Time for Lime**

$$ | **THAI** | Time for Lime is a large, open-air restaurant right off the beach. Each night there is a different three-course set menu, and reclining chairs are placed on the recessed sandbar while music plays and wonderful cocktails (try the chili margarita) are served. **Known for:** changing menus; cooking classes; lovely location. [$] *Average main: B200* ✉ *72/2 Klong Dao Beach, Lanta Yai, Saladan* ☎ *075/684590, 089/967–5017* 🌐 *www.timeforlime.net.*

OLD TOWN

Caoutchouc

$ | **THAI** | This lovely restaurant is situated at the end of a small dirt road in a wooden, traditional house with high ceilings from which colorful Chinese lanterns hang, swaying in the sea breeze. The Thai chef has a culinary vision and style that differs from the standard southern fare, so expect food a bit more sophisticated than elsewhere. **Known for:** lovely setting; creative food; in-season fare. [$] *Average main: B145* ✉ *Moo 1, Old Town* ☎ *075/697060, 084/629–0704.*

Pinto Restaurant

$ | **INTERNATIONAL** | This delightful sea view restaurant in Lanta Old Town is known for its fresh seafood and Thai cuisine, but also serves great burgers and has a separate vegetarian menu. The staff are quick to recommend favorite Thai dishes, in particular the tamarind prawns and the tart pomelo salad. **Known for:** extensive menu; friendly staff; fun atmosphere. [$] *Average main: 180* ✉ *65 Moo 2 Lanta Old Town, Koh Lanta* ☎ *085/883–4049* 🌐 *www.facebook.com/pintorestaurantkohlanta* 💳 *No credit cards.*

PHRA AE

★ Cook Kai

$ | **THAI** | From the outside, this restaurant looks like a standard, wooden Thai beach restaurant, but the creative cooking elevates it from the ordinary. Sizzling "hot pan" dishes of seafood in coconut cream, stir-fried morning glory, and sweet-and-sour shrimp are delicious. **Known for:** duck curry when it's available; creative cooking; sizzling seafood. [$] *Average main: B115* ✉ *Moo 6, Klong Nin Beach, Koh Lanta* ☎ *081/606–3015* 🌐 *www.cook-kai.com.*

Lap Royet

$ | **THAI** | This extremely casual, roadside street-food restaurant serves delicious, basic, and inexpensive food that everyone loves. Try the Isaan (northeastern) catfish *larb,* the zingy *som tam* (spicy papaya salad), or the fat noodles cooked in a thick pork broth, and sticky barbecue chicken. **Known for:** very casual setting; superb street food; Isaan catfish. [$] *Average main: B50* ✉ *Klong Dao Rd., Koh Lanta* ✣ *Toward northern end of Klong Dao Beach* ☎ *No phone.*

Tides

$$ | **THAI** | On a romantic seafront terrace of the Layana Resort, this restaurant is a romantic spot for sophisticated dinner. Look for daily specials like grilled giant prawns, as well as more traditional Thai dishes like green curry and a selection of international classics. **Known for:** excellent wine list; fun cocktails; sophisticated setting. [$] *Average main: B250* ✉ *272 Moo 3, Saladan, Phra Ae Beach, Koh Lanta* ☎ *075/607100* 🌐 *www.layanaresort.com.*

KLONG NIN

★ Otto Bar & Grill

$ | **INTERNATIONAL** | This is one of the most popular beach bar/restaurants in Koh Lanta, mostly owing to its vibrant owner, Otto, a been-there, done-that, rocker-hippie-type with an infectious joie de vivre. It's open all day, serving delicious, fruity cocktails and a variety of barbecued meats (burgers have a following) and salads. **Known for:** great burgers; Otto is a character; beachside location. [$] *Average main: B130* ✉ *Klong Nin Beach, Koh Lanta* 💳 *No credit cards.*

Roi Thai

$ | **INTERNATIONAL** | With tables facing out to the horizon, and fresh, flavorful seafood and fish barbecues, this is an idyllic spot for dinner by the beach. It's a simple but charming restaurant; the food certainly attracts a loyal clientele, but the service can be slow. ■ **TIP→ You can take a cooking class organized by Roi Thai, which also teaches the traditional art of fruit and vegetable carving.** **Known for:** laid-back vibe; pretty beach setting; cooking classes offered here, too. [$] *Average main: B100* ✉ *75/1 Moo 6, Klong Nin Beach* ☎ *083/636–0470.*

Salty Fish Beach Bistro

$ | **ASIAN** | With a back terrace that overlooks the beach and a pleasant atmosphere, this is a good spot for fresh seafood, classic Thai favorites, and specialities from northern Thailand. The chicken satay here is particularly good. **Known for:** good seafood dishes; chicken satay; nice views. [$] *Average main: 180* ✉ *Moo 5 Klong Tob, Koh Lanta* ☎ *082/473–3497* 🌐 *www.facebook.com/saltyfishlanta/* ⏲ *Tues.* 💳 *No credit cards.*

SOUTHERN LANTA

Drunken Sailors

$ | **AMERICAN** | **FAMILY** | This is one of those quintessential backpacker-friendly cafés with a laid-back vibe, eclectic seating (including beanbags and hammocks), and all kinds of comfort food. Try the tuna wasabi sub, the DK veggie samosas in puff pastry, or a burger. **Known for:** backpacker popularity; chill vibe; they also sell funky clothes. [$] *Average main: B100* ✉ *116 Moo 5, Koh Lanta Yai, Kantiang Bay* ☎ *075/665076.*

Phad Thai Rock n' Roll

$ | **THAI** | It's all in the name at this tiny roadside eatery presided over by the talented musician-owner who also plays local gigs. There are several varieties of delicious pad Thai. **TIP→ Ask the owner when his next gig is.** **Known for:** good smoothies; really good pad Thai; musician crowd. [$] *Average main: B70* ✉ *92 Moo 5, Kantiang Bay* ☎ *080/784–8729.*

Hotels

KLONG DAO

Costa Lanta

$$$ | **RESORT** | One of the coolest things about this boutique resort is that the rooms are "convertible": If you're too hot you can open up the "walls" and allow the breeze to blow through. **Pros:** fun amenities from a pool table to snorkeling; quiet location; cool design. **Cons:** not on best beach; limited dining options; not great value. [$] *Rooms from: B4,250* ✉ *212 Klong Dao Beach, Lanta Yai, Koh Lanta* ☎ *075/618092, 075/668186* 🌐 *www.costalanta.com* 💳 *No credit cards* 🛏 *22 rooms* 🍴 *Free Breakfast.*

Southern Lanta

$ | **RESORT** | **FAMILY** | With a fun slide plunging into a big pool and several two-bedroom villas (each with large multibed rooms), Southern Lanta is understandably popular with families. **Pros:** family-friendly; good location; pleasant restaurant. **Cons:** limited views; pool crowds easily; needs redecoration. [$] *Rooms from: B1,000* ✉ *105 Klong Dao Beach, Lanta Yai, Koh Lanta* ☎ *075/684175 up to 77* 🌐 *www.southernlanta.com* 💳 *No credit cards* 🛏 *100 bungalows* 🍴 *Free breakfast.*

Twin Lotus Resort and Spa

$$$ | **RESORT** | This resort is as much an architectural and interior-design exhibition as it is a sophisticated and tranquil retreat. **Pros:** stunning location; quality dining; appealing in-room facilities. **Cons:** service can be lax; decor not for everyone; may be too quiet for families. [$] *Rooms from: B4,200* ✉ *199 Moo 1, Klong Dao Beach, Koh Lanta Yai, Koh Lanta* ☎ *075/560–7000, 02/361–1946 up to 49 in Bangkok* 🌐 *www.twinlotusresort.com* 💳 *No credit cards* 🛏 *81 rooms* 🍴 *No Meals.*

OLD TOWN

Mango House

$$ | **HOTEL** | In the laid-back and increasingly trendy Old Town, or Sri Raya, Mango House is a home away from home, with three seafront suites and three villas, all in Chinese-style wooden houses that stand on stilts over the water. **Pros:** comfortable rooms; welcoming atmosphere; a great base for exploring the Old Town. **Cons:** no air-conditioning; private property next to rooms is shabby. [$] *Rooms from: B2,500* ✉ *45 Sriraya Rd., Moo 2, Old Town* ☎ *089/867-1067* 🌐 *www.mango-houses.com* 🍴 *No Meals* 🛏 *6 rooms.*

PHRA AE

Best House

$ | **B&B/INN** | The Best House lobby, an inviting high-ceilinged room with comfortable chairs, white tile floors, and wooden beams, offers a good sense of what you can expect from the accommodations. **Pros:** friendly service; inexpensive; near the beach. **Cons:** no pool; rooms are basic; no in-room amenities. $ *Rooms from: B1,000* ✉ *5/1 Moo 3, Phra Ae Beach, Lanta Yai, Koh Lanta* ☎ *075/684560, 084/464–1500* ⊕ *www.besthouselantaguesthouse.com* ☾ *Closed Apr.–Oct.* ➥ *30 rooms* ❍❘ *No Meals.*

Fruit Tree Lodge

$ | **HOTEL** | **FAMILY** | This budget-friendly resort is made up of basic bungalows on stilts, in a tropical garden. **Pros:** great coffee shop attached; lovely garden setting; great sightseeing tips. **Cons:** basic bungalows; Wi-Fi is sporadic; not on the beach. $ *Rooms from: 700* ✉ *557 Moo 2, Koh Lanta* ☎ *089/697–8379* ⊕ *www.facebook. com/FruitTreeLodge* ❍❘ *No Meals* ➥ *10 bungalows* ▭ *No credit cards.*

Lanta Sand Resort and Spa

$ | **RESORT** | There are large ponds with water lilies and fountains, and brick paths meander from the villas to the pool to the spa—it's all very chic. **Pros:** near beach; spacious rooms; romantic. **Cons:** noisy air-conditioning in some rooms; far from any town; prices are high for what you get. $ *Rooms from: B1,750* ✉ *279 Moo 3, Phra Ae Beach, Lanta Yai, Koh Lanta* ☎ *075/684633, 089/724–2682* ⊕ *www.lantasand.com* ➥ *78 rooms* ❍❘ *No Meals.*

★ Layana Resort and Spa

$$$$ | **RESORT** | Guests repeatedly return to the Layana for the pampering, understated luxury, and a relaxed, peaceful environment. **Pros:** lovely beach; varied breakfast buffet includes healthy juice bar; many activities organized in-house. **Cons:** some bungalows lack sea views; no children; not much in the way of nightlife. $ *Rooms from: B7,500* ✉ *272 Moo 3, Saladan, Phra Ae Beach, Koh Lanta, Koh Lanta* ☎ *075/607100, 02/713– 2313 in Bangkok* ⊕ *www.layanaresort. com* ❍❘ *Free Breakfast* ➥ *50 rooms.*

Nakara Long Beach Resort

$$ | **RESORT** | If you're staying in a resort on a beautiful, white-sand beach with crystal-clear, blue water, you should treat yourself to a room with a view— and at Nakara, you'll have one, even if you end up in a room at the back. **Pros:** friendly staff; great views; good location near the beach. **Cons:** free Wi-Fi only in lobby; could use some renovations; bland design. $ *Rooms from: B3,700* ✉ *172 Moo 3, Phra Ae Beach, Saladan* ☎ *075/684198* ⊕ *www.lantalongbeach. com* ❍❘ *Free Breakfast* ➥ *41 cottages.*

KLONG NIN

Lanta Miami Resort

$ | **B&B/INN** | The affordable, beachside bungalows at the Lanta Miami are clean, spacious, and with big beds, and have nicely sized, tiled bathrooms. **Pros:** nice pool; great location; comfortable. **Cons:** staff can be unaccommodating; some rooms lack hot water; rooms without sea views are a bit stuffy. $ *Rooms from: B1,000* ✉ *13 Moo 6, Klong Nin Beach, Lanta Yai, Koh Lanta* ☎ *075/662559* ▭ *No credit cards* ☾ *Closed June–Sept.* ➥ *26 rooms* ❍❘ *Free Breakfast.*

Lanta Paradise Beach Resort

$ | **RESORT** | Bungalows here come in all permutations, from fan-cooled and cold-water-only to air-conditioned, with hot water and all the standard amenities. **Pros:** impressive Western food at restaurant; nice pool; prime location. **Cons:** lack of amenities; very basic rooms; not the best value. $ *Rooms from: B1,100* ✉ *67 Moo 6, Klong Nin Beach, Lanta Yai, Koh Lanta* ☎ *075/662569, 082/801–2036* ⊕ *www.lantaparadisebeachresort.com* ☾ *Closed June–Sept.* ❍❘ *Free Breakfast* ➥ *34 rooms.*

Rawi Warin Resort and Spa

$$ | **RESORT** | **FAMILY** | This enormous, lively resort with luxuriously outfitted rooms and high-tech amenities stretches gracefully across an entire hillside along the road from Klong Khong Beach to Klong Nin. The resort features, among many other things, a 24-seat minitheater, a music room, a video game room, a dive shop, and a beautiful private beach. **Pros:** family-friendly; many amenities; helpful staff. **Cons:** beach is rocky; not great value; activities are limited. [$] *Rooms from: B4,000* ✉ *139 Moo 8, Lanta Yai Island, Krabi, Koh Lanta* ☎ *026/643490 up to 48, 02/434–5526 in Bangkok* 🌐 *www.rawiwarin.com* 🍴 *Free Breakfast* 🛏 *185 rooms.*

SriLanta

$$ | **RESORT** | One of the first upscale resorts in the area to market the "less is more" philosophy, SriLanta remains an island getaway for edgy urbanites. **Pros:** nice pool; great in-room amenities; yoga classes. **Cons:** attention to detail is slack; staff a bit standoffish; no sea views. [$] *Rooms from: B2,200* ✉ *111 Moo 6, Klong Nin Beach, Lanta Yai, Koh Lanta* ☎ *075/697288* 🌐 *www.srilanta.com* 🛏 *52 rooms* 🍴 *No Meals.*

SOUTHERN LANTA

Narima Bungalow Resort

$$ | **B&B/INN** | Most of the bungalows at this chill resort have views of Koh Ha and balconies where you can sway in a hammock or kick back in a palm-straw rocking chair. **Pros:** professional dive school; panoramic views; pleasant hosts. **Cons:** bathrooms are rough around the edges; rocky beach; restaurant could be better. [$] *Rooms from: B3,937* ✉ *98 Moo 5, Klong Nin Beach, Lanta Yai, Koh Lanta* ☎ *075/662668, 075/662670* 🌐 *www.narima-lanta.com* 🍴 *No Meals* 🛏 *32 rooms* 💳 *No credit cards.*

★ **Pimalai Resort and Spa**

$$$$ | **RESORT** | The rain forest meets the stunning beach at Pimalai, where the seductive yet unpretentious luxury attracts the likes of royalty and celebrities. **Pros:** gorgeous Andaman beach with crystal-clear water; beautiful architecture; friendly, helpful management and staff. **Cons:** prices also exclusive; can be a bit too see-and-be-seen for some; fills up fast. [$] *Rooms from: B7,000* ✉ *99 Moo 5, Bakantiang Beach, Lanta Yai, Koh Lanta* ☎ *075/607999* 🌐 *www.pimalai.com* 🍴 *No Meals* 🛏 *109 rooms.*

🍸 Nightlife

Bob Bar

BARS | Is this spot named after the owner, or Bob Marley? We might never know but the music is great, the beer is cold, and the atmosphere is friendly. ✉ *Klong Dao, Ban Koh Lanta.*

Funky Monkey

LIVE MUSIC | Designed to look like the inside of a jungle, this roadside bar-club is the venue for live gigs that get locals, expats, and tourists dancing together until the late hours. Outside, benches offer respite from blaring music and a place to snack from nearby street food stalls. It's not as lively on nights when there isn't a live performance. ✉ *Klong Dao Rd., Koh Lanta.*

The Frog Wine Cellar and Restaurant

WINE BARS | In Saladan port town, near the pier, this wine bar with an atmospheric garden setting is a nice change of scene for those interested in sampling wines and accompanying appetizers. They have labels from 12 countries. ✉ *295/19 Moo 3, Klong Dao Beach* 🌐 *www.thefroglanta.com.*

🏃 Activities

Diving, snorkeling, hiking, and cooking are just a few activities available on Koh Lanta and the nearby islands.

Diving Koh Lanta

DIVING & SNORKELING | Diving and snorkeling activities are available on Koh Lanta

and the nearby islands. Trips can be arranged through dive and tour operators, though most people choose to book through their own resort. Popular nearby dive sites are **Koh Ha** and **Koh Rok,** off Koh Lanta. ⊠ *Koh Lanta.*

Emerald Cave

BOAT TOURS | A boat trip to the famous **Emerald Cave** on **Koh Mook** is a worthwhile experience. You can swim and snorkel through a dark water cave to an idyllic lagoon, though get here early to avoid the flotilla of boats taking others to do the same thing. ⊠ *Koh Lanta.*

★ Time for Lime Cooking Classes

COOKING CLASSES | You can learn to cook fresh, seasonal, and creative Thai food (with Chinese, Malaysian, and Indian twists), under fun, expert instruction at this popular restaurant by the beach. Their excellent classes include a valuable theoretical introduction to Thai food and a five-hour option, during which you will prepare, and learn to beautifully present, your own feast. ⊠ *2/2 Klong Dao Beach, Koh Lanta* ⊕ *www.timeforlime.net.*

Koh Phi Phi

48 km (30 miles) or 90 mins by boat southeast of Phuket Town, 42 km (26 miles) or 2 hrs by boat southwest of Krabi.

Phi Phi is the Thailand you've probably seen in movies and it IS undeniably gorgeous, even if tourism has taken a toll. It's actually six islands. The largest, Phi Phi Don, is shaped like a butterfly: the "wings" are covered by limestone mountains, and connected by a flat 2km (1 mile) narrow land mass with a sandy beach on each side. This is also the only inhabited island. On Phi Phi Don, the main access point is Tonsai Pier, in Tonsai Bay, which also has a Tonsai Beach. This is different from the Tonsai Beach in Railay.

The islands of Koh Phi Phi were once idyllic retreats, with secret silver-sand coves, unspoiled stretches of shoreline, and limestone cliffs dropping precipitously into the sea. After *The Beach* (2000) was filmed here, though, Phi Phi became a hot (overcrowded) property. The beaches on Phi Phi are still stunning and are some of the most accessible in Thailand, though the famed Maya Bay (also called Maya Beach) is sometimes closed to tourists to allow it to recover from the crowds.

Luxury resorts have spread themselves across the sands here and a multitude of restaurants, bars, and smaller guesthouses fill the demand for lodging. Many of the budget accommodations that dominated the island for years have upgraded their facilities (and their prices) in a hit-and-miss process of development—some have achieved grandeur, or class, others are tacky and overpriced for what they offer.

Sadly, it seems that unchecked development is the norm, and the buildings are creeping higher each year. The resorts have generally become more high-end; but beware, the terms "resort" and "deluxe" are used liberally and don't necessarily reflect reality. Note also that the tsunami of 2004 has not had any lasting impact and, if you were unaware that such a catastrophe had taken place, you would think it was a beautiful island under a lot of development, rather than one that was destroyed and has been rebuilt.

The popularity of the Phi Phi Islands stems from the outstanding scuba diving; leopard sharks, turtles, and seahorses are some species still frequenting popular reefs. As Phi Phi becomes more developed, people have been forced away from the center of Ao Dalerm Beach. Other beaches have been discovered and now bear the brunt of growing tourist numbers on the island.

Long Beach has become popular but still retains its charm.

GETTING HERE AND AROUND

The main pier for arriving and departing Phi Phi is Tonsai Pier. Ferries depart from Ratsada Pier on Phuket five times daily and reach Phi Phi Don two hours later. PP Cruiser also takes two hours to reach Phi Phi Don, but departs from Phuket's Makham Pier. A one-way ticket is B650, and a round-trip ticket is B1,000. Ferries traveling to Phuket from Ao Nang or Koh Lanta stop at Koh Phi Phi in the high season (November to April) as well. From Krabi, boats depart four times each day and cost B650. A few years ago local authorities implemented a B20 "clean-up" tax, collected upon arrival at the dock. It's not clear, however, how this money is being used, as there have been no immediately apparent improvements to the island's environment.

Beaches

Bamboo Island

ISLAND | It's a 45-minute trip by longtail boat to Bamboo Island, but there's a superb beach and the colors of the fish and the coral are brilliant. You can sometimes spot reef sharks, too. There are several places to get food and drinks. **Amenities:** food and drink. **Best for:** swimming; snorkeling; solitude. ⊠ *Koh Phi Phi.*

Laem Tong Beach

BEACH | Accessible by boat only, Laem Tong Beach is more secluded than some of the other Phi Phi beaches. The turquoise waters are warm and the beach is bordered by jungle. All this gives Laem Tong more of a tropical-island-paradise feel than other busier Phi Phi beaches. ■ **TIP→ Local fishermen can bring you here and take you to other nearby destinations on their longtail boats for less money than organized trips. Amenities:** food and drink; toilets. **Best for:** snorkeling; sunrise; swimming. ⊠ *Northern Phi Phi, Koh Phi Phi.*

Loh Dalum Beach

BEACH | On the other side of the Phi Phi Don Island from Tonsai Village, Loh Dalum has all the hallmarks of a tropical paradise: clear emerald waters, views onto the beautiful bay, and a white sandy beach. However, it's also touristy, busy, and noisy—an unfortunate symptom of Phi Phi's popularity. Beach bars put on spectacular fire shows at night, and the partying lasts well into the early hours. Swimming is best at high tide. **Amenities:** food and drink; showers; toilets; water sports. **Best for:** partiers; swimming. ⊠ *Koh Phi Phi Don, Koh Phi Phi.*

Long Beach

BEACH | Long Beach, a few minutes' longtail boat ride from Tonsai Pier, affords visitors a calmer and more relaxing experience away from the madding crowds. The white sands are almost silky underfoot and there are gorgeous views of Phi Phi Leh. Day-trippers often only stay for a dip and lunch, so the rest of the time it's pretty peaceful. **Amenities:** food and drink; toilets. **Best for:** snorkeling; swimming. ⊠ *Long Beach, Koh Phi Phi, Koh Phi Phi.*

Phi Phi Lae

ISLAND | Phi Phi Lae, where Maya Bay is located, is a popular day trip from Phi Phi Don via longtail or speedboat. The first stop is Viking Cave, a vast cavern of limestone pillars covered with crude drawings. Most boats continue on for an afternoon in Maya Bay, aka "The Beach," (though note the government has taken to closing Maya Bay periodically to allow the area's nature to recover from mass tourism). If you don't mind thronging crowds (snorkelers practically outnumber the fish), Maya Bay is a spectacular site. If you get a really early jump on everyone, cruise into a bay and leave first tracks along the powdery sand beach; otherwise, head to Loh Samah Bay, on the opposite side of the island. Loh Samah Bay may, in fact, be the better option. Though smaller, it is as beautiful as Maya Bay but receives less attention. ⊠ *Koh Phi Phi.*

Tsunami Memorials

On the eastern end of Loh Dalam Beach is the Phi Phi Tsunami Memorial Park, a tiny garden with a small plaque listing some of the names of those who lost their lives in the 2004 tsunami. Several benches have been dedicated to the memory of others lost in the disaster. The memorial is a little sad, because it seems so small in relation to the devastation that claimed 5,395 lives. Regardless, it is a nice little park, and looking out across the beach and sea, one cannot help but be moved.

Another memorial, this one under-water, is 66 feet deep, off the coast of Monkey Beach. The granite memorial consists of three pyramid-shaped plaques arranged in the shape of an equilateral triangle; the plaques are the exact number of centimeters apart as the number of victims taken by the sea. The bases of the pyramids contain philosophical quotations, and the three markers symbolize the elements of land, water, and air in which humans must learn to live in balance. In the center of the triangle rests a single granite stand that describes the tsunami's occurrence. In addition, 2,874 (the number of missing persons) centimeters from the memorial is a traditional Thai sala made from tsunami debris. It is the first underwa-ter memorial monument on Earth.

Tonsai Beach

BEACH | Not to be confused with the Tonsai, in Railay, this Tonsai Beach is not a place for the fainthearted; it's crowded, noisy, and not the cleanest. The best time to visit is in the early morning when most of the young revelers are sleeping off the excesses of the previous night. **Amenities:** showers; toilets; water sports. **Best for:** partiers. ✉ *Ton Sai, Koh Phi Phi, Koh Phi Phi.*

Chao Koh Restaurant

$$ | **SEAFOOD** | As you stroll Tonsai's walking path, it's hard to miss the catch of the day on display in front of Chao Koh Restaurant (opposite the Chao Koh Resort). Kingfish, swordfish, and barra-cuda are some of the usual options, and are served grilled with garlic and butter, white wine, or marsala sauce; clams, crabs, shrimp, Phuket lobster, and live rock lobsters are priced by weight. **Known for:** seafood display; grilled barracuda; popular with day-trippers. $ *Average*

main: B230 ✉ *Tongsai Bay, Tonsai Beach Rd. at Chao Koh Rd., Koh Phi Phi* ☎ *075/620800* ▭ *No credit cards.*

Ciao Bella

$ | **ITALIAN** | It's not a local haunt in Napoli or Rome, but for Phi Phi, the Italian food is tasty and the candlelit seaside setting is magical. The pizza and focaccia come from a wood-fired oven, and inventive pasta dishes and classic appetizers such as bruschetta, caprese salad, and prosciutto di Parma round out the menu. **Known for:** good pizza; simple Italian cuisine; candlelit setting. $ *Average main: B145* ✉ *9 Koh Phi Phi Muu, Loh Dalum Beach, Koh Phi Phi* ☎ *081/894–1246.*

Hippies Bar

$$ | **INTERNATIONAL** | On the eastern end of Tonsai Beach, Hippies serves a mixture of international food, from burgers and steaks to pasta and pizza. The staff at both the restaurant and seaside bar are friendly. **Known for:** international cuisine; live entertainment; beach views. $ *Aver-age main: B200* ✉ *Tonsai Beach, Koh Phi Phi* ▭ *No credit cards.*

Phi Phi Bakery

$ | **CAFÉ** | If you've been craving fresh-baked doughnuts, croissants, mouth-watering eggs Benedict, and real coffee rather than the instant stuff, you'll fall in love with the family-run Phi Phi Bakery, which serves American, continental, and Thai breakfast and brunch specials and freshly baked pastries (the cinnamon buns are especially good). They also serve Thai and Western standards for lunch (it closes at 5 pm). **Known for:** family atmosphere; fresh baked goods; Thai brunch specials. [$] *Average main: B150* ✉ *97 Moo 7, Tonsai Village, Koh Phi Phi* ☎ *075/601017.*

Hotels

Arayaburi Resort

$$ | **RESORT** | The rooms here are modern and clean, and all have tile floors, which keeps the resort looking fresh. **Pros:** quiet away from the noise of Tonsai Beach; great views out to sea; private beach. **Cons:** 25-minute walk to the pier; resort is on hilly terrain; sometimes slippery access when it rains. [$] *Rooms from: B2,200* ✉ *69 Laem Hin Beach, Koh Phi Phi* ☎ *076/281360* 🌐 *www.arayaburiphi-phi.com* 🍴 *No Meals* 🛏 *38 rooms.*

Bay View Resort

$$ | **RESORT** | Every bungalow here has a large deck with a great view of both Phi Phi Lae and Tonsai Bay, though the rooms are bit dated. **Pros:** great views; quiet location; breakfast included. **Cons:** not on best beach; removed from main village; could use a refresh. [$] *Rooms from: B2,200* ✉ *69 Laem Hin Beach, Koh Phi Phi* ☎ *075/601127 up to 30* 🌐 *www.phiphibayview.com* 🛏 *109 bungalows* 🍴 *Free Breakfast.*

Paradise Resort

$ | **RESORT** | Despite having undergone renovations and pushing up its prices, the Paradise Resort continues to offer great value for money but make sure to book ahead (it's popular), and don't settle for less than beachfront. **Pros:** great beach massage service; budget rooms in idyllic location; clean rooms. **Cons:** Wi-Fi at extra charge; some rooms lack air-conditioning; may be too quiet for some. [$] *Rooms from: B1,700* ✉ *Long Beach, Koh Phi Phi* ☎ *091/968–3982 up to 89* 🌐 *www.paradiseresort.co.th* 🍴 *No Meals* 🛏 *25 rooms.*

P. P. Erawan Palms Resort

$$ | **RESORT** | This is a small, comfortable resort in the middle of Laem Tong Beach, next to the sea gypsy village. **Pros:** nice beach bar; relaxed resort feel; nice location. **Cons:** restaurant prices high; boat ride away from main village; decor shows some age. [$] *Rooms from: B3,100* ✉ *Moo 8, Laem Tong Beach, Koh Phi Phi* ☎ *075/818713 up to 4, 082/645–8549* 🌐 *www.pperawanpalms.com* 🍴 *No Meals* 🛏 *18 cottages.*

★ **Phi Phi Holiday Resort**

$$ | **RESORT** | This resort couldn't have a better location—it's on a beach shared with just three other resorts, where the gorgeous blue water has a sandy sea floor and you can swim and snorkel year-round. **Pros:** attentive staff; secluded, private beach; very peaceful. **Cons:** jungle setting means some creepy crawlies; set away from the main part of Koh Phi Phi; not walking distance to many restaurants or shops. [$] *Rooms from: B3,600* ✉ *Laem Tong Beach, Koh Phi Phi* ☎ *075/627300* 🌐 *www.ihg.com/holidayinnresorts/hotels/us/en/phi-phi-island/phupb/hoteldetail?cm_mmc=GoogleMaps-_-RS-_-TH-_-PHUPB* 🍴 *No Meals* 🛏 *130 bungalows.*

Phi Phi Natural Resort

$$ | **RESORT** | Beautiful sunrise views from the seaside bungalows are this resort's biggest draw. **Pros:** daily boat service to Phuket and Krabi; has good budget rooms; lovely views at moderate prices. **Cons:** lacks amenities compared to other resorts in price range; remote; can get busy. [$] *Rooms from: B2,200* ✉ *53 Moo 8, Laem Tong Beach, Koh Phi Phi*

☎ *075/613000* 🌐 *www.phiphinatural.com* 🛏 *70 rooms* 🍴 *Free Breakfast.*

Phi Phi ViewPoint Resort
$ | **RESORT** | On the western hillside overlooking Loh Dalam Bay, the hillside bungalows here are stacked pretty tightly next to and on top of each other, but the six beachfront bungalows will give you a little more breathing room and privacy. **Pros:** nice location overlooking bay; all bungalows have a terrace; beachfront bungalows have amazing views. **Cons:** some huts are basic for the price; steep gradient to some areas; not much privacy around the property. [$] *Rooms from: B1,900* ✉ *107 Loh Dalam Bay, Koh Phi Phi* ☎ *075/601200* 🌐 *www.phiphiview-point.com* 🛏 *55 huts* 🍴 *No Meals.*

Phi Phi Villa Resort
$$ | **RESORT** | Large thatch-covered huts in a natural setting give Phi Phi Villa a relaxing island feeling quite different from bustling Tonsai Bay, a short walk away. **Pros:** close to the action; budget prices; yoga. **Cons:** rocky beach not great for swimming; noise from nearby bars; service is hit-and-miss. [$] *Rooms from: B2,200* ✉ *Tonsai Bay, Koh Phi Phi* ☎ *075/601100* 🌐 *www.phiphivillaresort.com* 🍴 *Free Breakfast* 🛏 *55 bungalows.*

SAii Phi Phi Island Village
$$$ | **RESORT** | **FAMILY** | This eco-friendly retreat has secluded bungalows and villas all with bright, contemporary interiors. **Pros:** several good restaurants; stunning location; luxurious pool area. **Cons:** how you get there depends on the tide; a little remote; staff can be a little lax. [$] *Rooms from: B5,000* ✉ *49 Moo 8, Loh Bagao Bay, Koh Phi Phi* ☎ *075/628900* 🌐 *www.saiiresorts.com/phiphiisland/village/* 🍴 *Free Breakfast* 🛏 *156 bungalows.*

★ **Zeavola**
$$$$ | **RESORT** | This resort takes its name from a flower, the name of which translates to "love of the sea," which certainly is fitting, since the water off the powdery white-sand Laem Tong Beach is simply stunning. **Pros:** stunning beach location; tasteful design; private. **Cons:** expensive service charge on food; jungle setting means some creepy crawlies; reachable only by boat. [$] *Rooms from: B8,600* ✉ *11 Moo 8, Laem Tong, Koh Phi Phi, Koh Phi Phi* ☎ *075/627000* 🌐 *www.zeavola.com* 🛏 *52 villas* 🍴 *Free Breakfast.*

🍸 Nightlife

Many people come to Phi Phi for two reasons only: to go to Maya Bay during the day, and to party in Tonsai Bay at night. Once you head down the side streets away from the beach there are mazes of bars and clubs competing in stereo wars, filled with young travelers eager to drink and dance the night away. If you like Khao San Road in Bangkok, you will love Tonsai Bay at night.

Reggae Bar
BARS | There are several bars dotted around this complex but it's the boxing ring that tends to draw the crowds, eager for some Muay Thai action. ✉ *Tonsai Bay, Koh Phi Phi.*

Slinky Beach Bar
DANCE CLUBS | If you're young, restless, and like to party all night, Slinky is the place for you. They regularly host theme parties and fire shows, and it does tend to get pretty rowdy. ✉ *Loh Dalum Bay, Koh Phi Phi.*

Sunflower Bar
BARS | On the eastern end of Loh Dalam Beach, the Sunflower Bar is a laid-back beach bar next to the Tsunami Memorial Park. It's built almost entirely out of driftwood and old wooden bungalows, with scenic sea views and local reggae bands jamming beneath the stars. ✉ *Loh Dalum Bay, Koh Phi Phi.*

Chapter 7

CHIANG MAI

7

Updated by
Marisa Marchitelli

◉ Sights	🍴 Restaurants	🛏 Hotels	🛍 Shopping	🍸 Nightlife
★★★★☆	★★★★☆	★★★★☆	★★★★☆	★★★☆☆

WELCOME TO CHIANG MAI

TOP REASONS TO GO

★ **History:** Chiang Mai's history is vividly on display in the temples and architecture of the Old City; there are also two excellent museums chronicling the city.

★ **Temples and Monastery Gardens:** The Old City alone has more than 30 ancient temples, where monks are happy to chat with visitors about the principles of Buddhism and their not-so-cloistered lives.

★ **Local Eating:** Restaurants and street stalls serve delicious northern Thai cuisine and dishes, often costing no more than three dollars.

★ **Views for Miles:** Chiang Mai has easy access to spectacular mountain scenery, crisscrossed by trekking trails that lead to remote hill tribe villages where visitors are welcome guests. The mountainous region north of the city beckons adventure seekers with actvities like white-water rafting, waterfall swimming, and rock climbing.

Modern Chiang Mai is expanding on all sides, but the Old City is relatively compact. First-time visitors would do well to find accommodations within this square mile of busy roads and quiet lanes containing reminders of the eight centuries Chiang Mai served as a citadel and bulwark against invasion from Burma. A stroll through the backstreets and lanes—known as *sois*—is one of the top pleasures of a visit. Two ring roads with underpasses keep traffic flowing around the city center.

1 The Old City. An 800-year-old moat surrounds the Old City. Much of the wall that once encircled the city has been restored, and the most important of its five original gates, called Thapae, fronts a broad square where markets and festivals are constantly in full swing. Most of Chiang Mai's principal attractions, including its oldest temples, lie within this square mile and are easily accessible on foot.

2 Beyond the Old City. The Old City's compact size means that there are also many hotels, guesthouses, restaurants, and commercial premises beyond the moat.

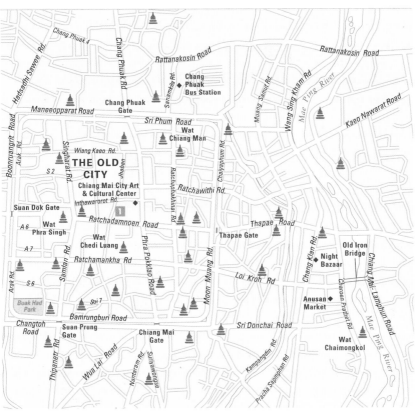

3 Greater Chiang Mai.
Two ring roads and a "Super Highway" allow easy access to the rapidly growing residential suburbs and to the mountains that rise east, west, and north of the city. Day trips to the mountains, including Thailand's highest peak, Doi Inthanon, or the city's "guardian mountain," Doi Suthep, can include white-water rafting or jungle hikes and still leave time for a leisurely evening back in Chiang Mai.

Cosmopolitan Chiang Mai, Thailand's second city, is regarded by many as its rightful, historic capital. It's a fascinating and successful mix of old and new, where 1,000-year-old temples and quiet meditation gardens exist side by side with glittering new hotels and shopping malls. Delectable street food options abound, along with sophisticated restaurants.

The city is enjoying boom times and expanding at a giddy rate as it continues to develop into one of Thailand's must-visit cities and a gateway to Myanmar and Laos. Luxury hotels are popping up all over the city, attracting more business and leisure travelers. The country's main highway, Highway 1, bypasses Chiang Mai as it runs between Bangkok and Chiang Rai, but the city is at the center of a spider's web of highways reaching out in all four directions of the compass, with no major city or town more than a day's drive away.

Granted, first impressions of modern Chiang Mai can be disappointing. The immaculately maintained railroad station and the chaotic bus terminal are in so-so areas, and the drive into the city center is not all that scenic. First-time visitors ask why they can't see the mountains that figure so prominently in the travel brochures. But as you approach the Ping River, Chiang Mai begins to take shape. Enter the Old City, and Chiang Mai's brooding mountain, Doi Suthep, is in full view—except in the month of March, when it's shrouded in heavy air pollution caused by farmers burning their fields after the harvest.

Whenever you visit, there's often a festival in progress, and with guesthouses and restaurants in the Old City vying with each other for the most florid decoration, it feels like a party year-round. In the heart of the Old City, buildings more than three stories high have been banned, and many of the streets and sois have been paved with flat, red cobblestones. Strolling these narrow lanes, lingering in the quiet cloisters of a temple, sipping hill tribe coffee at a wayside stall, and fingering local fabrics in one of the many boutiques are among the chief pleasures of a visit to Chiang Mai.

Planning

When to Go

The best time to visit is during the dry season between November and February, when days are pleasantly sunny and evenings refreshingly cool. From March to June the weather can be uncomfortably hot, and pollution is heavy in March and April. From July to October the monsoon rains drench the city.

■ TIP→ **Pollution has become so bad that travelers with breathing problems are advised to avoid the city in March and April, the hottest months of the year, and should check pollution levels before coming in other months.**

Planning Your Time

Most visitors come to Chiang Mai for only a few days, so to sample all the city has to offer, your itinerary will be jam-packed. Be sure to allow a day for exploring the surrounding countryside.

FESTIVALS AND ANNUAL EVENTS

April sees Thailand's New Year, Songkran, known for its water festivals, which can offer a refreshing opportunity to cool off in the scorching heat. Book accommodation months in advance for Songkran and expect to pay high-season rates. Songkran is wild and fun, but Loy Kratong in November, a combination of thanksgiving and prayers for future prosperity, is a quieter occasion. Small boatlike receptacles called *kratong* are launched into the Ping River, surrounding lakes, and even ponds. The simultaneous release of thousands of hot-air lanterns into the night sky above Chiang Mai as part of the celebration, usually around the middle of November, is an awesome sight. Awesome, too, is the annual flower festival in February, at which you will likely encounter exotic shrubs and flowers you've never seen before, many of them decorating the huge floats that wend their way through the city in one of its most spectacular processions.

Getting Here and Around

AIR

There are more than 50 flights, most daily, from Bangkok to Chiang Mai (1 hour 10 minutes); six daily direct from Phuket (1 hour 50 minutes); and two daily direct from Krabi (1 hour 45 minutes). In peak season flights are heavily booked. Thai Budget airline VietJet flies from BKK and Air Asia and Nok Air from Bangkok's Don Mueang airport.

Chiang Mai International Airport is about 5 km (3 miles) south of the Old City. A taxi ride to the Old City costs B150, a trip in a songthaew about B60.

AIRPORTS AND TRANSFERS Bangkok Airways. ☎ 02/706699 ⊕ *www.bangkokair.com.* **Chiang Mai International Airport.** ⊕ *www.chiangmaiairportonline.com.* **Thai Airways.** ☎ 02/356–1111, 02/545–3691 ⊕ *www.thaiairways.com.*

BUS

VIP buses travel between Bangkok's Northern Bus Terminal and Chiang Mai, stopping at Lampang on the way. For B400 to B850 you get a comfortable 10- to 12-hour ride in a modern, air-conditioned bus with reclining seats, blankets and pillows, TV, onboard refreshments, and lunch or dinner at a motorway stop.

■ TIP→ **Sometimes the buses are downright chilly; keep a sweatshirt with you.**

You can take cheaper buses, but the faster service and comfort are well worth the few extra baht.

Chiang Mai's Arcade Bus Terminal serves Bangkok, Chiang Rai, Mae Hong Son, and destinations within Chiang Rai Province.

Chang Phuak Bus Terminal serves Lam-phun, Chiang Dao, Tha Ton, and destinations within Chiang Mai Province.

CAR

The well-paved roads around Chiang Mai are no problem for most drivers—even the mountainous Mae Sa route north of Chiang Mai is perfectly drivable. Nevertheless, if you are not familiar with driving on the left, it may be better to hire a driver. Two major car-rental agencies in Chiang Mai are Avis and Hertz; Budget has a good range of four-wheel-drive vehicles. Motorcycle and scooter rentals shops abound.

Avoid driving in the city during rush hours, which start as early as 7 in the morning and 3 in the afternoon, and pay attention to no-parking restrictions (usually from 9 am to noon and 3 pm to 6 pm). Parking is prohibited on many streets on alternate days, but the explanatory signs are mostly in Thai. Your best bet is to note on which side of the street vehicles are parking. Chiang Mai's traffic police clamp and tow away vehicles parked illegally. Parking lots are numerous and charge as little as B20 for all-day parking.

Hiring a driver with a car is the most convenient way to visit the hard-to-find temples outside the city. This option can be expensive for solo travelers though, and can start at B1,500 ($50) for a half day to B3,000 ($100) for a day trip. It is more affordable to drive yourself or hop in a shared cab. Car-rental agencies also handle car-and-driver hires.

TAXI, TUK-TUK, AND SONGTHAEW

Metered taxis, which can be flagged down on the street, are being introduced gradually in Chiang Mai but are still not as common as tuk-tuks (auto rickshaws) and songthaews (shared rides with bench seating). The basic taxi charge is B30; you'll pay about B100 for a ride across the Old City. Ride-sharing app Grab is very popular and easy to use. Tuk-tuks are generally cheaper than taxis, but

you are expected to bargain—offer B20 or so less than the driver demands. The songthaews that trundle around the city on fixed routes are the cheapest form of transportation—from B25 per person if traveling with other people, but more if you hire the whole vehicle. If the driver has to make a detour, you'll be charged an extra B20 or so. Settle on the fare before you get in. To confirm a price just hold up the relevant number of fingers. If you hold up three and your gesture evokes the same response from the driver, you'll be paying B30.

TRAIN

The State Railway links Chiang Mai to Bangkok and points south. As the uninteresting trip from Bangkok takes about 13 hours, overnight sleepers are the best choice. The overnight trains are well maintained and comfortable, with clean sheets on rows of two-tier bunks.

■ TIP → **Spending a few extra baht for a first-class compartment is strongly recommended. In second class you may be kept awake by partying passengers.**

Trains for the north depart from Bangkok's Hualamphong Railway Station and arrive in the Chiang Mai Railway Station. First-class fares from Bangkok to Chiang Mai range from B1,650 for a sleeper to B700 or B900 for a day train.

Safety and Precautions

Motorcycle accidents are a daily occurrence. Though rentals are easily available, riding a motorbike or scooter is inadvisable unless you have ample experience riding on the left side. If you do ride, cover your skin and wear a good helmet.

Incidents of street crime involving foreign visitors are rare, and when they do occur they are energetically investigated by the police. Nevertheless, the usual precautions should be taken when walking the city streets, and particularly the sois, at night. Leave your valuables in your hotel. If you leave your passport in the hotel, make sure to carry a copy—though you are very unlikely to be stopped, it's required to carry some form of ID. Also be sure to have your international driver's license handy as there are checkpoints all over town. Carry handbags on the side of the sidewalk that's farthest from the street.

Restaurants

All of the city's top hotels serve reasonably good food, but for the best Thai cuisine go to the restaurants in town. The greatest variety—from traditional Thai to Italian—are to be found within the Old City, and Nimmanhaemin Road, about 2 km (1 mile) northwest of downtown, is packed with great places to eat. For street stall fare, get to Anusan Market and the nearby Night Bazaar, the Sunday night market, and Warorot Market.

What It Costs in Baht

$	$$	$$$	$$$$
RESTAURANTS			
under B200	B200– B300	B301– B400	over B400

Hotels

Soaring tourist numbers—particularly young Chinese visitors with newly acquired wealth and the urge and freedom to travel—have fueled an unprecedented hotel building boom in recent years. Most of the new properties are in the traditional so-called Lanna style, and the most luxurious of them rival hotels in Bangkok. Except for the high season, from December to February, prices are far lower than in the capital. Charming, modestly priced guesthouses and small hotels abound, and some are right on the water.

What It Costs in Baht

$	$$	$$$	$$$$
HOTELS			
under B2,200	B2,200– B4,000	B4,001– B6,000	over B6,000

Nightlife

Chiang Mai has dozens of places where you can grab a beer or a cocktail, listen to live music, or both. Two centers of action are the Riverside area, where restaurants like the Good View double as bars later in the evening, and Nimmanhaemin Road heading south from Huay Kaew Road. As with elsewhere in Thailand, there are many easy-to-find hostess bars, most notably at the western end of Loi Kroh Road, the southern end of Moon Muang Road, and the Bar Beer Center next to the Top North Hotel on Moon Muang Road.

Tours and Classes

Every other storefront in Chiang Mai seems to be a tour agency, but professionally run. Pick up a list of agencies approved by the Tourism Authority of Thailand before choosing one (*www.tourismthailand.org/About-Thailand/About-TAT/TAT-Local-offices*).

Prices vary quite a bit, so shop around, and carefully examine the offerings. Many hotels have their own travel desk with ties to a tour operator. The prices are often higher, as the hotel adds its own surcharge. If spending time in monasteries makes you wonder about the lives of the monks, or if you find yourself so enthralled by delicious dishes that you want to learn how to prepare them, you're in luck. Chiang Mai has hundreds of schools offering classes in anything from aromatherapy to Zen Buddhism. The city also has dozens of cooking classes—some in the kitchens of guesthouses, others at fully accredited schools—teaching the basics of Thai cuisine. Courses cost from B800 to B1,000 a day.

Cooking courses are listed in this chapter under Activities.

Alternative medicine, cooking, and massage are the other most popular courses.

CLASSES

American University Alumni
The alumni group has been offering Thai language courses for more than two decades. Charges vary according to the duration of the course and the number of pupils. ⊠ *24 Ratchadamnoen Rd.* ☎ *053/214120, 053/211973* ⊕ *www.learnthaiinchiangmai.com.*

TOUR OPERATORS

Nathlada Boonthueng
A TAT-registered English-speaking guide with a deep knowledge of the region, Nathlada "Timmy" Boonthueng is one of the best local independent operators. She conducts half-day, full-day, and multiday tours for groups and individuals. ⊠ *Chiang Mai* ☎ *081/531–6884* ⊕ *www.chiangmaidestination.com* ✉ *From B600 for ½-day group tours.*

Tours by Locals
This worldwide organization pairs travelers with freelance tourism-board-licensed local guides. Hire a personal guide in Chiang Mai for any specific interest or area of focus or choose from more than 15 group tours in and around the city. These range from bird-watching at Doi Inthanon to cycling around the Old City. Prices vary; guides can be contacted directly and group tours booked through the website. ⊠ *Chiang Mai* ☎ *866/844–6783* ⊕ *www.toursbylocals.com.*

Temple Tips

Most temple complexes open around 6 am and don't close until 6 or 8 pm, although the hours can be irregular and the doors may be locked for no apparent reason. If that's the case, approach any monk and explain that you'd like to visit. He'll normally open up the temple, and might even chat with you. There's no admission charge at most temples, except at Wat Phra That Doi Suthep (B50 if you take the tram, B30 if you choose to walk), the viharn (assembly hall) of Wat Phra Singh (B20) and the viharn of Wat Chedi Luang (B20).

Visitor Information

CONTACTS Tourist Authority of Thailand (Chiang Mai). ⊠ *105/1 Chiang Mai–Lamphun Rd.* ☎ *053/248604, 053/241466* ⊕ *www.tourismthailand.org/Chiang-Mai.*

The Old City

Covering roughly 2½ square km (1 square mile) and crisscrossed by winding lanes, Chiang Mai's Old City is bounded by the restored remains of the original city wall and framed by a wide, water-filled moat. The compact Old City can be explored easily on foot or by bike. The system of one-way streets can be confusing—though not a problem for pedestrians—but the plan keeps traffic moving quite effectively around the moat, which is crossed by bridges at regular intervals.

The moated "one square mile" of the Old City contains 38 of Chiang Mai's temples, including its oldest and most historic ones. The so-called Lanna style of architecture—stepped eaves, dark teak, and gleaming white stucco construction—has been adopted by the owners of boutique hotels in the Old City, where high-rise buildings are banned.

Sights

Chiang Mai City Arts & Cultural Center

HISTORY MUSEUM | The handsome city museum is housed in a colonnaded palace that was the official administrative headquarters of the last local ruler, Chao (Prince) Inthawichayanon. Around its quiet central courtyard are 15 rooms with exhibits documenting the history of Chiang Mai. In another small, shaded courtyard is a delightful café. The palace was built in 1924 in the exact center of the city, the site of the ancient city pillar that now stands in the compound of nearby Wat Chedi Luang. In front of the museum sit statues of the three kings who founded Chiang Mai. ✉ *Phrapokklao Rd., Old City* ☎ *053/217793, 053/219833* 🌐 *cmocity.com/* 🎟 *B90; B180 includes admission to Lanna Folklife Museum and Chiang Mai Historical Centre* 🕓 *Closed Mon. and Tues.*

★ Wat Chedi Luang

RELIGIOUS BUILDING | In 1411 King Saen Muang Ma ordered his workers to build a chedi "as high as a dove could fly." He died before the structure was finished, as did the next king. During the reign of the following king, an earthquake knocked down about a third of the 282-foot spire, and it's now a superb ruin. The parklike grounds contain assembly halls, chapels, a 30-foot-long reclining Buddha, and the ancient city pillar. The main assembly hall, a vast, pillared building guarded by two *nagas,* mythical snakes believed to control the irrigation waters in rice fields, was restored in 2008. ✉ *103 Phrapokklao Rd., between Ratchamankha and Ratchadamnoen Rds., Old City* 🎟 *B40.*

Wat Chiang Man

RELIGIOUS BUILDING | Chiang Mai's oldest monastery, dating from 1296, is typical of northern Thai architecture. It has massive teak pillars inside the bot, and two important images of the Buddha sit in the small building to the right of the main viharn (assembly hall). The Buddha images are supposedly on view only on Sunday, but sometimes the door is unlocked. ✉ *Ratchaphakhinai Rd., 1.5 blocks south of the moat, Old City.*

★ Wat Phra Singh

RELIGIOUS BUILDING | Chiang Mai's principal monastery was extensively renovated in 2020. In the western section of the Old City, the beautifully decorated wat contains the Phra Singh Buddha, with a serene and benevolent expression that is enhanced by the light filtering in through the tall windows. Also of note are the temple's facades of splendidly carved wood, the elegant teak beams and posts, and the masonry. Don't be surprised if a student monk approaches you to practice his English. ✉ *2 Samlarn Rd., Old City* 🎟 *B20.*

Restaurants

★ Akha Ama Coffee

$ | **CAFÉ** | Founder Lee Ayu Chuepa studied the art of roasting and brewing coffee in Italy, then brought his knowhow back to his home village on the outskirts of Chiang Mai, where he grows organic coffee. The vibe is casual, with a few seats to hang out and enjoy your beverage. **Known for:** coffee blossom honey; single origin monthly selections; homemade cold brew. [$] *Average main: 60* ✉ *175/1 Rachadamnoen Rd., Old City* ☎ *088/267–8014* 🌐 *www.akhaamacoffee.com* 💳 *No credit cards.*

Dash Teak House

$$ | **THAI** | **FAMILY** | In a beautiful, traditional, two-story teak house with a balcony overlooking a garden, Dash is one of the

The Old City

Sights ▼

1 Chiang Mai City Arts &
  Cultural Center **F4**
2 Wat Chedi Luang **F6**
3 Wat Chiang Man **G3**
4 Wat Phra Singh **D5**

Restaurants ▼

1 Akha Ama Coffee **D5**
2 Dash Teak House **H7**
3 The House by Ginger **I3**
4 Khao Soi Khun Yai **D2**
5 Rachamankha **C6**
6 SP Chicken **D5**
7 Writer's Club & Wine Bar **F5**

Hotels ▼

1 Banjai Garden Guesthouse **G7**
2 Kiri Hotel **H4**
3 Lamphu House **G5**
4 99 The Gallery Hotel **D5**
5 Rachamankha **C6**
6 Tamarind Village **G5**
7 U Chiang Mai **F5**

KEY

🔵 Sights
🔴 Restaurants
🟠 Hotels
⛩ Temple

Old Town's best midrange restaurants. Guests receive a warm welcome from the Thai mother–son team who returned to Thailand to open the restaurant after living for many years in the United States. **Known for:** tasty Western fare for those tired of Thai; tranquil garden seating; Lanna dishes like gaeng hang lay (pork curry). [$] *Average main: B300* ✉ *38/2 Moon Muang Rd., Soi 2, Old City* ✣ *One block in from the city wall* ☎ *053/279230* 💳 *No credit cards.*

★ The House by Ginger

$$ | ECLECTIC | Trendy locals have been loving this iconic restaurant that serves creative Thai and pan-Asian fare since it opened in 2004. The walls are adorned with tropical motif wallpaper, the plush furniture is finished with dark velvets, and traditional Chinese pottery in bold colors sits on display, while the banquette seating is topped with colorful throw pillows that you can purchase in the shop. **Known for:** international cuisine; long-standing favorite; trendy atmosphere. [$] *Average main: B250* ✉ *199 Moon Muang Rd., Old City* ☎ *053/287681* 🌐 *www.thehousebygingercm.com.*

Khao Soi Khun Yai

$ | THAI | The colorful plastic stools and small wooden tables at this open-air *khao soi* spot are packed with a mix of locals and tourists slurping egg noodles in curry soup. Get yours with beef, chicken, or pork, each bowl topped with an addictive handful of crunchy noodles. **Known for:** fresh-pressed longan juice; heaping bowls of khao soi; spicy and more moderate khao soi options. [$] *Average main: B50* ✉ *Sri Poom Rd., Soi 8, Chiang Mai* ✣ *Right at the moat, near Wat Kuan Kama. Restaurant is on the left* 🕒 *Closed Sun.* 💳 *No credit cards.*

★ Rachamankha

$$ | THAI | A meal at the Rachamankha hotel's elegant restaurant is a must whether you're a guest or not. The menu focuses on Lanna, Burmese, and Shan cuisine, a sensible approach given the entwined history of these northern neighbors. **Known for:** live Lanna folk music and other entertainment; romantic courtyard; not the typical Asian dishes. [$] *Average main: B250* ✉ *6 Ratchamankha, Soi 9, Old City* ☎ *053/904111* 🌐 *www.rachamankha.com.*

SP Chicken

$ | THAI | This family business is famous for their juicy charcoal-grilled rotisserie chicken, stuffed with generous amounts of fragrant local garlic. Papaya salad, sticky rice, and other Northeastern/Isan favorites such as pork *larb* and grilled beef with sweet, spicy, tart *jaeow* dipping sauce are all recommended, too. **Known for:** can accommodate your preferred level of spiciness; around the corner from Wat Phra Singh; no MSG. [$] *Average main: 90* ✉ *8/1 Samlarn Road Soi 1, Old City* ☎ *805–005035.*

Writers Club & Wine Bar

$ | ECLECTIC | You don't have to be a journalist to dine at Chiang Mai's unofficial press club—the regulars include not only media types but artists and eccentric local characters. Expect the typical pan-Thai dishes, including salads, stir-fries, and curries, as well as decent and sensibly priced house wines. **Known for:** a respite from the Sunday Market; popular with media types; some of the best value wine in Chiang Mai. [$] *Average main: B150* ✉ *141/3 Ratchadamnoen Rd., Old City* ☎ *053/814187* 🕒 *Closed Sat.*

🛏 Hotels

99 The Gallery Hotel

$$ | HOTEL | Elegant for the price, this midrange hotel with a fantastic location near the Sunday night market and other attractions has rooms to suit most budgets. **Pros:** fantastic location; saltwater swimming pool; elegant for the price. **Cons:** staff doesn't speak much English; many rooms are small; beds

Elephants flank the ruined chedi at Wat Chedi Luang.

are hard. $ *Rooms from: B3,000* ✉ *99 Intrawarorot Rd., Old City* ☎ *053/326338* ⊕ *99thegalleryhotel.com* ⇋ *53 rooms* ⦿︎ *No Meals.*

★ Banjai Garden Guesthouse

$ | B&B/INN | A French restaurateur and his Thai wife renovated this sturdy old Chiang Mai residence into a clean and comfortable guesthouse. **Pros:** easy access to bars and restaurants; shaded garden; delightful owners. **Cons:** books up far ahead in high season; some rooms share a bath; some street noise. $ *Rooms from: B900* ✉ *43 Phrapokklao Rd., Soi 3, Old City* ☎ *085/716–1635* ⊕ *www.banjai-garden.com* ⦿︎ *No Meals* ⇋ *7 rooms.*

Kiri Hotel

$ | HOTEL | Two old shophouses were renovated into this sleek and modern boutique hotel that's a serene oasis in the heart of old town. **Pros:** roof deck with stunning views; connected family rooms available; excellent SOMM restaurant. **Cons:** pool is small; no gym; can be noisy at night because of nearby bars. $ *Rooms from: 2,000* ✉ *8 Mun Mueang Rd., Old City* ☎ *052-005-799* ⊕ *kiri-hotel. com* ⦿︎ *No Meals* ⇋ *23 rooms.*

Lamphu House

$ | HOTEL | An excellent choice for first-time visitors, this Old City budget boutique hotel is a short stroll from Wat Chedi Luang and several other star attractions. **Pros:** good-size saltwater swimming pool; near star attractions; balconies. **Cons:** few amenities; compact rooms; inconsistent service. $ *Rooms from: B950* ✉ *1 Phrapokklao Rd., Soi 9, Old City* ☎ *053/274966* ⊕ *lamphu-housechiangmai.com* ⦿︎ *No Meals* ⇋ *41 rooms.*

★ Rachamankha

$$$ | HOTEL | The luxurious rooms at this small hotel on a quiet lane near Wat Phra Singh straddle a series of hushed brick courtyards enclosed by triple-eave Lanna-style buildings. **Pros:** peaceful setting; helpful staff; pool. **Cons:** noisy temple dogs; rooms too spartan

Old City Tour

A good place to start a tour of the Old City is at the Thapae Gate, near the Warorot Market. Heading west on Ratchadamnoen Road and turning north on Ratchaphakhinai Road brings you to Wat Chiang Man, the oldest temple in Chiang Mai, just on the outside of the moat. Backtracking down Ratchaphakhinai Road and heading west on Ratchadamnoen Road brings you to Wat Chedi Luang and Wat Phra Singh. Several other worthwhile temples are outside the city walls. Wat Chaimongkhon is an easy walk from the Thapae Gate. Wat Suan Dok is pretty far outside the city gates and best reached by tuk-tuk. Wat Umong is a 30-minute walk from there.

for some; children under age 12 not permitted. $ *Rooms from: B5,500* ✉ *6 Ratchamankha Rd., Soi 9, Chiang Mai* ☏ *053/904111* ⊕ *www.rachamankha.com* ❖ *No Meals* ⇆ *25 rooms.*

Tamarind Village

$$$ | B&B/INN | Set around an ancient tamarind tree, this serene oasis in the heart of the old city has white stucco walls and terra-cotta roofs evoking the image of a French-Indochinese mansion. **Pros:** excellent restaurant; famous Sunday market is right outside; three leading temples within walking distance. **Cons:** street noise on Sundays; Wi-Fi inconsistent; pool area small. $ *Rooms from: 6,000* ✉ *50 Rachadamnoen Rd. Soi 1, Chiang Mai* ☏ *02/301–1861* ⊕ *www.tamarindvillage.com* ❖ *No Meals* ⇆ *46 rooms.*

U Chiang Mai

$$$ | HOTEL | A Lanna-style boutique hotel in the center of the Old City, the U Chiang Mai was built around a century-old teak house, the home of a former governor. **Pros:** helpful tour desk; 24-hour room rate, so if you arrive at 10 pm, you don't have to leave until 10 pm the next day; prime location in center of town. **Cons:** no parking; exposed pool that's open to view from most rooms; high bar and restaurant prices. $ *Rooms from: B4,200* ✉ *70 Ratchadamnoen Rd., Old City* ☏ *053/327000* ⊕ *www.uhotels-resorts.com/uchiangmai* ⇆ *41 rooms* ❖ *Free Breakfast.*

##

BARS

Namton's House Bar

Beer lovers come to this Chiang Mai restaurant-bar for its selection of local and imported craft beers, dozens bottled and 18 on tap. ✉ *196/2 Chiangmai-Lamphun Rd, Chiang Mai* ❖ *Opposite the Gymkhana Club* ☏ *086/911–1207.*

Ram Bar

CABARET | The city's most popular gay bar runs a drag show every night from 10 pm, though seats fill up far earlier with a wide mix of travelers and local LGBTQ community members. The costumes are stunning, the dancers' stamina impressive, and the routines a hoot, leaving the audience laughing up a storm (it's mostly Western music, so you don't need to speak Thai to enjoy yourself). There's no cover charge, drinks are reasonably priced (expect to pay B180 for a local beer), and everyone is welcome. ✉ *48 Charoenprathet Rd., Soi 6, Chiang Mai* ❖ *One block west of the river.*

King Saen Muang Ma designed Wat Chedi Luang to house his father's ashes.

Yellow Pug

BARS | The Weave Artisan Society, in a renovated ice factory, includes an art gallery, a craft shop, a café, an open-kitchen restaurant with a massive wood-fired oven, and the Yellow Pug, a bar known for its selection of craft beers. The choices are constantly rotating but you can expect selections from the U.S., Europe, and elsewhere. You can also take your beer over to the restaurant to enjoy with a wood-fired pizza. ⊠ *700 Tambon Hai Ya, Old City.*

LIVE MUSIC

★ North Gate Jazz Co-Op

LIVE MUSIC | This is the city's most popular bar for jazz music. Doors open at 7 pm and seats on the first floor and mezzanine fill up soon afterwards with a mix of expats, locals, and tourists eager to hear covers of jazz, folk rock, and pop. Tuesdays are jam-session nights, but the place, on the northern edge of the Old City, is packed every night of the week. The bar is super casual—shorts

and flip-flops are welcome—and there's no cover, with drinks moderately priced (stick to beer and cider; the cocktails and wine aren't worth the price). ⊠ *91/1-2 Sriphum Rd., opposite Chang Phuak Gate, Old City* ☎ *081/765–5246.*

Shopping

CRAFTS

★ Kalm Village

CRAFTS | This collection of modern buildings constructed in Lanna-style and connected by walkways around an inner courtyard has the aesthetic of a small village and is part cafe-restaurant, part art gallery, part textile studio, and part retail shop. The clothing, accessories, and home decor items for sale are all handmade and local, with the Kalm brand. ⊠ *14 Soi 4 Phra Sing, Old City* ☎ *093/320–9809* ⊕ *www.kalmvillage. com* ☯ *Closed Wed.*

Continued on page 312

SILK-MAKING IN THAILAND

by Dave Stamboulis

According to legend, the Chinese empress His-Ling discovered silk nearly 5,000 years ago when a cocoon fell into her teacup, and she watched it unwind into a fine filament. As China realized the value of these threads, the silk trade was born, spreading through Asia, along what became known as the Silk Road.

For centuries, the Chinese protected the secret of silk production, beheading anyone who tried to take silkworm eggs out of the country. But, eventually, smuggled worms, along with silk-making knowledge, made it to other parts of Asia. As the demand for silk grew, Chinese traders searched for the best climates in which to cultivate worms; historians believe that these traders brought sericulture, or silk-making, to Thailand about 2,000 years ago. Archaeologists have found silk remnants in the ruins of Baan Chiang near Udon Thani.

Though silkworms thrived, the silk business did not take on a large scale in Thailand, because Buddhist Thais were reluctant to kill the silkworms—an unavoidable part of the process. But a few families in Isan did continue to produce silk, using native plants like Palmyra Palm and jackfruit to make natural bleaches and dyes. After World War II, American businessman Jim Thompson discovered Thailand's cottage industry and helped expand it, founding the Thai Silk Company in 1951. Queen Sirikit, King Bhumibol's wife, has also been a long-term supporter of sericulture through her SUPPORT organization, which teaches traditional crafts to rural Thais.

Silk cocoons in the final stage of incubation, Surin.

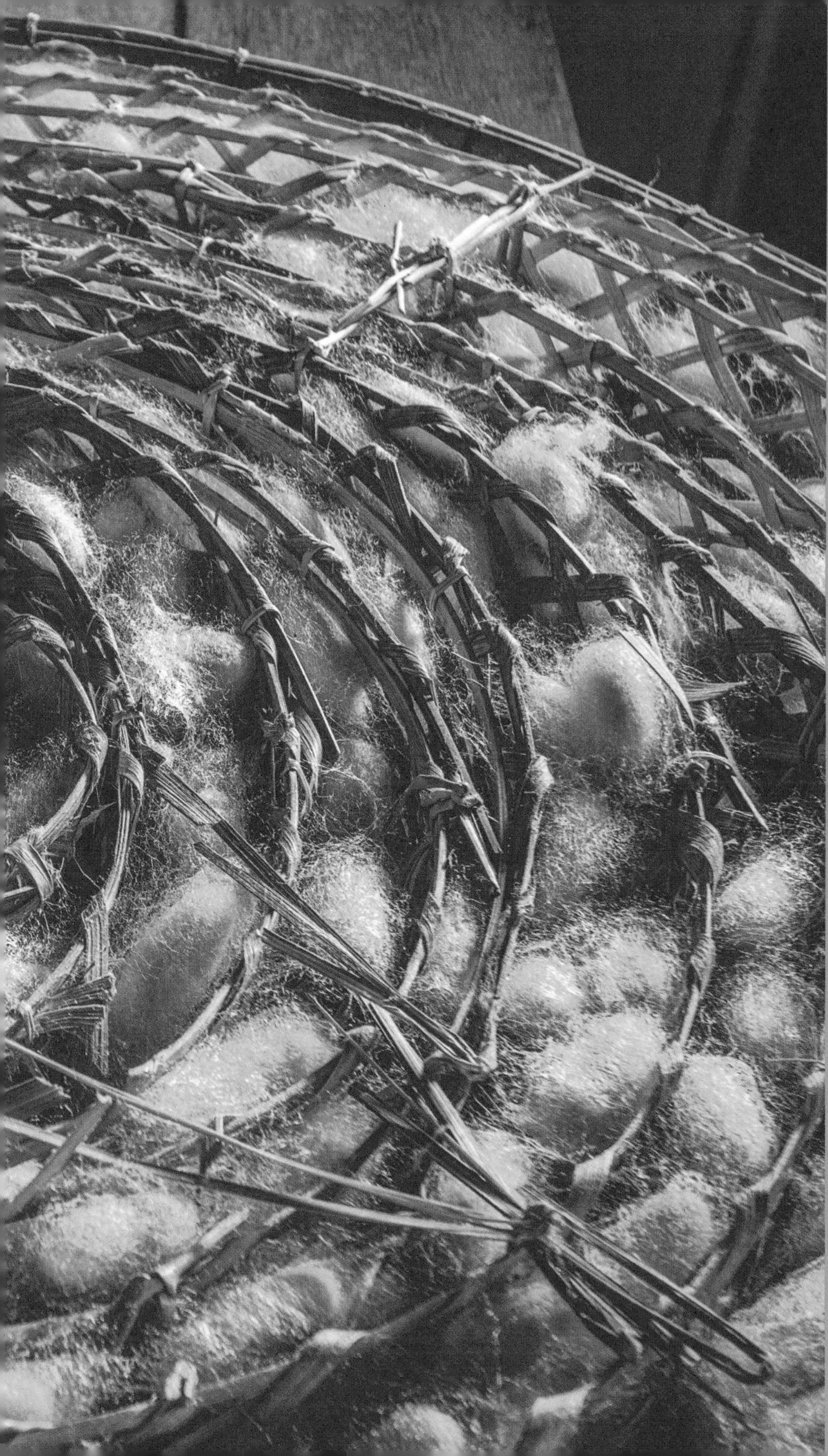

HOW SILK IS MADE

20mm

Adult female bombyx mari.

Female moth laying eggs.

Larvae eating mulberry leaves.

Silkworms are really the caterpillars of bombyx mari, the silk moth. The process begins when a mature female moth lays eggs—about 300 at once. When the eggs hatch 10 days later, the larvae are placed on trays of mulberry leaves, which they devour. After this mulberry binge, when the worms are approximately 7 cm (2.75 in) long, they begin to spin their cocoons. After 36 hours the cocoons are complete.

Before the worms emerge as moths—destroying the cocoons in the process—silk makers boil the cocoons so they can unravel the intact silk filament. The raw silk, which ranges in color from gold to light green, is dried, washed, bleached, and then dyed before being stretched and twisted into strands strong enough for weaving. The coarse, knotty texture of Thai silk is ideal for hand-weaving on traditional looms—the final step to creating a finished piece of fabric.

Silk cocoons.

Boiling cocoons to remove silk.

DID YOU KNOW?

Thai silk moths reproduce 10 or more times per year—they're much more productive than their Japanese and Korean counterparts, which lay eggs only once annually.

A worm can eat 25,000 times its original weight over a 30-day period, before encasing itself in a single strand of raw silk up to 900 m (3,000 ft) long.

Woman sifting through cocoons.

CHECK IT OUT

In Bangkok, the Naj Collection has an excellent reputation and top quality products, and the Jim Thompson outlets are quite good, as are Shinawatra's.

Naj Collection

✉ 42 Convent Rd. (Opposite BNH Hospital), Silom, Bangkok ☎ 662/632–1004-6 ⊕ www.najcollection.com.

Jim Thompson Outlet

✉ 9 Surawong Rd., Suriyawong, Bangrak, Bangkok ☎ 02/632–8100, 02/234–4900 ⊕ www.jimthompson.com.

Shinawatra Thai Silk

✉ 94 Sukhumvit Soi 23, North Klong Toei, Wattana, Bangkok ☎ 02/258-0295-9 ⊕ www.shinawatrathaisilk.com

Man works a traditional loom.

VARIETIES OF THAI SILK

Most Thai silk is a blend of two different colors, one for the warp (threads that run lengthwise in a loom) and the other for the weft (strands that are woven across the warp). Smoother silk, made with finer threads, is used for clothing, while rougher fabric is more appropriate for curtains. To make "striped" silk, weavers alternate coarse and smooth threads. Isan's famous mudmee silk, which is used mainly for clothing, consists of threads that are tie-dyed before they are woven into cloth.

Mudmee silk.

SHOPPING TIPS

Appraising silk quality is an art in itself. But there are a few simple ways to be sure you're buying pure, handmade fabric.

■ Examine the weave. Hand-woven, authentic silk has small bumps and blemishes—no part of the fabric will look exactly like any other part. Imitation silk has a smooth, flawless surface.

■ Hold it up to the light. Imitation silk shines white at any angle, while the color of real silk appears to change.

■ Burn a thread. When held to a flame, natural fibers disintegrate into fine ash, while synthetic fabrics melt, smoke, and smell terrible.

■ Though this isn't a foolproof method, consider the price. Genuine silk costs five to 10 times more than an imitation or blended fabric. You should expect to pay between B250 and B350 a meter for high-quality, clothing-weight silk. Men's shirts start at B800 but could be more than B2,000; women's scarves run from B350 to B1,500. At Bangkok shops that cater to westerners, you'll pay considerably more, though shops frequented by Thais have comparable prices throughout the country.

Fine Thai silk on bobbins.

Activities

SPAS

Vocational Training Center Of Chiang Mai Women's Correctional Institution

SPAS | If you want to do a good deed for Thai society while you enjoy a great massage, come by this vocational training center for women who have been in the correctional system. Female inmates trained in Thai massage are allowed to practice their trade at a purpose-built spa. A two-hour Thai massage costs B200—money well spent in helping to assure that these remarkably cheerful women have a solid foundation for life outside the prison walls. After the massage, relax over tea, coffee, or a Thai meal in the neighboring restaurant, also staffed by women prisoners. ⊠ *Ratvithee Rd., Old City* ☎ *053/122340.*

COOKING CLASSES

Baan Thai Cookery School

COOKING CLASSES | The classes at this cooking school are among Chiang Mai's best, with lovely, encouraging teachers. A one-day course costs B1,000, including transportation, snacks, and a cookbook to take home; the shorter four-hour evening course is B800. ⊠ *9 Prapokklao Rd., Soi 9, Old City* ☎ *053/206388, 053/206315* ⊕ *www.cookinthai.com.*

Chiang Mai Thai Cookery School

COOKING CLASSES | Sompon Nabnian, an internationally recognized TV chef, runs this school, where students learn to make dishes like fish cakes and curries. A one-day beginner's course costs B1,450. The five-day master class costs B6,700. Price includes round-trip transportation. ⊠ *47/2 Moon Muang Rd., Old City* ☎ *053/206388* ⊕ *www.thaicookery-school.com.*

Thai Farm Cooking School

COOKING CLASSES | The one-day classes at this popular school run by a genial husband-and-wife team take place at its working farm. Participants visit a food market before heading to the farm, where dishes are prepared by the participants and then enjoyed all together as a sit-down meal. The B1,500 fee includes transportation to and from lodgings or other points in or near the Old City. ⊠ *Office, 38 Moon Muang Rd., Soi 9, Old City* ☎ *081/288–5989, 087/174–9285* ⊕ *www.thaifarmcooking.com.*

Beyond the Old City

Outside the borders of the Old City, Chiang Mai expands into urban sprawl, although there are several worthy sights and a handful of identifiable areas that have preserved or developed some individual style. Shoppers must venture outside the moat and make for the famous Night Bazaar or Nimmanhaemin Road, both a 10-minute tuk-tuk ride away from the city center. Chiang Mai's best and liveliest nighttime scene is to be found in the Riverside quarter bordering the Ping River.

Sights

Chiang Mai Tribal Museum (Highland People Discovery Museum)

HISTORY MUSEUM | The varied collection at this museum, more than 1,000 pieces of traditional crafts from the hill tribes living in the region, is one of the finest in the country and includes farming implements, hunting traps, weapons, colorful embroidery, and musical instruments. The museum was extensively renovated in 2021. It's off the road to Mae Rim, about 1 km (½ mile) from the National Museum. ⊠ *Rama IX Lanna Park, enter on Chotana Rd., Chiang Mai* ☎ *053/210872* 🎫 *Free* ⊗ *Closed weekends.*

Night Bazaar

MARKET | Sandwiched between the Old City and the riverside, this market opens for business every evening at around 6 pm. More than 200 stalls—selling food, fake fashion brands, knickknacks, and some pretty handicrafts—line a half-mile section of Chang Klan Road. Some people find the scene a bit too chaotic and commercial, but many love it, especially for the many food purveyors and souvenir opportunities. The area is also a major nighttime entertainment zone. Loi Kroh Road, which bisects the market, is Chiang Mai's (perfectly safe) red-light district. ⊠ *Chang Klan Rd., between Thapae and Sri Donchai Rds., City Center* 🖾 *Free.*

Nimmanhaemin Road

NEIGHBORHOOD | Chiang Mai's version of Bangkok's hip Sukhumvit area is simply called Nimman (the full Nimmanhaemin is a bit of a mouthful), a mile-long strip west of the Old City. Cafés, pubs, bars, restaurants, art galleries, boutiques, and the trendy One Nimman shopping plaza line the street, which is usually packed with students from the nearby Chiang Mai University. It's definitely worth exploring the jumble of side streets off the main drag, too, where hipper restaurants, shops, and nightlife venues jostle for space. ⊠ *Nimmanhaemin Rd., between Huay Kaew and Suthep Rds., Chiang Mai* ⊹ *Also accessible via Super Hwy.*

Ploen Ruedee Night Market

GATHERING PLACES | Part–night market, part–outdoor food hall, Ploen Ruedee is a great place to get a bite to eat, drink a cold Chang or Singha beer, and listen to the bands that perform nightly. This is the trendiest of the night markets, with tables made of reclaimed wood, pretty string lights, and a cocktail kiosk. Two or three local bands perform nightly, with the music ranging from folk to pop to rock. Food-wise you'll find stands selling pizza, dumplings, satay, pad Thai, sashimi bowls, crepes, and ice cream. ⊠ *Chang Klan Rd. near Thanon Charoen Mueang,*

Chiang Mai ⊹ *One block west of the Night Bazaar, next to the Dusit D2 Hotel.*

Riverside

NEIGHBORHOOD | Chinese traders originally settled this area 1½ km (1 mile) east of the Old City, and some of their well-preserved homes and commercial premises now house upscale and midrange restaurants, guesthouses and hotels, galleries, boutiques, and antiques shops. Unlike in Bangkok where many of the riverfront spots tend to be full of foreigners, the restaurants, hotels, and bars along the river are enjoyed by Thai couples and families on evenings out. ⊠ *Charoen Prathet Rd., at Nawarat Bridge, Chiang Mai.*

Warorot Market

MARKET | Chiang Mai's oldest market is a great place to explore during the day. This is where locals actually do their shopping so prices and quality tend to be better than what you'll see at the more tourist-oriented markets. ⊠ *Wichayanon Rd., Old City.*

Wat Chaimongkhon

RELIGIOUS BUILDING | Although rarely visited, this small temple is well worth the journey. Its little chedi contains holy relics, but its real beauty lies in the serenity of the grounds. Outside the Old City near the Mae Ping River, it has fewer than 20 monks in residence. ⊠ *133 Charoen Prathet Rd., just behind Central Chiang Mai Memorial Hospital, Chiang Mai.*

Wat Ched Yot

RELIGIOUS BUILDING | Wat Photharam Maha Viharn is more commonly known as Wat Ched Yot, or Seven-Spired Monastery. Built in 1455, it's a copy of the Mahabodhi temple in Bodh Gaya, India, where the Buddha is said to have achieved enlightenment. The seven intricately carved spires represent the seven weeks that he subsequently spent there. The sides of the chedi have striking bas-relief sculptures of celestial figures, most of

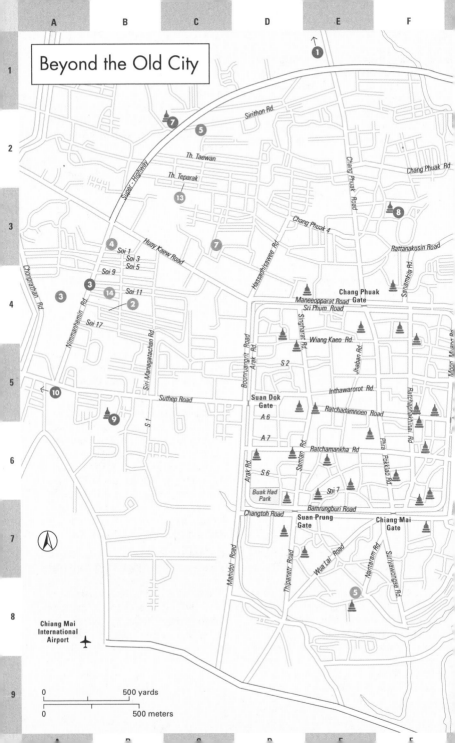

Sights ▼

1 Chiang Mai Tribal Museum (Highland People Discovery Museum).............**E1**
2 Night Bazaar **H6**
3 Nimmanahaemin Road...........**A4**
4 Riverside............................**H9**
5 Warorot Market...................**H5**
6 Wat Chaimongkhon **I7**
7 Wat Ched Yot.....................**C2**
8 Wat Ku Tao **F3**
9 Wat Suan Dok.....................**B5**
10 Wat Umong.........................**A5**

Restaurants ▼

1 Aroon Rai **G6**
2 Beast Burger......................**B4**
3 Chez Marco **G6**
4 Ginger Farm Kitchen **B3**
5 Greensmoked **E8**
6 Hinlay Curry House................**I5**
7 Huen Muan Jai.....................**C3**
8 Maadae Slow Fish Kitchen.......**H5**
9 Ploen Ruedee Night Market **H6**
10 Raming Tea House Siam..........**H5**
11 River Market **H6**
12 Rustic & Blue Farm.................**J6**
13 Tikky Cafe...........................**C2**
14 Tong Tem Toh......................**B4**

Hotels ▼

1 Anantara Chiang Mai Resort & Spa **I7**
2 dusitD2 Chiang Mai...............**H6**
3 Kantary Hills.......................**A4**
4 Ping Nakara Boutique Hotel & Spa.........................**I7**
5 Ruen Come In **C2**

KEY

1 *Sights*
1 *Restaurants*
1 *Hotels*
▲ *Temple*

them in poor repair but one bearing a face of hauntingly contemporary beauty. The temple is just off the highway that circles Chiang Mai, but its green lawns and shady corners are strangely still and peaceful. ✉ *Super Hwy., between Huay Kaew and Chang Phuak Rds., Chiang Mai.*

Wat Ku Tao

In the heart of Chiang Mai's Shan Burmese community, this rarely visited temple was built in 1613 to inter the remains of Tharawadi Min, son of King Bayinnaung, who ruled the then-Lanna kingdom from 1578 to 1607. The temple incorporates Burmese design elements and has a distinctive chedi (stupa) made up of five stone spheres, rising largest to smallest. With its bulbous shape, it's been nicknamed "the watermelon stupa" ("tao" is the word for watermelon in Northern Thai dialect). Every spring, the festive Poy Sang Long coming-of-age ceremony takes place here, drawing most of the Shan community. ✉ *Lang Sanam Kila Road, Chiang Mai* ☎ *053–211–842.*

Wat Suan Dok

RELIGIOUS BUILDING | One of Chiang Mai's largest temples, Wat Suan Dok is said to have been built on the site where bones of Lord Buddha were found. Some of these relics are believed to be inside the chedi; others were transported to Wat Phra That Doi Suthep. At the back of the viharn is the bot housing Phra Chao Kao, a superb bronze Buddha figure cast in 1504. Chiang Mai aristocrats are buried in stupas in the graveyard. ✉ *Suthep Rd., west of the Old City, at Suan Dok Rd., Chiang Mai* 🎫 *Donations welcome.*

Wat Umong

RELIGIOUS BUILDING | One of the most unusual temples in Chiang Mai, Wat Umong dates from 1296 and is set in a forest near Chiang Mai University—this style of temple is usually far from urban areas and hard to access. According to local lore, a monk named Jam liked to go wandering in the forest. This irritated King Ku Na, who often wanted to consult with the sage. So he could seek advice at any time, the king built this wat for the monk in 1380. Along with the temple, tunnels were carved out and decorated with paintings, fragments of which may still be seen. Beyond the chedi is a pond filled with hungry carp. If you come early enough in the morning you might see people on mediation retreats clad in white doing their walking meditation around the vast property. Throughout the grounds the trees are hung with snippets of Buddhist wisdom such as "Time unused is the longest time."

■ TIP→ Within the Old City is a small temple with the same name. For the bigger Wat Umong, tell your driver you're going to Wat U Mong Thera Jan. ✉ *Off Suthep Rd., past Wat Suan Dok, Chiang Mai* 🌐 *www.watumong.org* ☞ *Meditation Center open to tourists.*

🍴 Restaurants

Aroon Rai

$ | **THAI** | This simple, open-sided restaurant just outside the city walls has been preparing such traditional northern dishes as frogs' legs fried with ginger for more than 30 years. Try the *tabong* (boiled bamboo shoots fried in batter) and *sai ua* (pork sausage with herbs). **Known for:** cheap and cheerful northern Thai fare; zesty sai ua (fermented pork sausages); packets of curry mix to go. [$] *Average main: B160* ✉ *45 Kotchasarn Rd., Chiang Mai* ☎ *053/276947* 💳 *No credit cards.*

Beast Burger

$$ | **BURGER** | **FAMILY** | If you find yourself craving Western fast food, skip the global franchises and make a beeline for this restaurant, which grew out of a popular food truck. Run by two young Thai siblings and open from 11 am until 10 pm or when sold out, Beast's burgers are made with premium-quality ingredients and are perfectly cooked. **Known for:** good

value; cool crowd; house-made sauces, like Korean ketchup and blue cheese. [$] *Average main: B200* ✉ *14 Nimmanhaemin, Soi 17, Chiang Mai* ☎ *080/124–1414* 🌐 *beast-burger.com* 🕒 *Closed Wed.*

Chez Marco

$$$ | **FRENCH** | This French restaurant, located in Chiang Mai's perfectly safe "red-light district," is consistently full of locals and foreigners enjoying excellent coq au vin and creamy pâtés. It's run with Gallic flair by Franco-Japanese chef Marco, and has doubled in size with the acquisition of neighboring premises, but still has a tiny, stylishly intimate, street terrace. [$] *Average main: B400* ✉ *15/7 Loi Kroh Rd., Chiang Mai* ☎ *053/207032* 🕒 *Closed Sun.*

★ **Ginger Farm Kitchen**

$$ | **THAI** | **FAMILY** | The cuisine is eclectic Thai, with ingredients sourced from Ginger's own farm on the outskirts of Chiang Mai, at this vibrant Thai bistro decorated with vintage furniture, large patterned cushions, and hanging plants. Nothing is too-too spicy, and everything, including rich curries, refreshing salads, and vegetable-packed summer rolls, is served in pretty ceramic bowls and plates. **Known for:** zingy cocktails with fresh herbs; eclectic Thai-boho decor; pretty presentation. [$] *Average main: 200* ✉ *One Nimman, Nimmanhemin Rd, City Center* ☎ *052/080928* 🌐 *www.gingerfarmkitchen.com.*

Greensmoked

$$ | **BISTRO** | The focus at this stylish modern restaurant in an old ice factory is the wood-fired oven in the open kitchen, visible throughout the dining room. The menu tours the globe, with popular dishes including the fire-grilled pork jowl with spicy pineapple glaze and arguably the most authentic tacos in town. **Known for:** mouth-watering beef brisket; homemade tortillas; a favorite of trendy locals. [$] *Average main: 300* ✉ *12/8 Wualai Soi 3, Chiang Mai* ✥ *Inside Weave Artisan Society* ☎ *062/449–9425.*

Hinlay Curry House

$$ | **ASIAN** | Tucked away in a corner of a former businessman's mansion, this small, open-sided restaurant specializes in inexpensive curry dishes from India, Burma, and Thailand, with some Japanese-inspired dishes as well. Daily specials, accompanied by two varieties of rice or a selection of Indian breads like pillowy naan, are written on a blackboard. **Known for:** homemade sorbets and ice creams; airy, plant-filled dining room; great Indian breads. [$] *Average main: B200* ✉ *8/1 Na Watket Rd., Soi 1, Wat Ket* ☎ *053/242621.*

Huen Muan Jai

$ | **THAI** | On a backstreet in an increasingly cool local neighborhood dotted with cafés and small eateries, this restaurant in a traditional teak house serves authentic Lanna cuisine. Try the *nam prik ong* (tomato, minced-pork dip) served with crispy vegetables, the *larb moo* (a rich minced-pork salad), or the locally revered *gaeng hang lay* (pork belly curry). **Known for:** fried bamboo shoots filled with minced pork; open-air dining room surrounded by greenery; solid vegetarian options. [$] *Average main: B100* ✉ *24 Ratchpruek Rd., Chiang Mai* ☎ *053/404998* 🌐 *www.huenmuanjai.com* 🕒 *Closed Wed.* 💳 *No credit cards.*

Maadae Slow Fish Kitchen

$$ | **THAI** | Born from Chef Yaowadee's desire to keep artisanal fisherman in business down south, this casual eatery features Thai comfort food with an emphasis on the freshest catch of the day—something not that common in this landlocked region. The menu features stir-fried squid, crab ceviche, and an impressive array of fish dishes, including charcoal-grilled trevally, mackerel curry, and brown-sugar-cured sardine jerky, all accompanied by local organic rice and stir-fried vegetables. **Known for:** charcoal grilled fish; sustainable seafood; local flavors. [$] *Average main: 250* ✉ *88 Thapae Rd., Chiang Mai* ☎ *098/248–2446.*

Raming Tea House Siam

$ | **ECLECTIC** | The menu at this tranquil teahouse is fairly short, with a selection of curries, salads, sandwiches, satay, and desserts, but the cool interior of this exquisitely restored century-old Chinese merchant's house is a wonderful respite from the bustle of the city. It doubles as a showroom of fine celadon pottery and has an adjoining courtyard with a shop selling Lanna fabric and the pottery used in the restaurant. **Known for:** housemade tea blends; pretty home goods in its shop; peaceful garden tables. $ *Average main: B180 ⊠ 158 Thapae Rd., Chiang Mai ☏ 053/234518 ⊗ No dinner.*

River Market

$$$ | **ECLECTIC** | This handsome Lanna-style restaurant complex is next to Chiang Mai's historic Iron Bridge, and the spacious outside terrace has lovely views of the bridge and the Ping River. The chefs prepare the full range of authentic, if pricey, Thai dishes, along with a couple of continental options, including a cheeseburger. ■TIP➡ **Although the restaurant is fairly family-friendly, with a lawn on which kids can run around, there's not much on the menu for picky eaters.** **Known for:** high prices to match the setting; pretty setting overlooking the Ping River; modern twists on pan-Thai fare. $ *Average main: B310 ⊠ 33/12 Charoen Prathet Rd., Chiang Mai ☏ 053/234493 ⊕ therivermarket.com/menu.*

Rustic & Blue Farm

$$ | **AMERICAN** | **FAMILY** | Chiang Mai's farm-to-table pioneer Chef Radee Timsuren realized her dream of opening a restaurant right on the family farm, just about a 15-minute drive outside Chiang Mai. The casual daytime menu features impeccably made sandwiches, pizzas, and an array of colorful salads, while at night the options veer toward fine dining, with an impressive selection of imported wine and craft beer. **Known for:** homemade ice-cream, breads, and pastries;

sunset views; seasonal produce from the farm. $ *Average main: 250 ⊠ 73/8 Buak-Klog-Luang, Moo 1, Soi 10, Tambol Tasala, Amphur Muang, Chiang Mai ☏ 086/654–7178 ⊕ www.rusticandblue.com.*

Tikky Cafe

$ | **THAI** | **FAMILY** | At rough-hewn wooden tables surrounded by hill tribe textiles, hungry lunch-goers at this casual spot dig into heaping plates of colorful, vegetable-filled pan-Thai fare. The fruit shakes, especially mango and watermelon, are a cooling balm after a morning of sightseeing. **Known for:** fresh fruit shakes; pretty textiles on tables and chairs; pan-Thai fare that skews healthy. $ *Average main: B90 ⊠ 20 Taeparak Road, City Center ☏ 098/796–2182 ⊗ Closed Mon.*

Tong Tem Toh

$ | **THAI** | Follow your nose to the street-side barbecue at this cool and casual Lanna restaurant that's popular with young Thais, who love the great, affordable food and the beer-garden atmosphere. Start with the northern Thai hors d'oeuvre platter that includes fermented pork sausages, pork crackling, spicy relishes, and raw vegetables. **Known for:** northern dishes like larb and sai ou (pork sausages); long lines for dinner; you order dishes by number as you wait for a table. $ *Average main: B100 ⊠ 11 Nimmanhaemin Rd., Soi 13, Chiang Mai ☏ 053/894701 ▭ No credit cards.*

 ## Hotels

★ Anantara Chiang Mai Resort & Spa

$$$$ | **HOTEL** | The former grounds of the British Consulate now house this waterfront oasis whose rooms and suites have private terraces overlooking either the Mae Ping River or the verdant gardens. **Pros:** historic setting but contemporary feel; riverside location; renowned restaurant. **Cons:** some find the metallic, rust-colored facade off-putting; blackout shades don't fully cover window; when

property full, breakfast a bit chaotic. $ *Rooms from: B10,000* ✉ *123 Charoen Prathet Rd., Chiang Mai* ☏ *053/253333* ⊕ *www.chiang-mai.anantara.com* �‖○�‖ *No Meals* ⤢ *84 rooms.*

dusitD2 Chiang Mai

$$ | **HOTEL** | Although a bit dated, this overall contemporary hotel makes a complete break from the traditional Lanna style so prevalent in Chiang Mai. Clean lines, brushed-steel-and-glass surfaces, and cubist upholstery set the tone in the interiors, from the airy lobby to the bright rooms, where a wealth of cushions compensates for the somewhat minimalist look. **Pros:** comfortable mattresses; in the thick of the shopping scene; short stroll to Night Bazaar. **Cons:** small rooms; small pool for the size of the hotel; modern style might not appeal to those seeking traditional Thai charm. $ *Rooms from: B3,500* ✉ *100 Chang Klan Rd., T. Chang Klan, A. Muang, Chiang Mai* ☏ *053/999999* ⊕ *dusitd2chiangmai.dusit. com* ⤢ *131 rooms* �‖○�‖ *No Meals.*

Kantary Hills

$$ | **HOTEL** | **FAMILY** | A showpiece of the Thailand-based Cape & Kantary Hotels collection, this large and stylish complex dominates the glitzy Nimmanhaemin Road district. **Pros:** whirlpool and regular pool; one-bedroom suites have washing machines; huge selection at breakfast. **Cons:** lacks character; noisy neighborhood; gridlock at night. $ *Rooms from: B3,300* ✉ *44 Nimmanhaemin Rd., Soi 12, Chiang Mai* ☏ *053/222111* ⊕ *www. kantarycollection.com* ⤢ *152 rooms* �‖○�‖ *No Meals.*

Ping Nakara Boutique Hotel & Spa

$$ | **HOTEL** | It's hard to believe that this stunning riverside property was built in 2009; a masterpiece of colonial-style architecture, it's furnished throughout with exquisite antiques. **Pros:** garden teatime service; peaceful setting; big rooms. **Cons:** drab, main-road neighborhood; some rooms get road noise;

so-so restaurant. $ *Rooms from: B2,000* ✉ *135/9 Charoen Prathet Rd., A. Muang, City Center* ☏ *053/252999* ⊕ *www.ping-nakara.com* �‖○�‖ *No Meals* ⤢ *19 rooms.*

Ruen Come In

$$ | **B&B/INN** | An extremely hospitable (English-speaking) Thai couple runs this two-story teak-timbered hotel whose main building was the family home before the children left the nest. **Pros:** massive rooms; swimming pool; superb food. **Cons:** street and airport noise; Old City not within walking distance; few facilities. $ *Rooms from: B2,200* ✉ *79/3 Sirithorn Rd., Chiang Mai* ☏ *086/664–1532* ⊕ *www.ruencomein.com* ⤢ *13 rooms* �‖○❼ *No Meals.*

Nightlife

BARS

Wine Connection

WINE BARS | Although it's predominantly a retail shop, this well-stocked spot in a shopping plaza has outside bistro tables where customers can sample wines until late. Wine buffs, still a newish breed here, crowd the tables on most evenings. Food can be ordered from a neighboring bistro. ✉ *Nim City Daily, 197 Mahidol Rd., Chiang Mai* ☏ *053/201252* ⊕ *www. wineconnection.co.th.*

Looper Co.

COCKTAIL LOUNGES | An espresso bar by day and a cocktail bar by night, this sleek spot takes both sides of its persona very seriously. The barista offers several styles of coffee-making, such as Aeropress, Japanese drip, and cold brew. Later, the bartender takes over with a list of creative options that includes the Jackie Kennedy, a surprising but delicious combination of passion fruit, tomato, and mustard flavors. ✉ *151 Ratchawong Rd., Chiang Mai* ☏ *087/177–2640* ⊕ *www. facebook.com/looperandcompany.*

DANCE CLUBS
Warm Up
DANCE CLUBS | Young Thais, many of whom are students at nearby universities, love the discos and music bars of the Nimmanhaemin Road area, a major nightlife scene. Visiting ravers under 40 won't feel out of place in haunts like Warm Up, where local bands play Thai pop music and, in between sets, a DJ spins house and EDM. If you don't want to put in earplugs, enjoy a drink at the low-key outdoor tables. ⊠ *40 Nimmanhaemin Rd., Chiang Mai ✥ One block east of Chiang Mai University* ☎ *053/400677.*

KHANTOKE
Old Chiang Mai Cultural Center
THEMED ENTERTAINMENT | This fine ensemble of old-style teak-built houses offers a multicourse dinner accompanied by traditional music and dancing. Take a seat on the floor to experience the show up close. ⊠ *185/3 Wualai Rd., Chiang Mai* ☎ *053/202–9935* ⊕ *www.oldchiangmai.com.*

MUSIC
The Good View
LIVE MUSIC | This longtime popular live music venue on the east bank of the Ping River, resounds after dark with live rock, jazz, and Motown oldies played by cover bands. The Thai fare and extensive cocktail list are above average, too. The Riverside Restaurant & Bar is another good option for a laid-back evening of music. ⊠ *13 Charoen Rat Rd., Chiang Mai* ☎ *053/241–866* ⊕ *www.goodview.co.th.*

Shopping

ART
The Gallery
ART GALLERIES | Beautiful traditional Thai paintings, carvings, sculptures, and other artworks are displayed and sold at the fine gallery attached to The Gallery restaurant. ⊠ *25–29 Charoen Rat Rd.,*

Five-Star Products

To encourage each *tambon* (community) to make the best use of its special skills, the Thai government set up a program called OTOP, which stands for "One Tambon, One Product." It's been a great success. More than 25,000 community-based artisans and manufacturers have joined the program, and nearly 600 products have been given five-star ratings. About half are food or beverage items, but there are also clothes, housewares and decorations, handicrafts, and souvenirs. Look for the OTOP symbol when you shop.

Chiang Mai ☎ *053/248–601* ⊕ *thegallery-restaurant.com/art-gallery.*

★ Wattana Art Gallery
ART GALLERIES | The celebrated Thai artist Wattana Wattanapun runs this gallery whose eclectic artworks—textiles and works on paper—represent the full range of Thailand's artistic expression. Gallery staff are welcoming and knowledgeable. ⊠ *100/1 Soi Wat Umong, Chiang Mai* ☎ *053/278–747, 089/429–1883* ⊕ *www.wattana-art.com.*

C.A.P Studio
ART GALLERIES | Specializing in contemporary works on paper in a variety of techniques, from etching to woodblock prints, this studio is part gallery and part printmaking workshop. It's run by local artist and professor Kitikong Tilokwattanotai, who works with emerging and established Thai and international artists. ⊠ *368/13 Nimmanhemin Rd Soi 17, Chiang Mai* ☎ *087/810–8860* ⊕ *www.chiangmaiartonpaper.com* ☽ *Closed Mon.*

Shopping 101

The best items to buy if you're shopping around Chiang Mai are vibrant hill tribe textiles and products made from them, such as handbags and shoes; handicrafts, from handmade paper to pretty parasols (great for the sun); hippie clothes; knockoff bags; and accessories and jewelry.

Antiques

True antiques are hard to find. If you find something you like, examine it for signs of counterfeiting—new paint or varnish, tooled damage marks—and ask for certificates of provenance and written guarantees that the goods can be returned if proved counterfeit. The Night Bazaar has two floors packed with plenty of nice pieces and trinkets claiming to be "antiques," most of which are certainly not.

The road south to Hang Dong (take the signposted turn before the airport) is lined with antiques shops. Just outside Hang Dong is the craft village of Ban Tawai, which specializes in woodwork. You could spend hours rummaging through the shops and storerooms.

Handicrafts

For two of Chiang Mai's specialties, lacquerware and paper products, take a taxi or songthaew to any of the outlets along San Kamphaeng Road. Large emporiums that line the 10-km (6-mile) stretch sell a wide variety of items. Whole communities here devote themselves to their traditional trades. One community rears silkworms, for instance, providing the raw product for the looms humming in workshops.

Outside the city center, the highways running south and east of Chiang Mai are lined for several miles with workshops stocked with handicrafts of every description. They're a favorite destination for tuk-tuk drivers, who receive a commission on goods bought by their passengers.

For local handicrafts, head to Thapae Road and Loi Kroh Road. Across the Nawarat Bridge, Charoen Rat Road is home to a handful of boutiques selling interesting crafts. Farther afield, along Nimmanhaemin Road, a slew of crafts and home goods shops has developed. Start from Soi 1 and work your way south.

Jewelry

Chiang Mai is well known for its shops selling gems and semiprecious stones. If gold is your passion, make your way to the Chinese district. All the stores that jostle for space at the eastern end of Chang Moi Road are reliable, invariably issuing certificates of authenticity. The city's silver district, Wualai Road, is lined for several hundred yards with shops where you can sometimes see silversmiths at work.

■TIP→ **If you want trinkets, the Night Market is fine, but it's not the place to find authentic jewelry and gems.**

Textiles

Chiang Mai and textiles, both silk and woven cotton, go hand in hand. Here you can buy products and see them being manufactured. Several companies along San Kamphaeng Road open their workrooms to visitors and explain the process of making silk.

■TIP→ **Factory shops are favorite destinations of package tours, so prices will be higher than in other parts of town or at the Night Market.**

HANDICRAFTS

Baan Tawai Village

CRAFTS | Four kilometers (2½ miles) after the turnoff from highway 108 to Baan Tawai, lies this community of workshops dealing in antiques and handicrafts. Expect to see teak, mango, rattan, and water hyacinth being worked into attractive and unusual items. If you end up buying a heavy piece of teak furniture, the dealer will arrange for its shipping. ⊠ 90 Moo 2 Tambon Baan Tawai, in Hang Dong, Chiang Mai ☎ 081/882–4882 ⊕ www.ban-tawai.com.

Northern Village

CRAFTS | Chiang Mai's largest handicrafts retail outlet has an astounding selection of ceramics, jewelry carvings, and silks and other textiles. ⊠ CentralPlaza Airport Chiangmai, 2 Mahidol Rd., Chiang Mai ✛ Near Thipanet Rd. ☎ 053/999199.

Thai Tribal Crafts

CRAFTS | Operated by the Baptist Christian Service Foundation, the nonprofit Thai Tribal Crafts has more than 25 years' experience in retailing the products of northern Thailand's hill tribe people. The organization prides itself on its fair trade policy and the authenticity of its products like clothing, accessories, and home goods. They also run weaving classes suitable for beginners, including kids. ⊠ 208 Bamrungrat Rd., Chiang Mai ✛ Near Kaeo Nawarat Rd. ☎ 053/241043 ⊕ www.ttcrafts.co.th.

Umbrella Making Center

CRAFTS | Among the crafts you can find at this large sales outlet in the village of Bo Sang, 10 miles east of Chiang Mai, are hand-painted umbrellas made from lacquered paper and tree bark. Hundreds of these are displayed at the center. You can watch the whole process here, as artists paint traditional designs on anything from a T-shirt to a suitcase—travelers have discovered that this is a handy way of helping identify their luggage on an airport carousel. ⊠ 11/2 Moo 3 Tambon Bo Sang, Chiang Mai ✛ On Hwy. 1014 just northeast of Hwy. 1006 ☎ 053/338195 ⊕ handmade-umbrella.com.

JEWELRY

Nova

JEWELRY & WATCHES | This stunning jewelry shop has an attached studio where striking contemporary pieces are created in gold, silver, platinum, and stainless steel. Some pieces incorporate common materials, such as stone and rosewood, into their designs. ⊠ 179 Thapae Rd., Chiang Mai ☎ 053/273058 ⊕ www.nova-collection.com.

Royal Orchid Collection

JEWELRY & WATCHES | This shop specializes in jewelry featuring all sorts of flowers, including orchids and roses, set in gold and silver. The Siam Royal Orchid booth at Northern Village has a spectacular selection. ⊠ 94-120 Charoen Muang Rd., Chiang Mai ✛ One block from the river ☎ 053/245598 ⊕ www.royalorchidcollection.com ⊗ Closed Sun.

Shiraz

JEWELRY & WATCHES | This small shop specializes in loose gemstones and made-to-order rings of all types (especially engagement rings), and has an unchallenged reputation for reliability, expertise, and good value. If the owner, Mr. Nasser, is behind the counter or at work in his office workroom, you're in luck—you won't find a more knowledgeable gems expert in Chiang Mai. ⊠ 170 Thapae Rd., Chiang Mai ✛ Near Kampangdin Rd. ☎ 053/252382 ⊕ www.shirazjewelrychiangmai.com ⊗ Closed Sun.

STREET MARKETS

Kalare Night Bazaar

MARKET | This bazaar, in a big entertainment complex on the eastern side of the Night Bazaar on Chang Klan Road (clearly marked), is packed with boutiques, food and souvenir stalls (and seating), and inexpensive restaurants. There is often live music, too, mostly Thai pop bands. ⊠ Chang Klan Rd., Chiang Mai ✛ One block north of Loi Kroh Rd.

★ Night Bazaar

MARKET | The justifiably famous Night Bazaar (also called the Night Market), on Chang Klan Road, is a kind of open-air department store filled with stalls selling everything from inexpensive souvenirs to pricey antiques. In the late afternoon and evening, traders set up tented stalls along Chang Klan Road and the adjoining streets. This is a market for tourists; you're expected to bargain, so don't be shy. But remain polite, and don't haggle over tiny sums. ✉ *Chang Klan Rd., Chiang Mai* ✛ *Near Loi Kroh Rd.*

Walking Streets

MARKET | Chiang Mai has two so-called walking streets, closed off to traffic to make way for weekly markets. One is held on **Wualai Road** (the "silver street") on Saturday evening. The other, much larger one, takes up the whole of **Ratchadamnoen Road** and surrounding streets on Sunday evenings. Although the Night Bazaar sells good food and plenty of souvenirs, you will usually find more local handicrafts at the walking street markets. ✉ *Chiang Mai*

TEXTILES

Shinawatra Thai Silk

FABRICS | Silk and other local textiles can be purchased at this company's shops, where you can also buy made-to-order clothing and home-decor items. This is a good place to learn about how silk is made and how the industry has evolved in Thailand. There are several branches around the city. ✉ *18 Huay Kaew Rd., Chiang Mai* ☎ *053/221076* ⊕ *shinawatrathaisilk.co.th.*

★ Studio Naenna

CRAFTS | Patricia Cheesman has been working with local textiles since 1988, though she first encountered them in the 1970s, when working for the UN in Laos. Today she and her daughter Lamorna run a collective of female weavers, designers, and embroiderers called Weavers for the Environment (WFE). There's another branch on Soi 1 Nimmanhaemin Road.

✉ *138/8 Soi Chang Khian, Chiang Mai* ☎ *053/226042* ⊕ *www.studio-naenna. com.*

 # Activities

BOATING

Mae Ping River Cruise

BOAT TOURS | If you're looking for a low-key river cruise, this outfitter offers languid boat rides upriver with an optional bowl of *khao soi* at a local farmer's house. The longtail journey departs hourly starting at 9 am from the landing at Wat Chai Mongkol, just down from the Iron Bridge, but prices include hotel pickup. ✉ *133 Charoen Prathet Rd., Chiang Mai* ☎ *053/274822* ⊕ *www.maepingrivercruise.com.*

HORSEBACK RIDING

Pong Horse Park

HORSEBACK RIDING | **FAMILY** | Beginners and experienced riders can gallop across rolling green hills, dirt trails, and grassy fields, just a half hour outside the Old City. Lessons (45 minutes) are B700 for ages three to adult. Trail rides are B1,000/hour; a six-hour trek, including lunch, is B,5000. ✉ *119 Moo 1, Chiang Mai* ☎ *081/882–8899.*

SPAS

Ban Sabai Village Resort and Spa

SPAS | At this spa you can get your massage in a wooden Thai-style house or a riverside sala. The steamed herb massage, with soothing herbs placed on the body, is especially recommended. ✉ *219 Moo 9 San Pee Sua, Chiang Mai* ☎ *053/854778 and 79, 082/762–8310* ⊕ *bansabairesorts.com/ban-sabai-village-chiang-mai/.*

Chetawan Thai Traditional Massage School

SPAS | The Chetawan Thai Traditional Massage School is affiliated with Bangkok's famous Wat Po massage school. A 30-minute Thai massage costs B220; a 60-minute oil massage is B400. ✉ *7/1-2 Soi Samut Lana, Chiang Mai*

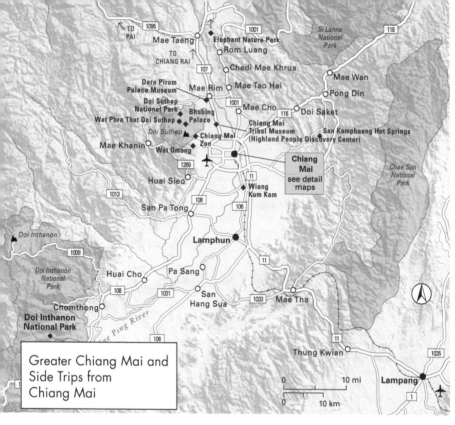

Greater Chiang Mai and
Side Trips from
Chiang Mai

☎ 053/410360 ⊕ www.watpomassage.
com.

Oasis Spa At Nimman

SPAS | Oasis has three locations in Chiang
Mai and all offer a full range of massage
styles, from Swedish to traditional Thai.
The body scrubs make use of ingredients like coconut butter, Himalayan salt,
and rose sugar. ✉ 11 Nimmanhaeminda
Rd Lane 7, Chiang Mai ☎ 053/920111
⊕ www.oasisspa.net/destination/
chiangmai.

Thai Massage School Shivagakomarpaj

SPAS | This school, one of Thailand's
oldest such establishments, is author-
ized by the Thai Ministry of Education.
A 30-hour, five-day, Level 1 introductory
course costs B5,000 (including lunches).
✉ 238/1 Wualai Rd., Chiang Mai ✢ Near
Thipanet Rd. ☎ 053/275–085 ⊕ thaimas-
sageschool.ac.th.

Thapae Boxing Stadium

BOXING | Professional Muay Thai boxing
contestants square off most nights at
this stadium just outside the Old City's
Thapae Gate. Matches start at 8 pm and
tickets cost from B400 to B600. ✉ 1
Moon Muang Rd., Chiang Mai ✢ Just
south of Thapae Gate ☎ 081/164–8784.

Greater Chiang Mai

There are a number of sights to see
outside Chiang Mai, most famously Wat
Phra That Doi Suthep, the mountaintop temple that overlooks the city. The
mountain road that skirts Doi Suthep,
winding through the thickly forested Mae
Sa Valley, is lined with touristy attractions, including bungee-jumping towers
and orchid farms. Several operators have

created a network of ziplines through the forest, enabling more adventurous visitors to swing Tarzan-style for more than a mile at treetop level.

 Sights

Bhubing Palace

CASTLE/PALACE | The summer residence of the royal family is a serene mansion that shares an exquisitely landscaped park with the more modest mountain retreats of the crown prince and princess. The palace itself cannot be visited, but the gardens are open to the public. Flower enthusiasts swoon at the sight of the roses—among the blooms is a variety created by the king himself. A rough, unpaved road to the left of the palace brings you after 4 km (2½ miles) to a village called Doi Pui Meo, where many of the Hmong women are busy creating finely worked textiles (the songthaew fare there and back is B300). On the mountainside above the village are two tiny museums documenting hill tribe life and the opium trade. *No shorts or short skirts, no bare shoulders.* ⊠ *Chiang Mai* ⊹ *Off Huay Kaew Rd., 6 km (4 miles) past Wat Phra That Doi Suthep* ☎ ⊕ *bhubingpalace.org* ⊠ *Gardens B50* ⊗ *Closed Jan.–Mar.*

Chiang Mai Zoo

There aren't a lot of activities in Chiang Mai geared toward kids, so this is a good bet if you're traveling with children. The enclosures of this zoo on the lower slopes of Doi Suthep are spaced out along paths that wind leisurely through shaded woodlands. If the walk seems too strenuous, you can hop on a shuttle that stops at all the sights. The most popular animals are the giant pandas and and the koala bears. ■TIP→ **The aquarium is within the zoo (additional cost) but is not worth a visit.** ⊠ *100 Huay Kaew Rd., Chiang Mai* ☎ *053/221179* ⊕ *www.chiangmai.zoothailand.org/en/index.php*

⊠ *B150; pandas B100 additional; B60 shuttle; aquarium B450 additional.*

Dara Pirom Palace Museum

HISTORIC HOME | This Lanna-style mansion was the last home of Jao Dara Rasamee, daughter of a late-19th-century ruler of Chiang Mai and the favorite wife of King Chulalongkorn. The low-eaved and galleried building has been restored and furnished with many of the princess's antiques, including clothes she designed herself. It's a living museum of 19th-century Lanna culture and design, and if you have extra time in Chiang Mai, it's worth the 35-minute drive. ⊠ *Chiang Mai–Mae Rim Rd., Chiang Mai* ☎ *053/299-175* ⊕ *www.museumthailand.com/en/museum/DARAPIROM-MUSEUM* ⊠ *B20* ⊗ *Closed Sun. and Mon.*

Doi Suthep National Park

NATIONAL PARK | **FAMILY** | You don't have to head to the distant mountains to go trekking during your stay in Chiang Mai. Doi Suthep, the 3,542-foot peak that broods over the city, lends its name to a national park with plenty of hiking trails to explore. One of these, a path taken by pilgrims over the centuries preceding the construction of a road, leads up to the gold-spired Wat Phra That Doi Suthep (see that listing for details). There's also an easy hiking trail (about 45 minutes) that'll bring you to one of Chiang Mai's least known but most charming temples, Wat Pha Lat. This modest ensemble of buildings is virtually lost in the forest. Make sure to explore the compound, which has a weathered chedi and a grotto filled with images of Buddha. After you leave Wat Pha Lat, the path becomes steeper. After another 45 minutes you emerge onto the mountain road, where you can flag down a songthaew if you can't take another step. Otherwise, follow the road for about 200 yards; a break in the forest marks the uphill trail to Wat Phra That. Keep a sharp lookout for snakes; they thrive on the mountain, and some of them are highly venom-ous. ✉ *Huay Kaew Rd., Chiang Mai* ☎ *053/210244* ⊕ *www.thainationalparks. com/doi-suthep-pui-national-park* ✉ *B200* ⊗ *Closed June–Sept.*

Elephant Nature Park

NATURE PRESERVE | FAMILY | There are several elephant reserves north of Chiang Mai, but there are few where elephants are not ridden. Here more than 100 rescued elephants, including a few youngsters, roam freely in the natural enclosure formed by a narrow moun-tain valley an hour's drive away. Visitors can volunteer to care for the elephants or simply stroll among the elephants, observing them in the river that runs through the park. There are no elephant rides or circuslike shows; Sangduen ("Lek") Chailert, a Ford Foundation laure-ate who runs the reserve, insists that the animals in her care live as close to nature as possible. Visits, which last a full day, can be arranged online or at the park's Old City office; the rate includes pickup at your Chiang Mai hotel and your return. Longer overnight volunteer packages are also available. ✉ *Old City office, 1 Ratchamankha Rd., Phra Singh, Old City* ☎ *053/272855, 053/208246* ⊕ *www. elephantnaturepark.org* ✉ *B2,500.*

San Kamphaeng Hot Springs

HOT SPRING | FAMILY | Among northern Thailand's most spectacular hot springs, these include two geysers that shoot water high into the air. The spa complex, set among beautiful flowers, includes an open-air pool and several bathhouses of various sizes. There's a rustic restaurant with a view over the gardens, and small chalets with hot tubs are rented either by the hour (B300) or for the night (B1,000). Tents and sleeping bags can also be rent-ed for B150. The spa is 56 km (35 miles) north of Chiang Mai, beyond the village of San Kamphaeng. Songthaews bound for the spa leave from the riverside flower market in Chiang Mai; be sure to negotiate return transportation. ✉ *Moo 7,*

The Mae Sa Valley

This beautiful upland valley winds behind Chiang Mai's Doi Suthep and Doi Pui mountain ranges. A well-paved 100-km (60-mile) loop that begins and ends in Chiang Mai is lined by resorts, country restau-rants, hill tribe villages, orchid hothouses, and the Queen Sirikit Botanical Gardens (Dara Pirom Palace is within 30 minutes' drive). The route follows Highway 107 north from Chiang Mai, turning left at Mae Rim onto Highway 1096 and then 1269, returning to Chiang Mai from the south on Highway 108.

Tambon Ban Sahakorn, Mae-On, Chiang Mai ☎ *053/037101* ⊕ *www.skphot-springs.com* ✉ *B100.*

★ Wat Phra That Doi Suthep

RELIGIOUS BUILDING | As in so many chapters of Thai history, an elephant is closely involved in the legend surround-ing the foundation of the late-14th-cen-tury Wat Phra That, northern Thailand's most revered temple and one of only a few enjoying royal patronage. The elephant was dispatched from Chiang Mai carrying religious relics from Wat Suan Dok. Instead of ambling off into the open countryside, it stubbornly climbed up Doi Suthep. When the elephant came to rest at the 3,542-foot summit, the decision was made to establish a temple to contain the relics at that site. Over the centuries the temple compound grew into the glittering assembly of chedis, bots, viharns, and frescoed cloisters you see today. The vast terrace, usually smothered with flowers, commands a breathtaking view of Chiang Mai. Constructing the temple was quite a feat—until 1935 there was no paved road to the temple. Workers and pilgrims alike had to slog through thick jungle. The road was the result of a large-scale community project: individual villages throughout the Chiang Mai region contributed the labor, each laying 1,300-foot sections. **Getting here and around:** In Chiang Mai, you can find songthaews at Chang Phuak Gate, the Central Department Store (Huay Kaew Road), and outside Wat Phra Singh to take you on the 30-minute drive to this temple. When you arrive, you are faced with an arduous but exhilarating climb up a broad, 304-step staircase. Flanking it are 16th-century tiled balustrades that take the customary form of nagas, the mythical snakes believed to control irrigation waters. A funicular railway provides a much easier way to the top, but the true pilgrim's path is up the majestic steps. ✉ *Huay Kaew Rd., Chiang Mai* ☎ *053/295-003* 🎫 *B30; B50 with tram ticket* ☞ *Wheelchair accessible (by elevator).*

Wiang Kum Kam

RUINS | When King Mengrai decided to build his capital on the Ping River, he chose a site a few miles south of present-day Chiang Mai. He selected a low-lying stretch of land, but soon realized the folly of his choice when the river flooded during the rainy seasons. Eight years after establishing Wiang Kum Kam, he moved to higher ground and began work on Chiang Mai. Wiang Kum Kam is now being excavated, and archaeologists have been amazed to uncover a cluster of buildings almost as large as Chiang Mai's Old City. Several agencies run trips to Wiang Kum Kam, with some taking visitors by boat and then horse-drawn carriage. You can book with one, or simply hire a horse and carriage in downtown Chiang Mai (or ask your hotel to; expect to pay around B500 to B650). Horse and carriages hired at the ruins cost B300. ✉ *Chiang Mai* ✣ *4 km (2½ miles) south of Chiang Mai on old Chiang Mai–Lamphun Rd.* ☎ *053/140–322* 🌐 *www.facebook.com/WiangKumKam* 🎫 *Free.*

🍴 Restaurants

★ Bombay Hut

$$$ | **ASIAN FUSION** | A charming courtyard garden leads to the cozy dining room of this predominantly Indian restaurant, where you'll be welcomed as if you were at a friend's home. The menu focuses on Indian selections, with a few Thai and Western options, but everything is delicious. **Known for:** accommodates dietary restrictions; tasting menu; vibrant decor. [$] *Average main: 650* ✉ *94 Moo 2 Donkaeo, Chiang Mai* ☎ *090/252–0563.*

Huen Jai Yong

$ | **THAI** | Ask a Thai chef where to find Chiang Mai's finest and most authentic Lanna food, and you'll likely be directed to this rustic restaurant a 30-minute drive south of the Old City. The place occupies an old timber house and several air-conditioned rooms in a contemporary building that wraps around the back garden. **Known for:** cheerful groups of Thai families; lunch only; big bowls of fermented pork sausage sai ua. [$] *Average main: B80* ✉ *65 Moo 4 San Kamphaeng Rd., Tambon Buak Khang, off Hwy. 1317, Chiang Mai* ☎ *086/671–8710* ⏲ *Closed Mon.*

🛏 Hotels

Four Seasons Resort Chiang Mai

$$$$ | **RESORT** | **FAMILY** | The magnificent Four Seasons commands 20 acres of tropical countryside above the lush Mae Rim Valley. **Pros:** peaceful mountain setting; impeccable, attentive service; idyllic pool. **Cons:** rooms and public areas starting to show age; 40-minute drive from town; limited access for those with mobility problems. [$] *Rooms from: B21,000* ✉ *Mae Rim–Samoeng Old Rd., Chiang Mai* ☎ *053/298-181, 800/545–4000 in U.S.* 🌐 *www.fourseasons.com/chiangmai* 🔑 *99 suites and villas* 🍽 *Free Breakfast.*

The History of Chiang Mai

Chiang Mai's rich history stretches back more than 700 years to the time when several small tribes, under King Mengrai, banded together to form a new nation called Anachak Lanna Thai. Their first capital was Chiang Rai, but after three decades they moved it to the fertile plains near the Mae Ping River to a site they called Nopburi Si Nakhon Ping Chiang Mai.

The Lanna Thai eventually lost their independence to Ayutthaya and, later, to expansionist Burma. Not until 1774—when the Burmese were finally driven out—did the region revert to the Thai kingdom. After that, the region developed independently of southern Thailand. Even the language is different, marked by a more relaxed tempo. In the last 50 years the city has grown well beyond its original moated city walls, expanding far into the neighboring countryside.

★ **Raya Heritage**

$$$ | RESORT | Simple, modern, and relaxing are the words that come to mind when describing the Raya Heritage, where guests can sip evening cocktails while sitting on the bank of the sleepy Ping River. **Pros:** spa treatments; total seclusion; beautiful grounds. **Cons:** no activities for kids; surrounding neighborhood has little activity; it can take 30 minutes to reach the Old City. [$] *Rooms from: 8,000* ✉ *157 Moo 6, Donkaew, Chiang Mai* ☎ *02/301–01861* 🌐 *www.rayaheritage.com* 🍴 *Free Breakfast* 🛏 *33 rooms.*

Activities

ROCK CLIMBING

★ **Chiang Mai Rock Climbing Adventures**

ROCK CLIMBING | Enthusiasm and safety standards are both high at CMRCA, which runs caving and rock-climbing excursions for all levels of experience. The guides are passionate about climbing and do everything to make sure guests feel safe, comfortable, and are having a wonderful time. All outings are full-day, and prices vary; the intro-to-climbing day course is B750. A day on CMRCA's climbing wall is B250 (shoes and chalk bag B75). ■ TIP→ **Kids can be accommodated, but be sure to let CMRCA know in advance.** ✉ *55/3 Ratchapakhinai Rd., Chiang Mai* ☎ *053/207102* 🌐 *www.thailandclimbing.com.*

ZIP LINING

Flight of the Gibbon

ZIP LINING | FAMILY | Flying Tarzan-style through the jungle of northern Thailand is the ultimate adventure trip for many visitors. Several operators maintain ziplines in stretches of thick forest north of Chiang Mai. Flight of the Gibbon has been established the longest and is reputedly the most reliable. It has more than 7 km (4½ miles) of lines. As you glide along on them, chances are slim you'll see a gibbon, but you'll certainly feel like one. ✉ *Mae On, Chiang Mai* ☎ *089/970-5511* 🌐 *www.flightofthegibbon.com* 🎫 *B4,199.*

Side Trips from Chiang Mai

Doi Inthanon National Park

100 km (62 miles) southwest of Chiang Mai.

Doi Inthanon, Thailand's highest mountain (8,464 feet), rises majestically over a national park of staggering beauty. Many have compared the landscape—thick forests of pines, oaks, and laurels—with that of Canada. Only the tropical vegetation on its lower slopes, and the 30 villages that are home to 3,000 Karen and Hmong people, remind you that this is indeed Asia. The reserve is of great interest to nature lovers, especially birders who come to see the 362 species that nest here. Red-and-white rhododendrons run riot, as do plants found nowhere else in Thailand.

Hiking trails penetrate deep into the park, which has some of Thailand's highest and most beautiful waterfalls. The Mae Klang Falls, just past the turnoff to the park, are easily accessible on foot or by vehicle, but the most spectacular are more remote and involve a trek of 4 to 5 km (2½ to 3 miles). The Mae Ya Falls are the country's highest falls, but even more spectacular are the Siribhum Falls, which plunge in two parallel cataracts from a 1,650-foot-high cliff above the Inthanon Royal Research Station. The station's vast nurseries are a gardener's dream, filled with countless varieties of tropical and temperate plants. Rainbow trout—unknown in the warm waters of Southeast Asia—are raised here in tanks fed by cold streams plunging from the mountain's heights, then served at the station's restaurant. The national park office provides maps and guides for trekkers and bird-watchers. Accommodations are available: B1,000 for a two-person chalet, B6,500 for a villa for up to eight people. The park admission fee is collected at a tollbooth at the start of the road to the summit.

GETTING HERE AND AROUND

Although there are minibus services from the nearest village, Chom Tong, to the summit of Doi Inthanon, there is no direct bus route from Chiang Mai. The most convenient way to access the park is either to book a tour with a Chiang Mai operator or hire a car and driver in Chiang Mai for around B3,000 return. If you're driving a rental car (about B2,000 per day), take Highway 108 south (the road to Hot), and after 36 km (22 miles) turn right at Chom Thong onto Road 1099, a sinuous 48-km (30-mile) stretch winding to the mountain's summit.

■TIP→ **The ashes of Chiang Mai's last monarch, King Inthawichayanon, are contained on Road 1099 in a secluded stupa that draws hundreds of thousands of pilgrims annually.**

SAFETY AND PRECAUTIONS

The regular flow of visitors to the mountain ensures that it's a perfectly safe destination, although you should stick to marked paths and forest trails. A guide (obtainable at the national park headquarters) is recommended if you plan a long hike on the thickly forested mountain slopes.

TIMING

Doi Inthanon is a full day's outing from Chiang Mai. Chalets near the national park headquarters are available if you plan to stay overnight. Dawn on the mountain is an unforgettable experience, with the tropical sun slowly penetrating the upland mist against a background of chattering monkeys, barking deer, and birdsong.

Lamphun

20 km (12 miles) south of Chiang Mai.

Two of northern Thailand's most important monasteries, dating back more than 1,000 years, are in Lamphun. The smallest of them, Wat Chamthewi, holds the remains of the city's fabled 8th-century ruler, Queen Chamthewi. The other, Wat Phra That Hariphunchai, is a walled treasure house of ancient chapels, chedis, and gilded Buddhas.

Lamphun claims to be the oldest existing city in Thailand, but so does Nakhon Pathom. Originally called Nakhon Hariphunchai, it was founded in AD 660. Its first ruler was a queen, Chamthewi, who has a special place in Thailand's pantheon of powerful female leaders. Two striking statues of her are in the sleepy little town, and one of its wats bears her name. Queen Chamthewi founded the eponymous dynasty, which ruled the region until 1932. Today the compact little city is the capital of Thailand's smallest province and also a textile and silk production center.

Several Chiang Mai travel agencies offer day trips to Lamphun, and any hired tour guide will go with you. A vehicle isn't strictly necessary—you can easily take a bus and then walk or take a tuk-tuk around.

GETTING HERE AND AROUND

Buses from Chiang Mai to Lampang stop at Lamphun, a 40-minute drive south on Highway 106, a busy but beautiful road shaded by 100-foot-tall rubber trees. The buses leave every 20 to 30 minutes from Chiang Mai's city bus station (Chang Phuek Bus Station, not Arcade) and from a stop next to the Tourism Authority of Thailand office on Chiangmai-Lamphun Road. Blue minibus songthaews also operate a service to Lamphun. They leave from in front of Warorot Market, and you can flag them down anywhere

Lamphun's Native Fruit

The countryside surrounding Lamphun is blanketed with orchards of longan, aka *lamyai*, a sweet cherry-size fruit with a thin, buff-colored shell. The annual lamyai festival brings the town to a halt in the first week of August with parades, exhibitions, a beauty contest, and copious quantities of lamyai wine. The lamyai-flower honey is reputed to have exceptional healing and aphrodisiacal powers. You can buy lamyai at the market stalls along the 100-yard covered wooden bridge opposite Wat Phra That Hariphunchai.

on Chiangmai-Lamphun Road. Fares for all services to Lamphun are about B50. Lamphun has no bus station; buses stop at various points around town, including at the TAT office and outside Wat Hariphunchai.

Lamphun is a compact city, easy to tour on foot, although Wat Chamthewi is on the outskirts and best visited by tuk-tuk or songthaew.

TIMING

One day is sufficient for Lamphun, which is less than an hour's drive from Chiang Mai.

Sights

Hariphunchai National Museum

HISTORY MUSEUM | Just outside Wat Phra That Hariphunchai, the National Museum has a fine selection of Dvaravati-style stuccowork. The collection of Lanna antiques is also impressive. ⊠ *Chai Mongkol Rd., Lamphun* ✢ *At Chiang Mai-Lamphun Rd.* ☏ *053/511186* 🎫 *B100* ⊘ *Closed Mon. and Tues.*

Ku Chang Ku Ma

CEMETERY | Lamphun has one of the region's most unusual cemeteries, an elephant's graveyard called Ku Chang. The rounded chedi is said to contain the remains of Queen Chamthewi's favorite war elephant. On the same grounds is Ku Ma, a chedi containing the remains of the same queen's most revered horse. ⊠ *38 Soi Ku Chang, Lamphun* ✢ *Enter from Chittawongphan Rangsan.*

★ Wat Chamthewi

RELIGIOUS BUILDING | About 2 km (1 mile) west of Lamphun's center is Wat Chamthewi, often called the "topless chedi" because the gold that once covered the spire was pillaged sometime during its history. Work began on the monastery in AD 755, and despite a modern viharn added to the side of the complex, it retains an ancient, weathered look. Suwan Chang Kot, to the right of the entrance, is the most famous of the two chedis, built by King Mahantayot to hold the remains of his mother, the legendary Queen Chamthewi. The five-tier sandstone chedi is square; on each tier are Buddha images that get progressively smaller. All are in the 9th-century Dvaravati style, though many have obviously been restored. The other chedi was probably built in the 10th century, though most of what you see today is the doings of King Phaya Sapphasit, who reigned during the 12th century. You'll probably want to take a samlor down the narrow residential street to the complex. This is not an area where samlors generally cruise, so ask the driver to wait for you. ⊠ *Chamadevi Rd., Lamphun* ✢ *Adjacent to Lamphun Hospital.*

★ Wat Phra That Hariphunchai

RELIGIOUS BUILDING | The temple complex of the 11th-century Wat Phra That Hariphunchai is dazzling. Through gates guarded by ornamental lions lies a three-tier, sloping-roof viharn, a replica of the original that burned down in 1915.

Inside, note the large Chiang Saen–style bronze image of the Buddha and the carved *thammas* (Buddhism's universal principals) to the left of the altar. As you leave the viharn, you pass what is reputedly the largest bronze gong in the world, cast in 1860. The 165-foot Suwana chedi, covered in copper and topped by a golden spire, dates from 847. A century later King Athitayarat, the 32nd ruler of Hariphunchai, added a nine-tier umbrella, gilded with 14 pounds of gold. At the back of the compound—where you can find a shortcut to the center of town—there's another viharn with a standing Buddha, a sala housing four Buddha footprints, and the old museum. ⊠ *Chai Mongkol Rd., Lamphun* ✢ *At Chiang Mai-Lamphun Rd.* 🚌 *B40.*

🍴 Restaurants

Lamphun Ice Restaurant

$ | ASIAN | The name of this restaurant derives from its origins as an ice-cream parlor—and nine flavors are served—though the menu these days is much more expansive, covering Chinese, Thai, and Indian food as well as some Western favorites. The interior is modern with two private dining rooms and is surprisingly quiet for being on a main highway. **Known for:** good coffee, hot or iced; air-conditioned respite with free Wi-Fi; ice cream sundaes and banana splits. $ *Average main: B200* ⊠ *37/9 Moo 2 Lamphun-Doi-ti Road, Lamphun* ☎ *090/891–8708* ⊕ *www.facebook.com/lamphunice* ⊗ *Closed Wed.*

★ Temple House Lamphun

$ | ECLECTIC | This airy shophouse-turned-café, art gallery, and boutique is the kind of warm, homey space that makes you want to linger. The selection of pastries and cake are enticing and the barista makes excellent coffee. **Known for:** good coffee; rotating art exhibits upstairs; hummingbird cake (banana-pineapple spice cake). $ *Average main: B100* ⊠ *102*

*Intharayongyot Rd., Lamphun ✛ Soi
Rotkaew near Chiang Mai-Lamphun Rd.
☎ 065/056–9839 ⊕ www.facebook.com/
templehouselamphun ⊘ Closed Tues.*

Shopping

Lamphun's silk brocade and other textiles
are an added reason to make a visit to
this small but charming town. A handful
of vendors set up shop, selling silk,
textiles, and local handicrafts, daily from
roughly 9 am to 6 pm by the 91-meter-
long (100-yard-long) covered wooden
pedestrian bridge. The bridge is opposite
the main entrance to Wat Phra That Hariphunchai, Inthayongyot Road.

Lamphun Thai Silk

FABRICS | Lamphun is famous for their
intricate silk brocade textiles worn by royals for over a hundred years and at Lamphun Thai Silk, one of the area's largest
silk businesses, located along the river,
you can watch women weave at wooden
looms dating back generations. Eight
kilometers (5 miles) from Lamphun on
the main Lampang highway is a second
outlet. ⊠ *8/2 Panangjitawong Rd., Tambon Nai-Muang, Lamphun* ☎ *053/510329*
⊕ *www.lamphunthaisilk.com.*

Lampang

*65 km (40 miles) southeast of Lamphun,
91 km (57 miles) southeast of Chiang
Mai.*

At the end of the 19th century, when
Lampang was a thriving center of the
teak trade, well-to-do local elders gave
the city a genteel look by buying a fleet
of English-built carriages and a stable of
nimble ponies to pull them through the
streets. Before that, elephants had been
a favored means of transportation—a
century ago the number of elephants
here, who were employed in the nearby
teak forests, nearly matched the city's
population. The carriages arrived on the

first trains to steam into Lampang's fine
railroad station, which still looks much
the same as it did back then. More than
a century later, the odd sight of horse-
drawn carriages still greets visitors to
Lampang. The brightly painted, flower-be-
decked carriages, driven by hardened
types in Stetson hats and cowboy boots,
look touristy, but the locals also use them
to get around the city, albeit for considerably less than the B10 visitors are usually
charged for a short city tour (B200 for a
longer tour, or B300 per hour).

Apart from some noteworthy temples
and a smattering of fine teak shophouses and private homes, not much
else remains of Lampang's prosperous
heyday. An ever-dwindling number of
sturdy 19th-century teak houses can
be found among the maze of concrete.
Running parallel to the south bank of the
Wang River is a narrow street of ancient
shops and homes that once belonged to
the Chinese merchants who catered to
Lampang's prosperous populace.

■ **TIP →** **The riverfront promenade is a
pleasant place for a stroll; some of the
cafés and restaurants along it have terraces
overlooking the water.**

GETTING HERE AND AROUND

Lampang Airport, which handles domes-
tic flights, is just west of downtown.
Songthaews run to the city center for
around B60. Bangkok Airways and Nok
Air each have three flights a day from
Bangkok.

Buses from Chiang Mai to Lampang,
leave every half hour, often more frequently, from Chiang Mai's Arcade Bus
Station. Like the train, it takes about
2 or 2 1/2 hours, depending on if the
route is direct. You are unlikely to have
to wait more than 20 minutes. Expect
to pay B40 to B150. The VIP buses that
run Bangkok to Chiang Mai also stop in
Lampang.

Within Lampang, songthaews are the cheapest way of getting around, though traveling via the city's horse-drawn carriages is delightfully retro. Carriages are at various city stands, outside the old town hall, and outside Wienglakor Hotel and Wiengthong Hotel.

All Bangkok-to-Chiang Mai trains stop at Lampang, where a samlor or tuk-tuk can take you the 3 km (2 miles) into town for about B40. By train Lampang is 2 to 2½ hours from Chiang Mai and 11 to 13 hours from Bangkok depending on which train you choose. First-class fares from Bangkok range from B1,700 for a sleeper to B700 to B900 for a day train.

TOURS
Lampang Holiday Tours
This travel agency arranges tours of the temples and Lampang's old quarter. ✉ *260/17 Chatchai Rd., Lampang* ☎ *054/310403.*

TIMING
Lampang is worth at least one overnight stay. It has a large selection of comfortable hotels and a few restaurants where a pleasant evening can be spent.

 Sights

Wat Phra Kaew Don Tao
RELIGIOUS BUILDING | Near the banks of the Wang River, this temple is dominated by its tall chedi, built on a rectangular base and topped with a rounded spire. More interesting, however, are the Burmese-style shrine and adjacent Thai-style sala. The 18th-century shrine has a multi-tier roof. The interior walls are carved and inlaid with colored stones; the ornately engraved ceiling is painted with enamel. The sala, with the traditional three-tier roof and carved-wood pediments, houses a Sukhothai-style reclining Buddha. Legend has it that the sala was once home to the Emerald Buddha, which now resides in Bangkok. In 1436, when King Sam Fang Kaem was transporting the

Shopping Secrets

Before setting off on a shopping expedition, buy a copy of *Shopping Secrets of Chiang Mai*, a comprehensive 280-page visitors' guide containing in-depth information on virtually everything the city has to offer. It's available in most bookstores. Or page through the local English-language monthlies *Guidelines* (⊕ *guidelineschiangmai.com*) and *Art & Culture Lanna*, available free of charge in most hotels. Both are packed with information and feature local crafts by trustworthy dealers.

statue from Chiang Rai to Chiang Mai, his elephant reached Lampang and refused to go farther. The Emerald Buddha is said to have remained here for the next 32 years, until the succeeding king managed to get it to Chiang Mai. ✉ *Phra Kaew Rd., Lampang* 🎫 *B20.*

★ Wat Phra That Lampang Luang
RELIGIOUS BUILDING | One of the most venerated temples in the north, Wat Phra That Lampang Luang is also one of the most striking. Surrounded by stout laterite defense walls, the temple, near the village of Ko Khang, has the appearance of a fortress, exactly what it was when the legendary Queen Chamthewi founded her capital here in the 8th century. The Burmese captured it two-and-a-half centuries ago but were ejected by the forces of a Lampang prince—a bullet hole marks the spot where he killed the Burmese commander. The sandy temple compound has much to hold your interest, including a tiny chapel with a hole in the door that creates an amazing, inverted photographic image of the wat's central, gold-covered chedi. The temple's

Thailand's Elephants

The United States has its eagle. Britain acquired the lion. Thailand's symbolic animal is the elephant, which has played an enormous role in the country's history through the ages. It even appeared on the national flag when Thailand was Siam. It's a truly regal gentle giant—white elephants enjoy royal patronage, and several are stabled at the National Elephant Institute's conservation center near Lampang.

But the elephant is also an animal of the people, domesticated some 2,000 years ago to help with the heavy work and logging in the teak forests of northern Thailand. Elephants were in big demand by the European trading companies, who scrambled for rich harvests of teak in the late 19th and early 20th centuries. At one time there were nearly as many elephants in Lampang as people.

Early on, warrior rulers recognized their usefulness in battle, and "Elephants served as the armored tanks of pre-modern Southeast Asian armies," according to the late American historian David K. Wyatt. The director of the mahout training program at the Lampang conservation center believes he is a reincarnation of one of the foot soldiers who ran beside elephants in campaigns against Burmese invaders.

Increasing Threats

Though a few elephants enjoy royal status, most are under threat. The International Union for Conservation of Nature (IUCN) Red List includes Asian elephants as endangered. Ivory poaching, cross-border trade in live elephants, and urban encroachment have reduced Thailand's elephant population from about 100,000 a century ago to just 2,500 today. Despite conservation efforts, even these 2,500 face an uncertain future as mechanization and a 1989 government ban on private logging threw virtually all elephants and their mahouts out of work. Elephants eat roughly 200 kilograms (440 pounds) of food a day, a huge expense for mahouts.

What's a Tourist to Do?

Elephant tourism in Thailand is a contentious issue. With the ban on private logging, mahouts and their elephants have been left with no options for livelihood. The various elephant camps in northern Thailand, sometimes called conservation centers, are a response to this. Here tourists can interact with elephants, feeding, bathing, and sometimes riding them. Whether or not these camps are good for elephants is hotly debated. One side argues that without tourism dollars, the mahouts and by proxy their elephants will be destitute. The other says this treatment of elephants is inhumane. Both sides are correct. The best and most considerate (to both sides of the argument) course of action for a visitor is to choose elephant conservation centers that do not allow rides, where elephants do not perform routines, and where elephants—social creatures just like humans—can roam freely and spend time with other elephants. Elephant Nature Park is a place where elephants are not ridden, and tourists can just spend time with the graceful beasts.

ancient viharn has a beautifully carved wooden facade; note the intricate decorations around the porticoes. A museum has excellent wood carvings, but its treasure is a small emerald Buddha, which some claim was carved from the same stone as its counterpart in Bangkok. ⊠ *Lampang ✛ 15 km (9 miles) south of Lampang in Koh Kha district.*

Wat Srichum

RELIGIOUS BUILDING | Workers from Myanmar were employed in the region's rapidly expanding logging business, and these immigrants left their mark on the city's architecture. Especially well preserved is Wat Sri Chum, a 19th-century Burmese temple. Pay particular attention to the viharn (assembly hall), as the eaves are covered with beautiful carvings. Inside you can find gold-and-black lacquered pillars supporting a carved-wood ceiling. To the right is a bronze Buddha cast in the Burmese style. Red-and-gold panels on the walls depict temple scenes. ⊠ *211 Tippawan Rd, Lampang ✛ Opposite Ramkhamhaeng National Museum 🖾 B100.*

🍴 Restaurants

★ Butterhead Kitchen & Bake Shop

$$ | **MEDITERRANEAN** | **FAMILY** | Lampang native, Achareeya Chapin, studied baking and pastry at the Culinary Institute of America, and worked at a highly acclaimed restaurant in Napa Valley before returning home to set up shop. The restaurant, on a sleepy little river evoking the feeling of times gone by, has a selection of Thai and Western dishes, all prepared to perfection. **Known for:** roast chicken; macadamia cheesecake; riverside dining. $ *Average main: 200* ⊠ *80/2 Monkrating Soi 15 Bo Haew, Lampang* 🕾 *086/345–8514* ⊕ *butterheadkitchen-bakeshop.business.site* 🕙 *Closed Wed.* ▭ *No credit cards.*

Hotels

The Coconut Hotel

$ | **HOTEL** | Ten minutes by tuk-tuk outside downtown Lampang, this pristine hotel has good air-conditioning, comfortable beds, strong Wi-Fi, and most guest rooms have balconies. **Pros:** most rooms have balconies; spacious rooms; family rooms available. **Cons:** 30 minutes' walk downtown; few choices at breakfast; some noise carries through doors and walls. $ *Rooms from: B790* ⊠ *124/9, Prabath Rd., Soi 3, Lamphun* 🕾 *054/821789, 089/988–6027* ⊕ *www.thecoconuthotel. com* 🛏 *50 rooms* ¶◎¶ *Free Breakfast.*

Lampang River Lodge

$$ | **RESORT** | Nature lovers are well catered to at this remote lodge, a simple riverside resort isolated in woodland and a 15-minute drive south of Lampang's bright lights. **Pros:** ample parking; beautifully landscaped grounds; magical riverside bar. **Cons:** shuttle bus to Lampang infrequent; far from city center; patchy restaurant service. $ *Rooms from: B2,400* ⊠ *330 Moo 11, Tambol Chompoo, off Chiang Mai–Lampang Hwy. 11, Lampang* 🕾 *054/209777* ⊕ *www.lampangriverlodge.com* 🛏 *60 rooms* ¶◎¶ *No Meals.*

★ Riverside Guest House

$ | **B&B/INN** | Each of the wooden Thai houses on stilts that make up the lodgings at this property have a rustic coziness, making for an utterly enchanting place to stay. **Pros:** river views; homey atmosphere; garden hammocks. **Cons:** no restaurant on-site; noisy neighborhood dogs; some rooms share baths. $ *Rooms from: B700* ⊠ *286 Talad Kao Rd., Lampang* 🕾 *054/227005* ⊕ *www. theriverside-lampang.com* 🛏 *7 rooms* ¶◎¶ *No Meals.*

Shopping

Lampang is known for its blue, white, and orange pottery, much of it incorporating the image of a cockerel, the city's emblem. There is a weekend evening street market (Kad Kong Ta), on Talad Kao Road, where vendors sell food and drink, as well as pottery, fabrics, and handicrafts.

■TIP➜ You can find the best bargains at markets like Thung Kwian Market, a few miles south of the city on the highway to Bangkok, or north of the city on the road to Chiang Mai.

Indra Ceramic

CERAMICS | Lampang's biggest pottery outlet is west of the city center on the road to Phrae. You can see the ceramics being made and even paint your own designs. The extensive showrooms feature a ceramic model city. ✉ 382 Vajiravudh Damnoen Rd., Lampang–Phrae Hwy., Lampang ✛ 2 km (1 mile) west of city center ☎ 054/315083 ⊕ www.indraceramic.com.

★ Kad Kong Ta Market

MARKET | The alternately handsome and crumbling colonial-, Burmese- and Chinese-style houses along Old Market Road date to the late 1860s, when British and Burmese teak companies and Chinese traders lived here. Today the street is again a hub of trade when a market sets up every Saturday and Sunday from 4 to 9 pm. The 1.2-mile area is lined with stalls selling tasty street food (noodles, summer rolls, satay, sweets, fresh fruit), textiles, contemporary and traditional clothing, artwork, jewelry, and assorted souvenirs. There's always live music, too, which adds to the atmosphere.

■TIP➜ Unlike Chiang Mai markets, this market is not crowded, and you can make your way down the road at a more leisurely pace. ✉ Talad Gao Rd., Lampang ✛ At Tippawan Rd. ☉ Closed Mon.–Fri.

Chapter 8

NORTHERN THAILAND

8

Updated by
Marisa Marchitelli

 Sights
★★★★☆

 Restaurants
★★★★☆

 Hotels
★★★☆☆

 Shopping
★★★★☆

 Nightlife
★☆☆☆☆

WELCOME TO NORTHERN THAILAND

TOP REASONS TO GO

★ **Natural Wonders:** Northern Thailand is mountain country. Beyond Chiang Mai, the peaks rise to the borders of Myanmar and Laos, criss-crossed by deep valleys and fast-flowing rivers. National parks welcome hikers and campers to wild areas of outstanding natural beauty and hill tribe villages lost in time. At the southern edge lie the ruins of Sukhothai, a cradle of Siamese civilization.

★ **Shopping:** The region is world-famous for its silks, and the night markets of Mae Hong Son and Chiang Rai have an astonishing range of handicrafts, many of them from hill tribe villages.

★ **Eating:** Many people consider northern Thai cuisine the country's tastiest. Excellent restaurants can be found throughout the region, and even the simplest food stall can serve up delicious surprises.

★ **Temples:** The golden spires of thousands of temples dot the region. Each can tell you volumes about Buddhist faith and culture.

1 **Nan.**

2 **Phrae.**

3 **Pai.**

4 **Mae Hong Son.**

5 **Khun Yuam.**

6 **Mae Sariang.**

7 **Chiang Dao.**

8 **Doi Ang Khang.**

9 **Tha Ton.**

10 **Chiang Rai.**

11 **Chiang Saen.**

12 **Ban Sop Ruak.**

13 **Chiang Khong.**

14 **Sukhothai.**

15 **Si Satchanalai.**

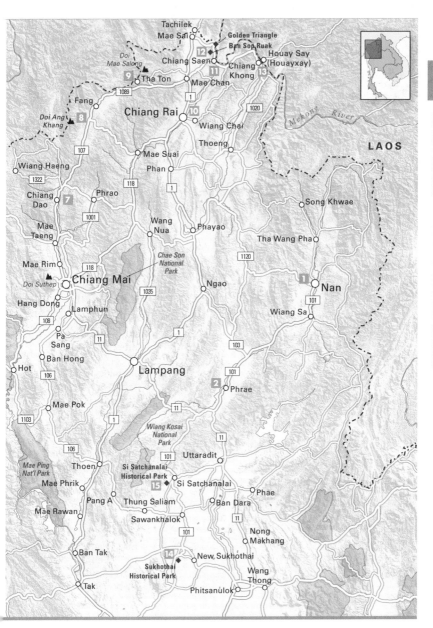

EATING AND DRINKING WELL IN NORTHERN THAILAND

To most food lovers, Thailand's northern reaches are a culinary hot spot, literally and figuratively. The distinctive Laotian and Burmese influences, as seen in the spicy salads, grilled river fish, and other delicacies prepared here likely resemble no Thai food you've tasted back home. Here, a healthy peasant's diet of fresh river fish, sticky rice, sausage, and spicy salads replaces the richer shellfish and coconut curries of Thailand's center and south.

Thailand's expansive north encompasses various ethnicities and immigrant groups, making it hard to pigeonhole the food. Universal, however, are searingly sour curries centering on sharp herbs and spices rather than coconut milk; river fish grilled over open coals; and salads integrating lime and fermented shrimp.

CLEVER COOKING IN NORTHERN THAILAND

The food of the far north is distinctly different from that of the rest of Thailand. In this mountainous region of the country, cooks are often inspired by whatever's on hand and you won't see as much coconut milk or fish sauce in the food. Fermentation is also popular. Take salted eggs, for example: They're soaked in salt and then pickled, preserving a fragile food in the hot environment and adding another tasty briny element to dishes.

PLA DUK YANG

You'll find grilled river fish throughout the north, and snakehead fish is one of the region's specialties. As opposed to the south, where fish is often deep-fried or curried, here it is usually stuffed with big, long lemongrass skewers and grilled over an open fire, searing the skin. Add the spicy, sour curry that's served atop the fish—and throw in *som tam* salad and sticky rice for good measure—and you've got a quintessential northern meal.

SOM TAM

Som tam, a ragingly hot green-papaya salad prepared with a mortar and pestle, originated from the northeastern Isaan region but is popular throughout Thailand. Tease out the differences between three versions: *som tam poo,* integrating black crab shells (a challenging texture, to say the least); *som tam pla,* an Isaan version with salted fish and long bean; and the traditional Thai *som tam,* ground with peanuts and tiny dried shrimp.

KHAO LAM

On highways, meandering rural roads, and at most markets you'll find women selling tubes of bamboo filled with sticky rice and coconut. The rice is grilled over smoky coals, which adds a woodiness to the rice's rich, sweet,

salty flavor. (Slowly peel off the bamboo to eat it.) The rice can be black or white, and sometimes is cooked with minuscule purplish beans. In mango season, *khao neaw ma muang* (mango with sticky rice) is the ultimate salty-sweet dessert.

KHAO SOI

This comforting noodle dish, believed to have Chinese Muslim origins, is ubiquitous in the north. Egg noodles and chicken pieces (generally a leg per serving) swim in a hearty stock fortified by coconut milk, flavored with turmeric and ginger, and topped with deep-fried noodles. Add your own chilli paste and lime to taste. Cheap and hearty, it's a street stall favorite in Chiang Mai.

GAENG HANG LAY

Another northern favorite, most likely of Burmese origin, is a rich and complex slow-cooked pork curry (usually pork belly and ribs). It owes its unique flavor to the Indian-influenced use of dried spices such as coriander and cumin seeds, cardamom pods, star anise, and ground nuts (peanuts). It's best served with a side dish of sticky rice that is used to mop up the sauce.

Northern Thailand begins where the flat rice-growing countryside above Bangkok rises north toward the mountains bordering Myanmar and Laos.

The vast region is strikingly different, both culturally and geographically, from the south. The north has its own language (Khum Muang), cuisine, traditional beliefs and rituals (many of them animist), and a sturdy architectural style these days called Lanna (literally "a million rice fields" because "lan" means "million" and "na" is "rice paddies"). The north's distinguishing physical feature, the mountains, contributed to the development of distinctive cultures and subcultures by isolating the mostly rural residents. Even today the daunting terrain is protecting them from too rapid an advance of outside influences.

Although Chiang Mai is the natural capital of northern Thailand it's not the only city in the region deserving inclusion in a Thailand itinerary. Chiang Rai, Chiang Saen, Mae Hong Son, Phrae, and Nan have enough attractions, particularly historic temples, to make at least overnight visits worthwhile. The ancient city of Sukhothai, with its stunning ensemble of temple ruins, is a stand-alone destination in its own right but can be easily integrated into a tour of the north. The mountains and forested uplands that separate these fascinating cities are studded with simple national park lodges and luxury resorts, hot-water spas, elephant camps—the list is endless.

Chiang Rai is a particularly suitable base for exploring the region further—either on treks to the hill tribe villages that dot the mountainsides or on shorter jaunts by elephant. The fast-flowing mountain rivers provide ideal conditions for white-water rafting and canoeing. The truly adventurous may want to head for one of the national parks, which offer overnight accommodations and the services of guides.

From Chiang Rai, circular routes run through the city's upland surroundings and deep into more remote mountains, where descendants of Chinese soldiers who fled after the Communist takeover of their country grow coffee and tea. Nan is tucked away in the mountainous corner bordering Laos, and Myanmar lies just over the nearest range from Mae Hong Son and Mae Sariang. The so-called Mae Hong Son Loop, a spectacular road starting and ending in Chiang Mai, runs through a small market town, Pai, that has developed over the years into a major tourist destination. The area was made popular by backpackers doing the "Loop," and the town's simple guesthouses are now making way for smart resorts designed for Bangkok businesspeople seeking a quiet weekend in the north.

MAJOR REGIONS

A journey through northern Thailand feels like venturing into an entirely different country than what you'll find within the frenzied streets of far-off Bangkok: the landscape, language, architecture, food, and even the people are all quite distinct.

Chiang Mai is the area's natural capital and main draw, but Chiang Rai is also developing rapidly. Both cities are not smaller versions of Bangkok, either;

they're bustling commercial and cultural centers in their own right. Just beyond each of them rises the mountain range that forms the eastern buttress of the Himalayas. The region's northernmost section borders Myanmar and Laos, and improved land crossings into Laos from here have made forays into that country a popular side trip.

Visitors looking for off-the-beaten-track territory usually head north from Chiang Mai and Chiang Rai to the Golden Triangle or west to Mae Hong Son. Relatively few venture east, toward Laos, but if time permits **Nan and nearby** is a region well worth exploring. At its center, some 70 km (42 miles) from the Laotian border, is Nan, the provincial capital and ancient royal residence. The city is very remote; roads to the border end in mountain trails, and there are no frontier crossings, although there are ambitious, long-term plans to run a highway through the mountains to Luang Prabang in Laos. Two roads link Nan with the west and the cities of Chiang Mai, Chiang Rai, and Lampang—they are both modern highways that sweep through some of Thailand's most spectacular scenery, following river valleys, penetrating forests of bamboo and teak, and skirting upland terraces of rice and maize. Hill tribe villages sit on the heights of the surrounding Doi Phu Chi (Phu Chi Mountains), where dozens of waterfalls, mountain river rapids, and revered caves beckon travelers with time on their hands. Here you can find Hmong and Lahu villages untouched by commercialism, and jungle trails where you, your elephant, and mahout beat virgin paths through the thick undergrowth. The southern route from Chiang Mai to Nan passes through the ancient town of Phrae, the center of Thailand's richest teak-growing region and a pleasant overnight stop.

Set two or three days aside for traveling Thailand's famous tourist trail **The Mae Hong Son Loop,** which begins and ends in Chiang Mai, winding through spectacular mountain scenery for much of the way. Although the route is named after its principal town, Mae Hong Son, the quiet village of Pai has become a major destination. The "Loop" route runs from Chiang Mai to Mae Hong Son via Pai if you take the northern route which is considered the most attractive route (about six hours); the southern route (eight hours) is easier to drive and takes you through the area's mountain village of Khun Yuam and the market town of Mae Sariang.

The northernmost region of Thailand, **Chiang Rai and the Golden Triangle,** is known mostly for its former role as the center of the opium trade. This fabled area is a beautiful stretch of rolling uplands that conceal remote hill tribe villages and drop down to the broad Mekong, which is backed on its far side by the mountains of Laos. Although some 60 km (37 miles) to the south, Chiang Rai is its natural capital, a city equipped with the infrastructure for touring the entire region. Winding your way from Chiang Mai to Chiang Rai will take you past Chiang Dao, best known for its astonishing cave complex; Tha Ton, a pretty riverside town on the Myanmar border, which has many outdoor activities; and Doi Ang Khang, a small, remote settlement—with a fancy resort. The Golden Triangle's apex is the riverside village of Ban Sop Ruak, once a bustling center of the opium trade. An archway on the Mekong riverbank at Ban Sop Ruak invites visitors to step symbolically into the Golden Triangle, and a large golden Buddha watches impassively over the river scene. In a nearby valley where poppies once grew stands a huge museum, the Hall of Opium, which describes the history of the worldwide trade in

Great Itineraries

To really get a feel for northern Thailand, plan on spending at least a week here.

If You Have 2 Days. Spend your first day exploring the streets of Chiang Mai. On the second day rise early and drive up to Wat Phra That Doi Suthep. In the afternoon, visit Chiang Rai and its mountainous surroundings.

If You Have 5 Days. Begin your stay in the north in Chiang Mai, flying from there to Mae Hong Son, and take a tour of a nearby Karen village. Set out the next day by hired car or bus for Chiang Rai, stopping over for one night at Pai. On the third day, en route for Chiang Rai, you might consider overnighting in Tha Ton or Chiang Dao. On the fourth and fifth days, make a circular tour to Chiang Saen to see its excavated ruins and meet the

Mekong River, then to Ban Sop Ruak to visit the magnificent Hall of Opium museum.

If You Have 7 Days. If you're lucky enough to have a week or more in northern Thailand, you'll have plenty of time to stay a night with a hill tribe family. Treks to these mountain villages can be arranged from Chiang Mai, Chiang Rai, Mae Hong Son, and other communities. Sukhothai, a must-see destination, is a day's journey to the south, so the best way to include it in your itinerary is to return to Chiang Mai and catch a long-distance VIP bus to Sukhothai, where a tour of the well-preserved ruins of ancient Siam's most advanced and most civilized kingdom will take up one day. From Sukhothai, another six-hour bus ride returns you to Bangkok.

narcotics. South of Bang Sop Ruak is Chiang Saen which sits on the banks of the Mekong and is an embarkation point for river trips to Myanmar, Laos, and China. East of Ban Sop Ruak, the Mekong river town of Chiang Khong offers magnificent vistas from the riverside towpath to the hills of Laos across the Mekong.

To history buffs, the soul of the country is to be found in the cities of **Sukhothai and nearby** where architecture and culture evoke Thailand's ancient civilizations. In the valley of the Yom River, protected by a rugged mountain range in the north and richly forested mountains in the south, lies Sukhothai. The many ruins here mark the birthplace of the Thai nation and its emergence as a center for Theravada Buddhism. North of Sukhothai 80 km (50 miles) is quieter Si Satchanalai, whose historical park contains the remnants of more temples and monuments.

Planning

When to Go

Northern Thailand has three seasons. The region is hottest and driest from February to May. The rainy season is from June to October, with the wettest weather in September. Unpaved roads are often impassable at this time of year. The best time to visit is between November and March, when the days are warm, sunny, and generally cloudless, and the nights are pleasantly cool. (At higher altitudes, it can be quite cold in the evening.) Book hotel accommodations a month or two ahead of the Christmas and New Year holiday periods and the Songkran New Year's celebration, in mid-April.

Getting Here and Around

Northern Thailand appears to be a very remote area of Asia, around 700 km (420 miles) from the country's capital, Bangkok, and far from other major centers. In fact, this region—bounded on the north, east, and west by Myanmar and Laos—is easily accessible. Chiang Mai and Chiang Rai are northern Thailand's major centers.

AIR

Main cities and towns are linked to Bangkok by frequent and reliable air service. There are dozens of flights a day from Bangkok to Chiang Mai and Chiang Rai, and regular flights from the capital to Mae Hong Son and Nan. Flight schedules to these two towns change with frustrating regularity, so check with your airline or travel agent for the latest information.

BUS

An excellent regional bus service links towns and remote villages via a network of highways. The main north-to-south artery, Highway 1, connects Bangkok with Chiang Rai and the Golden Triangle. Highway 11 branches off for Chiang Mai at Lampang, itself a major transport hub with a long-distance bus terminal, a railroad station, and an airport. From Chiang Mai you can reach the entire region on well-paved roads, with travel times not exceeding eight hours or so. The journey on serpentine mountain roads to Mae Hong Son, however, can be very tiring, requiring a stopover in either the popular resort town of Pai or quieter Mae Sariang. Chiang Rai is a convenient stopover on the road north to the Golden Triangle.

CAR

Driving in Thailand is not for the faint of heart; hiring a car and driver is usually a better option *(See Car Travel in Travel Smart Thailand)*.

■ TIP→ **On Thai New Year's (April 13–15), the highway between Chiang Mai, Chiang Rai, Pai, and Mae Hong Son may be packed with bumper-to-bumper traffic.**

MOTORCYCLE

Motorcycles are a cheap and popular option for getting around cities and towns. Rental agencies are numerous, and most small hotels have their own. Do not rent a motorcycle unless you are an experienced rider. Tourists are involved in motorcycle accidents on a daily basis.

Restaurant and Hotel Prices

What It Costs in Baht			
$	$$	$$$	$$$$
RESTAURANTS			
under B200	B200–B300	B301–B400	over B400
HOTELS			
under B2,000	B2,000–B4,000	B4,001–B6,000	over B6,000

Nan

318 km (198 miles) southeast of Chiang Mai, 270 km (168 miles) southeast of Chiang Rai, 668 km (415 miles) northeast of Bangkok.

Near the border of Laos lies the city of Nan, a provincial capital founded in 1272. According to local legend, Lord Buddha, passing through the Nan Valley, spotted an auspicious site for a temple to be built. By the late 13th century, Nan was brought into Sukhothai's fold, but, largely because of its remoteness, it maintained a fairly independent status until the last few decades.

Nan is rich in teak plantations and fertile valleys that produce rice and superb oranges. The town of Nan itself is small; everything is within walking distance. Daily life centers on the morning and evening markets. The Nan River, which flows past the eastern edge of town, draws visitors at the end of Buddhist Lent, in late October or early November, when traditional boat races are held. Each longtail boat is carved out of a single tree trunk, and at least one capsizes every year, to the delight of the locals. In mid-December Nan honors its famous fruit crop with a special Golden Orange and Red Cross Fair—there's even a Miss Golden Orange contest. It's advisable to book hotels well ahead of time for these events.

Tourist information about Nan Province, Nan itself, and Phrae is handled by the Tourism Authority of Thailand's regional office in Chiang Rai.

GETTING HERE AND AROUND
AIR
Nok Air runs at least a couple of 95-minute flights daily from Bangkok to Nan. Schedules and fares vary with the season. Songthaews meet incoming flights. It costs about B50 for the 3-km (2-mile) drive south into central Nan.

BUS
Several air-conditioned buses leave Bangkok and Chiang Mai daily for Nan, stopping en route at Phrae. The 11-hour journey from Bangkok to Nan costs from B400 to B600; the journey from Chiang Mai to Nan takes 6 hours and costs between B300 and B400. Air-conditioned buses also make the five-hour journey from Lampang to Nan. There's local bus service between Nan and Phrae.

CAR
Hiring a car and driver is the easiest way to get to Nan from Lampang or Chiang Mai. It costs about B1,500 per day.

TAXI AND TUK-TUK
City transport in Nan is provided by tuk-tuks, songthaews, and samlors. All are cheap, and trips within the city should seldom exceed B30.

TRAIN
Nan is not on the railroad route, but a relatively comfortable way of reaching the city from Bangkok is to take the Chiang Mai–bound train and change at Den Chai to a local bus for the remaining 146 km (87 miles) to Nan. The bus stops en route at Phrae.

TOURS
Trips range from city tours of Nan and short cycling tours of the region to jungle trekking, elephant riding, and white-water rafting. Nan is the ideal center from which to embark on treks through the nearby mountains, as well as raft and kayak trips along the rivers that cut through them. Khun Chompupach Sirsappuris has run Nan's leading tourist agency, Fhu Travel and Information, for more than 30 years. She speaks fluent English and knows the region like her own backyard.

CONTACTS Fhu Travel. ✉ *453/4 Sumond-hevaraj Rd., Nan* ☎ *081/287–7209* ⊕ *www.facebook.com/fhutravel/.*

 # Sights

National Museum
HISTORY MUSEUM | To get a sense of the region's art, visit the National Museum, which occupies a mansion built in 1923 for the prince who ruled Nan, Chao Suriyapong Pharittadit. The house itself is a work of art, a synthesis of overlapping red roofs, forest-green doors and shutters, and brilliant-white walls. There's a fine array of wood and bronze Buddha statues, musical instruments, ceramics, and other works of Lanna art. The revered black elephant tusk is also an attraction. The tusk, about a meter (3 feet) long,

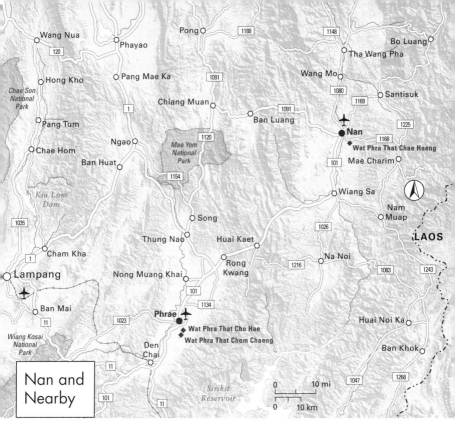

Nan and Nearby

weighs 18 kg (40 pounds). It's actually dark brown in color, but that doesn't detract at all from its special role as a local good-luck charm. ⊠ 42 Suriyapong Rd., Nan ☎ 054/710561 🎫 B100.

Wat Hua Wiang Tai

RELIGIOUS BUILDING | Small yet spectacular, the rather gaudy Wat Hua Wiang Tai has a splashy naga snake coiled along the edges of its roof and boldly colored murals painted across the viharn's exterior. Come by in the morning to experience the hustle and flow of a nearby market as well. ⊠ Sumonthewarat Rd., Nan.

Wat Ming Muang

RELIGIOUS BUILDING | With its all-white exterior Wat Ming Muang strikes a dramatic pose offset slightly by the exterior's surfeit of intricate carvings (photo ops galore). The wat contains a stone pillar erected at the founding of Nan, some 800 years ago. Don't miss the interior murals, some of which depict life here in days gone by. ⊠ Suriyaphong Rd., Nan.

Wat Phra That Chae Haeng

RELIGIOUS BUILDING | This 14th-century wat draws worshippers from all over Thailand, particularly those born in the year of the rabbit; Lanna people believe that traveling to pay respect to the Phra That of their lunar year of birth brings great prosperity. Others are attracted to a hillside location that looks down on the town of Nan and its main river, an iconic reclining Buddha image, and a tall gold chedi said to store a holy Buddha hair that once belonged to King Lithai. ⊠ Nan ♁ 4 km (3 miles) southeast of central Nan off Hwy. 1168.

Wat Phra That Chang Kham

RELIGIOUS BUILDING | One of Nan's oldest and most historically significant wats, Wat Chang was built at the turn of the 15th century, right across from what is now a National Museum. True to its title, the "elephant temple," its large chedi is propped up by 24 stone pachyderms, protecting the country's largest *ho trai* (scripture library) and a rare solid gold Buddha image from the Sukhothai period. ✉ *Suriyaphong Rd., Nan.*

★ **Wat Phumin**

RELIGIOUS BUILDING | Nan has one of the region's most unusual and beautiful temples, Wat Phumin, whose murals alone make a visit to this part of northern Thailand worthwhile. It's an economically constructed temple, combining the main shrine hall and viharn, and qualifies as one of northern Thailand's best examples of folk architecture. To enter, you climb a short flight of steps flanked by two superb *nagas* (mythological snakes), their heads guarding the north entrance and their tails the south. The 16th-century temple was extensively renovated in 1865 and 1873, and at the end of the 19th century murals picturing everyday life were added to the inner walls. Some have a unique historical context—like the French colonial soldiers disembarking at a Mekong River port with their wives in crinolines. A fully rigged merchant ship and a primitive steamboat are portrayed as backdrops to scenes showing colonial soldiers leering at the pretty local girls corralled in a palace courtyard. Even the conventional Buddhist images have a lively originality, ranging from the traumas of hell to the joys of courtly life. The bot's central images are also quite unusual—four Sukhothai Buddhas locked in conflict with the evil Mara. ✉ *Phakong Rd., Nan.*

🍴 Restaurants

Ruen Kaew

$$ | **THAI** | The name of this riverside restaurant means Crystal House, which is rather fitting, since it's such a gem. Pass through a profusion of bougainvillea flowers to find a wooden deck overlooking the Nan River, the perfect vantage point for taking in the lush scenery and enjoying the Thai menu with some original touches. **Known for:** chicken in honey sauce; original takes on Thai food; nightly live music. [$] *Average main: B240* ✉ *1/1 Sumondhevaraj Rd., Nan* ☎ *054/710631, 080/604–6454.*

Suriya Garden

$$ | **THAI** | This large restaurant has a wooden deck overlooking the Nan River banks and live music every night. Get here early, as it's often full of diners looking for authentic food at fair prices and a prime spot along the water. **Known for:** a peerless atmosphere; Chinese-style white bass and pig's trotters; spicy and sour northern Thai notes. [$] *Average main: B220* ✉ *9 Sumondhevaraj Rd., Nan* ☎ *054/710687.*

🛏 Hotels

Dhevaraj Hotel

$ | **HOTEL** | Built around an attractive interior courtyard, which is lighted for evening dining, the Dhevaraj supplies comfortable accomodations within a short walk of all the sights. **Pros:** large rooms; interior courtyard; central location. **Cons:** service a bit erratic; so-so breakfast; dated decor. [$] *Rooms from: B1,200* ✉ *466 Sumondhevaraj Rd., Nan* ☎ *054/710212* 🌐 *www.dhevarajhotel.com* 🛏 *160 rooms* 🍴 *Free Breakfast.*

Nan Boutique Hotel

$ | **HOTEL** | Boutique hotels are rare in rural Thailand, so this small and modern space is very much in a class of its own. **Pros:** friendly service; free bicycles; restaurant with Western breakfast. **Cons:** long walk to town center; no pool; rooms with double beds not always available. $ *Rooms from: B1,400* ✉ *1/11 Kha Luang Rd., Nan* ☎ *054/775532* ⊕ *www.nanboutique.com* ⊖ *No Meals* ⇆ *32 rooms.*

Pukha Nanfa Hotel

$$ | **HOTEL** | Named after the first Nan dynasty, this restored two-story hotel is a teak-lined trip back to the early 1900s, with old-world charm alongside modern amenities. **Pros:** immaculately maintained ; centrally located; traditional yet trendy. **Cons:** no elevator; sleepy in the off-season; rooms can be rather small. $ *Rooms from: B2,600* ✉ *369 Sumon Thewarat Rd., Nan* ☎ *054/771111* ⊕ *pukhananfahotel.co.th/* ⇆ *14 rooms* ⊖ *Free Breakfast.*

Phrae

110 km (68 miles) southeast of Lampang, 118 km (73 miles) southwest of Nan.

A market town in a narrow valley well off the beaten path, Phrae is renowned in northern Thailand for its fine teak houses. It's a useful stopover on the 230-km (143-mile) journey from Lampang to Nan, but has little to offer the visitor apart from ruined city walls, some attractive and historic temples, and the sturdy teak buildings that attest to its former importance as a center of the logging industry.

GETTING HERE AND AROUND

The domestic airline Nok Air flies daily between Bangkok and Phrae. The flight takes about 90 minutes. Daily air-conditioned buses from Bangkok and Chiang Mai headed for Nan stop at Phrae; it's a 10-hour journey from Bangkok and a five-hour one from Chiang Mai. There are also air-conditioned buses that travel between Lampang and Phrae (three hours) daily. There's local bus service between Phrae and Nan, an uncomfortable but cheap journey of two to three hours between each center. Hiring a car and driver in

Lampang or Chiang Mai is the easiest way to get here, but doing this costs about B3,000 per day.

Sights

Ban Prathap Chai

HISTORIC HOME | There are many teak houses to admire all over Phrae, but none match this large one near the city's southern edge. Like many such houses, it's actually a reconstruction of several older houses—in this case nine of them supported on 130 huge centuries-old teak posts. The result is remarkably harmonious. A tour of the rooms open to public view provides a glimpse of bourgeois life in the region. The space between the teak poles on the ground floor of the building is taken up by stalls selling handicrafts, including carved teak. ✉ *Tambon Pa Maet, Phrae* ✛ *Hwy. 1022, 10 km (6 miles) east of Phrae* ☎ 🚪 *B40.*

Wat Chom Sawan

RELIGIOUS BUILDING | Teak plays a prominent role in this beautiful monastery, which was designed by a Burmese architect and built by migrants from the country's Shan State during King Rama V's reign (1868–1910). The bot and viharn combine to make one giant structure, supported by stilts and housing statues made of marble and bamboo. ✉ *Yantarak-itkosol Rd., Phrae* ✛ *On northeastern edge of town.*

Wat Luang

RELIGIOUS BUILDING | Phrae's oldest structure lies within the Old City walls. Although the wat was founded in the 12th century, renovations and expansions completely obscure so much of the original design that the only section visible from that time is a Lanna chedi with primitive elephant statues. A small museum on the grounds contains sacred Buddha images, swords, and texts. ✉ *Kham Lue Rd., Phrae.*

★ **Wat Phra That Cho Hae**

RELIGIOUS BUILDING | On a hilltop in Tambon Pa Daeng, this late-12th-century temple is distinguished by its 33-meter-tall (108-foot-tall) golden chedi and breathtaking interior. The chedi is linked to a viharn, a later construction that contains a series of murals depicting scenes from the Buddha's life. The revered Buddha image is said to increase a woman's fertility. Cho Hae is the name given to the cloth woven by the local people, and in the fourth lunar month (June) the chedi is wrapped in this fabric during the annual fair. A fairly steep multitier staircase leads up to the temple. ✉ *Hwy. 1022, Phrae* ✣ *8 km (5 miles) east of Phrae.*

Wat Phra That Chom Chaeng

RELIGIOUS BUILDING | In a woodland setting about 2 km (1 mile) east of the more famous Wat Phra That Cho Hae, this smaller wat has a chedi said to contain a strand of Lord Buddha's hair. A large standing Buddha stands watch over the gate, and the grounds contain an enormous reclining Buddha. ✉ *Hwy. 1022, Phrae* ✣ *10 km (6 miles) east of Phrae.*

🍴 Restaurants

Pan Jai

$ | **THAI** | For authentic Lanna cuisine, you can't do better than this simple but superb restaurant, with an extensive menu. Try the *kanom jin* (Chinese noodles) served with a spicy meat sauce, raw and pickled cabbage, and various condiments, or the *satay moo,* thin slices of lean pork on wooden skewers, served with a peanut sauce dip. **Known for:** pork dishes; relaxed environment; popular lunch spot. [$] *Average main: B100* ✉ *2 Wira Alley, Phrae* ☎ *054/620727* 💳 *No credit cards.*

🛏 Hotels

Maeyom Palace Hotel

$ | **HOTEL** | It may not be palatial—despite the name—but the Maeyom Palace does have comfortable rooms with Lanna touches like distinctive carvings on the walls. **Pros:** close to the bus station; mountain views from some rooms; reliable Wi-Fi. **Cons:** traffic noise; impersonal, chain-hotel atmosphere; decor a bit dated. [$] *Rooms from: B1,200* ✉ *181/6 Yantarakitkosol Rd., Phrae* ☎ *054/521028* 🌐 *www.maeyompalace.com* 🛏 *104 rooms* 🍴 *No Meals.*

Must Come Boutique Hotel

$ | **B&B/INN** | In the heart of Phrae's Old Town, this modern bed-and-breakfast is basic but convenient and clean, and they have free bicycles for exploring the neighborhood. **Pros:** large beds and good water pressuer; free bicycle rentals; well-stocked drinks and snacks in the common area. **Cons:** many rooms don't have windows; no elevator; brick and concrete can feel a bit austere. [$] *Rooms from: 790* ✉ *20/4 Rong Sor 2 Alley, Phrae* ☎ *054/531456* 🌐 *www.facebook.com/profile.php?id=100018903427732* 🍴 *Free Breakfast* 🛏 *37 rooms.*

Pai

160 km (99 miles) northwest of Chiang Mai, 110 km (68 miles) east of Mae Hong Son.

Although Pai lies in a flat valley, a 10-minute drive in any direction brings you to a rugged upland terrain with stands of wild teak, groves of towering bamboo, and clusters of palm and banana trees hiding out-of-the-way resorts catering to visitors who seek peace and quiet. At night the surrounding fields and forest seem to enfold the town in a black embrace.

As you enter Pai from the direction of Chiang Mai, you'll pass by the so-called

World War II Memorial Bridge, which was stolen from Chiang Mai during the Japanese advance through northern Thailand and rebuilt here to carry heavy armor over the Pai River. When the Japanese left, they neglected to return the bridge to Chiang Mai. Residents of that city are perfectly happy, as they eventually built a much more handsome river crossing.

Exhausted backpackers looking for a stopover along the serpentine road between Chiang Mai and Mae Hong Son fell in love with Pai in the late 1980s. In 1991 it had seven modest guesthouses and three restaurants; now its frontier-style streets are lined with restaurants and bars of every description, cheap guesthouses and smart hotels, art galleries, and chic coffeehouses, while every class of resort, from back-to-nature to luxury, nestles in the surrounding hills. Thus far, Pai has managed to retain its slightly off-the-beaten-path appeal, but that may change as Bangkok property investors pour money into its infrastructure.

GETTING HERE AND AROUND
BUS
Buses traveling between Mae Hong Son and Chiang Mai stop in Pai. They take four hours for the 120-km (75-mile) journey from Chiang Mai and an additional five hours to cover the 130 km (81 miles) from Pai to Mae Hong Son. Fares for each stretch vary from about B100 to B200. Buses stop in the center of Pai.

CAR
A hired car does the trip from Chiang Mai to Pai one hour faster than the buses, and cuts the journey time from Pai to Mae Hong Son by about the same margin. Cars and four-wheel-drive vehicles can be hired from many companies in Chiang Mai from B1,000 and upward a day. A driver costs about B3,000 per day.

Pai Etiquette

Pai has a sizable Muslim population, which is why some of the guesthouses post notices asking foreign visitors to refrain from public displays of affection. Immodest clothing is frowned on, so bikini tops and other revealing garb are definitely out. The music bars close early, meaning that by midnight the town slumbers beneath the tropical sky. Nevertheless, quiet partying continues behind the shutters of the teak cabins that make up much of the tourist lodgings. This is, after all, backpacker territory.

SAFETY AND PRECAUTIONS
Pai had a crime problem, but it was caused by drug-taking young foreign visitors, not the locals. A police crackdown appears to have cleaned up the town, but keep your wits about you when visiting the local bars.

TIMING
Some foreign visitors come to Pai intending to stay a few days and never leave. It's that kind of place. There's not much to do in Pai besides exploring the surrounding countryside by day and partying by night, so if trekking, bike tours, river rafting, and late nights are not your thing, you'll want to get going again after one or two days.

TOURS
Thai Adventure Rafting
This outfit organizes wild-water rafting on the Pai River, as well as sightseeing, elephant riding, mountain biking, and bamboo rafting tours. Prices start at about B1,150 per person for 2 people for ½-day cycling tour. ✉ *39 Moo 3 Chaisongkram Rd., Tambon Viang Tai, Mae Hong Son* ☎ *053/699111* ⊕ *www.thairafting.com.*

Sights

Pai Canyon

VIEWPOINT | Backpackers came to this scenic spot back in the '90s and spread the word: it quickly became the sunset thing-to-do in Pai. What were dirt paths are now properly paved and lined with touristy vendors selling elephant pants. Once you climb the stairs and arrive at the viewpoint, intrepid hikers can walk at their own risk alongside skinny, unstable trails lined with slippery red sandstone and steep drop-offs. Proper footwear is an absolute must here. Also of note in the area is Pam Book Waterfall, about a 20-minute drive west on Route 1095, and the nearby Memorial Bridge many pass through on their way to Chiang Mai. ⊠ *Hwy. 1095, Pai* ✛ *8 km (5 miles) south of Pai.*

Restaurants

Cafecito

$ | **MEXICAN** | In an increasingly hip neighborhood on the edge of town, this taqueria serves authentic Mexican food including homemade tortillas (flour and corn), salsa, and hot sauce. The chicken mole is delicious and the margaritas are spot on, too. **Known for:** overstuffed burritos; breakfast all day; coffee that's locally sourced and roasted on-site. Ⓢ *Average main: B150* ⊠ *258 Moo 8 Vieng Tai, Pai* ☎ *053/699055.*

The Jazz House Pai

$ | **ECLECTIC** | At this Pai institution, the crowd-pleasing international menu matches the diversity of the live jazz music performed here. There's lots of seating and hammocks keep the vibe laid-back. **Known for:** weekly open mic nights; everything from pad Thai to pizza; cheap yet tasty cocktails. Ⓢ *Average main: B150* ⊠ *24/1 Chaisongkram Rd., Vieng Tai, Pai* ☎ *095/197–1656* ⊟ *No credit cards.*

Om Garden Cafe

$ | **ECLECTIC** | Fragrant with incense, this hippie-chic café is set in an idyllic, shaded courtyard garden with mismatched rattan furniture, colorful cushions, sheer curtains, and Buddha statues. The food is healthy, hearty, and wholesome. **Known for:** khao soi salad; fresh juices and fruit shakes; house-baked cake. Ⓢ *Average main: B175* ⊠ *4 Wiang Tai, Pai* ☎ *082/451–5930* ☽ *Closed Mon.* ⊟ *No credit cards.*

★ Pai Siam Bar & Bistro

$ | **FUSION** | Husband-wife duo Carlo and Supaporn man this perfectly situated indoor-outdoor bar, bistro, and guesthouse at one of the busiest intersections in Pai, just at the end of the walking street. The menu is expansive with Thai-fusion tapas, all-day breakfast, large pizzas, and Thai staples. **Known for:** passion fruit cheesecake; great people-watching; cozy ambience. Ⓢ *Average main: 150* ⊠ *Tedsaban Rd., Pai* ☎ *097/947–9060.*

★ Silhouette

$$ | **MEDITERRANEAN** | Widely acknowledged as Pai's best restaurant, Silhouette serves outstanding Thai-inspired European cuisine, made with fresh, mostly organic, local produce. Panoramic mountain views, the quirky house sense of style, and live jazz music all add to the pleasure of having a meal here. **Known for:** solid wine selection; charcuterie and cheese boards; plentiful small plates. Ⓢ *Average main: B250* ⊠ *Reverie Siam Resort, 476 Moo 8, Vieng Tai, Pai* ☎ *053/699870* ⊕ *reveriesiam.com.*

Hotels

Brook View

$ | **B&B/INN** | The brook babbles right outside your cabin window if you ask for a room with a view at this little resort. **Pros:** pretty breakfast gazebo; near town, but still "away from it all"; ample parking.

Did You Know?

Though forest still clothes the mountainsides, decades of illegal logging have endangered Thailand's prized old-growth teak trees. These days artisans are turning to alternative woods like bamboo and mango to make ornaments and furnishings.

Cons: staff keeps a low profile; some cabins are small, with no river view; uninteresting neighborhood. $ *Rooms from: B400* ☒ *132 Moo 1, Vieng Tai, Pai* ☏ *081/992–4900* ▭ *No credit cards* ⤴ *19 rooms and villas* ¶⊙¶ *No Meals.*

Cave Lodge

$ | **B&B/INN** | The chatter of gibbons wakes you up at this remote mountain lodge between Pai and Mae Hong Son. The cave after which it is named, just a short walk from the lodge, is one of the region's most spectacular caverns, with wall paintings and prehistoric coffins. **Pros:** Shan herbal sauna on-site; bread and pastries from the wood-fired oven; tucked away in a tropical forest. **Cons:** more than an hour away from Pai and Mae Hong Son; basic rooms and lots of bugs; cave tours can be quite challenging for beginners. $ *Rooms from: B600* ☒ *15 Moo 1, Pang Mapha, Pai* ☏ *053/617203* ⊕ *www.cavelodge.com* ▭ *No credit cards* ⤴ *17 rooms* ¶⊙¶ *No Meals.*

Pai Treehouse Resort

$$ | **RESORT** | The rooms with the best views at this riverside lodging outside Pai are only for the most adventurous travelers—they're in the upper branches of an enormous rain tree. **Pros:** peaceful location; terrace bar-restaurant; fine river views. **Cons:** popular for seminars; 20-minute drive from town; can get crowded. $ *Rooms from: B2,300* ☒ *90 Moo 2, Tambon Maehee, Pai* ☏ *081/911–3640* ⊕ *www.paitreehouse.com* ⤴ *19 rooms* ¶⊙¶ *No Meals.*

Paivimaan Resort

$ | **HOTEL** | *Vimaan* means "heaven," and this fine resort commands a celestial spot on the banks of the Pai River. **Pros:** pleasant and peaceful; family-friendly; close to town center. **Cons:** noise from nearby developments; villa rooms are small; irksome insects. $ *Rooms from:*

B1,500 ☒ *73 Moo 3, Tedsaban Rd., Pai* ☏ *053/699403* ⊕ *www.paivimaan.com* ¶⊙¶ *No Meals* ⤴ *17 rooms.*

★ Reverie Siam Resort

$$$ | **RESORT** | This boutique resort has beautiful rooms decorated with antiques and vintage pieces, and there are two stunning swimming pools. **Pros:** fantastic low-season rates; hospitable staff and on-site owners; elegant rooms with style to spare. **Cons:** on the edge of town; pricey in high season; Wi-Fi can be weak. $ *Rooms from: B5,000* ☒ *476 Moo 8, Vieng Tai, Pai* ☏ *053/699870* ⊕ *reveriesiam.com* ⤴ *20 rooms* ¶⊙¶ *No Meals.*

 # Nightlife

Beat Roots

LIVE MUSIC | This tiny, open-air bar is home to Pai's biggest disco ball, which sets the upbeat tone. The lineup is eclectic, with a mix of reggae and jazz, some of it local and some not. Late in the evening the crowed usually spills onto the street. ☒ *133 Moo 3 Viangtai, Pai* ☏ *093/317–7705.*

Jikko Cocktail Bar

BARS | Dedicated to the craft beer revolution, this casual spot is run by a mother-daughter duo who stock the bar with pilsners, IPAs, and strong ales from such popular international breweries as Hitachino Nest, Stone, Deschutes, and Rogue. If hops and heady flavor profiles aren't your thing, Chang's always on tap, too, and the cocktails are exceptional. There are also breakfast and lunch basics, too. ☒ *63 Moo 3 Pai, Pai* ⤊ *Near the end of Pai's main walking street* ☏ *083/616–6545* ⊕ *www.facebook.com/pg/JikkoBeer/.*

Mae Hong Son

245 km (152 miles) northwest of Chiang Mai via Pai, 368 km (229 miles) via Mae Sariang.

The remote, mountain-ringed market town of Mae Hong has been transformed into one of northern Thailand's major resort areas, with handsome hotels gracing the landscape here.

For a small town, Mae Hong Son has a surprising number of noteworthy temples, many erected by the Burmese. Two of the temples, Wat Chong Kham and Wat Kham Klang, sit on the shore of a placid lake in the center of town, forming a breathtaking ensemble of golden spires. Within a short drive are dozens of villages inhabited by the Karen, the so-called "longneck" people. Fine handicrafts are produced in these hamlets, whose inhabitants trek daily to Mae Hong Son to sell their wares at the lively morning market and along the lakeside promenade.

Although Mae Hong Son offers a welcome cool retreat during the sometimes unbearably hot months of March and April, the mountains can be obscured during that part of the year by the fires farmers set to clear their fields. One of the local names for Mae Hong Son translates as "City of the Three Mists." The other two refer to the clouds that creep through the valleys in the depths of winter and the gray monsoons of the rainy season.

GETTING HERE AND AROUND
AIR
Bangkok Airways offers one daily 45-minute flight between Chiang Mai and Mae Hong Son. The Mae Hong Son Airport is at the town's northern edge. Songthaews run to the city center for around B50. In March and April, smoke from slash-and-burn fires often causes flight cancellations.

BUS
Chiang Mai's Arcade Bus Terminal serves Mae Hong Son. Several buses depart daily on an eight-hour journey that follows the northern section of the Loop, via Pai. Buses stop in the center of town.

CAR
The most comfortable way to travel the route and enjoy the breathtaking mountain scenery is to let somebody else do the driving. The Loop road brings you here from either direction: the northern route through Pai (six hours) is a more attractive trip; the southern route through Mae Sariang (eight hours) is easier driving.

If you choose to rent a car, you'll probably do it in Chiang Mai, but if needed Avis has an office at Mae Hong Son Airport.

TOURS
A tourist info kiosk with erratic hours stands on the corner of Khunlum Prapas and Chamnansathit roads. An efficient travel agency, Amazing Mae Hong Son, has an office at the airport. In the center of town, Discover Mae Hong Son books day tours of local hill tribe villages.

TRAVEL AGENCIES Mae Hong Son Holidays. ✉ *Mae Hong Son* ☎ *061/310–9789* ⊕ *www.maehongsonholidays.com/.* **Discover Mae Hong Son.** ✉ *Mae Hong Son* ☎ *053/611537.*

Sights

Tham Pla–Namtok Pha Suea National Park
NATIONAL PARK | FAMILY | About 28 km (17 miles) north of Mae Hong Son on the Pai road, this park has one of the region's strangest sights—a grotto with a dark, cisternlike pool overflowing with fat mountain carp. The pool is fed by a mountain stream that is also full of thrashing fish fighting to get into the cave. Why? Nobody knows. It's a secret that draws thousands of Thai visitors a year. Some see a mystical meaning in

the strange sight. The cave is a pleasant 10-minute stroll from the park's headquarters. ✉ *70 Moo 1 Huay Pa, Mae Hong Son* ☎ *085/706–6663* ⊙ *Closed Jul.–Aug.*

Wat Chong Kham

RELIGIOUS BUILDING | A wonderfully self-satisfied Burmese-style Buddha, the cares of the world far from his arched brow, watches over this temple from 1827, which has a fine pulpit carved with incredible precision. It's located on a small lake, right next to the equally important Wat Chong Klang. ✉ *Chamnansathit Rd., Mae Hong Son.*

Wat Chong Klang

RELIGIOUS BUILDING | Completed in 1871, this striking white-and-gold structure features a rarely seen wicker Buddha, gorgeous stained glass, and teak figurines that depict the various stages of the Lord Buddha's life. It's one of two Burmese temples built on a small lake in the middle of Mae Hong Son—the other being the similarly named Wat Chong Kham. ✉ *Chamnansathit Rd., Mae Hong Son.*

Wat Hua Wiang

RELIGIOUS BUILDING | Built in 1863, this temple, with it's multitiered wooden roof structure adorned with detailed carvings in zinc, is an excellent representation of Shan-Burmese architecture. It is also noted for housing Mae Hong Son's most celebrated Buddha image, and one of the most revered in northern Thailand, which is now the centerpiece in the main sermon hall. Its origins are clear: note the Burmese-style long earlobes, a symbol of the Buddha's omniscience. ✉ *Singhanat Bamrung Rd, Mae Hong Son* ☎ *053/612003.*

Wat Phra That Doi Kong Mu

RELIGIOUS BUILDING | On the top of Doi Kong Mu, this temple has a remarkable view, especially at sunset, of the surrounding mountains. The temple's two chedis contain the ashes of two major 19th-century monks, Phra Moggallana (one of the Buddha's closest disciples) and Phaya Singhanat Racha (Mae Hong Son's first governor, who built the building). ✉ *Mae Hong Son* ✣ *2 km (1 mile) west of Mae Hong Son* ☎ *053/612–982.*

Sunset Views

For a giddy view of Mae Hong Son and the surrounding mountains, hike up Doi Kong Mu, a hill on the western edge of town. It's well worth the effort. From here you can see the mountains on the border of Myanmar. The view is particularly lovely at sunset. This is also where you'll find the white-marble Buddha at Wat Phra That Doi Kong Mu.

🍴 Restaurants

Bai Fern

$ | THAI | Mae Hong Son's main thoroughfare, Khunlumprapas Road, is lined with inexpensive restaurants serving local cuisine, but this one is one of the best. You can eat in the spacious dining room with solid teak columns, under whirling fans, or there's an adjoining café that has free Wi-Fi and strong coffee. **Known for:** steamed whole snakehead fish; pork ribs with pineapple; roast chicken in pandan leaves. [$] *Average main: B150* ✉ *87 Khunlum Prapas Rd., Mae Hong Son* ☎ *053/611374.*

Baan Song Thai

$ | THAI | This charming restaurant just a bit south of town is nestled in a lush tropical garden and has a vast menu of Thai specialties. Locally grown sesame is featured in a variety of dishes. **Known for:** adjoining shop selling local food products; sesame fried chicken wings; smoothies. [$] *Average main: 120* ✉ *138 Moo 5 Baan Ta Pong Daeng, Mae Hong Son* ☎ *090/316–3176* 🌐 *www.baansongthaimhs.com.*

Sights

1 Tham Pla-Namtok Pha Suea National Park **C1**
2 Wat Chong Kham........ **C5**
3 Wat Chong Klang........ **C5**
4 Wat Hua Wiang....... **B3**
5 Wat Phra That Doi Kong Mu........... **A4**

Restaurants

1 Bai Fern..... **B5**
2 Baan Song Thai.......... **C5**

Hotels

1 Fern Resort....... **D5**
2 Imperial Mae Hong Son Resort....... **C5**
3 Rim Nam Klang Doi ... **C5**

Hotels

Fern Resort

$$ | **RESORT** | The room rate at Fern is relatively expensive, but it'll get you one of the spacious bungalows built in steep-eaved Shan style, set over a valley of former rice paddies. **Pros:** friendly owners; access to hiking trails; fine mountain views. **Cons:** mosquitoes; 15-minute drive from town, though there's a shuttle bus; small bathrooms. [$] *Rooms from: B2,000* ✉ *64 Moo 10 Ban Hua Nam, Tambon Pha Bong, Mae Hong Son* ☎ *053/686110, 053/686111* 🌐 *www.fernresort.info* 🛏 *30 rooms* 🍴 *No Meals.*

Imperial Mae Hong Son Resort

$$ | **HOTEL** | Set among mature teak trees, this fine hotel was designed to blend in with the surroundings—bungalows in landscaped gardens have both front and back porches, giving the teak-floored and bamboo-furnished rooms a light-and-airy feel. **Pros:** satellite TV; pleasant walks in the grounds; large rooms. **Cons:** long walk from town, though there is shuttle service; some rooms need refurbishing; insects. [$] *Rooms from: B2,550* ✉ *149 Moo 8, Tambon Pang Moo, Mae Hong Son* ☎ *053/684444* 🌐 *www.imperial-maehongson.com/* 🛏 *104 rooms* 🍴 *No Meals.*

Rim Nam Klang Doi

$ | **RESORT** | This retreat about 7 km (4 miles) outside Mae Hong Son is an especially good value. **Pros:** good restaurant; helpful tour service; fine local walks. **Cons:** small bathrooms; shuttle service to town is erratic; unreliable plumbing. [$] *Rooms from: B1,020* ✉ *108 Ban Huay Dua, Mae Hong Son* ☎ *053/612142* 🛏 *39 rooms* 🍴 *No Meals.*

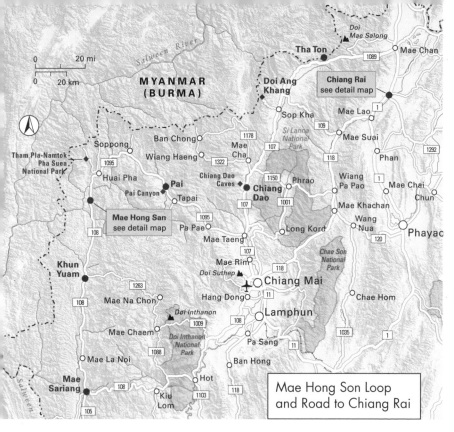

Mae Hong Son Loop
and Road to Chiang Rai

Khun Yuam

64 km (40 miles) south of Mae Hong Son, 100 km (62 km) north of Mae Sariang.

In the mountain village of Khun Yuam, along the southern route of the Loop between Mae Hong Son and Mae Sariang, you can find one of the region's most unusual and, for many, most poignant museums, the Thai–Japan Friendship Memorial Hall.

GETTING HERE AND AROUND

Most visitors to Khun Yuam stop here on their southern Loop travels by bus or car along winding mountain roads (so the going can be slow). The village is small and can be covered easily on foot and it only takes an hour or so to tour the

town's main attraction, the Thai–Japan Friendship Memorial Hall.

Sights

Thai–Japan Friendship Memorial Hall (*aka World War II Memorial Museum*)˙
HISTORY MUSEUM | This museum goes by two different names and commemorates the hundreds of Japanese soldiers who died here during a chaotic retreat from the Allied armies in Burma. Locals took in the dejected and defeated men, and a local historian gathered the belongings they left behind: rifles, uniforms, cooking utensils, personal photographs, and documents. They provide a fascinating glimpse into a little-known chapter of World War II. ⊠ *Mae Hong Son Rd.* 🚇 *B100.*

Hotels

Khun Yuam Resort

$ | RESORT | A friendly couple runs this hotel, which offers basic rooms in its main building and larger, more luxurious options in a separate two-story villa. **Pros:** fast Wi-Fi for the area; even the grand deluxe rooms are fairly priced; large balconies overlooking the valley below. **Cons:** can be hard to find; 10 minutes outside town; the drive up to the property is on a dirt road. $ *Rooms from: B800* ⊠ *139 Moo 1, Ban Tor Phae* ☎ *086/421–3287* ❍| *No Meals* ⌁ *10 rooms.*

Mae Sariang

175 km (109 miles) southwest of Chiang Mai, 140 km (87 miles) south of Mae Hong Son.

The southern route of the Loop runs through Mae Sariang, a neat little market town that sits beside the Yuam River. With comfortable hotels and a handful of good restaurants, the town makes a good base for trekking in the nearby Salawin National Park or for boat trips on the Salawin River, which borders Myanmar.

GETTING HERE AND AROUND

Buses from Chiang Mai's Chang Phuak bus station take about four hours to reach Mae Sariang. Fares range from B200 to B300. A few songthaews ply the few streets of Mae Sariang, but the town is small and compact, and can be covered easily on foot.

Tours of the border region around Mae Sariang are offered by travel agencies in Mae Hong Son. Two of the leading ones are Amazing Mae Hong Son and Discover Mae Hong Son.

TIMING

Mae Sariang is a beautiful, laid-back little town. If you're looking for relaxation, a stay of two or three days provides a welcome break on the long Mae Hong Son Loop route.

Sights

Mae Sariang and Nearby

SCENIC DRIVE | Near Mae Sariang the road winds through some of Thailand's most spectacular mountain scenery, with seemingly endless panoramas opening up through gaps in the thick teak forests that line the route. You'll pass hill tribe villages where time seems to have stood still, and Karen women go to market proudly in their traditional dress. Salawin National Park is west of Mae Sariang on Highway 1194, though the road doesn't proceed very far into this beautiful wilderness area that has hiking and biking trails. ⊠ *Hwy. 108, Mae Sariang.*

Restaurants

★ Coriander in Redwood

$$ | THAI | This century-old log trader's home was transformed into a warm, redwood-lined restaurant—part of the Riverhouse Hotel group—that serves very good Thai cuisine and well-executed Western dishes. There are tables arranged under the trees of a leafy garden for a nice view of the Yuam River. **Known for:** romantic setting; locally sourced beef; ample wine options. $ *Average main: B200* ⊠ *12 Moo 2, Langpanich Rd., Mae Sariang* ☎ *053/683309* ⊕ *www.riverhousehotelgroup.com/coriander-in-redwood.*

Inthira

$ | THAI | Family run since Inthira Tansuhaj first opened it in 1964, this Mae Sariang favorite sticks to Thai staples like curries, soups, and stir-fries. English menus are available, and service is actually quite efficient for an ever-expanding space that now seats up to 300 people. **Known for:** seasonal specialties like chayote greens, red ant eggs, and giant crickets; fried fish with garlic; cold bottles of Chang. [$] *Average main: B100* ✉ *170/1 Wiangmai Rd., Mae Sariang* ☎ *053/681441, 053/681529* 🌐 *inthira.wordpress.com.*

🛏 Hotels

Riverhouse Hotel

$ | **HOTEL** | Cooling breezes from the Yuam River waft through the open-plan areas of this attractive teak hotel, with rooms a simple but elegant synthesis of white walls, dark woods, and handwoven textiles from Sop Moei Arts, an initiative that supports local Pwo Karen artisans. **Pros:** sesame pulled chicken noodles; homey public lounge area; timber-walled bathrooms. **Cons:** traffic noise; no nightlife; limited restaurant menu. [$] *Rooms from: B1,000* ✉ *77 Langpanich Rd., Mae Sariang* ☎ *053/621201* 🌐 *www.riverhousehotelgroup.com/hotel* 💳 *No credit cards* 🛏 *12 rooms* 🍴 *No Meals.*

Riverhouse Resort

$ | **HOTEL** | This modern hotel is a stylish contrast to the nearby teak-built River House, under the same ownership, but the smart interior is welcoming and comfortable. **Pros:** ample parking; riverside garden; fine views. **Cons:** pool is next door; limited breakfast; insects. [$] *Rooms from: B1,200* ✉ *6/1 Moo 2 Langpanich Rd., Mae Sariang* ☎ *053/683066* 🌐 *www.riverhousehotelgroup.com/resort* 🍴 *No Meals* 🛏 *42 rooms.*

Chiang Dao

72 km (40 miles) north of Chiang Mai.

The area around the quaint village of Chiang Dao has two claims to fame: Thailand's third-highest mountain, 7,500-foot Doi Chiang Dao, which leaps up almost vertically from the valley floor; and the country's most spectacular caves, which penetrate more than 10 km (6 miles) into the massif. If you want to explore more of the mountain, hire a guide.

GETTING HERE AND AROUND

Buses bound for Chiang Dao depart regularly from Chiang Mai's Chang Phuak Bus Terminal. The fare is between B100 and B200, depending on the type of service (express, air-conditioned, etc.). Buses stop on the main road in town.

If you need information about Chiang Dao, the best source is Khun Wicha of the Chiang Dao Nest. The innkeeper knows the town and its attractions so well that she has produced a charming map for visitors.

TIMING

Chiang Dao's famous caves can be explored in a couple of hours, but many visitors are so captivated by the mountain scenery that they stay for a few days. The hike to the top of Chiang Dao mountain takes at least six hours, and most trekkers bivouac overnight at the top.

TOURS

CONTACT Khun Wihataya, Chiang Dao Nest. ✉ *Chiang Dao* ☎ *053/456612* 🌐 *www.chiangdao.com/nest.*

CONTACT William Lemas, Dek Doi. ✉ *Chiang Dao* ☎ *065/418–9417.*

👁 Sights

Chiang Dao Caves

CAVE | Caves have a mystic hold over Buddhist Thais, so foreign visitors to Chiang Dao's famous caverns find themselves vastly outnumbered by the locals. The caves are thought to penetrate more than 10 km (6 miles) into the small town's guardian mountain, Doi Luang, but the sights in the lighted portion, which is only a few hundred yards, include spectacular stalagmites and stalactites, along with hundreds of Buddha statues and other votive items placed there by devout Buddhists. If you want to explore past the lighted areas, you can hire a local guide with a lantern for about B100. The mountain itself can be scaled in a day, but even just an hour or two of tough walking can bring you to viewpoints with amazing panoramas. ✉ *Chiang Dao* ✥ *About 3 km (2 miles) west of town* ☎ *053/248604* 🎟 *B40.*

Hotels

★ **Chiang Dao Nest**

$ | **RESORT** | Describing itself as a mini-resort, the Nest consists of two groups of chalets, a mile apart from each other, nestled at the foot of Chiang Dao mountain. **Pros:** bicycles available; total seclusion; great food. **Cons:** Western dishes can be pricey; dim lighting makes bedtime reading difficult; unheated pool water can be cold in winter. [$] *Rooms from: B695* ✉ *144/4 Moo 5, Ban Tham, Chiang Dao* ☎ *086/017–1985* 🌐 *www.chiangdao.com/nest* 🛏 *26 chalets* 🍴 *No Meals.*

Rim Doi Resort

$ | **RESORT** | *Rim Doi* means "on the edge of the mountain," so it's fitting that two extraordinary peaks loom over this peaceful little resort near Chiang Dao. After a day exploring the nearby caves or venturing into the mountains, it's just the place to relax and prepare for the journey farther north. **Pros:** open-air restaurant; pleasant walks on the grounds; well-stocked lake for perch fishing. **Cons:** rooms could use a refresh; staff has limited English-language skills; chalet accommodation is very basic. [$] *Rooms from: B850* ✉ *46 Moo 4 Muang Ghay, Chiang Dao* ☎ *052/010016* 🌐 *www.rimdoiresort.com* 🛏 *40 rooms* 🍴 *No Meals.*

Doi Ang Khang

60 km (36 miles) north of Chiang Dao.

Ang means "bowl," and that sums up the mountaintop location of this remote corner of Thailand. A tiny, two-street settlement shares the small valley with the orchards and gardens of a royal agricultural project, which grows temperate fruits and vegetables found nowhere else in Thailand.

GETTING HERE AND AROUND

From Chiang Dao take Highways 1178 and 1340 north to Doi Ang Khang. Local bus services connect the two towns, stopping in the center of Doi Ang Khang.

TIMING

Doi Ang Khang is for nature lovers, who tend to relax for a few days amid its orchards and gardens. It's a long drive from either Chiang Mai or Chiang Rai, so at least an overnight stay is recommended. There's no nightlife, however, and after 9 pm the small community is wrapped in slumber.

TOURS

Wandering Star and Bens Taxi offer private tours and day trips to Doi Ang Khang.

TRAVEL AGENCY Bens Taxi. ☎ *089/853–7527* 🌐 *www.benstaxiserviceandtours.com/.* **Wandering Star Tour.** ☎ *089/951–8996 mobile* 🌐 *wanderingstarchiangmai-tour.com/.*

Sights

Royal Agricultural Station Angkhang (*Doi Ang Khang*)

FARM/RANCH | A project of the royal family, this mountainside facility at 1,400 m (4,593 ft) elevation has both agricultural and political objectives. Developing new and more efficient farming practices is one goal; fruit, tea, and coffee research is another; and a third is to wean northern

Northern Thailand Then and Now

As late as 1939, northern Thailand was a semiautonomous region of Siam, with a history rich in tales of kings, queens, and princes locked in dynastic struggles and wars. The diversity of cultures you find here today is hardly surprising, because the ancestors of today's northern Thai people came from China, and the point where they first crossed the mighty Mekong River, Chiang Saen, became a citadel-kingdom of its own in around 773. Nearly half a millennium passed before the arrival of a king who was able to unite the citizens of the new realm of Lanna.

That fabled ruler, King Mengrai (1259–1317), established a dynasty that lasted two centuries. Mengrai's first capital was Chiang Rai, but at the end of the 13th century he moved his court south and in 1296 founded a new dynastic city, Chiang Mai. Two friendly rulers, King Ngarm Muang of Phayao and King Rama Kampeng of Sukhothai, helped him in the huge enterprise, and the trio sealed their alliance in blood, drinking from a chalice filled from their slit wrists. A monument outside the city museum in the center of Chiang Mai's Old City commemorates the event. Nearby, another monument marks the spot where King Mengrai died, in 1317, after being struck by lightning in one of the fierce storms that regularly roll down from the neighboring mountains.

Lanna power was weakened by waves of attacks by Burmese and Lao invaders, and for two centuries—from 1556 to the late 1700s—Lanna was virtually a vassal Burmese state. The capital was moved south to Lampang, where Burmese power was finally broken

and a new Lanna dynasty, the Chakri, was established under King Rama I.

Chiang Mai, nearby Lamphun (also at the center of Lanna-Burmese struggles), and Lampang are full of reminders of this rich history. Lampang's fortified Wat Lampang Luang commemorates with an ancient bullet hole the spot where the commander of besieging Burmese forces was killed.

To the north is Chiang Rai, a regal capital 30 years before Chiang Mai was built. This quieter, less-developed town is evolving into a base for exploring the country's northernmost reaches. In the far north Chiang Saen, site of the region's first true kingdom, is being excavated, its 1,000-year-old walls slowly taking shape again. Chiang Saen is on the edge of the fabled Golden Triangle. This mountainous region, bordered by Myanmar to the west and Laos to the east, was once ruled by the opium warlord Khun Sa, whose hometown, Ban Sop Ruak, has a magnificent museum that traces the story of the spread of narcotics.

Chiang Mai and Chiang Rai are ideal bases for exploring the hill tribe villages, where people live as they have for centuries. The communities closest to the two cities have been overrun by tourists, but if you strike out on your own with a good map, you may still find some that haven't become theme parks. Most of the villages are bustling crafts centers, where the colorful fabrics you see displayed in Bangkok shop windows take shape before your eyes. The elaborately costumed villagers sell their wares in the night markets of Chiang Mai and Chiang Rai.

farmers off opium production. Remote and fascinating, the station is beloved by bird-watchers for its numerous rare species, and there are many flower gardens. The orchards, gardens, and hothouses are open to the public, and at various times of the year you can buy pears, apples, plums, and peaches harvested on-site. ✉ *Off Hwy. 1249, Angkhang* ✣ *From Chiang Dao, north on Hwy. 1178, east and then north on Hwy. 1340, and north on Hwy. 1249* 🎟 *B50.*

Tha Ton

90 km (56 miles) north of Chiang Dao.

North of Chiang Dao lies the pretty resort town of Tha Ton, on the River Kok right across the border from Myanmar. The local temple, Wat Tha Ton, is built on a cliff overlooking the town. From the bridge below boats set off for trips on the River Kok, some of them headed for Chiang Rai, 130 km (81 miles) away.

Tha Ton is a pleasant base for touring this mountainous region. The 1089 and 1130 highways that run north, close to the Myanmar border, pass through villages that are more Chinese than Thai. The largest of these, Mae Salong, is on Highway 1234. Most of the Chinese in the area are descendants of the Nationalist forces who fled their homeland after the Communists' 1949 victory in the civil war that gave birth to the People's Republic of China. Based at first mostly in Burma, the Nationalists arrived in Chiang Rai Province in large numbers in the early 1960s. Many of these families have prospered cultivating tea, coffee, and fruit.

GETTING HERE AND AROUND

Six buses a day leave Chiang Mai's Chang Phuak station for the four-hour journey to Tha Ton. Fares range from B150 to B250. Boats leave Chiang Rai for the four-hour upstream journey to Tha Ton. The single fare is B350.

ESSENTIALS

TOURS AND ACTIVITIES

Maekok River Village Resort

For information about Tha Ton and its beautiful surroundings, inquire at this resort, where proprietors Bryan and Rosie Massingham are knowledgeable and helpful hosts. Their travel desk can arrange everything from on-site classes and activities lasting an hour or two to multiday off-site treks for guests and nonguests. ✉ *Tha Ton–Chiang Rai Rd., Tha Ton* ☎ *053/053628* 🌐 *www.maekok-river-village-resort.com.*

Hotels

Mae Salong Flower Hills Resort

$ | **RESORT** | The border hills of Myanmar lie just beyond the grounds of this resort hotel whose timber-built chalets have fine views of tea plantations and the surrounding mountains. **Pros:** tropical gardens; ceremonial teatime on the resort terrace; authentic Chinese food. **Cons:** long walk to village center; erratic bathroom plumbing; no nightlife. [$] *Rooms from: B1,000* ✉ *779 Moo 1, Doi Mae Salong Nok, Mae Salong* ☎ *053/765–4957, 091/850–6262* 🌐 *www.maesalongflowerhills.com* 🛏 *45 chalets* 🍴 *Free Breakfast.*

★ **Maekok River Village Resort**

$$ | **RESORT** | **FAMILY** | This remarkable resort, a combination of hotel and outdoor education center, is in a beautiful Kok River location with sweeping views of the winding waterway, rice paddies, maize fields, orchards, and mountains beyond. **Pros:** snug bar with open fireplace for winter evenings; friendly and knowledgeable British management; fine open-sided restaurant. **Cons:** some rooms are cramped; kids at the education center can be noisy; tour buses call regularly. [$] *Rooms from: B3,250* ✉ *333 Moo 4, Tha Ton* ☎ *053/053628* 🌐 *www.maekok-river-village-resort.com* 🛏 *36 rooms* 🍴 *Free Breakfast.*

Chiang Rai

180 km (112 miles) northeast of Chiang Mai, 780 km (485 miles) north of Bangkok.

Chiang Rai attracts more and more visitors each year. Many come for massive, modern, Wat Rong Khun, also known as the "White Temple" built by artist *Chalermchai Kositpipat. People also come to learn more about the* six hill tribes—the Akha, Yao, Meo, Lisu, Lahu, and Karen—that live within Chiang Rai Province. Each tribe has different dialects, customs, handicrafts, and costumes, and all still venerate animist spirits despite their increasing acquaintance with the outside world. You can learn about their cultures and lives at a museum in town, and as in Chiang Mai, they make daily journeys to the markets of Chiang Rai, where you can meet them and enjoy their handiwork. The best of the markets is a night bazaar, just off Phaholyothin Road, which has a cluster of small restaurants and food vendors.

Despite having luxury hotels and sufficient restaurants and bars to keep night owls happy, Chiang Rai comes off as quieter and less flashy than Chiang Mai, and therein many find its charm. It's also a city with far more greenery, a pleasant contrast to Chiang Mai.

■ TIP→ **Climbing to the top of Doi Tong, a modest hill on the northeastern edge of Chiang Rai, is a great way to learn the lay of the land.**

From the grounds of the 13th-century Wat Doi Tong, you'll have a fine view of the Mae Kok River and the mountains beyond.

GETTING HERE AND AROUND
AIR
Thai Airways has several daily flights from Bangkok to Chiang Rai. Chiang Rai International Airport is 6 km (4 miles) northeast of the city. Incoming flights are

Chiang Rai's Origins

Legend has it that a royal elephant ran away from its patron, the 13th-century king Mengrai, founder of the Lanna kingdom. The beast stopped to rest on the banks of the Mae Kok River. The king regarded this as an auspicious sign, and in 1256 built his capital, Chiang Rai, on the site. Little remains from those heady days: the Emerald Buddha that used to reside in Wat Phra Keo is now in Bangkok's Grand Palace, and a precious Buddha image in the 15th-century Wat Phra Singh has long since disappeared.

met by songthaews and tuk-tuks, whose drivers charge about B50 for the journey to central Chiang Rai.

BOAT AND FERRY
Longtail boats and rafts set off daily from Tha Ton for the 130-km (81-mile) trip downstream to Chiang Rai.

BUS
Chiang Rai is served by buses that leave regularly from Chiang Mai's two terminals. The trip takes from three to four hours and costs between B80 and B200. Buses to Chiang Rai also leave regularly between 8 am and 7:15 pm from Bangkok's Northern Bus Terminal (12 hours; from B600 to B700). Express buses (B180) leave hourly from Chiang Mai's Arcade Terminal.

CAR
Roads are well paved throughout the Golden Triangle, presenting no problem for drivers. The area is bisected by the main north-to-south road, Highway 110, and crisscrossed by good country roads. In Chiang Rai the most prominent car-rental companies are Avis, National, and Budget.

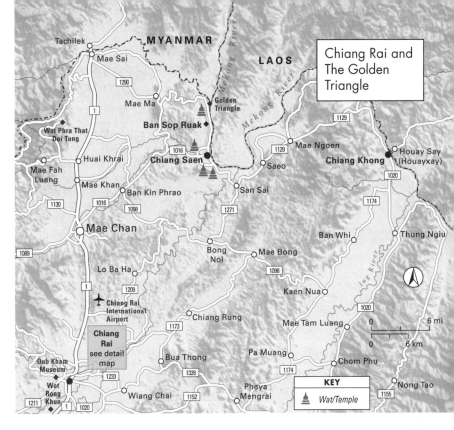

Chiang Rai and The Golden Triangle

TAXI AND TUK-TUK

Tuk-tuks are the common way of getting around Chiang Rai. A trip across town costs from B40 to B50. Songthaews can also be hailed on the street and hired for trips to outlying areas. The fare inside the city is B15. To go anywhere farther afield is a matter of negotiation.

Travel desks are found in all Chiang Rai hotels and they are generally efficient and reasonably priced.

ESSENTIALS
TIMING

Chiang Rai has few sights of note, so a leisurely walk around town will take at most a few hours. The city makes an ideal base for exploring the surrounding upland countryside and mountains, though, so a stay of at least two or three days is recommended.

TOURS

Chiang Rai is an excellent base from which to set out trekking through the nearby mountains or canoeing and rafting on the region's rivers.

Golden Triangle Tours

The major hotels in Chiang Rai and the Golden Triangle Resort in Chiang Saen organize minibus tours of the region, and the hotel travel desks will arrange treks to the hill tribe villages. ✉ 590 Phahol-yothin Rd., Chiang Rai ☏ 053/740478 ⊕ www.goldenchiangrai.com.

VISITOR INFORMATION
CONTACT Tourist Authority of Thailand (Chiang Rai). ✉ 448/16 Singhaklai Rd., Chiang Rai ☏ 053/744674, 053/717434 ⊕ www.tourismthailand.org/chiang-rai.

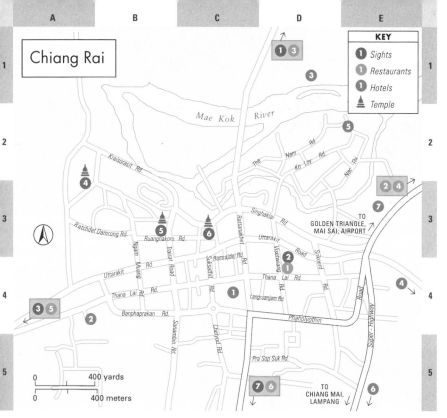

Chiang Rai

	A	B	C	D	E

KEY
- ① Sights
- ① Restaurants
- ① Hotels
- ▲ Temple

TO GOLDEN TRIANGLE, MAI SAI, AIRPORT

TO CHIANG MAI, LAMPANG

0 — 400 yards
0 — 400 meters

Sights

Baan Dam Museum (*The Black House*)
One of Thailand's most unusual architectural and artistic displays, the Baan Dam Museum, also known as the Black House, is essentially a vast outdoor art gallery, dominated by macabre and rather sinister imagery. It was conceived of by celebrated national artist Thawan Duchanee over the course of 36 years, and includes the work of a number of other artists. The sprawling compound has multiple buildings and artworks spread over the grounds, including monumental wood carvings, black thrones made of buffalo horns, and the artists' likeness transformed into Buddhist imagery. It's creepy and fascinating and is a stark contrast to the nearby White Temple. ⊠ *333 Moo 13 Nang-Lee, Muang* ⊕ *www. thawan-duchanee.com* ⊠ *B80.*

Hilltribe Museum & Education Center
HISTORY MUSEUM | The cultures, ways of life, and crafts of the many hill tribe people that populate the Chiang Rai region are explained with extensive displays at this exemplary museum in the city center. The museum also supports its own travel service, PDA Tour, which organizes visits to hill tribe villages under the motto "We don't support human zoos." ⊠ *PDA Bldg., 620/25 Thanalai Rd., 3rd fl., Chiang Rai* ☎ *053/719167* ⊕ *www. pdacr.org.*

Oub Kham Museum
HISTORY MUSEUM | Lanna history and culture are vividly chronicled at this jewel of a facility on the outskirts of Chiang Rai. The museum, in an attractive complex of historic buildings, displays several centuries' worth of local artifacts, including the throne and coronation robes of a 16th-century Lanna ruler. ⊠ *81/1 Rai Mai Luang Rd., Chiang Rai* ☎ *053/713349* ⊕ *www.oubkhammuseum.com/* ⊠ *B300.*

Wat Phrathat Doi Chom Thong
RELIGIOUS BUILDING | Near the summit of Doi Tong, this temple overlooks the Mae Kok River. The ancient pillar that stands here once symbolized the center of the universe for devout Buddhists. The sunset view is worth the trip. ⊠ *ArjAmnuay Rd, Chiang Rai.*

Wat Phra Kaew
RELIGIOUS BUILDING | The Emerald Buddha, which now sits in Thailand's holiest temple, Wat Phra Keo in Bangkok, is said to have been discovered when lightning split the chedi housing it at this similarly named temple at the foot of the Doi Tong in Chiang Rai. A Chinese millionaire financed a jade replica in 1991, and though it's not the real thing, the statuette is still strikingly beautiful. ⊠ *19 Trairat Rd., Chiang Rai.*

Wat Phra Singh
RELIGIOUS BUILDING | This 14th-century temple is worth visiting for its viharn, distinguished by some remarkably delicate wood carving and for colorful frescoes depicting the life of Lord Buddha. A sacred Indian Bhodhi tree stands in the peaceful temple grounds. ⊠ *Singhaclai Rd., Chiang Rai.*

★ **Wat Rong Khun (The White Temple)**
RELIGIOUS BUILDING | One of Thailand's most astonishing buildings, Wat Rong Khun stands like a glistening, sugar-coated wedding cake beside the A-1 Chiang Rai–Bangkok motorway south of Chiang Rai. Popularly called the White Temple because of its lustrous exterior, the extraordinary structure was built by internationally renowned Thai artist Chalermchai Kositpipat, assisted by a team of more than 40 young artists, craftsmen, and construction workers, as a Buddhist act of winning merit. The glistening effect comes from thousands of reflective glass mosaics set into the white stucco. In addition to the Buddhas, there are images from contemporary culture, including

Mae Salong Nok

[eye icon]

Visit this remote mountain village northwest of Chiang Rai, and you could be excused for believing you'd strayed over a couple of borders and into China. The one-street hamlet—the mountainside leaves no room for further expansion—is the home of the descendants of Chinese Nationalist troops who arrived here in the 1960s after spending a dozen or so years in Burma following the Communists' ascension to power in China. The settlers established orchards and tea and coffee plantations that now drape the mountainsides; in December and January, visitors crowd the slopes to admire the cherry blossoms and swaths of sunflowers. Stop in at any of the numerous tea shops for a pot of refreshing oolong. A local bus service runs from Chiang Rai to Mae Salong (the village's official Thai name is Santikhiri), and most Chiang Rai travel agents offer day tours for about B3,000.

spaceships and Superman. A songthaew ride to the temple from Chiang Rai costs about B50. ✉ *A-1 Chiang Rai–Bangkok motorway, Chiang Rai* ✥ *13 km (8 miles) south of Chiang Rai* 🎫 *Free.*

🍴 Restaurants

Cabbages & Condoms

$$ | **THAI** | Most of the modest price of your meal at this quirkily named restaurant, one of three in Thailand, goes toward the country's leading nongovernmental organization that specializes in HIV/AIDS education. The food is Thai, geared somewhat to Western tastes. **Known for:** fairly priced Thai food; condoms as parting gifts; lightly applied chilies. [$] *Average main: B220* ✉ *620/1 Thanalai Rd., City Center* ☎ *053/719167* 🌐 *www.cabbagesandcondoms.net/.*

Chivit Thamma Da

$$ | **THAI** | Classically trained baker Nattamon Holmberg puts an emphasis on slow and sustainable food at this cozy café on the Kok River that serves a mix of Western favorites like avocado toasts, along with Thai food. The prices are a little higher than other restaurants in Chiang Rai, but the quality of its locally sourced ingredients more than make up for it. **Known for:** art exhibitions and books you can borrow; draft beer of the month; a serious tea selection and expansive menu of Thai and Western food. [$] *Average main: B250* ✉ *179 Moo 2, Rim Kok, Chiang Rai* ☎ *053/166967* 🌐 *www.chivitthammada.com.*

Give Green Farm House Restaurant

$ | **THAI** | Although it's located right down the street from a major attraction (Thawan Duchanee's "Black House" museum), this family-run business keeps its prices low and its traditional dishes noticeably fresh and delicious. Much of what they make is straight off the Give Green Farm, and operates as a master class in sustainable comfort food. **Known for:** vegetarian options; organic without the sticker shock; farm-to-table fare that tastes like it. [$] *Average main: B40* ✉ *300 Moo 13, Chiang Rai* ☎ *081/090–1805.*

Leelawadee

$$ | **THAI** | The name of this attractive open-sided restaurant signifies the strongly perfumed frangipani trees that frame its riverside setting. The

gargantuan menu embraces Chinese, Thai, and Japanese cuisine, but the specialty is northern Thai food, including fresh fish from the Kok and Mae Kong rivers. **Known for:** its prime location; big crowds; frog legs and jellyfish for adventurous eaters. $ *Average main: B200* ✉ *58 Moo 19 Kaew Wai Rd., Chiang Rai* ☎ *053/600–0000, 089/999–8444* ⊕ *leela-wadeechiangrai.com.*

Moommai

$ | **THAI** | A garden panorama of ceramic dolls and other tiny figurines greets you at this enchanting restaurant, where the tables are distributed among the shrubs and ornamental trees. The locals love the place for its excellent lineup of northern Thai specialties and Chinese-influenced dishes. **Known for:** fantastic Lanna food; nightly folk music; laid-back vibes. $ *Average main: B150* ✉ *64 Sankhongluang Rd. Moo 16, Tambon Robwiang, Chiang Rai* ☎ *053/716416* ▭ *No credit cards.*

Toke Tong

$ | **THAI** | Chinese and northern Thai dishes dominate the extensive menu at this timber-built traditional restaurant in a lovely garden. They're known for *khantoke* dinners (northern Thai set meals, served on a tray) and their delicious khao soy noodles. **Known for:** intimate garden; set meals; spicy curries. $ *Average main: B150* ✉ *45/12 Phaholyothin Rd., Chiang Rai* ☎ *088/260–2069* ⊕ *www.toke-tong. com/* ▭ *No credit cards.*

Hotels

Baan Bua Guesthouse

$ | **B&B/INN** | This basic but comfortable homestay is a lovely garden oasis in the heart of Chiang Rai town. **Pros:** central location; lovely gardens; home feel. **Cons:** can be noisy at night; thin walls; some rooms could use an update. $ *Rooms from: 200* ✉ *879/2 Jetyod Rd., City*

Center ☎ *053/718880* ⊕ *baanbua-guest-house.business.site/* ¶◎¶ *No Meals* ⇦ *17 rooms* ▭ *No credit cards.*

Ben Guest House

$ | **B&B/INN** | This family-run inn has comfortable, reasonably priced accommodations that attract a backpacker crowd. **Pros:** pool; friendly staff with deep knowledge of the region; lively evening scene. **Cons:** young clientele can be noisy; least expensive rooms are very basic and have thin walls; 10- to 15-minute walk to town center. $ *Rooms from: B700* ✉ *351/10 San Khong Noi Soi 4, Chiang Rai* ☎ *053/716775* ⊕ *www.ben-guesthousechiangrai.com* ⇦ *30 rooms* ¶◎¶ *No Meals.*

Imperial River House Resort and Spa

$$ | **RESORT** | A large glass-enclosed lobby with high ceilings and a permanent art gallery sets the stylish tone at this riverside hotel. **Pros:** near the Blue Temple; tropical gardens and a picturesque swimming pool; spa treatments. **Cons:** breakfast is nothing special; far from town; some decor is a bit dated. $ *Rooms from: B3,780* ✉ *482 Moo 4 Mae Kok Rd., Muang, Chiang Rai* ☎ *053/750830* ⊕ *www.imperialriverhouse.com* ⇦ *36 rooms* ¶◎¶ *No Meals.*

Le Meridien

$$$ | **RESORT** | Large and luxurious, this hotel commands a stretch of the Mae Kok River and views of the northern mountain range. **Pros:** helpful tour desk; shuttle bus service until 10 pm; special activities like bonfires and yoga. **Cons:** slow room service; shabby neighborhood; limited breakfast options. $ *Rooms from: B5,780* ✉ *221/2 Moo 20 Kwaewai Rd., Chiang Rai* ☎ *053/603333* ⊕ *lemeridienchiangrai.com* ⇦ *159 rooms* ¶◎¶ *No Meals.*

8

Northern Thailand CHIANG RAI

Continued on page 377

THAILAND'S
HILL TRIBES

Thailand's hill tribes populate the remote, mountainous regions in the north. They welcome visitors, and their villages have become major attractions—some are even dependent on tourist dollars. But other villages, especially those that are harder to reach, have retained an authentic feel; a knowledgeable guide can take you to them.

Hill tribes are descendants of migratory peoples from Myanmar (Burma), Tibet, and China. There are at least 10 tribes living in northern Thailand, and they number a little over half a million, a mere 1% of Thailand's population. The tribes follow forms of ancestral worship and are animists: that is, they believe in a world of spirits that inhabit everything—rivers, forests, homes, and gardens. Historically, some tribes made a living by cultivating poppies for opium, but this practice has mostly died out.

Many tribespeople claim to be victims of official discrimination, and it is indeed often difficult for them to gain full citizenship. Although the Thai government has a program to progressively grant them citizenship, the lack of reliable documentation and the slow workings of the Bangkok bureaucracy are formidable obstacles. However, Thais normally treat hill tribe people with respect; in the Thai language they aren't called "tribes" but Chao Khao, which means "Owners of the Mountains."

Visiting the Chao Khao is a matter of debate. Some of the more accessible villages have become Disneyland-like, with tribespeople, clad in colorful costumes, who are eager to pose in a picture with you—and then collect your baht. In general, the farther afield you go, the more authentic the experience.

Even if you don't visit a village, you'll likely encounter tribespeople selling their crafts at markets in Chiang Mai, Chiang Rai, and Mae Hong Son.

The four tribes you're likely to encounter in northern Thailand are the Karen, Hmong, Akha, and Lisu.

(left) Long neck woman, Chiang Mai; (top) Akha girls wearing ornate headdresses.

KAREN

ORIGINS: Myanmar
POPULATION: 400,000
DID YOU KNOW? The famous "long necks" are actually the Paduang tribe, a subdivision of the Karen.
CRAFTS THEY'RE KNOWN FOR: weaving, beaded jewelry, handmade drums.

The majority of Thailand's hill tribe population is Karen, and there are an estimated 7 million of them living in Myanmar as well. The Karen are the most settled of the tribes, living in permanent villages of well-constructed houses and farming plots of land that leave as much of the forest as possible undisturbed. Though Karen traditionally hold Buddhist and animist beliefs, many communities follow Christianity, which missionaries introduced in colonial Burma.

(top) Karen woman weaving; (bottom) Padaung girls.

LONG NECKS

Traditionally, Paduang women have created the illusion of elongated necks—considered beautiful in their culture—by wrapping brass coils around them. The process begins when a girl is about 5 years old; she will add rings each year. The bands, which can weigh up to 12 lbs, push down on the collarbone, making the neck appear long.

Some human rights groups call the Paduang villages "human zoos" and say that you should not visit because tourism perpetuates the practice of wearing neck coils, which can be harmful. But, most of Thailand's Paduang are refugees who have fled worse conditions in Myanmar, and Thailand's three Paduang villages depend on tourism. Some Paduang women object not to tourism but to the fact that they earn as little as $50 a month from tour operators who profit handsomely. If you go, try to find an operator who treats the Paduang equitably.

HMONG

ORIGINS: China

POPULATION: 80,000

DID YOU KNOW? The Hmong wear elaborate silver lockets to keep their souls firmly locked into their bodies.

CRAFTS THEY'RE KNOWN FOR: needlework, batik, decorative clothing and headdresses.

At the night markets of Chiang Mai and Chiang Rai, you'll recognize Hmong women by their colorful costumes and heavy silver jewelry. There are two divisions of Hmong, White and Blue; White Hmong women wear baggy black pants and blue sashes, while Blue Hmong women wear knee-length pleated skirts. But the divisions "white" and "blue" don't refer to traditional Hmong costumes. "Blue" is a translation of the Hmong word "ntsuab," which also means "dark," a description given to a branch of Hmong whose members once practiced cannibalism. Hmong communities that rejected cannibalism were described as "dlawb," which means "innocent" or "white."

(right) Hmong children.

AKHA

ORIGINS: Tibet

POPULATION: 33,000

DID YOU KNOW? Akha villages are defined by a set of wooden gates, often decorated with charms meant to ward off evil spirits.

CRAFTS THEY'RE KNOWN FOR: silver belt buckles and bracelets, decorative hats and clothing, *saw oo* (fiddles).

The Akha once thrived on opium production, shielded from outside interference by the relative inaccessibility of the remote mountaintop sites they chose for their settlements. Today, all but the most remote communities grow alternative crops, such as rice, beans, and corn. They're a gentle, hospitable people whose women wear elaborate headdresses decorated with silver, beads, and feathers. Akha men wear hollow bracelets containing a silver bead, which they believe keeps them in touch with ancestral spirits.

Akha women wearing traditional headdresses.

LISU

ORIGINS: Tibet

POPULATION: 25,000

DID YOU KNOW? The Lisu pass their history from generation to generation in the form of a song.

CRAFTS THEY'RE KNOWN FOR: silver belt buckles, saw oo, large beaded hats.

Though they're not the most numerous, the businesslike Lisu are the tribe you're most likely to meet on day trips out of Chiang Mai and Chiang Rai. More than any other hill tribe, the Lisu have recognized the earning power of tourism. As tourist buses draw up, women scramble to change from their everyday clothes into the famous multicolored costumes they normally wear only on high days and holidays.

Lisu women.

THE SHAN

Though sometimes referred to as a hill tribe, the Shan, who live predominantly in Myanmar, are actually a large minority (there are an estimated 6 million) who have been fighting for their own state for decades. They have lived in the area for 1,000 years and are believed to be descendents of the Tai people, the original inhabitants of the region. The Shan who reside in Thailand have fled persecution in Myanmar. Unlike the hill tribes, the Shan are predominantly Buddhist. Shan craftspeople make some of the silver jewelry and ornaments you'll find at markets.

Shan woman wearing a traditional bamboo hat.

VISITING HILL TRIBE COMMUNITIES

(top) Akha woman with children; (bottom) Karen woman.

ETIQUETTE

Hill-tribe people tend to be conservative, so do follow a few simple guidelines on your visit.

- Dress modestly.
- Keep a respectful distance from religious ceremonies or symbols, and don't touch any talismans without asking first.
- Avoid loud or aggressive behavior and public displays of affection.
- Always ask permission before taking a person's picture.

TREKKING

Meeting and staying with tribespeople is one of the main attractions of trekking in northern Thailand. Some day trips include brief stops at villages, which are often little more than theme parks. But if you book a trek of three days or more you're sure to encounter authentic hill tribes living as they have for centuries.

Chao Khao are hospitable to westerners, often organizing spontaneous parties at which home-brewed rice whiskey flows copiously. If you stay overnight, you'll be invited to share the community's simple food and sleep on the floor in one of their basic huts.

Virtually all travel operators offer tours and treks to hill tribe villages. The **Mirror Foundation** (✉ *106 Moo 1, Ban Huay Khom, T. Mae Yao, Chiang Rai,* ☎ *053/737412* ⊕ *www.themirrorfoundation.org*), an NGO that works to improve the lives of hill tribes near Chiang Rai, can arrange culturally respectful tours. The foundation's current projects include bringing volunteer teachers to tribal villages and preventing the exploitation of hill tribe women and children.

■ TIP➔ **To avoid being taken to a tourist trap instead of an authentic village, ask the operator to identify the tribes you'll visit and to describe their culture and traditions.** It's a good sign if the operator can answer your questions knowledgeably; the information will also add greatly to the pleasure of your trip.

DAY TRIPS

You can also take daytrips to see hill tribes from Chiang Mai, Chiang Rai, or Mae Hong Son. The villages appear on few maps, so it's not advisable to set out on your own; a guide or driver who knows the region well is a better bet. You can easily hire one for about B1,000 per day; ask the TAT in Chiang Mai or Chiang Rai for recommendations.

Several Chiang Mai operators offer "three country" one-day tours of the Golden Triangle: a boat trip to a Laotian island in the Mekong River; a brief shopping trip to the tax-free Myanmar border town of Tachilek; and a stop at a Thai hill tribe village on the way home. The fare of B800 to B1,000 includes lunch. These tours are likely to feel fairly touristy.

SHOPPING FOR HILL TRIBE CRAFTS

Embroidered textiles at a market near Chiang Mai.

Over the past few decades, the Thai royal family has worked with the government to wean hill tribe farmers off cultivating opium poppies. One initiative has been financing workshops for manufacturing traditional handicrafts, such as basketry, weaving, and woodworking. Some of these royal projects, located near hill tribe villages, offer both employment and on-site training. The workshops also prevent the crafts from dying out and create a market for products that were originally only distributed within the tribal communities.

WORKSHOPS

The Doi Tung mountain, 40 km (25 mile) north of Chiang Rai, is home to 26 hill tribe villages as well as the **Doi Tung Development Project** (⊕ *www. maefahluang.org* and ⊕ *www.doitung. com*), a royal project based at the late Queen Mother's former summer palace. The tribes living in the mountain villages produce handicrafts; the project workshops also employ hill tribe craftsmen and women. Both the villages and the project welcome visitors. Tribespeople sell crafts at a shop and at stalls on the grounds.

Though it's not for the faint of heart, a very curvy 16-km (10-mile) road leads to the top of Doi Tung from the village of Huai Krai, 20 km (12 mile) south of Mae Sai via Highway 101. Local buses and songthaews from Huai Krai will take you here; you can also hire a driver or a guide.

MARKETS & STORES

Although hill tribe crafts are abundant at the night markets in Chiang Mai, Chiang Rai, and Mae Hong Son, serious collectors prefer government-run stores whose products come with certificates of authenticity. Prices are fixed at these stores but are comparable to what you'll pay at markets (upscale hotel boutiques, however, inflate prices substantially). Expect to pay at least B500 for a silver ring or belt buckle and as much as B2,500 for a bracelet or necklace; around B300 for a meter of woven cloth; and B300 to 400 for a simple wooden instrument like a bamboo flute.

★ The Legend

$$$ | RESORT | Large, tastefully furnished rooms, vast bathrooms, secluded terraces, an open-air gourmet restaurant, and unrestricted views of the distant mountains make it easy for The Legend to live up to its name. **Pros:** reliable airport pickup; elegant and peaceful; impeccably designed. **Cons:** city center is a 10-minute drive away; standard rooms have no bathtubs; confusing signposting can make it difficult to find your room at night. $ *Rooms from: B4,410* ⊠ *124/15 Kohloy Rd., Amphoe Muang, Chiang Rai* ☎ *053/910400* ⊕ *www.thelegend-chiangrai.com* ⊃ *76 rooms* ⧍ *No Meals.*

The Mantrini

$$ | HOTEL | Only the tropical vegetation hints that this highly stylish, modern hotel is in Thailand and not a boutique establishment in central Milan or Munich. **Pros:** friendly staff; beautifully designed; shady pool area. **Cons:** noisy bars nearby; drab neighborhood; 5-minute drive to city center. $ *Rooms from: B2,400* ⊠ *292/13 Moo 13, Chiang Rai* ☎ *053/601555* ⊕ *www.mantrini.com* ⧍ *No Meals* ⊃ *63 rooms.*

Rasa Boutique Hotel

$ | HOTEL | Rich hues, warm lighting, and grand Moroccan architectural flourishes set a distinctly exotic tone at this boutique hotel well away from the city center. **Pros:** romantic setting; secluded swimming pool; good restaurant. **Cons:** far from city center; shabby neighborhood; noisy at night. $ *Rooms from: B1,500* ⊠ *789/7 Phaholyothin Rd., Chiang Rai* ☎ *053/717454* ⊕ *www.rasaboutiquehotelchiangrai.com* ⧍ *Free Breakfast* ⊃ *30 rooms.*

Nightlife

Bear Grill

BARS | Slightly off the main drag, this bar is part beer house and part hot-pot restaurant, though the main attraction is the imported beer, on top and in bottles. ⊠ *869, 138 Thai Viwat Alley, Chiang Rai* ☎ *062/526–9666.*

Reggae Home & Bar

BARS | This relaxed temple to all things reggae sums up Chiang Rai's laid-back attitude. Whether you're playing Jenga with strangers, listening to a live band, or talking to the friendly Rastafarian owner, this is the perfect place to spend a chill evening. ⊠ *869/39 Thai Viwat Alley, Chiang Rai* ☎ *087/273–1432.*

Shopping

There's a good **night market** on Robviang Nongbua Road—although it's much smaller than the one in Chiang Mai, there are lots of handicrafts and textiles for sale, including modern boutiques like Dek Ban Suan's home decor shop El Jardin. A central section of Thanalai Road is closed to traffic on Saturday nights for a "walking street" market, and San Khon Noi Road becomes a pedestrian-only area for a Sunday market.

Doy Din Dang Pottery

Head out 12 km (7.4 mi) north of the city center to the serene, Japanese-influenced ceramics studio of Chiang Rai native Somluk Pantibooner to browse the lovely traditional and contemporary stoneware bowls, cups, teapots, vases, and original art pieces. The studio was established in 1991 and there's a café and small exhibition space. Want a closer look at northern Thailand's burgeoning art scene beyond all those cups, bowls, and plates? Stop at the Art Bridge gallery that Pantiboon co-founded on the way back

Doi Tung

If you're traveling north from Chiang Rai on Highway 110, watch for the left-hand turn at Km 32 that will take you to Doi Tung. The road winds 42 km (26 miles) to the summit, where an astonishing view opens out over the surrounding countryside. The temple here, Wat Phra That Doi Tung, founded more than a millennium ago, is said to be the repository of some important relics of Lord Buddha, including a collarbone. The shrine attracts pilgrims from as far away as India and China, for whom its huge Chinese Buddha figure is an important symbol of good fortune. On the mountain slopes below the temple is the summer home built for the king's late mother. The fine mansion is closed to the public, but the gardens, an explosion of color in all seasons, are open unless particularly important guests are staying.

into town. ⊠ *Rte. 1, Chiang Rai* ✛ *About 6 km (3.7 mi) north of the airport* ☎ *081/764–3205* ⊕ *www.facebook.com/doydindangpotter/* ⊙ *Closed Sun.*

Activities

BOATING

For a little something adventurous, catch a bus to the border town of Tha Ton where you can board a high-powered longtail boat and ride the rapids 130 km (81 miles) to Chiang Rai. Boats leave from a pier near the town bridge at noon and take about three to four hours to negotiate the bends and rapids of the river, which passes through thick jungle and past remote hill tribe villages. The single fare is B350. For a more leisurely ride to Chiang Rai, you can take a raft, which takes two days and nights to reach the city, overnighting in hill tribe villages. Fares start at B1,000.

◼ TIP→ **Take bottled water and a hat or umbrella to shade you from the sun.**

The best time to make the trip is during October and November, when the water is still high but the rainy season has passed.

Bamboo Tours
BOATING | ⊠ *22 Moo 18 Tambol Wiang, Chiang Rai* ☎ *086/115–3980* ⊕ *www.facebook.com/bambootrekkingtour.*

Coconuts Tours
BOATING | ⊠ *1016/2 Jed-Yod Rd., Chiang Rai* ☎ *080/677–0375* ⊕ *www.coconutstourschiangrai.com/.*

HIKING

Phu Sang National Park
Some 90 km (56 miles) east of Chiang Rai is the region's most beautiful national park, Phu Sang, which has one of Thailand's rarest natural wonders, cascades of hot water. The temperature of the 85-foot-high falls never drops below 33°C (91°F), and a nearby pool is even warmer. The park has some spectacular caves and is crisscrossed by nature trails teeming with bird life. One hour's drive north lies the mountainous border with Laos, straddled by 5,730-foot-high Phu Chee Fah, a favorite destination for trekkers and climbers. You reach Phu Sang National Park via Thoeng, 70 km (43 miles) east of Chiang Rai on Highway 1020. The park rents cabins for B500 a night. Entrance to the park costs B100, and B30 for a vehicle. ⊠ *National Hiwy. 1093 Phu Sang, Chiang Rai* ☎ *093/293–5099.*

Chiang Saen

59 km (37 miles) north of Chiang Rai, 239 km (149 miles) northeast of Chiang Mai, 935 km (581 miles) north of Bangkok.

A one-road town on the banks of the Mekong River, Chiang Saen was home to the future King Mengrai, who built a citadel here in the 12th century. Two ancient chedis are all that remain standing to remind the visitor of Chiang Saen's ancient glory, but government-financed excavation is gradually uncovering evidence of the citadel. The ancient flooring and walls that have been exposed are providing tantalizing clues about one of the region's first royal palaces. Little of the citadel survived the incursion by the Burmese in 1588, and the remaining fragments were ravaged by fire when the last of the Burmese were ousted in 1786.

The embarkation point for river trips to Myanmar, Laos, and China, Chiang Saen is being developed as a major Mekong River port.

GETTING HERE AND AROUND

Two buses daily run between Chiang Mai's Chang Phuak bus station and Chiang Saen, taking 4½ hours. The fare is about B150; buses stop in the center of town and at the boat piers. Songthaews provide the local transportation. Rides cost B20.

TIMING

Chiang Saen is an ideal base from which to explore the Golden Triangle, so plan on staying two or three days—longer if the town's ancient ruins and museum attract your interest.

Sights

National Museum

HISTORY MUSEUM | Next door to Wat Phra That Luang, the National Museum exhibits artifacts from the Lanna period, as well as some Neolithic discoveries. The museum also has a good collection of carvings and traditional handicrafts from the hill tribes. ✉ *Chiang Saen Rd. to Chiang Rai, 1 km (½ mile) from town center* ☎ *053/777102* 🌐 *www.museumthailand.com/en/museum/Chiang-Saen-National-Museum* 🎟 *B100* 🕒 *Closed Mon. and Tues.*

Wat Pa Sak

RELIGIOUS BUILDING | The name of this wat, Chiang Saen's oldest chedi, refers to the 300 *ton sak* (teak trees) planted in the surrounding area. The stepped temple, which narrows to a spire, is said to enshrine holy relics brought here in the 1320s, when the city was founded by King Saen Phu. The chedi itself predates that, however; it was built by Phu in 1295, right around the arrival of Lanna's first ruler—and Phu's grandfather—King Mangrai. ✉ *Chiang Saen.*

Wat Phra That Luang

RELIGIOUS BUILDING | Some scholars attribute this imposing octagonal wat inside Chiang Saen's city walls to its founder and namesake, King Saen Phu (1325–34), though others speculate that it predates him. Regardless of where its roots lie, Wat Phra That Luang is the tallest religious building in the Chiang Rai region, reaching towards the heavens at 88 meters high right next to the National Museum. ✉ *Chiang Saen.*

Hotels

Athita

$$ | **HOTEL** | This chic and sleek designer property takes a modern approach to local architecture with terra-cotta bricks framing the mostly teak wood house, and the interior sprinkled with mid-century furnishings. **Pros:** free parking; short walk to the river; helpful and friendly staff. **Cons:** Ban Sop Ruak a 15-minute drive away; street noise; no transportation. [$] *Rooms from: 3,500* ✉ *984 Wiang, Chiang Saen* ☎ *063/426–9464* 🌐 *athitahotel.com* 🍴 *Free Breakfast* 🛏 *9 rooms.*

Viang Yonok
$ | **HOTEL** | Although it's not a well-oiled machine like nearby resorts from the Four Seasons and Anantara, this small husband-and-wife-run hotel offers laid-back luxury at a fraction of the price. **Pros:** free kayaks, bikes, and surprisingly strong Wi-Fi; discounts for extended stays; luxury that doesn't require a bank loan. **Cons:** hosts are hospitable but can feel like they're hovering over you; far from other food options; not as lavish as its corporate competitors. [$] *Rooms from: B1,200* ✉ *201 Moo 3, Dtumbon Yonok, Chiang Saen* ☎ *053/650444, 081/862–8727* 🌐 *www.viangyonok.com* 🛏 *6 bungalows* 🍴 *No Meals.*

Ban Sop Ruak

8 km (5 miles) north of Chiang Saen.

The borders of Myanmar, Thailand and Laos meet at Ban Sop Ruak, a scenic village in the heart of the Golden Triangle with views over the confluence of the Mae Sai, Ruak, and Mekong rivers. This was once the domain of the opium warlord Khun Sa, until Thai and Burmese troops pushed him out in 1996. He spent the remaining years until his death in 2007 under house arrest in Yangon, where he lived comfortably in the company of a personal seraglio of four young Shan women. His picaresque reputation still draws those eager to see evidence of the man who once held the region under his thumb.

This simple riverside town has one main street, 1 km (½ mile) in length, that winds along the southern bank of the Mekong River. It's lined with stalls selling souvenirs and textiles from Laos. Waterfront restaurants serve fresh catfish and provide vantage points for watching the evening sun dip over the mountains to the west.

GETTING HERE AND AROUND

Songthaews (about B50) are the only transport service from Chiang Saen to Ban Sop Ruak. A taxi service is operated by Golden Shan Travel (*587 Ban Sop Ruak High St. 053/784198*), which also offers tours of the Golden Triangle, Mae Salong, Doi Tung, and hill tribe villages for B3,000 and B3,500.

TIMING

Ban Sop Ruak is the Golden Triangle, with enough points of interest to warrant a stay of at least two or three days. The Hall of Opium alone is extensive enough to take up a whole day, and boat trips to Laos beckon.

Sights

★ **Hall of Opium**
OTHER MUSEUM | The magnificent Hall of Opium is a white stucco, glass, marble, and aluminum building nestled in a valley above the Mekong. The site is so close to former poppy fields that a plan is still being considered to extend the complex to encompass an "open-air" exhibit of a functioning opium plantation. The museum traces the history of the entire drug trade, including a look at how mild stimulants like coffee and tea took hold in the West. It even attempts to give visitors a taste of the "opium experience" by leading them through a long tunnel where atmospheric music wafts between walls bearing phantasmagoric bas-relief scenes. The synthetic smell of opium was originally pumped into the tunnel but the innovation was dropped after official complaints. It's an arresting introduction to an imaginatively designed and assembled exhibition, which reaches back into the murky history of the opium trade and takes a long look into a potentially darker future. ✉ *Hall of Opium Golden Triangle Park, Ban Sop Ruak* ☎ *053/784–4446* 🌐 *www.maefahluang.org* 🎟 *B200* 🕒 *Closed Mon.*

House of Opium

OTHER MUSEUM | Opium is so linked to the history of Ban Sop Ruak that the small town now has two museums devoted to the subject. This smaller one is in the center of town. A commentary in English details the growing, harvesting, and smoking of opium. Many of the exhibits, such as carved teak opium boxes and jade and silver pipes, are fascinating. *✉ 212 Moo 1, Wiang Subdistrict, Ban Sop Ruak ☎ 053/784060 🎫 B50.*

🍴 Restaurants

Mekong Pizza

$$ | PIZZA | This laid-back pizza spot where the tables are laid with checkered tablecloths is a welcome break from all the fancy resort dining options in the Sop Ruak area. The crispy, thin-crust pies are topped with traditional and Thai ingredients ranging from pepperoni and Parma ham to a tom yum–tinged seafood and northern-style sausage. **Known for:** a prime location near both opium museums; inventive flavor combos and custom pies; baked-to-order cookies for dessert. *[$] Average main: B250 ✉ 301/5 Rt. 1290, Ban Sop Ruak ☎ 083/915–4750 🌐 www.mekongpizza.com ⏲ Closed Mon. 💳 No credit cards.*

Sala Mae Nam

$$$ | THAI | The Anantara resort's main breakfast buffet room turns into a reputable Thai restaurant during the lunch and dinner hour, offering northern specialities like *khao soi, geang ho* (dry curry pork with glass noodles and vegetables), and a duo of dips made with minced pork and green chilies. **Known for:** full-bodied flavors; surreal elephant spottings; open-air dining. *[$] Average main: B390 ✉ 229 Moo 1 Weng, Chiang Saen ☎ 053/784084 🌐 www.anantara.com/en/golden-triangle-chiang-rai/restaurants/sala-mae-nam.*

🛏 Hotels

★ Anantara Golden Triangle Elephant Camp & Resort

$$$$ | RESORT | The Anantara is one of the Golden Triangle's greatest hits, a symphony of styles created by Thailand's leading interior designer and architect, Bill Bensley. **Pros:** service on par with the rest of Anantara's five-star portfolio; stunning place to stay; peerless views from nearly every vantage point. **Cons:** isolated from village center; access to some rooms involves much stair climbing; steep bar prices. *[$] Rooms from: B43,200 ✉ 229 Moo 1, Ban Sop Ruak ☎ 053/784084, 02/476–0022 in Bangkok 🌐 goldentriangle.anantara.com 🛏 61 rooms 🍴 All-Inclusive.*

★ Four Seasons Tented Camp Golden Triangle

$$$$ | RESORT | Set near the borders of Laos and Burma, and about a 90-minute drive from Chiang Rai, this property is an unparalleled member of the Four Seasons portfolio, with sixteen tents spread around the edges of a riverside bamboo jungle and designed to evoke luxury safaris. **Pros:** luxury with a touch of adventure; up-close experiences with humanely treated elephants; wonderful regional activities. **Cons:** some tents may not be suitable for guests with mobility issues; location is a bit remote (requires car and boat rides); the occasional creepy-crawler. *[$] Rooms from: B75,000 ✉ 499 Moo 1 Tambon Wiang, Chiang Saen ☎ 053/910200 🌐 www.fourseasons.com/goldentriangle 🍴 All-Inclusive ☞ 2-night stay minimum 🛏 16 rooms.*

Imperial Golden Triangle Resort

$$ | HOTEL | It's all about the views at this high-eaved, Lanna-style hotel, where the rooms and restaurant have magnificent vistas of three rivers rushing together. **Pros:** spectacular sunsets over the Mekong; excellent travel service; pleasant restaurant terrace. **Cons:** service staff can be offhand; poor language skills; many rooms involve flights of stairs. $ *Rooms from: B3,025* ✉ *222 Ban Sop Ruak, Ban Sop Ruak* ☎ *053/784001* ⊕ *www.imperialgoldentriangleresort.com* ⇥ *73 rooms* ❖ *No Meals.*

Activities

Longtail excursion boats

BOAT TOURS | Longtail excursion boats captained by experienced rivermen tie up at the Ban Sop Ruak jetty, and the B500 fee covers a 90-minute cruise into the waters of Laos and a stop at a Laotian market. ✉ *Ban Sop Ruak.*

Chiang Khong

64 km (40 miles) east of Ban Sop Ruak, 53 km (33 miles) northeast of Chiang Rai.

Chiang Khong is a convenient overnight stop before heading across the river to Houay Say (Houayxay), in Laos, where daily boats set off for the two-day trip to the World Heritage town of Luang Prabang in Laos. Chiang Khong itself has little to attract the visitor apart from the magnificent vistas from the riverside towpath to the hills of Laos across the Mekong. The town's one 300-year-old temple has an interesting Chiang Saen–style chedi but is in need of repair. Textiles from China and Laos can be bought cheaply in Chiang Khong's market.

GETTING HERE AND AROUND

The paved road east out of Chiang Saen parallels the Mekong River for much of the way en route to Chiang Khong and a halfway point commands a magnificent view of the wide river valley far below. A refreshment stall and tables cater to thirsty travelers. Songthaews ply the route for about B100, but you can also hire a speedboat (B500) to go down the river, a thrilling three hours of slipping between the rocks and rapids. Not too many tourists make the journey,

especially to villages inhabited by the local Hmong and Yao tribes. The rugged scenery along the Mekong River is actually more dramatic than that of the Golden Triangle.

ESSENTIALS

TIMING

Chiang Khong is the official border crossing to Laos, and few visitors linger longer than one night, waiting for the Mekong River ferry.

TOURS

Chiang Khong is the embarkation point for the Laotian pier where boats for Luang Prabang are moored. Most Chiang Khong guesthouses have travel desks where tickets for the river cruise to the Laotian World Heritage site can be bought.

Restaurants

7he Vow

$ | **CAFÉ** | This trendy riverside café has an extensive menu of Thai and international foods, homemade baked goods, and the best local coffee. They also sell housemade and locally sourced items including tall bottles of wild honey and bags of lightly roasted Thai coffee beans. **Known for:** fresh-baked bagels; all-day breakfast; its sister hostel Sleeping Well. $ *Average main: B100* ✉ *10/8 Moo 8, Chiang Khong* ☎ *088/600–0599.*

Hotels

Nam Khong Riverside Hotel

$ | **HOTEL** | This hotel edges the south bank of the Mekong River, and most of the rooms—which are decorated in northern Thai style, using local woods and fabrics—have unobstructed views to the hills of Laos on the other side. **Pros:** rooftop Thai and European restaurant; central location; helpful travel desk can organize boat trips to Luang Prabang. **Cons:** traffic noise; drab neighborhood; small bathrooms. $ *Rooms from:*

B1,000 ✉ 174–176 Moo 8, Wiang Sub-district, Chiang Khong ☎ 053/791796, 053/791801 🌐 www.namkhongriverside.com 🍴 Free Breakfast 🛏 40 rooms.

Sleeping Well

$ | HOTEL | The hostel attached to the 7he Vow café is bright and modern and has room types for every budget, from shared bunk-bed rooms to suites with terraces and private bathrooms. **Pros:** close to the river; variety of room options; lively area. **Cons:** some rooms have shared bathrooms; hostel rooms are pretty basic; it's in the center of the action so expect some street noise. *[$] Rooms from: 700 ✉ 108/8 Moo 8 Wiant, Chiang Khong ☎ 097/280–4040 🍴 No Meals 🛏 12 rooms.*

Sukhothai

293 km (180 miles) southeast of Chiang Mai, 427 km (265 miles) north of Bangkok.

Most people come to Sukhothai to see the astounding, extensive ruins of the kingdom that flourished here in the mid 13th to 14th centuries—it's probably the most-visited ancient site in Thailand. The name Sukhothai means "the dawn of happiness" and this period is often referred to as the golden age of Thai civilization, when Thai art and architecture flourished.

The Sukhothai Historic Park has more than 190 ruins, spread across a 70-square-km (27-square-mile) area. It's divided into five zones. The central zone—the most visited—is the site of the royal palace (now collapsed) and the spiritual center, Wat Mahathat. Because the park is so large it's best explored by bicycle.

New Sukhothai, where all intercity buses arrive, is a quiet town where most inhabitants are in bed by 11 pm. Its many guesthouses are a magnet for tourists coming to see the ruins. New Sukhothai's night market is sleepy by the region's standards—don't expect much of an urban cultural experience here. If you've come specifically to visit the Historical Park, seek accommodation at one of the guesthouses or hotels that ring the Old City, rather than making the uncomfortable B50 songthaew or samlor journey there every day from the newer part of town.

GETTING HERE AND AROUND

AIR

Bangkok Airways flies daily from Bangkok to Sukhothai Airport, which is north of town. The airline owns and operates the airport and is its exclusive occupant. You can also fly into Phitsanulok Airport. Served by Nok Air, Thai, and Asian, that airport is 72 km (45 miles) southeast of Sukhothai.

CONTACTS Sukhothai Airport. *✉ Sawankhalok ⊕ 31 km (19 miles) north of Sukhothai, off Hwy. 1195 ☎ 02/134–3960 🌐 www.sukhothaiairport.com/.*

BICYCLE

Because the sights are so spread out, getting around by bike is a great way to explore the Historical Park; you can rent one for about B40 a day from outlets opposite the entrance.

BUS

Buses to Sukhothai depart from Bangkok's Northern Bus Terminal (Mo Chit) daily from 7 am to 11 pm, leaving roughly every 20 minutes. There are five main companies to choose from, but all charge about the same, most with prices under B300. One company, Win Tours, operates "super VIP" buses that offer comfort and service comparable to business-class air travel. The journey takes about seven hours. Buses from Sukhothai's new bus terminal on the bypass road depart at the same times and for the same prices.

Continued on page 392

THE BUDDHA IN THAILAND

Buddhism plays a profound role in day-to-day Thai life. Statues of the Buddha are everywhere: in the country's 30,000 *wats* (temples), in sacred forest caves, in home shrines, and in cafés and bars. Each statue is regarded as a direct link to the Buddha himself and imparts its own message—if you know what to look for.

by Howard Richardson

The origins of Buddhism lie in the life of the Indian prince Siddhartha Gautama (563 BC– 483 BC), who became the Buddha (which simply means "awakened"). Statues of the Buddha follow ancient aesthetic rules. The Buddha must be wearing a monastic robe, either covering both shoulders or leaving the right shoulder bare. His body must display sacred marks, or laksanas, such as slender toes and fingers, a full, lion-like chest, and long eyelashes. Many statues also have elongated earlobes, a reminder of the Buddha's original life as a prince, when he wore heavy earrings. Buddha statues are in one of four positions: sitting, standing, walking, or reclining.

Statues of the Buddha have their hands arranged in a mudra or hand position. The mudras, which represent the Buddha's teachings or incidents in his life, were created by his disciples, who used them to enhance their meditation. There are about 100 mudras, but most are variations on six basic forms.

Reclining Buddha,
Wat Po, Bangkok.

Detail of Reclining Buddha's head.

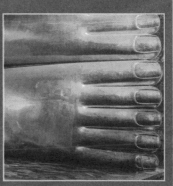
Detail of top of Reclining Buddha's feet.

Detail of bottom of Reclining Buddha's foot.

WHAT THE BUDDHA TAUGHT

Gautama taught that there are three aspects to existence: *dukkha* (suffering), *anicca* (impermanence), and *anatta* (the absence of self). He believed that unfulfilled desire for status, self-worth, and material possessions creates dukkha, but that such desire is pointless because anicca dictates that everything is impermanent and cannot be possessed. Therefore, if we can learn to curb desire and cultivate detachment, we will cease to be unhappy.

The ultimate goal of Buddhism is to reach enlightenment or nirvana, which is basically the cessation of struggle—this happens when you have successfully let go of all desire (and by definition, all suffering). This signals the end to *samsara,* the cycle of reincarnation that Buddhists believe in. Buddhists also believe in karma, a law of cause and effect that suggests that your fate in this life and future lives is determined by your actions. Among the ways to improve your karma—and move toward nirvana—are devoting yourself to spirituality by becoming a monk or a nun, meditating, and *tham boon,* or merit making. Making offerings to the Buddha is one form of tham boon.

Thai painting of monks listening to the Buddha speak at a temple.

THE MIDDLE WAY

Gautama's prescription for ending dukkha is an attitude of moderation towards the material world based on wisdom, morality, and concentration. He broke this threefold approach down further into eight principles, called the Noble Eightfold Path or the Middle Way.

Wisdom:

Right Understanding: to understand dukkha and its causes.

Right Thought: to resist angry or unkind thoughts and acts.

Morality:

Right Speech: to avoid lying, speaking unkindly, or engaging in idle chatter.

Right Action: to refrain from harming or killing others, stealing, and engaging in sexual misconduct.

Right Livelihood: to earn a living peacefully and honestly.

Concentration:

Right Effort: to work towards discipline and kindness, abandoning old, counterproductive habits.

Right Mindfulness: to be aware of your thoughts, words, and actions; to see things as they really are.

Right Concentration: to focus on wholesome thoughts and actions (often while meditating.)

Did You Know?

Burmese invaders damaged many Buddha statues when they sacked Ayutthaya in 1767. The head of one statue became lodged in the roots of a tree at Wat Phra Mahathat, where it remains today.

THE BUDDHA'S POSITIONS

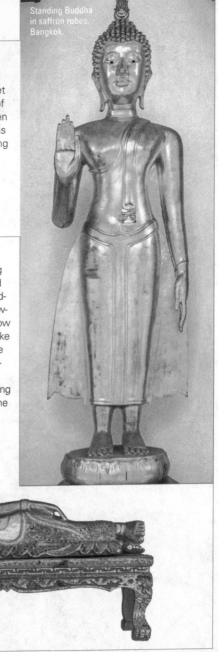

Standing Buddha in saffron robes, Bangkok.

STANDING

The Buddha stands either with his feet together or with one slightly in front of the other. The standing posture is often accompanied by certain hand positions to signify driving away fear or appealing to reason.

⇨ Wat Phra Mahathat, Sukhothai; Wat Benjamabophit, Bangkok.

RECLINING

Many scholars believe that reclining sculptures depict the Buddha dying and simultaneously reaching nirvana. According to another story, the Buddha is showing a proud giant who has refused to bow to him that he can lie down and still make himself appear larger than the giant. The Buddha then took the giant to the heavens and showed him angels that made the Buddha himself appear small, teaching the giant that there are truths beyond the realm of our own experience.

⇨ Wat Po, Bangkok.

Reclining Buddha ornament.

In Focus | THE BUDDHA IN THAILAND

SITTING

Seated Buddhas are the most common. The Buddha can sit in three different postures: adamantine or lotus, with legs crossed and feet resting on opposite thighs; heroic, a half-lotus position with one leg folded over the other; or western, with legs hanging straight down, as if sitting in a chair.

⇨ Wat Suthat, Bangkok (heroic style).

THE LAUGHING BUDDHA

The Laughing Buddha, whose large belly and jolly demeanor make him easy to recognize, is a folkloric character based on a 9th century Chinese monk known for his kindness. The Laughing Buddha does not figure into Thai Buddhism but you may see him at temples in Bangkok's Chinatown. And because he represents good fortune and abundance, some Thai shops sell Laughing Buddhas as lucky charms. Laughing Buddha statues often carry sacks full of sweets to give to children.

Seated Buddha, Wat Suthat, Bangkok.

WALKING

Walking statues represent the Buddha going into the community to spread his teachings. Traditionally, walking Buddhas were constructed in relief. The first walking-Buddha statues were created in Sukhothai, and you can still see a few in the city's ruins.

⇨ Wat Sra Sri, Sukhothai and Wat Phra Phai Luang, Sukhothai.

Walking Buddhas, Wat Phra Mahathat, Sukhothai.

WHAT DO THE BUDDHA'S HANDS MEAN?

MEDITATION

The Buddha's hands are in his lap, palms pointing upwards. This position represents a disciplined mind.

⇨ National Museum, Bangkok; Phra Pathom Chedi, Nakhon Pathom.

SETTING THE WHEEL IN MOTION

In this mudra, the Buddha's thumbs and forefingers join to make a circle, representing the Wheel of Dharma, a symbol for Buddhist law.

⇨ Cloisters of Wat Benjamabophit, Bangkok; Phra Pathom Chedi, Nakhon Pathom.

REASONING

This posture, which signifies the Buddha's preference for reason and peace rather than hasty or thoughtless action, is similar to the absence of fear mudra, but the Buddha's thumb and forefinger are touching to form a circle.

⇨ Cloisters of Wat Benjamabophit, Bangkok; Sukhothai Historical Park.

IN FOCUS | THE BUDDHA IN THAILAND

THE BUDDHA IN THAILAND

SUBDUING MARA

Mara is a demon who tempted the Buddha with visions of beautiful women. In this posture, the Buddha is renouncing these worldly desires. He sits with his right hand is on his right thigh, fingers pointing down, and his left hand palm-up in his lap.

⇨ Wat Suthat, Bangkok; Wat Mahathat, Sukhothai; Phra Pathom Chedi, Nakhon Pathom.

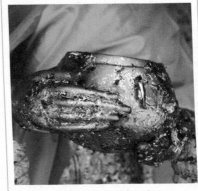

Hand and alms bowl detail; Nakhon Pathom Chedi, Nakon Pathom.

CHARITY

Buddhas using this mudra are usually standing, with their right arm pointing down, palm facing out, to give or receive offerings. In some modern variations, the Buddha is actually holding an alms bowl.

⇨ National Museum, Bangkok.

ABSENCE OF FEAR

One or both of the Buddha's arms are bent at the elbow, palms facing out and fingers pointing up (like the international gesture for "Stop!") In this attitude the Buddha is either displaying his own fearlessness or encouraging his followers to be courageous.

⇨ Cloisters of Wat Benjamabophit, Bangkok.

CONTACTS Sukhothai Bus Station. ✉ *Bypass Rd., Sukhothai ✛ Off Hwy. 101* ☎ *055/614529.*

CAR

Highway 12 from Phitsanulok leads to Sukhothai and is a long, straight, and reasonably comfortable 59-km (37-mile), one-hour drive. Car rentals are available at Sukhothai Airport. The drive from Bangkok, along the four-lane Highway 117, is about 440 km (273 miles), or roughly seven hours. From Chiang Mai, take the M1 and head to the town of Tak, where Highway 12 branches east to Sukhothai.

SAMLOR AND SONGTHAEW

Sukhothai does not have local buses, and most of the population gets around in souped-up samlors or songthaews.

ESSENTIALS
SAFETY AND PRECAUTIONS

When touring the Historical Park, bring a bottle of water with you—the day will get hotter than you think.

TIMING

At least two days are needed to tour the magnificent Sukhothai Historical Park, and even a glancing survey of the Ramkhamhaeng National Museum's holdings requires an additional morning or afternoon. Depending on your means of transportation, touring the rest of the city could take a few hours or the better part of a day. It's best to tour Sukhothai in the late afternoon to avoid the midday sun and enjoy the late evening's pink-and-orange hues.

If you use Sukhothai as a base for exploring the ruins of Si Satchanalai and the potteries and museum of Sawankhalok, at least an additional two days are mandatory.

TOURS AND INFORMATION

In the Old City the main travel agency is run by the Vitoon guesthouse, whose owner, Kuhn Michael, is a knowledgeable guide who speaks English well. The

The Traces of a Nation

The optimism that accompanied the birth of the nation at Sukhothai is reflected in the art and architecture of the period. Strongly influenced by Sri Lankan Buddhism, the monuments left behind by the architects, artisans, and craftsmen of those innovative times had a light, often playful touch. Statues of the Buddha show him as smiling, serene, and confidently walking toward a better future. The iconic image of the walking Buddha originated in Sukhothai. Note also the impossibly graceful elephants portrayed in supporting pillars.

guesthouse has fleets of bicycles and motorbikes and runs a taxi service.

TRAVEL AGENCY Vitoon Guesthouse. ✉ *49 Moo 3 Jarodvithithong Rd., Old City* ☎ *055/633397.*

VISITOR INFORMATION Tourism Authority of Thailand Sukhothai Office. ✉ *130 Jarodvithithong, Sukhothai* ☎ *055/616228* ⊕ *www.tourismthailand.org/sukhothai.*

Sights

Royal Palace (*Noen Prasat*)
RUINS | Across from Wat Mahathat, there's not much left of Noen Prasat, which translates as "Palace Hill," but you can get an idea of the size from what remains of the square base. In the 19th century a famous stone inscription of King Ramkhamhaeng was found among the ruins of the palace. Now in the National Museum in Bangkok, it is sometimes referred to as Thailand's Declaration of Independence. The inscription's best-known quote reads: "This city

Sukhothai declined in power in the 15th century, but its temples and palaces were left intact.

Sukhothai is good. In the water there are fish, in the field there is rice. The ruler does not levy tax on the people who travel along the road together, leading their oxen on the way to trade and riding their horses on the way to sell. Whoever wants to trade in elephants, so trades. Whoever wants to trade in horses, so trades." Essentially, Thais imagine Sukhothai's government as a monarchy that served the people, stressing social needs and justice. Slavery was abolished, and people were free to believe in Hinduism and Buddhism (often simultaneously), and to pursue their trades without hindrance. ⊠ Old City ☎ 055/697241 ✉ B100 (includes all Historical Park sites).

Ramkhamhaeng National Museum

HISTORY MUSEUM | The region's most significant artifacts are in Bangkok's National Museum, and the many pieces on display at this fine facility demonstrate the gentle beauty of the Sukhothai era. One of several impressive exhibits reveals how refinements in the use of bronze enabled artisans to create the graceful walking Buddhas. ⊠ Muang Kao Sub-District, Old City ☎ 55/697–367 ✉ B150.

★ Sukhothai Historic Park

HISTORIC SIGHT | The 193 sights historic sites within the Sukhothai district are considered part of the historic park and are covered in the single entrance fee. Most of the key sites such as Noen Prasat (the Royal Palace) and Wat Mahathat are within the moated city walls but it's worth heading farther afield to Wat Saphan Hin, which offers an elevated vista of the valley below, dotted with Sukhothai's signature ruins. Until the 13th century most of Thailand consisted of small vassal states under the thumb of the Khmer Empire based in Angkor Wat. But the Khmers had overextended their reach, allowing the princes of two Thai states to combine forces. In 1238 one of the two princes, Phor Khun Bang Klang Thao, marched on Sukhothai, defeating the Khmer garrison commander in an

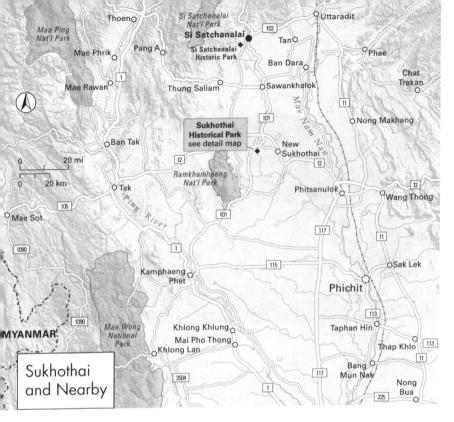

elephant duel. Installed as the new king of the region, he took the name Sri Indraditya and founded a dynasty that ruled Sukhothai for nearly 150 years. His youngest son became the third king of Sukhothai, Ramkhamhaeng, who ruled from 1279 to 1299. Through military and diplomatic victories, he expanded the kingdom to include most of present-day Thailand and the Malay Peninsula. By the mid-14th century Sukhothai's power and influence had waned, and Ayutthaya, once its vassal state, became the capital of the Thai kingdom. Sukhothai was gradually abandoned to the jungle, and a new town grew up about 14 km (9 miles) away. A decade-long restoration project costing more than $10 million created ths 70-square-km (27-square-mile) Sukhothai Historical Park. Sukhothai is busiest during the Loi Krathong festival, which

is celebrated in the Historical Park each year on the full moon in November. Its well-orchestrated, three-day light-and-sound show is the highlight. ✉ *Old City* 🎫 *B100.*

Wat Chang Lom

RUINS | Due east of the park is one of Sukhothai's oldest monasteries. Its bell-shape pagoda, thought to have been built in the latter part of the 14th century, is of Sri Lankan influence. The pagoda is perched on a three-tier square base atop damaged elephant buttresses. In front of the chedi are a viharn and solitary pillars; the remains of nine other chedis have been found within this complex. ✉ *Old City* ✛ *2 km (1 mile) east of park entrance, behind Legendha Sukhothai Resort (west of resort, turn north on small lane, cross bridge, and make first right)* ☎ *055/697241* ✉ *B100 (includes all Historical Park sites).*

★ Wat Mahathat

RUINS | Sitting amid a tranquil lotus pond, Wat Mahathat is the largest and most beautiful monastery in Sukhothai. Enclosed in the compound are some 200 tightly packed chedis, each containing the funeral ashes of a member of the royal family. Towering above them is a large central chedi, notable for its bulbous, lotus-bud prang. Wrapping around the chedi is a frieze of 111 monks, their hands raised in adoration. Probably built by Sukhothai's first king, Wat Mahathat owes its present form to King Lö Thai, who in 1345 erected the lotus-bud chedi to house two important relics brought back from Sri Lanka by the monk Sisatta. This Sri Lankan–style chedi became the symbol of Sukhothai and classical Sukhothai style. Copies of it were made in the principal cities of its vassal states, signifying a magic circle emanating from Sukhothai, the spiritual and temporal center of the empire. ✉ *Old City* ☎ *055/697241* ✉ *B100 (includes all Historical Park sites).*

Wat Phra Phai Luang

RUINS | This former Khmer structure, once a Hindu shrine, was converted to a Buddhist temple. Surrounded by a moat, the sanctuary is encircled by three laterite prangs, similar to those at Wat Sri Sawai—the only one that remains intact is decorated with stucco figures. In front of the prangs are the remains of the viharn and a crumbling chedi with a seated Buddha on its pedestal. Facing these structures is the *mondop*, a square structure with a stepped pyramid roof, built to house religious relics. ✉ *Donko Rd., Old City* ✚ *North of Old City walls, opposite Tourist Information Center* ☎ *055/697241* ✉ *B100 (includes all Historical Park sites).*

Wat Saphan Hin

RUINS | This pretty wat is reached by following a slate pathway and climbing a 200-meter (656-foot) hill. An amazing standing Buddha, nearly 12 meters (40 feet) tall, gazes down on the mere mortals who complete the climb. ✉ *Old City* ✚ *West of Old City walls* ✉ *Free.*

Wat Sra Sri

RUINS | This peaceful temple sits on two connected islands within a lotus-filled lake that supplied the monks with water and served as a boundary for the sacred area. A Sri Lankan–style chedi dominates six smaller chedis, and a large stucco seated Buddha looks down a row of columns, past the chedis, and over the lake to the horizon. Especially notable is the walking Buddha beside the Sri Lankan–style chedi. The walking Buddha is a Sukhothai innovation, and the most ethereal of Thailand's artistic styles. The depiction of the Buddha is often a reflection of political authority, and is modeled after the ruler. Under the Khmers, authority was hierarchical, but the kings of Sukhothai represented the ideals of serenity, happiness, and justice. The walking Buddha is the epitome of Sukhothai's art; he appears to be floating in air, neither rooted on Earth nor placed on a pedestal above the reach of the common people. ✉ *Old City* ☎ *055/697241* ✉ *B100 (includes all Historical Park sites).*

★ Wat Sri Chum

RUINS | Like many other sanctuaries, Wat Si Chum was originally surrounded by a moat, and the main structure is dominated by a statue of the Buddha in a seated position. The huge but elegant stucco image is one of the largest in Thailand, measuring 11¼ meters (37 feet) from knee to knee. Enter the mondop, a ceremonial structure, through the passage inside the left inner wall. Keep your eyes on the ceiling: more than 50 engraved slabs illustrate scenes from the *Jataka,*

The Festival of Loi Krathong

On the full moon of the 12th lunar month, when the tides are at their highest and the moon at its brightest, Thais head to the waterways to celebrate Loi Krathong, one of Thailand's most anticipated and enchanting festivals.

Indian Influences

Loi Krathong was influenced by Diwali, the Indian lantern festival that paid tribute to three Brahman gods. Thai farmers adapted the ceremony to offer tribute to Mae Khlong Kha, the goddess of the water, to thank her for blessing the land with water.

Ancient Sukhothai is where the festival's popular history began, with a story written by King Rama IV in 1863. The story concerns Naang Noppamart, the daughter of a Brahman priest who served in the court of King Li-Thai, grandson of King Ramkhamhaeng the Great. She was a woman of exceptional charm and beauty who soon became his queen. She secretly fashioned a *krathong* (a small float used as an offering), setting it alight by candle in accordance with her Brahmanist rites. The king, upon seeing this curious, glimmering offering, embraced its beauty, adapting it for Theravada Buddhism and thus creating the festival of Loi Krathong.

Krathong were traditionally formed by simply cupping banana leaves. Offerings such as dried rice and betel nut were placed at the center along with three incense sticks representing the Brahman gods. Today krathong are more commonly constructed by pinning folded banana leaves to a buoyant base made of a banana tree stem; they're decorated with scented flowers, orange candles (said to represent the Buddhist monkhood), and three incense sticks, whose meaning was changed under Li-Thai to represent the three forms of Buddhist existence.

Modern Meanings

Contemporary young Thai couples "loi" their "krathong" to bind their love in an act almost like that of a marriage proposal, while others use the ceremony more as a way to purge any bad luck or resentments they may be harboring. Loi Krathong also commonly represents the pursuit of material gain, with silent wishes placed for a winning lottery number or two. The festival remains Thailand's most romantic vision of tradition, with millions of Thais sending their hopes floating down the nearest waterway.

Although it's celebrated nationwide, with events centered around cities such as Bangkok, Ayutthaya, Chiang Mai, and Tak, the festival's birthplace of Sukhothai remains the focal point. The Historical Park serves as a kind of Hollywood back lot, with hundreds of costumed students and light, sound, and pyrotechnic engineers preparing for the fanfare of the annual show, which generally happens twice during the evening. With the Historical Park lighted and Wat Mahathat as its stage, the show reenacts the story of Sukhothai and the legend of Loi Krathong. Following this, governors, dignitaries, and other celebrity visitors take part in a spectacular finale that includes sending off the krathong representing the king and queen, and fireworks.

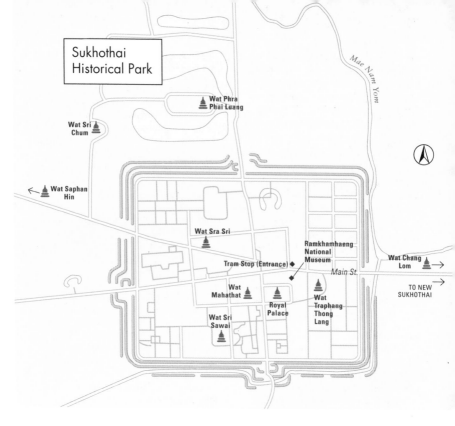

which are stories about the previous lives of Lord Buddha. ⊠ *Old City ✛ Northwest of Old City walls* ☎ *055/697367* 💷 *B100*.

Wat Sri Sawai

RUINS | Sukhothai's oldest structure may be this Khmer-style one with three prangs—similar to those found in Lopburi—surrounded by a laterite wall. The many stucco Hindu images and scenes suggest that Sri Sawai was probably first a Hindu temple, later converted to a Buddhist monastery. ⊠ *Old City* 💷 *B150 (includes all Historical Park sites).*

Wat Traphang Thong Lang

RUINS | The square mondop of Wat Traphang Thong Lang is the main sanctuary, the outer walls of which contain beautiful stucco figures in niches—some of Sukhothai's finest art. The north side depicts the Buddha returning to preach to his wife. On the west side he preaches to his father and relatives. Note the figures on the south wall, where the story of the Buddha is accompanied by an angel descending from heaven. ⊠ *Sukhothai ✛ East of park entrance opposite Ramkhamhaeng museum.*

🍴 Restaurants

In the new city, some of the best food is found at the local food stalls that line the main street before and after the Phra Ruang Bridge.

Dream Café

$ | THAI | Part of the appeal at this lovely, longtime favorite restaurant is the decor, extraordinary antiques that have filled its weathered space for decades. The Thai food is good, too, though be sure to ask for things spicy if that's your preference. **Known for:** crowd-pleasing flavor profiles; rustic but romantic guest rooms at the adjacent Cocoon House; stellar ginger salad. $ *Average main: B150* ⊠ *86/1 Singhawat Rd., Old City* ☎ *092/191–0449.*

Mai Krang Krung

$ | **THAI** | This pretty, family-run lunch spot is known for the local specialty "Sukhothai noodles"—a clear pork broth with rice noodles, chili flakes, toasted peanuts, and lime, topped with roasted and minced pork. The restaurant doubles as a boutique selling jewelry and silk textiles. **Known for:** pad Thai that's nothing like what you've had back home; butterfly pea dumplings (chor muang) for dessert; delightful herbal drinks. $ *Average main: B60* ⊠ *139 Jarovithi Thong Rd., Sukhothai* ☎ *081/971–4406* 🗖 *No credit cards.*

Sweet Rice Café

$ | **INTERNATIONAL** | Just 5 minutes from the main historic park by car, this bright, colonial-style café is in a lovely manicured garden. The menu offers a mix of Thai staples and Western comfort foods, but they're really known for their noodle soup with roast pork. **Known for:** Thai noodle soup; interesting ice cream flavors; pretty setting. $ *Average main: 150* ⊠ *91/4 Moo 2 Muangkao, Old City* ☎ *0813772071* ⊘ *Closed Tues. and Wed.*

Hotels

★ Legendha

$ | **HOTEL** | This attractive resort blends so well with the outskirts of Sukhothai's Historical Park that it could easily pass for a creation of King Ramkhamhaeng himself. **Pros:** chlorine-free pool; welcome fruit basket; friendly, helpful staff. **Cons:** expensive hotel transportation; inconvenient location between Historical Park entrance and the new city center; some rooms need refurbishing. $ *Rooms from: B1,500* ⊠ *214 Moo 3, Tambon Muangkao, Old City* ☎ *055/697214,* ⊕ *www.*

legendhasukhothai.com 🗗 *65 rooms* ⦿| *Free Breakfast.*

★ Sukhothai Heritage Resort

$ | **RESORT** | **FAMILY** | *Swank* is the word for this luxury resort at just about the midpoint between the historical parks in Sukhothai and Si Satchanalai. **Pros:** countryside setting; gracious service; elegant design. **Cons:** not convenient to historical parks; location near Sukhothai Airport may be too remote for some guests; mosquitoes could be controlled better. $ *Rooms from: B1,700* ⊠ *900 Moo 2, Tambon Klongkrajong, Sawankhalok* ☎ *055/647567* ⊕ *www.mosaic-collection. com/sukhothai-heritage* 🗗 *68 rooms* ⦿| *Free Breakfast.*

Sriwilai Sukhothai

$$ | **RESORT** | Sriwilai Sukhothai has redefined the concept of luxury lodging in Sukhothai, with a somewhat minimalist design and local crafts alongside sweeping views of rice paddies and the ruins of Chedi Sung. **Pros:** good on-site restaurants; gorgeous views; fine furnishings. **Cons:** 25-minute walk to town; not much in the area; limited dining options nearby. $ *Rooms from: 3,500* ⊠ *214/4 Moo 2, Old City* ☎ *055/697445* ⊕ *sriwilaisukhothai.com/*⦿| *Free Breakfast* 🗗 *54 rooms.*

Si Satchanalai

80 km (50 miles) north of Sukhothai.

Si Satchanalai, a sister city to Sukhothai, was governed by a son of Sukhothai's reigning monarch. Despite its secondary position, the city grew to impressive proportions, and the remains of about 200 of its temples and monuments survive, most of them in a ruined state, but many well worth seeing.

Sukhothai, with its expanse of neatly mowed lawns, is sometimes said to be too well groomed, but Si Satchanalai, spread out on 228 acres on the banks of the Mae Yom River, remains a quiet place with a more ancient, undisturbed atmosphere. It isn't difficult to find the ruins of a temple where you won't be disturbed for hours. Accommodations near the park are limited, so most visitors stay in Sukhothai, but Si Satchanalai Historical Park has plenty of casual dining spots where you can get lunch.

GETTING HERE AND AROUND

Most visitors to Si Satchanalai reach it as part of a tour from Sukhothai (most hotels can set you up with a guide). If you want to go on your own, hop on a bus bound for the town of Sawankhalok. The ride from Sukhothai takes 1½ hours and costs around B40. Take a taxi from Sawankhalok to the Historical Park, asking the driver to wait while you visit the various temples. You can also tour the site by bicycle or on top of an elephant. The Vitoon Guesthouse in Sukhothai also offers day trips to Si Satchanalai and Sawankhalok; it's opposite the entrance to the Sukhothai Historical Park.

TIMING

Si Satchanalai Historical Park is a day's outing from Sukhothai.

TOUR INFORMATION Vitoon Guesthouse.
✉ 49 Moo 3 Jarodvittiong Rd., Old City ☎ 055/633397.

 ## Sights

Si Satchanalai Historic Park

RUINS | Si Satchanalai was a sister city to Sukhothai back in their heyday; it was almost a mini Sukhothai. The historic park consists of eight main sites that can be explored by bicycle or on foot. Wat Chang Lom, with its unique stupa, is adorned with figures of 39 standing elephants around the base. ✉ Si Satchanalai ▨ B100.

Sawanworanayok National Museum

ART MUSEUM | Sukhothai grew wealthy on the fine ceramics it produced from the rich earth around the neighboring town of Sawankhalok. The ceramics were so prized that they were offered as gifts from Sukhothai rulers to the imperial courts of China, and they found their way as far as Japan. Fine examples of 1,000-year-old Sawankhalok wares are on display at this museum. The exhibits include pieces retrieved from the wrecks of centuries-old vessels that were headed to China and Japan but sank in typhoons and storms. Sukhothai Historical Park contains the ruins of many kilns used to fire the types of pottery on view here. ✉ Wang Phinphat, Sawankhalok ☎ 055/641571 ▨ B50.

Wat Chang Lom

RUINS | Near the entrance to the Historic Park, Wat Chang Lom shows strong Sri Lankan influences. The 39 elephant buttresses are in much better condition than their counterparts at the same-named temple in Sukhothai. The main chedi was completed by 1291. As you climb the stairs that run up the side, you'll come across seated images of the Buddha. ✉ Mueang Kao, Si Satchanalai ▨ Free.

Wat Chedi Jet Thaew

RUINS | This complex to the south of Wat Chang Lom has seven rows of ruined chedis, some with lotus-bud tops that are reminiscent of the larger ones at Sukhothai. The chedis contain the ashes of members of Si Satchanalai's ruling family. ✉ Si Satchanalai ▨ B100 (includes admission to entire Historical Park).

Wat Nang Phaya

RUINS | To the southeast of Wat Chedi Jet Thaew, this temple has well-preserved floral reliefs on its balustrade and stucco reliefs on the viharn wall. ✉ Si Satchanalai ▨ B100 (includes admission to entire Historical Park).

Wat Suan Kaeo Uthayan Yai

RUINS | As you leave the park, stop at this wat to see a Si Satchanalai image of Lord Buddha, one of the few still remaining. ⊠ *Si Satchanalai* 🎫 *B100 (includes admission to entire Historical Park).*

 Restaurants

Ran Sam Sai Noodles

$ | **THAI** | This family-run noodle shop serves bowls of Sukhothai's namesake noodle dish, mai krang krung, with roast pork and heaping piles of crushed peanuts and dried chili flakes. Don't expect anyone here to speak anything other than Thai, but pointing can get you pretty far. **Known for:** good stir-fries; local clientele; noodle soup. 💲 *Average main: 60* ⊠ *205/13 Tha Chai, Si Satchanalai.*

Chapter 9

CAMBODIA

Updated by
Simon Ostheimer

👁 Sights	🍴 Restaurants	🛏 Hotels	👜 Shopping	🍸 Nightlife
★★★★★	★★★★☆	★★★★☆	★★★☆☆	★★☆☆☆

WELCOME TO CAMBODIA

TOP REASONS TO GO

★ **Angkor temple complex:** Hands-down Southeast Asia's most magnificent archaeological treasure, Angkor has hundreds of ruins, many still hidden deep in the jungle.

★ **Education and enlightenment:** You'll learn a heap about history, warfare, human tragedy, science, and archaeology.

★ **Off-the-beaten-path beaches:** Along the Gulf of Thailand lie a few of Southeast Asia's most unspoiled beaches and (generally) unpolluted waters. There's delicious seafood, too.

★ **Philanthropy:** Work with street kids, give blood, buy a cookie to support the arts—if you're looking to do good while you travel, you'll find plenty of meaningful opportunities here. Scams abound, though, so make sure organizations are reputable.

★ **Southeast Asia's rising star:** Siem Reap is developing into one of the hippest cities in Southeast Asia.

1 **Phnom Penh.** The lively capital city.

2 **Tonle Bati.** Small lake with a beach and temples.

3 **Phnom Chisor.** Gorgeous countryside.

4 **Koh Dach.** Beach-day destination and home to silk weavers.

5 **Udong.** An important pilgrimage destination for Cambodians.

6 **Kampong Cham.** Temple ruins and temple-topped hills.

7 **Kompong Thom Ruins.** Pre-Angkorian ruins.

8 **Kratie.** Freshwater Irrawaddy dolphins.

9 **Ratanakkiri Province.** A remote destination with a mystical lake.

10 **Battambang.** City known for its temple ruins.

11 **Siem Reap.** Gateway to Angkor Wat.

12 **Tonle Sap.** The biggest freshwater lake in Southeast Asia.

13 **Kulen Mountain.** A sacred place for modern Cambodians.

14 **Sihanoukville.** A base to explore islands.

15 **Kampot.** Lively riverside town.

16 **Kep.** A beautiful seaside getaway.

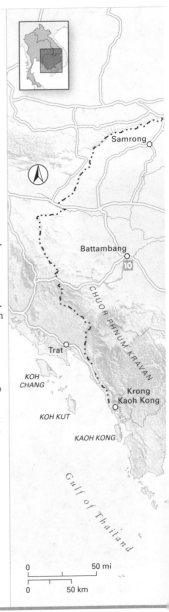

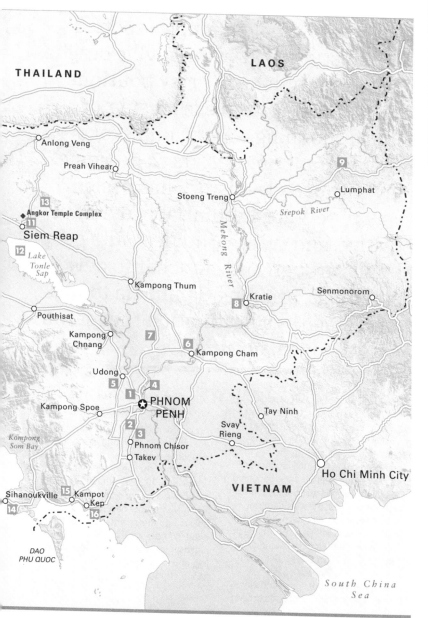

THAILAND

LAOS

Anlong Veng

Preah Vihear

9

Stoeng Treng

Lumphat

Srepok River

13
Angkor Temple Complex

Mekong River

11
Siem Reap

12 *Lake Tonle Sap*

Kampong Thum

8 Kratie

Senmonorom

Pouthisat

Kampong Chnang

7

6 Kampong Cham

Udong

5

4

1

Kompong Som Bay

Kampong Spoe

★ PHNOM PENH

Tay Ninh

2

3

Svay Rieng

Phnom Chisor

Takev

Ho Chi Minh City

VIETNAM

Sihanoukville

15 Kampot

14

Kep

16

DAO PHU QUOC

South China Sea

It's not by chance that Cambodia has become highly popular among eclectic travelers of all sensibilities, whether they're seeking lush jungles spotted with dusty temple ruins, idyllic beaches with an air of luxury, artsy boutique hotels, exciting nouvelle cuisine, or ethical shopping, among numerous other vibrant options. Its rich—some may say loaded—history has peeled away to reveal the admirably dynamic, positive, and creative ability of its people to pull through and launch into new beginnings, bringing Cambodia to the world stage as a destination that stands on its unique identity.

Phnom Penh is the bustling capital, where visitors can dip into the darkest corners of the country's traumatized past by walking through the Killing Fields one day, and the next exploring the hip, edgy, new design boom exemplified by the city's new hotels, restaurants, bars, and shops. Siem Reap is still a leading draw because it's the base for visiting the country's architectural crown jewel, the stunning Angkor Wat, which continues to epitomize the merging of spirituality and symbolism. Then there's the south, where once-sleepy beach coastlines are being transformed, sometimes into tasteless seaside gambling and partying zones, but in other cases into enchanting havens of stylish seaside chic.

An interesting trend with which tourists are met when exploring Cambodia is the support given to local communities by NGOs, the creation of which blossomed in the early 1990s. In the aftermath of Cambodia's civil war, foreign aid groups and governments have poured billions of dollars into the country, but not without coming under scrutiny. Many have faced criticism for lack of structure, profiteering, and the commercialization of humanitarian efforts.

In most cases the nonprofit organizations are working toward a better Cambodia, addressing a wide range of humanitarian, cultural, and environmental issues. Many nonprofits now run accommodations, restaurants, and travel agencies that provide the visitor with more than they expect to receive on vacation—the chance to help and an education. But it's worth checking out the legitimacy of an organization before parting with your money.

MAJOR REGIONS

Phnom Penh and Nearby. In the capital, Phnom Penh, you'll find a great deal to see and do: a palace and war monuments, great food and fine wine, and ample opportunities for people-watching along the breezy riverfront. Roads heading out of the capital lead to day-trip destinations like the beaches of Tonle Bati, a small lake with a couple of temples nearby, the lovely temple at Phnom Chisor to the south, and the pagoda-topped hill of Udong and the Mekong island of Koh Dach in the north.

North of Phnom Penh. As you travel north, you'll see some of Asia's last remaining, but ever-decreasing jungles, where some wildlife populations are actually increasing. For pre-Angkorian ruins, visit the ancient temple ruins at Kampong Cham and the Kompong Thom ruins, halfway between Phnom Penh and Siem Reap, which date to the 7th-century capital of Zhen La. Get a glimpse of the rare freshwater Irrawaddy dolphin at Kratie. There are still seven ethnic hill tribes, and some of the country's last remaining wild elephants, in the far north in Ratanakkiri Province. The city of Battambang (Cambodia's second largest) is a thriving center for the arts with exquisite colonial buildings, and is only three hours away from Siem Reap on a new road. Note that even if many of these destinations are quite removed from one another,

it's now possible to visit most of them by simply hopping on and off buses between Phnom Penh, Siem Reap, and the Laos border.

Siem Reap and Angkor Temple Complex. Siem Reap, which means "Siam defeated," based on a 15th-century battle with Cambodia's neighbors to the west, has emerged as a modern, friendly, and elegantly low-key city with highly sophisticated shopping, dining, and nightlife options. It's a rapidly growing place, and the gateway to the Angkor Temple Complex, the largest religious structure ever built, and just one temple in a complex of hundreds. **Around Siem Reap**, Tonle Sap is the biggest freshwater lake in Southeast Asia while Kulen Mountain, considered a holy mountain during the Angkor Dynasty, has the ruins of ancient temples.

Southern Cambodia. The once-sleepy coast has perked up. Whether you stay at a high-end resort, in a hillside bungalow, or in an island hut, it's a treat to enjoy the laid-back, beach-ambience setting. Sihanoukville is some 230 km (143 miles) southwest of Phnom Penh, a four-hour bus ride from the capital, and has suffered the dire consequences of Chinese-backed investments, becoming a grimy casino-strewn construction site. Don't linger: use it as a base to take boats to the offshore islands, which still remain relatively unexploited. Kampot, east of Sihanoukville, has become the place to linger and, with its caves, views, and pepper plantation, is worth a couple of days. The next province over, Kep has reemerged as a stylish getaway, where you can find some of the world's best pepper plantations.

At a Glance

Capital: Phnom Penh

Population: 17 million

Currency: Riel

Money: ATMs in cities; U.S. dollars widely accepted (even preferred), credit cards only in tourist places.

Language: Khmer

Country Code: 855

Emergencies: Call local police

Driving: On the right

Electricity: 230v/50 cycle; plugs are either U.S. standard two-prong, European standard with two round prongs, or U.K. standard three-prong. Power adapter needed.

Time: 11 hours ahead of New York during daylight savings; 12 hours otherwise

Documents: 30 days or more with valid passport; visa on arrival

Mobile Phones: GSM (900 and 1800 bands)

Major Mobile Companies: Smart, Cellcard

Websites
Ministry of Tourism: *www.tourismcambodia.org*

Move to Cambodia: www.movetocambodia.com

Tourism Cambodia: *www.tourismcambodia.com*

Planning

When to Go

Cambodia has two seasons, both affected by the monsoon winds. The northeastern monsoon blowing toward the coast ushers in the cool, dry season in November, which lasts through February, with temperatures between 65°F (18°C) and 80°F (27°C). December and January are the coolest months. It heats up to around 95°F (35°C) and higher in March and April, when the southwestern monsoon blows inland from the Gulf of Thailand, bringing downpours that last an hour or more most days. This rainy, humid season runs through October, with temperatures ranging from 80°F (27°C) to 95°F (35°C). The climate in Phnom Penh is always very humid. Thanks to climate change, Cambodia now experiences rainstorms in the dry season, cool temperatures in the hot season, and a lot of unpredictability. Bring your umbrella, although higher-end resorts usually offer one along with your bathrobe and slippers.

It's important to book in advance if you plan on visiting during mid-April's New Year celebrations, or for the Water Festival in Phnom Penh in November. Strangely, the New Year is one of the best times to see the capital—at least in terms of lower rates and crowds—because the majority of Phnom Penh residents come from somewhere else and they all go home for the holidays.

Plan Your Time

HASSLE FACTOR
Limited. There are no direct flights from the United States to Cambodia, but flights to nearby Asian hubs are frequent.

3 DAYS

Fly into Siem Reap. Explore the many temples of Angkor. By night visit Siem Reap's night markets and downtown.

1 WEEK

You have time to explore the temples of Angkor in more depth (there are some 300, but only the largest have been excavated). Then head to Phnom Penh and take a river cruise down the Mekong. If time permits, hit the beaches of Kep or spend a day in the emerging gourmand town of Kampot.

2 WEEKS

Explore Angkor and Siem Reap in depth, followed by a trip to Battambang, Cambodia's second-largest city and a developing hub of arts and culture. Then head to Phnom Penh and a day trip up the Mekong to Koh Dach (aka Silk Island). Relax at the beaches of Koh Rong, then check out Kep and Kampot.

Getting Here and Around

AIR

After many years of "semi–aviation isolation" Phnom Penh has opened up to the rest of the world, with regular flights to other Asian capitals and easy transit onward.

There are half a dozen flights from Vietnam's Ho Chi Minh City each day to Phnom Penh (prices start at $69 one way) and the travel time is about 45 minutes. Carriers that fly direct include Vietnam Airlines, Qatar Airways, and Cambodia Angkor Air.

You can also fly to Siem Reap from Ho Chi Minh City with Cambodia Angkor Air. The flight takes about an hour and 15 minutes and costs from $79 one way. There are about a dozen flights a day from Hanoi to Siem Reap; these take about 2 hours, and fares start at $80 one way on VietJet Air.

Regular air service links Phnom Penh and Siem Reap to Bangkok and Vientiane. Domestic flights run between Phnom Penh and Siem Reap. Air Asia, Bangkok Airways, Lao Airlines, and Thai Airways have flights to Cambodia.

BOAT

Boats do travel from Ho Chi Minh City to Phnom Penh, but they take three days and are a sightseeing option rather than quick A-to-B travel. From Phnom Penh, ferries called "bullet boats" travel along the Tonle Sap to reach Siem Reap and Angkor; they no longer ply waters between Sihanoukville and Koh Kong, however, so the only way to go is by road. You can buy tickets from a tour operator, your hotel's concierge, or at the port in Phnom Penh.

■ TIP → **Bullet boats, though fast, can be dangerous.**

Smaller (but noisy) ferries travel daily between Siem Reap's port and Battambang, on the Sangker River. Ask about water levels before booking a ticket; in dry season the water can get so low the boat may get stuck for hours at a time or be cancelled. For those who like to sit atop in the fresh air, take lots of suntan lotion.

BUS

Cambodia has a comprehensive bus network, and bus travel is cheap and generally of a good standard. It's also usually the safest cross-country transportation, aside from flying, especially since many highways have been recently upgraded. Travel from neighboring countries is easy, reliable, and cheap. Buses from Thailand and Vietnam operate daily.

BUS CONTACTS Giant Ibis. ⊠ *7E0, Rd. 106, Sangkat Daun Penh, Khan Daun Penh* ☎ *096/999–3333* ⊕ *giantibis.com.*

CAR

If you want to get to a destination quickly, hiring a driver with a car is probably the most effective way, but it can be a hair-raising ride if you choose the wrong company. A hired car with a driver costs about $50 a day, but agree on the price beforehand.

■ TIP→ **We strongly advise against driving yourself.**

Foreign drivers licenses are not valid here, rules of the road aren't observed, most drivers drive dangerously, and most of the main roads, apart from in Phnom Penh, are not in good condition.

MOTO AND TUK-TUK

Within cities and for shorter journeys, rickshaws (three-wheeled cabs) and tuk-tuks (two-wheeled carriages pulled by motorcycle) are the best and cheapest ways of getting around. Tuk-tuk drivers used to greet (or hassle) you at every street corner, but these days most people use taxi apps like Grab and PassApp with pre-set fees. These work great in most Cambodian cities, and start at just $0.10 per kilometer. Safe and reliable, you can either use cash or attach your credit card to your account for cash-free payment.

TRAIN

Cambodia's train system was revamped in 2018. Trains run south between Phnom Penh, Takeo, Kampot, and Sihanoukville ($8) on Friday, Saturday, Sunday, Monday, and on public holidays (though the schedule does change). On alternate days, a second line runs west and south of the Tonle Sap to Poipet and the Thai border. The main stops are at Pursat and Battambang, and the journey takes about 10 hours through serene countryside. For more information, check royal-railway. com.

BORDER CROSSINGS

There are five main border crossings between Vietnam and Cambodia, the busiest and most popular being Moc Bai–Bavet, with regular bus service between Ho Chi Minh City and Phnom Penh; this is the recommended way to go. When getting on the bus to return to Vietnam from Phnom Penh, the driver's assistant will ask you for your passport, which will be kept until you reach the border. This may appear strange, but it's the standard procedure, so don't worry. Other crossings include Ving Xuong to Kaam Samnor, on the river from Chau Doc, if you're traveling by boat; Tinh Bien to Phnom Den, if you are traveling to or from Kep; and O Yadao to Le Thanh, if you want to cross into the north of the country. All border crossings have become more regulated over the past few years, but corruption and minor bribery remains. Travelers have reported the borders at Koh Kong, between Cambodia and Thailand, and Dom Kralor, between Cambodia and Laos, to be particularly stressful. Don't listen to any tout asking for money to "facilitate" your visa process, and don't be surprised if even the border officials will ask for a $2 "stamping fee" when entering or leaving the country, or as much as $5 extra for issuing a tourist visa on arrival. Don't lose your cool: smiling and insisting on the correct price may help, but don't expect it.

The following border points are open with Thailand (Thai border towns in parentheses): Koh Kong (Hat Lek), Pailin (Ban Pakard), Duan Lem (Ban Laem), Poipet (Aranyaprathet), O'Smach (Chong Jom), and Anlong Veng (Chong Sa Ngam). From Laos you can cross at Dom Kralor (Voeung Kam). Overland crossings through Poipet and Koh Kong are the most popular, but bear in mind that Cambodian roads remain arduous, particularly in the rainy season. Coming from Laos overland, the best way to continue into Cambodia is by catching one of the many bus services plying the route Pakse/Si Phan Don/Stung Treng. Asia Van Transfers connects the Laos/Cambodia border to Siem Reap daily for $20. Book your tickets online at least a day in advance.

BORDER CROSSING CONTACTS Asia Van Transfer. ⊕ *www.asiavantransfer.com.*

Passports and Visas

One-month single-entry tourist visas, which cost $30, are available at all land border crossings and at the airports. You may need a passport photo—if you don't have one with you, it's an added $2 to have it made there (no added wait; sometimes you might not even be asked for a photo). When crossing on the bus from Vietnam, bus operators will ask for a fee of $5 for helping "fix" your visa. This is not compulsory and you can arrange your own visa at the border, but it does make the crossing slightly less of a hassle. Don't forget that you must have your visa for Vietnam in advance, and the dates must be relevant to your entry. You can also get your visa in advance on the Kingdom of Cambodia's e-visa website. This service takes a maximum of three days, costs $30 plus $6 service charge, but it saves a passport page as no visa sticker is applied at the border, and can prevent overcharging at land borders. ⊕ www.evisa.gov.kh.

Money Matters

The Cambodian currency is the riel, but the U.S. dollar is widely accepted everywhere, a legacy of the post-civil war 1990s United Nations peacekeeping mission, which helped run the country.

Although there is a strong government push for the population to use riel (and smaller U.S. notes have been phased out locally), both currencies are still used equally, though expect change in riel.

Most prices are given in dollars in this chapter.

Thai baht are sometimes accepted in bordering provinces.

The official exchange rate is approximately 4,000 riel to one U.S. dollar. It's possible to change dollars to riel just about anywhere.

ATMs are available in all major cities and towns, some major banks to look out for are ABA and Canadia. Credit cards are accepted at major hotels, restaurants, and at some boutiques. Cambodian banking hours are generally from 8 am until 4 pm. ATMs, often with full self-service options, are available 24 hours.

What It Costs in U.S. Dollars			
$	$$	$$$	$$$$
RESTAURANTS			
under $8	$8–$12	$13–$16	over $16
HOTELS			
under $50	$50–$100	$101–$150	over $150

Health and Safety

If a real health emergency arises, evacuation to Bangkok is always the best option, but the Thai-owned Royal Phnom Penh Hospital also offers excellent care.

Cambodia is far safer than many people realize, but you still need to always exercise common sense. Most violence occurs against Cambodians, but opportunist "snatch" thieves are often on the lookout for phones and bags, so keep your belongings close.

Keep most of your cash, valuables, and your passport in the hotel safe, and avoid walking on side streets after dark—and it's best to just avoid abrupt or confrontational behavior overall. Siem Reap has less crime than the capital, but that's starting to change.

■ TIP→ **Late at night use more secure ride-hail services like Grab and PassApp, whose vehicles and drivers are automatically tracked.**

Land mines laid during the civil war have been removed from most major tourist destinations. Unexploded ordnance is a concern, however, around off-the-beaten-track temples, where you should only travel with a knowledgeable guide. As a general rule, never walk in uncharted territory in Cambodia, unless you know it's safe.

Although better than Thailand, Cambodia still has one of Asia's most atrocious road records. Accidents are common in the chaotic traffic of Phnom Penh and on the highways, where people drive every which way. If you travel by car or coach, always wear a seat belt if they're available, and if you rent a moto, make sure you wear a helmet (if it has any cracks, ask for another). If you are in a tuk-tuk, just hold on tight—this is a once in a lifetime experience.

Royal Phnom Penh Hospital. ⊠ *Phnom Penh*

Tours and Packages

5oceans Travel
This company has been at the forefront of tourism in Cambodia for more than a decade and is the official representative for most of the carriers flying to Cambodia. 5oceans arranges various trips ranging from comprehensive daylong tours of Phnom Penh to bespoke one-month adventures around the country. ⊠ *139, St. 136 (Oknha In), Khan Daun Penh* ☎ *023/221537* ⊕ *www.5oceanscambodia.com.*

Beyond. Unique Escapes
Expert and ethical, this tour operator for the Siem Reap area offers the usual Angkor Temple tours, but also some more unusual experiences like spotting sunrise or sunset at a remote ruin far from the crowds, or hiking to a waterfall in the jungle of Kulen National Park. Other highly rated options include trips to villages and volunteering at their own NGO project HUSK, a rural literacy and development program. ⊠ *717 St. 14, Old Market* ⊹ *Near J Trust Royal Bank* ☎ *077/562565* ⊕ *beyonduniqueescapes.co.*

Beggars

Beggars will sometimes approach you in Cambodia. Many NGO workers who work with the homeless advise against giving handouts on the street. Instead, you should acknowledge the people who greet you, politely decline, and make a donation to an organization that operates larger-scale programs to aid beggars and street kids.

Osmose
An agent of positive change in the area, Osmose, a nonprofit organization, has been fighting to conserve the unique biosphere of Tonle Sap and Prek Toal by reeducating local villagers from poachers to protectors of the environment that sustains them. They also lobby against big commercial interests that have been involved in short-term exploitation of the ecosystem, and have successfully helped to reharmonize many aspects of human coexistence with nature. On their exceptional tours you get to visit a bird sanctuary with an expert guide and also experience floating villages in a fascinating and respectful way. ⊠ *House 0203, Group 8, Phum Wat Damnak, Sangkat Salakamreuk* ☎ *012/832812, 063/765506* ⊕ *www.osmosetonlesap.net.*

Visitor Information

Once you arrive, pick up one of the commercial visitor's maps, which are widely available free at airports, hotels, and restaurants.

Move to Cambodia (*www.movetocambodia.com*), updated by long-term expats, offers a wealth of information on the best places to eat, drink, and party in all major Cambodian destinations.

The two main English-language newspapers, relative newcomer *Khmer Times* (*www.khmertimeskh.com*) and longer standing *Phnom Penh Post* (*www. phnompenhpost.com*) are also good sources of information, offering unique insight into your destination.

Phnom Penh

The capital of Cambodia, Phnom Penh is strategically positioned at the confluence of the Mekong, Tonle Sap, and Bassac rivers. The city dates back to 1372, when a wealthy woman named Penh, who lived at the eastern side of a small hill near the Tonle Sap, is said to have found four Buddha statues hidden in a large tree drifting down the river. With the help of her neighbors, she built a hill (a *phnom*) with a temple on top, and invited Buddhist monks to settle on its western slope. In 1434 King Ponhea Yat established his capital on the same spot and constructed a brick pagoda on top of the hill. The capital was later moved twice, first to Lovek and later to Udong. In 1866, during the reign of King Norodom, the capital was moved back to Phnom Penh.

It was approximately during this time that France colonized Cambodia, and the French influence in the city is palpable—the legacy of a 90-year period that saw the construction of many colonial buildings, including the grandiose post office and train station. Some of the era's art deco architecture remains, in varying degrees of disrepair. Much of Phnom Penh's era of modern development took place after independence in 1953, with the addition of tree-lined boulevards, modernist buildings, and the Independence Monument (built in 1958), all under the tutelage of state architect Vann Molyvann as "New Khmer Architecture."

Today Phnom Penh has a population of 2.3 million people. But during the Khmer Rouge's 1975 forced emigration of people from the capital, Phnom Penh had fewer than 1,000 residents. Buildings and roads deteriorated, and many side streets are still a mess. The main routes are now well paved, however, and the city's wats (temples) have fresh coats of paint, as do many homes. This is a city being reborn, and its vibrancy is in part due to the abundance of young people, most of whom were born after the war years. Its wide streets are filled with motorcycles, which weave about in a complex ballet, making it a thrilling achievement merely to cross the street. You can try screwing up your courage and stepping straight into the flow, which should part for you as if by magic, but if you're not quite that brave—and people have been hit doing this—a good tip is to wait for locals to cross and tag along with them.

There are several wats and museums worth visiting, and the Old City has some attractive colonial buildings scattered about, though many have disappeared as time goes on. The wide park that lines the waterfront between the Royal Palace and Wat Phnom is a great place for a sunset stroll, particularly on weekend evenings when it fills with Khmer families, as do the other parks around town, including the promenade between Independence Monument and the imposing NagaWorld casino. On a breezy evening you'll find hundreds of Khmers out flying kites, or just going for a stroll.

GETTING HERE AND AROUND
AIR
Vietnam Airlines flies direct to Phnom Penh from Ho Chi Minh City, four times a day. Flights take 45 minutes and prices start at $150. Qatar Air flies once every day and is slightly cheaper, with prices from $120.

Thai International Airways flies twice daily from Bangkok to Phnom Penh,

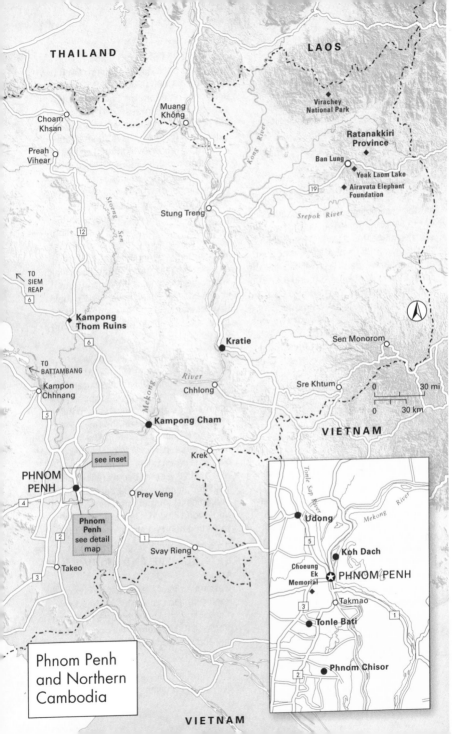

THAILAND

LAOS

Choam
Khsan

Muang
Khŏng

Preah
Vihear

Virachey
National Park

Ratanakkiri
Province

Ban Lung
Yeak Laom Lake

19

Airavata Elephant
Foundation

Stung Treng

Srepok River

12

TO
SIEM
REAP

6

Kampong
Thom Ruins

6

TO
BATTAMBANG

Kampon
Chhnang

5

Kampong Cham

Krek

Kratie

Sen Monorom

Sre Khtum

Chhlong

0   30 mi

0   30 km

VIETNAM

PHNOM
PENH

see inset

4

Phnom
Penh
see detail
map

Prey Veng

1

Takeo

Svay Rieng

2

3

Phnom Penh
and Northern
Cambodia

VIETNAM

Tonle Sap River

Mekong River

Udong

5

Koh Dach

Choeung
Ek
Memorial

PHNOM PENH

3

Takmao

Tonle Bati

1

Phnom Chisor

2

and Bangkok Airways has three flights a day. The trip takes about an hour and costs around $200 round-trip. Siem Reap Airways and AirAsia also have service between Bangkok and Phnom Penh. Lao Airlines flies from Vientiane and Pakse in Laos to Phnom Penh. Siem Reap Airways and Royal Khmer Airlines provide service between Cambodian cities.

(See Air Travel in Travel Smart Thailand for airline contacts.)

Phnom Penh's modern Pochentong Airport is 10 km (6 miles) west of downtown. A taxi from the airport to downtown Phnom Penh costs between $15 and $20 depending on your final destination, while motorcycles and tuk-tuks will set you back $4 and $8 respectively. There is also a convenient and air-conditioned Bus Line 3 (1,500 riel; prepare to have small change) that takes about 30 minutes to reach the Central Market. To find the bus stop to town, walk out of the airport's parking lot and turn left.

■TIP→ **If using motorcycles and tuk-tuks, Grab and PassApp Taxi ride-hail apps get lower fares.**

BUS
Phnom Penh has an efficient air-conditioned city bus system running from 5:30 am to 8:30 pm and costing only 1,500 riel per trip. The most useful line to tourists is number 3, which runs east to west from the night market, and stops at the Central Market and the Pochentong International Airport.

■TIP→ **Download the Stops Near Me smartphone app to see all routes, bus stops, and real-time position of available buses, all in English.**

There are also a half dozen or more private bus companies with regular service from all major Cambodian cities. Major bus stations include the Central Market, Sisowath Quay near the ferry port, and the Hua Lian Station near the Olympic Stadium. Giant Ibis charges a little more

than other bus companies, but routes are direct and buses are clean and comfortable, with onboard tour guides, Wi-Fi, and a bathroom (bring your own paper, which is a golden rule anywhere in Cambodia). Most long-distance bus tickets cost $6 to $25, depending on the destination and distance. Tickets can be purchased at the bus companies' offices or through hotels.

Note that some bus companies advertise a direct Phnom Penh–Bangkok ticket, but that trip takes around 20 hours on rough roads, including several bothersome stops, so it's not recommended.

Even though there are regular buses from Ho Chi Minh City to Phnom Penh, and the reverse, it's advisable to book ahead. The trip takes six to seven hours and is pretty straightforward. There are a couple of stops en route as well as the lengthier layover at the border crossing; prices range from $10 to $20. Get a Vietnam visa before you set off.

Minivans are an option but not a good one—though they go to all the major, and some minor, destinations within Cambodia they can get very cramped, and it's best to stick with the bigger buses. Minivans travel between the Lao border (at the Cambodian immigration point) and Stung Treng (about one hour), where you can catch a bus to Phnom Penh. **Asia Van Transfer** travels direct from the Lao border to Siem Reap daily at 11:30 am for $20 (*www.asiavantransfer.com*).

RICKSHAW, TUK-TUK, AND TAXI
The most common forms of transportation are rickshaws and tuk-tuks, best booked via the main taxi apps Grab or PassApp. They cruise the streets in abundance, and gather outside hotels and restaurants. Booking via the app means there's no arguing about your destination or the cost. While there are some official taxis at the airport, for getting around town in a car you're better off using Grab, though note that these are journeys in private vehicles.

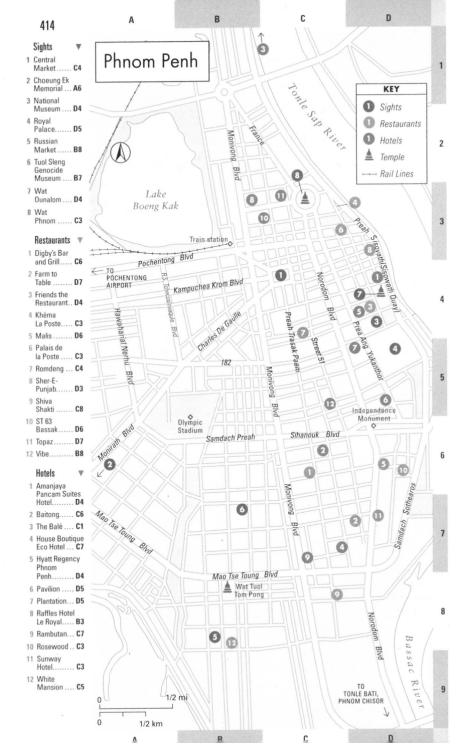

Phnom Penh

KEY

- ① Sights
- ① Restaurants
- ① Hotels
- ▲ Temple
- — Rail Lines

Tonle Sap River

Monivong Blvd

France

Lake Boeng Kak

Train station

Pochentong Blvd

TO POCHENTONG AIRPORT

Kampuchea Krom Blvd

R.S Tchecoslovaque Blvd

Charles De Gaulle

Jawaharlal Nehru Blvd

182

Monivong Blvd

Preah Trasak Paem

Street 51

Norodom Blvd

Preah Ang Yukanthor

Preah Sisowath / Sisowath Quay

Olympic Stadium

Samdach Preah

Sihanouk Blvd

Independence Monument

Monivong Blvd

Monirath Blvd

Mao Tse Toung Blvd

Samdach Sothearos

Mao Tse Toung Blvd

▲ Wat Tuol Tom Pong

Norodom Blvd

Bassac River

TO TONLE BATI, PHNOM CHISOR

0   1/2 mi

0   1/2 km

Touring Phnom Penh

Start your tour early, just as the sun rises over the Tonle Sap. Take a tuk-tuk to **Wat Phnom**, then climb the staircase and head for the temple where King Ponhea Yat is venerated. After descending the hill, head east to the Tonle Sap and walk south along the riverfront promenade. Across the street you are greeted by a plethora of breakfast options; pick the restaurant of your choice. After eating, return to the riverfront, where you have a fine view of the Chroy Changvar Peninsula. The cobbled riverside path leads you to **Wat Ounalom**, one of Phnom Penh's largest and oldest pagodas.

After visiting the wat, continue south on Sisowath Quay, past a busy strip of bars and restaurants, and on to a huge lawn in front of the cheerful yellow **Royal Palace**. On the grounds of the palace is the must-see **Wat Preah Keo Morokat**, aka the Silver Pagoda. The palace closes for lunch from 11 am to 2 pm, so plan accordingly. On the northern side of the palace a side street leads to the traditional-style **National Museum**, which is a peaceful and quiet place to spend an hour or two.

By now you might be hungry again. As you exit the museum, head north on Street 13 to **Friends the Restaurant** for a light lunch and tasty drink. From there, if you think you can hack it, catch a tuk-tuk to the **Tuol Sleng Genocide Museum**, which will require an hour or more with a clear head. It's a somber, sobering experience, and most locals wouldn't dream of visiting. Afterward head to the trendy Street 240 for some good food and interesting shopping.

VISITOR AND TOUR INFORMATION

Guides can be hired at major sights like the Royal Palace and National Museum.

CONTACTS Diethelm Travel. ⊠ *3, St. 240* ☎ *023/219151* ⊕ *www.diethelmtravel.com/cambodia.* **Exo Travel.** ⊠ *111 Norodom Blvd., 2nd fl.* ☎ *023/218948* ⊕ *exotravel.com/destinations/cambodia.* **Tourist Information Center.** ⊠ *373 Preah Sisowath Quay, Khan Daun Penh* ⊹ *In front of Yisang Restaurant Riverside* ☎ *023/218585* ⊕ *tourismcambodia.com.*

 ## Sights

There are a number of markets, museums, and historical sites to visit in Phnom Penh and you can see the highlights in three to four days. You can explore on your own, or all hotels will be able to arrange a range of comfortable transportation options for you.

Central Market

MARKET | An inescapable sightseeing destination in Phnom Penh is the colonial-era Central Market, built in the late 1930s on land that was once a watery swamp. This wonderfully ornate building with a soaring dome retains some of the city's once prominent art-deco style. The market's Khmer name, Phsar Thmei, translates as "new" market to distinguish it from Phnom Penh's original market, Phsar Chas, near the Tonle Sap River; it's popularly known as Central Market, however. Entry into the market is through one of four grand doors that face the directions of the compass. The main entrance, facing east, is lined with souvenir and textile merchants hawking everything from cheap T-shirts and postcards to expensive silks, handicrafts, and silverware. Other stalls sell electronic goods, cell phones, watches, jewelry, household items, shoes, secondhand clothing, flowers, and just about anything else you can imagine. ⊠ *Kampouchea Krom Blvd. and St. 130.*

Choeung Ek Memorial (*Killing Fields*)
MONUMENT | Under Pol Pot's rule from 1975 to 1979, thousands of Khmer Rouge prisoners who had been tortured at the infamous Tuol Sleng prison were taken to the rural Choeung Ek extermination camp for execution. Today the camp, 14 km (9 miles) southwest of downtown Phnom Penh, is a memorial, and the site consists of a monumental glass stupa built in 1989 and filled with 8,000 skulls, which were exhumed from mass graves nearby. It's an extremely disturbing sight: many of the skulls, which are grouped according to age and sex, bear the holes and slices from the blows that killed them. The site is at the end of a rough and dusty road, and can be reached in 30 minutes by motorbike, tuk-tuk ($12 is a reasonable price), or car. ■ TIP→ **The audio tour, available in English, is excellent and well worth the small additional fee.** ⊠ *Sangkat Cheung Ek* 🔁 *$3, $6 with audio tour.*

National Museum
HISTORY MUSEUM | **FAMILY** | This is one of Cambodia's two main museums and, although threadbare, it houses impressive relics that have survived war, genocide, and widespread plundering. More than 5,000 artifacts and works of art chronicle the various stages of Khmer cultural development, from the pre-Angkor periods of Fu Nan and Zhen La (5th to 8th century) to the Indravarman period (9th century), the classical Angkor period (10th to 13th century), and post-Angkor period. A palm-shaded central courtyard with lotus ponds houses the museum's showpiece: a sandstone statue of the Hindu god Yama, the Leper King, housed in a pavilion. ■ TIP→ **Guides, who are usually waiting just inside the entrance, can add depth to a visit here.** ⊠ *Sts. 13 and 178* ☎ *023/211753* ⊕ *www.cambodiamuseum.info* 🔁 *$10 adults.*

★ **Royal Palace**
CASTLE/PALACE | **FAMILY** | A walled complex that covers several blocks near the river, the official residence of current King Sihamoni and former residence of the late King Sihanouk and Queen Monineath Sihanouk (who also still lives here), is a 1913 reconstruction of the timber palace built in 1866 by the former King Norodom. The residential areas of the palace located to the west are strictly off limits to the public, but within the pagoda-style compound are several structures worth visiting, including **Wat Preah Keo Morokat, aka the Silver Pagoda**; the Throne Hall, with a tiered roof topped by a 200-foot-tall tower; and a pavilion donated by the Emperor Napoléon III and shipped here from France. The Temple of the Emerald Buddha, built from 1892 to 1902 and renovated in 1962, is one of Phnom Penh's greatest attractions. It's referred to as the Silver Pagoda because of the 5,329 silver tiles—more than 5 tons of pure silver—that make up the floor in the main vihear (temple hall). At the back of the vihear is the venerated Preah Keo Morokat (Emerald Buddha)—some say it's carved from jade, whereas others maintain that it's Baccarat crystal. In front of the altar is a 200-pound solid-gold Buddha studded with 2,086 diamonds. Displayed in a glass case are the golden offerings donated by Queen Kossomak Nearyreath in 1969; gifts received by the royal family over the years are stored in other glass cases. The gallery walls surrounding the temple compound are covered with murals depicting scenes from the Indian epic, the Ramayana. Pride of place outside is given to a bronze statue of King Norodom on horseback, completed in Paris in 1875 and brought here in 1892. ⊠ *Sotheros* ✛ *Between Sts. 184 and 240* ☎ 🔁 *$6.50, plus $2 for a camera, $5 for a video camera* ☞ *Guides can be hired at the entrance for $10.*

The Royal Palace's Throne Hall is used today for ceremonies like coronations and royal weddings.

Russian Market

MARKET | This popular covered market earned its nickname in the 1980s, when the wives and daughters of Russian diplomats would often cruise the stalls on the lookout for curios and antiques. Today the market has a good selection of Cambodian handicrafts and produce for sale. Wood carvings and furniture abound, as do "spirit houses" used for offerings of food, flowers, and incense. Colorful straw mats and hats, as well as baskets, are in high demand. The market is one of the city's best sources for art objects, including statues of the Buddha and Hindu gods; you can also buy old Indochinese coins and paper money printed during different periods of Cambodia's history—though note sometimes these are just replicas. A jumble of stalls concentrated at the market's south side sells DVDs, videos, and electronics. It's also a great place to buy overstock clothes from Cambodia's numerous garment factories at a fraction of their official retail price.

✉ Phnom Penh ✛ South of Mao Tse Tung Blvd., between Sts. 155 and 163.

Tuol Sleng Genocide Museum

HISTORY MUSEUM | This museum is a horrific reminder of the cruelty of which humans are capable. Once a neighborhood school, the building was seized by Pol Pot's Khmer Rouge and turned into a prison and interrogation center, the dreaded S-21. During the prison's four years of operation, some 14,000 Cambodians were tortured here; most were then taken to the infamous Killing Fields for execution. The four school buildings that made up S-21 have been left largely as they were when the Khmer Rouge left in January 1979. The prison kept extensive records and photos of the victims, and many of the documents are on display; particularly chilling are the representations of torture scenes painted by S-21 survivor Vann Nath. ✉ St. 113 (Boeng Keng Kang) and St. 350 ☎ 077/252121 ⊕ www.tuolsleng.gov.kh/en 🎟 $5.

Wat Ounalom

TEMPLE | On the riverfront, a little way north of the National Museum, the 15th-century Wat Ounalom is now the center of Cambodian Buddhism. Until 1999 it housed the Institute Buddhique, which originally contained a large religious library destroyed by the Khmer Rouge in the 1970s. Wat Ounalom's main *vihear* (temple hall), built in 1952 and still intact, has three floors; the top floor holds paintings illustrating the lives of the Buddha. The central feature of the complex is the large stupa, Chetdai, which dates to Angkorian times and is said to contain hair from one of the Buddha's eyebrows. Four niche rooms here hold priceless bronze sculptures of the Buddha. The sanctuary is dedicated to the Angkorian king Jayavarman VII. ✉ *Sisowath Blvd.* 🎟 *Free.*

Wat Phnom

TEMPLE | According to legend, a wealthy woman named Penh found four statues of the Buddha hidden in a tree floating down the river, and in 1372 she built this hill and commissioned this sanctuary to house them. It is this 90-foot knoll for which the city was named: Phnom Penh means "Penh Hill." Sixty years later, King Ponhea Yat had a huge stupa built here to house his ashes after his death. You approach the temple by a flight of steps flanked by bronze friezes of chariots in battle and heavenly *apsara* (traditional Khmer dancing figures). Inside the temple hall, the vihear, are some fine wall paintings depicting scenes from the Buddha's lives, and on the north side is a charming Chinese shrine. The bottom of the hill swarms with vendors selling devotional candles and flowers, food stands serving local street food, and some beggars. ✉ *Norodom Blvd. and St. 94* 🎟 *$1.*

🍴 Restaurants

Phnom Penh is rapidly becoming one of the top culinary cities in Asia. There is delectable Khmer food at everything from street stands to five-star establishments, plus an influx of international restaurants. The country's colonial history means you'll find many French-inspired restaurants, too.

Digby's Bar & Grill

$$ | **AMERICAN** | **FAMILY** | If it's meat you're after, this restaurant, coffee shop, butcher shop, and deli—all rolled into one—is the place for you. The locally sourced animal products are all certified (a rarity in Cambodia) and the gourmet sausages and cold cuts are prepared, cured, and smoked on the premises. **Known for:** hearty breakfasts; popular happy hour; club sandwiches. [$] *Average main: $10* ✉ *197, 63 St., Boeung Keng Kang 1* ☎ *077/772326.*

Farm to Table

$ | **INTERNATIONAL** | **FAMILY** | Focusing on a mostly Western menu packed with organic, locally sourced ingredients, this restaurant does what the name says, featuring fresh, seasonal produce from farmers across Cambodia. There is indoor seating, but the best place to be is in the lovely leafy garden, which also hosts regular farmers' markets. **Known for:** sustainability focus; wonderful garden; good cocktails. [$] *Average main: $7* ✉ *16 St. 360* ☎ *078/899722.*

★ Friends the Restaurant

$ | **TAPAS** | This popular nonprofit eatery just a short walk from the National Museum serves a huge range of tapas, fruit juices, salads, and international dishes. You can admire the colorful artwork, then visit the Friends Futures Factory (F3) next door, an open-air creative space with regular markets, exhibitions, and concerts. **Known for:** international clientele and atmosphere; falafel burger; attentive staff

Cambodian Cuisine

Although relatively unknown outside its borders, Cambodian cuisine is distinct from that of neighbors Thailand, Laos, and Vietnam, although some dishes are common throughout the region. Fish and rice are the mainstays, and some of the world's tastiest fish dishes are to be had in Cambodia. The country has the benefit of a complex river system that feeds Southeast Asia's largest freshwater lake (the Tonle Sap), plus a coastline famous for its crab. Beyond all that, Cambodia's rice paddies grow some of the most succulent fish around. (Besides fish, Cambodians also eat a lot of pork, more so than beef, which tends to be tough.)

Be sure to try *prahok*, the Cambodian lifeblood—a stinky, cheeselike fermented fish paste that nourishes the nation. *Amok*, too, is a sure delight: Done the old-fashioned way, it takes two days to make this fish-and-coconut concoction, which is steamed in a banana leaf.

Down south, Kampot Province grows world-renowned aromatic pepper. If you're coming from a northern climate, try a seafood dish with whole green peppercorns on the stalk. You won't find it (not fresh, anyway) in your home country.

Generally, the food in Cambodia is far tamer than that of Thailand or Laos, but comes seasoned heavily with fresh herbs. Curried dishes, known as *kari*, show the ties between Indian and Cambodian cuisine. As in Thailand, it is usual in Cambodian food to use fish sauce in soups, stir-fry, and as a dipping sauce. There are many variations of rice noodles, which give the cuisine a Chinese flavor. Beef noodle soup, known simply as *kuyteav*, is a popular dish brought to Cambodia by Chinese settlers. *Banh chiao*, a crepe-like pancake stuffed with pork, shrimp, and bean sprouts and then fried, is the Khmer version of the Vietnamese *bánh xèo*, a crispy, stuffed rice pancake . Cambodian cuisine uses many vegetables. Mushrooms, cabbage, baby corn, bamboo shoots, fresh ginger, Chinese broccoli, snow peas, and bok choy are all found in Cambodian dishes from stir-fry to soup.

Meals in Cambodia usually consist of three or four different dishes, reflecting the tastes of sweet, sour, salty, and bitter. The dishes are set out and you take from which dish you want and mix with your rice. Eating is usually a communal experience, and it is appropriate to share your food with others.

and service. $ *Average main: $5* ✉ *215 St. 13* ☎ *012/802072* ⊕ *www.tree-alliance.org.*

Khéma La Poste

$ | FRENCH | There are two branches of Khéma in the city, but this one, with its French colonial stylings, heritage building, and location in the heart of the old quarter, is the one to go to. Expect modern French cuisine served at all times of the day, but weekend brunch is probably the most popular meal. **Known for:** classical interior stylings; excellent French cuisine; weekend brunch. $ *Average main: $6* ✉ *41 St. 13, Khan Daun Penh* ✚ *Corner of St. 98* ☎ *015/841888* ⊕ *khema-restaurant.com.*

Malis

$$$ | **CAMBODIAN** | The Phnom Penh elite frequent this upscale, traditional Khmer restaurant in a peaceful garden, as its chef Luu Meng is a Cambodian celebrity who has worked on TV with the likes of Gordon Ramsay. The long menu features a variety of fresh fish and seafood, soups, curries, and grilled meats. **Known for:** creative curries; fish prahok; rotating seasonal menu. [$] *Average main: $13* ✉ *136 St. 41 (Preah Norodom)* ☎ *015/814888* 🌐 *www.malis-restaurant.com/phnompenh.*

Palais de la Poste

$$$$ | **FRENCH** | In the elegant setting of the beautifully restored 1880s Indochina Bank Building, next to the historical main post office, you can dine on exquisite French cuisine. The roof terrace above the restaurant has a swanky cocktail bar-lounge. **Known for:** set lunch specials; duck confit paupiette with duck liver; fillet of grouper with a matelote sauce. [$] *Average main: $25* ✉ *5 St. 102* ☎ *011/735576* 🌐 *www.palais-restaurant.com.*

Romdeng

$ | **CAMBODIAN** | Some of the country's tastiest provincial Khmer dishes are served at this gorgeously redesigned house in a residential area. Romdeng (which means "galangal" in Khmer) offers plenty of piquant soups, curries, salads, and meat dishes. **Known for:** fried insects; Cambodia's signature fermented fish paste; pomelo salad. [$] *Average main: $7* ✉ *74 St. 174* ☎ *070/519565* 🌐 *www.tree-alliance.org.*

Sher-E-Punjab

$ | **INDIAN** | Follow the aroma of pungent spices into this restaurant and prepare for a hearty curry and all the essential sides at one of the capital's best Indian restaurants. The accommodating staff and exotically spiced fare more than compensate for the modest appearance. **Known for:** perfectly cooked kebabs; wide selection of naan breads; tandoori chicken. [$] *Average main: $6* ✉ *16 St. 130* ☎ *023/216360.*

Shiva Shakti

$$ | **INDIAN** | Succulent samosas, vegetable *pakoras* (fritters), spicy lamb masala, butter chicken, and prawn *biryani* (with rice and vegetables) are among the favorites served at this small Indian restaurant. In the pleasant dining room a statue of the elephant-headed Hindu god Ganesha stands by the door, and reproductions of Mogul art line the walls. [$] *Average main: $9* ✉ *17 St. 63, Khan Chamkarmon* ☎ *012/813817.*

★ ST 63 Bassak

$ | **CAMBODIAN** | ST 63 Bassak is run by a young Cambodian couple who aim to make international cuisine accessible and affordable for a local crowd, and at the same time showcase the best of Cambodian cuisine for foreign crowds. The result is a mix of local favorites like beef *loc lac* (stir-fried beef with fried egg and lime pepper sauce), alongside French-inspired dishes such as slow-cooked oxtail with a red wine *jus*. **Known for:** creamy smoothies; Cha Kdao Sach Maon (spicy hot chicken with basil); refreshing cocktails. [$] *Average main: $5* ✉ *2 St. 308, Boeung Keng Kang 1* ☎ *015/647062.*

Local Eats 🍴

For a local treat, try the afternoon **noodle shops** on Street 178 near the National Museum. These street-side eateries pack in the Khmer crowds, serving quick-fried noodles and rice-flour-and-onion cakes. They're popular among locals and cheap (less than a dollar per serving). You won't find the cleanest of restaurants, but everything is well cooked, and you'll get a tasty snack with an eye for what it's like to eat Khmer-style. Don't get here before 4 pm.

Topaz

$$$$ | **FRENCH** | The first-class French specialties at this fine restaurant make it a longtime Phnom Penh favorite. Imported cuts of beef from Cape Grim in Tasmania and other highest-quality ingredients cooked to perfection mean that Topaz remains one of the most feted places to dine in the city, a great choice for an intimate meal. **Known for:** three-course set lunch menus; peaceful courtyard garden; extensive wine list. $ *Average main: $25* ✉ *162 Norodom Blvd.* ☎ *015/821888,* ⊕ *www.topaz-restaurant.com.*

Vibe

$ | **VEGETARIAN** | This small spot is probably the best vegan restaurant in Phnom Penh, possibly in the whole country. The menu is packed with vegetable, plant, and grain dishes, with options for all dietary needs (nut, dairy, gluten), and delivers on flavor. **Known for:** quality vegan food; cold-pressed juices; laid-back atmosphere. $ *Average main: $7* ✉ *26 St. 446* ☎ *061/764937* ⊕ *vibecafeasia. com.*

 ## Hotels

These days the capital offers plenty of accommodations for all budgets, from world-class hotels such as the storied Raffles to mid-range brand-name offerings, unique boutiques, and trendy guesthouses.

◼ **TIP→ When booking a hotel, check for special offers and promotions—many establishments offer deals.**

Amanjaya Pancam Suites Hotel

$$$ | **HOTEL** | With chic rosewood furnishings and Khmer silk textiles in the rooms, Amanjaya is the classiest hotel on the banks of the Tonle Sap River. **Pros:** balcony views; glorious riverside location; great restaurant and bar. **Cons:** no pool; faces one of Phnom Penh's busiest streets; small elevator. $ *Rooms from: $140* ✉ *1 St. 154, Sisowath Quay* ☎ *023/214747* ⊕ *www.*

amanjaya-suites-phnom-penh.com ⤶ *21 suites* ⦿| *Free Breakfast.*

Baitong

$$ | **HOTEL** | This downtown hotel has a streamlined modern aesthetic focused on water features, open air spaces, and plants. **Pros:** central location; full service on-site spa; lots of greenery. **Cons:** some rooms lack privacy; Skybar menu is limited; rooms have thin walls. $ *Rooms from: $65* ✉ *10 St. 282, Boeung Keng Kang 1* ☎ *023/223838* ⊕ *baitonghotel. asia* ⦿| *Free Breakfast* ⤶ *105 rooms.*

The Balé

$$$$ | **HOTEL** | While technically still in Phnom Penh, this lovely design resort is a 45-minute drive upriver from the city along the banks of the Mekong. **Pros:** pool; serene atmosphere; great breakfast. **Cons:** expensive; only one restaurant on-site; distance from the city. $ *Rooms from: $350* ✉ *National Rd. 6A, Bridge No. 8* ☎ *023/900425* ⊕ *thebalephnompenh. com* ⦿| *Free Breakfast* ⤶ *18 suites.*

House Boutique Eco Hotel

$ | **HOTEL** | This quiet and airy ecohotel offers large, solar-powered rooms, some with balconies, fitted with upcycled wooden furniture. **Pros:** quiet environment; good value; close to nightlife. **Cons:** not all rooms have balconies; ground floor rooms lack privacy; pool is a little small. $ *Rooms from: $30* ✉ *76 St. 57, Boeung Keng Kang 1* ☎ *023/220884* ⊕ *www.houseboutiquehotel.com* ⤶ *32 rooms* ⦿| *Free Breakfast.*

Hyatt Regency Phnom Penh

$$$$ | **HOTEL** | While some Hyatt hotels have a generic, could-be-anywhere feel, this smart property in the heart of the old city seamlessly blends a historical French colonial home (it once belonged to a princess) with a sleek modern building that incorporates some of the best dining and drinking outlets in Phnom Penh. **Pros:** views overlooking the palace; easy walking distance to sights; one of the city's best sky bars. **Cons:** gets busy with outside guests; not all rooms have good views; outdoor pool can be quite cold. [$] *Rooms from: $200* ✉ *55 St. 178* ☎ *023/6001234* 🌐 *hyatt.com/en-US/hotel/cambodia/hyatt-regency-phnom-penh/pnhrp* 🍴 *Free Breakfast* 🛏 *247 rooms.*

★ Pavilion
$$ | **HOTEL** | A discreet green oasis in the heart of bustling Phnom Penh, the Pavilion is in a lovingly restored building dating from the raging 1920s, with a swimming pool surrounded by palm, banana, and jackfruit trees. **Pros:** great location; limo pickup service; good spa. **Cons:** no children under 16 allowed; rooms and bathrooms are a little small; fills quickly. [$] *Rooms from: $65* ✉ *227 St. 19, Khan Daun Penh* ☎ *023/222280* 🌐 *www.maads.asia/pavilion* 🛏 *36 rooms* 🍴 *Free Breakfast.*

★ Plantation
$$ | **HOTEL** | This large boutique hotel is built around a grand 1930s villa in the heart of the city, with an open yard with a lotus-filled pond in the middle. **Pros:** good location; super restaurant; the larger of the two pools is only for guests. **Cons:** slight overcharging for outsourced activities and transportation booked through reception; only one shower at the main pool; insects can be a nuisance in the garden. [$] *Rooms from: $90* ✉ *28 St. 184* ☎ *023/215151* 🌐 *theplantation.asia* 🛏 *70 rooms* 🍴 *Free Breakfast.*

Raffles Hotel Le Royal
$$$$ | **HOTEL** | Phnom Penh's ritziest hotel, first opened in 1929, was practically destroyed during the Khmer Rouge years and was meticulously restored by the Raffles group in 1996. **Pros:** large swimming pool; great location; old-world luxury. **Cons:** service has become quite lackadaisical; style may not be to everyone's tastes; old premises start looking a bit worn out. [$] *Rooms from: $200* ✉ *92 Rukhak Vithei Daun Penh* ☎ *023/981888, 800/17233537 international access* 🌐 *www.raffles.com/phnom-penh* 🛏 *133 rooms* 🍴 *Free Breakfast.*

★ Rambutan
$$ | **HOTEL** | This refurbished 1960s Khmer villa brings a touch of arty chic to Phnom Penh's central suburbs. **Pros:** bathtub on the balcony; excellent breakfast; great location. **Cons:** popular with the young flashpacker crowd; pool area can be busy; tucked in a side alley and not always easy to find tuk-tuks. [$] *Rooms from: $50* ✉ *29 St. 71, Boeung Keng Kang 1* ☎ *023/993400* 🌐 *www.rambutan-cambodia.com* 🍴 *Free Breakfast* 🛏 *16 rooms.*

Rosewood
$$$$ | **HOTEL** | Atop Phnom Penh's tallest building, the Rosewood offers luxury lodgings with sky-high views to match. **Pros:** amazing room views; fully equipped spa; varied dining options on-site. **Cons:** indoor pool is cold; not much close by; expensive. [$] *Rooms from: $270* ✉ *Vattanac Capital Tower, 66 Monivong Blvd., Khan Daun Penh* ☎ *023/936888* 🌐 *rosewoodhotels.com/en/phnom-penh* 🍴 *Free Breakfast* 🛏 *175 rooms.*

Sunway Hotel
$$ | **HOTEL** | Located right next to Wat Phnom and opposite the U.S. embassy, this is a popular choice among business travelers. **Pros:** no smoking in all rooms; in the heart of the business district; excellent lounge bar. **Cons:** only the suites have balconies; slightly dated architecture; adjoining rooms can get noisy. [$] *Rooms from: $60* ✉ *1 St. 92* ☎ *023/430333* 🌐 *www.sunwayhotels.com/sunway-phnompenh* 🛏 *138 rooms* 🍴 *Free Breakfast.*

White Mansion
$$ | **HOTEL** | This glossy boutique hotel on the hip Street 240 has suites on the top floors with balconies overlooking great vistas of the city, while rooms on the ground floor have terraces that lead directly to the pool. **Pros:** nice monochrome design; spacious rooms with espresso machines; child-friendly. **Cons:** elevator only goes up to third floor; open showers can be messy; set breakfast

Cambodia's Festivals

Like many Southeast Asian nations, Cambodia celebrates a lot of important festivals. Quite a few of them are closely tied to Buddhism, the country's predominant religion.

Meak Bochea: On the day of the full moon in February, this festival commemorates the Buddha's first sermon to 1,250 of his disciples. In the evening, Buddhists parade three times around their respective pagodas.

Khmer New Year: Celebrated at the same time as the Thai and Lao lunar new year (mid-April), it's a new-moon festival spread over the three days following the winter rice harvest. People celebrate by cleaning and decorating their houses, making offerings at their home altars, going to Buddhist temples, and splashing lots and lots of water on each other. Be forewarned: foreigners are fair game.

Visakha Bochea: This Buddhist festival on the day of the full moon in May celebrates the Buddha's birth, enlightenment, and death.

Chrat Preah Nongkol: The Royal Plowing Ceremony, a celebration of the start of the summer planting season, is held in front of the Royal Palace in Phnom Penh in May. The impressive ceremony includes soothsaying rites meant to predict the outcomes for the year's rice harvest.

Pchum Ben (All Souls' Day): In mid-October the spirits of deceased ancestors are honored according to Khmer tradition. People make special offerings at Buddhist temples to appease these spirits.

Bonn Om Touk: The Water Festival ushers in the fishing season, and marks the "miraculous" reversal of the Tonle Sap waters. It's celebrated in November throughout the country: longboat river races are held, and an illuminated flotilla of *naga*, or dragon boats, adds to the festive atmosphere. The biggest races are held in Phnom Penh in front of the Royal Palace, and the king traditionally presides.

can be hit or miss. [$] *Rooms from: $100* ✉ *26 St. 240* ☎ *092/254300* 🌐 *www.whitemansion.asia* 🛏 *30 rooms* 🍴 *Free Breakfast.*

Nightlife

What makes the nightlife here so enjoyable is how easy it is to get from place to place in this compact city. Many of the dusk-to-dawn nightspots are near the Tonle Sap riverside, but there are great bars and clubs spread all over town, including a cluster in Bassac Lane. A useful website for upcoming events and venue information is www.lengpleng.com, which is usually updated every Thursday.

⚠ **Always keep your bags and phones close to you when out after dark in Phnom Penh (during daytime too)—snatch thefts are common, although foreigners aren't specifically targeted.**

BARS AND PUBS

Bassac Lane

GATHERING PLACES | Once a sleepy residential lane, this road has been transformed in recent years into a highly celebrated local drinking destination, with many tiny boutique bars next to each other, each with its own peculiar style. From the biker Americana of **Hangar 44**, to the stylish vibes of **Cay Bar**, or the post-drink beef noodles and handmade dumplings at **Mama Wong's**, there's a bit of everything. ⊠ *Bassac La., Boeung Keng Kang 1.*

Le Moon Rooftop

GATHERING PLACES | Opened back in 2010, this rooftop bar is an ideal spot for a night of cocktails accompanied by sparkling views of both the Tonle Sap and Mekong rivers, as well as Wat Ounalom. It's on the roof of the Amanjaya Pancam Hotel, and also serves finger food. ⊠ *1 St. 154, Sisowath Quay* ☎ *087/600768* ⊕ *www.le-moon-rooftop.com.*

Long After Dark

BARS | The name somewhat gives it away, but this cool cocktail and whisky bar is one of *the* places to head when everywhere else is closing down but that said, you don't have to be a late-night owl to enjoy a drink here. The atmospheric lighting and speakeasy vibe are complemented by a surprisingly comprehensive menu. ⊠ *86 St. 450* ☎ *093/768354.*

★ Samai Distillery

BARS | Difficult to find but well worth the effort, this microdistillery-bar, near the Aeon Mall, is one of the trendiest joints in Phnom Penh. Their excellent Samai rum is distilled on-site in 200-year-old copper stills and makes a great base for the Moorish-Asian-inspired cocktails. The downside: it's only open on Thursday nights. ⊠ *9b St. 830* ⊹ *Off Sothearos Blvd.* ☎ *023/212548* ⊕ *www.samaidistillery.com.*

Score Sports Bar & Grill

BARS | Open until 2 am on weekends, Phnom Penh's largest sports bar is a favorite of expats, locals, and tourists alike, who all want to catch a sports game live on one of many TV screens while enjoying a tipple among the enthusiastic crowd. There's pub grub and a British-style weekend roast. ⊠ *Wat Lanka, 5 St. 282* ☎ *089/371803* ⊕ *www.scorekh.com.*

Sundown Social Club

BARS | It may not have a riverside vista of the Mekong, but this cocktail bar somehow manages to top that with a view of the kaleidoscopic-colored tin roofs of its noisy neighbor, Russian Market. The cool factor continues with the tiki theme, cocktails made with local spirits, craft beer, and a menu of tapas-style Asian fusion. ⊠ *86, St. 440* ⊹ *North side of Russian Market* ☎ *015/526373.*

DANCE CLUBS

Blue Chilli

CABARET | Blue Chilli, behind the National Museum, is one of the most popular and oldest gay-friendly bars in the city, for locals and expats. They host entertaining drag shows and other performances throughout the week, as well as DJ sets that will keep you dancing until the early hours. ⊠ *36 St. 178* ☎ *012/566353* ⊕ *www.bluechillicambodia.com.*

Epic

DANCE CLUBS | As the name implies, this place is for big nights out—it's a high-tech dance club near the Russian embassy that caters to the young high-fliers of the capital, including jet-setters, A-list celebrities, and serious ravers. The nightly party usually goes until 5 am. Check the website for details of upcoming events. ⊠ *122B, Sangkat Tonle Bassac* ⊹ *Nr. Russian Embassy* ☎ *010/600608* ⊕ *www.epic.com.kh.*

Love Lounge

DANCE CLUBS | Every night, this cosmopolitan dance club packs in guest DJs and a motley crew of expats and locals. ⊠ *3 St. 278, Boeung Keng Kang 1* ⊹ *Above Duplex* ☎ *010/833363* ⊕ *www.lovephnompenh.com.*

Pontoon

DANCE CLUBS | This older club brings top DJs from around the world for happening live sets, drawing an accidental as well as a dedicated music-loving crowd. Visit the website for an up-to-date list of events. ✉ *80 St. 172* ☎ *010/300400* ⊕ *www.pontoonclub.com.*

WINE BARS

Bouchon Wine Bar

WINE BARS | Bouchon serves a dapper selection of more than 40 French wines and accompanying light meals (well, light by French standards) and finger food, in a buzzy, nouveau-pub atmosphere that attracts an eclectic international crowd. You can sample different varieties by bottle or by the glass. ✉ *82, St. 174* ☎ *077/881103.*

🎭 Performing Arts

Various Phnom Penh theaters and restaurants offer programs of traditional music and dancing, many organized by nonprofit groups that help Cambodian orphans, disadvantaged kids, and individuals with disabilities. Siem Reap perhaps has more venues, but most there are run by for-profit companies in the tourism industry.

Chaktomuk Conference Hall

CONCERTS | This architectural landmark, built in 1960 by Vann Molyvann in the modernist "New Khmer Architecture" style, hosts performances of traditional music and dance organized by the Ministry of Culture, and is also a venue for business events such as conferences. Ask your hotel to check for upcoming concert details. ✉ *Sisowath Quay* ✛ *North of St. 240.*

Meta House

ARTS CENTERS | Since 2007, Meta House has been a trendy one-stop for culture in the capital, and a significant supporter of the development of the Cambodian arts scene. Their calendar of events includes movie screenings, live music, DJ sets, theater performances, arts exhibitions, and media festivals. ✉ *St. 228, Sangkat Tonle Bassac* ☎ *023/218987* ⊕ *www.meta-house.com.*

Katy Peri's Pizza

🍴

9

Cambodia PHNOM PENH

Though not a bar, this pizza oven attached to a moped is an essential part of Phnom Penh nightlife. It's usually stationed at popular nightlife hub Street 51, serving hot pizzas and Peri Peri chicken to hungry patrons, keeping them fueled into the night.

🛍 Shopping

In addition to the the numerous malls springing up around the city, there are a great many shops and markets selling everything from fake antiques to fine jewelry, while polished boutiques sell items made with local materials and often supporting socially disadvantaged individuals. Prices are generally set at shops, so save your bargaining skills for the markets. The best shops are to be found on Streets 178 and 240.

ANTIQUES AND FINE ART

Le Lezard Bleu

ANTIQUES & COLLECTIBLES | A boutique gallery selling creations inspired by Cambodian culture and made by local artisans, Le Lezard Bleu stocks items such as Khmer posters, sculptures, prints, and silks. ✉ *61 St. 240* ☎ *023/986978* ⊕ *lelezardbleu.business.site.*

BOOKS AND RECORDS

D's Books

BOOKS | Located down Street 240, a leafy thoroughfare close to the Royal Palace, this unassuming secondhand bookstore is one of the city's foremost purveyors of English-language tomes. There are books in a broad range of categories, from novels to cooking to home design, plus an excellent selection of Cambodian literature. ✉ *79 St. 240* ☎ *012/726355.*

Wang Dang Doodle by Space Four Zero

RECORDS | It doesn't get more groovy than this record store, usually just called Space Four Zero. As well as vintage vinyl (including an impressive and rare collection of Cambodian prints from the '60s "Golden Era of Cambodian Pop"), they also sell limited edition artworks and concert posters. ✉ *30EA, St. 240 1/2* ☎ *069/571100* ⊕ *spacefourzero.com.*

CLOTHING AND ACCESSORIES

Amboh

SHOES | Espadrilles are the ultimate casual and comfortable summer footwear and the concept has been adopted at Amboh, where they create shoes with fun designs that combine trendy patterns with the country's signature *krama* (a multiuse checkered scarf). New collections are regularly released, meaning this is a place you can come back time and time again for a cool new pair. ✉ *45 St. 21 (Abdul Carime St.)* ☎ *070/572094* ⊘ *Closed Sun.*

Ambre

WOMEN'S CLOTHING | After studying at the Paris School of Fine Arts and the Esmod School of Fashion Design, Romyda Keth made a name for herself abroad. Since returning to her native Cambodia, she opened her own fashion boutique in an old colonial villa and showcases her stylish women's fashion in the elegant venue. ✉ *37 St. 178* ☎ *023/217935* ⊕ *ambreshop.business.site.*

Clothesline Resale Boutique

SECOND-HAND | Run by a friendly Khmer-American couple, this thrift shop is a bit hard to find, down a tiny alleyway, but rewards the adventurous with a treasure trove of vintage threads. After you've discovered a new outfit, check out the secondhand shoes, bags, and books. ✉ *186E St. 122z* ☎ *012/382402* ⊘ *Closed Mon. and Tues.*

Krama Scarves

The *krama* is a uniquely Cambodian item: it's essentially a check-patterned scarf, but its use extends far beyond keeping your neck warm. Farmers in the field tie it around their head to keep the sun off, ladies wrap it around their middle as a decorative belt, babies are rocked to sleep in it as a hammock, martial arts fighters wear it as a bandanna, and the list goes on. It's the perfect useful souvenir. Note that the patterns don't signify a particular tribe or location, they're just aesthetically pleasing.

CRAFTS

★ Daughters of Cambodia Visitor Centre

SOUVENIRS | Providing new opportunities to victims of sex trafficking, this boutique sells men's and women's clothing and accessories, children's toys, and home decor items. There is also a lovely café and a spa. ✉ *63C St. 456* ☎ *077/657678* ⊕ *www.daughtersofcambodia.org.*

Friends 'N' Stuff

CRAFTS | Trendy, playful, and eco-friendly accessories can be found here, next to the ultrapopular Friends restaurant. Check out the cool, locally crafted laptop cases made from recycled bicycle tires, handbags made from food packets, hardback books about Cambodia, Khmer cookbooks, and lots of other fun stuff—all for the worthy cause of helping street children achieve a better quality of life. ✉ *215 St. 13, Khan Daun Penh* ⊹ *Inside Friends Futures Factory (F3)* ☎ *010/886968* ⊕ *www.mithsamlanh.org.*

★ Trunkh

CRAFTS | For a unique souvenir, browse the interesting found-item crafts that the creative Australian owners of this shop put together. They take pieces of Cambodian design, such as old toys, signage, and patterned tiles, and turn them into one-of-a-kind pieces of art. They also make their own fabric prints, spinning them into shirts, shorts, and pillows. ⊠ *126 St. 19* ☎ *017/886440* ⊕ *trunkh.com* ☾ *Closed Mon.*

MARKETS

Central Market

MARKET | Psar Thmei, popularly known as Central Market, is a 1930s art-deco-style structure in the center of the city that sells foodstuffs, household goods, fake antiques, and some silver and gold jewelry. You're expected to bargain—start off by offering half the named price and you'll probably end up paying about 70%. Take your time to find what you want, as the vendors can sometimes be a little pushy. It's busiest in the morning. ⊠ *Blvd. 128 (Kampuchea Krom)* ✣ *At St. 76 and Neayok Souk St.*

Phnom Penh Night Market

MARKET | This lively riverfront market attracts locals and tourists alike for basic clothing, traditional handmade souvenirs, accessories, and gift shopping until midnight. Several stands sell freshly made local dishes as well as drinks like sugarcane and bean juices, and there is a large sitting area covered in rattan mats. ⊠ *Sisowath Quay* ✣ *Between St. 106 and St. 108.*

Russian Market

MARKET | A popular location for discovering some of the best bargains in town, the Psar Tuol Tom Pong, or Russian Market (it was named after the Russian diplomats who used to shop here in the 1980s), sells a huge variety of Cambodian handicrafts, local *krama* scarves, Khmer wood carvings, baskets, and much more. Located in a trendy district, there's plenty of options for dinner and drinks once you finish your shopping. ⊠ *Sts. 155 and 440.*

SILK

Sayon Silkworks

FABRICS | There's an excellent collection of silk accessories, quilts, and other items for the home, such as cushions, all adorned in exquisite colors and patterns, at this shop that offers employment to impoverished women from remote regions. ⊠ *79 St. 240.*

FOOD

Veggy's

FOOD | This cute shop sells fine wines, cheeses, and meats from around the world. It also supplies imported dry goods and fresh veggies, as the name indicates. ⊠ *23 St. 240* ☎ *023/211534* ⊕ *veggyscambodia.com.*

Tonle Bati

33 km (20 miles) south of Phnom Penh.

On weekends, many Phnom Penh residents head for this small lake a half-hour drive south on Highway 2. It has a beach with refreshment stalls and souvenir stands. Note that you'll encounter many beggars and children clamoring for attention here. The nearby but more remote **Ta Phrom,** a 12th-century temple built around the time of Siem Reap's Angkor Thom and Bayon, is less chaotic. The five-chambered laterite temple has several well-preserved Hindu and Buddhist bas-reliefs. Nearby is an attractive, smaller temple, **Yeah Peau.** Admission to Ta Phrom and Tonle Bati is $3 and open to the public at all times. The **Phnom Tamao Wildlife Rescue Centre**, which houses animals rescued from the illegal wildlife trade, is about 11 km (7 miles) farther south. Tours can be booked via the Wildlife Alliance (*www.wildlifealliance.org*).

Cambodia Then and Now

Internationally, Cambodia is best known for two contrasting chapters of its long history. The first is the Khmer Empire, which in its heyday covered much of modern-day Southeast Asia. Today the ruins of Angkor attest to the nation's immutable cultural heritage.

The second chapter is the country's recent history and legacy of Khmer Rouge brutality in the late 1970s, which left at least 1.7 million Cambodians dead. In 1993 the United Nations sponsored democratic elections that failed to honor the people's vote. Civil war continued until 1998, when another round of elections was held, and violent riots ensued in the aftermath. Although much more settled than previously, Cambodia's long-standing political turmoil—once on the battlefield and now in much more subtle displays—continues to shape the nation's day-to-day workings.

Through decades of war, a genocide, continued widespread government corruption, high rates of violence and mental illness, the provision of billions of dollars in international aid, and the disappearance of much of that money, Cambodia has suffered its demons. Yet Cambodians are a forward-thinking, sharp-minded, and friendly people, whose warm smiles are not yet jaded by global tourism and do not belie the inordinate suffering their nation has so recently endured. Though practically destroyed by the regional conflict and homegrown repression of the 1970s, individual Cambodians have risen from those disasters, and a new, hardworking, creative, and young middle class has blossomed.

Ecology and Wildlife

Until relatively recently, more than half of Cambodia was blanketed in forests, but the landscape has changed in recent decades as a result of ruthless and mercenary deforestation. The country is blessed with powerful waters: the Mekong and Tonle Sap rivers, and Tonle Sap Lake, which feeds 70% of the nation. The surrounding mountain ranges, protecting Cambodia's long river valleys, are still home to a variety of indigenous hill tribes and—at least for now—some of the region's rarest remaining wildlife.

Historically, the three ranges of low mountains—the northern Dangkrek, the exotically named Elephant Mountains in the south, and the country's highest range, the Cardamoms, in the southwest—formed natural barriers against foreign invasion and were used as fortresses during the war years. Among these ranges is a depression in the northwest of Cambodia connecting the country with the lowlands in Thailand; by allowing communication between the two countries, this geographic feature played an important part in the history of the Khmer nation. In eastern Cambodia the land rises gradually into a forested plateau that continues into the Annamese Mountains, the backbone of neighboring Vietnam.

Colonization, War, and Invasion

As the seat of the Khmer Empire from the 9th to the 13th century, Cambodia developed a complex society based first on Hinduism and then, later, on Buddhism. After the decline of the Khmers and the ascendancy of the

Siamese, Cambodia acceded to becoming a French protectorate; they ruled from the mid-1860s until 1953.

Shortly after the end of World War II, during which the Japanese had occupied Cambodia, independence became the rallying cry for all of Indochina. Cambodia soon became a sovereign power with a monarchy, ruled by King Norodom Sihanouk, who surprisingly abdicated in favor of his father in 1955 and took the opportunity to enter the public stage as a mercurial politician and the leader of an emerging state.

In the early 1970s the destabilizing consequences of the Vietnam War sparked a horrible chain of events. The U.S. government secretly bombed Cambodia, arranged a coup to oust the king, and invaded parts of the country in an attempt to rout the Viet Cong. Civil war ensued and in 1975 the Khmer Rouge, led by French-educated Pol Pot, emerged as the victors. A regime of terror followed. Under a program of extreme Mao Tse-tung–inspired reeducation centered on forced agricultural collectives, the cities were emptied and hundreds of thousands of civilians were tortured and executed. Hundreds of thousands more succumbed to starvation and disease. During just four short years of incredibly brutal Khmer Rouge rule, somewhere between 1 and 2 million Cambodians—almost one-third of the population—were killed.

By 1979 the country lay in ruins. Vietnam, now unified under the Hanoi government, invaded Cambodia in response to a series of cross-border attacks and massacres in the Mekong Delta by the Khmer Rouge. The invasion swept the group from Phnom Penh and forced them into the hills bordering Thailand, where they remained entrenched for years. United Nations–brokered peace accords were signed in 1991. International mediation allowed the return of Norodom Sihanouk as king and the formation of a coalition government that included Khmer Rouge elements after parliamentary elections in 1993. But civil war still continued.

Reconciliation and Recovery

In 1997, Second Prime Minister Hun Sen toppled First Prime Minister Norodom Ranariddh (son of the King) in a coup. During the following year's national elections, Hun Sen won a plurality and formed a new government, despite charges of election rigging. Pol Pot died of natural causes in his mountain stronghold in April 1998, and the remaining Khmer Rouge elements lost any influence left.

It took years for the United Nations and the Cambodian government to establish a tribunal that brought to justice the few surviving key leaders of the Khmer Rouge regime. Proceedings began in 2007, but only one former Khmer Rouge leader, Duch, the infamous head of Tuol Sleng, was put in jail (he died in 2020); Ta Mok, the so-called Butcher, was the only other Khmer Rouge leader to be imprisoned, but he died in 2006. Most others have now passed away, but it's remarkable how many blended with ease into modern society and remained within the government.

Foreign investment and the development of tourism have been very strong in recent years, but it remains to be seen whether domestic problems can truly be solved by Prime Minister Hun Sen (a former Khmer Rouge commander) and his hard-line rule.

GETTING HERE AND AROUND
Hiring a car and driver in Phnom Penh
is perhaps the easiest way to visit Tonle
Bati (around $50 including waiting time),
and if you do this, you can easily combine
the trip with Phnom Chisor. The drive
takes about 30 minutes.

Diethelm Travel *(see Cambodia Planner)*
arranges tours to Tonle Bati.

Phnom Chisor

55 km (34 miles) south of Phnom Penh.

A trip to Phnom Chisor is worth the drive
just for the view from the top of the hill
of the same name. There's a road to the
summit, but most visitors prefer the
20-minute walk to the top, where stunning vistas of the Cambodian countryside
unfold. At the summit the 11th-century
temple is a Khmer masterpiece of
laterite, brick, and sandstone. Admission
is $3.

GETTING HERE AND AROUND
Though the (decent) bus ride is cheap,
you can combine Tonle Bati and Phnom
Chisor in one trip if you hire a car and
driver (about $50 per day), perhaps the
easiest way to visit Phnom Chisor. The
drive takes about 20 minutes from Tonle
Bati or 40 minutes from Phnom Penh.
Takeo-bound GST and Neak Krorhorm
buses (departing from Phnom Penh every
hour) stop at Prasat Neang Khmau; from
there you can hire a moto to take you up
the hill. The whole trip should take no
more than an hour.

Diethelm Travel and Hanuman Travel
(see Cambodia Planner) arrange tours to
Phnom Chisor.

Koh Dach

30 km (19 miles) north of Phnom Penh.

This Mekong River island's main
attractions are its beach and its handicrafts community of silk weavers, wood
carvers, potters, painters, and jewelry
makers. The beach isn't spectacular by
Southeast Asian standards, but it is convenient for Phnom Penh getaways. In all,
the trip over to the island is quick; most
people spend about half a day on this
excursion, which you can visit by tuk-tuk,
motorcycle, or by boat from the Phnom
Penh waterfront.

GETTING HERE AND AROUND
Any tuk-tuk or moto driver can take you
to Koh Dach from Phnom Penh. Alternatively, you can hire a car and driver for the
day (about $50 per day). The trip takes
approximately two hours each way, and
involves a ferry trip to the island.

Diethelm Travel and Hanuman Travel *(see
Cambodia Planner)* arrange tours to Koh
Dach.

Udong

45 km (28 miles) north of Phnom Penh.

It may seem surprising, but this small
town served as the Khmer capital from
the early 1600s until 1866, when King
Norodom, under French guidance, moved
the capital south to Phnom Penh. Today
it's an important pilgrimage destination
for Cambodians paying homage to their
former kings. You can join them on the
climb to the pagoda-studded hilltop,
site of the revered Vihear Prah Ath Roes
assembly hall, which still bears the scars
of local conflicts from the Khmer Rouge
era. At its foot is a small market and food
stalls.

GETTING HERE AND AROUND

Udong is best reached by catching a Sorya bus to Kampong Chhnang from the Central Bus Station and getting off at the junction at the Km 37 mark. Motos and tuk-tuks will then take you to the temples. The bus costs around $2.

You can also take a boat from Phnom Penh; this can be arranged through your hotel or any travel agent.

Diethelm Travel and Hanuman Travel *(see Cambodia Planner)* arrange tours to Udong.

Kampong Cham

125 km (78 miles) northeast of Phnom Penh.

Cambodia's third-largest city was also an ancient Khmer center of culture and power on the Mekong River, and it has a pre-Angkorian temple, **Wat Nokor.** (Sadly, the temple itself is in a state of disrepair and the $2 entry fee is unmerited.) Just outside town are the twin temple-topped hills, Phnom Pros and Phnom Srei (included in the price). Ask a local guide to explain the interesting legend surrounding their creation. In the ecotourism village of Cheungkok, about 5 km (3 miles) south of town, you can see silk making, carving, and other traditional crafts in progress and also buy the wares directly from villagers. All profits are reinvested in the village. Kampong Cham can be visited in a few hours, but with Cheungkok it is an all-day trip.

GETTING HERE AND AROUND

You can get to Kampong Cham from Phnom Penh by taxi or bus; the trip takes about three hours. Any guesthouse or hotel can arrange for a taxi. Expect to pay $6 for a single bus ticket and $50 for a taxi from Phnom Penh. The buses (Giant Ibis provides the best service) leave hourly from the bus station at the Central Market.

 Restaurants

Kampong Cham has the usual local food stalls and shophouses, but few restaurants of note.

Smile

$ | **CAMBODIAN** | Buddhism for Social Development Action runs this experiential training restaurant. Even so, the dining experience (Khmer and Western, leaning heavily towards Italian, food served) on the whole is better than many professional setups. $ *Average main: $3* ⊠ *6 Mort Tunle St. (aka Riverside St.)* ☎ *017/997709* ⊕ *www.bsda-cambodia.org.*

 Hotels

LBN Asian Hotel

$ | **HOTEL** | This 11-story hotel on the bank of the Mekong has great views, either over the city or the Mekong River. **Pros:** views; centrally located; understated decor. **Cons:** occasional hot water issues; sometimes loud music from rooftop bar; price high for location. $ *Rooms from: $35* ⊠ *#11, Preah Sihanouk Blvd.* ☎ *012/999942* ⊕ *lbnasian.com* ⊙ *Free Breakfast.*

Monorom VIP Hotel

$ | **HOTEL** | The heavy, sculpted wooden furniture of the large rooms may be too much for some, but it's apparent that the owners of this hotel have made a real effort to create a pleasant and polished environment. **Pros:** nice views; central, riverside location; comfortable beds. **Cons:** no breakfast; bored, inattentive staff; not all rooms have views. $ *Rooms from: $20* ⊠ *Mort Tunle St. (aka Riverside St.)* ☎ *092/777102* ⊕ *www.monoromviphotel.com* ⤴ *50 rooms, 1 suite* ⊙ *No Meals.*

Religion in Cambodia

As in neighboring Thailand, Laos, and Vietnam, Buddhism is the predominant religion in Cambodia, but animism and superstition continue to play strong roles in Khmer culture and society. Many people believe in powerful *neak ta*, or territorial guardian spirits. Spirit shrines are common outside Khmer houses as well as on temple grounds and along roadsides. The Khmer Loeu hill tribes, who live in the remote mountain areas of Ratanakkiri and Mondulkiri provinces, and some tribes of the Cardamom Mountains are animists, believing in spirits living in trees, rocks, and water.

The main layer of Cambodian religion is a mix of Hinduism and Buddhism. These two religions both reached the country from India about 2,000 years ago and played a pivotal role in the social and ideological life of the earliest Khmer kingdoms. After Hinduism, Buddhism flourished in Cambodia in the 12th to 13th century, when King Jayavarman VII embraced Mahayana Buddhism. By the 15th century, influenced by Buddhist monks from Siam and Sri Lanka, most Cambodians practiced Theravada Buddhism.

Cambodian religious literature and royal classical dance draw on Hindu models, such as the *Reamker*, an ancient epic about an Indian prince searching for his abducted wife and fighting an evil king. Brahman priests still play an important role at court rituals.

Cambodia's Muslim Chams, who number a few hundred thousand, are the descendants of the Champa Kingdom that was based in what is today Vietnam. They have had a presence in this area since the 15th century, when they were forced from the original kingdom. The country's 60,000 Roman Catholics are mainly ethnic Vietnamese, while a small Chinese minority follows Taoism.

Kompong Thom Ruins

160 km (99 miles) north of Phnom Penh, 144 km (90 miles) southeast of Siem Reap.

These ruins, exactly halfway between Phnom Penh and Siem Reap, are even older than those at Angkor. They are all that remain of the 7th-century Sambor Prei Kuk, the capital of Zhen La, a loose federation of city-states. The ruins, which are free and open to the public at all times, are near the Stung Sen River, 35 km (22 miles) northeast of the provincial town of Kampong.

GETTING HERE AND AROUND
The ruins are a day trip by taxi from Siem Reap (two hours; $50) or Phnom Penh (three hours; also $50, or $10 per person, shared). The journey can be dusty and hot in the dry season and muddy and wet in the rainy season. All buses between Phnom Penh and Siem Reap stop in Kompong Thom, but you will pay the full fare (about $10) regardless. Arrange local transportation via tuk-tuk or moto (about $25 for the full tour of the ruins).

Kratie

340 km (217 miles) northeast of Phnom Penh.

Kratie is famous for the colony of freshwater Irrawaddy dolphins that inhabit the Mekong River about15 km (9 miles) north of town in the village of Kampi.

TIP→ **The dolphins are most active in the early morning and late afternoon.**

Tuk-tuks and hired cars with driver from Kratie charge about $10 for the journey to the stretch of river where the dolphins can be observed. You will likely have to hire a local boatman to take you to where the dolphins are, as they move up and down the river. The trip costs $9 for two people, and $7 for three or more.

GETTING HERE AND AROUND

Several bus companies from Phnom Penh's Central Bus Station offer regular service to Kratie (six to seven hours; $10). Expect delays in the wet season. You can also get a shared taxi or hire your own driver, but as always buses are a far safer option.

Diethelm Travel *(see Cambodia Planner)* arranges tours to Kratie.

🍴 Restaurants

Kratie has an abundance of local food shops. Most guesthouses have simple menus, and there is a lively food-stall scene in town.

The C+ Kratie
$ | CAFÉ | This charming cafe right on the river is a lovely spot to relax with a coffee. They also serve some of the best bubble tea in town, as well as fruity treats such as the blueberry frappe. **Known for:** outdoor and indoor seating; fruit teas and coffee blends; contemporary design. [$] *Average main: $2* ✉ *Preah Soramarith Quay* ☎ *017/961964* 💳 *No credit cards.*

🛏 Hotels

Soriyabori Resort
$$ | RESORT | After the long bus or taxi trip to Kratie, it is another 20 minutes by boat and tuk-tuk to get to Soriyabori Resort, tucked on the northern end of the blissful island of Koh Trong. **Pros:** nature all around; free bikes for exploring the island; peaceful location (no cars). **Cons:** getting to and from the resort can be challenging; food and drinks on the expensive side; nonguests pay $5 to use the pool. [$] *Rooms from: $60* ✉ *Koh Trong* ☎ *012/770650* 🌐 *soriyabori.com* 🛏 *15 bungalows* 🍴 *Free Breakfast.*

★ **Le Relais de Chhlong**
$$ | HOTEL | Once the home of a French trader, this historic property on the banks of the Mekong has been immaculately restored to its former splendor, with the addition of a large pool and a new wing. **Pros:** French breakfast; Old World charm; riverside views. **Cons:** limited local activities; 45 minutes from Kratie; some neighborhood noise at times. [$] *Rooms from: $78* ✉ *Road 308, Chhlong* ☎ *012/347309* 🌐 *lerelaisdechhlong.com* 🍴 *Free Breakfast* 🛏 *10 suites.*

Ratanakiri Province

Ban Lung is 635 km (395 miles) northeast of Phnom Penh.

Both Ratanakkiri and neighboring Mondulkiri provinces are mountainous and once covered with dense jungle, which is rapidly giving way to mainly rubber plantations, and together they are home to 12 different Khmer Loeu ethnic-minority groups. The government has developed four community-based projects in the region. The eventual aim is to reinvent large sections of the area as ecotourism destinations, making them self-sufficient and helping the communities reduce the impact on the natural resources.

GETTING HERE AND AROUND

From Phnom Penh there are buses to Banlung (10 hours; $8 to $14) on Virak Buntham bus lines. The journey is much improved from a few years ago with the opening of a paved road all the way there. Taxis are also always an option.

Diethelm Travel *(see Cambodia Planner)* arranges tours to Ratanakiri.

In Ban Lung you can hire a jeep with a driver-guide or, if you're very adventurous, rent a motorcycle, to visit the fascinating destinations an hour or two away.

 # Sights

Ratanakkiri Province is remote, but it is slowly building a reputation as an eco-tourism destination, and the government is trying hard to promote tourism to this part of Cambodia. Intrepid travelers will find natural and cultural attractions, including waterfalls, jungle treks, lakes, villages, and the Airavata Elephant Foundation.

Airavata Elephant Foundation

NATURE PRESERVE | FAMILY | Located a few kilometers south of Ratanakiri's capital Banlung, Airavata is a "new generation" elephant camp following responsible and ethical alternatives to mass tourism. In an effort to help save some of Cambodia's dwindling population of 300-odd elephants, they work under patronage of Cambodia's King Norodom Sihamoni. Travelers meet the animals in optimal natural conditions, guided by highly selected indigenous mahouts who treat elephants in the best possible way, as they enjoy their work. ☒ ✢ *10 km south of Banlung, past Okatieng waterfall* ☎ *012/770650* ⊕ *www.airavata-cambodia.com.*

Ban Lung

TOWN | The provincial capital is a small, sleepy town that holds a certain romance as a far-flung capital, away from the influence of Phnom Penh, but otherwise offers little more than slow-paced local life and clouds of red dust in the dry season—or mud in the wet season. Arrive with everything you need, as Western goods are sometimes difficult to obtain. Most of the decent hotels are located around Kan Seng lake.

Bokeo

MINE | A visit to the gem mines of the Bokeo area, 30 km (20 miles) east of Ban Lung, can be arranged through your hotel, or any moto driver in Ban Lung can take you there. Some of the mines are increasingly deep, man-sized potholes, and mining is for semiprecious stones such as zircon. As you drive through the villages in the area, the villagers line up to sell you their finds. *Bokeo* literally means "gem mine."

Virachey National Park

NATIONAL PARK | This lush and scenic jungle, 35 km (22 miles) northeast of Ban Lung, is home to the two-tiered Bu Sra Waterfall and lots of wildlife. Tuk-tuks and motos will take you here from Ban Lung ($15), but all treks and eco-activities should be prearranged in Ban Lung at the park's visitor information center. The best way to discover the area and possibly spot rare species found here is through one of the local tour operators. ☒ *Banlung* ☒ *$5.*

Yeak Laom Lake

BODY OF WATER | FAMILY | Lodged in a volcanic crater 5 km (3 miles) east of Ban Lung, this mystical lake, bordered by jungle, is sacred to the Khmer Loeu hill tribes. It's a half mile in diameter and 154 feet deep, and there are wooden jetties from which to launch yourself into the cool waters. Swing from a hammock in one of the huts lining the shore—these cost $3 to rent for the day, but if you order food it's free. The local specialty is *prung*, bamboo stuffed with vegetables, meat, and local herbs and spices which are cooked over an open fire. Stalls at the entrance sell jungle honey, as well as Cambodian *krama* scarves. Take a tuk-tuk ($3) or moto from Ban Lung. ✉ *Banlung* 🎫 *$1.50.*

🍴 Restaurants

Chantrea

$ | **CAMBODIAN** | This roadside open-air restaurant serves large helpings of excellent local dishes at bargain prices. **Known for:** very budget friendly; fried beef salad (lok lak); generous portions. [$] *Average main: $2* ✉ *Crossroads of St. 29 and St. 514, Banlung* ☎ *088/728–2878* 💳 *No credit cards.*

The Green Carrot

$ | **INTERNATIONAL** | In the center of sleepy Banlung, this popular open-air restaurant serves a mixed menu of simple Western and Asian dishes. There are burgers (fish and beef options), ham and cheese sandwiches, and fried noodles, as well as a large selection of tasty vegetarian options, including Greek salad and tofu curry. **Known for:** $2 happy hour cocktails; large vegetarian menu; cozy atmosphere. [$] *Average main: $4* ✉ *78A Krong Ban Lung, Banlung* ☎ *071/929–3278* 💳 *No credit cards.*

🛏 Hotels

Morokotratanak Hotel

$$ | **HOTEL** | It doesn't have the rustic country vibes of the simpler homestays that dot the area, but this modern hotel in the center of Banlung provides a comfortable stay while you plan your forays around the area. **Pros:** on-site cafe and rooftop bar; convenient central location; walking distance to restaurants. **Cons:** service is hit or miss; mattresses are hard; limited breakfast buffet. [$] *Rooms from: $50* ✉ *St. 78A, Banlung* ☎ *088/5828555* 🌐 *morokotratanakhotel.com* 🍽 *Free Breakfast.*

Terres Rouge Lodge

$$ | **HOTEL** | The former residence of the governor of Ratanakiri Province has been transformed into a scenic resort with a beautifully landscaped tropical garden. **Pros:** good restaurant and bar; spacious rooms, some with lake views; beautiful colonial building. **Cons:** some rooms are showing a little wear and tear; sporadic service; a little out of the town center. [$] *Rooms from: $75* ✉ *Boeung Kan Siang Lake, Banlung* ☎ *012/856242* 🌐 *www.ratanakiri-lodge.com* 🛏 *22 rooms, 7 suites* 🍽 *Free Breakfast.*

Battambang

GETTING HERE AND AROUND

All the major bus companies depart daily from Phnom Penh's Central Market to Battambang (five hours; $9), and in some cases, on to Poipet. There is also a train service leaving Phnom Penh Railway Station at 6:30 am every other day, stopping at Pursat and Battambang (eight hours) en route to Poipet. Buses also leave from Siem Reap (three hours; $6). For the more adventurous, lovely but lengthy boat trips are a good option. The ride to Siem Reap can take anywhere between five and 10 hours ($20). A hired car with a driver costs about $50 a day, but settle on the price before setting off.

👁 Sights

The few sights to see in and around town include some Angkor-era temple ruins and the Khmer Rouge "killing caves." The town is walkable and full of vibrant art galleries and cafés, and strolling down to the river in the evening is a pleasant way to pass the time. Most of the out-of-town sights, including the bamboo train, can be visited in a day, renting a tuk-tuk with driver for about $25.

Heritage Walk

NEIGHBORHOOD | The cluster of blocks between Street 1, parallel to the Sanker River, and Street 3, and all the way down to Street 127, house a great variety of historic architecture representing diverse phases of the city's legacy. Ask your hotel for one of the annotated walking maps by Khmer Architecture Tours and explore on foot. ■ TIP→ **Don't miss the very interesting and free museum at the Governor's Mansion, itself an exquisite piece of colonial architecture.** ☒ *Sangkat* ⊕ *www.ka-tours.org.*

Phnom Banan

RUINS | In the countryside 25 km (15 miles) south from the city, this 11th-century hilltop temple has five impressive towers and is sometimes referred to as "the mini Angkor Wat." Reaching the temple involves a hike up 350 or so steps, so go after lunch when it's less hot. Tuk-tuks from Battambang charge $10 to $15 for the round-trip. There is a mystical little cave round the side of the hill whose waters are supposed to induce visions. ☒ *Banan Hill* ⊠ *$2.*

Phnom Sampeou

HISTORIC SIGHT | In addition to being the site of a temple, this hill, 10 km (7 miles) southwest of Battambang, was also used by the Khmer Rouge to execute prisoners in a group of killing caves. In one, which contains the skeletal remains of some of the victims, you can stand on the eerily dark floor and look up to a hole in the cave roof, with sunlight streaming through. The Khmer Rouge reportedly pushed their victims through that hole to their deaths on the rocks below. ☒ *Hwy. 57.*

Psar Nath Market

MARKET | This historic central market, built in the art deco style during French rule, is a great spot to buy fresh foods, gems, and Battambang's famous fruit—lime-green oranges. Vendors sell everything from tourist souvenirs to electronics imported from China. Some stalls have textiles, but most of these are imported. ☒ *On the Sangker River.*

Romcheik5 Art Space

ART GALLERY | This hip art gallery hosts rotating exhibits of local artists on the ground floor. Upstairs a museum collects the best work from the four young co-founders, all graduates of the Phare Ponleu Selpak School, who were expelled from Thailand during childhood and shelterd by an NGO. ☒ *St. 201A* ☎ *092/304210* ⊠ *$2.*

Wat Ek Phnom

RUINS | Long before the French arrived, Battambang was an important Khmer city, and among its many temples is this 11th-century Angkorian structure. Even though it has been heavily looted over the centuries, the temple still has a few fine stone carvings in excellent condition. In front of the ruins stands a newly built pagoda. It's 10 km (7 miles) north of the city and getting here via tuk-tuk or moto will cost around $10. ■ TIP→ **Admission is free with a ticket to Wat Banan, but only on the same day.** ☒ *St. 1734* ⊠ *$3.*

🍴 Restaurants

There's a good selection of restaurants in town, including some spots serving excellent Western cuisine. Most places to eat are at the lower end of the price range. A Khmer food market down by the river is open in the late afternoon or early evening.

Jaan Bai

$ | CAMBODIAN | The name means "rice bowl" in Khmer and this social enterprise restaurant curated by the Cambodian Children Trust dishes up tasty Khmer and Thai mains in a cozy and artsy atmosphere—rotating exhibits of local artworks hang from the wall, and it's often packed with young creatives in the evenings. Jaan Bai provides skills development and employment for disadvantaged Cambodians, and a share of the profits goes

towards community development work.
Known for: no MSG in the food; good
set meals for sharing; locally brewed
organic coffee. $ *Average main: $4* ⊠ *St.
2* ✛ *Next to Psar Nat* ☎ *078/263144*
⊕ *www.cambodianchildrenstrust.org/
review-jaan-bai-restaurant.*

Kinyei Cafe

$ | **CAFÉ** | A tiny, hip coffee shop in the
historical district strewn, Kinyei is decorated with potted plants and managed by
knowledgeable local baristas who serve a
robust blend of beans from Thailand, Vietnam, and Cambodia. The lunch options,
such as the veggie rolls, are perfect
for a quick bite. **Known for:** gluten-free
choices; strong coffee; good breakfast
sets. $ *Average main: $3* ⊠ *229 St. 1.5*
☎ *069/734745* ⊕ *www.kinyei.org.*

 # Hotels

★ Battambang Resort

$$ | **RESORT** | A small paradise, this
tranquil resort has a lush garden where
you can relax in a hammock among
exotic fruit trees and organically grown
herbs, flowers, and vegetables, all used
by its restaurant to create healthy Asian
and European dishes. **Pros:** free shuttle
service to town; lovely pool; free use
of bikes. **Cons:** not many local dining
options; a little out of the way; nearby
high-rises spoil the charm. $ *Rooms
from: $70* ⊠ *Wat Ko Village* ☎ *012/510100*
⊕ *www.battambangresort.com* ⊋ *10
rooms* ❍ *Free Breakfast.*

★ La Villa

$$ | **HOTEL** | This boutique hotel is in a
beautifully restored 1930s colonial house,
with well-maintained, spacious rooms
that have an old-world charm and quaint
art deco feel. **Pros:** large, clean pool;
beautiful architecture; lovely riverfront
location. **Cons:** service can lack attention
to detail; not many facilities; starting to
show some wear and tear. $ *Rooms
from: $80* ⊠ *185 Pom Romchek, 5 Kom,*

Rattanak Commune ☎ *053/730151*
⊕ *www.lavilla-battambang.net* ⊋ *3
rooms, 4 suites* ❍ *Free Breakfast.*

Maisons Wat Kor

$$ | **RESORT** | The traditional Khmer villas
here, set in lush garden surroundings,
with a swimming pool, spa, and an excel-
lent restaurant, are about 3 km south
of the Old Town. **Pros:** great value for
the money; attentive service; beautiful
natural setting. **Cons:** basic continental
breakfast; 10-minute drive from town;
not many activities in the area. $ *Rooms
from: $70* ⊠ *221 St. 800* ✛ *Wat Kor Vil-
lage* ☎ *017/555377* ⊕ *www.maisonswat-
kor.com* ❍ *Free Breakfast* ⊋ *8 rooms.*

Bambu

$$ | **HOTEL** | This heritage-inspired property
oozes charm, with a combination of
wood Khmer and colonial French styles,
even if the building is not actually as
old as it looks. **Pros:** selection of room
styles; welcoming poolside bar; charming vintage design. **Cons:** limited free
breakfast; not on the riverside; no shade
at the pool. $ *Rooms from: $90* ⊠ *St.
203, Rattanak Commune* ☎ *053/953900*
⊕ *bambuhotel.com* ❍ *Free Breakfast*
⊋ *16 rooms.*

 # Nightlife

Vintage Wine Bar Mezze

WINE BARS | The nondescript exterior
makes this spot easy to pass by but it's
actually one of the friendliest bars in
Battambang, with a wide range of beers,
cocktails, and wine, as well as excellent
value tapas. ⊠ *Pub St.* ☎ *071/202–6527.*

 # Performing Arts

★ Phare Ponleu Selpak

ARTS CENTER | **FAMILY** | The famous Phare
circus in Siem Reap actually originated in
Battambang, and for more than 15 years,
the Phare Ponleu Selpak center has
offered quality arts training to locals. Their

daily shows ($14) combine dance, theater, live music, and circus performances with Cambodian narratives. Shows start at 7 pm, and there are also guided visits of the campus ($5) from Monday to Friday until 3:30 pm. ✉ *Anh Chanh Village, Ochar Commune* ☎ *077/554413* ⊕ *www.phareps.org.*

Shopping

Tep Kao Sol

ART GALLERIES | This is a good place to buy watercolors, reproductions, and postcards by leading Cambodian artists. On the first floor, co-owner and artist Loeum Lorn exhibits his peculiar artworks created by printing photographs of ice on canvas. ✉ *129 St. 2* ☎ *017/982992.*

Siem Reap

315 km (195 miles) north of Phnom Penh.

Siem Reap, which means "Siam defeated," based on a 15th-century battle with Cambodia's neighbors to the west, has emerged as a modern, friendly, and elegantly low-key city with sophisticated shopping, dining, and nightlife options. After a long day at the Angkor Temple Complex, you can spend the evening strolling the Siem Reap River and dining at an outdoor table on a back alley in the hip old French quarter or Alley West off the more boisterous Pub Street, which is closed to traffic in the evening.

The Old Market area is a big draw and the perfect place to shop for souvenirs; dig through the silk, wood, and silver ornaments and accessories. A lot of the colonial buildings in the area were destroyed during the Khmer Rouge years, but many others have been restored and turned into upmarket resorts and restaurants.

You could spend an entire afternoon in the Old Market area, wandering from

shop to shop, café to café, gallery to gallery. It changes every month, with ever more delights in store. Long gone are the days when all the high-end souvenirs came from Thailand. Today numerous shops offer high-quality Cambodian silks, the famous Kampot pepper and other Cambodian spices, and herbal soaps and toiletries made from natural Cambodian products.

GETTING HERE AND AROUND

AIR

Angkor Air has five daily flights from Phnom Penh to Siem Reap costing about $100 each way and taking 40 to 45 minutes. Vietnam Airlines have five direct flights daily to and from Hanoi's Noibai Airport ($160 each way) and six daily flights direct to and from Ho Chi Minh City ($145 each way). There are also daily charter flights, which may offer a cheaper alternative.

Bangkok Airways flies six times daily between Siem Reap and Bangkok (one hour; $300 round-trip). Lao Air flies three times a week to Siem Reap from both Pakse (50 minutes; $150 one-way) and Vientiane (80 minutes; also $150 one-way), in Laos.

Royal Khmer Airlines and Angkor Air fly between Phnom Penh and Siem Reap (one hour; from $65 and up one-way). Siem Reap International Airport is 6 km (4 miles) northwest of town. The taxi fare to any hotel in Siem Reap is $5.

BOAT

The road to Phnom Penh was upgraded several years ago, but some tourists still prefer the six-hour boat trip on the Tonle Sap. High-speed ferries, or "bullet boats," depart from Phnom Penh for Siem Reap daily.

A daily boat travels from Battambang to Siem Reap (5 to 10 hours; $20) on the Tonle Sap.

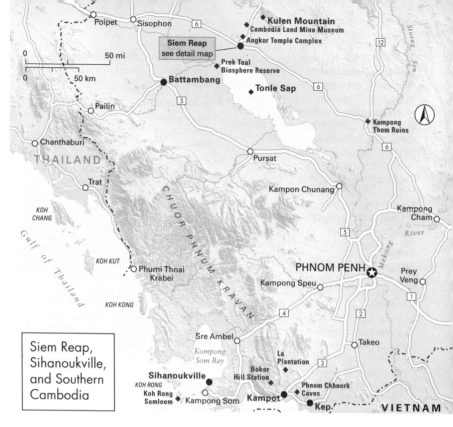

Siem Reap, Sihanoukville, and Southern Cambodia

■ TIP→ **In the dry season, the water level on the Tonle Sap is often low. Passengers may be required to switch boats, or boats might get stuck—a long ordeal.**

Boats arrive at the ferry port at Chong Khneas, 12 km (7½ miles) south of Siem Reap.

BUS

Siem Reap is accessible by direct bus from Phnom Penh (five to six hours; $5 to $13) on all major lines. Minvans also connect it to Kratie, Kampong Thom, and Battambang.

Travel agencies can help you arrange all bus trips.

CAR

The road to Siem Reap from Phnom Penh has greatly improved in recent years, and the trip by taxi takes four hours.

Nevertheless, if you hire a cheap driver, you'll be putting your life in the hands of a daredevil. Splurge a little for a more upmarket taxi company like Oudong Express (*oudongexpress.com*), or take the bus instead.

MOTO AND TUK-TUK

Tuk-tuk and moto drivers have kept apace with the growing number of tourists visiting Siem Reap: they'll find you—you won't need to find them. They charge about $2 to $4 for a trip within town, but be sure to settle on the fare before setting off, or use a ride-hail app like Grab and PassApp to secure a reasonable and fixed fare. There are no cruising taxis, but hotels can order one.

TOURS

Indochine Exploration

Bespoke ecotourism options are offered throughout Cambodia by this company whose partners are conservationists and expert explorers. Many of the employees here previously worked for other conservation groups, and this has become the preferred tour operator for all the established high-end hotels. A tour with Indochine Exploration could be a highlight of your trip to Siem Reap. ⊠ *Siem Reap* ☎ *092/650096* ⊕ *www.indochineex.com.*

Osmose

An agent of positive change in the area, Osmose, a nonprofit organization, has been fighting to conserve the unique biosphere of Tonle Sap and Prek Toal by reeducating local villagers from poachers to protectors of the environment that sustains them. They also lobby against big commercial interests that have been involved in short-term exploitation of the ecosystem, and have successfully helped to reharmonize many aspects of human coexistence with nature. On their exceptional tours you get to visit a bird sanctuary with an expert guide and also experience floating villages in a fascinating and respectful way. ⊠ *House 0203, Group 8, Phum Wat Damnak, Sangkat Salakamreuk* ☎ *012/832812, 063/765506* ⊕ *www.osmosetonlesap.net.*

◉ Sights

Siem Reap is the base to use for exploring the temples at Angkor, but it's also much more than that. It has its own great places to see, and there is something seductive about this city that makes visitors want to linger. You can wander around the contemporary Angkor National Museum, take a cooking class, visit a rural village, explore myriad art galleries, try a gourmet restaurant, or take a stroll down the central Pub Street. There's plenty to keep the temple-weary traveler occupied for two or three days, or even a week or more.

★ Angkor National Museum

HISTORY MUSEUM | This modern, interactive museum, which opened in 2008, gracefully guides you through the rise and fall of the Angkorian empires, covering the religions, kings, and geopolitics that drove the Khmer to create the monumental cities whose ruins are highly visible in modern-day Cambodia. With more than 1,300 artifacts on glossy display, complemented by multimedia installations, this museum experience helps demystify much of the material culture that visitors encounter at the archaeological parks and sites. The atmosphere is set in the impressive gallery of a thousand Buddhas, which plunges you into the serene spirituality that still dominates the region. Seven consequent galleries, set up chronologically, highlight the Funan and Chenia pre-Angkorian epochs, followed by the golden age of the Angkorian period led by the likes of King Soryavarman II, who built Angkor Wat. The final two galleries showcase stone inscriptions documenting some of the workings of the empires, and statues of Apsara, shedding light on the cult and fashions of these celestial dancers. The audio tour is excellent and well worth the extra cost. ⊠ *968, Vithei Charles de Gaulle, Khrum 6, Phoum Salakanseng, Khom Svaydangum* ☎ *063/966601* ⊕ *www.angkornationalmuseum.com* 💲 *$12.*

★ Angkor Temple Complex

RUINS | The temples of Angkor, hailed as "the eighth wonder of the world" by some, constitute the world's great ancient sites and Southeast Asia's most impressive archaeological treasure. The massive structures, surrounded by tropical forest, are comparable to Central America's Mayan ruins—and far exceed them in size. Angkor Wat is the world's

Hiring an Angkor Guide

A guide can greatly enrich your appreciation of Angkor's temples, which are full of details you might miss on your own. English-speaking guides can be hired through the tourism office on Pokambor Avenue, across from the Raffles Grand Hotel d'Angkor. But the best way to find a guide is through your hotel or guesthouse. Ask around. Most guides who work for tour companies (and the tourism office) are freelancers, and often when you book through a tour company, you'll pay a higher price. Find a young staffer at your hotel or guesthouse and tell him or her what you want—the type of tour, what you hope to learn from your guide, your particular interests in the temples.

Prices usually run around $45 a day, not including transportation, for a well-informed, English-speaking guide. Your guide will meet you at your hotel, along with a tuk-tuk or car driver, whom you'll need to pay separately ($12 to $15 per day for a tuk-tuk; $25 for a car). Guides, who are almost always men, will typically cater to your interests and know how to avoid crowds. You aren't expected to join your guide for lunch. Usually your driver will drop you and your guide at a temple and pick you up at another entrance, meaning you won't have to double back on yourself.

Hanuman Travel If you feel more comfortable booking through a travel company, Hanuman Travel is an excellent choice. The expert company, which works throughout Cambodia and surrounding countries, has established a foundation to help eradicate poverty in Cambodia's hinterlands. Your tourist dollars will go toward wells, water filters, mosquito nets, and other amenities that can greatly improve a rural family's life. ✉ 165, St. 110, Sangkat Tonle Bassac ⊕ hanuman-travel.com.

largest religious structure—so large that it's hard to describe its breadth to someone who hasn't seen it. And that's just one temple in a complex of hundreds. In all, there are some 300 monuments reflecting Hindu and Buddhist influence scattered throughout the jungle, but only the largest have been excavated and only a few of those reconstructed. Most of these lie within a few miles of each other and can be seen in one day, though two or three days will allow you to better appreciate them. Most people visit the temples of Bayon and Baphuon, which face east, in the morning—the earlier you arrive, the better the light and the smaller the crowd—and west-facing Angkor Wat in the late afternoon, though this most famous of the temples can also be a stunning sight at sunrise. The woodland-surrounded Ta Prohm can be visited any time, though it is best photographed when cloudy, whereas the distant Banteay Srei is prettiest in the late-afternoon light. With so many temples to see, the choice is yours. The entrance to the complex is 4 km (2½ miles) north of Siem Reap; you'll need to arrange transportation to get here and around. Most independent travelers hire a car and driver ($35 to $50 per day), moto (motorcycle) driver ($12 to $18), or tuk-tuk ($20 to $35, seats up to four). Renting bicycles ($3 to $5) or electric bikes ($5 to $8) is also an option if you're up for the exertion in the heat. Tourists

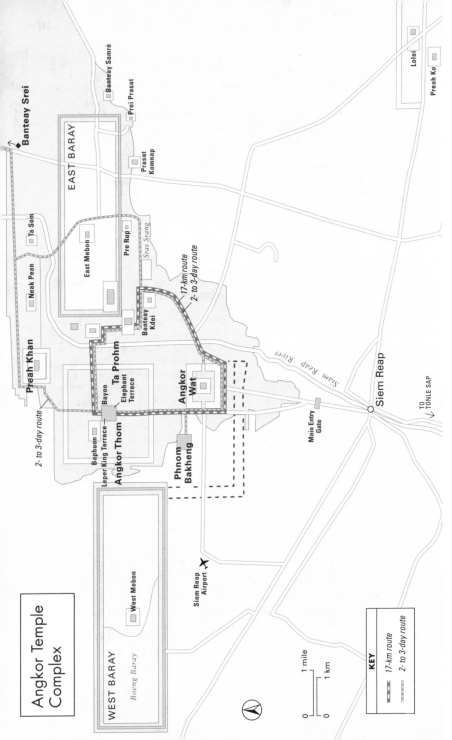

may not drive motorized vehicles in the park. If you hire a driver, he'll stick with you for the whole day. Going with a guide is strongly recommended. The Angkor complex is open from 5:30 am to 6 pm. You'll receive a ticket with your photo on it, which you'll need at each site and to access the restrooms. If you buy your ticket at 5 pm, you'll be admitted for the remaining open hour, in time to see the sunset from Phnom Bakeng to catch the last rays setting Angkor Wat aglow. Your ticket will also count for the following day. Consider swinging back to Siem Reap for lunch or to your hotel for an afternoon rest so you don't get templed out. Make sure to drink plenty of water. ✣ *5½ km (3½ miles) north of Siem Reap* ☎ *063/965414* 🌐 *www.angkorenterprise.gov.kh* 🎫 *$37 for 1 day, $62 for 3 days, $72 for 1 wk* ☞ *Revealing clothing violates the dress code; shield yourself from the sun with light fabrics, and bring a wide-brimmed hat or an umbrella for shade.*

Cambodia Land Mine Museum

HISTORY MUSEUM | Be sure to visit this museum, established by Aki Ra, a former child soldier who first fought for the Khmer Rouge, then the Vietnamese, and finally the Cambodian Army. Now he dedicates his life to removing the land mines he and thousands of others laid across Cambodia. His museum is a must-see, a sociopolitical eye-opener that portrays a different picture of Cambodia from the glorious temples and five-star hotels. Any tuk-tuk or taxi driver can find the museum, your entry ticket helps landmine victims go to college. **TIP→ As it is a decent distance from Siem Reap, it's best to combine this with a visit to the Banteay Srey Temple complex.** ✣ *Off road to Angkor, 6 km (4 miles) south of Banteay Srey Temple, 25 km (15 miles) from Siem Reap* ☎ *015/674163* 🌐 *www.cambodialandminemuseum.org* 🎫 *$5.*

🍴 Restaurants

Abacus

$$$$ | INTERNATIONAL | Ideal for a romantic garden dinner, Abacus offers an eclectic choice of French-international fusion cuisine. The restaurant also has a pleasant bar that welcomes guests for an aperitif or an after-dinner digestif. **Known for:** impeccable service; foie gras; Abacus burger. [$] *Average main: $17* ✉ *Off Rd. 6* ✣ *Take Rd. 6 toward the airport, pass Angkor Hotel, and turn right at ACLEDA Bank. After 100 meters turn left* ☎ *012/644286* 🌐 *www.restaurantabacus.com.*

★ **Elia Greek Kitchen**

$ | GREEK | FAMILY | There's a sophisticated yet casual vibe at this airy, white and brick restaurant that, along with its sister branch in Phnom Penh, serves probably the best Greek food in the country. You'll find all the classics here, including tzatziki, hummus, gyros, calamari, and moussaka; it's all just great. **Known for:** excellent service; authentic and delicious Greek food; romantic atmosphere. [$] *Average main: 7* ✉ *31-34 St. 9, Old Market* ☎ *089/325245* 🌐 *eliagreekkitchen.com.*

Il Forno

$$ | ITALIAN | Hidden away down a small alleyway, this small, welcoming trattoria turns out delicious thin-crust pizza and calzone from a wood-fire oven, as well as wonderful homemade pasta, all using locally-sourced ingredients. The filling portions and menu of Italian wines makes this spot especially appealing after a long day's sightseeing. **Known for:** four-cheese gnocchi; good Italian wines; friendly atmosphere. [$] *Average main: $10* ✉ *Pari's Alley, 16 The Lane, Old Market* ☎ *063/763380* 🌐 *www.ilforno.restaurant/siem-reap.*

Continued on page 453

ANGKOR

by Christina Knight

The scale of the ruins, the power of the encroaching jungle, and the beauty of the architecture have made Angkor one of the world's most celebrated ancient cities. This was the capital of the mighty Khmer empire (present-day Thailand, Laos, Vietnam, and Cambodia). The vast complex contains more than 300 temples

and monuments that four centuries of kings built to honor the gods they believed they would become after they died. It's not just the size of the structures that takes your breath away; it's the otherworldly setting and a pervading sense of mystery.

THE CITY OF ANGKOR

Silk-cotton tree roots growing over the ruins at Ta Prohm.

CONSTRUCTION

Angkor, which simply means "city," was founded in 839 AD when King Jayavarman II completed the first temple, Phnom Bakheng, using sandstone from the Kulen mountains, northeast of Angkor. Jayavarman II had established the empire in 802, uniting various principalities, securing independence from Java (in present-day Indonesia), and declaring himself the world emperor as well as a "god who is king," or *devaraja*.

Over the next 400 years, each successive Khmer emperor added to Angkor, erecting a *wat*, or temple, to worship either Shiva or Vishnu. The Khmer empire was Hindu except during the rule of Jayavarman VII (1181–1220), who was a Mahayana Buddhist. Theravada Buddhism became the dominant religion in Cambodia after the decline of the Khmer empire, in the 15th century.

Kings situated buildings according to principles of cosmology and numerology, so the center of the city shifted over the centuries. Only the wats, built with reddish-brown laterite, ochre brick, or gray sandstone, have survived; wooden structures perished long ago.

Historians estimate that the royal city had a population of 100,000 in the late 13th century; at that time, London's population was roughly 80,000. The royal city was ringed by a larger medieval city about 3,000 square km (1,150 square mile)—the world's largest pre-industrial settlement and more than twice the size of present-day Los Angeles, with an estimated population of 1 million. At its height, the Khmer empire covered about 1 million square km (400,000 square mile), stretching east from the Burmese border to southern Vietnam and north from Malaysia to Laos.

Archaeologists have only excavated the largest of the hundreds of temples that once dotted the royal city, and even fewer have been restored. The most impressive and best preserved temple, Angkor Wat, is also the world's largest religious monument; it covers approximately 2 square km (¾ square mile), including its moat.

Apsara bas-relief on a wall of Angkor Wat.

DECLINE AND RENEWAL

In 1431, Thailand's Ayutthaya kingdom invaded and sacked Angkor. The following year, the declining Khmer empire moved its kingdom to Phnom Penh, 315 km (195 mile) south. Though a handful of foreign adventurers visited Angkor in the following centuries, it wasn't until 1861, when Frenchman and naturalist Henri Mouhot published a book about the site, that Angkor became famous. By this time, looting foreigners and the insistent forces of time and nature had taken a toll on the complex. Restoration efforts began in the early 20th century but were interrupted by the Cambodian Civil War in the 1960s and '70s; in 1992, UNESCO declared Angkor a World Heritage Site. Since that time the number of visitors has risen an average of 2 million annually. You won't have the place to yourself, but it's unlikely to feel crowded in comparison to famous European sites.

Angkor Wat.

ANGKOR WAT

A monk looking at Angkor Wat across the moat.

The best-preserved temple has become shorthand for the entire complex: Angkor Wat, built by King Surya-varman II in the early 12th century. The king dedicated Angkor Wat to Vishnu (the preserver and protector), breaking with tradition—Khmer kings usually built their temples to honor Shiva, the god of destruction and rebirth, whose powers the kings considered more cosmically essential than Vishnu's.

It helps to think of the ancient city as a series of concentric protective layers: a 190-m- (623-ft-) wide moat surrounds an outer wall that's 1,024 by 802 m (3,359 by 2,630 ft) long— walking around the outside of the wall is a more than 2-mi stroll. A royal city and palace once occupied the space inside the wall; you can still see traces of some streets, but the buildings did not survive. The temple itself sits on an elevated terrace that takes up about a tenth of the city.

APPROACHING THE TEMPLE

You'll reach the temple after crossing the moat, entering the western gateway (where you'll see a 10-foot, eight-armed Vishnu statue), and walking nearly a quarter of a mile along an unshaded causeway. Angkor Wat originally had nine towers (an auspicious number in Hindu mythology), though only

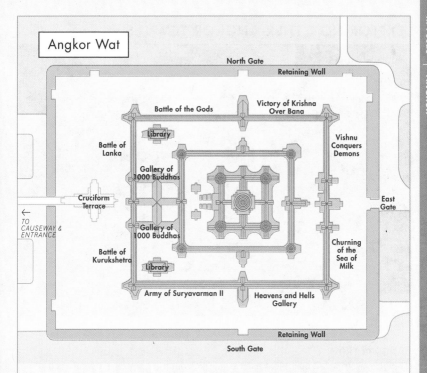

Angkor Wat

North Gate

Retaining Wall

Battle of the Gods

Victory of Krishna Over Bana

Library

Battle of Lanka

Vishnu Conquers Demons

Gallery of 1000 Buddhas

Cruciform Terrace

← TO CAUSEWAY & ENTRANCE

East Gate

Gallery of 1000 Buddhas

Battle of Kurukshetra

Library

Churning of the Sea of Milk

Army of Suryavarman II

Heavens and Hells Gallery

Retaining Wall

South Gate

---

five remain. These towers, which took 30 years to complete, are shaped like closed lotuses and form the center of the temple complex. Their ribbed appearance comes from rings of finials that also take the form of closed lotuses. These finials, along with statues of lions and multi-headed serpents called *nagas,* were believed to protect the temple from evil spirits.

Like the other major monuments at Angkor, the complex represents the Hindu universe. The central shrines symbolize Mt. Meru, mythical home of the Hindu gods, and the moats represent the seven oceans that surround Mt. Meru.

THE GALLERIES

Nearly 2,000 *Apsara*—celestial female dancers—are scattered in bas-relief on the outer entrances and columns of galleries. Inside the shaded galleries, 600 m

Bas-relief depicting a historical Khmer battle.

(2,000 ft) of bas-reliefs tell epic tales from the *Ramayana,* the *Churning of the Sea of Milk* (gods and demons join forces to find the immortality elixir), the punishments of the 32 hells, and the less-imaginative rewards of the 37 heavens.

EXPLORING OTHER ANGKOR TEMPLES

Banteay Srei temple complex.

ANGKOR THOM

King Jayavarman VII built the massive city known as Angkor Thom in 1181 and changed the state religion to Buddhism (although subsequent kings reverted to Hinduism). At the center of the city stands the 12th-century **Bayon,** a large, ornate state temple that rises into many towers (37 remain today), most of which are topped with giant, serene, smiling boddhisattva faces on four sides. These faces, the most photogenic and beatific in all of Angkor, resemble both the king and the boddhisattva of compassion—a Buddhist twist on the king-as-a-god tradition.

On the walls of Bayon's central sanctuary are 1½ km (1 mile) of marvelous bas-relief murals depicting historic sea battles scenes from daily life, and Hindu

King Jayavarman VII.

gods and mythical creatures. You can pick out the Khmers in the reliefs because they are depicted with long earlobes; they frequently warred with the Cham, whose warriors wear headpieces that curl towards the jawline. Jayavarman VIII, a later king, added the Hindu iconography and destroyed some of his predecessor's Buddhist statuary.

Just to the north of the Bayon is the slightly older **Baphuon,** which King Udayadityavarman II built in the mid-11th century as part of a small settlement that predated Angkor Thom. The king built the temple on a hill without proper supports, so it collapsed during a 16th-century earthquake. In that same century, a magnificent reclining Buddha was added to the three-tiered temple pyramid, which was originally a Shiva sanctuary. The temple is undergoing reconstruction and is not open to the public; however, the exterior gate and elevated walkway are open.

Once the foundation of the royal audience hall, the **Elephant Terrace** is adorned with carvings of *garudas* (bird-like creatures), lion-headed figures, and elephants tugging at strands of lotuses with their trunks.

Located at the north end of the Elephant Terrance, the **Terrace of the Leper King** area is named after a stone statue found here that now resides in the National Museum; a copy remains here. Precisely who the Leper King was and why he was so named remains uncertain, though several legends offer speculation. (One theory is that damage to the sculpture made the figure look leprous, leading people in later generations to believe the person depicted had been ill.) Today the terrace's two walls create a maze lined some seven layers high with gods, goddesses, and nagas.

TA PROHM

Jayavarman VII dedicated this large monastic complex to his mother. It once housed 2,700 monks and 615 royal dancers. Today the moss-covered ruins lie between tangles of silk-cotton and strangler fig trees whose gnarled offshoots drape window frames and grasp walls. This gorgeous, eerie spot gives you an idea of what the Angkor complex looked like when westerners first discovered it in the 19th century. Another famous mother—Angelina Jolie—shot scenes of *Lara Croft: Tomb Raider* here.

Two-storeyed pavilion at Preah Khan.

PHNOM BAKHENG

One of the oldest Angkor structures, dating from the 9th century, Bakheng temple was carved out of a rocky hilltop and occupied the center of the first royal city site. Phnom Bakheng is perhaps the most popular sunset destination, with views of the Tonle Sap Lake and the towers of Angkor Wat rising above the jungle. Climb a shaded trail or ride an elephant up the hill. You'll still have to climb steep stairs to reach the top of the temple.

PREAH KHAN

Dedicated to the Jayavarman VII's father, mossy Preah Khan was also a monastery. Its long, dim corridors are dramatically lit by openings where stones have fallen out. Preah Khan is the only Angkor site with an annex supported by rounded, not square, columns.

BANTEAY SREI

This restored 10th-century temple, whose name means "citadel of women," lies 38 km (24 mile) northeast of Siem Reap. Its scale is small (no stairs to climb), but its dark pink sandstone is celebrated for its intricate carvings of scenes from Hindu tales. The site is at least a 40-minute, somewhat-scenic drive from other Angkor sites; your driver will charge extra to take you here, but it's less crowded than other temples.

Sculptures of *devas* leading to Angkor Thom.

Did You Know?

Time has erased the red lacquer and gold leaf that originally accented Angkor's many bas-reliefs; oil from the hands of countless visitors has darkened the dancing *Asparas* and warring soldiers.

The Little Red Fox Espresso

$ | **CAFÉ** | Tucked away along Siem Reap's quiet Kandal Village shopping street, this charming cafe run by an Australian couple provides more than just espresso: there's a great menu of healthy breakfast and lunches (they're closed in the evening) such as the B.L.A.T bagel (a BLT with avocado) or the Tri Grain Bowl, a combination of red rice, chia seeds, and couscous, topped with kale and beetroot hummus. **Known for:** chill atmosphere; healthy breakfasts; great coffee beverages. Ⓢ *Average main: 5 ✉ 593 Hap Guan St., Kandal Village* ☎ *016/669724* ۞ *Closed Wed., no dinner.*

Tell Steak House

$$ | **GERMAN** | A selection of hearty sausages and schnitzel dishes, typically accompanied by sauerkraut, are served at this homey German-Swiss restaurant in an old villa, which has been serving great food since 1998. **Known for:** excellent Bavarian wheat beer; fancy fine dining atmosphere; superb Wiener schnitzel. Ⓢ *Average main: $8 ✉ Wat Bo Rd.* ☎ *063/963289* ⊕ *www.tellsteakhouse.com.*

 Hotels

Reliable chain hotels have opened along the road to Angkor, and both the dusty airport road and the town's noisy thoroughfares are clogged with upper-end accommodations—but why settle for a lousy location? Siem Reap offers a number of excellent lodging options in the quaint and quiet river area: booking a room in this quarter means that your view of the hotel pool won't include the neighbors' laundry line, and will delight you with natural splendor instead of traffic jams.

★ Amansara

$$$$ | **RESORT** | The jewel in the crown of Siem Reap hotels, Amansara offers exceptional service, atmosphere, and accommodations in surroundings of understated luxury. **Pros:** 10 minutes from Angkor; some suites have private plunge pool; impressive attention to detail by friendly management and staff. **Cons:** no in-room TV; pricey; feels very proper. Ⓢ *Rooms from: $760 ✉ Road to Angkor ⊹ Behind Tourism Dept.* ☎ *063/760333* ⊕ *www.aman.com/resorts/amansara* ⤴ *24 suites* ⦿l *Free Breakfast.*

FCC Angkor by Avani

$$$ | **HOTEL** | Just behind the official Royal Residence, this former colonial building has been transformed into an inviting retreat along the river, far removed from the noise of the city center. **Pros:** excellent on-site bar; contemporary design; riverside location. **Cons:** distance from downtown; poor lighting in some rooms; pool can get crowded. Ⓢ *Rooms from: $125 ✉ Pokambor Ave.* ☎ *063/760280* ⊕ *www.avanihotels.com/en/angkor-siem-reap* ⤴ *80 rooms* ⦿l *Free Breakfast.*

La Résidence d'Angkor

$$$$ | **RESORT** | **FAMILY** | Swathed in ancient Angkor style, this luxurious retreat is within a walled compound with lovely gardens beside the river. **Pros:** excellent restaurant; attractive riverside location; family-friendly services. **Cons:** River Road rooms can get traffic noise; some rooms have less than spectacular views; pricey room service. Ⓢ *Rooms from: $225 ✉ River Rd., Wat Bo* ☎ *063/963390* ⊕ *www.belmond.com/la-residence-d-angkor-siem-reap* ⤴ *59 rooms* ⦿l *Free Breakfast.*

Navutu Dreams

$$ | **RESORT** | **FAMILY** | A slightly different Siem Reap experience is offered at this countryside bungalow resort, where the concept of well-being is promoted via resident yoga instructors, holistic practitioners, and healthy eating options. **Pros:** tuk-tuk shuttle package available; free yoga classes; free airport pickup. **Cons:** limited breakfast options; about 10 minutes out of town; some public spaces showing wear. Ⓢ *Rooms from: $100 ✉ Navutu Rd.* ☎ *063/964864* ⊕ *www.*

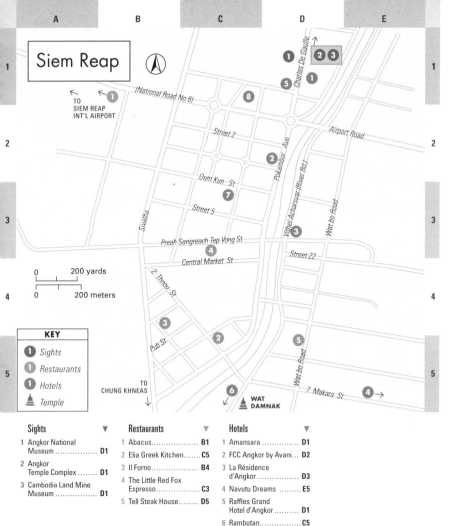

Siem Reap

(National Road No 6)
Street 2
Oum Kun St
Street 5
Preah Sangreach Tep Vong St
Central Market St
Street 22
Pub St
7 Makara St

Charles De Gaulle
Pokambor Ave
Vithei Achasvar (River Rd.)
Wat bo Road
Airport Road
Sivatha
2 Throu St
Wat bo Road

TO
TO
SIEM REAP
INT'L AIRPORT

TO
CHUNG KHNEAS

WAT DAMNAK

0   200 yards
0   200 meters

KEY

● Sights
● Restaurants
● Hotels
▲ Temple

Sights ▼

1 Angkor National
  Museum **D1**

2 Angkor
  Temple Complex **D1**

3 Cambodia Land Mine
  Museum **D1**

Restaurants ▼

1 Abacus.................. **B1**

2 Elia Greek Kitchen....... **C5**

3 Il Forno................. **B4**

4 The Little Red Fox
  Espresso................. **C3**

5 Tell Steak House........ **D5**

Hotels ▼

1 Amansara **D1**

2 FCC Angkor by Avani... **D2**

3 La Résidence
  d'Angkor **D3**

4 Navutu Dreams **E5**

5 Raffles Grand
  Hotel d'Angkor **D1**

6 Rambutan................ **C5**

7 Shinta Mani Angkor..... **C3**

8 Victoria Angkor **C1**

navuturesorts.com/siem-reap 🛏 *26 rooms, 4 suites* 🍴 *Free Breakfast.*

Raffles Grand Hotel d'Angkor
$$$$ | **HOTEL** | Built in 1932 and still featuring the original cage elevator from that year in the lobby, this grande dame was restored and reopened after near destruction by occupying Khmer Rouge guerrillas. **Pros:** Old World charm; picturesque gardens; excellent restaurant. **Cons:** more impersonal than smaller hotels; pricier than may be warranted, due to the name; outside the center of Siem Reap. [$] *Rooms from: $190* ✉ *1 Vithei Charles de Gaulle, Khom Svaydangum* ☎ *023/982598* 🌐 *www.raffles.com/siem-reap* 🛏 *99 rooms, 18 suites, 2 villas* 🍴 *Free Breakfast.*

★ **Rambutan**
$$ | **B&B/INN** | This gem is one of the better boutique accommodations around, with rooms (most have balconies and outdoor bathtubs) grouped around a stone-and-palm-enclosed saltwater pool. **Pros:** tasty breakfast; good prices; friendly staff. **Cons:** some rooms are accessed by steep stairs; front door closes early; small swimming pool. [$] *Rooms from: $90* ✉ *Krom 10, Rambutan La., Wat Damnak* ☎ *012/654638* 🌐 *www.rambutansiemreap.com* 🍴 *Free Breakfast* 🛏 *43 rooms.*

★ **Shinta Mani Angkor**
$$$$ | **HOTEL** | Not only will you sleep and eat in luxurious style here, your money will also help support community projects bringing clean water, transportation, and jobs to underprivileged communities, via the Shinta Mani Foundation. **Pros:** great facilities; good location; supports charitable causes. **Cons:** in-room wardrobe space could be bigger; not very family-friendly; no elevator, which limits some accessibility. [$] *Rooms from: $200* ✉ *Oun Khum and 14th Sts., Old French Quarter* ☎ *063/964123* 🌐 *angkor.shintamani.com* 🛏 *62 rooms* 🍴 *Free Breakfast.*

Victoria Angkor
$$ | **RESORT** | **FAMILY** | Just west of the Royal Gardens stands this sophisticated resort modeled on a strong colonial aesthetic. **Pros:** top-quality breakfast buffet; attentive service; friendly staff. **Cons:** spa is not so great; a bit of a commercial feel; can get crowded with tour groups. [$] *Rooms from: $100* ✉ *National Hwy. 6 and Sivatha Rd., Khom Svaydangum* ☎ *063/760428* 🌐 *www.victoriaangkorhotel.com* 🛏 *129 rooms* 🍴 *Free Breakfast.*

🍸 Nightlife

Most of Siem Reap's nightlife is concentrated around the Old Market, particularly on vibrant Pub Street, and in Kandal Village, where some of the most popular spots are found. Wander a little and you're sure to find a hangout that fits your style.

Laundry Bar
LIVE MUSIC | This local institution has a winning combination of cheap drinks and live music, with a popular pool table for entertainment and a bar where you can chat the night away, often until closing time at 3 am. ✉ *St. 26, Wat Bo* ☎ *017/843428.*

Picasso Bar
BARS | This cozy Spanish-run bar, distinctive for its barrel-shaped roof and horseshoe bar, draws a crowd of fun, young expats, who often spill out onto the tiled alley outside. ✉ *Alley West, Old Market.*

Scribe
BARS | With the venerable FCC hotel as its backdrop, the colonial-styled Scribe attracts a discerning crowd. There is seating under the trees, on the rooftop, or at the wraparound bar. ✉ *Pokambor Ave., Old French Quarter* ✥ *Behind Royal Residence* ☎ *063/760681* 🌐 *avanihotels.com/en/angkor-siem-reap/restaurants/scribe-bar-and-grill.*

Performing Arts

★ **Phare, The Cambodian Circus**

CIRCUSES | FAMILY | Cambodia's answer
to the Cirque du Soleil is truly a must-
see. It started as a traveling troupe, but
there are now nightly performances in
a high-top tent southwest of the city
center, though they continue to take the
show on the road internationally and
also to Phnom Penh. The high-energy
performances combine Cambodian story-
telling traditions with circus arts, dance,
acrobatics, and acting to captivate audi-
ences every night. The Phare School is a
charitable organization that has a positive
impact on poor communities. If you want
to learn more about the background,
visit the Phare Ponleu Selpak center
in Battambang. ■TIP➔ **Most seating is
first-come-first-served, so try to get there
early.** ✉ Ring Rd., south of Sok San Rd.
✛ 2 km from Old Market and Pub St.
☎ 015/499480 ⊕ www.pharecircus.org
✉ $35.

🛍 Shopping

Artisans Angkor

CRAFTS | With more than 30 workshops
in Siem Reap and over 800 craftspeople
employed throughout the country, the
Artisans Angkor shop offers a dazzling
selection of Cambodian arts and crafts,
accessories, and silverware from all
over Cambodia. You'll find work featuring
skills such as woodworking, silk painting,
and lacquering. ✉ Stung Thmey St.
☎ 063/963330 ⊕ www.artisansdangkor.
com.

Eric Raisina

WOMEN'S CLOTHING | Madagascar-born,
French-raised fashion designer Eric
Raisina presents his impeccably stylish
couture designs at this outlet in the
design-centric mall Aviary Square. The
world-acclaimed designer uses stunning
Khmer silks to create clothing and accessories that clearly stand a head above

Night Flights

Around sunset, the sky fills with
thousands of large bats, which
make their homes in the trees
behind the Preah Ang Chek Preah
Ang Chorm Shrine, near the
gardens in front of the Raffles hotel.

the rest. ■TIP➔ **You can also visit his
atelier, at 75–81 Charles de Gaulle Avenue,
by appointment only.** ✉ The Aviary Hotel,
Preah Sangreach Tep Vong St., Sangkat
Svay Dangkum ☎ 012/580283 atelier, for
appointment, 063/963208 Aviary Square
shop ⊕ www.ericraisina.com.

★ **Kandal Village**

NEIGHBORHOODS | This quiet lane near the
center of town is a go-to shopping destination for its range of upscale boutiques
and pleasant cafés. You can shop for elegant gifts from Louise Loubatieres, who
makes wonderful ceramics and jewelry
pieces; browse the clothing collection
of designer Sirivan Chak Dumas at the
namesake Sirivan; pick up exquisite handmade silks from Neary Khmer; or enjoy
the naturally scented candles from Saarti.
If all the shopping makes you weary, treat
yourself to a massage at Frangipani Spa
or a coffee at Little Red Fox Espresso.
✉ Hap Guan St.

Mekong Quilts

CRAFTS | A social enterprise offering
employment opportunities to disadvantaged women in both Cambodia and
Vietnam, Mekong Quilts sells beautiful
handmade, durable quilts of all designs,
colors, styles, and sizes. ✉ 5 Sivutha
Blvd., Old Market ☎ 063/964498 ⊕ www.
mekongquilts.com.

Psar Chas Old Market

MARKET | Perfect for last-minute souvenir
shopping, you'll find just about everything
here, from clothing to traditional

There are about 200 faces of Lokesvara, the bodhisattva of compassion, on Bayon's towers.

woodcrafts, fabrics, and ceramic home-style items, kitschy souvenirs, attractive silverware, and local foods. ✉ *Market St. and Pokombor Ave.*

Senteurs d'Angkor

OTHER SPECIALTY STORE | This store transforms traditional Cambodian spices and herbs into delightful cosmetics and food products. You'll find Kampot pepper, Rattanakiri coffee, soaps made with lemongrass, turmeric, jasmine, or mango, and lots more. All the products make excellent gifts. ✉ *Psaa Chas, 2 Thnou St., Old Market* ☎ *011/686217* ⊕ *www. senteursdangkor.com.*

Theam's Gallery

ART GALLERIES | This art gallery specializes in unique lacquerware designs such as polychrome paintings and trademark colored elephants, as well as elegant traditional wood-carved Buddha statues and homestyle items. ✉ *25 Phum Veal, Kokchak Commune* ☎ *078/208161* ⊕ *www.theamsgallery.com.*

Tonle Sap

10 km (6 miles) south of Siem Reap.

Covering 2,600 square km (1,000 square miles) in the dry season, Cambodia's vast Tonle Sap is the biggest freshwater lake in Southeast Asia. Its unique annual cycle of flood expansion and retreat dictates Cambodia's rice production and supplies of fish. During the rainy season the Mekong River backs into the Tonle Sap River, pushing waters into the lake, which quadruples in size. In the dry season, as the Mekong lowers, the Tonle Sap River reverses its direction, draining the lake. Boats make the river journey to the lake from Phnom Penh and Battambang, tying up at Chong Khneas, 12 km (7½ miles) south of Siem Reap. Two-hour tours of the lake, costing $15 to $20, set out from Chong Khneas, and you can tour the floating villages, with prices starting at $20.

Cambodia's Endangered Species 9

In an ironic contrast to the Khmer Rouge atrocities, much of Cambodia's wild lands and wildlife populations emerged from that period intact—a far different scenario than that faced by neighboring countries, where the rarest of species were expunged years ago. Unfortunately, however, much of Cambodia's wildlife is now under threat.

The Prek Toal Biosphere Reserve is Southeast Asia's most important waterbird nesting site, home to several endangered species. Near Sre Ambel, in what was a Khmer Rouge hotbed, conservationists are working to save the Cambodian royal turtle, which was thought extinct until the early

2000s. In Kratie, some of the world's last Irrawaddy dolphins swim the Mekong in another area long held by the Khmer Rouge, and in Mondulkiri, local conservationists report a recent increase in wildlife species.

The more tourists who express interest in Cambodia's natural environment, the better the outlook for these species and others. The jungles remain threatened by illegal logging (as you might see in Stung Treng and Ratanakiri) and plantation concessions, while poaching is still common. But if those in charge begin to see serious tourist dollars connected to conservation, there may be hope yet.

GETTING HERE AND AROUND

Boats make the river journey to the lake from Phnom Penh ($30) and Battambang ($20; usually during the wet season, May to October only), tying up at Chong Khneas, 12 km (7½ miles) south of Siem Reap.

Two-hour tours of the lake ($15) set out from Chong Khneas; arrange them at any travel agent in Siem Reap.

Transportation to and from the Tonle Sap can be arranged at any hotel or travel agent. Alternatively, ask any tuk-tuk or moto ($7 to $12).

 Sights

★ Prek Toal Biosphere Reserve
NATURE PRESERVE | Located between Chong Khneas and the city of Battambang, Prek Toal is mainland Southeast Asia's most important waterbird nesting site. It's a spectacular scene if you can visit at the start of the dry season (November and December), when water

remains high and thousands of rare birds begin to nest. To support their education and eco activities, tours can be booked through the Osmose conservation organization. Day tours and overnight stays at the Prek Toal Research Station can also be arranged. ⊠ *Siem Reap.*

Kulen Mountain

50 km (31 miles) north of Siem Reap.

King Jayavarman II established this mountain retreat 50 km (31 miles) northeast of Siem Reap in AD 802, the year regarded as the start of the Angkor dynasty. The area is strewn with the ruins of Khmer temples from that time, when the mountain was revered as holy, with a hallowed river and a waterfall. Admission to the area costs $20, and it is not included in the ticket price to Angkor.

GETTING HERE AND AROUND

Tuk-tuks, motos, and local taxis can take you to Kulen Mountain; negotiate a price prior to departure, or ask your hotel to handle it (expect to pay around $20 for the trip). The journey should take no more than 50 minutes. Siem Reap tour companies also go here.

Sihanoukville

230 km (143 miles) southwest of Phnom Penh.

A half a century ago, Cambodia's main port city, Sihanoukville, was a sleepy backwater called Kampong Som. Then a series of world-shattering events overtook it and gave rise to the busy industrial center and coastal resort now prominent on every tourist map.

The French laid the foundations of Kampong Som back in the mid-1950s, before they lost control of the Mekong Delta and its ports following their retreat after the French-Indochina War. The town was renamed Sihanoukville in honor of the then king. A decade later, Sihanoukville received a further boost when it became an important transit post for weapons destined for American forces fighting in the Vietnam War. In the mid-1970s Sihanoukville itself came under American attack by U.S. marines after Khmer Rouge forces captured the SS *Mayaguez*, a United States container ship.

During the 1990s, Sihanoukville developed into Cambodia's seaside playground. Its seven main beaches, all easily accessible from downtown by motorbike taxi or even a rented bicycle, attracted backpackers and foreign investors.

In recent years, though, with the arrival of increasing numbers of mainland Chinese investors, what was once a quiet, budget beach haven has been transformed into an open-air construction site. Chinese developers have built some 50 casinos, as well as hotels and karaoke bars to cater to their clientele. On the plus side, roads have been redone and the beaches cleared of illegal buildings, but all this

seems likely to be the prelude to yet more development.

If that was not enough, prostitution and crime rates are rising, and so are the prices of accommodations and food. The city has lost most of its local character, and is slowly morphing into the Macau of Cambodia (a comparison frequently made). All that said, there are still some beautiful places to stay on the islands offshore. We don't currently recommend a visit to Sihanoukville for more than what's necessary to catch a boat to the nearby islands.

GETTING HERE AND AROUND
Sihanoukville airport has undergone modernization over the past few years and has five daily flights to different cities in China, one flight to Kuala Lumpur in Malaysia, and Cambodia Angkor Air flights to Siem Reap and Phnom Penh.

Air-conditioned buses from Phnom Penh run several times daily ($8 to $10), departing from the Central Market or the Hua Lian Station near Olympic Stadium. Four hours later, they arrive a couple of kilometers outside of Sihanoukville, and getting off the bus you're enthusiastically greeted by the local tuk-tuk and moto drivers who jostle for your business. The farthest trip, to Otres, by tuk-tuk shouldn't cost more than $8, and going anywhere else shouldn't be more than $6 (there is a board with price suggestions at one end of the bus station). Prices for motos are half that of tuk-tuks, and taxis will cost double, but don't expect them to have a meter. Buses from Bangkok (10 hours; from $25) and other towns on Thailand's eastern seaboard connect to Sihanoukville via Koh Kong. At last, trains ($8) connect Phnom Penh to Sihanoukville, stopping at Takeo and Kampot, on Friday, Saturday, Sunday, Monday, and public holidays.

You can hire a private car and driver through your hotel or guesthouse for the trip to the coast from Phnom Penh (three

Khmer: A Few Key Phrases

A knowledge of French may once have gotten you somewhere in formerly francophone Cambodia, but these days it's far easier to find English speakers. The Cambodian language, Khmer, belongs to the Mon-Khmer family of languages, enriched by Indian Pali and Sanskrit vocabulary. It has many similarities to Thai and Lao, a reminder of their years as vassal lands in the Khmer Empire.

The following are some useful words and phrases:

Hello: joom reap soo-uh

Thank you: aw-koun

Yes: bah (male speaker), jah (female speaker)

No: aw-te

Excuse me: som-toh

Where?: ai nah?

How much?: t'lay pohn mahn?

Never mind: mun ay dtay

Zero: sohn

One: muay

Two: bpee

Three: bay

Four: buon

Five: bpram

Six: bpram muay

Seven: bpram pull

Eight: bpram bay

Nine: bpram buon

Ten: dop

Eleven: dop muay

Hundred: muay roi

Thousand: muay poan

Food: m'hohp

Water: dteuk

Expensive: t'lay nah

Morning: bprek

Night: youp

Today: tngay nee

Tomorrow: tngay sa-ik

Yesterday: mus'el mun

Bus: laan ch'nual

Ferry: salang

Village: pum

Island: koh

River: tonle

Doctor: bpet

Hospital: moonty bpet

Bank: tia-nia-kia

Post Office: praisinee

Toilet: baan tawp tdeuk

to four hours; starting at $50 excluding gas).

■ TIP→ **The highway to Sihanoukville is much improved and is now one of the better roads in Cambodia, but it is still hazardous to drive for anyone who is not familiar with roads in Cambodia. Buses are almost as fast, and usually safer.**

Taxis make the trip to and from Sihanoukville and Phnom Penh. The charge is $10 per person for five people, but if you want to be a little less cramped you can pay $13 to have only three seated in the back, or try and get the coveted front seat.

Sights

Sihanoukville is a beach town without a real center. There's a market area with a surrounding business area that has all the banks and other basic facilities; however, the town's accommodations are spread out along the coast.

★ Koh Rong Samloem

ISLAND | The Sihanoukville coast is flanked by several islands, many of them untouristed and lightly populated by Khmer fishermen, and some are accessible by boat. **Koh Rong Samloem, Koh Tas, Koh Ta Kiev,** and **Koh Russei** are popular day-trip destinations for snorkeling and picnicking, but local guides can arrange overnight stays in rustic bungalows if you'd like to linger for a few days. Koh Rong Samloem is about 2½ hours by boat from the mainland (or 40 minutes in a speedboat), and there are some quiet and isolated beaches with a few basic bungalow options. The amenities vary depending where you go. ⚠ **The jungle interior of the island is home to some of the deadliest snakes in Cambodia. They are more afraid of you, of course, but be aware.** ✉ *Sihanoukville.*

Restaurants

The most inexpensive guesthouses, restaurants, and other tourist services are on Victory (Weather Station) Hill, Serendipity Beach, and Ochheuteal Beach. Some of the lodgings in these areas are quite attractive, although over the years these locations have become somewhat blighted by mass tourism.

Curry King

$ | **INDIAN** | This small restaurant serves big portions of Indian favorites at a great price, from paneer biryani rice to chicken masala and onion bhajis. You can accompany your meal with a mango lassi or a local beer, if you must. **Known for:** vegetarian options; thali platter meals; casual atmosphere. [$] *Average main: 7* ✉ *Serendipity Beach Road, Sihanoukville* ☎ *098/609030.*

The Deck Tapas Bar

$$ | **INTERNATIONAL** | In the Sokha Beach Resort, this outdoor beachfront restaurant is an idyllic dinner-and-drinks spot, from the dreamy sunset hour to late at night. The tapas menu is innovative and trendy and there's a nice selection of international wines to choose from. **Known for:** fresh seafood; duck and vegetable spring rolls; happy hour. [$] *Average main: $12* ✉ *Sokha Beach Resort, 2 Thnou St., Sokha Beach* ☎ *034/935999* 🌐 *www.sokhahotels.com.kh/sihanoukville/dining* 🕒 *No lunch.*

Manoha

$ | **CAMBODIAN** | Though it doesn't have the sea views, the simple and unpretentious Manoha serves excellent French-Khmer cuisine with a sophisticated air, prepared by a Cambodian chef who utilizes the best of fresh local ingredients and the fresh fish. Delicate dishes like fish carpaccio and tartare are recommended, as is the *bai cha Manoha* (prawns in a spicy sauce, with rice served in a pineapple). **Known for:** open 24 hours; big portions and extensive menu; hearty breakfast. [$] *Average main: $5* ✉ *1035 Rd., Sihanoukville* ☎ *096/440–1586.*

Rendez-Vous

$$ | **ASIAN FUSION** | This trendy downtown restaurant serves a blend of Khmer and Chinese dishes—which makes sense given Sihanoukville's demographics—so expect choices like roast pork and rice, chicken curry, whole salted fish, and even durian pizza. The large two-level space has plenty of seating choices. **Known for:** varied menu; modern decor; open all day. [$] *Average main: $8* ✉ *28 Mithona St., Sihanoukville* ☎ *098/268005.*

★ Sandan

$ | **CAMBODIAN** | Operated by the Tree Alliance charity, this is a vocational training restaurant that demonstrates just how good the training is—the service

The Road to the Coast

The four-hour bus journey from Phnom Penh to Sihanoukville along Highway 4 is an interesting one, winding through uplands, rice paddies, and orchards. Once you drive past Phnom Penh's Pochentong Airport and the prestigious Cambodia Golf & Country Club, and on through the area of Kompong Speu, the landscape turns rural, dotted with small villages where a major source of income seems to be the sale of firewood and charcoal. Somewhere around the entrance to Kirirom National Park all buses stop for refreshments at a roadside restaurant.

The halfway point of the journey lies at the top of the **Pich Nil mountain pass,** guarded by dozens of colorful spirit houses. These spirit houses were built for the legendary deity Yeah Mao, guardian of Sihanoukville and the coastal region. Legend has it that Yeah Mao was the wife of a village headman who worked in far-off Koh Kong, an island near today's border with Thailand. On a journey to visit him, Yeah Mao died when the boat transporting her sank in a storm—an all-too-believable story to anyone who has taken the boat from Sihanoukville to Koh Kong. Her spirit became the guardian of local villagers and fisherfolk.

At the small town of Chamcar Luang, a side road leads to the renowned smuggling port of Sre Ambel. The main highway threads along **Ream National Park,** with the Elephant Mountains as a backdrop. The national park is a highlight of Sihanoukville, with its mangroves, forests, waterfalls, and wildlife. The park is, unusually for Cambodia, well protected from the vagaries of modern development. The sprawling Angkor Beer brewery heralds the outskirts of Sihanoukville and the journey's end.

Getting Here and Around

You can easily hire a private car and driver through your hotel or guesthouse for the trip to the coast from Phnom Penh. The price varies, but starts at approximately $50, and can be split with other passengers if you prefer. The drive takes around four hours, but will go down to just two once the new Chinese-built expressway (Cambodia's first) to the capital city is completed, which is currently expected to happen in 2022.

is attentive and the food exceptional. New and inventive Cambodian dishes are constantly being added, the specials change regularly, and the cocktails are pretty decent, too. **Known for:** great value and taste; your meal supports youth training; Cambodian panfried noodles. *[$] Average main: $5 ✉ St. 10311, Krong Preah ✣ One block south of 7 Makara St. ☎ 098/454400 🌐 www.tree-alliance.org/our-restaurants/sandan.php.*

Hotels

Don Bosco Hotel School

$ | HOTEL | FAMILY | As the name implies, this lodging doubles as a school for trainees in the service industry, who are selected from a pool of local underprivileged young adults, but far from feeling like a guinea pig at a training facility, guests enjoy a high level of service and care. **Pros:** excellent food; big swimming pool; shuttle service to town and beaches three times a day. **Cons:** part of a larger complex; inconvenient location; somewhat impersonal. $ *Rooms from: $35* ⊠ *Group 13, Sangkat 4, Ou 5, Sihanoukville* ☏ *016/919834* ⊕ *www.hotel-sihanoukville.com* ⇱ *31 rooms* ⦿ *Free Breakfast.*

★ **Lazy Beach**

$$ | **B&B/INN** | Jump on the hotel's boat at Ochheuteal Beach at midday and two hours later you'll be marveling at this beautiful tropical hideout, made up of wooden bungalows stretched along the powdery beige sand. **Pros:** peaceful getaway; friendly management and staff; pretty, natural setting. **Cons:** not much to do (except relax); no electricity (but a generator supplies power in the evening); a two-hour boat ride. $ *Rooms from: $60* ⊠ *Lazy Beach, Koh Rong Sanloem, Sihanoukville* ☏ *016/214211* ⊕ *lazybeach-cambodia.com* ⇱ *10 rooms* ⦿ *Free Breakfast.*

The One Resort

$$ | **RESORT** | **FAMILY** | In the middle of the most popular beach on Cambodia's most popular island, The One is a step up from the usual backpacker lodgings. **Pros:** very clean beach; bungalows with a/c; swimming pool. **Cons:** breakfast is small; expensive meals; service is slow. $ *Rooms from: 54* ⊠ *Saracen Bay, Koh Rong Sanloem, Sihanoukville* ☏ *016/676700* ⊕ *theone-resort.com* ⦿ *Free Breakfast* ⇱ *20 rooms.*

★ **Six Senses Krabey Island**

$$$$ | **RESORT** | The Six Senses is a splurge but if you're ever going to do it, this private island, where the 40 private pool villas blend into the jungle, is the place to do it. **Pros:** all-inclusive activities; complete privacy; full spa. **Cons:** limited dining options; expensive; facilities are spread out. $ *Rooms from: $500* ⊠ *Koh Krabey, Sihanoukville* ☏ *069/944888* ⊕ *sixsenses.com/en/resorts/krabey-island* ⦿ *Free Breakfast* ⇱ *40 suites.*

Sokha Beach Resort

$$$ | **RESORT** | **FAMILY** | This is a huge, first-class resort hotel with all the facilities required for a fun-filled beach holiday. **Pros:** nice location; great for families; private beach. **Cons:** a bit short on the luxury status it claims; not geared to romantic getaways; close to a casino. $ *Rooms from: $120* ⊠ *2 Thnou St., Sihanoukville* ☏ *034/935999* ⊕ *www.sokhahotels.com.kh/sihanoukville* ⇱ *268 rooms, 20 suites, 79 villas* ⦿ *Free Breakfast.*

★ **Song Saa Private Island**

$$$$ | **RESORT** | Barefoot luxury are the buzzwords most used to describe this multiple-award-winning resort (the name Song Saa is Khmer for "sweet hearts"), set on two small islands a 40-minute speedboat trip from Sihanoukville. **Pros:** all-inclusive packages available; created with sustainability in mind; surrounding waters are part of a marine park. **Cons:** stepping off the speedboat at Port 1, Gate 1 (Sihanoukville's harbor) at the end of your stay; limited accommodations so book early; surrounding waters have many sea urchins. $ *Rooms from: $1,400* ⊠ *Koh Ouen, Sihanoukville* ☏ *092/609488* ⊕ *www.songsaa-private-island.com* ⇱ *27 villas* ⦿ *Free Breakfast.*

🎣 Activities

Most hotels and guesthouses can arrange boat trips, which include packed lunches, to the many offshore islands. Several companies offer diving and snorkeling; two of the most popular dive centers are EcoSea Diver and Scuba Nation.

EcoSea Dive

DIVING & SNORKELING | Eco-friendly instruction comes at very competitive prices here. Dives start from $30. ⊠ *M'Pai Bay, Koh Rong Samloem, Sihanoukville* ☏ *016/976431.*

Jayavarman VII built Preah Khan in 1191 to commemorate the Khmers' victory over Cham invaders.

Scuba Nation

DIVING & SNORKELING | This was Cambodia's first certified PADI dive center and is still probably the best around, taking trips out to good underwater sites. They offer all the courses, up to advanced levels, and have fun options for children. ✉ *Saracen Bay, Koh Rong Sanloem, Sihanoukville* ☎ *071/781–9266* ⊕ *www. divecambodia.com.*

Kampot

110 km (68 miles) east of Sihanoukville, 150 km (93 miles) south of Phnom Penh.

With the drastic changes happening in nearby Sihanoukville, this attractive riverside town at the foot of the Elephant Mountain range, not far from the sea, is luring more and more tourists and expats, and is fast becoming the new "place to be" on the southern coast. Kampot is known for its French colonial architectural remnants—and for salt and pepper. In the dry season laborers can be seen along the highway to Kep, working long hours in the salt fields; pepper plantations are scattered around the province. Kampot is also the departure point for trips to the seaside resort of Kep and Bokor Hill Station. The coastal road from Sihanoukville to Kampot has been sealed and offers spectacular views. Several limestone caves speckle the landscape from Kampot to Kep to the Vietnam border. Plan at least a morning or afternoon excursion to see the cave and Hindu temple at Phnom Chhnork.

GETTING HERE AND AROUND
To get here, take a taxi or bus, or hire a car and driver through your hotel. The journey from Phnom Penh takes approximately three hours. A single bus ticket on Sorya Transport costs $7 from Phnom Penh's Central Market. Prices for a taxi or a car with driver start at $50. Hotels are the best source for tour information in and around Kampot.

Sights

Kampot has enough to keep the intrepid traveler busy for a couple of days. The town is artsy and relaxed, with a wide river marking the center of the town's dining and lodging area, whose epicenter is the cluster of streets around the Old Market. Kampot is the stepping-off point for nearby Kep, and it has rapids and a few caves to explore. Don't forget the world-renowned salt and pepper production. The remains of Bokor Hill Station are probably the largest draw for visitors.

Bokor Hill Station

RUINS | In the early 20th century, the French built this hill station as a retreat from the heat and humidity of the coast. Aside from the once derelict casino, which has been restored as a hotel, it's now mostly a collection of ruins but it's worth visiting for the spectacular sea views from its 3,000-foot heights. It's 35 km (22 miles) west of Kampot, and easily reachable by rented motorbike. Or you can hire a car with a driver for more comfort (and local knowledge). Besides the hotel, the abandoned church and former royal residences are highlights. ✉ *Kampot*.

★ La Plantation

FARM/RANCH | **FAMILY** | Kampot's world-renowned aromatic pepper is sold all around the country and was once the go-to spice for upmarket kitchens in Paris, but there's nothing quite like visiting where it's grown, sampling it right off the plant, and paying its producers in person for a certified 100% organic product. La Plantation is one of the most respectable producers, where you can buy white, red, or black pepper after a free tour of the pepper plantation itself. You can also explore its numerous heritage buildings, which were rescued and restored from the surrounding villages (the main one, where you can have lunch, was once a hall for monks). They also offer fun water buffalo–led cart rides, which take

you into the waters of the nearby Secret Lake, a beautiful stretch of water that hides a dark past; it was built by forced labor during the Khmer Rouge years.
■ **TIP** → **As most pepper plantations are in the countryside along dusty, rocky roads, it's best to arrange a taxi ride—tuk-tuks across this kind of terrain can be exhausting.** ✉ *Secret Lake, Bosjheng Village, Domnak Er district* ☎ *17/842505* ⊕ *www.kampotpepper.com* ⌖ *Bookings 24 hours in advance.*

Phnom Chhnork Caves

CAVE | These limestone caves shelter a pre-Angkorian Hindu ruin (before it was Buddhist, the Khmer empire was Hindu), over which the stalagmites and stalactites are gradually growing. The less appealing cave of Phnom Sia (flashlight required) is mostly about exploring in the depths of a cave but the white elephant cave, or Cave of Sasear, has a shrine where worshippers pray to an elephant-shaped limestone formation. Tuk-tuks from town cost around $10 for the round-trip. Locals will ask $4 to guide you into the caves. ✉ *On road from Kampot to Kep* ⌖ *$1.*

 Restaurants

Cafe Espresso Kampot

$ | **CAFÉ** | Caffeine can lovers rejoice, for at the Australian-run Cafe Espresso you are guaranteed to find an excellent cup of coffee. Beans are locally sourced, regionally grown, home roasted, and ground fresh to order. **Known for:** family-friendly environment; vegetarian options; Western comfort food. $ *Average main: $5* ✉ *Highway 33* ⌖ *On main road to Kep* ☎ *092/388736* ⊕ *www.kampotcoffee.wixsite.com/espresso* ☾ *No dinner.*

★ Epic Arts Cafe

$ | **CAFÉ** | **FAMILY** | Created to raise awareness and generate work opportunities for deaf and disabled people, many of whom it now employs, Epic Arts Cafe serves a selection of tasty breakfast and lunch dishes, as well as desserts, fresh-fruit smoothies, and coffee brewed from local beans. There's a shop upstairs, too, selling local goods. **Known for:** known for its BLT sandwich and carrot cake; provides work opportunities for deaf and disabled; very pleasant atmosphere. $ *Average main: $3* ✉ *1st May Rd., Kompong Kandal* ✛ *Across from new Kampot Market* ☎ *092/922069* ⊕ *www.epicarts.org.uk* ⊘ *No dinner.*

The Fish Market

$$ | **ASIAN FUSION** | Kampot's 1930s fish market has been upgraded into a luxe riverfront bistro that's the perfect spot for a stylish sundowner: cocktails use local flavors so you'll find a Kampot pepper Bloody Mary and lychee martinis. The seafood-focused menu mixes Asian and international flavors, from Cajun Salmon steaks to Sicilian-style squid, to perfection. **Known for:** variety of seafood options; creative cocktails; sunset views. $ *Average main: $10* ✉ *Riverside Rd.* ✛ *Opposite the Old Market* ☎ *012/728884.*

Rikitikitavi

$ | **INTERNATIONAL** | This cheery second-floor terrace restaurant above a guesthouse serves European and American favorites such as burgers, bruschetta, and salads, as well as Khmer dishes: try the creamy Saraman beef curry with peanuts, local herbs, and spices. Many ingredients are seasonal and locally sourced, though there aren't a lot of vegetarian options. **Known for:** extensive menu; local ingredients; great riverside views. $ *Average main: $7* ✉ *Riverside Rd.* ✛ *Next to post office* ☎ *017/306557* ⊕ *www.rikitikitavi-kampot.com.*

DeliCious

$ | **FRENCH FUSION** | Despite its small size, Kampot has some of the best restaurants in the kingdom and this tiny French-run deli-café is one of the standouts. The fare is relatively simple—salads, sandwiches, and homemade pastries and pies, but it's all top quality and made using natural, locally sourced ingredients. **Known for:** fun evening happy hour; great food; daily changing specials. $ *Average main: 4* ✉ *34 St. 724, French Quarter* ☎ *095/952106.*

Hotels

Amber Kampot

$$$$ | **RESORT** | **FAMILY** | If you like the idea of a villa with your own private pool this upmarket retreat across the river from Kampot's old French Quarter is for you. **Pros:** private pools and larger shared one; secluded; full wellness spa on-site. **Cons:** limited on-site dining options; pools are not heated; boat needed to reach town. $ *Rooms from: $348* ✉ *Ta Ang Village* ☎ *078/775542* ⊕ *amber-kampot.com* ❖ *Free Breakfast* ⤣ *26 villas.*

Kampot View Boutique Hotel

$$ | **HOTEL** | This river-view boutique hotel next to Kampot's new bridge has three floors of minimalist-chic rooms, some with river views and some with garden views. **Pros:** convenient to center but still private; modern design; swimming pool. **Cons:** next to a trafficked road and can get noisy; 1 km (half mile) from the Old Market; ground-floor rooms next to the pool are less private. $ *Rooms from: $50* ✉ *National Rd. 3, Thvi Village, Andong* ✛ *Next to the new bridge, on the opposite side of the river from town* ☎ *017/294120* ✉ *kampotviewboutique-hotels@gmail.com* ⤣ *22 rooms* ❖ *Free Breakfast.*

Gecko Village

$ | **RESORT** | **FAMILY** | A few miles upriver from Kampot, this lovely French-run resort is surrounded by nature: it's on the water, with the mountains looming behind. **Pros:** nature all around; saltwater swimming pool; bicycle and kayak rentals. **Cons:** little else in the area; far from Kampot city; limited breakfast. $ *Rooms from: $25* ✉ *Wat Teuk Beul, Kampong Kreang Village* ☎ *096/726–2157*

Cambodia's Early History

The earliest prehistoric site excavated in Cambodia is the cave of Laang Spean in the northwest. Archaeologists estimate that hunters and gatherers lived in the cave 7,000 years ago. Some 4,000 years ago this prehistoric people began to settle in permanent villages. The Bronze Age settlement of Samrong Sen, near Kampong Chhnang, indicates that 3,000 years ago people knew how to cast bronze axes, drums, and gongs for use in religious ceremonies; at the same time, they domesticated cattle, pigs, and water buffaloes. Rice and fish were then, as now, the staple diet. By 500 BC ironworking had become widespread, rice production increased, and moats and embankments were being built to enclose their circular village settlements. It was at this stage that Indian traders and missionaries arrived—in a land then called Suvarnabhumi, or Golden Land.

Legend has it that in the 1st century AD the Indian Brahman Kaundinya arrived by ship in the Mekong Delta, where he met and married a local princess named Soma. The marriage led to the founding of the first kingdom on Cambodian soil. Archaeologists believe that the kingdom's capital was at Angkor Borei in Takeo Province.

In the 6th century the inland kingdom of Zhen La emerged. It comprised several small city-states in the Mekong River basin. A period of centralization followed, during which temples were built, cities enlarged, and land irrigated. Power later shifted to Siem Reap Province, where the history of the Khmer Empire started when a king of uncertain descent established the Devaraja line by becoming a "god-king." This royal line continues today.

✉ geckovillage.kampot@gmail.com
🍴 Free Breakfast ⇆ 10 rooms.

Villa Vedici

$ | **RESORT** | **FAMILY** | One of the original riverside resorts in Kampot, Villa Vedici sprawls over its four hectares, with two pools and a mix of accommodation options, including rooms upstairs in the main house as well as private villas. **Pros:** plenty of activities; beautiful scenery; variety of room options. **Cons:** property in need of some renovations; a bit far from town; insects. 💲 Rooms from: 40 ✉ Kampot River ☎ 089/290714 ⊕ villavedici.com 🍴 Free Breakfast.

Kep

25 km (16 miles) east of Kampot, 172 km (107 miles) south of Phnom Penh.

You'll never find another seaside getaway quite like Kep, with its narrow pebble-and-sand coastline bordered by the ghostly villa ruins of the Khmer Rouge era. What was once the coastal playground of Cambodia's elite and the international glitterati was destroyed in decades of war but ever so slowly investors are refurbishing what's salvageable; most of the villas now being turned into resorts were bought for next to nothing in the early 1990s. If you arrive by bus, tuk-tuk drivers and tour guides are sure to find you. Not much traffic comes through Kep, so the locals know the bus schedule.

They're sure to offer you a tour of a nearby pepper plantation, which can be a rewarding experience but also a long, bumpy ride along dusty rural roads (a 4x4 or regular car is the best option). Kep grows some of the world's best pepper, which you can enjoy in its green, red, black, and white phases in a multitude of traditional dishes—the crab with Kampot pepper is especially good.

The beach in town is small and a popular picnic spot for locals who come to relax at the water's edge. Offshore, beautiful Rabbit Island has attracted a lot of tourists over the last few years, and the unfortunate result is that it has become somewhat polluted. You can hire a boat to take you there for $7 to $10. If you are a true nature adventurer and choose to stay at one of the 30 or so bungalows here, be warned—there are snakes in the interior of the island and there is only sporadic electricity.

GETTING HERE AND AROUND

To get here, take a taxi or bus, or hire a car and driver through your hotel. The journey from Phnom Penh takes approximately 3½ hours. A single bus ticket is $7 from Phnom Penh's Central Market. Hiring a taxi or a car with driver will cost at least $50. Given the good condition of the coastal road and the distance of the sights, renting a scooter (around $6 per day) is the best way to move around town.

🍴 Restaurants

A strip of simple eateries mainly run by local fishermen and their families can be found in the seafront Crab Market area. Here you can take your pick of these good-value local haunts, each serving fresh seafood dishes for around $6. Choices range from fresh salads and crunchy patties to succulent, spicy curries starring the famously flavorsome green, red, or black pepper from neighboring Kampot. Ideally, arrive around sunset to watch the fishermen returning with their catch, and to enjoy the mesmerizing colors play on the ocean before tucking into your dinner.

Kep Coffee

$ | AMERICAN | FAMILY | This small restaurant is a popular with the chic weekenders from Phnom Penh and it's the perfect spot to stop in before catching a boat to Koh Tonsay (Rabbit Island). The handwritten chalk menu features quesadillas, burgers, and grilled sandwiches, served in large, tasty portions. **Known for:** friendly atmosphere; ham and cheese cold sandwich; freshly made cakes and desserts. [$] *Average main: 5* ✉ *St. 33A* ✥ *Next to Koh Tonsay (Rabbit Island) Pier* ☎ *097/2607472* 🕒 *Closed Mon.* 💳 *No credit cards.*

★ Sailing Club

$$ | INTERNATIONAL | FAMILY | A great way to combine seaside eating and fun, especially for families, the Knai Bang Chatt hotel's Sailing Club welcomes all for seafood barbecues, a popular Sunday brunch, and light meals as well as beach volleyball, sailing, Hobie Cat rentals, and kayaking. Linger on until the evening to sip a cocktail and take in the stunning sunset views from this beautifully restored wooden fisherman's cottage. **Known for:** romantic location; sunset dinners; fresh seafood. [$] *Average main: $10* ✉ *Phum Thmey, Sangkat Prey Thom* ☎ *078/737995* 🌐 *www.knaibangchatt.com.*

🛏 Hotels

★ Knai Bang Chatt

$$$$ | RESORT | At this scenic, luxurious resort you can experience the laissez-faire glamour of Kep in the 1960s and 1970s, when it was the fashionable seaside escape known as Kep-Sur-Mer and attracted Cambodian royalty and the international elite. Accommodations are in four villas, three of which were built in the 1970s, and a seamlessly integrated fourth, completed in 2012. **Pros:** old-fashioned elegance; exclusive and luxurious; close to the crab market. **Cons:** not the best beach in Cambodia; not much else around; not all rooms have good natural light. [$] *Rooms from: $190* ✉ *Phum Thmey, Sangkat Prey, Thom Khan, Kampot* ☎ *078/333684* 🌐 *www.knaibangchatt.com* 🛏 *18 rooms* 🍴 *Free Breakfast.*

Atmaland

$$ | RESORT | FAMILY | While not as fancy as some of other offerings in town, this small, cozy resort offers great value in comfortable surrounds, with its complimentary breakfast of Khmer and French standards. **Pros:** walking distance to crab market; clean and comfortable rooms; homemade bread and pizza. **Cons:** road not lit at night; rooms lack natural light; pool can get crowded. [$] *Rooms from: $70* ✉ *St. 33A* ☎ *012/204155* 🌐 *atmaland.com* 🍴 *Free Breakfast* 🛏 *8 rooms.*

Raingsey Bungalow

$ | RESORT | FAMILY | "Hidden retreat" is an apt description for this little oasis, located as it is down a small lane of a quiet road. **Pros:** crab market close by; specialist massages; nice pool area. **Cons:** limited car park; lacks sea views; small pool. [$] *Rooms from: $35* ✉ *Hillside Rd.* ☎ *085/560294* 🌐 *raingsey.com* 🍴 *Free Breakfast* 🛏 *9 rooms.*

★ **Samanea Beach Resort**

$$$ | RESORT | FAMILY | Twelve Khmer-style villas, all with their own private verandas and charming open-roofed Balinese baths filled with plants and trees, fan around a large blue-tiled pool set amid peaceful gardens at this seafront resort. **Pros:** private beach and jetty; family-size pool; quiet atmosphere. **Cons:** open-roofed bathrooms; far from town; limited dining options nearby. [$] *Rooms from: $175* ✉ *33A Kep Rd.* ☎ *088/240–0600* 🌐 *www.samanea-resort.com* 🛏 *12 villas* 🍴 *Free Breakfast.*

Veranda Natural Resort

$$$ | RESORT | FAMILY | Perched on a hill above Kep, this resort eschews the seaside to instead offer guests lofty ocean views and a nature-filled environment. **Pros:** two saltwater pools; easy access to hiking trails; peaceful environment. **Cons:** restaurant is outdoors; distance from the beach; some rooms have no view. [$] *Rooms from: 130* ✉ *Kep Hillside Rd.* ☎ *012/888619* 🌐 *veranda-resort.asia* 🍴 *Free Breakfast* 🛏 *40 rooms.*

Chapter 10

LAOS

Updated by
Jason Rolan

👁 Sights   🍴 Restaurants   🛏 Hotels   🛍 Shopping   🍸 Nightlife

★★★★☆   ★★★☆☆   ★★★★☆   ★★☆☆☆   ★★☆☆☆

WELCOME TO LAOS

TOP REASONS TO GO

★ **Natural Beauty:** Laos is a beautiful country. Take a multiday trek or bike ride, or enjoy the fantastic mountain scenery from Luang Prabang to Vang Vieng. The far north from Luang Nam Tha to Phongsaly offers the best trekking and nature options.

★ **Archaeological Wonders:** The country's most unusual attraction is the Plain of Jars, which has 5-ton stone-and-clay jars of mysterious origin. Wat Phou, pre-Angkor Khmer ruins, is Laos's most recent UNESCO World Heritage site.

★ **Buddhist Customs:** Observing or participating in morning alms in Luang Prabang is a magical experience; so, too, is sitting in a temple to chat with a novice monk, surrounded by the sounds of chanting and chiming bells.

★ **The Mekong:** The Mekong River is the lifeline of Laos. You can travel down the mighty tributary on a slow cruise, or stop at one of 4,000 Islands for a chance to spot freshwater dolphins.

1 Vientiane.

2 Nam Ngum Lake.

3 Phou Khao Khouay.

4 Plain of Jars.

5 Vang Vieng.

6 Luang Prabang.

7 Tad Kouang Si Waterfall.

8 Tad Sae Waterfall.

9 Pak Ou Caves.

10 Ban Meuang Ngoi.

11 Luang Nam Tha.

12 Meuang Sing.

13 River Journey to Houay Xai.

14 Phongsaly.

15 Tha Khek.

16 Highway 13 South Along the Mekong.

17 Savannakhet.

18 Pakse.

19 Bolaven Plateau.

20 Tad Fane.

21 Champasak.

22 Si Phan Don and the 4,000 Islands.

Despite a limited infrastructure, Laos is a wonderful country to visit. Laotians are some of the friendliest, gentlest people in Southeast Asia—devoutly Buddhist and traditional in many ways—and the country has a rich culture and history. Though it's been a battleground many times in the past, this is a peaceful, stable country today. Roughly 7 million people live in this landlocked nation and, not yet inured to countless visiting foreigners, locals volunteer assistance and offer a genuine welcome.

Luang Prabang and its historic sites are the country's primary claim to fame and the reason most tourists visit, but as a travel destination, Laos also excels with its abundant nature and the chance to visit small towns and villages and escape normally overcrowded Southeast Asia. In many ways, a visit to Laos is a placid throwback to what travel in Thailand was like two decades or so ago. Many parts of the country—among them 4,000 Islands in the Mekong, or Phongsaly, Meuang Ngoi, and Luang Nam Tha in the north—offer a fabulous opportunity to unwind, relax, and get away from the stresses of big cities and must-see-everything travel. Most visitors to Laos enter via Vientiane, but even here the rhythm of life is calmer than in its regional counterparts. As you venture forth from the capital city, as nearly all visitors do and should, the vibe becomes mellower still.

MAJOR REGIONS

Vientiane and Nearby. Vientiane is not only the capital of Laos but also the logical gateway to the country, as it's much more accessible to the outside world than Luang Prabang. Sitting along the Mekong River, the city is a curiosity—more like a small market town than a national capital—but it has some fine temples, many French colonial buildings, and a riverside boulevard unmatched elsewhere in Laos. North of Vientiane, you'll find beautiful day trip destinations including Nam Ngum Lake, Phou Khao Khouay National Park, the archaeological wonder Plain of Jars, and Vang Vieng with its beautiful mountains, caves, waterfalls, and a laid-back, rural vibe.

Luang Prabang and Northern Laos. For all its popularity as a tourist destination, Luang Prabang remains one of the most isolated cities in Southeast Asia. Although a highway now runs north to the Chinese border, the hinterland of Luang Prabang is mostly off-the-beaten-track territory, a mountainous region of impenetrable forests and deep river valleys. Pleasant day trips from the city include Tad Kouang Si Waterfall, Tad Sae Waterfall, and Pak Ou Caves. For trekking, ecotourism, gorgeous scenery, and visits to ethnic minorities, the towns of Ban Meuang Ngoi, northeast of Luang Prabang, and Meuang Sing and Luang Nam Tha, north of Luang Prabang, are good bases. Despite Luang Prabang's air links to the rest of the country and the outside world, the Mekong River is still a preferred travel route, with various cruise and ferry boats departing Luang Prabang for the leisurely River Journey to Houay Xai. Farther north of Luang Prabang, Phongsaly offers even more adventure and trekking through forest-covered mountains.

Southern Laos. In some ways, Laos is really two countries: the south and north are as different as two sides of a coin. The mountainous north was for centuries virtually isolated from the more accessible south, where lowlands, the broad Mekong Valley, and high plateaus were easier to traverse and settle. The south does have its mountains, however: notably the Annamite range, called Phou Luang, home of the aboriginal Mon-Khmer ethnic groups who lived here long before Lao farmers and traders arrived from northern Laos and China. The Lao were followed by French colonists, who built the cities of Tha Khek, Savannakhet, and Pakse. Although the French influence is still tangible, the southern Lao cling tenaciously to their old traditions, making the south a fascinating destination. The far southern region sees fewer tourists than other parts, but Pakse is an interesting town and a convenient base from which to explore the fabulous Wat Phou in Champasak and other ancient Khmer ruins, or explore the waterfalls and coffee plantations of the Bolaven Plateau. Fishing villages line the lower reaches of the Mekong River, a water wonderland with Si Phan Don and the 4,000 Islands and waterfalls at Tad Fane.

Planning

When to Go

Laos has a tropical climate with three distinct seasons: the cool season, from October through February; the hot season, from March through May; and the rainy season, from June through September. The cool season is a comfortable time to tour Laos but by March temperatures begin to soar. The country becomes baking hot, and because farmers burn their fields in spring, the air turns brown and hazy. In the rainy season, road travel can be slower, but quick rain showers can bring cool evenings; August and September see the most rain. On the upside, the country is greener and less crowded during the rains and prices are lower.

The yearly average temperature is about 82°F (28°C), rising to a maximum of 100°F (38°C) in April and May. In the mountainous areas around Luang Nam Tha, Phonsavan, and Phongsaly, however, daytime temperatures can drop to 59°F (15°C) in winter and sometimes hit the freezing point at night.

Laos has a busy festival calendar and Vientiane and Luang Prabang, in particular, can get very crowded during the most important of these festivals, among them Lao New Year, in April, and Vientiane's That Luang Festival, in November. Book your hotel room well in advance during these periods.

Planning Your Time

Given distances in Laos and its mountainous terrain, if you've only got a week to spend here, you'll have to choose between visiting the north or south. A popular strategy in the north would be to enter Laos in Houay Xai from Chiang Mai/Chiang Rai in Thailand, then take the two-day boat trip on the Mekong to Luang Prabang.

If you're a mountain lover, you could skip the boat ride and take a minivan to Luang Nam Tha, and spend a couple of days here kayaking or trekking in the Nam Ha Reserve or visiting ethnic minority hill tribes. From here it takes a long day's journey to get to Luang Prabang, where you can relax in a colonial resort and enjoy the UNESCO World Heritage city. Luang Prabang is more about the atmosphere than actual sights, so a few days can be enough for a quick visit. Afterward, take a bus south to Vang Vieng, or else a van to the Plain of Jars, and spend a few days in either of these spots, with Vang Vieng the best option for nature and scenery lovers, and the Plain of Jars of interest for history and archaeology buffs.

From Vang Vieng, an hour's drive by car will get you to Vientiane; from the Plain of Jars you can fly. Spend your last night in Vientiane, which has all services and connections out of the country. If you opt for seeing the 4,000 Islands and southern Laos, it's best to head here from Ubon Ratchathani in Thailand, crossing over to Pakse (or else flying from Vientiane if you have been up north). Pakse isn't worth more than a day, so head down to Champasak for a day exploring Wat Phou and staying in the quiet river town or else across on Don Daeng Island. Then head to Don Khong, Don Khon, or Don Det for a few days, where you can investigate the Irrawaddy dolphins in the Mekong, check out the spectacular waterfalls, and enjoy the sleepy island life. It's worth it

from here to make a side trip up to the Tad Fane waterfall and the coffee-growing region on the Bolaven Plateau. With all these side trips, you'll need at least four days here.

Getting Here and Around

AIR

There are no direct flights from the United States to Laos but it is easily accessed by plane through other points in Asia, including Seoul, Bangkok, Hanoi, and Kuala Lumpur.

Most of Laos's mountainous terrain is impenetrable jungle, and road travel here is very slow; the only practical way to tour the country in less than a week is by plane. Bangkok Airways has daily flights from Bangkok to Luang Prabang and Vientiane; Thai Airways flies to Vientiane; and Lao Airlines runs frequent flights from Bangkok to Luang Prabang and Vientiane, as well as provincial cities including Pakse and Savannakhet. Lao Skyway offers cheaper fares on major domestic routes and also operates the country's only flight options to remote areas, like Phongsaly, on 15-seat Cessnas. (See Air Travel in Travel Smart Thailand).

■ TIP→ **An inexpensive and convenient option is to fly Air Asia, Thai Smile, or Nok Air from Bangkok to either Udon Thani or Ubon Ratchathani and then cross the border by land, putting you in Vientiane or Pakse in less than an hour.**

BOAT

Running virtually the entire length of the country, the Mekong River is a natural highway. Because all main cities lie along the Mekong, boats are an exotic yet practical means of travel. Mekong Cruises operates two luxury cruise routes: the Luang Say (River Journey between Houay Xai and Luang Prabang) and the Vat Phou (a circular route starting and ending in Pakse). The Shompoo Cruise (River Journey from Houay Xai to Luang Prabang) is a mid-range alternative to the Luang Say cruise.

BUS

A network of bus services covers almost the entire country. Though cheap, bus travel is slow and not as comfortable as in Thailand. VIP buses, which connect Vientiane, Luang Prabang, and Pakse, are somewhat more comfortable—they have assigned seats and more legroom, and make fewer stops, but all buses in Laos are aging second- or thirdhand imports. Minivan service, common between cities, costs slightly more than the bus, but it's quicker and some companies pick up passengers at their hotels.

■TIP→ **Sleeper buses travel between Vientiane and Pakse, but beds are less than 6 feet long, so tall folks may want to buy both spots in what is essentially one shared small bed.**

CAR

Although it's possible to enter Laos by car and drive around on your own, this is not recommended as driving conditions are difficult: nearly 90% of the country's 14,000 km (8,700 miles) of roads are unpaved, road signs are often indecipherable, and accidents will invariably be considered your fault. A better alternative is to hire a car and driver for about $70 per day.

SONGTHAEW, TUK-TUK, AND TAXI

Tuk-tuks and songthaews cruise the streets and are easy to flag down in most towns. Songthaews are usually small pickup trucks with a roof over the bed and two rows of seats running down the sides. They generally run along fixed routes like a bus, but can also just be privatized. Tuk-tuks are a bit smaller, have three wheels and are only for private hire. Tuk-tuk drivers can be unscrupulous about fares, especially in Luang Prabang

and Vientiane. ■TIP→ **Use the ride-hailing app, LOCA, to avoid the tuk-tuk hustlers.**

While Uber never made it to Laos, a home-grown ride-hailing app has become popular in Vientiane, Luang Prabang, and Pakse. Download the LOCA app (*loca.la*) and you can get around without the tuk-tuk hassle and in air-conditioned comfort.

Border Crossings

In addition to the international airports in Vientiane, Luang Prabang, and Pakse, there are numerous land and river crossings into Laos. The busiest is the Friendship Bridge, between Laos and Thailand, which spans the Mekong River 18 km (12 miles) east of Vientiane. Other border crossings from Thailand to Laos are: Chiang Khong to Houay Xai (by bridge across the Mekong River); Nakhon Phanom to Tha Khek; Mukdahan to Savannakhet; and Chongmek to Vang Tao. There are also several new open crossings from the more remote Loei and Phrae provinces in northern Thailand. You can also enter Laos from Cambodia at Nong Nok Khien, and from Mohan, in China's Yunnan Province, at Boten. There are seven crossings between Laos and Vietnam, including Cau Treu to Nam Phao (from near Vinh, Vietnam, to Lak Xao in Laos); Nam Can to Nam Khan (Vinh to Phonsavan); and Lao Bao to Dansavan (on the Hue to Savannakhet route).

Border crossings are open daily from 8:30 to 5, except for the Friendship Bridge, which is open daily from 6 am to 10 pm.

Money Matters

The currency is the Lao kip (LAK), which comes in relatively small notes (the largest denomination equals about $10). Most prices in this chapter are listed in kip, sometimes with the U.S. dollar equivalent for reference. The Thai baht is accepted in Vientiane, Luang Prabang, and border towns. It's best to carry most of your cash in dollars or baht and exchange relatively small amounts of kip as you travel. At this writing, the official exchange rate is approximately 300 kip to the Thai baht and around 10,000 kip to one U.S. dollar.

There are ATMs throughout the country so changing money is not a big issue.

Credit cards are accepted in most hotels and some restaurants but few shops. Banks in major tourist destinations will provide a cash advance on a MasterCard or Visa, typically for a 5% service charge. Western Union has branches in Vientiane and other major towns.

Health and Safety

■TIP→ **Health care in Laos is nowhere near as good as in Thailand. If you will be traveling extensively, consider buying international health insurance that covers evacuation to Thailand.**

Take the same health precautions in Laos that you would in Thailand.

(see Health in Travel Smart Thailand)

Pharmacies are stocked with Thai antibiotics and are often staffed with assistants who speak some English. Vientiane is malaria-free, but if you're visiting remote regions, consider taking prophylactics. HIV is more widespread in border areas. Reliable Thai condoms are available in Laos.

Laos is fairly free of crime in tourist areas. Pickpocketing is rare, but you should still be careful in crowded areas. Never leave luggage unattended.

Penalties for drug possession are severe. Prostitution is illegal, and $500 fines can be levied against foreigners for having sexual relations with Lao citizens to

whom they are not married (how this is enforced is unclear, but even public displays of affection may be interpreted as shady behavior).

■TIP→ **In the countryside, trekkers should watch out for unexploded ordnance left over from the Vietnam War, especially in Xieng Khouang (Plain of Jars) and Houa Phan provinces, and in southern Laos.**

Don't wander off well-traveled trails. Better yet, trek with a qualified guide. Do not photograph anything that may have military significance, such as airports or military installations.

Passports and Visas

You'll need a passport and a visa to enter Laos. Visas can be obtained on arrival at most entry points, but if you're taking the cross-border bus to Vientiane from Udon Thani or Nong Khai in Thailand, you'll need to get a visa in advance. You can do this at the Lao embassy in Bangkok or consulate in Khon Kaen in an hour or through an embassy or travel agency before you leave home. Tourist visas are good for 30 days, cost $35 for Americans ($42 for Canadians), and can be paid for in U.S. dollars (if you are buying a visa at the Lao border or in a Lao embassy or consulate in Thailand, you can pay in baht, but you will be charged B1,500, which is much more than $35). You'll need to have two passport-size photos (one photo if buying at the border) with you. Bring photos from home, get them in Bangkok, or pay an extra $1 at the border for a photo. Occasionally immigration officials ask to see evidence of sufficient funds and a plane ticket out of the country. Showing them credit and ATM cards should be proof enough of funds.

■TIP→ **Regulations change without warning, so check with the Lao embassy in your home country before setting out.**

At A Glance

Capital: Vientiane

Population: 7,123,205

Currency: kip

Money: ATMs in cities; U.S. dollar and Thai baht widely accepted; credit cards only in resort areas.

Language: Lao

Country Code: 856

Emergencies: Call local police, tel: 191

Driving: On the right

Electricity: 230v/50 cycle; plugs are either U.S. standard two- and three-prong or European standard with two round prongs. Power converter needed.

Time: 11 hours ahead of New York

Documents: Up to 30 days with valid passport; visa on arrival

Mobile Phones: GSM (900 and 1800 bands)

Major Mobile Companies: Lao Telecom, Unitel, T-Plus, ETL Mobile

Websites

The Ministry of Information, Culture and Tourism: *tourismlaos. org*

Love Laos: *love-laos.com*

We Are Lao: *wearelao.com*

EMBASSY Lao Embassy (Bangkok).
✉ *502/502/1–3 Soi Sahakarnpramoon, Pracha Uthit Rd., Wangthonglang, Bangkok* ☎ *02/539–6667.*

Tours

EXO Travel
One of Laos's most creative and respected travel agencies, EXO Travel offers package trips and is a good source for information and tours in Laos. The agency's "Laos, a Journey Within" tour takes you deep into remote areas to showcase the best the country has to offer. Multiday tours to Wat Phou also take in other major attractions in southern Laos. Headquartered in Vientiane, they maintain offices throughout the country. ✉ *15 Kaysone Rd., Phonsa-at Village,* ☎ *021/454640* ⊕ *exotravel.com* ✇ *Daytours start from $70 per person for 2 travelers (higher rate for 1 person, lower for more than 2).*

Green Discovery Laos
The top eco- and adventure-tour operator in Laos, Green Discovery offers a staggering array of adventure, eco, and cultural tours, from one day to one week, throughout the country. The company, which trains its guides well, is also the best source for local information. ✉ *059, Unit 15 Rue Hengboun, Vientiane* ☎ *021/264528* ⊕ *greendiscoverylaos.com* ✇ *From 1,000,000 kip ($123) per person for 2 travelers.*

Ministry of Information, Culture and Tourism
The official government tourist information office has branches in all provinces of Laos. The staff provides some printed materials and tries to be helpful, but you are probably better off going to private travel agencies for more detailed information. ✉ *Box 3556, Ave. Lane Xang, Vientiane* ✛ *East side of street near Dongpalane Rd.* ☎ *021/212248* ⊕ *tourismlaos.org.*

Restaurants

Restaurant choices in Luang Prabang and Vientiane are endless, among them high-end French restaurants; Japanese, Thai, Indian, and pizza places; and fantastic bakeries and coffee shops. In smaller locales, you might have to make do with sticky rice and grilled meats or fish, but most towns have at least one or two fancier places with decent menus. Lao food is similar to Thai but relies more heavily on herbs. Vietnamese pho noodles are widely available, as are baguette sandwiches.

Hotels

Luang Prabang has some of the most elegant resorts in the world. Vientiane has a classic colonial luxury hotel (the Settha Palace), a few boutique options, and several international-caliber business-style hotels. Upscale options have opened around Champasak in the south. Otherwise, fancy resorts in Laos are few and far between, though there are perfectly adequate facilities in Pakse and the Plain of Jars. In Phongsaly, Meuang Ngoi, 4,000 Islands, and other out-of-the-way places, amenities such as Wi-Fi connections and even basics like hot water may not be up to par.

What It Costs in Lao Kip

$	$$	$$$	$$$$
RESTAURANTS			
under 81,000 kip	81,000–122,000 kip	122,001–162,000 kip	over 162,000 kip
HOTELS			
under 410,000 kip	410,000–820,000 kip	820,001–1,230,000 kip	over 1,230,000 kip

Vientiane

Laos's capital is a low-key, pleasant city thanks to its small size, relative lack of traffic, and navigable layout. The pace here is as slow as the Mekong River, which flows along the edge of town. Aside from the magnificent lotus-shaped stupa Pha That Luang, there aren't a lot of must-see sights, but the town has a vibrant international food and café scene, and the promenade along the Mekong and the many wats scattered about are great to explore by bicycle.

Being the center of commerce and government, the city attempts to be the centerpiece of modernity and development for the country—with mixed results—but this makes the remnants of elegant French colonial architecture stand out all the more. There are also dozens of temples—ornate, historic Buddhist structures that stand amid towering palms and flowering trees. First-time visitors often overlook Vientiane's subtle charms, but stay longer and dive deeper to understand that first impressions can be misleading.

GETTING HERE AND AROUND

AIR

Vientiane's Wattay International Airport is about 4 km (2½ miles) from the city center. You can take a metered taxi from the airport into the city for 80,000 kip; get a taxi voucher from the kiosk in the arrivals hall. The ride to the city center takes about 15 minutes. Alternatively, if you don't have much luggage, walk out the airport gate and take a tuk-tuk for 40,000 kip. The cheapest option is the air-conditioned Airport Shuttle bus to Talat Sao (Vientiane's morning market), which costs 15,000 kip.

BUS

Vientiane's city bus system was upgraded in 2018 and provides a few useful routes for the traveler. Note however that most services stop running at around 5 or 6 pm. The city bus station is next to Talat Sao and only handles city routes, the Airport Shuttle Bus, and international buses to Thailand. The Airport Shuttle Bus (#44) leaves roughly every 40 minutes from 8 am to 10:20 pm, and also stops in the city center next to several accommodation options. The Northern Bus Terminal for trips to and from northern Laos is 10 km (6.2 miles) northwest of the center, and is served from Talat Sao by Bus #8 (5,000 kip; every 30 minutes from 6 am to 5 pm). Buses bound for points in southern Laos leave from the Southern Bus Station, which is far out on the northern reaches of the city near Highway 13, and is served by Bus #23 or #29 (5,000 kip; every 20 minutes from 6 am to 6 pm). Another useful route is Bus #20 (5,000 kip; every 30 minutes from 6:30 am to 5:20 pm) which stops at Wat That Luang. Check updated schedules at fb.com/VientianeCity2Bus.

The best way to get to Vientiane from Thailand via bus is to take one of the hourly buses from either Udon Thani (two hours; B80) or Nong Khai (one hour; B55).

■ TIP→ **These buses take you straight to Talat Sao, Vientiane's morning market, but you cannot board them unless you already have a Lao visa.**

If you don't have an advance visa, you can take a bus from Udon Thani to Nong Khai, then a tuk-tuk to the border (from B30 to B50), cross the Friendship Bridge on a B20 shuttle bus, and take a taxi (B350), tuk-tuk (B150), or public bus #14 (8,000 kip; every 15 minutes from 6 am to 6 pm) from the Lao side of the border into Vientiane's morning market. B14 also stops at the interesting Buddha Park in the opposite direction of the city.

TAXI AND TUK-TUK

You can cover Vientiane on foot, but tuk-tuks and jumbos, their larger brethren, are easy to flag down. Negotiate the price before setting off; you can expect to pay about 20,000 to 40,000 kip for a ride within the city if you are a firm negotiator. Taxis are best used through the ride-hailing app, LOCA (download it at loca.la): you'll save the hassle of haggling with tuk-tuks and get a seamless, air-conditioned experience. For day trips outside the city, ask your hotel or guesthouse to book a car with a driver.

SAFETY AND PRECAUTIONS

Vientiane is very safe, but beware of being fleeced by tuk-tuk drivers. Use the LOCA app to hail a ride at a set price. Bag snatching is rare, but be aware of your surroundings and don't hand a potential thief an opportunity.

TIMING

Most people stay in Vientiane a few days, time enough to tour That Luang and a few other monuments, soak up the sleepy ambience, and enjoy some creature comforts and a Beerlao on the Mekong before heading out into the wilds. If you throw in day trips to Nam Ngum or nearby national parks, you could make it a few more. Vientiane is also the place to take care of any business (onward visas, consular affairs, etcetera).

EMERGENCIES

The new Alliance International Medical Centre Clinic, affiliated with the Wattana Hospital in Thailand, is the best medical center in Laos. Most expats and embassy personnel head here to attend to their health needs.

■ TIP→ **For anything major, consider crossing the border to Thailand and going to Wattana Hospital in Nong Khai or Udon Thani.**

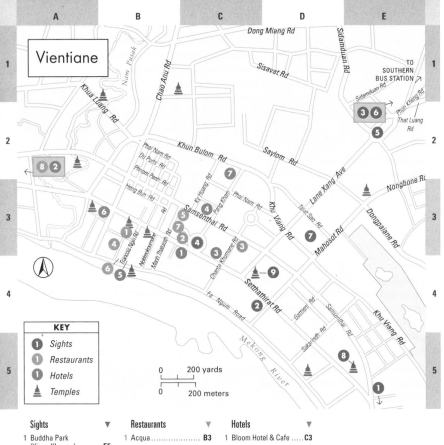

Sights ▼

1 Buddha Park
(Xieng Khouan).......... **E5**
2 Ho Phra Keo............. **C4**
3 Lao National
Museum **E2**
4 Nam Phou Square....... **C3**
5 Patouxay Monument.... **E2**
6 Pha That Luang **E2**
7 Talat Sao................. **D3**
8 Wat Si Meuang **E5**
9 Wat Sisaket **C4**

Restaurants ▼

1 Acqua **B3**
2 Khop Chai Deu **B3**
3 Kualao.................... **C3**
4 La Signature............. **B3**
5 Noy's Fruit Heaven..... **B3**
6 Sticky Fingers **B4**
7 Taj Mahal **B3**
8 Villa Opera.............. **A2**

Hotels ▼

1 Bloom Hotel & Cafe **C3**
2 Crowne Plaza
Vientiane................. **A2**
3 Ibis Vientiane
Nam Phu.................. **C3**
4 Lao Plaza Hotel **C3**
5 Le Charme
Vientiane Hotel.......... **B4**
6 Salana
Boutique Hotel **B3**
7 Settha Palace **C2**

Etiquette

Laotians are generally gentle and polite, and visitors should take their lead from them—avoiding any public display of anger or impolite behavior. Even showing affection in public is frowned on.

Laotians traditionally greet others by pressing their palms together in a sort of prayer gesture known as a *nop*; it is also acceptable for men to shake hands. If you attempt a nop, remember that it's basically reserved for social greetings; don't greet a hotel or restaurant employee this way. The general greeting is *sabaidee* ("good health"), invariably said with a smile.

Avoid touching or embracing a Laotian, and keep in mind that the head has spiritual significance; even patting a child affectionately on the head could be misinterpreted. Feet are considered "unclean," so when you sit, make sure your feet are not pointing directly at anyone, and never use your foot to point in any situation. Shoes must be removed before you enter a temple or private home, as well as some restaurants and offices.

Short-shorts and sleeveless tops should not be worn in temple compounds. Some places will have wraparound skirts for women to borrow. When visiting a temple, be careful not to touch anything of spiritual significance, such as altars, Buddha images, or spirit houses. Ask permission from anyone before taking a photograph of him or her.

Sights

Buddha Park (Xieng Khouan)
PUBLIC ART | The bizarre creation of an ecumenical monk, Luang Pou Boun-leua Soulilat, who dreamed of a world religion embracing all faiths, this park is "peopled" by enormous Buddhist and Hindu sculptures spread across an attractive landscape of trees, shrubs, and flower gardens. Keep an eye out for the remarkable 165-foot-long sleeping Buddha. The park was laid out by the monk's followers in 1958 on a strip of land along the Mekong, opposite the Thai town of Nong Khai. After the revolution, the monk escaped across the river, where he began building anew. Visit Xieng Khouan by taking B14 from the Talat Sao bus station. ⊠ *Thadeua Rd., Vientiane ✛ Km 27–28, northeast of Thai-Lao Friendship Bridge* ☎ 5,000 kip, 15,000 kip for audio tour.

Ho Phra Keo
RELIGIOUS BUILDING | There's a good reason why Ho Phra Keo, one of the city's oldest and most impressive temples, has a name so similar to the wat in Bangkok's Grand Palace (there it's Wat Phra Kaew, the temple of the Emerald Buddha). The original Ho Phra Keo here was built by King Setthathirat in 1565 to house the Emerald Buddha, which he had taken from Chiang Mai in Thailand. The king installed the sacred statue first in Luang Prabang and then in Vientiane at Ho Phra Keo, but the Siamese army recaptured the Buddha in 1778 and it was installed in Bangkok. The present temple, restored in 1936, is a national museum. On display are Buddha sculptures of different styles, some wonderful chiseled images of Khmer deities, and a fine collection of stone inscriptions. The masterpiece of the museum is a 16th-century lacquered door carved with Hindu images. ⊠ *Setthathirat Rd. and Mahosot Rd., Vientiane* ☎ 021/212621 ☎ 5,000 kip.

Lao National Museum

HISTORY MUSEUM | Recently relocated to the outskirts of the city, this building aims to outline the "official" version of Lao history with some interesting geological and historical displays. Exhibits touch on Laos's ancient past, its colonial years, and its struggle for liberation. Other highlights include details about the country's 50 main ethnic groups, along with indigenous instruments that illustrate how they make music. ⊠ *KM 5, Avenue Kaysone Phomvihane, Vientiane* ☎ *021/212460* ✉ *10,000 kip.*

Nam Phou Square (*Fountain Square*)

PLAZA/SQUARE | The main square in Vientiane's tourist area used to reflect more emphatically the city's French influence, reinforced further by a cadre of very Gallic restaurants around the perimeter. Unfortunately, a recent renovation saw Nam Phou's namesake central fountain incorporated into a fancy new restaurant complex, including a skate park, visually disrupting the plazalike feel. The fountain is lit up multicolor at night, and bands perform for a crowd dominated on most days by tourists and Lao youth hanging out. The square and surrounding streets still contain many restaurants. ⊠ *Nam Phou Fountain, Rue Pangkham, Vientiane.*

Patouxay Monument

MONUMENT | An ersatz Arc de Triomphe, this monument is a prominent landmark, if minor attraction, between the city center and Pha That Luang. During the war years, America donated concrete for a new airport runway, but it was used to build this monument, instead. You can climb the stairs of its seven stories for a decent photo op and stroll the souvenir stalls on the second floor. ⊠ *Avenue Lang Xang, Vientiane* ✢ *2½ km (1½ miles) southeast of Pha That Luang* ☎ ✉ *5,000 kip.*

★ Pha That Luang

MONUMENT | The city's most sacred monument, this massive, 147-foot-high, gold-painted stupa is also the nation's most important cultural symbol, representing the unity of the Lao people. King Setthathirat had it built in 1566 to guard a piece of the Buddha's breastbone and to represent Mt. Meru, the holy mountain of Hindu mythology, the center and axis of the world. Surrounding the lotus-shaped stupa are 30 pinnacles on the third level and a cloistered square on the ground with stone statues of the Buddha. Two brilliantly decorated temple halls, the survivors of four temples originally here, flank That Luang. On the avenue outside the west gate stands a bronze statue of King Setthathirat erected in the 1960s by a pious general. That Luang is the center of a major weeklong festival during November's full moon. The stupa is on the north end of town, a 10-minute tuk-tuk ride from the city center. ⊠ *That Luang Rd., Vientiane* ✢ *End of That Luang Rd., northeast of Patouxay Monument* ✉ *5,000 kip.*

Talat Sao (*Morning Market*)

MARKET | To immerse yourself in Vientiane, visit this indoor bazaar, named for the local morning market that once stood here. Shops within the bright and orderly space sell everything from handwoven fabrics and wooden Buddha figures to electric rice cookers and sneakers. Most vendors cater to locals, but there is plenty to interest travelers: fabric, handicrafts, intricate gold-and-silver work, jewelry, T-shirts, and bags and suitcases, though many products are imported from abroad. Local restaurants and noodle soups are upstairs. It's also worth crossing Nong Bone Road to the Khoua Din market for a look at Vientiane's largest wet market. ⊠ *Ave. Lane Xang and Khou Vieng St., Vientiane.*

Laos Festivals

Laos has many fascinating festivals, most of them steeped in Buddhism. Book hotels well in advance if you're planning on visiting during festival time, particularly in the big cities.

Boun Bang Fai: Rocket Festivals are held throughout May in villages across the country. Rockets are fired and prayers are said in the paddy fields to bring rain in time for the planting of the rice seedlings.

Boun Khao Padab Din: This special rice ceremony takes place in August/September; the exact date depends on the new moon. People make offerings at temples to keep alive the memory of spirits who have no relatives. Lively boat races are held in Luang Prabang.

Boun Khao Salak: This rice ceremony occurs on the full moon a fortnight after Boun Khao Padab Din. For this one, people visit temples to make offerings for their ancestors.

Boun Ok Pansa: The full moon in October marks the end of Buddhist Lent, and is celebrated with donations to local temples. Candlelight processions are held, and colorful floats set adrift on the Mekong River. There's a huge parade of candlelit floats down Luang Prabang's main street and the following day, there are boat races in Vientiane and Pakse.

Boun Pimai: Lao New Year officially takes place from April 14 to 16. At this water festival similar to Thailand's Songkran, the important Buddha images are cleaned with scented water, and the public gets wet in the bargain. Festivities are particularly lively in Luang Prabang, where the holiday is celebrated for nearly a week.

Boun Visakhabouxa (Buddha Day): On the day of the full moon in May, candlelight processions are held in temples to mark the birth, enlightenment, and death of the Buddha.

That Ing Hang Festival: In December, on the grounds of the ancient Wat That Ing Hang, just outside the city, this festival lasts several days, with events including sports contests, performances of Lao music and dance, and a spectacular drumming competition.

That Luang Festival: This weeklong event in Vientiane in November is the largest festival in Laos, with processions, a traditional hockey game, a market showcasing regional products, and concerts. Hundreds of monks gather in the morning to accept alms.

Wat Phou Festival: Also known as Makhabouxa Day, this festival is held during the day of the first full moon in February at Wat Phou, near Champasak. Elephant races, buffalo fights, cockfights, and traditional Lao music-and-dance performances are on the schedule.

Wat Si Meuang

RELIGIOUS BUILDING | This wat that dates to 1563—its last major renovation was in 1956—guards the original city pillar, a revered foundation stone also from the 16th century. Throughout the day, this temple receives a steady stream of local visitors seeking blessings for themselves—and their new vehicles! In a small park in front of the monastery stands a rare memorial to Laos's royal past: a large bronze statue of King Sisavang Vong, which survived the revolution as it had been cast by a Soviet

Thai invaders destroyed That Luang in 1828; it was restored in the 20th century.

artist. ✉ *Samsenthai Rd. at Setthathirat Rd., Vientiane* ✥ *Near eastern end of Setthathirat Rd.* 🎫 *Free.*

Wat Sisaket

RELIGIOUS BUILDING | A courtyard with 6,840 Buddha statues stops the show at this intriguing temple-monastery complex across from Ho Phra Keo. Built in 1818 by King Anou, the temple survived Vientiane's 1828 destruction by the Siamese army, and the monastery, still active, remains intact in its original form. The courtyard contains little niches and large platforms with Buddhas of all sizes. The impressive temple hall underwent some restoration in 1938. The intricately carved wooden ceiling and doors still impress, but time has taken its toll on the paintings that once covered the hall's walls. ✉ *Setthathirat Rd. at Ave. Lane Xang, Vientiane* ☎ *021/212622* 🎫 *10,000 kip.*

🍴 Restaurants

★ Acqua

$$ | **ITALIAN** | All the usual Italian stalwarts grace the menu at this upbeat spot, along with imported oysters and Wagyu beef. The same owners also run the more casual Ai Capone next door, a traditional pizzeria. **Known for:** extensive wine list; pizzas; lunch buffet. [$] *Average main: 108,000* ✉ *007/078 Rue Francois Ngin, Ban Mixay* ☎ *020/599–10888.*

Khop Chai Deu

$$ | **LAO** | A popular downtown restaurant and bar in a French colonial building, this is an excellent stop for happy-hour cocktails or dinner. For a tasty introduction to traditional Lao cuisine, try the Discovery Lao, a set menu including *larb* (a semi-spicy salad of ground meat), a zesty sour fish soup, *khao niaw* (Lao sticky rice), and a glass of *lao-lao* (rice whisky). **Known for:** live music; Lao, Asian, and international dishes; happy-hour cocktails. [$] *Average main: 96,000* ✉ *54*

Setthathirat Rd., Vientiane ✛ Near Nam Phou Sq. ☎ 021/263829 ⊕ www.inthira.com/restaurants-bars/khop-chai-deu.

Kualao

$$ | LAO | The Lao food at this restaurant inside a fading mansion is among Vientiane's best. Favorites include *mok pa fork* (steamed fish wrapped in banana leaves and cooked with eggs, onions, and coconut milk), and *gaeng panaeng* (a thick red curry with chicken, pork, or beef). **Known for:** larb and black sticky rice; classy ambience; Lao folk dancing evening performances. $ *Average main: 85,000* ✉ 134 Samsenthai Rd., Vientiane ✛ One block northeast of Nam Phou square ☎ 021/214813 ⊕ www.kualaorestaurant.com.

★ La Signature

$$$ | FRENCH | The charming restaurant of the boutique Ansara Hotel serves authentic French cuisine in a romantic garden setting. Appetizers on the varied menu might include anything from fish carpaccio or a warm goat cheese salad to the over-the-top combo of fried duck and duck foie gras. **Known for:** refined atmosphere; daily chef's plates; superb wine selection. $ *Average main: 150,000* ✉ Ansara Hotel, Quai Fa Ngum, Ban Vat Chan, Hom 5, Muang Chanthabury ✛ 100 meters up from river road on small side lane just past Wat Chan ☎ 021/213514 ⊕ www.ansarahotel.com.

Noy's Fruit Heaven

$ | CAFÉ | The family that runs this cute little café prepares various breakfasts and gourmet sandwiches that include imported feta, Camembert, or goat cheese melted onto fresh baguettes. They also whip up just about any tropical fruit smoothie you can imagine. **Known for:** Instagrammable ambience; fruit shakes; baguette sandwiches. $ *Average main: 30,000* ✉ Vientiane ✛ Near the corner of Rue Hengboun and Rue Hengboun Noy ☎ 021/253577 ▭ No credit cards.

Beware: Happy Meals

When you see a sign for "Happy Pizza" or "Happy Shakes" in Vang Vieng, you might imagine there's a jolly local cook whipping up that pizza or shake. Well, the chef might indeed be jolly but you won't be if you are caught ingesting what is in actuality pizza or shakes laced with marijuana or mushrooms. These drugs are illegal in Laos (but you'd never know the way restaurants openly advertise happy meals) so you need to know that you can be fined and even jailed. Bummer.

★ Sticky Fingers

$ | INTERNATIONAL | An institution on Vientiane's culinary landscape for several decades, this restaurant serves modern Australian and international comfort foods and a revolving weekly menu of specials showcases the dexterity of the Lao chef. The twice-weekly happy hours are great for meeting local expats. **Known for:** fall-off-the-bone pork ribs; tom yum martinis; half-price happy hours. $ *Average main: 70,000* ✉ 10/3 Francois Nginn, Vientiane ☎ 021/215972 ⊕ stickyfingers-laos2001.com.

Taj Mahal

$ | INDIAN | A nondescript eatery tucked behind the Lao National Culture Hall, Taj Mahal serves Indian food at ridiculously cheap prices. Excellent tandoori naan bread, a good selection of dal and meat and fish curries, and other northern Indian favorites are among the many menu choices. **Known for:** central location; savory chicken tikka masala; fresh naan. $ *Average main: 30,000* ✉ Setthathirat Rd., Vientiane ✛ Off Nokkeokoumane Rd., behind Lao National Culture Hall ☎ 020/5561–1003.

Lao Cuisine 🍴

It may not be as famous as Thai food, but Lao cuisine is similar and often just as good, though usually with more herbal, earthy, and sour notes, consistent with ingredients largely foraged from the jungles. Chilies are used as a condiment, but Lao cuisine also makes good use of ginger, lemongrass, coconut, tamarind, and fermented fish sauce. Because so much of the country is wilderness, there's usually game, such as venison or wild boar, on the menu. Fresh river prawns and fish—including the famous, massive Mekong catfish, the world's largest freshwater fish—are also standard fare, along with chicken, vegetables, and sticky rice.

As in Isan, *larb* (meat salad with shallots, lime juice, chilies, garlic, and other spices) is a staple, as are sticky rice and *tam mak houng*, the Lao version of green-papaya salad. Grilled chicken, pork, and duck stalls can be found in every bus station and market in the country. Northern Laos, especially Luang Prabang, is noted for its distinctive cuisine. Specialties include grilled Mekong riverweed, a type of algae that's pounded, sprinkled with sesame, tomato, and garlic and then laid flat to dry in the sun. It's then cut into pieces and flash-fried, and the crispy chips are served with a spicy chili dip for a great snack. There's also *or lam*, an eggplant-and-meat stew with bitter herbs. Sticky rice, served in bamboo baskets, is the bread and butter of Laos. Locals eat it with their hands, squeezing it into a solid ball or log and dipping it in other dishes.

Throughout the country you'll find *pho*, a Vietnamese-style noodle soup, served for breakfast. Fresh baguettes, a throwback to the French colonial days, are also available everywhere, often made into sandwiches with meat pâté, pickled vegetables, and chili sauce. Laotians wash it all down with extra-strong Lao coffee sweetened with condensed milk, or the ubiquitous Beerlao, Asia's tastiest lager.

★ **Villa Opera**

$$$ | **ITALIAN** | This longtime Italian restaurant, in a beautiful colonial villa with a garden, is a bit out of the main tourist center but still reigns as one of Vientiane's steady grande dames. Villa Opera serves authentic pasta, baked entrées, and fresh salads along with items like the Pizza de Laos, made with chilies and Lao sausage. **Known for:** homely but high-end; homemade pasta; longtime Italian favorite. [$] *Average main: 150,000* ✉ *42 Rue Panya Si, Si Thane Nuea, Vientiane* ☎ *021/215099.*

🛏 Hotels

Bloom Hotel & Cafe

$$ | **HOTEL** | This small boutique hotel above the namesake Euro-inspired bistro offers a few good-value, squeaky-clean rooms that range from basic-but-stylish doubles to larger mini-studio apartments. **Pros:** central; intimate; stretches the budget in style. **Cons:** no swimming pool; no views; dining options somewhat limited. [$] *Rooms from: 500,000* ✉ *Wat Xieng Yeun Alley, Sethathirath Road, Vientiane* ☎ *021/216140* 🌐 *fb.com/bloomhotelandcafe* 🍴 *Free Breakfast* 🛏 *16 rooms.*

★ Crowne Plaza Vientiane

$$ | **HOTEL** | **FAMILY** | Vientiane's newest, and arguably best, chain hotel blends traditional Lao touches with modern conveniences like super-fast Wi-Fi. **Pros:** excellent staff; sunset views from the infinity pool; chic dining at Three Merchants. **Cons:** busy on weekdays with meeting guests; location a bit far on foot; on the pricey side. $ *Rooms from: 740,000 ⊠ 20 Samsenthai Rd, Nong Douang Neua Village, Vientiane ☎ 021/908888 ⊕ ihg.com* ¶○¶ *Free Breakfast ⌁ 198 rooms.*

Ibis Vientiane Nam Phu

$$ | **HOTEL** | This is a good choice if you're after a trusted brand with clean and comfortable facilities, right next to the Nam Phou Fountain and the adjoining restaurant and bars. **Pros:** trusted brand; central Nam Phou Fountain location; blackout curtains on windows. **Cons:** small rooms; no gym or pool; breakfast not included. $ *Rooms from: 600,000 ⊠ Box 2359, Nam Phou Sq, Setthathirath Rd., Vientiane ☎ 021/262050 ⊕ accor. com ⌁ 64 rooms* ¶○¶ *No Meals.*

Lao Plaza Hotel

$$$ | **HOTEL** | Something of a local landmark, the Lao Plaza stands six stories tall in the center of town. **Pros:** large swimming pool and terrace; three restaurants; enormous beds. **Cons:** constant hassle from tuk-tuk drivers outside; on very busy street; overpriced for what you get. $ *Rooms from: 1,347,000 ⊠ 63 Samsenthai Rd., Vientiane ☎ 021/218800, 021/218801 ⊕ laoplazahotel.com* ¶○¶ *Free Breakfast ⌁ 134 rooms.*

Le Charme Vientiane Hotel

$ | **HOTEL** | With a convenient location in the heart of town near the Mekong River, and comfort at competitive rates, this hotel is popular with business travelers. **Pros:** great location near river and restaurants; fitness center and Jacuzzi; quiet pool area. **Cons:** no views; small pool; rooms feel slightly worn. $ *Rooms from: 336,000 ⊠ 2–12 Francois Ngin Rd., Ban Mixay, Vientiane ☎ 021/216226 ⊕ lecharmevientiane.com* ¶○¶ *Free Breakfast ⌁ 44 rooms.*

Salana Boutique Hotel

$$$ | **HOTEL** | Rooms with Lao textiles and decor, finely crafted wood floors, and modern amenities like flat-screen TVs and fast Wi-Fi make this boutique hotel on a quiet downtown street a splendid choice. **Pros:** in the heart of the city center; chic, with fine wood floors and Lao decor; temple views from some rooms. **Cons:** tends to book up in busy periods; expensive for downtown; no swimming pool. $ *Rooms from: 1,100,000 ⊠ Chao Anou Rd., 112 Ban Wat Chan, ☎ 021/254254 ⊕ www. salanaboutique.com ⌁ 42 rooms* ¶○¶ *Free Breakfast.*

★ Settha Palace

$$$$ | **HOTEL** | Rooms at this landmark property have high ceilings, hardwood floors, Oriental rugs, and period pieces that reflect its many histories—from its inception in the French colonial period to its life as a hotel in the 1930s and again in the 90s (with a period of expropriation by the Communist government in between). **Pros:** beautiful pool garden; elegant and private; gorgeous furnishings. **Cons:** no elevator; often fully booked; only four standard rooms. $ *Rooms from: 1,800,000 ⊠ 6 Pang Kham Rd., Vientiane ☎ 021/217581, 021/217582 ⊕ www.setthapalace.com ⌁ 29 rooms* ¶○¶ *Free Breakfast.*

◍ Nightlife

The after-dark scene in Vientiane is very subdued, mostly confined to certain expensive hotels and a handful of bars and pubs along the Mekong River boulevard.

Bor Pen Yang

BARS | This popular bar and restaurant occupies a prime spot on the Mekong, with great views from the rooftop setting for sunsets as the night market starts up down below. On most nights it's packed with locals and travelers—often an assortment of ladyboys and bar girls—but the views, music, and camaraderie are good enough to prevent it from becoming too seedy. It's open from 10 am to midnight. ⊠ *Fah Ngum Quay, Ban Wat Chan, Vientiane* ☎ *021/261373* ⊕ *borpennyangvientiane.com.*

Cocoon

COCKTAIL LOUNGES | This classy speakeasy behind a nondescript exterior is tiny—15 people would be a full house—and it can be tricky to locate, but well worth it if you can get a place to sit. The cocktail menu includes classics as well as a selection of in-house creations. ⊠ *Hengboun Noy Rd., Vientiane* ✛ *In a small alley opposite Vayakorn Inn* ☎ *030/575–9992* ⊕ *fb.com/cocoonbarvientiane.*

Chokdee Café Belgian Beer Bar

BARS | With an interesting Tintin-inspired decor and beers imported from Belgium (14 on tap and much more bottled), it's no wonder this casual bar is as popular as it is, albeit a little expensive for Vientiane. Dishes like the excellent mussels in garlic butter sauce greatly exceed pub-grub expectations. ⊠ *Quai Fa Ngum, Vientiane* ✛ *On the riverside* ☎ *021/263847.*

★ Gallery 38

COCKTAIL LOUNGES | Perched above an unassuming liquor shop and cafe is one of the city's best speakeasy bars. It's a stylish yet welcoming place that serves cocktails as creative as they are delicious, with jazz playing at a comfortable volume and local art adorning the walls. You can rub shoulders with Vientiane's jet set until after midnight. ⊠ *Xieng Yeun, Vientiane* ☎ *020/559–57388* ⊕ *fb.com/gallery38.societyofdrinkers.*

Shopping

Carol Cassidy Lao Textiles

CRAFTS | American-born textile expert Carol Cassidy runs this beautiful weaving studio inside a renovated French Colonial mansion. She and her team of local artisans, mostly women, create high-quality textiles and scarves, shawls, and wall hangings. ⊠ *84–86 Nokkeokoumane Rd., Vientiane* ☎ *021/212123* ⊕ *laotextiles. com* ⊗ *Closed Sun.*

Caruso Lao

CRAFTS | For exquisite handwoven Lao silk and fine wood carvings, head to this workshop and showroom, one of the best in Laos. It's a bit outside the city center, but the craftsmanship is heirloom-quality. ⊠ *Unit 49, Hom 14, Nongbouathong Neua Village, Vientiane* ☎ *020/555–15450* ⊕ *carusocreations.com* ⊗ *Closed Sun.*

Phaeng Mai Silk Gallery

CRAFTS | This shop in Vientiane's old weaving district sells naturally dyed handwoven silk products. ⊠ *110 Ban Nongbuathong Tai, Vientiane* ☎ *020/22226599* ⊕ *fb.com/phaengmai* ⊗ *Closed Sun.*

TaiBaan Crafts

CRAFTS | A fair-trade business that works with traditional artisans to preserve and promote Lao village crafts and empower local women, this shop sells silk and cotton textiles, recycled bomb products, bags, jewelry, and other items. ⊠ *Chao Anou Rd., 97/1 Ban Watchan, Vientiane* ✛ *Near Wat Ong Teu* ☎ *021/241835* ⊕ *taibaancrafts.com* ⊗ *Closed Sun.*

Talat Sao (*Morning Market*)

SOUVENIRS | With crafts, jewelry, T-shirts, mobile phone sellers, and more, this indoor complex satisfies most Lao shoppers' needs. A visit here provides perspectives on modern Lao life and the lifestyles of the younger generation. ⊠ *Lane Xang Ave. at Khao Vieng St., Vientiane.*

Vientiane and Nearby

Nam Ngum Lake

90 km (56 miles) north of Vientiane.

This vast lake of deep green water, with secluded beaches and swimming spots, is actually a reservoir created when Laos's first hydropower project opened in 1971—what were once mountain peaks are now islands. Floating restaurants ply the waters (some with karaoke) and there are now also a few resorts along the shore.

GETTING HERE AND AROUND
Getting to Nam Ngum Lake by public transportation involves taking 3 buses and at least 3 hours; it's recommended, instead, to take a full-day Green Discovery Laos (Tours, in Planning, above) adventure tour, which includes a boat ride on the lake. Another option is to hire a car and driver for the day (costs about 600,000 kip or $60).

TIMING
This trip is best done as a day tour, but if you have extra time, spend the night in one of the area's resorts, which are found on both the north and south sides of the reservoir.

Phao Khao Khouay

100 km (62 miles) northeast of Vientiane.

Not far from Vientiane and yet still quite undeveloped, this national park is home to several stunning waterfalls and has good opportunities for trekking through the jungle. With a good guide, it may also be possible to spot some beautiful orchids and interesting wildlife.

GETTING HERE AND AROUND

This National Park is about three hours from Vientiane, via Highway 13 south to Tha Bok, and then via a side road north from there. Green Discovery Laos (Tours, in Planning, above) runs reasonably priced one- to two-day treks and homestays; this is a good way to see the park, because hiring a car and driver is pricey. It's not recommended to go without a tour operator because the park itself no longer offers scheduled activities, and accommodations are almost nonexistent. Should you decide to venture out on your own, buses run from the Southern Bus Station to Tha Bok (35,000 kip); from there, songthaews go to Ban Hat Khai, where you can arrange treks.

TIMING

One day or an overnight trip is enough time to see the area.

Plain of Jars

350 km (217 miles) northeast of Vientiane, 270 km (162 miles) southeast of Luang Prabang.

"How did they get here!?" is the question you will ask as you consider the hundreds of megalithic jars clustered together across the plains and throughout the province of Xieng Khouang. Interspersed between all the stone jars are trenches and bomb craters. From the early 19th century until 1975, the area was a recurring battle zone. Literal tons of unexploded ordnance have been cleared from the area to make way for it being designated as a UNESCO World Heritage site, but tread carefully outside of these zones.

Phonsavan, the capital city of the Xieng Khouang, is the jumping-off point for for visiting the Plain of Jars (Jar Site 1 is only 6 miles away).

GETTING HERE AND AROUND

It's a long day's drive along Highway 7 from either Vang Vieng or Luang Prabang (about seven or eight hours)—the vast plain is difficult to reach but a wonder to behold. Travel agencies in Vientiane and Luang Prabang, among them EXO Travel *(see Laos Planner)*, offer tours. You'll fly into Xieng Khouang Airport in Phonsavan, which is 3 km (2 miles) outside town. Lao Airlines flies daily from Vientiane for about $100 and Lao Skyway offers regular flights from Luang Prabang (in 15-seat Cessnas) for about $50. There is also an excellent paved road between Phonsavan and Pakxan, on the highway south of Vientiane. A trip on this road takes seven hours by bus. Most hotels and guesthouses in Phonsavan can arrange trips to the jar sites for 120,000 kip per person in a shared minivan; you can also take a taxi to the sites for about 250,000 kip.

The bus to Phonsavan from Luang Prabang costs 120,000 kip, and takes seven hours. From Vientiane's Southern Bus Station the cost is 150,000 kip and the trip takes about 8 hours.

SAFETY AND PRECAUTIONS

Stay on marked paths, and don't stray off into the countryside without a guide; Plain of Jar sites 1, 2, and 3 are totally cleared of unexploded ordnance, but other areas may still have danger hiding underground.

TIMING

One day is enough to see the jar sites and visit some local villages. Nevertheless, Phonsavan is a friendly place that doesn't see many tourists other than visitors to the jars, and it may be worthwhile to spend an extra day exploring the pretty surrounding countryside, hot springs, and local villages.

Who created the ancient jars on the Plain of Jars, and why, remains a mystery.

TOURS

Sousath Travel

This is the best tour operator in town. Run by the Maly Hotel family, it conducts many different trips around the area, from basic Plain of Jars tours to Luang Prabang boat trips. The day trips to the jars and local villages and overnight treks to visit Hmong villages are an excellent way to experience rural Laos. ✉ *Xaysana Rd. (Hwy. 7), Phonsavan* ☎ *020/229–67213* 🎫 *From 120,000 kip.*

🍴 Restaurants

★ Cranky-T Cafe and Bar

$ | **BISTRO** | This charming restaurant dishes up savory Western comfort foods, delicious cocktails, and the best coffee in town. The well-traveled owner is also a vivacious fountain of knowledge about the area. **Known for:** Korean-style chicken wings; all-day breakfasts; extensive wine selection. [$] *Average main: 50,000* ✉ *049 Ban Phonsavanh Xay* ☎ *030/538–8003* 🌐 *fb.com/CrankyTLaos* 💳 *No credit cards.*

Nisha

$ | **INDIAN** | Here's a double surprise: some of the best food in Laos can be found in remote Phonsavan, and it's Indian to boot. Hole-in-the-wall Nisha, presided over by its amiable owners from Tamil Nadu, serves fantastic Indian cuisine, including delicious chicken tikka or tandoori. **Known for:** naan bread; chicken lessani; full vegetarian menu. [$] *Average main: 45,000* ✉ *7th Rd., Ban Thai, Phonsavan* ✥ *At eastern end of Phonsavan's main street (Hwy. 7)* ☎ *030/984–8435* 💳 *No credit cards.*

🛏 Hotels

Anoulack Khenlao Hotel

$ | **HOTEL** | **FAMILY** | This hotel is clean, comfortable, and centrally located to the heart of the action in Phonsavan. **Pros:** good Wi-Fi; not far from the small tourist strip; both heating and cooling systems, good for all seasons. **Cons:** fine but not worth a long stay; VIP rooms not worth the added cost; breakfast buffet a bit uninspiring. $ *Rooms from: 360,000* ✉ *059/4 Ban Phonsavanxay, Phonsavan* ☎ *061–213599* ⊕ *anoulackkhenlao.com* ❑ *Free Breakfast* ↝ *78 rooms.*

Maly Hotel

$ | HOTEL | FAMILY | With nice enough rooms to let, a good restaurant, and a respected tour agency, the Maly Hotel may not be as well looked after as it used to be but it's still good value in Phonsavan. **Pros:** discounts often available when hotel isn't full; excellent in-house tour agency; good restaurant. **Cons:** a bit of a hike to center of town; deluxe rooms overpriced; not the best value for Phonsavan. $ *Rooms from: 284,000* ✉ *Muang Phouan Rd., Phonsavan* ✛ *East of Phonsavan Hospital* ☎ *020/555–06255* ⊕ *www.malyhotel.com* ▭ *No credit cards* ↝ *26 rooms* ❑ *Free Breakfast.*

Pukyo Guesthouse

$ | B&B/INN | This relaxing Lao-Belgian-run guesthouse set in a quiet neighborhood about 2 miles out of town offers five clean and large rooms, some with balconies, in an authentic Lao mansion. **Pros:** free tea, coffee, and fruit all day; good breakfast included; authentic Lao house. **Cons:** tiny en suite bathrooms; out of town; far from other dining options. $ *Rooms from: 300,000* ✉ *56 Saylom Village, Phonsavan* ✛ *4 km from Phonsavan's center* ☎ *020/595–56275* ⊕ *fb.com/ Pukyophonsavanh* ❑ *Free Breakfast* ↝ *5 rooms.*

Vang Vieng

128 km (80 miles) north of Vientiane.

Set on the banks of the Nam Song (Song River), with limestone peaks towering overhead, sparkling lagoons and caves below, and luscious green rice paddies beyond, Vang Vieng has some of the most attractive scenery and countryside in Laos. In the mid-1990s backpackers traveling between Vientiane and Luang Prabang on Highway 13 were dazzled by the town's natural beauty and what had been a laid-back spot soon became famous for its rope-swing party bars along the river. In 2012, however, due to a huge number of deaths caused by drinking, drugs, and drowning, the Lao government closed the bars along the river. Today Vang Vieng is starting to move slightly more upscale and trying to disassociate itself from the backpacker party scene, and it attracts a steady number of Korean and Chinese package tour groups. With the opening of the Vientiane–Vang Vieng Expressway, it is now a popular weekend getaway for domestic tourists.

These days the town center is jam-packed with bars and backpacker hangouts, but you can escape the noise and the crowds by making for the river, which is lined with guesthouses and restaurants catering to both backpackers and those on a more flexible budget. During the Vietnam War, the United States maintained an airstrip in the town center and there are rumors that the abandoned tarmac may be converted into a very out-of-place shopping complex.

GETTING HERE AND AROUND
BUS

From Vientiane you can take a minibus (80,000 kip), which takes about one hour to reach Vang Vieng via the Expressway.

VIP buses (110,000 kip) headed back to Vientiane from Luang Prabang stop here three times a day. Minivan rides to Vang Vieng can be arranged at travel agencies in both cities for roughly the same price as a VIP bus ticket and often include a pickup at your hotel.

A daily bus (110,000 kip) goes to Phonsavan (Plain of Jars), a six-hour ride.

SONGTHAEW

Songthaews run from the bus station, 2 km (1 mile) north of town to all hotels for 20,000 kip per person. They can also be hired for excursions farther afield; prepare to bargain.

The pretty village of Vang Vieng is surrounded by spectacular limestone cliffs.

SAFETY AND PRECAUTIONS

Always double-check prices in Vang Vieng, as merchants are notorious for overcharging. Make sure to shop around and compare, as quotes for identical services may vary wildly.

The river can be fast flowing during the rainy season, and all but the strongest swimmers are advised to wear a life vest and take the necessary precautions when inner tubing or kayaking.

Do not under any circumstances accept offers for smoking marijuana or doing other drugs in Vang Vieng. Dealers are usually informants for the police, and visitors who are caught face paying a very large bribe or jail time.

TIMING

Vang Vieng itself is not all that pleasant, but the surrounding countryside merits exploration. One day to explore the caves and go farther afield to a blue lagoon, and one day to relax on the river should be plenty.

EMERGENCIES

HOSPITAL Vang Vieng District Hospital.
✉ *Ban Vieng Keo, Vangviang* ✛ *Across from Inthira Vang Vieng, along river* ☎ *023/511604.*

TOURS

Green Discovery Laos

This established tour operator offers a variety of full and half-day tours exploring Vang Vieng's surroundings. Choose between kayak excursions on the Nam Song River, visits to the caves, experiences in local villages, or a combination of the three. ✉ *Vangviang* ✛ *Inside Inthira Vang Vieng Hotel* ☎ *023/511230* ⊕ *greendiscoverylaos.com* ✉ *Kayaking trip 592,000 kip ($73) per person for 2 people, less for larger groups.*

Restaurants

Khop Chai Deu

$ | **INTERNATIONAL** | An incredibly scenic branch of a Vientiane restaurant mainstay, Khop Chai Deu offers Lao, Thai, and Western food options served on the pool deck of Inthira Vang Vieng hotel. Try the duck *laab*, a zesty minced duck salad tossed with herbs. **Known for:** quality cigar menu; romantic sunset views; tom yum seafood spaghetti. $ *Average main: 50,000* ✉ *Vangviang* ✛ *Inside Inthira Vang Vieng Hotel* ☎ *023/511088* ⊕ *inthirahotels.com.*

Restaurant du Crabe d'Or

$$ | **ECLECTIC** | Vang Vieng's haute cuisine restaurant offers an eclectic choice of Lao, traditional Asian, and French dishes—the Laotian sampling menu is the top draw. The indoor and outdoor dining areas command majestic views of the river and towering limestone cliffs. **Known for:** strong Lao coffee; buffet breakfast; salmon carpaccio and glazed duck breast. $ *Average main: 95,000* ✉ *Riverside Boutique Resort, Ban Viengkeo,* ☎ *023/511726* ⊕ *riversidevangvieng.com/restaurant/.*

 # Hotels

Amari Vang Vieng

$$ | **RESORT** | Towering above the river in close proximity to Vang Vieng's tourist enclave, the Amari is popular with tour groups, but sleek rooms with walls of windows and attractive river-view balconies offset that nuisance. **Pros:** spacious reception hall; trusted brand; large pool next to the river. **Cons:** close to a noisy and ugly part of town; breakfast is $15 extra; not all rooms have views. $ *Rooms from: 760,000* ✉ *Song River Road, Savang Village, Ban Savan* ☎ *023/511800 up to 09* ⊕ *amari.com/vang-vieng* ⤴ *160 rooms* ⦿ *No Meals.*

Inthira Vang Vieng

$$ | **HOTEL** | This central hotel's well-appointed rooms have wood floors, large and modern en suite bathrooms, and balconies offering stunning views of the Nam Song River and mountain backdrop. **Pros:** private river views; good restaurant; large pool. **Cons:** some bathrooms less

modern; lacks a spa; close to a busy part of town. $ *Rooms from: 600,000* ✉ *Ban Viengkeo, Vangviang* ☎ *023/511088* ⊕ *inthirahotels.com/vangvieng* ⤴ *38 rooms* ⦿ *Free Breakfast.*

★ Riverside Boutique Resort

$$$$ | **RESORT** | With the best riverside viewpoint in town, overlooking fabulous mountain scenery and an atmospheric wooden bridge, this upscale boutique hotel is blissfully, beautifully serene. **Pros:** quiet and away from the backpacking crowd; best viewpoint in Vang Vieng; best swimming pool. **Cons:** rooms fill up in busy periods; not all rooms have good river views; expensive for the area. $ *Rooms from: 1,570,000* ✉ *Ban Viengkeo, Vangviang* ☎ *023/511726* ⊕ *riversidevangvieng.com* ⦿ *Free Breakfast* ⤴ *34 rooms.*

Silver Naga

$$ | **HOTEL** | **FAMILY** | Tastefully put together by a Lao/Australian couple, Silver Naga has well-planned, spacious rooms with all the modern conveniences and an infinity pool that overlooks the Song River. **Pros:** on-site branch of Naked Espresso for great coffee; sunset yoga; family suites. **Cons:** riverside restaurants opposite can be noisy; poor views in city-facing rooms; can book up on long weekends. $ *Rooms from: 500,000* ✉ *Ban Savang, Vangviang* ☎ *023/511822* ⊕ *silvernaga.com* ⦿ *Free Breakfast* ⤴ *84 rooms.*

Activities

River trips and caving expeditions are organized by every guesthouse and hotel in Vang Vieng. Treks to the caves can be fairly arduous, and some are only accessible by motorbike or bicycle, a popular alternative. Go via the toll bridge next to Riverside Boutique Hotel (4,000 kip on foot; 6,000 kip by bicycle; 10,000 kip by motorbike) and expect to pay between 10,000/20,000 kip to enter most caves. Those with sturdy legs will

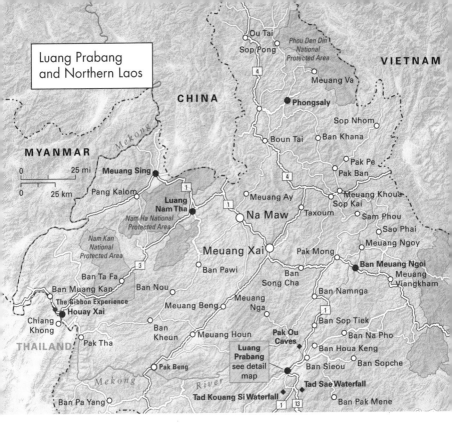

VIETNAM

CHINA

MYANMAR

THAILAND

also enjoy near-vertical hikes up to various viewpoints over the area. Well worth the effort, but carry water and avoid the hottest part of the day. Less adventurous types can rent an inner tube for 70,000 kip and float down the river for a few hours.

Luang Prabang

310 km (193 miles) north of Vientiane by road and 220 km (134 miles) by air.

Luang Prabang is Laos's religious and artistic capital, and its combination of impressive natural surroundings, historic architecture, and friendly inhabitants make it one of the region's best stopovers. The abundance of ancient temples led UNESCO to declare Luang Prabang

a World Heritage Site in 1995, and since then it's been bustling with construction and renovation activity.

The charm of Luang Prabang has a lot to do with the people, who seem to spend as much time on the streets as they do in their homes. Children play on the sidewalks while matrons gossip in the shade, young women in traditional dress zip past on motor scooters, and Buddhist monks in saffron robes stroll by with black umbrellas, which protect their shaven heads from the tropical sun. There's also some 36 temples scattered around town, making Luang Prabang a fine place to explore, on a rented bicycle or on foot. And when you need a break from temple-hopping, there are plenty of appealing eateries and fashionable boutiques. Waking early one morning to watch the throngs of monks make their alms runs at dawn is highly recommended. Your hotel should be able to tell you what time to get up and suggest a good viewing spot.

■TIP➜ **Locals may approach you to buy food from them to serve to the monks, but this is not wise. The locals often give packs of unsuitable rice or other junk to turn a profit. Speak to someone at your lodging or a reputable agency in town about how best to donate to the monks.**

GETTING HERE AND AROUND
AIR
There are direct flights to Luang Prabang from Bangkok and Chiang Mai. Lao Airlines operates two flights daily from Bangkok and one from Chiang Mai, and Bangkok Airways flies twice daily from Bangkok. There is also service between Luang Prabang and Singapore, Hanoi, and Siem Reap.

Lao Airlines also operates three flights a day between Vientiane and Luang Prabang, and one between Pakse and Luang Prabang. Lao Skyway also offers several flights daily to Vientiane, as well as several times per week to Xieng Khouang (Plain of Jars).

Luang Prabang International Airport is 4 km (2½ miles) northeast of the city. The taxi ride to the city center costs 50,000 kip.

BIKE
Biking is one of the best ways to visit all the interesting sights within Luang Prabang, and many hotels provide bicycles for guests. If yours does not, you can rent one from shops in town for 20,000 to 30,000 kip per day.

BOAT AND FERRY
Boats for hire can be found just about anywhere along the entire length of the road bordering the Mekong River; the main jetty is on the riverside of Wat Xieng Thong.

BUS AND MINIVAN
Buses from Vientiane arrive four or five times daily; the trip to Luang Prabang takes between 9 and 11 hours. You have your choice of VIP (usually with air-conditioning and toilets aboard), express, and regular buses; prices range from 130,000 to 150,000 kip. You'll pay more if you buy your ticket from an agency in town, though it is convenient. There are also buses to Phonsavan (eight hours; 100,000 kip), Vang Vieng (seven hours; 105,000 kip), Oudomxay (four hours; 60,000 kip), and Luang Nam Tha (nine hours; 100,000 kip), among other places. There are two bus terminals in Luang Prabang, the Northern Bus Terminal, out near the airport, and the Ban Naluang Southern Bus Terminal, in the south of town, with services to respective destinations.

■TIP➜ **For about the same price as a bus, minivans make the trip to Luang Prabang and many other destinations far more comfortably and quickly, and service usually includes pickup from your hotel. There is a minivan station opposite the Southern Bus Terminal.**

CAR
Although you can drive from Vientiane to Luang Prabang, it takes from six to eight hours to make the 310-km (193-mile) trip along the meandering, but paved, road up into the mountains.

TAXI, TUK-TUK, AND SONGTHAEW
Tuk-tuks and songthaews make up Luang Prabang's public transport system. They cruise all the streets and are easy to flag down, but the drivers are a pain to negotiate with and will attempt to charge extortionate prices. Plan on paying around 20,000 kip for a trip within the city. Taxis are best used through the ride-hailing app, LOCA (download it at *loca.la*). Save the hassle of haggling with tuk-tuks and download the app for a seamless, and air-conditioned, experience.

A Good Walk (or Ride)

Touring the city's major sights takes a full day—maybe longer if you climb Phou Si Hill, which has particularly lovely views at sunset. The evening bazaar on Sisavangvong Road starts around 6 pm. Though the distances between these attractions are walkable, you may not want to do this all on foot if it's really hot out. Rent a bike, or break this into a few shorter walks, and stay out of the sun during the heat of the day. Make use of Luang Prabang's many cafés for a break from the heat.

Start your tour of Luang Prabang at the bustling **Morning Market,** where goods are laid out along the small alley that runs from Wat Phonxay to the Royal Palace. From here head northeast along Sisavangvong, stopping at one of the city's most beautiful temples, **Wat Mai.** Magnificent golden relief murals decorate the portico entrance to the temple. Continue down Sisavangvong to the compound of the **Royal Palace,** with its large bronze statue of King Sisavangvong. After leaving the palace grounds by the main entrance, climb the 328 steps up **Phou Si Hill.** The climb is steep and takes about 15 minutes, but you'll be rewarded with an unforgettable view of Luang Prabang and the surrounding countryside.

Back in front of the Royal Palace, follow Sisavangvong toward the confluence of the Mekong and Nam Khan rivers, where you can find another fascinating Luang Prabang temple, **Wat Xieng Thong.** Leaving the compound on the Mekong River side, walk back to the city center along the romantic riverside road, which is fronted by several French colonial houses and Lao traditional homes. Passing the port area behind the Royal Palace, continue on to the intersection with Wat Phonxay; turn left here to return to the main intersection of town. Every evening there's a local night market, stretching from this intersection to the Royal Palace.

■ TIP→ **Use the ride-hailing app, LOCA, to avoid tuk-tuk hustlers.**

SAFETY AND PRECAUTIONS

For medical and police emergencies, use the services of your hotel or guesthouse. The higher-end resorts have a doctor on call from Luang Prabang Provincial Hospital. For serious emergencies, one needs to fly to Bangkok or Vientiane.

Luang Prabang is safe, but beware of unscrupulous tuk-tuk drivers. Bag snatching is rare, but be aware of your surroundings, and don't hand a potential thief an opportunity.

TIMING

Even if you aren't a temple addict, three or four days in Luang Prabang is enjoyable, although with the waterfalls and cave side trips, it's easy to stay longer. If you have the extra time, try to get farther north, where there are fewer tourists and fantastic nature.

■ TIP→ **Despite scores of guesthouses, finding accommodations here can be a challenge in the peak season and during holidays such as Lao New Year or Chinese New Year. When you visit the top attractions, be prepared for crowds of tourists.**

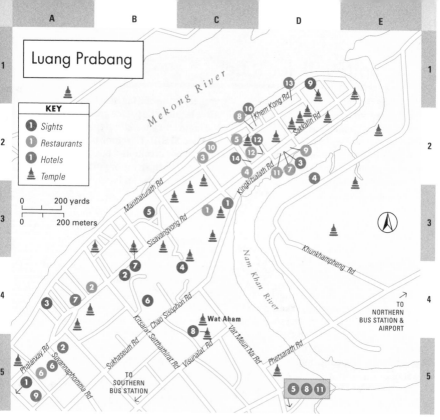

Luang Prabang

KEY
- ● Sights
- ● Restaurants
- ● Hotels
- ▲ Temple

0 — 200 yards
0 — 200 meters

Mekong River

Khem Kong Rd
Sakkalin Rd
Manthaturath Rd
Sisavangvong Rd
Kingkitsalath Rd
Nam Khan River
Khunkhampheng Rd
Kitsarat Chao Sisophon Rd
Wat Aham
Sukhaseum Rd
Setthathirat Rd
Visunalat Rd
Vat Meun Na Rd
Phetsarath Rd
Phalanxay Rd
Souvannaphomma Rd

TO NORTHERN BUS STATION & AIRPORT

TO SOUTHERN BUS STATION

TOURS

Tiger Trail

Established in 2000, this tour operator focuses on sustainable tours, offering one-day to weeklong tailored itineraries through the country's most famous and remote reaches. ⊠ *Sisavangvong Rd., Luang Prabang* ✛ *Across the road from Luang Prabang Bakery* ☏ *071/212311* ⊕ *laos-adventures.com* ✉ *From 400,000 kip (50$) per person.*

Green Discovery Laos and EXO Travel

(see Laos Planner) have Luang Prabang branches.

Mandalao

Since Laos was formerly the Kingdom of a Million Elephants, you should definitely take the opportunity to interact with some of them in a safe, humane, and mutually respectful manner. Animal welfare is at the forefront of this unique experience, where former logging elephants have been rescued and rehabilitated. Visitor numbers are kept at a minimum, and interactions are limited to walking with elephants in the forest (but not riding them). A hike into the lush Lao jungle with one of these magnificent creatures as your guide, accompanied by a mahout, is memorable. ⊠ *No. 82 Sisavangvong Rd., Luang Prabang* ☏ *030/566–4014* ⊕ *mandalaotours.com* ✉ *100 USD.*

 Sights

★ Laos Buffalo Dairy

FARM/RANCH | FAMILY | Opened by a group of expats who complained that the cost of cheese in Luang Prabang was too high, this full-fledged water buffalo farm started as a social enterprise and also now welcomes visitors. Laos Buffalo Dairy helps local farmers by renting their pregnant buffaloes, taking care of them, and returning them healthier to their owners, who are also welcome to join a series of practical workshops. Guests can try their hand at farming and milk-making

activities while learning about the challenges that local farmers face every day. Make sure to taste the delicious ricotta, feta cheeses, and cheesecakes on offer. Admission includes a cake of the day and tea. ⊠ *Ban Muang Khay, Luang Prabang* ✛ *On the way to Kouang Si Waterfall* ☏ *030/969–0487* ⊕ *laosbuffalodairy.com* ✉ *100,000 kip.*

★ Night Market

MARKET | The night market is a hub of activity—full of colorful local souvenirs and cheap, delicious food—and also a meeting place for locals and tourists. Starting in the late afternoon, Sisavangvong Road is closed to vehicles from the tourist office down to the Royal Palace, and a tented area is set up, thronged with vendors selling lanterns, patterned cushion covers, Lao coffee and tea, hand-stitched bags, and many other local crafts. Side streets are lined with food stalls selling everything from fried chicken to Mekong seaweed and other treats at a fraction of the price you'll pay in a restaurant. It's worth strolling the market just for the atmosphere. ⊠ *Sisavangvong Rd., from Kitsarat Rd. to Royal Palace, Luang Prabang.*

Pha Tad Ke Botanical Garden

GARDEN | Set on 40 hectares of land on the opposite side of the Mekong, a 15-minute boat ride south of town, the centerpiece of these botanical gardens is the ethno-botanic garden, where Laos's flora and its uses in daily life, rituals, and cuisine are richly explained. Gravel pathways bring visitors through an arboretum, a limestone habitat, and a ginger garden. This green oasis also has a restaurant/café, a plant retail store, and a souvenir shop. A dedicated jetty near Wat Mahathat has hourly departures to and from the gardens until 4 pm. ⊠ *Luang Prabang* ✛ *Ticket office on the Mekong near Wat Mahathat* ☏ *071/261000* ⊕ *pha-tad-ke.com* ✉ *210,000 kip* ☾ *Closed Wed.*

Phou Si Hill

VIEWPOINT | Several shrines and temples and a golden stupa crown this forested hill, but the best reason to ascend its 328 steps is to enjoy the view from the summit: a panorama of Luang Prabang, the Nam Khan and Mekong rivers, and the surrounding mountains. It's a popular spot for watching the sunset (bring insect repellent), but there are huge crowds (watch for pickpockets), so the view here might be better appreciated at sunrise, when you will have it all to yourself. If you're not game for the steep climb up the staircase, there's a less strenuous hike up the trail on the "back" side of the hill behind the Traditional Arts and Ethnology Centre; there aren't really views on the way up but the view from the top is the same. ⊠ *Luang Prabang* ✛ *Between Sisavangvong and Phousi Rds.* ⚐ *20,000 kip.*

Royal Palace

CASTLE/PALACE | In a walled compound at the foot of Phou Si Hill stands this palace, the former home of the royal family. Built by the French at the beginning of the 20th century, the palace served as the royal residence until the Pathet Lao took over Laos in 1975 and exiled King Savang Vatthana, Queen Khamphoui, and Crown Prince Vong Savang to a remote region of the country (their fate has never been fully confirmed). It still has the feel of a large family home—a maze of teak-floor rooms surprisingly modest in scale. The largest of them is the Throne Room, with its gilded furniture, colorful mosaic-covered walls, and display cases filled with rare Buddha images, royal regalia, and other priceless artifacts. The walls of the King's Reception Room are decorated with scenes of traditional Lao life painted in 1930 by the French artist Alix de Fautereau. The Queen's Reception Room contains a collection of royal portraits by the Russian artist Ilya Glazunov. The room also has cabinets full of presents given to the royal couple by visiting heads of state; a model moon lander and a piece of moon rock from U.S. president Richard Nixon share shelf space with an exquisite Sèvres tea set presented by French president Charles de Gaulle and fine porcelain teacups from Chinese leader Mao Tse-tung. Other exhibits in this eclectic collection include friezes removed from local temples, Khmer drums, and elephant tusks with carved images of the Buddha. The museum's most prized exhibit is the Prabang, a gold image of the Buddha slightly less than 3 feet tall and weighing more than 100 pounds. Its history goes back to the 1st century when it was cast in Sri Lanka; it was brought to Luang Prabang from Cambodia in 1359 as a gift to King Fa Ngum. This event is celebrated as the introduction of Buddhism as an official religion to Laos, and the Prabang is venerated as the protector of the faith and the most important Buddha image in the country. An ornate temple called Haw Prabang, near the entrance to the palace compound, has been constructed to house the image. Tucked away behind the palace is a crumbling wooden garage that houses the aging royal fleet of automobiles, including an Edsel. You'll need about two hours to work through the Royal Palace's maze of rooms. ⊠ *Sisavangvong Rd., Luang Prabang* ✛ *Across from Phu Si Hill* ☎ *071/212470* ⚐ *30,000 kip.*

★ Traditional Arts and Ethnology Centre

ARTS CENTER | **FAMILY** | This small but informative museum gives an in-depth introduction to the ethnic minorities of Laos in an easy-to-understand manner. In showcasing certain ethnic groups through the craftsmanship of their textiles and other arts, you can get a firm grasp of the ethnic diversity that exists in the country. This is a must-see, especially if you will spend any time in Laos outside of urban areas. The Centre is also active in research into and advocacy for the minority peoples of Laos. Guided tours and workshops are available and there is an activity center especially for children to engage in hands-on learning. There's a museum shop on the premises, as well as a boutique on Sisavangvong Road, both of which sell authentic high-quality fair-trade souvenirs. ⊠ *Ban Khamyong, Luang Prabang* ☎ *071/253364* ⊕ *taecla-os.org* 🖃 *25,000 kip* 🕑 *Closed Mondays.*

Wat Mai

TEMPLE | This small but lovely temple next to the Royal Palace compound dates from 1796. Its sweeping four-tier roof is characteristic of Luang Prabang's religious architecture, but more impressive are the magnificent wood carvings and gold-leaf murals on the main pillars and portico entrance to the temple. These intricate panels depict the last life of the Buddha, as well as various Asian animals. During the Boun Pimai festival (Lao New Year), the Phra Bang sacred Buddha image is carried from the Royal Palace compound to Wat Mai for ritual cleansing ceremonies. ⊠ *Sisavangvong Rd., Luang Prabang* ⊹ *Near Royal Palace Museum* 🖃 *10,000 kip.*

Wat Visoun (Wat Wisunarat)

TEMPLE | The 16th-century Wat Visoun and neighboring Wat Aham play a central role in Lao New Year celebrations, when ancestral deities, called *Pou Nyeu Nya Nyeu* emerge from Wat Aham and dance in the processions down Sisavangvong Rd. Wat Visoun was built in 1503, during the reign of King Visounarat, who had the temple named after himself. Within the compound is a large and unusual watermelon-shaped stupa called That Makmo (literally "Watermelon Stupa"). The 100-foot-high mound is actually a royal tomb, where many small, precious Buddha statues were found when Chinese Haw marauders destroyed the city in the late 19th century (these statues have since been moved to the Royal Palace). The temple hall was rebuilt in 1898 along the lines of the original wooden structure, and now houses an

impressive collection of Buddha statues, stone inscriptions, and other Buddhist art. ⊠ *Visounalat Rd., Luang Prabang* 🖃 *10,000 kip.*

★ Wat Xieng Thong

TEMPLE | Luang Prabang's most important and impressive temple complex is Wat Xieng Thong, a collection of ancient buildings near the tip of the peninsula where the Mekong and Nam Khan rivers meet. Erected in 1560, the main temple is one of the few structures to have survived centuries of marauding Vietnamese, Chinese, and Siamese armies, and it's one of the region's best-preserved examples of Buddhist art and architecture. The intricate golden facades, colorful murals, sparkling glass mosaics, and low, sweeping roofs of the entire ensemble of buildings (which overlap to make complex patterns) all combine to create a feeling of harmony and peace. The interior of the main temple has decorated wooden columns and a ceiling covered with wheels of dharma, representing the Buddha's teaching. The exterior is just as impressive thanks to mosaics of colored glass that were added in the 1950s. Several small chapels at the sides of the main hall are also covered with mosaics and contain various images of the Buddha. The bronze 16th-century reclining Buddha in one chapel was displayed in the 1931 Paris Exhibition. The mosaic on the back wall of that chapel commemorates the 2,500th anniversary of the Lord Buddha's birth with a depiction of Lao village life. The funerary carriage house near the compound's east gate, with a gilded facade, contains the royal family's funeral statuary and urns, including a 40-foot-long wooden funeral carriage. ⊠ *Sisaleumsak Rd., Luang Prabang* ⊹ *Between Suvannakhamvong Rd. and Sakkarin Rd., where Mekong and Nam Khan rivers meet* 🖃 *20,000 kip.*

The Prabang Buddha

But for a few simple facts, the Prabang Buddha image, the namesake of Luang Prabang, is shrouded in mystery. This much is known: the Prabang image is approximately 33 inches tall and weighs 110 pounds. Both hands of the Buddha are raised in double *abhaya mudra* position (the meaning of which has predictably ambiguous symbolic interpretations, including dispelling fear, teaching reason, and offering protection, benevolence, and peace). Historically, the Prabang Buddha has been a symbol of religious and political authority, including the legitimate right to rule the kingdom of Laos.

It is believed that the image was cast in bronze in Sri Lanka between the 1st and 9th centuries, although it has also been suggested that it is made primarily of gold, with silver and bronze alloys. Regardless of its composition, the double-raised palms indicate a later construction (14th century), and a possibly Khmer origin.

Nonetheless, in 1359 the Prabang was given to Fa Ngum, the son-in-law of the Khmer king at Angkor, and brought to Meuang Swa, which was subsequently renamed Luang Prabang, the capital of the newly formed kingdom of Lang Xang. The Prabang Buddha became a symbol of the king's legitimacy and a means of promoting Theravada Buddhism throughout Laos.

In 1563 the Prabang image was relocated to the new capital city of Vientiane. In 1778 Siamese invaders ransacked Vientiane and made off with both the Prabang and Emerald Buddhas. The Prabang was returned to Laos in 1782 after political and social unrest in Siam was attributed to the image. Similar circumstances surrounded the subsequent capture and release of the Prabang by the Siamese in 1827 and 1867.

Following its return to Laos, the Prabang was housed in Wat Visoun, Luang Prabang's oldest temple, and then at Wat Mai. In 1963, during the reign of Sisavang Vatthana, Laos's final monarch, construction began on Ho Prabang, a temple to house the Prabang on the grounds of the palace.

But in 1975 the Communist Pathet Lao rose to power, dissolved the monarchy, and installed a Communist regime. The Communist government, having little respect for any symbol of royalty *or* Buddhism, may have handed over the Prabang to Moscow in exchange for assistance from the Soviet Union. Other accounts of the image have it spirited away to Vientiane for safekeeping in a bank vault, where it may still reside today.

Regardless, there is a 33-inch-tall Buddha statue, real or replica, housed in the Haw Prabang. Every April 17th, the image is ferried via chariot to Wat Mai, where it is cleansed with water by reverent Lao people for three days before making the return journey to the palace.

As for its authenticity, the saying goes that "People believe that it is real because the Prabang Buddha belongs in Luang Prabang."

🍴 Restaurants

★ Bouang

$ | **FUSION** | The decor of this colorful, French-owned restaurant is a throwback to the Asia of 50 years ago, but the constantly changing menu of Asian, Western, and fusion comfort foods is quite modern. The cinnamon pork stew in particular is a crowd favorite with both the Lao and expat clientele and perfectly accompanied by one of Bouang's signature cocktails. **Known for:** people-watching from the patio; fun atmosphere; gnocchi green curry. [$] *Average main: 60,000* ✉ *Sisavangvong Rd., Luang Prabang* ☎ *020/552–68098* 🌐 *fb.com/bouang.asianeatery* 💳 *No credit cards.*

Joma Bakery Cafe

$ | **CAFÉ** | Canadians run this inexpensive self-service restaurant, where the in-house bakery turns out delicious pastries, bagels, sandwiches, and salads. The homemade soups are excellent, as are the breakfast burritos and wraps, and there are all the typical coffee and espresso drinks. **Known for:** social atmosphere; good coffee; Western comfort food. [$] *Average main: 30,000* ✉ *Chao Fa Ngum Rd, Houa Xieng, Luang Prabang* ✣ *Near post office on Chao Fa Ngum* ☎ *071/252292* 🌐 *joma.biz* 💳 *No credit cards.*

Khaiphaen

$ | **LAO** | A TREE Alliance training restaurant for marginalized youths, Khaiphaen's menu might include anything from tofu with *Khaiphaen* crispy river weed and green mango dip to fusion Lao staples such as grilled buffalo steak with pickled daikon. The food is great and you'll also be helping young Lao people build their hospitality skills. **Known for:** pineapple and chili margarita; humanitarian concept; chocolate mousse with rosella syrup. [$] *Average main: 45,000* ✉ *100 Sisavang Vatana Rd., Ban Wat Nong, Luang Prabang* ☎ *030/515–5221* 🌐 *khaiphaen-restaurant.org* ⏲ *Closed Sat. and Sun.*

Le Bistro Ban Vat Sene

$ | **FRENCH** | Sidewalk seating and the retractable brown-striped awning contribute to the atmosphere of a traditional French café at this café on the northern end of town. Freshly made quiche, baguettes, and *grandes tartines* (large slices of homemade bread with various toppings) are menu highlights for lunch and dinner. **Known for:** upstairs lunchtime salad bar; organic garden; fully homemade menu. [$] *Average main: 50,000* ✉ *Sakkarin Rd., Ban Wat Sene* ✣ *Across from Villa Santi Hotel* ☎ *071/212517* 🌐 *elephant-restau.com/bistrobanvatsene.*

★ L'Elephant Restaurant Français

$$$ | **FRENCH** | One of Luang Prabang's finest restaurants offers traditional French food, with a dash of Lao influence, such as the *chevreuil au poivre vert* (local venison in a pepper sauce) and the several daily specials usually include fish fresh from the Mekong. Seating is available in the bright, airy dining room or on the sidewalk, behind a barrier of plants. **Known for:** prix-fixe menus; tartare; lovely setting. [$] *Average main: 150,000* ✉ *Ban Wat Nong, Kounxoua Rd., Luang Prabang* ☎ *071/252482* 🌐 *elephant-restau.com.*

★ Manda de Laos

$$ | **LAO** | With an unbeatable location over a UNESCO-classified lotus pond, this impressive wooden restaurant only serves traditional Lao food, all based on the owner's family recipes. The dishes, such as fish *Hor Mok* steamed in banana leaves or the delicious jungle honey-glazed spareribs, are presented with a panache that helps emphasize the venue's authenticity. **Known for:** creative cocktails; authentic Lao cuisine; beautiful setting. [$] *Average main: 90,000* ✉ *10 Norrassan Rd, Ban That Luang, Luang Prabang* ✣ *Down the road from Satri House's back entrance* ☎ *071/253923* 🌐 *mandadelaos.com.*

★ Paste at the Apsara

$$$$ | **LAO** | As at the original location of Paste, a Michelin-starred restaurant based in Bangkok, the menu here is built on the traditional recipes of the Lao royal family, but with a slight update for modern tastes. The preparation, presentation, and taste are second-to-none in Luang Prabang. **Known for:** Or Lam, a Luang Prabang ratatouille; dinner set menus; flavorful slow-roasted duck curry. *[$] Average main: 385,000 ✉ Ban Wat Sene, Kingkitsarath St., Ban Wat Sene ☎ 071/254251 🌐 pastelaos.com.*

★ Popolo Cantina

$ | **MEDITERRANEAN** | This hip restaurant in the heritage home of a former French official serves refreshing Mediterranean fare such as huge salads, excellent wood-fired pizzas, and platters of beef carpaccio. Many dishes also feature savory local buffalo burrata cheese. **Known for:** el cubanito sandwich; mosquito mai tai; belle burrata pizza. *[$] Average main: 70,000 ✉ 201 Khounxoua Rd., Luang Prabang ☎ 020/778–01767 🌐 fb.com/popolocantina.*

Rosella Fusion

$ | **LAO** | This humble restaurant under a tent awning overlooking the Nam Khan River doesn't really churn out fusion food so much as superb Lao and Western dishes without overlapping influences. Chef Dith also makes frozen margaritas and mojitos that rival any in town, as well as iced tea with rosella, the restaurant's namesake and an edible species of the hibiscus plant. **Known for:** crunchy bruschettas; mok pa steamed fish; green curry. *[$] Average main: 45,000 ✉ Kingkitsarat Rd., Ban Wat Sene ✥ 100 ft after Apsara on riverside ☎ 020/777–75753 🌐 fb.com/rosellafusion ▭ No credit cards.*

★ Saffron Coffee

$ | **CAFÉ** | Contrary to popular belief, fine Lao coffee doesn't only come from southern Laos, it's also grown here in the northern part of the country, and this charming café, started over a decade ago, has helped change the lives of highland farmers in the surrounding rural areas. There are great sandwiches and pastries, but the absolute highlight is the artisanal coffee and the amazing views of the Mekong from their riverside terrace. **Known for:** ask about the Cherry to Cup tours; cheesecake brownies; cascara, a tea made from coffee cherry husks. *[$] Average main: 40,000 ✉ Khemkhong Rd., Wat Nong Village, Luang Prabang ☎ 071/212915 🌐 saffroncoffee.com ▭ No credit cards.*

★ Tamarind Restaurant and Cooking School

$ | **LAO** | **FAMILY** | This riverside restaurant is *the* place to experience and understand Lao cuisine in Luang Prabang. The various tasting menus feature five traditional types of *jeow*, or dips, to be eaten with vegetables or sticky rice; there's also a "five-bites" selection that includes dried buffalo, *sai oua* (flavored local sausage), and other delicacies. **Known for:** well-trained local staff; lemongrass stuffed with chicken; watermelon and chili granita. *[$] Average main: 50,000 ✉ Kingkitsarath Rd., Ban Wat Sene ✥ Just before Apsara on Nam Khan River ☎ 071/213128 🌐 tamarindlaos.com ▭ No credit cards.*

3 Nagas Restaurant

$$ | **LAO** | Crispy river weed with spicy buffalo jam and steamed mushrooms in an herbal mousse are just two of the local specialties served at this atmospheric restaurant on the front terrace of 3 Nagas Luang Prabang hotel. Set menus are available from 200,000 kip, though you can also order à la carte. **Known for:** sampler menus perfect for Lao food novices; grilled buffalo with coffee sauce; mango sticky rice with banana and rosella ice cream. *[$] Average main: 85,000 ✉ Sakkarin Rd., Ban Wat Nong, Luang Prabang ☎ 071/253 888 🌐 3-nagas.com.*

Hotels

New hotels are shooting up in Luang Prabang to accommodate the growing numbers of tourists. Many of the most attractive of them are in converted buildings dating from French colonial days, and several hotels are former royal properties.

Amantaka
$$$$ | **RESORT** | The queen of resorts in Luang Prabang, this gorgeous and tranquil oasis occupies the old French colonial hospital and is surrounded by leafy gardens and shaded verandas. **Pros:** huge pool; spacious and private suites; excellent food served in the atmospheric restaurant. **Cons:** rooms near a local school can be noisy at times; decor a bit too minimalist; absurdly expensive. [$] *Rooms from: 14,500,000* ✉ *55/3 Kingkitsarath Rd., Ban Thongchaleun, Luang Prabang* ☎ *071/860333* 🌐 *amanresorts.com* 🍴 *Free Breakfast* ☞ *Rates also include lunch or dinner* 🛏 *24 rooms.*

Angsana Maison Souvannaphoum
$$ | **HOTEL** | The former residence of Prince Souvannaphoum, prime minister in the 1960s, has been transformed into one of Luang Prabang's top hotels. **Pros:** spa; exclusive, private feel; large claw-foot tubs in some rooms. **Cons:** small bathrooms in some rooms; on a fairly busy road; views not inspiring. [$] *Rooms from: 700,000* ✉ *Chao Fa Ngum Rd., Luang Prabang* ☎ *071/254609* 🌐 *angsana.com/en/laos/maison-souvannaphoum* 🛏 *24 rooms* 🍴 *Free Breakfast.*

Apsara
$$ | **B&B/INN** | With its white facade and balustrades and riverside location, this former shophouse complex is now a trendy boutique hotel. **Pros:** rain-style showerheads in some bathrooms; quiet riverside location; beautifully furnished rooms. **Cons:** standard rooms a bit dark; downstairs rooms have no views; often fully booked. [$] *Rooms from: 760,000* ✉ *Kingkitsarat Rd., Ban Wat Sene* ✥ *Between Tamarind and Rosella restaurants* ☎ *071/254670* 🌐 *theapsara.com* 🛏 *13 rooms* 🍴 *Free Breakfast.*

Apsara Rive Droite
$$$$ | **B&B/INN** | For those looking for something glamorous and exclusive, this sister property of the Apsara, across the Nam Khan River, has a swimming pool, private verandas, and a free 24-hour shuttle-boat service to take guests across the river. **Pros:** nice swimming pool; luxurious isolation; quiet. **Cons:** little atmosphere in this neighborhood; across the river; only nine rooms, so often full. [$] *Rooms from: 1,350,000* ✉ *Ban Phanluang, Luang Prabang* ✥ *Across Nam Khan River from Apsara* ☎ *071/213053* 🌐 *theapsara.com* 🛏 *9 rooms* 🍴 *Free Breakfast.*

★ **Belmond La Résidence Phou Vao Hotel**
$$$$ | **RESORT** | Its prime position on Phou Vao (Kite Hill) gives this sumptuous hotel the best views in town. **Pros:** discounts for longer stays; infinity pool; excellent restaurant. **Cons:** a bit far to walk to town; garden rooms do not have great views; not the best value. [$] *Rooms from: 3,230,000* ✉ *Phou Vao Hill 3, Luang Prabang* ☎ *071/212530* 🌐 *belmond.com* 🛏 *34 rooms* 🍴 *Free Breakfast.*

★ **Maison Dalabua**
$$$ | **HOTEL** | **FAMILY** | Situated around UNESCO-protected ponds, Maison Dalabua is a peaceful escape, while still in the city. **Pros:** free bicycle use for guests; quiet location; swimming pool. **Cons:** rooms can book up; mosquitos enjoy the garden areas; maze-like layout of the hotel. [$] *Rooms from: 1,100,000* ✉ *Ouphalat Khamboua Rd., Luang Prabang* ☎ *071/255588* 🌐 *maisondalabua.com* 🍴 *Free Breakfast* 🛏 *40 rooms.*

Rattana Guest House
$ | **B&B/INN** | Family-run guesthouses are common in Luang Prabang, but this one stands out for making patrons feel right at home. **Pros:** firm mattresses; spotlessly clean; new building with teak floors. **Cons:** very basic; no views; smallish

rooms in new wing. $ Rooms from: 125,000 ✉ Koksack St., 3/2 Ban What That, Luang Prabang ☎ 071/252255 ⌁ 14 rooms ⑩ No Meals.

Rosewood Luang Prabang

$$$$ | RESORT | Situated outside the city by a pleasant waterfall, the Rosewood is a romantic sanctuary, that takes its decor cues from the heritage architecture of the city and traditional Lao art. **Pros:** relaxing waterfall views from the bar; gorgeous property; excellent restaurant. **Cons:** rather pricey; location a bit out of town; quite a hike up to the luxury tents. $ Rooms from: 11,600,000 ✉ Ban Nadueay Village, Luang Prabang ☎ 071/211115 ⊕ rosewoodhotels.com ⑩ Free Breakfast ⌁ 23 rooms.

★ Satri House

$$$$ | HOTEL | Formerly a prince's residence, this century-old property has been refurbished and expanded into a series of French colonial homes surrounded by pools and gardens and is one of Luang Prabang's best-kept secrets. **Pros:** superior furnishings; beautiful colonial residence; quiet neighborhood but not far from night market. **Cons:** a bit removed from the action; not all rooms have terraces; no TVs but available upon request. $ Rooms from: 1,300,000 ✉ 057 Photisarath Rd., Ban Thatluang, Luang Prabang ⊹ About 500 ft past Maison Souphannaboum on left ☎ 071/253491 ⊕ satrihouse.com ⌁ 31 rooms ⑩ Free Breakfast.

Sayo River Guest House

$$ | B&B/INN | A white colonial-style hotel with green shutters, the Sayo River Guest House is chic yet unpretentious. **Pros:** some rooms have balconies; serene riverside location; spacious, well-furnished rooms. **Cons:** often full in high season; some rooms lack big windows; a walk from central area. $ Rooms from: 490,000 ✉ Khem Khong Rd., Ban Phonheuang, Luang Prabang ☎ 071/254710 ⊕ sayoguesthouse.com/sayo-river-eng ⌁ 13 rooms ⑩ Free Breakfast.

Sofitel Luang Prabang

$$$$ | HOTEL | Though some say this elegant hotel was a French governor's mansion, in actuality it was the colonial-era prison (complete with guard towers); regardless, it's now one of Luang Prabang's most exclusive resorts. **Pros:** spacious rooms all with plunge pools or hot tubs in their own private gardens; exquisite spa; exclusive retreat. **Cons:** a bit on the pricey end; a trek to the town center; not many shops or restaurants nearby. $ Rooms from: 4,800,000 ✉ Ban Mano, Luang Prabang ⊹ Off Manomai Rd. just past Lao Airlines office ☎ 071/260777 ⊕ sofitel-luangprabang. com ⑩ Free Breakfast ⌁ 25 rooms.

3 Nagas Luang Prabang - MGallery

$$ | HOTEL | This complex of historical mansions stands under official UNESCO World Heritage site protection, thanks in no small measure to the efforts of the former owner to retain its weathered but handsome look. **Pros:** spacious bathrooms with claw-foot tubs; private patios; gorgeous garden. **Cons:** wooden floors can be creaky; often fully booked; some rooms have no view. $ Rooms from: 780,000 ✉ Sakkarin Rd., Ban Wat Nong, Luang Prabang ☎ 071/253 888 ⊕ 3-nagas.com ⌁ 15 rooms ⑩ Free Breakfast.

Victoria Xiengthong Palace

$$$$ | HOTEL | The final residence of Laos's royal family has been renovated into one of the Old Town's most luxurious addresses. **Pros:** elegant room furnishings; fantastic location; extremely quiet. **Cons:** not all rooms have Mekong views or plunge pools; tight spaces in some rooms; no swimming pool. $ Rooms from: 2,245,000 ✉ Khounxoua Rd., Ban Phonehueng ⊹ Just downstream from Wat Xieng Thong ☎ 071/213200 ⊕ victoriahotels.asia ⑩ Free Breakfast ⌁ 26 rooms.

Villa Santi Hotel
$$$ | **B&B/INN** | A local princess's son-in-law converted this 19th-century royal residence in the heart of Luang Prabang into a boutique hotel. **Pros:** opulent Royal Suite rooms; central location; restaurant in pleasant garden. **Cons:** no balconies or views; tiny bathrooms; rooms in new wing seem a bit dated. [$] *Rooms from: $1,122,000* ✉ *Sakkarin Rd., Ban Wat Sene* ☎ *071/212267* 🌐 *villasantihotel.com* 🍴 *Free Breakfast* 🛏 *20 rooms.*

Nightlife

Luang Prabang's nightlife is somewhat sedate and most places close by 11.

525 Cocktails and Tapas
COCKTAIL LOUNGES | This British-owned speakeasy has a delightful outdoor patio and sleek minimal-chic interior design with excellent black-and-white photography from Southeast Asia on the walls. Cocktails are strong and well mixed, and there's an eclectic menu of tapas, ranging from Mexican empanadas to lemon meringue tartlets. The lively mixed crowd of locals and expats makes this an enjoyable spot for a night out. ✉ *100 Kingkitsarath Rd, Luang Prabang* ☎ *020/566–65046* 🌐 *525cocktailsandtapas.com.*

★ **Icon Klub**
COCKTAIL LOUNGES | This laid-back, bohemian-style hangout in a*tiny, eclectically decorated white house*is a good spot for a well-mixed whisky sour or mojito and a perhaps a chat about life in Luang Prabang with the crowd of expats who hang out here. There are even theme nights with swing music or book discussions to keep things stimulating. ✉ *Sisavang Vatthana Rd., Ban Xiengmouane 51/4, Luang Prabang* ✥ *Uphill from Saynamkhan Hotel between Nam Khan River and Sakkarin Rd., across from Chez Matt* ☎ *071/254905, 020/525–54646* 🌐 *iconklub.com.*

The Spirit House Luang Prabang
COCKTAIL LOUNGES | On a side street just off the Mekong this charming bar stocks a selection of spirits and beers, and mixes excellent artisanal gin and tonics, as well as tasty Western and Asian food. There's seating inside the lovingly restored old Lao house, but the enchanting tiki garden is also a draw. ✉ *Ban Houa Xieng, Luang Prabang* ☎ *020/777–87619* 🌐 *fb.com/thespirithouselp.*

Performing Arts

Royal Ballet Theater Phralak-Phralam
FOLK/TRADITIONAL DANCE | Three times a week this troupe performs at the Royal Palace Museum. The program includes a *baci* welcoming ceremony, local folk songs, classical dances enacting episodes from the Indian *Ramayana* epic, and outdoor presentations of the music and dances of Lao minorities. ✉ *Royal Palace Museum, Sisavangvong Rd., Luang Prabang* ✥ *Across from Phou Si Hill* ☎ *071/253705* 🌐 *phralakphralam.com* 🎫 *From 100,000 kip.*

Shopping

Luang Prabang has two principal markets where you can find handicrafts: the Dara Market, on Setthathirat Road, and the Night Market, on Sisavangvong Road. In the evening, most of Sisavangvong Road turns into an open bazaar, similar to Thailand's night markets. It's a pleasant place to stroll, bargain with hawkers, and stop for a simple meal and a beer at one of many roadside stalls.

Caruso Lao
CRAFTS | The well-regarded Vientiane boutique noted for its fine wood carvings and high-end Lao silks also operates a Luang Prabang branch. All the products are handwoven and carved by master artisans. ✉ *60 Sakkarin Rd., Ban Wat Sene* ✥ *Near Le Bistro Ban Vat Sene* ☎ *071/254574* 🌐 *www.carusolao.com.*

Ock Pop Tok Heritage Shop

CRAFTS | This central boutique sells exquisite textiles produced with the help of more than 500 women in rural Laos. Browse among silk scarves, shirts, and even handmade dolls. Fifty percent of the proceeds go back to the weavers. You can also take their tuk-tuk out to the Living Crafts Center to learn even more about how Lao silk is produced with informative classes in a beautiful riverside garden setting. ⊠ *Sakkarin Rd., Ban Wat Sene* ☎ *071/254761* ⊕ *ockpoptok.com.*

Passa Paa

CRAFTS | A contemporary twist on ethnic traditional textiles, this boutique is a one-stop shop for unique and fashionable handmade products including favorites like infinity scarves, shawls, handbags, and reusable face masks. Passa Paa is known for their creative take on Hmong patterns, stamping them onto Lao silk. ⊠ *Sakkalin Rd., Luang Prabang* ⊹ *Next door to Le Bistro Ban Vat Sene* ☎ *020/566–51565* ⊕ *passa-paa.com.*

Pathana Boupha Antique House

ANTIQUES & COLLECTIBLES | Functioning as an antiques and textile shop, and as a museum, Pathana Boupha has a dizzying array of goods on display, though many are not for sale. Shoppers can, however, purchase textiles produced by various Laotian ethnic groups. It is worth coming here just to check out the beautiful old building and antique collection. ⊠ *26/2 Ban Visoun, Luang Prabang* ☎ *071/212262.*

Tad Kouang Si Waterfall

29 km (18 miles) south of Luang Prabang.

A series of cascades surrounded by lush foliage, Tad Khuang Si is a popular day or half-day trip for Lao residents and foreigners. Many visitors merely view the falls from the lower pool, where picnic tables and food vendors invite lingering, but a steep path through the forest leads to pools above the falls that are perfect for a swim.

Two nearby diversions that most groups include on a waterfall outing are a rescue center that rehabilitates moon bears saved from poachers, and a recently opened butterfly park. The waterfall is great to visit any time as the crystal waters flow year-round. Do watch your footing around the falls.

GETTING HERE AND AROUND

Tour operators in Luang Prabang offer day trips that combine Tad Kouang Si with a visit to a Khmu tribal village nearby for 70,000 kip. The drive, past rice farms and small Lao Loum tribal villages, is half the adventure. Taxi and tuk-tuk drivers in Luang Prabang all want to take you to the falls, quoting around 200,000 kip roundtrip, but unless you have your own group, a tour is a better deal.

🍽 Restaurants

★ Carpe Diem

$$ | **FRENCH FUSION** | This excellent French and Lao restaurant has a serene garden and wooden decks overlooking the last stretch of the falls. There's also a cocktail bar, La Terrasse, that makes a scenic setting for a quiet drink before or after a visit to Tad Kouang Si Waterfall park. **Known for:** good choice of fish and meats; natural setting with swimming hole; vegan options. $ *Average main: 100,000* ⊠ *Kouang Si Waterfalls, Luang Prabang* ⊹ *Down a right-side lane before the park's main entrance* ☎ *020/986–76741* ⊕ *carpediem.la.*

Laos: Then and Now

Early Settlers

Prehistoric remains show that the river valleys and lowland areas of Laos were settled as far back as 40,000 years ago, first by hunters and gatherers and later by more developed communities. The mysterious Plain of Jars—a stretch of land littered with ancient stone and clay jars at least 2,000 years old—indicates the early presence of a sophisticated society skilled in the manufacture of bronze and iron implements and ceramics. Starting in the 3rd century BC, cultural and trading links were forged with Chinese and Indian civilizations.

Between the 4th and 8th centuries, farming communities along the Mekong River began to organize themselves into communities called *Meuang*—a term still used in both Laos and neighboring Thailand. This network of Meuang gave rise in the mid-14th century to the first Lao monarchy, given the fanciful name of Lan Xang, or the Kingdom of a Million Elephants, because elephants were equated with wealth and military power.

Colonization and Independence

At the start of the 18th century, following fighting over the throne, the kingdom was partitioned into three realms: Luang Prabang, Vientiane, and Champasak. Throughout the latter part of the 18th century, these kingdoms fell under the control of neighboring Siam. In the early 19th century Laos staged an uprising against the Siamese, but in 1828 an invading Siamese army under King Rama III sacked Vientiane and took firm control of most of Laos as a province of Siam. Siam maintained possession of Laos until the French established the Federation of French Indochina, which included Laos, Vietnam, and Cambodia, in 1893. In 1904 the Lao monarch Sisavangvong set up court in Luang Prabang, but Laos remained part of French Indochina until 1949. For a brief period during World War II Laos was occupied by Japan, but reverted to French control at the end of the war. In 1953 the Kingdom of Laos became an independent nation, which was confirmed by the passage of the Geneva Convention in 1954. The monarchy was finally dissolved in 1975, when the revolutionary group Pathet Lao, allied with North Vietnam's Communist movement during the Vietnam War, seized power after a long guerrilla war, establishing the Lao People's Democratic Republic, the official name of the country.

The Vietnam War and its Aftermath

During the Vietnam War the U.S. Air Force, in a vain attempt to disrupt the Ho Chi Minh Trail, dropped more tons of bombs on Laos than were dropped on Germany during World War II. Since the end of the Vietnam War, the Lao People's Democratic Party (formerly the Pathet Lao) has ruled the country, first on Marxist-Leninist lines and now on the basis of limited pro-market reforms. Overtures are being made to the outside, particularly to Thailand, Japan, and China, to assist in developing the country—not an easy task. There are four "Friendship Bridges" now spanning the Mekong River with Thailand, making

Laos more accessible to trade with neighboring countries, and China, through its Belt and Road Initiative, has become a major player in Laos, financing dams, roads, the Vientiane–Vang Vieng Expressway, and now a high-speed railway, along with starting a massive construction boom in Vientiane.

Gradual Growth

Decentralization of the state-controlled economy began in 1986, resulting in a steady annual growth rate of around 6%. The country has continued to grow steadily: Vientiane, Luang Prabang, and Pakse have new airports; visitors from most countries can now get a visa on arrival; new hotels are constantly opening; there's a new railway; communications technology and electricity are widespread throughout most of the country (cell phones outnumber landlines five to one); and many of the country's airports and airstrips are paved. Nevertheless, infrastructure in the country remains primitive in comparison to the rest of the world. The road from the current capital, Vientiane, to Laos's ancient capital, Luang Prabang, has been paved and upgraded—but it still takes six hours to make the hilly, 310-km (193-mile) journey north on the new Vientiane–Vang Vieng Expressway, and many of the nation's other roads are in poor condition or unpaved. The upgraded road running south from Vientiane can now accommodate tour buses going all the way to the Cambodian border. Other border crossings have also opened up, especially along the Vietnamese border.

A low standard of living (the GDP per capita of $2,600 is one of the world's lowest, and 22% of the population lives below the poverty line) and a rugged landscape that hampers transportation and communication have long made the countryside of Laos a sleepy backwater. But Luang Prabang, boosted by its status as a World Heritage site, has become a busy and relatively prosperous tourist hub. Vientiane, despite its new hotels and restaurants, remains one of the world's sleepiest capital cities, but is getting set for some dramatic changes.

Despite their relative poverty, Lao people are shy, friendly, and outwardly cheerful people. Although Laos certainly has far to go economically, it is currently a member of the ASEAN trade group, has Normal Trade Relations status with the United States, and has acquired WTO membership. Growing investment in Laos and expanding numbers of tourists to both the main tourist centers and more remote areas should continue to benefit the people of Laos.

Tad Sae Waterfall

15 km (9 miles) east of Luang Prabang.

This dramatic cascade makes a worthy side trip from Luang Prabang, with opportunities for ziplining, swimming, and more.

GETTING HERE AND AROUND
From Luang Prabang you can hire a tuk-tuk for about 150,000 kip for a return journey, but you're better of letting a travel agency arrange a trip by boat. Tiger Trail *(see Tour Information in Luang Prabang)* and Green Discovery *(see Laos Planner)* also organize kayaking day trips to the falls.

 Sights

Tad Sae Waterfall
WATERFALL | Most scenically reached by boat, this waterfall is best visited between June and December, when the rivers are high and their combined waters form a thundering cascade—in other months, the waterfall will most likely be dry. The waterfall has multilevel limestone formations divided into three steps with big pools beneath them, so don't forget your bathing suit. Old waterwheels and new ziplines add an adventure component. You can get here by road and then ferry to the falls by boat, but it's delightful to arrive here by boat all the way from Luang Prabang. Be careful on the slippery paths around the falls. ⌧ *Luang Prabang* ✢ *Southeast of Luang Prabang, accessed by road from Ban Aen village* 🎫 *20,000 kip.*

Pak Ou Caves

25 km (16 miles) up the Mekong from Luang Prabang.

While the caves themselves leave some visitors underwhelmed, the scenery en route by boat is a highlight and the area is worth spending a couple of hours exploring.

GETTING HERE AND AROUND
It takes 1½ hours to get to Pak Ou by boat from Luang Prabang. Many agencies in town organize tours for 100,000 kip per person, not including admission to the caves. Tours leave Luang Prabang around 8 am and include visits to riverside villages for a look at the rich variety of local handicrafts, a nip of *lao-lao* rice whiskey, and perhaps a bowl of noodles. You can also take a tuk-tuk to the village of Pak Ou, and then a quick boat ride across the Mekong, but few people use this option, as it is less scenic and pricier than taking a tour.

 Sights

Pak Ou Caves
CAVE | In high limestone cliffs above the Mekong River, at the point where it meets the Nam Ou River from northern Laos, lie two sacred caves filled with thousands of Buddha statues dating from the 16th century. The lower cave, Tham Ting, is accessible from the river by a stairway and has enough daylight to allow you to find your way around. The stairway continues to the upper cave, Tham Phoum, for which you need a flashlight. The admission charge of 30,000 kip includes a flashlight and a guide. Many visitors are not impressed by the caves or the tourist hordes but find that the scenery along the way makes the trip worth the effort. Ideally, it's best to visit the caves as part of a cruise tour to or from Houay Xai. Try to avoid visiting in the height of high tourist season, as it gets extremely crowded and unpleasant. The town of Pak Ou, across the river from the caves and accessible by ferry, has several passable restaurants. It is possible to get to the cave by tuk-tuk from town, but then you'd miss the scenery, and you'll still have to catch a boat

to reach the entrance. ✉ *Luang Prabang* ⚓ *At confluence of Nam Ou and Mekong rivers* 🖃 *30,000 kip.*

Ban Meuang Ngoi

150 km (93 miles) northeast of Luang Prabang.

This picturesque village, populated by Lao Loum and surrounded by unusual limestone peaks, has become a popular traveler hangout, with friendly locals, gorgeous scenery, and plenty of treks and river-touring options. It's on the eastern side of the Nam Ou River, which descends from Phongsaly Province in the north to meet the Mekong River opposite the Pak Ou Caves.

All-day electricity has only recently arrived in Meuang Ngoi, but Wi-Fi is now available and several decent restaurants line its one street. With these upgrades, the village looks poised to roll into the future, but accommodations remain pretty basic and may lack the amenities travelers desire.

As of 2021, Lao Youth Travel (youtheco@ laotel.com) is the only tour operator based in Meuang Ngoi. They can organize hiking trips to nearby villages (250,000 kip per day/two persons) and kayaking expeditions (150,000 kip per person). Their office is near the boat landing.

GETTING HERE AND AROUND
The journey here is an adventure in itself: a minivan takes you from Luang Prabang's Northern Bus Terminal to a pier at Nong Khiaw (four hours; 50,000 kip), where boats (25,000 kip) continue on a one-hour trip upstream to the village. Boats leave Nong Khiaw at 11 am and 2 pm, and return from Meuang Ngoi at 9:30 am daily, which means that you need to charter your own boat or go on a tour if you don't want to spend the night. Also, remember that scheduled

afternoon boats may not run if there are not enough passengers. Just about any travel agent in Luang Prabang can arrange a guide or a tour.

TIMING
Two or three days will give you a chance to go for some hikes or boat trips and just relax in one of Laos's most tranquil spots.

 ## Hotels

Ning Ning Guesthouse
$ | B&B/INN | Of Ban Meuang Ngoi's many simple guesthouses, this one is probably the best. **Pros:** quiet; good mosquito netting; good riverside restaurant. **Cons:** expensive for Meuang Ngoi; bungalows lack river views; crowded in high season. 💲 *Rooms from: 220,000* ✉ *Ban Muang Ngoi, Ban Ngoy Nua* ⚓ *Near boat landing* ☎ *020/238–80122* ⊕ *fb.com/ningningguesthouse* ⦿ *No Meals* ⇆ *10 bungalows.*

Luang Nam Tha

307 km (191 miles) northwest of Luang Prabang.

The capital of one of Laos's northernmost provinces is the headquarters of the groundbreaking Nam Ha Ecotourism Project. Nam Tha town itself isn't very exciting, but it's a great place to spend a few days doing an ecotour or a trek, kayak, or bicycle trip. You can explore the sights along the Nam Tha River and the Nam Ha Protected Area.

GETTING HERE AND AROUND
Luang Nam Tha is tiny, and can be navigated on foot, although many places rent bicycles (from 10,000 kip to 25,000 kip per day) for exploring the surrounding countryside.

AIR

Lao Airlines flies daily from Vientiane to Luang Nam Tha for $100. Lao Skyway flies two or three times per day for just 400,000 kip. Tuk-tuks run from the airport and bus station into town for about 30,000 kip.

BUS

The Luang Nam Tha bus station is 10 km (6 miles) south of town, past the airport. Buses go to Oudomxay three times a day (four hours; 40,000 kip); to Luang Prabang and Vientiane each morning (8 and 19 hours; 90,000 kip and 200,000 kip, respectively); and to Muang Sing every hour and a half (two hours; 25,000 kip).

SAFETY AND PRECAUTIONS

Be careful of snakes if trekking in the area, and know that leeches (harmless but very annoying) come out during the rainy season.

TOURS

Forest Retreat Laos

Run by several foreigners and their Lao counterparts, this local agency offers a variety of tours in the area, including kayaking and trekking in the Nam Ha Protected Area, along with visits to ethnic minorities. The services are professional and highly recommended. ✉ *Main St., inside Minority Restaurant, Louang Namtha* ☎ *020/555–60007* 🌐 *forestretreatlaos.com.*

👁 Sights

Nam Ha Ecotourism

NATURE PRESERVE | This ecotourism program, a model for Southeast Asia, actively encourages the involvement of local communities in the development and management of tourism policies. You can join a two- or three-day trek through the Nam Ha Protected Area, which provides some excellent opportunities for communing with nature, having outdoor adventures, and visiting ethnic minorities (Khmu, Akha, Lanten, and Yao tribes live in the dense forest). The Boat Landing Guesthouse, Forest Retreat Laos, Phou Iu Travel, and Green Discovery Laos (all in Luang Nam Tha) conduct or arrange tours. ✉ *Louang Namtha* 🌐 *namha-npa.org.*

🍴 Restaurants

★ **The Bamboo Lounge**

$ | **INTERNATIONAL** | A husband-and-wife team from New Zealand opened this restaurant that serves outstanding wood-fired pizzas, freshly baked bread, pasta, and other Western dishes you can enjoy with a real espresso or cappuccino. It's affiliated with Forest Retreat Laos, a trekking agency across the street that works with local people to create and promote sustainable tourism in the Nam Ha Protected Area. **Known for:** espresso drinks; eclectic range of pizzas; tasty burritos. [$] *Average main: 57,000* ✉ *The Green Building, Main St., Louang Namtha* ☎ *020/296–43190* 🌐 *bamboolounge-laos.com.*

Luang Nam Tha Night Market

$ | **LAO** | Local families mix with tourists under the night-market sky to eat grilled meats and fish served alongside papaya salad, noodle dishes, and other local specialties. For about 40,000 kip you can score an entire chicken, dip it in hot sauce along with a handful of sticky rice, and accompany it with a cold beer. **Known for:** local flavor; cheap eats; fun atmosphere. [$] *Average main: 40,000* ✉ *Nam Tha Rd., Louang Namtha* ✥ *Downtown next to Bank of Commerce, across street from Zuela Guesthouse* ☎ 💳 *No credit cards.*

🛏 Hotels

The Boat Landing

$ | **B&B/INN** | The timber-and-bamboo bungalows at this eco-friendly guesthouse, 4 miles south of town, are comfortably furnished in rattan. **Pros:** bicycles available;

open-air restaurant with traditional food; great source of local information. **Cons:** expensive for Luang Nam Tha; not convenient to town and restaurants; patchy Wi-Fi. [$] *Rooms from: 450,000* ✉ *Ban Kone, Louang Namtha* ✣ *Off Luang Rd.* ☎ *086/312398* 🌐 *theboatlanding.com* 🛏 *11 rooms* 🍴 *Free Breakfast.*

Meuang Sing

60 km (37 miles) north of Luang Nam Tha.

In the late 19th century this mountain-ringed town was the seat of a Tai Lue prince, Chao Fa Silino. Meuang Sing lost its regional prominence, however, when French colonial forces occupied the town and established a garrison here. These days, however, it's mostly known for its morning market, which draws throngs of traditional ethnic minorities, and for trekking.

Shoppers from among the 20 different tribes living in the area, and even traders from China, come to the market to buy locally produced goods and handicrafts. It's open daily and it's best to go from 6 to 8 before the ethnic minority people return to their villages.

GETTING HERE AND AROUND

The only way in and out of Meuang Sing is by bus from Luang Nam Tha. There are five to six departures each day; the two-hour journey costs 25,000 kip.

Hotels

Phou lu II Bungalows

$ | **B&B/INN** | Nestled on the southern edge of town, these bungalows of bamboo thatch are a simple and good enough base for exploring the area. **Pros:** helpful management; central location; nice garden area. **Cons:** Wi-Fi can be spotty; rooms only have fans; a bit far from the bus station. [$] *Rooms from: 200,000* ✉ *Meuang Sing, Muang Sing* ☎ *020/559–85557* 🍴 *Free Breakfast* 🛏 *24 rooms* 💳 *No credit cards.*

River Journey to Houay Xai

297 km (184 miles) up the Mekong from Luang Prabang.

The trip along the Mekong River between Luang Prabang and Houay Xai is a leisurely journey on one of the world's most famous stretches of the river. The boat drifts along the meandering Mekong, past a constantly changing scene of towering cliffs, huge mudflats and sandbanks, rocky islands, and riverbanks smothered in thick jungle, occasionally interrupted by swaths of cultivated land, mulberry trees, bananas, tiny vegetable gardens, and occasionally elephants. There are few roads, just forest paths linking dusty settlements where the boats tie up for refreshment stops.

There are several ways to make this journey: by regular "slow" boat, which holds about 50 passengers; by speedboat (not recommended), which seats about four; or on the midrange Shompoo Cruise boat or the luxury *Luang Say* boat of Mekong Cruises. All these trips can be arranged in Luang Prabang.

The only village of note is a halfway station, Pakbeng, which has many guesthouses and restaurants along its one main street and seems to exist solely to serve the boat passengers who arrive each night. Once you arrive in Houay Xai (which has little of interest in itself other than the Gibbon Experience), a good way to enter Thailand is to cross the river on the bridge to Chiang Khong and then take a bus to Chiang Rai, 60 km (37 miles) inland.

GETTING HERE AND AROUND

BOAT

You can journey from Luang Prabang to Houay Xai on a regular "slow" boat, a luxury cruise liner, or a speedboat.

The slow boat trip is a 12- to 14-hour journey spread over two days. Taking the slow boat allows you to soak in local color, but, unless you book a luxury option, you will be sitting on uncomfortable wooden seats for the duration. The night is spent in Pakbeng, in basic guesthouses whose owners come to greet the boats and corral guests. The fare is 250,000 kip per person; slow boats depart daily from a recently constructed pier 7 km (4½ miles) north of Luang Prabang.

Speedboats make the journey between Luang Prabang and Houay Xai in six hours.

■ TIP➜ **Speedboats may be fun for the first hour, but they are not safe, and become extremely uncomfortable after the novelty wears off.**

The seats are hard, the engine noise is deafening (earplugs are advised), the movement of the boat is jolting, and the wind and spray can be chilling. If you're determined to travel this way, bring a warm, waterproof windbreaker, and make sure the boat driver provides you with a life jacket and crash helmet with a visor. Speedboats cost 450,000 kip per person, and leave daily from a pier on the outskirts of Houay Xai.

SAFETY AND PRECAUTIONS

Speedboats are uncomfortable and unsafe.

TOURS

Luang Say Lodge & Cruises

The *Luang Say* luxury boat travels between Luang Prabang and Houay Xai along the Mekong River and it's a much more comfortable (and more expensive) option than the regular slow boats or the speedboats that make this journey. The

options are two days and one night, or three days and two nights, with meals and visits to a few sights included in the rates. English- and French-speaking guides accompany the voyages and overnight stays are at the attractive Luang Say Lodge in Pakbeng. The price is 5.3 million kip ($634) all-inclusive from October to March; 3.7 million kip ($443) April through September. ✉ *50/4 Sakkarin Rd., Luang Prabang* ☎ *071/252 553* ⊕ *luangsay.com* 🖃 *5.3 million kip ($634) all-inclusive Oct.–Mar.; 3.7 million kip ($443) Apr.–Sept.* ☞ *Oct.–Apr. cruises 3 times a wk in each direction, May–Sept. twice; no cruises in June.*

Shompoo Cruise

Providing a much-needed alternative to expensive cruises and the uncomfortable and crowded slow boats plying the Mekong River between Luang Prabang and Houay Xai, Shompoo operates affordable two-day journeys. Costs in high season range from $155, not including accommodations in Pakbeng, to $225 with higher-end lodgings. The boats travel with a maximum of 40 people, but will sail with as few as 10. Stops along the way include a local Khmu village and the Pak Ou Caves. ✉ *18/02 Ounkham Rd., Bat Wat Nong, Luang Prabang* ☎ *071/213189* ⊕ *shompoocruise.com.*

 Sights

The Gibbon Experience

NATURE PRESERVE | Popular and unique, this experience combines a visit to the Bokeo Nature Reserve with jungle trekking, sleeping in canopy-level tree houses, traveling among the trees by ziplines, and watching gibbons and other wildlife. Profits benefit gibbon rehabilitation and sustainable conservation projects. Be prepared to rough it a bit. Groups are small, so book the experience well ahead. ✉ *Saykhong Rd., Ban Houayxay* ☎ *084/212021* ⊕ *gibbonexperience.org* 🖃 *2.5 million kip ($310) for 3-day all-inclusive package.*

Religion in Laos

The overwhelming majority of Laotians are Buddhists, yet as in neighboring Thailand, spirit worship is widespread, blending easily with temple traditions and rituals. A common belief holds that supernatural spirits called *phi* have power over individual and community life.

Laotians believe that each person has 32 *khouan*, or individual spirits, which must be appeased and kept "bound" to the body. If one of the khouan leaves the body, sickness can result, and then a ceremony must be performed to reattach the errant spirit. In this ritual, which is known as *baci*, white threads are tied to the wrist of the ailing person in order to fasten the spirits. Apart from the khouan, there are countless other spirits inhabiting the home, gardens, orchards, fields, forests, mountains, rivers, and even individual rocks and trees.

Luang Prabang has a pair of ancestral guardian spirits, Pou Nyeu Nya Nyeu, who are lodged in a special temple, Wat Aham. In the south, the fierce guardian spirits of Wat Phou are appeased every year with the sacrifice of a buffalo to guarantee an abundance of rain during the rice-growing season.

Despite the common belief in a spirit world, more than 90% of Laotians are officially Theravada Buddhists, a conservative nontheistic form of Buddhism said to be derived directly from the words of the Lord Buddha. Buddhism arrived in Laos in the 3rd century BC by way of Ashoka, an Indian emperor who helped spread the religion. A later form of Buddhism, Mahayana, which arose in the 1st

century AD, is also practiced in Laos, more so in the cities. It differs from Theravada in that followers venerate the bodhisattvas. This northern school of Buddhism spread from India to Nepal, China, Korea, and Japan, and is practiced by Vietnamese and Chinese alike in all the bigger towns of Laos. The Chinese in Laos also follow Taoism and Confucianism.

Buddhism in Laos is so interlaced with daily life that you have a good chance of witnessing its practices and rituals firsthand—from the early-morning sight of women giving alms to monks on their rounds through the neighborhood to the evening routine of monks gathering for their temple recitations. If you visit temples on Buddhist holy days, which coincide with the new moon, you'll likely hear monks chanting texts of the Buddha's teachings.

Christianity is followed by a small minority of mostly French-educated, elite Laotians, although the faith also has adherents among hill tribe converts in areas that have been visited by foreign missionaries. Missionary activity has been curbed in recent years, however, as the Lao government forbids the dissemination of foreign religious materials.

Islam is practiced by a handful of Arab and Indian businesspeople in Vientiane. There are also some Muslims from Yunnan, China, called Chin Haw, in the northern part of Laos. More recently, a very small number of Cham refugees from Pol Pot's Cambodia (1975–79) took refuge in Vientiane, where they have established a mosque.

 Restaurants

Daauw Home

$ | LAO | Inside a thatched hillside bunga-low overlooking Houay Xai's main street, Daauw Home is run by a nongovernmental organization that helps local women and ethnic minorities empower themselves. Cooking over an open fire, the chefs prepare amazing dishes that diners enjoy with "mojitlao" cocktails. **Known for:** Hmong handicrafts for sale; gai baan grilled chicken; pizzas. ⑤ *Average main: 73,000* ✉ *Wat Jom Kao Manilat, Ban Houayxay* ☎ *030/904–1296* ⊕ *daauwvil-lagelaos.com.*

Terrasse Restaurant and Chill Place

$ | LAO | Next to the stairs of Wat Chom Kao Manilat, this no-frills bamboo-and-thatch restaurant is a good choice for French and Lao food that's cooked with market-fresh ingredients. The hammocks and beautiful views over the Mekong help stretch meals into lazy spells—a perfect pastime in this sleepy town. **Known for:** selection of wines; big portions; garlic chicken. ⑤ *Average main: 30,000* ✉ *Ban Houayxay* ☎ *030/469–7019* ⊟ *No credit cards.*

Hotels

Riverside Houayxay

$ | HOTEL | About a third of the wood-floor rooms in this midtown hotel (not to be confused with the similarly named Phon-evichith Riverside) have superb Mekong River views. **Pros:** good restaurant with memorable views; centrally located; Mekong views from some rooms. **Cons:** river-facing rooms get very hot in the afternoon; expensive for Houay Xai; often packed with noisy tour groups. ⑤ *Rooms from: 280,000* ✉ *168 Centre Rd., Ban Houayxay* ☎ *020/542–02222* ✎ *river-side_huayxai_laos_@hotmail.com* ⑩ *Free Breakfast* ⇄ *43 rooms.*

Phongsaly

425 km (264 miles) north of Luang Prabang.

If you're looking for an off-the-beaten-track adventure, head for the provincial capital Phongsaly, in the far north of Laos. It's a hill station and market town nearly 5,000 feet above sea level in the country's most spectacular mountain range, Phou Fa. Trekking through this land of forest-covered mountains and rushing rivers may be as close as you'll ever get to the thrill of exploring virgin territory.

Most people stop in Oudomxay on the way to or from Phongsaly to break up the long bus ride (unless you opt to fly, see below).

GETTING HERE AND AROUND

Buses from Oudomxay make the nine-hour run to Phongsaly (90,000 kip) daily at 8 am, with the journey taking slightly less time each year as the road receives upgrades. In town, tuk-tuks can take you wherever you need to go for 10,000 kip.

A faster, yet equally adventurous option is to take a flight from Vientiane on Lao Skyway (about 1,000,000 kip). The airport in Phongsaly is in Boun Neua (about 27 miles away), but the views from the 15-seat Cessna along the route are absolutely breathtaking. Lao Skyway also offers a daily shuttle service from the airport to Phongsaly town for only 30,000 kip.

SAFETY AND PRECAUTIONS

Always trek with a local guide. The terrain is mountainous jungle, and it's easy to get lost. It is also close to the Chinese border, which is not always clearly marked. English is not widely spoken here.

TIMING

The primary reason to come to Phongsaly is to go trekking, experience one of Laos's most untouched spots, and enjoy the cool weather and fabulous scenery. Plan on spending a minimum of three days to experience Phongsaly. If you're pressed for time, skip this area, as the journey is a difficult one.

TOURS

The Phongsaly Provincial Tourism office runs a good ecotourism program providing treks and homestays in hill tribe areas with English-speaking guides.The owner of Amazing Lao Travel (*explorephongsalylaos.com*), located near the market, knows the entire province like the back of his hand and can arrange travels to far-flung areas.

VISITOR AND TOUR INFORMATION

CONTACT Phongsaly Tourism Office. ✉ *Phôngsali* ✣ *Downhill from the morning market* ☎ *020/542–84600.*

Sights

Tribal Museum

OTHER MUSEUM | For a break from trekking, drop by this museum where the exhibits provide a glimpse into the lives and culture of the area's 25 different ethnic groups. The tribal costume display is delightfully kaleidoscopic. ✉ *Phôngsali* ✣ *Next to Agricultural Bank, near post office* ☎ *020/565–76050* 🎫 *5,000 kip.*

Restaurants

Laoper

$ | **CHINESE** | This restaurant near the market serves the best authentic Chinese food in Phongsaly, though ordering is a bit unusual as there is no menu and the owner speaks no English nor Lao, so she invites you into the kitchen, opens the refrigerators, and you simply point to what vegetables and meats you want. The rest is up to her culinary magic. **Known for:** hot green tea; stir-fried morning glory; inexpensive prices. [$] *Average main: 40,000* ✉ *Phôngsali* ✣ *On the west side of the market* ☎ *020/554–81444* 💳 *No credit cards.*

Hotels

Sengphachan Guesthouse

$ | **B&B/INN** | The large rooms here have flat-screen TVs, electric kettles, and large en suite bathrooms, elevating the Sengphachan above most other accommodations in town. **Pros:** balcony overlooking the main road; good Wi-Fi; good value. **Cons:** owners live on the ground floor; some rooms are showing wear; staff doesn't speak great English. [$] *Rooms from: 120,000* ✉ *Phôngsali* ✣ *On western side of the main road, west of the market and Amazing Lao Travel* ☎ *020/551–94111* 🔑 *10 rooms* 🍴 *No Meals.*

Viphaphone Hotel

$ | **HOTEL** | It might look a bit uninspiring from the outside, but the refurbished, spotless rooms here have all the bells and whistles that travelers come to expect, even in such a remote part of Laos. **Pros:** spacious rooms; Western toilets; air-conditioner units with heater for the colder months. **Cons:** the odd hallway's structure sacrifces space in some rooms; cheaper rooms are small; some staff speak little English. [$] *Rooms from: 100,000* ✉ *Phôngsali* ✣ *On main road, east of market* ☎ *088/210999* 🌐 *fb.com/viphaphonehotelphongsaly* 💳 *No credit cards* 🔑 *24 rooms* 🍴 *No Meals.*

Oudomxay

163 miles south of Phongsaly.

Restaurants

Souphailin's Restaurant

$ | **LAO** | Despite its humble appearance, this small thatched-roof eatery serves the best food in Oudomxay, and is itself a reason to slip into this otherwise colorless town. The owner, Mrs. Souphailin, specializes in northern Lao cuisine. **Known for:** books filled with travelers' recommendations; mok het khao (white mushrooms cooked in a

Southern Laos

banana leaf); kaeng naw som sai sin gai (bamboo soup with chicken). $ *Average main: 40,000* ✉ *Ban Vieng Hai, 13 Nua Rd., Muang Xay* ✛ *Across from Bank of Lao building, a few steps up side road* ☎ *020/560–62474.*

 Hotels

Litthavixay Guesthouse
$ | **HOTEL** | Rooms here are simple but clean, with comfortable beds, hot showers, TVs, air-conditioning, and fans—all luxuries in this neck of the woods. **Pros:** owners can speak English and assist tourists; centrally located; best Wi-Fi in town. **Cons:** west-facing rooms get quite hot in the afternoon; noisy street outside; rooms are starting to feel a bit worn out. $ *Rooms from: 80,000* ✉ *Na Wan Noi, 13 Nua Rd., Muang Xay* ✛ *400 meters*

north of northern bus station on right ☎ *081/212688* ⤹ *18 rooms* ⦿ *No Meals.*

★ Muang La Lodge
$$$$ | **RESORT** | It's well worth spending several nights at this luxurious lodge located above natural hot springs. **Pros:** very well-trained staff; luxurious spa treatments; free wine and beer with dinner. **Cons:** touring is included in the price, no options without; two-night minimum stay; limited number of rooms that fill up in busy periods. $ *Rooms from: 7,800,000* ✉ *Muang La District* ☎ *021/24 446* ⊕ *muangla.com* ⦿ *All-Inclusive* ☞ *Rate is per person for a 2-night stay with full day of touring* ⤹ *15 rooms.*

Namkat Yorla Pa Resort
$$$ | **RESORT** | Opened in 2016, this eco-focused resort 10 miles out of Oudomxay's center is set amid the natural beauty

around the Nam Kat waterfall and is quite popular with domestic tourists. **Pros:** sauna; pretty forest surroundings; spa and gym. **Cons:** nature activities are not included; far from anything; re-created Khmu village is rather kitsch. $ *Rooms from: 850,000* ✉ *Faen Village, Xay District, Muang Xay* ☎ *020/555–64359* ⊕ *namkatyorlapa.com* ❍ *Free Breakfast* ⇪ *60 rooms.*

Tha Khek

350 km (217 miles) south of Vientiane.

Tha Khek is a bustling Mekong River port in Khammouan Province with some of its ancient city wall still intact. Thailand's provincial capital of Nakhon Phanom sits across the Mekong River from Tha Khek: ferries and the third Thai-Lao Friendship Bridge over the Mekong connect the two cities. The main reason to linger here is the stunning countryside and karst (limestone caverns and sinkholes) surrounding the town, which can be visited as a popular counterclockwise motorbike loop that starts and ends in Tha Khek. The region contains dramatic limestone caves, most notably **Tham Khong Lor**, set about 180 km to the northeast. More than 6½ km (4 miles) long, this cave is so large that the Nam Hin Boun River runs through it. There is a 75,000-kip entry fee, which includes an adventurous two-hour-long guided tour in a wooden longboat that fits a maximum of three people. The trip includes a stop on an exposed part of the cave so that visitors can walk among the impressive stalactites and stalagmites. When the boat reaches the other side of the cave, it turns and brings visitors back to the park's headquarters. It's recommended to use swimwear and rubber shoes or slippers as it's easy to get wet, especially in the rainy season, when water showers drip powerfully from holes in the cave's top.

GETTING HERE AND AROUND

To reach Tha Khek by air it is easier to fly to Nakhon Phanom in Thailand, which has a couple of daily flights from Bangkok, rather than backtrack from Savannakhet or Pakse's airports.

Several buses leave Vientiane's Southern Bus Station to Tha Khek (about eight hours; 60,000 kip), but if your final destination is Tham Kong Lor, it's easier to catch the direct bus (10 am, seven hours; 80,000 kip) to Kong Lor village.

The Kong Lor Loop is a popular 450-km motorbike circuit on completely sealed roads that starts and ends in Tha Khek. It's usually taken counterclockwise so that Tham Kong Lor remains one of the last highlights. Every hotel in town can rent motorbikes and hand out maps of the many caves and waterfalls to visit en route, but Wang Wang's, set in the town square by the river, and Mr Ku's, in-house at Thakek Travel Lodge, come recommended by travelers. For more info online: laosloop.info.

TIMING

The Kong Lor Loop can be done in three days, but a more leisurely four will help better enjoy the surroundings.

 ## Hotels

Spring River Resort & Restaurant

$$ | HOTEL | Neatly arranged in a lush meadow that faces a blue lagoon sheltered by an impressive karst formation, this series of squeaky-clean bamboo bungalows is set 2 km from Kong Lor's entrance. **Pros:** reliable Wi-Fi; picturesque location; excellent value. **Cons:** garden view rooms don't have air conditioning; a bit of a hike from Kong Lor; likely to fill up on Lao long weekends. $ *Rooms from: 673,000* ✉ *Near Konglor Cave, Ban Tiou Village* ☎ *020/596–36111* ⊕ *springriverresort.com* ❍ *Free Breakfast* ⇪ *16 rooms.*

Savannakhet

470 km (290 miles) south of Vientiane.

A former French colonial center, the riverside town of Savannakhet is, these days, the urban hub of a vast rice-growing plain. It's a good place to break the long journey between Vientiane and Pakse, as it's distinguished by some fine examples of French colonial architecture around Talat Yen Plaza and home to a night market and the iconic Catholic church Eglise Sainte Therese (free admission). Nearby Wat Xayaphoum dates back to the 16th century and has an interesting Buddha statue workshop. Savannakhet is waking up to the wonderful heritage it has and actively converting its old buildings into cozy cafes and bars, trendy boutiques, amazing restaurants, and unique accommodation.

GETTING HERE AND AROUND

Lao Airlines flies from Vientiane to Savannakhet several times daily for 850,000 kip ($100). From Pakse buses depart hourly until midday for Savannakhet from the northern bus station (five hours; 45,000 kip). VIP buses (120,000 kip) from Vientiane's Southern Bus Terminal to Savannakhet depart daily at 8:30 pm and arrive about seven hours later. There are also several daily buses from Thakhek (30,000 kip), which stop at the bus station along Highway 13, about 17 miles out of town. Most bus tickets include a songthaew transfer into town; otherwise, it will cost around 20,000 kip to most any point.

The Thai town of Mukdahan lies just across the Mekong River and is accessible by crossing the second of four bridges connecting Thailand and Laos. The bridge, one of several established to create an East-West Economic Corridor connecting the Vietnamese port of Da Nang with Laos, Thailand, and Myanmar (Burma), also greatly facilitates tourist travel between Thailand and Laos. Eight to twelve buses shuttle passengers the 10 miles in either direction; buses depart daily from 7 am to 5:30 pm, stopping briefly at the border, where passengers must pay a fee of 10 Thai baht.

Sights

Dinosaur Museum

OTHER MUSEUM | Dinosaur fossils were discovered in one of the villages around here, back in the 1930s and this museum pays tribute; however, the signs are not in English and the glass cases of dusty bones are a bit lackluster. ⊠ *Khanthabuli Rd. and Chaimeuang Rd., Savannakhet* ☎ *041/212597* 🖾 *10,000 kip.*

Talat Yen Plaza

PLAZA/SQUARE | Savannakhet's center develops around this old square, at whose upper end stands the iconic Catholic church Eglise Sainte Therese. One of the few churches in Laos, it is surrounded by peaceful gardens and can be visited throughout the day. All around Talat Yen Plaza, a grid of historical lanes boast several interesting yet crumbling art deco French buildings, perfect to explore on foot. From 5 pm Talat Yen Plaza fills up with a popular night market: you'll find souvenirs and stalls selling the usual Lao and Thai stir-fries and noodle-based dishes. The series of little bars and cafés that dot the square's perimeter are great spots to have a coffee or a drink in town. ⊠ *Savannakhet.*

Restaurants

Lin's Cafe

$ | **INTERNATIONAL** | This bistro occupies a 1930s historical building in the corner of Talat Yen Square and has a wide menu of Western-inspired comfort foods, including salads, pasta, rice dishes, and coffees. The good milkshakes, selection of beer, good coffee, and strong Wi-Fi make it popular with travelers. **Known for:** icy drinks; reasonable prices; exhibition of old Savannakhet on the first floor. [$] *Average main: 30,000* ✉ *Savannakhet* ✣ *Northeast corner of Talat Yen, in front of the Eglise Saint Therese* ☎ *030/533–2188* 🌐 *fb.com/lincafesavan* 💳 *No credit cards.*

Hotels

Aura Residence

$ | **HOTEL** | This modern and clean Thai-style flashpacker hotel within walking distance of the bus station has large rooms, most with small balconies; sturdy beds; and decent size bathrooms—all great perks at this price range. **Pros:** staff speak good English; very close to bus station and Thai consulate; good value. **Cons:** karaoke nearby can be noisy; a 25-minute walk to Talat Yen; breakfast unmemorable. [$] *Rooms from: 200,000* ✉ *Sisavangvong Rd., Savannakhet* ✣ *250 meters south of bus station, beside Avalon Residence* ☎ *041/252818* 🛏 *20 rooms* 🍴 *Free Breakfast.*

Savan Cafe

$ | **B&B/INN** | Inspired and decorated in a vintage Chinese style that hints at the old mercantile class of Indochina, this downtown option has a trendy ground-floor bistro and a rooftop bar and several good-value rooms, as well as a clean, functional dorm for those on a budget. **Pros:** hallways have been turned into art galleries; scenic and homely; rooftop terrace with Mekong views. **Cons:** reception staff speaks little English; few rooms so it can get booked solid; dorm rooms have shared bathrooms. [$] *Rooms from: 200,000* ✉ *37/1 Ban Xayaphoum, Savannakhet* ✣ *Old Town due west from Talat Yen Plaza* ☎ *020/765–60000* 🌐 *fb.com/savancafe* 💳 *No credit cards* 🛏 *5 rooms* 🍴 *Free Breakfast.*

Pakse

205 km (127 miles) south of Savannakhet, 675 km (420 miles) south of Vientiane.

Pakse is the transportation hub for all destinations in the south, including tours to the Khmer ruins at Wat Phou, the 4,000 Islands, and the Bolaven Plateau, which straddles the southern provinces of Salavan, Sekong, Attapeu, and Champasak. It's a former French colonial stronghold, now linked with neighboring Thailand 40 km (25 miles) away, and playing a central role in an ambitious plan for a trade and tourism community grouping Laos, Thailand, and Cambodia. There are few tourist attractions here but the most notable is the riverside Wat Luang, Pakse's biggest temple. It's home to a Buddhist Monk School, and probably the best place in the country to see a monk almsgiving ceremony—you'll be one of few visitors, compared to the throngs of tourists in Luang Prabang.

GETTING HERE AND AROUND

AIR

Domestic: There are several Lao Airlines flights each day from Vientiane to Pakse, sometimes routed via Savannakhet, and a daily service to Luang Prabang; both flights take just over an hour and cost about 900,000 kip ($90) one way. Lao Skyway also flies daily from Vientiane for about 490,000 ($49). **International:** Lao Airlines also flies daily to Siem Reap, Cambodia; to Ho Chi Minh City in Vietnam on Tuesdays, Thursdays and Saturdays (from 1,500,000 kip/$180); and to Bangkok on Mondays, Wednesdays, Fridays, and weekends (from 1,700,000 kip/$200). A tuk-tuk from Pakse International Airport, which is 4 km (2 miles) northwest of the city center, costs from 30,000 kip to 40,000 kip.

BOAT

Vat Phou Cruises

A luxurious double-decker houseboat, the *Vat Phou* plies the southern length of the Mekong between Pakse and Si Phan Don. The all-inclusive cruises, which last three days and two nights, stop at Champasak, Vat Phou, Don Khong Island, a small village containing the temple of Oup Moung, and the waterfall at Phapheng, near Laos's border with Cambodia. The cruise guide speaks English, French, and Thai. ⊠ *Mekong Cruises (tour operator), Box 24 Ban Lakmuang, Sedone Road, Pakse* ☎ *031/251446* ⊕ *vatphou.com* 🖅 *From 6 million kip ($739) all-inclusive Oct.–Mar., 4.5 million kip ($518) Apr.–Sept.* ⚅ *Oct.–Mar., Tues., Thurs., and Sat.; Apr.–Sept., Tues. and Sat.; no cruises in June.*

BUS

Pakse is the transportation hub for all destinations in the south. It has four bus stations: the Northern Bus Terminal, situated about 6 miles north of town, has hourly departures to Savannakhet (five hours; 40,000 kip) and other points north. The Southern Bus Terminal (aka KM8 Bus Terminal) is mostly used by locals to point south. The Kriang Kai Bus Terminal (aka Km2 Bus Terminal) has some night buses to Vientiane. At last, the most used bus station is the Chitpasong Bus Terminal next to the Sedone River in the center of town. From here, comfortable VIP bed buses make the overnight, 11-hour journey to and from Vientiane (200,000 kip from Vientiane, including transfer to bus station, 170,000 kip from Pakse to Vientiane). Buses leave Vientiane nightly at 8 or 8:30 pm and arrive in Pakse at 6:30 am; the times are the same from Pakse to Vientiane. If you're headed to Si Phan Don from Pakse, it's more convenient to take a minibus, which will pick you up at your hotel for 65,000 kip; all guesthouses sell tickets.

For international departures, you can get direct buses to Ubon in Thailand from Pakse as well as to Siem Reap and Phnom Penh in Cambodia.

CAR

Any travel agent in town can arrange car rental with a driver.

MOTORBIKE

Given the good quality of roads around Pakse, renting a scooter to visit the waterfalls, Champasak, or the Bolaven Plateau is a very popular option for the most adventurous.

TAXI, TUK-TUK, AND SONGTHAEW

Tuk-tuks around town cost 10,000 kip (although you will be hard-pressed to get this price as a tourist). Songthaews to Champasak (one hour; 30,000 kip) leave from the Dao Heuang market. Taxis are best used through the ride-hailing app, LOCA (download it at loca.la).

TIMING

Unless you are using Pakse as a base for visiting Champasak or elsewhere as a day tour, one night should be enough. The main city sights can be covered in a day, but allow for two if you decide to explore the countryside by motorbike. Pakse is also a perfect place to book tickets, go to the bank, and deal with any kind of communications or business before moving on to Champasak, Tad Fane, or the 4,000 Islands. Allow for two to three extra days if you decide to tackle the shorter or longer version of the Bolaven Plateau Loop.

TOURS

Miss Noy

This Belgian-Lao run motorbike rental shop (from 50,000 kip per day) also organizes tours and sells tickets for onward travel. ■TIP➜ **If you intend to explore the area independently, drop by Miss Noy at 6 pm for their daily brief on the best motorbike routes to Champasak and the Bolaven Plateau.** ⊠ *13 National Hwy., Pakse* ✛ *Right opposite Jasmine restaurant* ☎ *020/222–72278.*

Lao: A Few Key Phrases

The official language is Lao, part of the extensive Tai (not to be confused with Thai spoken in Thailand) family of languages of Southeast Asia spoken from Vietnam in the east to India in the west. Spoken Lao is very similar to northern and northeastern Thai language, as well as local dialects in the Shan states in Myanmar and Sipsongbanna in China. Lao is tonal, meaning a word can have several meanings according to the tone in which it's spoken.

Here are a few common and useful words:

Hello: sabai di (pronounced *sa-bye dee*)

Thank you: khop chai deu (pronounced *cop jai der*; use khop cheu neu in northern Laos)

Yes: chao (pronounced like jao)

No: bor

Where?: yoo sai?

How much?: taw dai?

Zero: soun (pronounced *soon*)

One: neung

Two: song

Three: sam

Four: si

Five: ha

Six: hok

Seven: jet

Eight: bpaet

Nine: kao (pronounced *gao*)

Ten: sip

Twenty: sao (rhymes with cow; different from Thai "yee sip")

Hundred: neung hoi (sometimes spoken as *neung loi*)

Thousand: neung phan

To eat: kin khao (pronounced *gi n cow*)

To drink: kin nam

Water: nam

Rice: khao

Expensive: phaeng

Bus: lot may

House: heuan

Road: thanon

Village: ban

Island: don

River: mae nam

Doctor: maw

Hospital: hohng maw

Post Office: paisani

Hotel: hohng haem

Toilet: hawng nam

Pakse Travel

This company arranges ecotours to Champasak, Si Phan Don, and farther afield, conducted by trained guides and with excellent transportation options. Day tours to the Bolaven Plateau, homestays on Don Daeng and in ethnic villages, and tea-and-coffee plantation tours are just some of the offerings. ⊠ *108 Ban Thaluang, Hwy. 13, Pakse* ✛ *Next to Phi Dao Hotel downtown* ☎ *020/222–77277, 020/777–34567.*

VISITOR AND TOUR INFORMATION

CONTACT Champasak Provincial Tourism. ✉ *Th. 11, Ban Thasalakham, Pakse* ✥ *Near BCEL bank* ☎ *031/212021* 🌐 *southern-laos.com.*

Sights

Historical Heritage Museum

HISTORY MUSEUM | Pakse's history museum displays stonework from the famous Wat Phou in Champasak, handicrafts from the Bolaven Plateau ethnic groups, and locally made musical instruments. ✉ *Hwy. 13, Pakse* ✥ *1 km (½ mile) before Dao Heung Market turnoff* ☎ *020/552–71733* 🎟 *10,000 kip.*

★ **Wat Phou Salao**

VIEWPOINT | Across the river on the way to Champasak, this hilltop temple was built in 2011 and has an impressive "Big Buddha" statue that dominates the peak. A long staircase flanked with nagas brings visitors to the top (allow 30 minutes for the climb) where there are great views of the river and the city, especially as they soak up the crimson sunsets. There is also a newer, concrete road to the top. ✉ *Pakse* ✥ *Adjacent to the Japanese bridge.*

Restaurants

★ **124 Thaluang Coffee**

$ | CAFÉ | This heritage shophouse in Pakse's old quarter has been lovingly converted by its Japanese owner into a warm café space infused with minimalism and Lao touches. The coffee here might be the best in Laos, and there are fresh homemade pastries, too. **Known for:** handicrafts for sale to support Lao communities; homemade brownies; artisanal drip coffee. [$] *Average main: 25,000* ✉ *124 Thaluang Village, Pakse* ☎ *020/968–90070* 🕒 *Closed Sat.* 💳 *No credit cards.*

Le Panorama

$ | ASIAN FUSION | The sixth-floor restaurant at the Pakse Hotel not only has the best view in town, but it also has some of the best food. Start with a sunset cocktail on the rooftop terrace, then move on to a romantic candlelight dinner under the stars. **Known for:** Pakse's best burgers; gai vat phou (chicken breast stuffed with crabmeat); international wines. [$] *Average main: 60,000* ✉ *Pakse Hotel, Th. 5, Ban Wat Luang, Pakse* ☎ *031/212131* 🌐 *hotelpakse.com* 🕒 *No lunch.*

Hotels

Athena Hotel

$$ | HOTEL | The old-world charm of this two-story building extends from spacious, vintage-styled rooms to a lovely pool area, enclosed by long wooden planks. **Pros:** unlimited a la carte breakfast; large bathrooms; swimming pool. **Cons:** patchy Wi-Fi; rooms facing main road can get noisy; central but not very close to the river. [$] *Rooms from: 600,000* ✉ *RN 13 South, Phabath Village, Pakse* ☎ *031/214888* 🌐 *fb.com/athenahotellaos* 🛏 *21 rooms* 🍴 *Free Breakfast.*

Pakse Hotel

$ | HOTEL | Pakse's oldest hotel was refurbished in 2018 and keeps offering well-maintained, centrally located rooms, though the deluxe ones are better value. **Pros:** fitness center; great central location; comfortable rooms with plenty of light. **Cons:** standard rooms don't have views; small elevator; busy with tour groups. [$] *Rooms from: 250,000* ✉ *Th. 5, Ban Wat Luang, Pakse* ☎ *031/212131* 🌐 *paksehotel.com* 🛏 *60 rooms* 🍴 *Free Breakfast.*

★ **Residence Sisouk**

$$ | HOTEL | A premier boutique hotel in a refurbished, historical corner building, Residence Sisouk is luxurious and charming, with original hardwood flooring and a mix of old and new furnishings.

Pros: good breakfast and café; close to everything; colonial charm. **Cons:** inconsistent service; not all rooms have river views; old staircase. $\boxed{\$}$ *Rooms from: 560,000* ✉ *Ban Lakmuang, Pakse* ☎ *031/214716* ⊕ *residence-sisouk.com* ❑❘ *Free Breakfast* ⇥ *16 rooms.*

Bolaven Plateau

23 km (14 miles) east of Pakse.

The volcanic soil of this plateau to the east of Pakse makes the vast region ideal for agriculture: it's the source of much of the country's prized coffee, tea, and spices. Despite its beauty and central role in the Lao economy, the plateau has minimal tourist infrastructure and is pretty much off-the-beaten-track territory. The Dong Houa Sao National Park is on the southwestern edge of the Bolaven Plateau.

GETTING HERE AND AROUND
Most tour agents and hotels organize day trips to the Bolaven Plateau from Pakse. These usually take in Tad Fane waterfall and the countryside around Paksong, but are just a mere teaser of the beauty that awaits farther east. The best way to go is to hire a car and driver for a few days, or rent a motorbike and strike on the well-established Bolaven Plateau Loop, starting and ending in Pakse. Miss Noy is a reliable rental company (*020/222–72278*).

SAFETY AND PRECAUTIONS
The main roads are paved, but any side trip requires caution. Motorbike theft is a problem in some areas: your rental company should be able to warn before you set off. Stick to normal precautions otherwise.

TIMING
Take a minimum of two days for the Small Loop and three for the Long Loop. Adding a few extra days makes the experience more enjoyable.

⊙ Sights

Bolaven Plateau Loop
SCENIC DRIVE | Travel around the Bolaven Plateau is unique in Laos due to its high altitude and cooler climate, and the sights focus primarily on waterfalls and coffee. The typical way to see the area is via the so-called Small Loop (200 km or 124 miles) or the Large Loop (320 km or 199 miles). The small loop, described here, is quite nice if your time is short: After your initial 35 km (22 mile) climb on a well-paved tollway, you'll arrive at a spot with several waterfalls. **Tad Fane** is the one mentioned most often for its lovely view of twin waterfalls dropping over a high cliff and potential ziplining for the brave (*greendiscoverylaos.com/ tours/fly-at-tad-fane 021/264528*). **Tad E-tu** is also nearby and has some decent accommodation. **Tad Yeuang** is just a little farther and has a local market, a scenic restaurant, and some unique photo spots. **Paksong** is the largest town on the Bolaven Plateau with a few basic accommodation options and some lovely cafes. Head northwest past several organic farms, including **Yamamoto Farm** (*fb.com/yamamotofarmlaos 030/957– 5237*) where visitors can pick (and eat) strawberries in the winter, then continue north to **Sinouk Coffee Resort** (*suansinouk. com 030/955–8960*), probably the nicest (and priciest) hotel on the plateau. Farther north still is **Captain Hook Homestay** (*fb.com/hook.23 020/989–30406*), where you can learn about the Katu ethnic group on day tours or stay overnight. **Tad Lo** is a series of three waterfalls with a village full of guesthouses. Continuing southwest, **Mr. Vieng Coffee & Homestay** (*020/998–37206*) can give you a look at organic farming and a coffee tasting. The final waterfall on this route is **Tad Pha Souam**, stunning in its own right, before the route returns to Pakse. ✉ *Pakse.*

Tad Fane

38 km (24 miles) east of Pakse.

Tad Fane is Laos's most impressive waterfall, pounding down through magnificent jungle foliage for almost 400 feet.

GETTING HERE AND AROUND

Buses and songthaews run from the Pakse bus station several times each morning. The trip up to Tad Fane and the Bolaven Plateau town of Paksong takes an hour and costs 20,000 kip.

SAFETY AND PRECAUTIONS

The trails around the falls are slippery and can be dangerous, especially during the rainy season (when the leeches come out). Proceed with caution and take a guide if you feel unsure about getting around on your own.

TIMING

Take one day for the falls and possibly another day to do some hiking in the park or explore the area around Paksong.

 Sights

Tad Fane Waterfall

WATERFALL | The waterfall is set on the border of the Dong Houa Sao National Park and up in the cool air of the Bolaven Plateau, Laos's premier coffee-growing region. There's good hiking here, and the cool temperatures are a relief from the heat and humidity down on the Mekong. The area is accessible as a day trip from Pakse, though there is a somewhat run-down and overpriced resort at the base of the falls should you care to stay. Aside from the easy stroll out to the viewing platform above the main falls, those who don't suffer vertigo can try the 400-meter-high zipline that soars over the falls, giving a bird's-eye view of the area ($40 per person). You can also take a guided walk down to the base of the falls, or venture onto one of the roundabout trails going up above the falls. These trails take in some minor falls and some fun swimming holes. Farther afield, the beautiful Tat Yeuang falls can be reached in about an hour via a trail from Tad Fane or from a turnout at Km 40 on the main road. Inquire at the resort about guides and trail information. ⊠ *Pakse.*

Champasak

40 km (25 miles) south of Pakse.

In the 18th and 19th centuries, Champasak, on the west bank of the Mekong River, was the royal center of a wide area of what is today Thailand and Cambodia. These days the small village is a gateway for visiting the ruins of Wat Phou.

The area's most unique lodging option, with a Robinson Crusoe feel, is La Folie on Don Daeng, an island near Champasak that remains largely untouched by tourism. The River Resort, just north of Champasak, is upscale and romantic.

GETTING HERE AND AROUND

Songthaews travel here from the Dao Heuang Market in Pakse three times each morning (one hour; 20,000 kip). Minibuses can be arranged through guesthouses and travel agencies in Pakse for 60,000 kip. While most tour agency minibuses take the road toward the 4,000 Islands and drop you off at the Ban Muang boat pier on the east bank of the Mekong—Don Daeng Island is accessed from here—a new road down the west side cuts out the need for a boat ride across if coming via local songthaew. A car with a driver can be hired from all tour agencies in Pakse for about 500,000 kip. Tuk-tuks run to Wat Phou from Champasak for 10,000 kip per person. You can also rent motorbikes (50/70,000 kip per day) as the road is perfectly sealed and sees sporadic traffic.

👁 Sights

Don Daeng Island

ISLAND | In the middle of the Mekong, opposite Wat Phou, this 9-km (5½-miles) long island has gorgeous views of the river and surrounding countryside. An ecotourism program and a long sandy beach have made it popular with visitors to Wat Phou as an alternative to staying in Pakse or Champasak. Bicycles can be rented on the island, and the Provincial Tourist Office in Pakse can arrange homestays. The upscale hotel, La Folie Lodge is located here. ✉ *Champasak.*

★ Wat Phou

TEMPLE | The ruins of this temple complex that predates Cambodia's Angkor Wat sit grandly on heights above the Mekong River, about 8 km (5 miles) south of Champasak. The strategic site was chosen by Khmer Hindus in the 6th century AD, probably because of a nearby spring of fresh water. Construction of the wat continued into the 13th century, at which point it finally became a Buddhist temple. Much of the original Hindu sculpture remains unchanged, including representations on the temple's lintels of the Hindu gods Vishnu, Shiva, and Kala. The staircase is particularly beautiful, its protective *nagas* (mystical serpents) decorated with plumeria, the national flower of Laos. Many of the temple's treasures, including pre-Angkor–era inscriptions, are preserved in an archaeology museum that is part of the complex. An impressive festival takes place at the temple each January. ✉ *Rd. 14, 8 km (5 miles) south of town, Champasak* ☏ *030/956–5325* ⊕ *vatphou-champassak.com* 🖆 *50,000 kip; 40,000 kip 6 am–8 am and 4:30–6, with no museum entry.*

🍴 Restaurants

★ The River Resort Restaurant

$ | **ECLECTIC** | The international team in the kitchen of the River Resort's elegant restaurant prepares fine Asian and Western dishes—the best food you will find in all southern Laos—with equal skill and panache. Highly recommended is the local Mekong fish, which can either be grilled and served with tamarind sauce and lime, or steamed in a banana leaf Lao-style. **Known for:** good prices for this quality; good wine list; Lao specialties. **$** *Average main: 80,000* ✉ *Ban Phaphinnoy, Rd. 14A, Champasak* ✛ *North of Champasak town, about 1 km (½ mile) north of boat-pier turnoff* ☏ *031/511055, 030/956–8306* ⊕ *theriverresortlaos.com.*

🛏 Hotels

★ La Folie Lodge

$$$$ | **B&B/INN** | For a luxury Robinson Crusoe experience, nothing surpasses La Folie. **Pros:** off-season discounts up to 40%; stunning views; unique escapist experience. **Cons:** very expensive; no other dining options nearby; most staffers do not speak English. **$** *Rooms from: 1,460,000* ✉ *Don Daeng, Pathoumphone, Champasak* ✛ *Opposite Champasak in middle of Mekong* ☏ *020/555–32004* ⊕ *lafolie-laos.com* ⇱ *27 rooms* ⦿ *Free Breakfast.*

★ The River Resort

$$$ | **RESORT** | This gorgeous riverfront boutique resort with outdoor rain-style showers and truly cool air-conditioning is the perfect spot to start or end a southern Laos excursion. **Pros:** free bicycles for guests; stunning Mekong River location and views; riverside swimming pool. **Cons:** no facilities near resort; outside town; not convenient to Wat Phou. **$** *Rooms from: 7,800,000* ✉ *Ban Phaphinnoy, Rd. 14A, Champasak* ✛ *North of Champasak town, about 1 km (½ mile) north of boat-pier turnoff* ☏ *031/511055, 030/9568306* ⊕ *theriverresortlaos.com* ⦿ *Free Breakfast* ⇱ *28 rooms.*

The Irrawaddy Dolphins

The freshwater Irrawaddy dolphin, *pa kha* in Lao, is one of the world's most endangered species; it's believed fewer than 100 now remain in the Mekong. The Irrawaddy has mythical origins. According to Lao and Khmer legend, a beautiful maiden, in despair over being forced to marry a snake, attempted suicide by jumping into the Mekong but the gods intervened, saving her life by transforming her into a dolphin.

Lao people don't traditionally hunt the dolphins, but they've been casualties

of overfishing, getting tangled in nets and new dams in the Mekong have altered their ecosystem, further threatening their survival.

Catching a glimpse of these majestic animals—which look more like orcas than dolphins—is thrilling. The least obtrusive way to visit is in a kayak or other nonmotorized boat. If you go by motorboat and do spot dolphins, ask your driver to cut the engine when you're still 100 yards or so away. You can then paddle closer to the animals without disturbing them.

Si Phan Don and the 4,000 Islands

80 km (50 miles) south of Champasak, 120 km (74 miles) south of Pakse.

If you've made it as far south as Champasak, then a visit to the Si Phan Don area—celebrated for its 4,000 Mekong River islands and freshwater dolphins—is a must. *Don* means "island," and two in this area are especially worth checking out: Don Khon (with its counterpart, Don Det) and the similarly named Don Khong.

The Khone Phapheng Falls, on the mainland near Don Khon, are a highlight, and visiting them can be combined with seeing the freshwater Irrawaddy dolphins. You'll find many boat operators happy to escort you. Don Det, connected to Don Khon by a bridge, attracts the backpacker crowd. Don Khong has scenic rice fields and more upscale lodging choices and is more peaceful than Don Khon, but is not as interesting or attractive.

GETTING HERE AND AROUND

Any travel agency in Pakse can help you make arrangements for getting to and from the islands.

From Pakse you can take a minibus, arranged at any travel agency or guesthouse, straight to Don Khong (it's connected to the mainland by a bridge) or the boat landing Nakasang (for Don Khon) with tickets for the small boat crossing to the island included. The journey takes from two to three hours and costs between 60,000 and 70,000 kip depending on which island you go to.

Boat crossings from the mainland to Don Khon (from Nakasang) cost 30,000 kip and take 15 minutes.

SAFETY AND PRECAUTIONS

Take care when kayaking on the Mekong. The water may appear still, but the currents are strong, as are the rapids; it's best to go with a guide. The name Liphi Falls means "spirit trap," and there's a lot of superstition surrounding them. It is considered offensive to swim here.

TIMING

The major sights can be seen in one day, but it would be a shame to not budget a few more days to relax and enjoy the local pace of life.

Sights

Don Khon Island

ISLAND | You can hike or bicycle to the beautiful Liphi waterfall on the island of Don Khon, though an even more stunning one, **Khone Phapheng,** is just east of Don Khon on the mainland. Day-trip tours that include visits to the Irrawaddy dolphins and the mainland's Phapheng fall set out from Don Khon. Also on Don Khon, and the connected Don Det, are the remains of a French-built railway. ⊠ *Don Khon Island.*

Don Khong Island

ISLAND | The largest island in the area, Don Khong is inhabited by a fisherfolk living in small villages amid ancient Buddhist temples. The best way to explore is by bicycle—this is a pretty big place. Far less visited than Don Det/Don Khon, it's also a great spot to chill out along the river. A bridge across the Mekong connects Don Khong to the mainland, but it hasn't yet spoiled the quiet pace of the island, which has beautiful rice fields in the interior. ⊠ *Don Khong Island.*

 Restaurants

Seng Ahloune Restaurant

$ | **LAO** | This rickety restaurant on wooden planks just above the Mekong may not look like much, but its cooks consistently deliver tasty and authentic Lao food. The setting is intimate and romantic, though the place can get busy with tour groups staying at the family's decent guesthouse. **Known for:** chicken biryani; river views; friendly staff. $ *Average main: 50,000* ✛ *Just west of bridge connecting Don Khon with Don Det* ☎ *020/538–31399* ▭ *No credit cards.*

Hotels

Pon Arena Hotel

$ | **HOTEL** | The enormous Mekong Riverview rooms with terraces are the way to go at this inviting riverside property. **Pros:** owner speaks fluent English; large Mekong-view rooms with fabulous vistas; beautiful riverside pool. **Cons:** standard and deluxe rooms lack views; disappointing breakfast; Mekong-view rooms cost twice as much as standard ones. $ *Rooms from: 400,000* ⊠ *Ban Kang Khong, Don Khong Island* ✛ *To right of boat pier on Don Khong* ☎ *031/515018 reservations, 020/222–70037 manager's cell* ⤴ *35 rooms* ⦿*Free Breakfast.*

Sala Done Khone

$$ | **B&B/INN** | There are three types of rooms at this charming resort: French colonial-style rooms, adobe-style rooms in a garden, and atmospheric "raftels" floating on the Mekong. **Pros:** swimming pool; beautiful riverside location; most upmarket hotel on the island. **Cons:** mosquitoes at sunset; rooms book up quickly in high season; rooms area a bit worn. $ *Rooms from: 600,000* ✛ *Just east of boat drop-off in Don Khon* ☎ *031/260940* ⊕ *salalaoboutique.com/saladonekhone* ⦿*Free Breakfast* ⤴ *30 rooms.*

Activities

Irrawaddy Dolphin viewing

BOAT TOURS | Downstream from Don Khon, at the border between Laos and Cambodia, freshwater Irrawaddy dolphins frolic in a protected area of the Mekong. Boat trips to view the dolphins set off from Hang Khon village, south of Liphi Falls. Even better, head out to see the dolphins by kayak. All the guesthouses in town can arrange trips. ✛ *Boats depart from southern tip of Don Khon Island* ▣ *70,000 kip per person, minimum of 3 people.*

Index

542

Photo Credits

*Every effort has been made to trace the copyright holders, and we apologize in advance for any accidental errors. We would be happy to apply the corrections in the following edition of this publication.

Fodor's ESSENTIAL THAILAND

Publisher: Stephen Horowitz, *General Manager*

Editorial: Douglas Stallings, *Editorial Director*; Jill Fergus, Amanda Sadlowski, Caroline Trefler, *Senior Editors*; Kayla Becker, Alexis Kelly, *Editors*; Angelique Kennedy-Chavannes, *Assistant Editor*

Design: Tina Malaney, *Director of Design and Production*; Jessica Gonzalez, *Graphic Designer;* Sophia Almendral, *Design and Production Intern*

Production: Jennifer DePrima, *Editorial Production Manager*; Elyse Rozelle, *Senior Production Editor;* Monica White, *Production Editor*

Maps: Rebecca Baer, *Senior Map Editor*; Henry Colomb and Mark Stroud (Moon Street Cartography), David Lindroth, *Cartographers*

Photography: Viviane Teles, *Senior Photo Editor;* Namrata Aggarwal, Payal Gupta, Ashok Kumar, *Photo Editors;* Rebecca Rimmer, *Photo Production Associate;* Eddie Aldrete, *Photo Production Intern*

Business and Operations: Chuck Hoover, *Chief Marketing Officer*; Robert Ames, *Group General Manager*; Devin Duckworth, *Director of Print Publishing*

Public Relations and Marketing: Joe Ewaskiw, *Senior Director of Communications and Public Relations*

Fodors.com: Jeremy Tarr, *Editorial Director;* Rachael Levitt, *Managing Editor*

Technology: Jon Atkinson, *Director of Technology;* Rudresh Teotia, *Lead Developer*; Jacob Ashpis, *Content Operations Manager*

Writers: Amy Benesma, Joe Cummings, Duncan Forgan, Marisa Marchitelli, Simon Ortheimer, Jason Rolan, Barbara Woolsey

Editor: Caroline Trefler

Production Editor: Jennifer DePrima

2nd edition

ISBN 978-1-64097-477-7

ISSN 2639-5967

SPECIAL SALES
This book is available at special discounts for bulk purchases for sales promotions or premiums. For more information, e-mail SpecialMarkets@fodors.com.

PRINTED IN CANADA

10 9 8 7 6 5 4 3 2 1

About Our Writers

Amy Benesma is a copywriter who has been based in Phuket since 2007. Adventurous by nature, she seeks out unique local experiences and off-the-beaten-path destinations that truly highlight the island's natural charm and Phuketian flavor. She also writes feature articles on travel, hospitality, leisure, and Phuket's dynamic dining scene. You can follow her on Instagram @phuketstagram.

Joe Cummings has written guidebooks on Thailand and other destinations around Southeast Asia for several publishers. He writes regularly for *CNN Travel, Conde Nast Traveler,* and *Travel & Leisure,* and has worked as a personal travel consultant with the likes of Anthony Bourdain, Mick Jagger, and Disney Studios. He makes his home in Bangkok. You can follow him on Instagram @joejcummings and on Twitter @joecummings.

As a result of frigid winters in his native Scotland, **Duncan Forgan** has worked his way closer to the equator. He arrived in Asia in 2010 on assignment, fell in love with the lifestyle, and didn't bother to redeem the return portion of his air ticket. Now based in Bangkok, he covers culture, cuisine, music, adventure, and anything else that takes his fancy around the region. Duncan has worked for *AFAR,* Channel News Asia, *TIME, Golf World, Esquire,* BBC, *The Guardian, Penthouse, Travel and Leisure,* CNN, and many others. Follow him on Instagram: @dunc1978.

Marisa Marchitelli is a Thai-Italian-American filmmaker and writer based in Chiang Mai. She's Thai-born, Hong Kong–raised, and completed her MFA at School of Visual Arts in New York City. Her work has appeared in *The New York Times, The Huffington Post,* BBC, and CNN. Follow her globe-trotting adventures on Instagram @chiangmaimarisa.

Raised in Hong Kong, **Simon Ostheimer** has been traveling and writing for much of his life. Currently based in Phnom Penh, he's found living in a place is the best way to get to know it, and has enjoyed discovering the many charms that come with life in Cambodia, the "Kingdom of Wonder."

Jason Rolan left his home in Texas nearly two decades ago for a tourism job in Thailand. Eventually relocating to Laos, he uses Vientiane as a base to explore the country and the rest of Southeast Asia. Now fluent in Thai and Lao, he is the editor-in-chief for two inflight magazines and assists the government on tourism matters. Have a sunset Beerlao on the Mekong with him or simply follow his travels on Instagram @jasonrolan.

Barbara Woolsey is a Canadian-Filipina journalist who has crisscrossed Asia by plane, train, and motorbike. She's lived in Thailand for several periods since 2010, including stints reporting for the *Bangkok Post* and hosting and producing for TrueVision. These days, she spends most of her time in Berlin, Germany, and is currently completing a Masters in Global Studies via Humboldt University of Berlin and Bangkok's Chulalongkorn University. Follow her on Instagram @barbara. woolsey